Raising the Bar

The Emerging Legal Profession in East Asia

Edited, with an introduction, by

William P. Alford

with the assistance of Emma Johnson,
Geraldine Chin, *and* Laura A. Cecere

Published by
East Asian Legal Studies
Harvard Law School

Distributed by Harvard University Press
Cambridge, Massachusetts
2007

Library of Congress Cataloging-in-Publication Data

Raising the bar : the emerging legal profession in East Asia / edited by William P.
Alford ; with the assistance of Emma Johnson, Geraldine Chin, and Laura A. Cecere.
   p. cm.
  ISBN-10 0-674-01452-9 (pbk.)
  ISBN-13 978-0-674-01452-7
 1. Lawyers—East Asia. 2. Lawyers—Asia, Southeastern.
 I. Alford, William P. II. Johnson, Emma. III. Chin, Geraldine. IV. Cecere, Laura A.
  KNC50.R35 2007
  340′.023′5—dc22   2004001750

This volume is published in memory of
my friend
Daniel S. Lev
a great scholar and an even greater person
and is dedicated to
my son
Benjamin Z. Alford
with my love and admiration.

TABLE OF CONTENTS

PREFACE

WILLIAM P. ALFORD

One of the many pleasures of academic life in a professional school setting lies in the ways in which one's teaching, research, and engagement with the profession have the potential to enrich one another. This book is a good example of that mutual enrichment. It is, to be sure, hard to pinpoint how my interest in the topic of this book first arose. In part, it is due to the presence in my classroom of aspiring lawyers from or deeply concerned about East Asia. It also was spurred by my research into the enormous changes that have characterized the Chinese legal system over the past quarter-century. And it is, no doubt, additionally attributable to the many stimulating conversations I have had with leading figures from all sectors of the region's legal world in my capacity as Director of Harvard's East Asian Legal Studies program (EALS). What is clear, however, is that each of these endeavors has benefited from my engagement in the others. The chance to teach a seminar on the legal profession in East Asia at Harvard in 1998 crystallized ideas that led to the conference from which this volume emerged, as well as providing me with the opportunity to co-teach with Setsuo Miyazawa and to teach Ben Liebman, two contributors to this project. My own research on the epochal transformations underway in China gave me an early exposure to what has proven to be history's most concerted effort to develop a legal profession. And my programmatic responsibilities at Harvard, in turn, brought me in contact with Sang-Hyun Song and JaeWon Kim, and through them, offered me a close-up window on Korea's attempts to re-think the legal profession.

Not surprisingly, in view of the foregoing, my debt of gratitude with respect to this volume is immense. First and foremost, I want to thank Harvard Law School and the people who comprise the institution. Too often, we take the institutions of which we are a part for granted—which is most unfortunate. Whatever merit there may be in my contribution to this volume is largely attributable to the abundant opportunities this institution provides—be it in the form of brilliant, hard-working students drawn from throughout the world; stimulating colleagues, many of whom participated in the conference on which this volume is based; the availability of faculty research support; the presence of the world's leading academic law library with its superb staff; and an extraordinary network of alumni and friends worldwide. In particular, I wish to thank Robert Clark, the Dean of the Law School at the time I embarked on this project and Elena Kagan, Dean at the time of its completion. It has been a privilege and a pleasure to be associated with them and the School.

Second, I am happy to be able to express my gratitude to the Abe Fellowship program for extending to me the honor of being an Abe Fellow in the late 1990s.

This wonderful program is sponsored by the Japan Foundation's Center for Global Partnership and is administered by the Social Science Research Council and the American Council of Learned Societies. I describe it as "wonderful" because the Abe program not only provided me with financial support to pursue my research interests regarding the legal profession in East Asia but also facilitated contacts with scholars across a wide range of disciplines from the United States and Japan both through its annual retreat for grantees and the good offices of its representatives. It is a fitting tribute to the individual after whom it was named, Shintaro Abe, the late foreign minister of Japan instrumental in building strong relations around the Pacific Rim.

Financial support for the conference from which this volume emerged came in important measure from the Pacific Basin Research Center headed by John Montgomery, Ford Foundation Professor of International Studies, Emeritus at the Kennedy School of Government at Harvard and aided by Virginia Kosmo. Harvard Law School also lent support through EALS.

Special thanks are also owed to Setsuo Miyazawa, Geraldine Chin, Esq., and Laura A. Cecere, Esq. Professor Miyazawa not only joined me in the teaching of the aforementioned seminar but also helped identify and recruit the Japanese participants for our conference. When Professor Miyazawa's other responsibilities precluded his playing a role in the editing of this volume, first Geraldine Chin (with Australian pluck) and then Laura Cecere (with its Long Island equivalent), both accomplished graduates of Harvard Law School's LL.M. program, brought their considerable talents to bear in the early stages of the editorial process. In addition to wishing to thank each author represented in this volume for their fine contributions and extraordinary patience (which included updating their chapters at least through 2005 and in some cases 2006, unless otherwise noted), I also wish to express my gratitude to a number of other individuals who made presentations or offered commentaries at the conference itself (which was held in December 1998). They include Dean Alfred Aman of the University of Indiana School of Law, Professor Robert Gordon of Yale Law School, Yoko Hayashi, Esq. of the Tokyo bar, Professor Takao Suami of Waseda University, and the following colleagues of mine on the Harvard Law School faculty—Andrew Kaufman, Mark Ramseyer, Anne-Marie Slaughter (now Dean of the Woodrow Wilson School at Princeton University), Detlev Vagts, Lucie White and David Wilkins. Others who also added valuably to the issues discussed at the conference include Dean Raul Pangalangan of the University of the Philippines College of Law, Assistant Professor John Ohnesorge of the University of Wisconsin School of Law (who, then a graduate student here, served as *rapporteur*), and Professor Louis Orzack of Rutgers University's Department of Sociology.

Thanks are additionally due to Dr. Zhang Nongji and Mariko Honshuku, Harvard Law School's splendid East Asian law librarians, and to Benedict Hur, Esq. who valuably reviewed the Korean chapters. Without Emma Johnson, with her excellent judgment and superb organizational skills, this book would still be a manuscript. I am also very appreciative for the very helpful involvement of Melissa Smith, Juliet Bowler, Timothy Locher, Julia Zhang, and Dr. Joanne Baldine, all of EALS. I am also grateful to Puritan Press and its able staff.

Naturally, notwithstanding the many hands that went into this project, responsibility for any and all errors is mine.

Usage Notes

The text, footnotes, and citations in this book principally conform to the guidelines for the author-date system found in *The Chicago Manual of Style*, 14th and 15th editions (1993 and 2003), save that in Works Cited, law journals are written in a modified Bluebook method.

Examples of the Chicago style that readers may not be familiar with include the following: for organizations or other proper nouns in Chinese, Japanese, and Korean, we use the English translation, capitalized, with the transliteration of the original given in italics and lower case in the first instance of use: "the Justice System Reform Council or JSRC (*shihō seido kaikaku shingikai*). . . ." An exception to the lower-case rule is the capitalization of a country name: "Japan Business Federation (*Nippon keidanren*)." Organizations that are primarily known outside of Asia by their original-language names are transliterated and translated once (per chapter), using the above rule, and thereafter are written as if in English, capitalized and not italicized: "the Japan Federation of Economic Organizations (*keizai dantai rengōkai* or *keidanren*, hereafter Keidanren). . . ." For citations in the text, English and non-English references are treated the same, capitalized and not italicized: ". . . (Shihō Seido Kaikaku Shingikai 2001)." Chinese words are Romanized using pinyin spellings unless they are commonly rendered in another way: "the Kuomintang." Titles of officeholders are not capitalized unless a specific person is named. For example: "the minister of justice," "the prime minister," "President Kim." The office itself is capitalized only if specific: "the Ministry of Justice," "various ministries," "the General Secretariat of the Supreme Court."

In the Works Cited sections, the English translation of a work is given in sentence case and brackets. Proper nouns such as publishers are capitalized and not italicized. Journal names are italicized but article titles are not (and are not in quotes). Article titles are given in sentence case, except that a country name is capitalized: "Tongguo sifa shixian shehui zhengyi: Dui Zhongguo faguan xianzhuang de yige toushi [The realization of social justice through judicature: A look at the current situation of Chinese judges]. In *Zou xiang quanli de shidai: Zhongguo gongmin fazhan yanjiu* [Toward a time of rights: A perspective on the development of civil rights in China], ed. Xia Yong. Beijing: Zhongguo Zhengfa Daxue Chubanshe."

In the text and notes, numbers one to one hundred and low round numbers are spelled out, unless they are near other numbers rendered as digits. In that case, they too may be rendered as digits for a consistent appearance.

Introduction

William P. Alford

We live at a time when the legal profession in East Asia is undergoing revolutionary change, if it is not an oxymoron to speak of lawyers doing anything in a revolutionary fashion. These changes are not simply the domain of lawyers. They are the product of intense struggles reaching, in many instances, to the highest levels of state, business, and society. Implicated in these battles are not only such obvious matters as the financial well-being of the bar or even the nature of the judicial system, but issues that are both far weightier and far thornier. These issues concern the openness and accountability of government, the allocation of power along the public-private continuum, the realization of justice for those historically disfavored (be it for reasons of gender, social status, or political position), and international competitiveness. Indeed, the Justice System Reform Council or JSRC (*shihō seido kaikaku shingikai*), a key commission reporting directly to the Japanese prime minister, has gone so far as to argue that at stake in changes proposed for the bar are the interplay between individual autonomy and social responsibility and, with it, the very character of Japanese society (Shihō Seido Kaikaku Shingikai 2001). Lawyers may historically have had a modest role to play in East Asia, but the legal profession has become both a spawning ground for national leaders (the president and vice president of Taiwan are lawyers, for example, as were both of the final candidates for the presidency of Korea in 2002) and a prime battleground on which some of the most important and difficult questions of our age are being contested.

The most obvious change underway regarding the legal profession involves its size—even if it remains small throughout the region relative to the bar in the United States in absolute terms and that of most nations on a per capita basis.[1] There were few lawyers in East Asia prior to 1900 and their number remained modest until the last two decades of the twentieth century (Ramseyer and Nakazato 1998; Alford 1995). The People's Republic of China, to take the most pronounced example, was home to little more than 3,000 lawyers at the start of the so-called Anti-Rightist Movement of the late 1950s and approximately the same number (and, for that matter, many of the same individuals) at the close of the Great Proletarian Cultural Revolution two decades later (Alford 1995). Today, some 150,000 individuals hold licenses to practice law in China and some national leaders have called for an expansion of the bar to 300,000 by 2010—which figure China should have no trouble meeting given that more

---

1. As Marc Galanter, among others, has suggested, the counting of lawyers for comparative purposes on a cross-national basis is a tricky business (Galanter 1992a, 1992b).

than 360,000 people took part in the first unified national examination for legal professionals (held in 2001).[2]

Much the same holds true for the Republic of Korea and Japan. As recently as 1980, Korea had fewer than 3,000 legal professionals—and was limiting new entrants to 100 people per annum. The yearly passage rate on the bar exam (known as the National Judicial Service Examination) has grown tenfold since that time, yielding a profession of close to 10,000 (Kim, in this volume). In Japan, fewer than 500 people passed the bar as recently as 1990. That number has more than doubled today, but far more substantial expansion is envisioned. The Justice System Reform Council recommended increasing the number of those passing the exam annually to 3,000 by 2010, as it believed that a private bar that still numbers below 25,000 is too small (Shihō Seido Kaikaku Shingikai 2001). And actors from such disparate points along the political spectrum as the Japan Federation of Economic Organizations (*keidanren*) and the Japan Civil Liberties Union are urging an even greater liberalization of admission to legal practice, while some distinguished practitioners and academics have gone so far as to call for an end altogether to any predetermined limit on the admission of qualified candidates to practice (Yanagida 2000).

As arresting as these statistics may be, they must share center stage with changes regarding the type of work lawyers do, for whom they do it, and their posture vis-à-vis the state. So it is, for instance, that even as attorneys in Japan and Korea and their counterparts elsewhere have generally worked to maintain their monopolies with respect to litigation and the provision of formal legal opinions, many have ventured well beyond (Kitagawa and Nottage, and Kim, both in this volume). For some, this has meant engaging in business planning, contractual negotiations, and lobbying, while for others it has grown to encompass deal-making and the assumption of full-time positions in business, government and activist groups in a manner heretofore rarely the case in East Asia (Kitagawa and Nottage, Miyazawa, and Kim, all in this volume). As this suggests, the clientele that lawyers serve has also expanded in a variety of senses, with domestic corporate actors making greater use of counsel, a rapidly expanding foreign presence requiring legal advice, and an increasing need for lawyers being voiced by women and others who have historically not been major consumers of legal services (Kitagawa and Nottage, and Miyazawa, both in this volume). And in some jurisdictions, these changes have been accompanied by a growing willingness of lawyers strenuously to advance positions adverse to those taken by the state.[3]

---

2. "Legal professionals" here means judges, procurators, and lawyers. Similarly, for Japan and Korea, the examinations referred to in this paragraph are unified and required for those aspiring to the bench, prosecutor's office, or private bar. For more on the number of legal professionals in China, see page 290, note 6.

3. I base this proposition on extensive interviews I conducted with practitioners and legal academics in Tokyo and Seoul between 1996 and 1999. To be sure, there are examples of lawyers taking strongly adversarial positions vis-à-vis the state from the Meiji era and from the late Yi dynasty. See Haley (1991) and Kim (in this volume).

No less prominent than these transformations concerning the activities, clients, and posture of the profession have been the associated changes regarding the profession's internal organization, legal education, and even its demographics. The most substantial and sustained growth in the legal profession has come in the region's larger law firms, as Ryo Hamano demonstrates with respect to Japan in his contribution to this volume, even if their size (topping out for now at fewer than 300 members of the bar) pales in comparison with major firms headquartered in the West (Hamano, in this volume).

In recent years, there has been extensive debate throughout the region, and particularly in Japan, Korea, China, and Taiwan, as to the adoption of what is described as American-style legal education. This would entail a radical departure from law training in these jurisdictions. Most potential lawyers in Japan, for example, first studied law in large undergraduate lecture classes focused chiefly on doctrine, supplemented by cram schools that overshadow American bar review courses in their importance and intensity. Those few who passed the bar examination (fewer than 4 in 100 and sometimes half that during the period from the 1960s through the 1990s) were then required to complete a further program (now of eighteen months duration) run by the judiciary that included both coursework and internships in law offices, during which time they were paid by the state (Ramseyer and Nakazato 1998).

The adoption of American-style legal education involves a shift to new, more practically oriented graduate level instruction of the type recently commenced at the University of Tokyo and other leading Japanese universities that would, in theory, utilize a "Socratic" approach involving active student participation[4] (Miyazawa, in this volume).[5] And with these other changes has come a diversification of the bar in terms of gender, educational background, and, to some degree, class. This is evidenced, for example, by the fact that women, who but a decade ago constituted appreciably less than 10 percent of the bar in virtually

---

4. This proposed shift is in keeping with the movement of members of the bar, particularly in large firms, into business counseling and the representation of foreign clientele, as it was felt that the relatively more abstract, passive nature of post-war legal education failed adequately to prepare students either to meet the challenges of new practice areas or to anticipate the expectations of clients accustomed to "full-service" advice from foreign law firms. The tendency of many proponents in East Asia of American-style legal education to see it as appreciably more practically focused than may well be the case, particularly in the elite U.S. law schools that are the purported models, may have as much to do with the ways in which such advocates would like to see their bar transformed as it does with their understanding (or misunderstanding) of the U.S. experience. For more on the proposed changes to the training of legal professionals in Japan and Korea, see the contributions in this volume of Miyazawa, Song, Kim, and Dezalay and Garth.

5. Korean universities have been authorized to launch new graduate law schools in 2008 and there are now efforts underway in the PRC to reinvigorate so-called Juris Master's programs aimed at students whose first degree is in a subject other than law.

every jurisdiction in the region, now account for 20 to 30 percent of all newly admitted lawyers in Korea, Japan, China, and Taiwan.

It is, of course, hardly a revelation that legal professionals within and perhaps even beyond East Asia would think such changes to be of consequence. What is far more intriguing is that these changes have become a prime focal point for some of the most significant and contentious political, social and economic challenges confronting East Asia, even if one discounts for the tendency of lawyers, legal scholars, and law-trained policy makers, particularly in the United States, to overstate the importance of their would-be colleagues elsewhere in the world (Alford, in this volume). So it is, for instance, that the seemingly arcane question of revising legal education was the subject in Japan of the high-profile blue-ribbon Justice System Reform Council and became an issue with serious national political implications (Miyazawa, in this volume). Similarly, in Korea, proposals by a presidentially appointed commission substantially to revamp the legal profession became the focus of intense jockeying involving leading politicians, major business groups, the highest levels of the judiciary, prominent activists, and the mass media, not to mention educators and the bar (Song and Kim, both in this volume). In Taiwan, the internal machinations of the Taipei Bar Association have long been national political fodder (Winn, in this volume). And major development banks, foundations, and governments outside the region (including the United States) have gone to substantial lengths to promote the growth of the legal profession in the PRC both in and of itself, and as the prime vehicle through which the "rule of law" is to be conveyed (Alford 2003 and in this volume).

That changes in the legal profession have begun to evoke interest beyond the world of lawyers ought not to be surprising if we ponder their implications. Consider their impact on governance. Arguably, at least in liberal democratic states in the region, the expanding number and roles of lawyers has been a significant factor in fostering a greater reliance on relatively visible rules, amenable (or so theory would have it) to reasoned interpretation and application, even as the increase in such rules has been a factor in the growth of the bar. This may be facilitating unprecedented constraints on state action, creating more space for the rise of interests other than those that have historically been dominant while leading, albeit gradually, to a diminution of particularistic practices such as reliance on *guanxi* (roughly, "relationships"), to use the Chinese term. Moreover, taken together with the potential that lawyers have to help those who have been at the periphery of power, such as women, minorities and dissidents, to articulate their concerns in terms of rights and to secure access to formal institutional avenues of redress, it augurs of possibilities for broader public participation in governance and greater accountability for those wielding public and private power. One need not fully embrace the sweeping language of the Justice System Reform Council in Japan, to the effect that lawyers are "doctors for the people's social lives," to appreciate that the changing legal profession may be helping the populace take on more responsibility for its own affairs vis-à-vis both the state and other citizens.[6] It may not be coincidental that the politically successful lawyers who have risen to the presidency of Taiwan and Korea (as well as the vice presidency of Taiwan) in the last few years all began their careers as human rights lawyers-activists and rose to prominence through opposition parties.

Not all changes in state administration that have been engendered (or accentuated) by lawyers, however, have been or will necessarily be in the direction of greater openness and citizen involvement. Arguably, it is possible even in relatively democratic states to understand the emergence of the bar as representing and reinforcing a privatization and commercialization of functions, some of which may previously have been performed by civil service, with results that may privilege those possessing the means and disposition to avail themselves of private legal services (particularly given the paucity of publicly funded or pro bono lawyering in the region). And as the Enron debacle suggests, for all the rhetoric to the contrary, lawyers may at times limit, rather than foster, transparency.

Furthermore, particularly in those states that are not liberal democracies, there is the possibility that some in the bar may form corporatist alliances with officials that shroud the exercise of power and rent-seeking behavior, creating an incentive structure that may work to impede, rather than promote, further legal, economic, and political liberalization (lest they lose their privileged positions), as my chapter on the PRC in this volume suggests. This may even lead to a cabining in legal channels of energies that might more fruitfully be devoted to fundamental political change of the very type needed for liberal legality to flourish.

The expansion in the bar's size and significance also has consequences for the judiciary and nonjudicial dispute resolution. The prime salutary effects include the growth of an additional constituency for legality, not to mention the widening of the pool (at least in some jurisdictions) from which jurists might be chosen.[7] But, as was the case with respect to state administration, the bar's growth also poses difficult challenges to the ways in which disputes have previously been resolved. With respect to informal means of dealing with disputes (such as mediation), the rise of lawyers has had the effect, intended or otherwise, of diverting attention, resources, and prestige away from such societally based mechanisms to more state-centered processes. This is not to romanticize informality, which clearly has problems of its own, but to note that traditional informal means of dispute resolution or redressing grievances may have been more accessible to some sectors of society (particularly in rural regions) than newer,

---

6. The full quote reads "for the people to actively form, maintain, and develop diversified social connections as autonomous being, the legal profession . . . [has the responsibility to] provide legal services in response to the specific living conditions of each individual . . . as the so-called 'doctors for the people's social lives.'" (Shihō Seido Kaikaku Shingikai 2001).

7. Japan, for instance, has endeavored to draw more jurists from the ranks of practitioners.

more formalized processes requiring lawyers are so far proving to be.[8] And conversely, particularly in countries with judicial systems that have yet firmly to establish themselves, one cannot assume that the courts will necessarily always benefit from the growth of a legal profession. Accounts abound of corrupt lawyers exacerbating the problems that plague China's fragile judicial system (Alford, in this volume). And the turn to arbitration, spurred in important part by the bar, in some jurisdictions arguably creates the equivalent of a private system of justice that absorbs cases involving major economic actors, especially from abroad, which might otherwise provide an impetus for improving the state's adjudicatory processes (Alford 1992; Dezalay and Garth 1996).

The development of the legal profession in East Asia also has had important implications in terms of integrating the region's nations into the international community, be it in an economic, political, or social sense. On the economic front, lawyers, particularly the increasing numbers who have been trained abroad, appear to have a vital bridging role to play. This manifests itself in their provision of opinion letters, contracts, and other documentation required for foreign investment, technology transfer, and an array of other transactions.[9] It is also evident in the role that lawyers play in constructing and staffing institutions that may harmonize with those found in economically advanced nations. And additionally, it is to be found in the broker-like functions that lawyers perform in facilitating the entry of foreign actors into societies perceived as relatively difficult to penetrate and in reassuring them once they have commenced business there (through the phenomenon of educated elites sharing a perceived commitment to legality). Politically, with the language of international relations increasingly taking on at least the visage of legality, lawyers are coming to play an enhanced role in both their nation's overall interface with the larger world and in conveying the norms and expectations of that broader community to a domestic audience. This was illustrated in Indonesia where, as Dan Lev and David Trubek have shown, lawyers in the early 1990s were a prime conduit for communicating international human rights norms and seeking their vindication at the national level, albeit with something less than full success (Lev 2000; Trubek et al. 1994). And this has been the case in a range of other areas touching on the fabric of society, as lawyers, in introducing international standards concerning the environment, gender and a range of other issues, have linked their societies to the world beyond their borders, consciously or otherwise.

---

8. As my work on debates surrounding the recent revision of China's marriage law suggests, endowing people with new rights in and of itself may be of limited utility in situations where access to formal institutions to vindicate said rights is curtailed, where facilitators such as lawyers have little incentive to be of help, and where the decisions of such institutions are likely to have little impact on distant defendants (Alford and Shen 2004).

9. The growing suppleness of the corporate form and the intentional fragmentation of production processes place an added responsibility on such documentation to address risks or otherwise fulfill functions that in earlier days might have been discharged within a single corporate entity or a single national setting.

Given this impact, it is unfortunate that the legal profession in East Asia has yet to be a prime topic for serious scholarly inquiry, either inside the region or outside. This is attributable to a number of factors, including the novel nature of many of the developments this volume treats and lingering perceptions among historians, social scientists and others of law as relatively insignificant in explaining either history or contemporary affairs in the region's major societies (Alford 1997). It may also be due to the ongoing formal doctrinal orientation of a good deal of legal scholarship throughout the area and the absorption in intense, short-term policy debates on these very issues of the energies of members of the bar and others who might otherwise be well positioned to write about such matters.

Yet a further reason for this inattention may lie in the fact that, to the extent that the profession in East Asia has been addressed, much of the scholarship focused on it and other pertinent writings (that might, for instance, discuss the legal profession in the course of examining broader issues of economic or political change), have operated on an assumption of convergence, typically toward a "western" and, especially more recently, an "American" model of lawyering (Alford, in this volume). This, ironically enough, may have diminished the impetus for an in-depth examination of the profession in East Asia, given the assumption, conscious or unwitting, that we are already familiar with its likely trajectory.

The most pervasive strand of such thinking about convergence is anchored in a socio-economic vision that associates the development of formal legal institutions with the movement of societies toward greater rationality, particularly as market economies industrialize (Alford, in this volume). Although its antecedents predate the twentieth century, the modern social scientific foundation of this understanding of the profession lies both in the historical sociology of Max Weber, who saw the presence of a legal profession as an important indication of the formation of a societal infrastructure that might foster the rationality and predictability needed to spur economic development, and in the functionalism of Talcott Parsons, who understood legal professionals as discharging what he identified as the vital function of bridging public and private interests (Weber 1954; Parsons 1954). It is perhaps no coincidence that the deans of the two most prominent American law schools at the dawn of the twenty-first century, Robert Clark of Harvard and Anthony Kronman of Yale, were multidisciplinary scholars whose most noted writing outside the law deals with Weber and Parsons, respectively, and who, in their institutional roles, evidenced a deep-seated faith in convergence, as both a descriptive and a normative matter (Alford, in this volume). This sense of an inevitable convergence toward an American model of the legal profession both permeates scholarly writing by leading American scholars concerned with the sociology of the profession and informs a great deal of developmental work (Alford, in this volume and 2000).

Without doubt, as earlier suggested in this chapter, the development of the legal profession in East Asia has been spurred by forces shaping the profession elsewhere, as is perhaps most powerfully evident with respect to economic considerations. In one sense, economic globalization is nothing new, as the Chinese, to take but one notable example, have for centuries been spreading capital, technology, labor, and more throughout the world. Yet, in another sense, particularly since the ebbing of the Cold War, the scope, nature and pace of this phenomenon has, arguably, taken on a different magnitude in which, for example, historically utilized clan, regional and other informal networks do not necessarily suffice to meet the demands of actors such as multilateral organizations and major financial institutions concerned about the conditions on which loans are made or multinational enterprises whose production, franchising or need for skilled workers may be near global in reach. Nor are such economic considerations wholly externally generated, as growing marketization in China and elsewhere, the rise of new industrial enterprises throughout the region, and the diffusion of corporate ownership in at least some jurisdictions have put more of a premium on arm's length transactions, greater transparency and accountability of the type that a growth of legalization, and with it lawyers, would seem to hold the promise of satisfying (Alford 1995).

As the experience of the overseas Chinese shows, globalization has long been about more than economic expansion alone. Considering our own era, one could well want to move beyond the disturbingly chauvinistic notion of an end of history while still acknowledging the impact throughout much of East Asia of political and social currents that have found expression throughout large parts of the world, be it as a product of the aforementioned economic forces or by virtue of the power of the ideas they embody. On the political side, the democratization and pluralization of public life felt in at least some jurisdictions in the region has typically generated a need for more public positive law to delimit, at least in theory, the role of the state and give voice to a growing range of actors which, in turn, appears to be requiring more lawyers to write, interpret, administer, and enforce (or avoid enforcement of) such rules. Socially, factors such as the breakdown of communities—as evidenced, for instance, by the fact that China today may have at least 150 million people living other than where the household registration system (*hukou*) would have them reside—and the not unrelated growing involvement of women in life beyond the family have weakened the foundation of "traditional" mediation and other informal modes of dispute resolution, bringing with it a larger role for the state's official norms and lawyers. And although the liberating potential of the Internet has been overstated (Zittrain and Edelman 2002; Zittrain and Palfrey 2005) in a way reminiscent of the unfettered enthusiasm that greeted the new technologies of earlier eras, the ideas that it and electronic media have spread about appropriate norms are not to be dismissed as one contemplates the rise of the legal profession.[10]

---

10. This was borne out amusingly, for example, by research in which I was engaged indicating that more than half of the respondents to a survey in rural Anhui, PRC expressed an admiration for lawyers even though none had yet met (and some, indeed, expressed real reservations about meeting) any legal professionals (Alford et al. 2002). This anomaly seemed to be explained by the respondents' exposure to popular television programs depicting lawyers in a highly favorable light.

Far from ending our inquiry (let alone history), however, the acknowledgment that there are powerful forces making their impact felt across much of the globe is, arguably, but the departure point for the more intriguing matter of how different societies—diverse in their histories, cultural backgrounds, institutional structures, and economic and other resources—have engaged such forces. This, in turn, opens up a raft of questions warranting our attention. For instance, to what degree have particular societies (or important segments within them) turned to law, rather than extralegal resources such as extended networks, cosmopolitan business consultants, joint ventures, or insurance, to address such challenges as the need to deal with (relative) strangers—and why so? Has this turn toward formal legality dictated a similar need for legal professionals throughout the region—and why so or why not? How have those actors embracing foreign models of a legal profession understood that upon which they are drawing and what expectations have they and their society more broadly had as they have done so? What has been the character of competition between different models of lawyering, given the discernible shift in recent years in Japan, Korea, China, Taiwan and other parts of the region away from the civil law example toward that of the common law? How compatible has the common law model of the profession been with public institutions framed more along continental lines, not to mention with the institutions and values of such societies more broadly? To what extent have foreign models had their desired impact and to what degree have they produced unintended consequences or willfully been used to generate results seemingly at odds with their stated purposes (as, for example, in legitimizing repression)? Who is winning, who is losing and who may believe (accurately or otherwise) that they are winning or losing by virtue of these developments? How have those from beyond the region advocating development of the legal profession and the adoption of foreign models thereof understood and presented their own experience? What impact is the development of the bar in East Asia having on the profession, both in those societies that may have provided models and in the articulation of transnational norms? What does this tell us about globalization in and beyond the law? And what does all this suggest about the nature and defining attributes of the legal profession and its relation to the development of the rule of law, market economies, and liberal democracy, be it in East Asia or elsewhere?

The chapters that comprise this volume do not purport, either individually or even collectively, to answer all these questions or the many others prompted by the changes underway regarding the legal profession in East Asia. They do, however, represent an effort by an eclectic group of scholars from the United States and East Asia trained in law, history, sociology, and economics, among other disciplines, to portray and understand this phenomenon from a variety of perspectives and so, we hope, to open it up for broader consideration. We have grouped the chapters geographically, given the different approaches that the contributors have, in some instances, taken toward events within the same jurisdiction, although reading them as a whole, one is struck by the ways in which developments in one part of the region echo those occurring in its other precincts, even if national pride, professional insularity, and linguistic, political and other differences have resulted in less explicit cross-border fertilization and intra-area comparison than might be optimal.

Korea was at the forefront of debates regarding a re-imagining of the bar in East Asia and this volume therefore commences with three contributions concerning the legal profession in that nation. The first chapter, by Professor Sang-Hyun Song of Seoul National University (SNU), entitled "The Education and Training of the Legal Profession in Korea: Problems and Prospects for Reform," offers a careful history of the ways in which the men and (relatively few) women who have filled the ranks of Korea's bar, judiciary and prosecutorial offices have been prepared for the responsible positions they have come to occupy in their nation's life. In so doing, Song, who was the first Korean to opt for a career in academe after passing the bar and who later became dean of his law faculty (as well as a visiting professor at Harvard and an inaugural member of the International Criminal Court), focuses both on pertinent dimensions of the personal background of Korea's legal professionals (examining, for instance, their regional and educational origins) and on the institutions involved in their education and professional certification, including universities, the so-called National Judicial Service Examination, and the state-sponsored Judicial Research and Training Institute (JRTI). Notwithstanding his eminence in the world of Korean legal education (leading to his being asked to play a central role in earlier efforts to rethink the academy's relation to the profession), Song remains critical of the current system, believing that it has limited access to the profession and encouraged schools and students to devote far too much time to rote exam preparation in lieu of learning to think critically. Meaningful improvement, he suggests, will come only with across-the-board reform that speaks to the size of the profession, the nature of legal education, and the role of the JRTI.

In "Legal Profession and Legal Culture during Korea's Transition to Democracy and a Market Economy," Professor JaeWon Kim, Dean of Dong-A University College of Law and a member of a major national commission charged with rethinking university legal education, argues that, for all its accomplishments, the Korean legal profession bears culpability (along, to be sure, with many other actors) both for the long period of authoritarian rule the country suffered commencing under President Park Chung-Hee and for the trauma of the Asian financial crisis of the late 1990s. In particular, he attributes this to what he terms the small size and parochial nature of the Korean legal profession. Prior to the current reforms, Korea's lawyers, he notes, overwhelmingly came from a relatively small circle, the vast majority being men who had graduated from a single university, SNU. This inbreeding, in turn, was heightened by the requirement that all bar-passers spend the next two years at the JRTI which, he suggests, immersed them in a curriculum oriented toward the judiciary's interests and provided an intense bonding experience. A prime consequence of all this, he contends, was to meld legal professionals too closely together, making it difficult for prosecutors to exercise independence and private lawyers to take on clients at odds either with the state or with major corporate interests linked closely to the government.

Legal academics, bemoans Kim (who earned a J.D. degree at American University in Washington, D.C.), have not been able to offset or even fruitfully criticize the ingrown nature of the legal profession, as "there exists little interaction in Korea between university law faculties and the realm of legal practice." Having no direct experience in practice, all too many faculty have been, in his mind, overly focused on a highly formalistic exposition of doctrine having too little appeal for university students who have already benefited from what, in Kim's view, is Korean "credentialism" and who have been more concerned with devoting their college years to mastering materials they believe will appear on the bar exam than to probing inquiry. Change, to be sure, has begun to come, both through what Kim sees as exemplary public-minded lawyers whose lives' work demonstrates alternative uses to which law may be put and through a new generation of legal academics having a greater interest in the law's societal implications. The introduction of so-called American-style approaches to legal education and with it, a marked expansion of the bar, has, he suggests, the potential to accelerate this trend and so transform the Korean profession in ways that would foster the further growth of political and economic democracy while also better equipping Korea to compete globally against foreign entities well served by adept legal professionals. Even though initial efforts to promote this agenda ran into considerable opposition from throughout the legal profession and legal academy, in Kim's view they have already shifted the focus of the reform "to reflect the perspective of the consumer, not of the supplier" (Kim, in this volume).

Yves Dezalay and Bryant Garth, authors of the third chapter concerned with Korea—"International Strategies and Local Transformations: Preliminary Observations of the Position of Law in the Field of State Power in Asia: South Korea"—share Kim's concerns about the Korean legal profession, but take an appreciably less sanguine view of the possibility that American and other foreign models and actors may have a constructive role to play in its reform. Having completed a major study of the ways in which lawyers, economists and other "national actors" in Latin America deployed "international strategies" in their "palace wars" (Dezalay and Garth 2002), Garth, who was until recently president of the American Bar Foundation, and Dezalay, who is a director at the Centre national de la recherché scientifique (CNRS) in Paris, use their contribution to this volume as a first step in launching a similar inquiry with respect to East Asia. Drawing on some thirty interviews conducted chiefly with Korean lawyers educated in the United States and American lawyers of Korean ancestry working in Seoul not admitted to the bar in Korea, Dezalay and Garth conclude that the "traditional position of legal professionals in Korea, therefore, provides a remarkable contrast to that seen in Latin America. Lawyers have higher prestige in Korea, but they are not connected to power and cannot even reproduce their own relatively prestigious position through their families" (Dezalay and Garth, in this volume).

Dezalay and Garth trace the seeming irony of lawyers enjoying high prestige but relatively limited power to what they characterize as "the fundamental historical illegitimacy of the law" emanating from the association of modern legality to the period of Japanese occupation during the first half of the twentieth century. This initial illegitimacy was only overcome, they suggest, through the establishment of a bar exam which, until recently, no more than 2 percent passed, thereby cultivating for the profession an image of merit-based accomplishment. This artificial scarcity, in turn, both legitimated the profession and helped generate considerable wealth for many of its members, but it has had attendant costs for lawyers, not to mention society more broadly. These include the near manic absorption of young prospective lawyers in preparation for the exam that diverts their energies from political affairs, an inability of those in the bar to ensure that their offspring would be able to follow in their shoes, and, most significantly, the irrelevance of this small group of actors to "the major family business groups, the *chaebol* [which] . . . did not need lawyers for their [all-important] relations with the state, since the major business leaders dealt directly and personally with state representatives" (Dezalay and Garth, in this volume).

In this mix, suggest Dezalay and Garth, "international strategies" have begun to "play an ambiguous role." While they have at times reinforced the existing examination-based structure of Korean society, foreign resources have also been used in two other respects that are, in effect, re-writing the rules even as they may be reinforcing hierarchy. The first, as Dezalay and Garth indicate, is that some Korean lawyers who have succeeded by traditional criteria have been able to utilize models taken from the U.S. to enhance the profession's power by making "places for the law and lawyers in major transactions involving the state and the economy," be it as political actors, advisors to *chaebol* leaders, or even as activists on behalf of nongovernmental organizations (Dezalay and Garth, in this volume). The second has been to provide a growing number of individuals who may have fallen short in their attempts to attain conventionally understood indicia of success in the law with an alternative path to remunerative and prestigious employment. Each of these uses of the foreign, the authors conclude, has eased some of the pressure that the established hierarchy might otherwise feel, thereby, ironically, facilitating its continuation.

The vast, intricate, and contentious political stakes involved in efforts to remake the Japanese bar are laid out in Setsuo Miyazawa's contribution to this volume, entitled "The Politics of Judicial Reform in Japan: The Rule of Law at Last?" In it, Miyazawa draws not only on a rich academic background (he holds doctoral degrees in law from Hokkaido and in sociology from Yale, and has taught in leading Japanese law faculties—including Waseda University and Kobe University—and at Harvard, NYU, Boalt Hall, and UCLA), but also takes advantage of his own active role in the debates (including his participation in two journals heavily focused on these issues—*Gekkan Shihō Kaikaku* (Journal of Judicial Reform) and *Kausa* (Cause) and his assumption of a senior leadership role in the newly established Omiya Law School). The result is a chapter that discusses in careful and heretofore unavailable detail the history of the substantive considerations and political factors at play in both the drive to revamp the Japanese system and resistance thereto.

Of particular interest is the insight Miyazawa sheds on the somewhat unusual alliances formed in the course of these debates. For instance, proponents of a large-scale revision of the prevailing system included major Japanese businesses and civil rights lawyers, each motivated by the hope that reform would both bring a considerable expansion of the bar (thereby providing cheaper and more accessible services) and also lead lawyers to take bolder stances vis-à-vis the state. On the other side, the prospect of such change has brought together many in the legal academy, the judiciary, and the bureaucracy who would not normally be aligned. They are drawn together, suggests Miyazawa, by their concerns about the deleterious impact that the proposed major adjustments may have on undergraduate law programs (which have heretofore been the principal locus of university-based legal education), on the role of the judiciary's Legal Training and Research Institute (both in and of itself and as a vehicle for socializing future lawyers into the norms preferred by the bench) and on the manner in which Japanese lawyers interact with the state. Notwithstanding the lines drawn in the Justice System Reform Council's report, the battle rages on in the process of implementation, which ought not to be surprising, given that at least some actors, according to Miyazawa, see this as involving a struggle for accountability, justice, and, even, the very soul of Japanese society.

Ryo Hamano's chapter, "The Turn Toward Law: The Emergence of Corporate Law Firms in Contemporary Japan," continues the impressive research he has been conducting for more than a decade on Japanese business lawyers. Drawing, inter alia, on survey data he compiled, Hamano, who is a professor of law at Rikkyō University, traces major trends in Japanese business-related practice. He notes, for instance, that large, internationally oriented firms in particular have grown more rapidly than other forms of legal practice in Japan, even if they remain modest by North American or British standards. With this, he suggests, has come increasing wealth, prestige and a growing degree of political and social influence.

Nonetheless, Hamano argues, the position of Japanese lawyers was a marginal one for much of the post-war era, subordinate to that of civil servants and technocrats much in the way, he intimates, that law was for much of this era itself secondary in importance to administration and to business in setting the course of Japanese development. The marginality of law and lawyers may even have intensified from the 1960s until the 1990s. This he attributes to what he characterizes as the marked self-restraint and deference of the bar to decision-making by the political branches of government following the Liberal Democratic Party's efforts to limit left-leaning judges in the 1970s and to the small size of the profession, which he sees as a product both of lawyers' concern with preserving their monopoly and of the appreciation by the state bureaucracy that an increase in the bar might "threaten their power and influence" (Hamano, in this volume).

Although Hamano argues that some of what he describes as "inertia is culturally influenced and systemically rooted" and so amenable to change "only little by little," he also is of the view that the situation is not necessarily a stable one. The Japanese "business and political elite," he suggests, "may have come to realize that the segmentation and marginalization of the legal domain is weakening the bases of their very power and rule, such as the sustained growth of the Japanese economy (Hamano, in this volume)." This, in turn, is leading them to be more supportive of attempts both to rethink the profession and to promote greater judicial independence, as evidenced, inter alia, in their support for the findings of the Justice System Reform Council.

Another manifestation of change that has begun to be felt in the Japanese legal profession lies in the substantial growth of the number and role of in-house counsel. This is the subject of "Globalization of Japanese Corporations and the Development of Corporate Legal Departments: Problems and Prospects" by Professor Toshimitsu Kitagawa of the Faculty of Law of Kyushu University and Professor Luke Nottage of the Faculty of Law of the University of Sydney. Drawing on the survey work done by the Business Management-Related Law Association, also known as the Association of Japanese Corporate Legal Departments (*keiei hōyūkai*), and the Japanese Association of Business Law, Inc., also known as the Commercial Law Center, Inc. (*shōji hōmu kenkyūkai*), Kitagawa, who worked as corporate legal counsel to Toshiba for some thirty years before becoming a full-time academic, and Nottage paint the most thorough picture to date in English of this heretofore little-publicized but now increasingly important phenomenon.

Prior to the 1970s, Japanese corporations had relatively small legal departments that typically had a negligible role in setting corporate policy. Generally staffed by some of the legion of law graduates who did not pass the bar exam, Japanese law departments, unlike their U.S. counterparts, offered scant prospect of promotion in the corporate hierarchy. In the 1980s and 1990s, legal departments began to take on broader responsibilities and assume increased prominence within the larger corporate structure. This, the authors suggest, was driven in important part by domestic concerns, most notably the growing pertinence and complexity of Japanese legislation, particularly in areas such as corporate governance, intellectual property, and product liability. External considerations, to be sure, also played a role, both as Japanese enterprises (especially trading companies) sought to enter into new types of cross-border transactions and as Japan increasingly became intertwined with global and foreign regulatory structures in areas such as trade and export controls (with respect to both of which Kitagawa draws on direct experience from his days at Toshiba).

As a consequence of such pressures, both domestic and foreign, Kitagawa and Nottage show that the legal departments of at least some major Japanese corporations have begun to change. Most significantly, they demonstrate that legal departments have begun to broaden their range of activity (reaching, for example, further into transactional work and preparations for events such as shareholders' meetings and even into areas such as antitrust). This, in turn, has led in some instances to a greater involvement of legal department personnel with senior management than had previously been the case. It is also leading a growing number of companies to "strengthen their departments by [inter alia] . . . employing . . . those qualified as *bengoshi* or other legal professionals," even as it is driving legal departments to a more business-oriented approach toward the retention of outside counsel, be they Japanese or foreign. All this, conclude Kitagawa and Nottage, is adding to the impetus for the type of reforms in the Japanese legal profession and legal training discussed in the Justice System Reform Council report and in the Miyazawa chapter in this volume.

This volume's three chapters concerning the Chinese world illustrate the need for caution in extrapolating generalizations about the role of lawyers from liberal democratic to more authoritarian settings. My own chapter, entitled "Of Lawyers Lost and Found: Searching for Legal Professionalism in the People's Republic of China," contends that most American (and other foreign) observers have seriously misjudged the character of China's rapidly expanding legal profession. Most often, they have assumed that lawyers in China will serve as a vanguard for major changes, including the rule of law, a market economy, and even liberal democracy. In the words of Anthony Kronman, Dean of Yale Law School from 1994 to 2004, "I was impressed by the extent to which lawyers had penetrated the process . . . . They are on their way to a very different system of adjudication" (quoted in Alford, in this volume). Such statements are of consequence not only in the academic arena, but also in the realm of affairs, as the United States government (among other important foreign actors) has made the development of the rule of law—which it is assumed Chinese lawyers will play a pre-eminent role in bringing about—a central tenet of policy toward China.

My own research, based in part on extensive interviewing of business lawyers in Beijing (who typically have had more education and greater exposure to international norms than the average Chinese practitioner) suggests that far from challenging the status quo, many PRC lawyers have, in fact, been reinforcing it. Too often, they appear to have entered into corporatist alliances with the regime, willing in the face of considerable pecuniary rewards to forego professional autonomy, let alone the possibility of using the law to press for systemic change in a party/state many know to be corrupt and authoritarian.

The failure of outside observers to be more discerning is in part explicable by the unwillingness of many foreign observers to examine Chinese conditions closely enough. It is further abetted both by the idealism of others who see law as providing an avenue for the "peaceful evolution" of Chinese society and by the cynicism of yet others for whom slogans regarding the rule of law provide a convenient way to avoid addressing China's authoritarianism. But more interestingly, as I endeavor to demonstrate through an examination of Kronman's work on the legal profession, this misreading emanates from a naïveté about the power of professionalism to overcome other values and institutions which, in turn, is premised on a flawed understanding of the history of our own legal profession in the U.S.

If my own chapter focuses chiefly on what Heinz and Laumann have described as the "upper hemisphere" of the legal profession, Benjamin Liebman's contribution to this volume—"Lawyers, Legal Aid, and Legitimacy in China"—concentrates principally on what they would term its "lower hemisphere" (Heinz and Laumann 1982). Liebman's chapter represents a departure from the bulk of prior work on these topics. That work has been largely descriptive—essentially chronicling legal aid and public interest law in the PRC with little, if any, self-consciousness as to the possible need to adjust the metric used in examining these activities in the United States. Liebman takes a far more thoughtful approach, exploring fundamental questions about such key issues as the meaning of "public interest" and of legal assistance in a setting in which the state continues to endeavor to define the public's interest and to reach into all sectors of society, including the bar.

Drawing on an extensive series of interviews with officials, lawyers and academics conducted in a number of Chinese cities throughout the late 1990s, Liebman identifies five models for the provision of legal aid, ranging from government-funded full-time legal aid lawyers to university-based legal assistance. Although he is cautious in extrapolating conclusions, given how new so much of this is, Liebman offers an intriguing and nuanced picture. The PRC has been appreciably more vigorous than many other nations, especially in the developing world, in mandating that lawyers provide legal aid. This has assisted a growing number of Chinese in securing legal protection—which, he suggests, is something that foreign actors concerned with international human rights should note. Yet, Liebman argues, we should not forget that the official mandate to engage in legal aid is, in the Chinese setting, indicative of the state's ongoing strong oversight of lawyers even as it offers one potential vehicle through which lawyers may in time come increasingly to find professional definition and assert themselves. And, he counsels, we should be mindful that "developing even a quasi-independent bar requires changing the attitudes of lawyers as much as it requires loosening state regulation of the legal profession" (Liebman, in this volume). In sum, it is simply too early even now to know the extent to which the involvement of lawyers in legal aid will foster the autonomy of lawyers and the the law.

This volume's final two chapters—dealing, respectively with Taiwan, and then Malaysia and Indonesia—further underscore the importance of the institutional context in defining the role of lawyers. Jane Kaufman Winn's chapter—entitled "The Role of Lawyers in Taiwan's Emerging Democracy"—continues her probing work into the nature of legality and lawyers on Taiwan. Winn sees the martial law and one-party rule that characterized the first four decades of the ROC on Taiwan as having had a searing effect on lawyers, preventing them from developing during that period into an autonomous profession of the type found in liberal democratic states. She does acknowledge that some members of the bar were able to play a role in the political transformation of the past two decades and that "the process of democratization and liberalization in Taiwan generally is creating more opportunities for lawyers to move the legal profession further in the direction of autonomy and the ideals of professionalism." Nonetheless, she remains concerned about possible impediments to continued "movement toward an independent profession that would enhance the rule of law in Taiwanese society" (Winn, in this volume).

One such impediment is what she describes as the excessive commercialization of the legal profession which she believes will be accentuated as Taiwan liberalizes its economy and further opens itself to international competition. These forces, she is quick to point out, are also posing significant challenges to professional ideals in the West, but with "less of a history of liberal professionalism to fall back on" and a less complete democratic state at home, she fears that the Taiwanese bar may be less well positioned to cope with this "rising tide of entrepreneurial thinking within the modern professions" (Winn, in this volume). The challenge confronting lawyers on Taiwan may yet be further exacerbated, she suggests, by opportunities that are opening for them on the Chinese mainland which, with its corruption and greater reliance on *guanxi*, may ironically reinforce the tendency to serve as "fixers" which the ROC profession might otherwise have been shedding, given Taiwanese society's movement toward greater, if still incomplete, democratization.

The volume's final chapter—"A Tale of Two Legal Professions: Lawyers and State in Malaysia and Indonesia"—is a thoughtful comparative exploration by Daniel Lev, the most distinguished western scholar of his generation of the law of those two nations. Lev's chapter revolves around the question of why the legal professions of these two nations—which share some features—have developed in such different ways. Although not without its own problems, particularly in recent years, Malaysia's profession, he suggests, "is well trained, highly organized, and influential," whereas its Indonesian counterpart has been "divided, not always well trained, weakly organized, and professionally only marginally influential" (Lev, in this volume).

It is tempting, Lev suggests, to attribute such differences to variables such as the common law/civil law divide, differing colonial experiences, and culture itself. But, he continues, there is obviously much more at stake. Ultimately, according to Lev, the most important variables are political structure and organization, economic organization, and the ideology and interests of political and professional elites. These, he concludes, have been the prime forces in shaping the legal profession which, in turn, has operated so as to reinforce these very variables.

A decade ago, when the idea for this conference first began to germinate, it was difficult to convince scholars either of East Asia or of the legal profession more generally that there was much of a rationale, other than professional self-interest, for studying lawyers in that part of the world. The events of the past decade have clearly shown that skepticism to have been unwarranted and the topic to be one providing a window into much broader changes underway throughout the region and in its relations with the world beyond. If lawyers have proven not to be as inconsequential a subject for study as the conventional wisdom a decade ago would have suggested, it, nonetheless, behooves us today not to fall into the opposite trap of assuming an easy path of convergence along the lines of an American model, as the conventional wisdom would suggest. Indeed, if there is any single lesson that emerges from the fascinating case studies that comprise the heart of this volume, it is that only through the careful study of the interplay of ideas and practice can one begin to discern how lawyers shape their society while simultaneously being shaped by it.

Works Cited

Alford, William P. 1992. International commercial arbitration: an idiosyncratic overview. *Korean Forum on International Trade and Business Law.*

———. 1995. Tasselled loafers for barefoot lawyers: Transformations and tensions in the world of Chinese lawyers. *China Quarterly* 141:22. Reprinted in *China's Legal Reforms,* ed. S.B. Lubman. 1996. New York: Oxford University Press.

———. 1997. Law, law, what law? Why Western scholars of Chinese history and society have not had more to say about its law. *Modern China* 23:398.

———. 2000. Exporting the 'pursuit of happiness.' 113 *Harvard Law Review* 1677.

———. 2003. The more law, the more . . . ? Measuring legal reform in the People's Republic of China. In *How far across the river? Chinese policy reform at the millennium,* eds. N. C. Hope, D. T. Yang, and M. Y. Li. Palo Alto: Stanford University Press.

——— and Yuanyuan Shen. 2004. Have you eaten? Have you divorced? Debating the meaning of freedom in marriage in China. In *Realms of Freedom in Modern China,* ed. W. Kirby. Palo Alto: Stanford University Press.

———, Robert P. Weller, Leslyn Hall, Karen R. Polenske, Yuanyuan Shen, and David Zweig. 2002. The human dimension of pollution policy implementation: air quality in rural China. *Journal of Contemporary China* 11 (32): 495.

Dezalay, Yves and Bryant G. Garth. 1996. *Dealing in virtue: International commercial arbitration and the construction of a transnational legal order.* Chicago: University of Chicago Press.

———. 2002. *The internationalization of palace wars: Lawyers, economists, and the contest to transform Latin American states.* Chicago: University of Chicago Press.

Galanter, Marc. 1992a. Pick a number, any number. *American Lawyer* (April): 82.

———. 1992b. Re-entering the Mythical Kingdom: Numbers on the world's lawyers are hard to come by. 18 *ABA Journal* 118 (November): 1.

Haley, John Owen. 1991. *Authority without power: Law and the Japanese paradox.* New York: Oxford University Press.

Heinz, John P. and Edward O. Laumann. 1982. *Chicago lawyers: The social structure of the bar.* New York: Russell Stage Foundation; Chicago: American Bar Association.

Lev, Daniel. 2000. *Legal evolution and political authority in Indonesia: Selected essays.* The Hague and Boston: Kluwer Law International.

Parsons, Talcott. 1954. *Essays in sociological theory.* 2nd edition. Glencoe, IL: Free Press.

Ramseyer, J. Mark and Minoru Nakazato. 1998. *Japanese law: An economic approach.* Chicago: University of Chicago Press.

Shihō Seido Kaikaku Shingikai [Justice System Reform Council]. 2001. *Recommendations of the Justice System Reform Council—For a justice system to support Japan in the 21st century.* Official English translation at the website of the Prime Minister of Japan at http://www.kantei.go.jp/foreign/judiciary/2001 /0612report.html.

Trubek, David, Yves Dezalay, Ruth Buchanan, and John Davis. 1994. The future of the legal profession: Global restructuring and the law: Studies in the internationalization of legal fields and the creation of transnational arenas. 44 *Case Western Reserve Law Review* 407.

Weber, Max. 1954. *Max Weber on law in economy and society.* Edited and annotated by Max Rheinstein; translated from Max Weber, *Wirtschaft und Gesellschaft,* 2nd ed. (1925) by Edward Shils and Max Rheinstein. Cambridge, MA: Harvard University Press.

Yanagida, Yukio. 2000. A new paradigm of legal training and education in Japan. 1 *Asian-Pacific Law & Policy Journal* 1. An electronic copy may be seen at the *Journal* website at http://www.hawaii.edu/aplpj/pdfs/01-yanagida.pdf.

Zittrain, Jonathan and Benjamin Edelman. 2002. *Empirical analysis of Internet filtering in China.* Berkman Center for Internet & Society, Harvard Law School. Http://cyber.law.harvard.edu/filtering/china.

——— and John Palfrey, Jr. 2005. *Documentation of Internet filtering worldwide: Country studies on Bahrain, China, Iran, Saudi Arabia, Singapore, the United Arab Emirates, Vietnam, and Yemen.* Cambridge, MA: Berkman Center for Internet & Society, Harvard Law School, and the OpenNet Initiative.

ONE

The Education and Training of the Legal Profession in Korea: Problems and Prospects for Reform

Sang-Hyun Song*

Introduction

It has become customary to begin academic papers dealing with the Republic of Korea with at least a cursory reference to the dramatic social, economic, and political changes that have occurred there during the past forty years. Indeed, it is almost impossible to discuss any aspect of Korea without reference to these changes, for they have left virtually no area of Korean life unaffected. The legal system and the legal profession are, of course, no exception, and the rapid changes that Korea has undergone have created special demands on legal professionals. Economic development has created a need for competent legal professionals to assist in the negotiation and drawing up of commercial contracts, to resolve or litigate economic disputes, and to assist clients as they navigate through increasingly complex economic regulations.

The rise of a middle class has been accompanied by an increased consciousness of rights, creating a demand for attorneys to represent clients in civil litigation and defense trials. Further, a more open political process and the transition from authoritarian rule to the rule of law has created the need for trained legal professionals[1] to administer the judicial organs of the state, to represent citizens addressing grievances against the state, and to otherwise participate in the democratic process. In addition, Korea's emergence as a major player on the world economic stage, notwithstanding the financial crisis of 1997, indicates the need for legal professionals who can competently advise both the government and Korean businesses on the legal aspects of international transactions, especially since Korea joined the World Trade Organization (WTO) in 1995 and the Organization for Economic Co-operation and Development (OECD) in 1996.

---

*Professor of Law at Seoul National University and Judge of the International Criminal Court. The views expressed in this chapter do not represent those of the ICC.

1. For the purposes of this chapter, the term "legal professional" is used to refer to all lawyers, including all judges, prosecutors, and private attorneys. The term "attorney" is used to refer only to those lawyers engaged in the private practice of law.

However, Korea's rapid economic progress was not initially accompanied by political liberalization. It has only been in the last decade that the legal system in Korea was allowed to develop in the direction of the open democratic processes that more appropriately correspond to the new economic and social realities in Korea. The development of the judiciary as an independent entity was stunted by the military dictatorships that governed Korea until the early 1990s. Judges and prosecutors served at the pleasure of the president, and judicial independence existed in name only.[2] This had several implications for the selection and training of legal professionals in Korea, the most important of which is that legal education was seen as a method of training judges and prosecutors as government bureaucrats in the service of the state.

Legal professionals have always been selected by an exam administered by the executive branch of the government, and their professional training focused almost exclusively on their roles as judges and prosecutors. There was no perceived need to train attorneys to represent clients in civil or criminal cases, since parties to lawsuits and even criminal defendants were expected to simply plead their cases to judges, who served as inquisitors as well as judges. In addition, since the government needed only enough apprentices to fill the small number of positions available as judges or prosecutors, less than 2 percent of aspiring law students passed the National Judicial Service Examination (judicial exam). The size of the Korean bar is still extremely small, especially when compared with the United States. Finally, since the training provided to young judges and prosecutors was primarily administrative and functional in nature, it had little in common with the academic education they had received as law majors at their respective universities.

These shortcomings of legal education evolved and were maintained during the authoritarian regimes of Korea's recent history. Although law professors and others have prepared several proposals for change, it has only been in the past decade that they have had any realistic chance of being properly addressed. The democratization of the political process, and the increased participation and transparency in corporate governance which accompanied the financial crisis of 1997, have provided many more avenues for the citizens of Korea to exercise their personal, political, and economic prerogatives. This increased consciousness has, in turn, led to an increased demand for the services of attorneys, and legal education must now be reformed to address these new demands. This

---

2. In the Korean context, judicial independence usually means independence from the influence of the executive branch of the government. Historically, Korea was very proud of its record of judicial independence as established by Mr. Kim Byung-Ro, an independence movement leader who was appointed the first chief justice in 1948. However, soon after General Park Chung-Hee seized power in 1961 through a military coup, the Supreme Court suffered from the Park regime's intervention and threats.

chapter will discuss the current state of legal education in Korea,[3] with special attention paid to formal legal education, the judicial exam, professional training at universities and at the Judicial Research and Training Institute (JRTI), and prospects for systemic reform.

I.   The Legal Education System in Korea

A.   The Role of Legal Education

One distinctive feature of legal education in Korea is that it has not been required for admission to the bar (this may change with the proposed introduction of graduate law schools in 2008). To become a judge, prosecutor, or attorney, one has only to pass the judicial exam (this too may change with the proposed phase-out of the current exam by 2013). Candidates who pass the judicial exam are then required to undertake the professional training program that is provided by the JRTI before they can be admitted to the bar. While there is no formal requirement that candidates for the exam be graduates of a law school, in practice, however, most candidates are undergraduate law school students or graduates, and it is extremely difficult for those with no legal educational background to pass the exam.[4] Therefore, the standard course of education for the vast majority of legal professionals typically includes an undergraduate law school.

B.   Law Schools in Korea

Law schools in Korea are four-year law colleges that admit high school graduates primarily on the basis of their college entrance exam scores. The first-year curriculum consists primarily of general studies, and the following three years are taken up mostly by law courses. There are around 90 law colleges and legal departments in Korea. The number of law school faculty members varies greatly, with the average number being 11. Seoul National University (SNU) was the largest in 2002 with 37 faculty members. The number of students admitted each year also varies from school to school, from 290 students at Korea University College of Law to around 40 at some small law departments. SNU College of Law had traditionally admitted 270 undergraduates each year, but the number was reduced to 205 in 2002.

   SNU College of Law is the most prestigious law school in Korea, and the majority of legal professionals are SNU graduates. This domination of the legal profession by SNU law graduates is slowly changing, however, as more and

---

3. The most comprehensive work in English on the education and training of the legal profession in Korea to date is *Education of the Legal Profession in Korea,* by James M. West (1991). Some details in this book are now out of date, but it remains a highly valuable and relevant introduction to legal education in Korea.

4. The educational background of successful candidates for the judicial exam is discussed further in Part II C of this chapter and illustrated by Table 1.4.

more non-law graduates of SNU and law majors at other universities pass the judicial exam. Until ten years ago, more than two-thirds of those who passed the exam were SNU law graduates, but in recent years, they have made up about half (Table 1.1). In May 2002, the total number of legal professionals in Korea was 9,285. As illustrated in Table 1.1, 43.1 percent of those legal professionals graduated from SNU.[5]

Table 1.1
Total Number of Legal Professionals in Korea by University, May 2002

University*	Number of successful candidates for judicial exam	Percentage of total
Seoul National University Law School	4,003	43.11
Seoul National University, non-law	1,090	11.74
Korea University	1,329	14.31
Yonsei University	555	5.98
Hanyang University	462	4.98
Sunggyungwan University	451	4.86
Kyungpook National University	174	1.87
Pusan National University	153	1.65
Chonnam National University	113	1.22
Ewha Woman's University	59	0.64
Other universities	690	7.43
High school diploma or below	45	0.48
Japanese exchange students**	104	1.12
Unknown	57	0.61
Total	**9,285**	**100%**

* Figure for each university except Seoul National University includes law graduates as well as non-law graduates.
** Japanese exchange students are Koreans studying in Japan.

Law school graduates go into many different professions following their graduation. Only several hundred out of the roughly 9,000 annual graduates enter the legal profession as judges, prosecutors, or attorneys. However, although only a small number of students are able to pass the judicial exam, the vast majority of law students at SNU and other major universities devote themselves to preparing for the exam and try to pass while they are still in law school

5. All tables in this paper, unless otherwise noted, were created by the author using information obtained from the *Law Times* (2000); the *Roster of Attorneys* (Korean Bar Association 2002); and several telephone conversations between the author and the Korean Bar Association conducted in mid-September 2002.

or immediately following graduation. Many end up toiling to pass the exam for several years after graduation. One of the problems with this system is that although law students are very intelligent and motivated, the psychological pressure to prepare for the exam, and the great potential rewards if they are fortunate enough to pass, tend to give them tunnel vision. Their perception of vital national and global issues is curtailed by their single-minded determination to pass the judicial exam. This also has a chilling effect on the academic environment at the law schools. Whatever new courses are developed to meet the needs of Korea's changing society, and however well the courses are designed and prepared, student enthusiasm and attendance is low unless the courses deal directly with the judicial exam topics. Only those who study law in such an exam-oriented manner pass it and can become judges, prosecutors, and attorneys.

Law school graduates who would like to pursue an academic career usually enter a master's degree program for two years and then a doctoral program for another three years. A doctoral degree is absolutely required for an aspiring law professor. Many students also choose to pursue advanced legal studies abroad. The number of students who choose to pursue academic careers in the law is very small, however, primarily as a result of the orientation of legal education toward the judicial exam. The exam-oriented curriculum limits students' opportunities to explore academic discourse and intellectual developments in legal scholarship, and their opportunities for achieving maximum growth are further limited by the availability of teachers who can teach subjects beyond such a limited curriculum. This is a circular problem, of course: the lack of diversity in the curriculum tends to produce scholars who are less than adequately prepared to address academic areas which were not taught or emphasized in their own legal education. The problem is exacerbated by a shortage of law professors in general, again as a result of the pervasive influence of the judicial exam on legal education.

While law professors are accorded great respect in Korean society generally, they are not members of the legal profession because they generally do not pass or even take the judicial exam. Many judges, prosecutors, and attorneys performed better academically than their counterparts who remained in academia, and often the best and brightest law students choose to take the exam because of the tremendous prestige and financial security attendant upon passing it. The salaries of law professors are very low when compared to their counterparts who are attorneys. It has thus been difficult to attract top students to academia. Another problem related to diversity in the curriculum is that law departments tend to choose law professors exclusively from their own alumni, which can lead to academic stagnation and complacency. This problem of inbreeding is intensified by the general lack of communication between legal scholars and the legal profession, mainly because very few teachers are members of the bar.

The national exam system adversely affects graduate programs in other ways as well. For example, the SNU College of Law admits ninety students or more to the LL.M. program and as many as twenty-five to the doctoral program each year, but about 90 percent of them have their names registered purely to secure deferment from the military draft while they study for the judicial exam.

Some of these problems stem from the fact that the purposes of legal education have not been completely agreed upon in Korea. However, most agree that legal education should consist of a professional education designed to produce both legal professionals and legal scholars. One of the main criticisms directed at legal education is that law colleges put too much emphasis on theoretical legal studies centering on the exegesis of black-letter law, and that the clinical legal studies which are necessary for professionals are thus neglected. Some argue that even theoretical legal studies are not adequately taught at the colleges of law, for two main reasons. First, the absence of the linkage between formal legal education and the national exam seriously paralyzes legal education. As mentioned above, formal legal education is not a prerequisite for becoming a lawyer, and legal scholars and the legal profession function independently with very little exchange between them. Second, law is an undergraduate major in universities where many subjects are taught, and consequently, degrees may be awarded to students who have taken only thirty-three credits in legal courses (this was raised to thirty-five credits for 2006).

C.   Study Abroad and the Influence of American Legal Norms

For years, a limited number of Korean law graduates and legal professionals were able to broaden their educational horizons by pursuing advanced legal studies abroad. Typically, in the early years of the Republic, Korean legal scholars went to Germany or Japan for graduate legal studies. This trend is a reflection of the historical influences on Korea's legal system. Following liberation from Japanese colonial rule in 1945, South Korea implemented a legal system very similar to the Japanese civil law system that had been in force during the colonial period. The Japanese, in turn, had borrowed heavily from the continental system of Germany and France, modeling most of their laws on the German civil code. Thus, it was natural for most Korean legal scholars to find their way to Germany or Japan. This pattern was repeated as professors who had studied in Germany and Japan returned to teach law and legal theory in Korean universities and as a result, influenced their students.

In recent years, however, there has been a strong tendency for Korean legal scholars and professionals to study in the United States. Some scholars still choose to pursue studies in Germany, but they are primarily academics who are interested in teaching about continental law or civil legal systems. Korea is a civil law country, and there will continue to be a demand for legal scholars with expertise in civil legal systems, but the pervasive influence of Anglo-American law, especially that of the United States, has made studying in the United States a more attractive and productive option for most law students and legal professionals. The American influence on corporation law, securities regulation, merger and acquisitions law, corporate bankruptcy law, banking law, antitrust and competition law, intellectual property law, and insurance law has been pro-found in Korea. Many statutes in these areas have been modeled on the corresponding statutes and regulations in the United States. This influence on domestic Korean law, combined with the strong American influence on international trade law, has been both a product of and an impetus for the increase in the number of Korean legal scholars studying in the United States. In fact, an increasing number of legal professionals now aspire to obtain an American J.D. degree rather than an LL.M. at home or abroad.

The Korean government, recognizing the importance of American legal concepts in the formation and administration of Korean and international law and legal institutions, sponsors one-year expense-paid sabbaticals for study abroad programs for judges and prosecutors after five years of service, and competition to study at prestigious American law schools is severe. Many large law firms also offer their associates the opportunity to study for one or two years in the United States, followed by practical training at an American law firm. In both cases, the students usually acquire an LL.M. degree from an American law school, and some pass one of the state bar exams, adding the prestige of an American law degree and membership in a U.S. state bar to an already rewarding educational and professional experience.

As will be seen below, the influence of this exposure to American legal education has had a significant impact on the nature of the proposals to reform the Korean legal education system. The most recent proposal by the presidential commission charged with formulating a comprehensive reform plan for graduate and professional education bears a striking resemblance to the American three-year graduate law school system.

II.   The National Judicial Service Examination

A.   The Structure and Content of the Examination

According to the National Judicial Service Examination Act (the Act), the judicial exam itself is composed of three stages. The first is a multiple-choice test that serves as a screening device to select a manageable number of about 4,500 candidates (from around 25,000 who take the test) for the second test. The second is a written essay test, and approximately 1,000 candidates pass each year. Only a few candidates are eliminated in the third stage, which consists of interviews, and the remaining 1,000 or so are announced as successful candidates.

Until 1997, the topics for the first and second tests included English, Korean history, cultural history, introductory economics, and many other subjects that were unnecessary if one assumes that the candidates are university graduates. Retaining these exam topics could only be justified if the assumption was that candidates were not university graduates. Preparation for these topics for the particular purpose of taking the test used to cost candidates considerable time and energy that could have been used more fruitfully to cultivate their intellectual and professional capabilities. The test was revised in 1997, and many of these extraneous subjects were removed.

The Act was most recently amended in March 2001. The first part of the exam now consists of five subjects, including constitutional law, civil law, criminal law, and two electives. The electives include English and a general legal subject such as international law, labor law, competition law, and several other specialized areas of law.

B. The Controversy over the Number of Successful Examination Candidates

The fundamental difference between the judicial exam in Korea and bar exams in the United States is that the Korean exam is used as a process for selecting an outstanding few, whereas U.S. bar exams are a minimum quality control mechanism. Thus, in Korea in 2002, there was one lawyer for approximately every 5,000 people, whereas in the United States in 1997, there was one lawyer for every 286 people.

Before 1981, any candidate who scored 40 percent or higher in every subject and whose average score was 60 percent or higher passed the exam. If no one met these two score requirements, there would be no successful candidates in that year. Due to this strict grading practice, there were very few successful candidates during those years. It was an important change of policy when the government decided to pass a fixed number of 80 candidates in 1981. Subsequently, the government allowed a stable number of approximately 300 candidates to pass up until 1995. Between 1981 and 1995, the passage rate was less than 2 percent, a severe and effective control on the number of legal professionals. However, as a result of an agreement reached in 1995 by the Supreme Court, the Korean Bar Association (KBA), and the Kim Young-Sam government in connection with legal education reform, 502 candidates passed in 1996. The Presidential Commission of Education Reform had called for an annual increase of 100 successful candidates until the year 2000, when the adequacy of the number was to be reviewed. The KBA, however, exerted great pressure to keep the number to a maximum of 500 per year. An unsteady compromise was reached in 1997 and the number was held at about 700 in 1998 and 1999. In late 1999, the government finally decided to increase the number to approximately 800 in 2000 and 1,000 in 2001. See Table 1.2 for the exact figures from 1991 to 2002.

Table 1.3 shows the age distribution of successful candidates in each of the years from 1994 to 2002. It is interesting to observe that when the government allowed up to 300 candidates to pass, the average age rose from twenty-five to twenty-eight years old. When the number of passers increased to 500 or more, the average age rose to about twenty-nine years old. This means that, after the two-year training period at the JRTI, most legal professionals started their legal career when they reached thirty-one.

As indicated earlier, there has been a great deal of controversy over the appropriate yearly number of successful candidates. Generally, judges, public

Table 1.2
Number of Applicants, Successful Candidates,
Minimum Score to Pass, and Passage Rate, 1991–2002

Year	The first part of the exam			The second part of the exam			The third part of the exam		Total exam passage rate (%)
	Number of applicants	Successful candidates	Score to pass (%)	Number of applicants	Successful candidates	Score to pass (%)	Number of applicants	Final number of successful candidates	
1991	12,925	741	78.75	1,468	288	56.29	287	287	2.2
1992	13,958	821	84.37	1,488	288	52.04	288	288	2.0
1993	15,516	777	82.50	1,492	288	51.75	288	288	1.8
1994	16,390	850	80.31	1,530	290	53.79	290	290	1.8
1995	16,879	1,052	81.87	1,856	308	54.20	308	308	1.8
1996	18,572	1,250	78.95	2,198	502	51.83	502	502	2.7
1997	15,568	1,865	83.20	2,949	604	50.92	604	604	3.9
1998	15,670	1,876	76.57	3,558	700	50.71	700	700	4.5
1999	17,301	1,842	81.75	3,554	709	48.50	709	709	4.1
2000	16,218	1,897	84.44	3,762	801	53.28	801	801	4.9
2001	22,365	2,406	87.96	4,578	991	50.57	991	991	4.4
2002	24,707	2,640	83.50	5,008	999	49.79	999	998	4.0

prosecutors, and particularly practicing attorneys regarded 1,000 per year as too many (as they do still in 2005, when the number is about 1,200). They argued that the quality of new legal professionals deteriorated considerably and that the annual increase saturated the already crowded legal services market. They pointed out that the forecast of an increase in demand for legal services turned out to be wrong, especially since the International Monetary Fund crisis hit Korea.[6]

Finally, legal professionals argued that the government decision to increase the number of successful candidates prompted many bright non-law students to prepare for the judicial exam with false expectations, abandoning their pre-

---

6. The government's decision to increase the number of passers from 300 to 1,000 was based on the prediction that Korea would need more lawyers as the country became more globalized and moved closer towards unification. In 1995, the government predicted that over the next ten years there would be a growth of litigation which would require approximately 10,000 to 13,000 total lawyers, plus an additional demand for new legal services which would require 3,500 to 4,000 lawyers, and a need for an additional 1,200 judges and prosecutors. The government argued that if Korea needed approximately 18,000 lawyers by 2005, more than 12,000 new lawyers should be produced by then.

Table 1.3

Age Distribution of the Successful Examination Candidates, 1994–2002

Year	Number of successful candidates	Age range (years old)							Average age
		20–21	22–23	24–25	26–27	28–29	30–35	Over 36	
1994	290	16	52	62	64	46	46	4	28.35
1995	308	3	29	76	69	59	64	8	28.48
1996	502	2	37	90	110	92	152	19	29.20
1997	604	–	57	103	99	121	190	34	29.48
1998	700	1	55	127	162	129	191	35	29.25
1999	709	2	48	140	152	139	192	36	29.25
2000	801	6	69	142	157	154	241	32	29.30
2001	991	3	52	126	200	184	353	73	29.22
2002	998	1	59	142	204	212	320	60	28.39

vious studies or jobs. And they pointed out that the JRTI, which was originally equipped to handle 300 new students annually, is overburdened by the 1,000 students that matriculate each year.

Law professors, however, reacted swiftly and in unison to stop the reduction proposal. The government's decision to increase the number to 300 or more in 1981 was a revolution for law and society in Korea. Previously, judges, public prosecutors, and attorneys who passed the exam formed an exclusive and privileged group, giving rise to parochialism on their part. They monopolized the small market for legal services in typical civil and criminal trials. Meanwhile, they largely neglected learning and developing skills in other important fields of modern law, such as intellectual property law and competition law, in which the legal services of qualified attorneys are desperately needed in an industrialized society.

The policy of keeping the number of attorneys as small as possible also blocked many law graduates, who could have been interested in important new fields of contemporary law, from becoming attorneys. In the meantime, the shortage helped many paralegal professionals such as judicial scriveners, tax specialists, labor specialists, and licensed realtors to thrive in areas where services from qualified attorneys have not been available unless litigation took place. The Korean legal profession is still too exclusive to allow ordinary citizens to seek the service of an attorney. Despite these concerns, an increase beyond 1,200 a year does not seem possible for the time being in view of the atmosphere prevailing in the bar, the judiciary, and the Ministry of Justice.

C.   The Educational and Social Costs of the Examination System

The lack of a formal legal educational requirement for the judicial exam and the enormous rewards for success, are two major reasons why most undergraduate law colleges and departments tend to look like private cram-course programs.[7] Since President Park Chung-Hee lifted the eligibility rule, in 1970, that only law graduates, or at least law school juniors, were allowed to take the exam, many young people with non-law majors have been taking it.

Table 1.4 shows that, although not common, it is possible to pass the exam with little or no formal education. The media trumpets such accomplishments loudly, causing more people to spend futile years preparing for the exam.

The focus on passing the exam without attending undergraduate law school and using cram-course programs threatens the integrity of legal education and entry to the legal profession in Korea. To address this situation, law profes-

Table 1.4
Educational Attainment of Successful Examination Candidates, May 2002

Level of education	Number of people	Percentage of total
College degree	5,457	58.77
Graduate school degree (Master's)	1,946	20.96
Completion of graduate school coursework*	1,534	16.52
Graduate school degree (Doctor's)	145	1.56
Graduate school dropout	82	0.88
High school diploma	36	0.39
College dropout	29	0.31
Elementary school diploma	12	0.13
Middle school diploma	11	0.12
Unknown	33	0.36
Total	**9,285**	**100%**

* This category means those who have completed all the coursework requirements, but obtained no degree, which is different from those who dropped out of the graduate school in the middle of the coursework.

sors proposed a revision of the Presidential Decree on the National Judicial Service Examination such that only law graduates may take it, with the establishment of a separate eligibility exam testing basic legal knowledge for non-law candidates. Others have suggested that the candidates' academic record in basic legal subjects should be reflected in their judicial exam scores.

To accommodate some of these ideas, the new legislation of March 2001 (see below) and its presidential decree provided that from January 2006 onward, only those who have completed at least thirty-five credits of law subjects will be allowed to take the exam. This provision was a political compromise between

---

7. Including all national exams, there are now roughly 50,000 professional preparers for the various state-administered exams, forming a big exam village in front of the SNU campus.

those who argued that only law graduates should be able to take the exam and the position that the exam should be open to everyone. Much debate, however, continues regarding more technical details, such as the kind of law subjects or the type of legal educational institutions that will be authorized to give thirty-five credits. Law professors are particularly worried that private cram-course programs might try to obtain qualification as a law school under the new decree.

D. Administration of the Examination

Until 2001, the government agency that administered the exam was the Ministry of Government Administration and Home Affairs. This structure implied that the exam was a mechanism for selecting government bureaucrats. Many argued that if the purpose of the exam was to select future members of the legal profession, including judges and prosecutors, the Supreme Court or an examination management committee composed of representatives of legal academia, the judiciary, the bar, and the prosecutor's office should administer the exam. The Supreme Court was perhaps best suited to undertake the job, but in the past it had been reluctant to assume the responsibility, claiming a shortage of personnel with experience in such matters. In addition, the Ministry of Government Administration and Home Affairs was reluctant to relinquish control over the exam, which it had administered without scandal for fifty years. In recent years, however, the ministry has suffered from frequent lawsuits filed by those who challenged the correctness of answers to some questions after taking the first part of the exam. Invoking a right to know, the lawsuits typically demanded to see the model answers for the multiple-choice questions as well as the claimant's individual score and contended that since there could be more than one right answer to some questions, the ministry's decision to fail them was wrong and should be overturned.

After much controversy and debate, the National Assembly under Kim Dae-Jung enacted the National Judicial Service Examination Act (the New Act) on March 28, 2001, replacing the Presidential Decree on the National Judicial Service Examination that had existed for fifty years. The New Act upgraded the legal norm for the exam, reflecting several important points of discussion. Under the New Act, the Ministry of Justice was put in charge of the administration of the exam. The Ministry of Justice formed the National Judicial Service Examination Management Committee (the Management Committee) in 2001, which included law professors, judges, public prosecutors, practicing attorneys, instructors at the JRTI, and a few others representing the public-interest sector.

The thirteen-person Management Committee, chaired by the minister of justice, deliberated on most of the important matters concerning the exam such as the number of candidates to pass; exam subjects, methods, schedules, and standards; and directions for exam questions and grading policies, among other things. The number of successful candidates in particular will be decided by the minister of justice based on the deliberations of the Management Committee as well as opinions submitted by the Supreme Court and the Korean Bar Association.

III. The Judicial Research and Training Institute (JRTI)

A. Background and History

Before 1962, there was no central institution coordinating the education and training of those who passed the judicial exam. Training consisted of loosely organized apprenticeships in which candidates for the bar served as judicial clerks to the court or the prosecutor's office, or, less frequently, in the offices of practicing attorneys. This system was possible because of the extremely small number of apprentices, usually not more than thirty each year, but it was widely criticized for its lack of organization and formal theoretical training.

In 1962, to remedy this situation, the Graduate School of Law was established at SNU as an addition to the normal graduate law programs. Only those who passed the exam could enter the new school. Students in the Graduate School of Law would first attend a year of lecture courses and then spend a second year in structured apprenticeships in judicial offices. Since SNU is a university authorized to grant graduate degrees, apprentices of the Graduate School of Law received a Master's degree in law (LL.M.) in addition to a license to practice law. Ironically, this arrangement was strongly criticized for its lack of practical focus, and in 1970, under the direction of the Supreme Court, the Graduate School of Law was replaced by the JRTI to provide a unified practical legal education and training program for prospective legal professionals.

As shown in Table 1.5, in May 2002, 85 percent of legal professionals in Korea were graduates of the JRTI and 3.5 percent of the SNU Graduate School of Law; 98 percent of judges and prosecutors and 80 percent of practicing attorneys were graduates of the JRTI.

B. The JRTI Training Program

The lucky few hundred that pass the judicial exam must enter the JRTI for a two-year apprenticeship, which consists of various lectures, exams, tours and supervised practice at the offices of judges, public prosecutors, attorneys and others. The faculty of the JRTI is entirely staffed by judges, prosecutors and practitioners, and all costs for training at the JRTI are covered by the government.

Table 1.5
Type of Training Received by Korean Lawyers, May 2002

Training institute	Number of lawyers	Percentage of total
Judicial Research and Training Institute	7,901	85.09
Graduate School of Law, SNU	616	6.63
Judge advocate training	442	4.76
Field apprenticeship program	326	3.51
Total	**9,285**	**100%**

In the first year, many legal courses and seminars are offered just as in any graduate school of law, and there are thus many occasions at the JRTI where the legal subjects that are taught are almost identical to those at the undergraduate and graduate levels in the leading colleges of law. Generally, more and more specialized courses are being offered, and the credit system, the semester system, a graduation thesis requirement, and other elements that make up any graduate program are being widely introduced.

C.   Problems at the JRTI

The most frequent criticism of the JRTI has been that it places too much emphasis on practical training, providing very little academic training to supplement the meager intellectual background of the apprentices who passed the exam through rote memorization and arduous toiling. Despite its emphasis on practical training, however, the JRTI does not provide apprentices with sufficient professional training to function as judges, prosecutors, or practicing attorneys. Young legal professionals who have completed the JRTI program still must undergo extensive on-the-job training when they begin their careers. The question that naturally arises, then, is whether the training at the JRTI is in fact useful, adequate, or necessary at all.

In addition, the training provided at the JRTI has long been oriented toward the training of judges and prosecutors, because in its earlier days almost all graduates served as judges or prosecutors prior to becoming private attorneys. Recently, however, most apprentices are commencing practice as attorneys immediately following their apprenticeship. In 2004, 72 percent of all lawyers had no experience as a judge or prosecutor. Therefore, the training that these apprentices receive at the JRTI is not necessarily as relevant to their private practice. Some have thus suggested that those apprentices who plan to go into private practice immediately after graduation from the JRTI should be exempted from the public-career-oriented curriculum so that they might invest more time studying subjects that will be more relevant to their area of practice.

A majority of apprentices would also like to see the supervised training program strengthened in order to prepare them better for private practice. Furthermore, they are strongly in favor of diversification of the JRTI curriculum for private practice by adding, for example, training on counseling techniques, negotiation skills, legal advice, contract drafting, and management of law offices. These requests raise an important related question, which is why the taxpayers should pay the educational expenses, including tuition and monthly stipends, for those apprentices who will become private attorneys immediately after graduation and earn a salary several times higher than that of judges and prosecutors.

Since a student's first-year performance, mainly based on the results of the exams that the apprentices take each semester, is crucial for subsequent appointment to the bench or the prosecutor's office, competition among the apprentices is so fierce that one student passed away in the middle of taking an exam.[8] A majority of the apprentices are worried about excessive competition and its subsequent adverse effects and have therefore demanded abolition of the first-year exams. Although the JRTI moved to a new facility in a northwestern suburb of Seoul to accommodate the increased number of apprentices, the question of whether or not the JRTI is capable of providing quality education and training for 2,000 to 2,500 apprentices is sometimes raised.

Finally, there are problems with the content of the instruction and training at the JRTI. Historically, very few constitutional, administrative, or labor law courses were provided, so the ability of the court adequately to deal with those issues in the judicial process could be called into question. Now, although one of the main purposes of the JRTI is to train judicial bureaucrats, it offers so many specialized courses that its full-time instructors cannot effectively teach them. The JRTI is even considering establishing a program leading to an LL.M. degree, which prompts one to suspect that it is becoming more and more like the academic graduate school it was established to replace.

IV. The Legal Profession

A. Career Patterns

Upon completion of the two-year apprenticeship program, male graduates who have not already completed compulsory military service must serve in the military as a judge advocate for three years. Women and those men who have completed or been exempted from military service are appointed as judges or public prosecutors, or go to work as private attorneys, depending on their individual desires and the results of their performance at the JRTI and on the judicial exam. Usually, those apprentices who finish at the top of their class at the JRTI decide to become judges, since generally a judge enjoys more prestige than an attorney or a prosecutor. Among these top students, the best and brightest are usually assigned to a district court in or around Seoul. As illustrated by Table 1.6, of the total number of legal professionals admitted to the bar as of May 2002, at least 26.6 percent commenced their careers as judges, 33.8 percent as private attorneys, and 20.3 percent as prosecutors.

The traditional career pattern for legal professionals in Korea has been to start a private law practice after serving as a judge or prosecutor for some years. It has long been customary that former colleagues and clerks in the court or the prosecutor's office refer some cases to retired judges or prosecutors when they open their law offices, as a matter of professional courtesy. This practice has become so excessive that recently, various measures to ban this practice have

---

8. A newspaper account stated that the student went to the restroom during the exam, collapsed there, and never regained consciousness. The strong implication was that she died of the stress and tension arising from the extremely competitive atmosphere. *Chosun Ilbo* (2001).

Table 1.6
Initial Appointments of Korean Lawyers, May 2002

Initial appointment	Number of lawyers	Percentage of total
Attorney	3,142	33.84
Judge	2,469	26.59
Public prosecutor	1,888	20.33
Military	421	4.54
Administration	93	1.00
Academia	25	0.27
Other	392	4.22
Unknown	855	9.21
Total	**9,285**	**100%**

been discussed. Interestingly, some of the loudest protests with regard to such collusion, if not corruption, in the bar have come from within the bar itself. With the production of a steady number of new young legal professionals each year, and with a majority choosing to practice law without first acquiring on-the-job training as a junior judge or public prosecutor, these young attorneys naturally resent the unfair advantage that judges or prosecutors have when they begin private practice.

B. Profile of Legal Professionals

In June 2002, there were 8,851 private attorneys, judges, and public prosecutors in Korea, not including those who passed the exam in 2000 and 2001. (Since those who passed the exam in those two years were then to be trained at the JRTI, they were not qualified as legal professionals in June 2002.) According to the Korean Bar Association, there were exactly 5,579 attorneys engaged in private practice in Korea as of June 2002 and 6,273 in May 2004 (see Table 1.7). There are also many legal professionals who are not engaged in active law practice, including professors like myself.

Geographically speaking, most legal professionals are concentrated in Seoul. In June 2002 the Seoul Bar Association had 3,731 private members. In May 2004 it had 4,116, and in 2005 it had 4,697. The distribution of attorneys among the other bar associations was as follows (2002; 2004; 2005): the Daegu Bar, 307; 317; 331; the Suwon Bar, 295; 353; 376; the Busan Bar, 288; 304; 320; the Daejeon Bar, 185; 208; 224; the Gwangju Bar, 182; 185; 196; the Incheon Bar, 148; 208; 246; the Changwon Bar, 121; 131; 136; the Jeonju Bar, 101; 94; 97; the Cheongju Bar, 73; 71; 71; the Chuncheon Bar, 67; 67; 67; the Ulsan Bar, 52; 59; 69; the Jeju Bar, 29; 27; 30; and the Uijeongbu Bar, 132 in 2004 and 151 in 2005. Including Seoul, the total number of the above members in 2002 was 5,579; in 2004 it was 6,272 members; and in 2005 it was 7,011 members.

Table 1.7
National Statistics on the Number of
Active Practitioners in Korea, 1994–2004

Date	Number of lawyers*
December 1994	2,852
December 1995	3,079
December 1996	3,188
December 1997	3,364
December 1998	3,521
December 1999	3,889
December 2000	5,073
December 2001	5,117
August 2002	5,593
May 2004	6,273

*This table is based on figures from the Korean Bar Association.

Among the cities and counties that have a branch court and a branch prosecution office in their territory, in 2002 Yeoungdong, Uiseong, Yeongdeok, and Namwon Counties had only one practicing attorney each, and Jangheung County had no one practicing law, which made it the only lawyer-less county in Korea. On the other hand, some Korean cities with no court or branch prosecution office do have practicing attorneys. In 2002 the figures were as follows: Pohang (12), Goyang (11), Ansan (8), Anyang (7), Gwangmyeong (3), Guri (1), Siheung (1), Dangjin (1), and Gimhae (1). Across the country in 2002 there were 226 incorporated law firms (258 in 2004) that employed 1,910 attorneys, and 76 joint law offices that were composed of 317 attorneys. The number of practicing attorneys will increase as more candidates pass the judicial exam and more judges and prosecutors retire and join law firms.

In light of the regionalism which plagues modern Korean politics, it is interesting to examine the success of candidates from different regions in Korea. The judicial exam is intended to establish a meritocracy in the selection of legal professionals, and it has its historical parallel in the government service examinations of the Choson Dynasty. Court historians kept careful records of those who passed government exams, and those records have provided valuable information about the social and political contours of the dynasty. During the Choson Dynasty, an inordinate number of exam-passers came from the Gyeongsang-do region. One may wonder what sort of regional distribution pattern exists among successful candidates of the modern judicial exam.

Since political power has been concentrated in the hands of people from the Gyeongsang-do region, and the Jeolla-do region has faced some measure of discrimination in terms of political and economic opportunities, one might suspect that a relatively higher number of people from Gyeongsang-do would pass the judicial exam. Because of the economic advantages they enjoy, they are more likely to have the time and resources necessary to devote to intensively studying for the exam. On the other hand, the fact that the outcome of the exam cannot be influenced by political connections or socio-economic status might motivate people from the Jeolla-do area to use the exam to open doors which are otherwise closed to them, since passing the judicial exam is a ticket to wealth and prestige for those who lack the family or political connections to the upper echelons of Korean society. The preliminary data in Table 1.8 would seem to indicate that the former rather than the latter has proven to be the case.

Table 1.8

Regional Origins of Successful Examination Candidates in Korea, May 2002

Region	Number of people	Percentage of total
Seoul	1,619	17.44
Busan	485	5.22
Daegu	456	4.91
Incheon	102	1.10
Gwangju	235	2.53
Daejeon	173	1.86
Ulsan	45	0.48
Gangwon	249	2.68
Gyeonggi-do	422	4.56
Gyeongsangnam-do	1,138	12.26
Gyeongsangbuk-do	1,215	13.09
Jeollanam-do	1,089	11.73
Jeollabuk-do	754	8.12
Chungcheongnam-do	637	6.86
Chungcheongbuk-do	378	4.07
Jeju-do	157	1.69
North Korea	96	1.03
Others	4	0.04
Unknown	31	0.33
Total	**9,285**	**100%**

Table 1.8 would seem to indicate that a relatively higher number of people from the Gyeongsang-do region pass the judicial exam compared to those from the Jeolla-do area. However, these statistics are preliminary, and further investigation must be conducted to determine if it is indeed the case that Gyeongsang-do is disproportionately represented.[9]

9. First, of course, the relative populations of each area must be taken into account. Gyeongsang-do is more heavily populated than Jeolla-do, for example. Second, there is some ambiguity in Korea as to the question, "Where are you from?" People who have lived in Seoul for all of their lives may say "Seoul" or they may still give the region of their ancestral home, such as Gyeongsang-do or Gyeonggi-do. Some clarification on this point is necessary before

C.   The End of the Legal Monopoly?

As the number of private attorneys gradually increases, the monopoly of the few legal professionals over the legal services market has begun to crumble. The number of new attorneys has exceeded the natural attrition rate each year, and many of them have begun to explore diverse areas of law such as international trade, intellectual property, corporate bankruptcy, mergers and acquisitions, and banking and financial law to deal with trans-border activities. Others specialize in complex litigation, alternative dispute resolution, and nongovernmental organization legal activities, and some have become advocates for social

the data in Table 1.8 can be taken as a true indication of disproportionate regional representation among the successful exam candidates. This ambiguity is highlighted by the data in Table 1.9, which show that although more successful candidates indicated Gyeongsang-do

Table 1.9		
Location of High School Attended by Successful Candidates, May 2002		
High school	Number of people	Percentage of total
Seoul	3,163	34.07
Busan	694	7.47
Daegu	816	8.79
Incheon	113	1.22
Gwangju	620	6.68
Daejeon	329	3.54
Ulsan	37	0.40
Gangwon	156	1.68
Gyeonggi-do	174	1.87
Gyeongsangnam-do	568	6.11
Gyeongsangbuk-do	550	5.92
Jeollanam-do	332	3.58
Jeollabuk-do	551	5.93
Chungcheongnam-do	181	1.95
Chungcheongbuk-do	174	1.87
Jeju-do	125	1.35
High schools in North Korea	49	0.53
High schools in Japan	21	0.23
Graduate equivalent examination	139	1.50
Others	2	0.02
Unknown	491	5.29
Total	**9,285**	**100%**

than Seoul as their place of origin, more of them actually attended high school in Seoul. This could mean that people raised and educated in Seoul still refer to their ancestral home areas as their place of origin, that many exam-passers moved to Seoul during their early years, or that the parents of many children in the provincial areas are sending their children to high school in Seoul where the schools are thought to provide a superior education. At any rate, it is safe to conclude that although the people of the Jeolla-do region do not seem to be underrepresented proportionate to their population, the judicial exam has not provided an effective way for them to gain ground on their cousins in Gyeongsang-do.

causes or human rights.[10] There have also started to be some in-house counsel teams within large business conglomerates such as Samsung and others.[11] Whether the use of in-house counsel will be successful depends largely upon the perception of top managers about the role of law and when and how to use attorneys in their businesses.

This diversification phenomenon has many implications. Access to the legal services of qualified attorneys is expected to be easily available in the future, even in diversified areas of law beyond typical civil litigation and criminal trials. The number of lawyers will increase, which is expected to help spread the rule of law in society. In addition, it will certainly stimulate the scholarly and teaching activities of many law professors, thereby propelling legal education reform.

The Korea Law Professors Association[12] has seized this opportunity to campaign for an amendment to the Lawyers Act so that law professors would be accorded a license to practice. If this position of the association becomes law, roughly 1,000 law professors who have not previously been licensed would be added to the size of the bar. There were several such attempts in past decades, but they were met with strong hostile reactions from the bar, the judiciary, and the ministry. The atmosphere is warm this time, but the technical details involved are very complex, and will be difficult to put into legislation.

V.   Prospects for Legal Education Reform

A.   Initial Attempts at Reform from the 1960s

The idea of extending legal education beyond the current four years of secondary education in order to solve the problem in legal education has been debated in Korea since the 1960s. The legal profession in general has opposed extending the legal education period in any way, viewing such efforts as a threat to their hegemony. But a five-year law college idea has been a pet project of SNU College of Law faculty members for many years. The basic idea behind such a plan would be to strengthen general education in the humanities and social sciences for the first two years of university education, and then emphasize professional education for the remaining three years.

Many faculty members believe that a two-year program of general education is needed for the formation of the personal qualities that lawyers should possess and that a three-year intensive law curriculum could equip law students with the level of legal knowledge and practical skills that they will need to become competent lawyers. But even many professors who are in favor of a five-year law school program have doubts about the feasibility of the idea, because parents

---

10. The human rights activities of lawyers in Korea are discussed in more detail in JaeWon Kim's chapter in this volume.

11. The trend toward in-house counsel teams in Japan is discussed in Toshimitsu Kitagawa and Luke Nottage's chapter in this volume.

12. The author is the president of this association.

and students would have to spend extra time and money on another year of education that would not necessarily help them pass the judicial exam. Thus, supporters of a five-year program also suggest that graduates from the program should be exempted from the first part of the judicial exam. Proposals for a five-year undergraduate law program have never materialized. In recent years, many law faculty members at SNU and other law colleges have advocated a three-year graduate law program similar to the one proposed by the Ministry of Education and Human Resources, discussed below.

The ministry in the past discussed plans to transform the present four-year College of Law at SNU, the most popular law college for high school graduates to enter, into a four-year law school after two years of college. SNU authorities in fact agreed to reorganize the College of Law in accordance with the ministry's guidelines. Under the plan, since the ministry would establish only a few such law schools (perhaps SNU and a few others), the entrance exam for new graduate law schools would be open to everyone who completes two years of college, and SNU Law School would be allowed to admit only 20 percent of its own students. Those who graduated from a new four-year law school would earn an LL.M. degree for their extra two years of study. This reform plan was criticized on the grounds that it would probably not solve the problem of excessive competition for entry to the SNU College of Law and the enormous private tutoring expenses that parents have to pay. It would only postpone such competition and expenditure for two years. Further, it was politically impossible for the ministry to establish only a few such law schools without involving the other seventy (now ninety) or more law colleges.

B.   Reform Efforts under the Kim Young-Sam Administration (1993–1998)

The office of the president, the Blue House, initiated an attempt to reform Korean legal education in early 1995, but the Presidential Commission on Education Reform could not reach any conclusions, mainly due to steadfast opposition by the judiciary and the bar. The most important and controversial idea considered by the commission was whether an American-style law school system should be introduced, with graduates of such law schools automatically qualified to practice, or easily qualified after a pro forma bar exam. However, after much debate, the commission decided merely to make minor changes in the subjects of the judicial exam and to increase the number of successful candidates as discussed above (Part II B).

In addition to strong resistance from existing legal professionals to increase their numbers, part of the problem is that such sudden and dramatic increases in the number of students created logistical problems for the JRTI, which saw its student body more than double in size in only a few years. In addition to more crowded classrooms and administrative adjustments, the JRTI is also struggling to revise its curriculum to reflect the diversity of the apprentices and their career goals.

C. Reform Proposals under the Kim Dae-Jung Administration (1998–2003)

When the Kim Dae-Jung administration was inaugurated in February 1998, the reform of professional schools such as law schools, medical schools, dental schools, divinity schools and business schools was high on its educational reform agenda. One of President Kim's political pledges was to alleviate the overheated competition for college entrance and thus eliminate the excessive financial burden of parents who pay for private tutoring to assist their children's preparation for college admission. The Ministry of Education perceived that this competition arises from the fact that almost every high school graduate wants to enter SNU in general and its Colleges of Law or Medicine in particular.

In May 1999, the Presidential Commission on Education Reform announced a proposal to initiate a three-year graduate professional law school system, similar to the American law school system, early in the twenty-first century. The proposal stated that universities that wish to establish a graduate law school under the new proposal must eliminate their undergraduate law departments, and that the faculty-to-student ratio must be at least one-to-twelve, with a minimum of twenty-five full-time faculty regardless of the number of students. Anyone with a bachelor's degree would be eligible to apply for law school regardless of their major, and admission would be based on undergraduate grades, foreign language ability, extra-curricular activities, and other factors. This was in stark contrast to the existing admission criteria for undergraduate law programs, based primarily on the college entrance exam score. Graduates of the new three-year program would receive a Juris Doctor (J.D.) and be exempt from the first part of the judicial exam.

The proposal also stated that students who do not attend the new law schools but who wish to take the judicial exam would be required to take at least twenty-four credits of law coursework in order to sit for the first round of the exam. In addition to the three-year J.D. program, the new law schools would be permitted to continue to operate two-year graduate programs for purely academic (nonprofessional) purposes.

This proposal, which seems to address many of the concerns that have been raised about legal education by law professors and even many legal professionals, was not been immune from criticism. Students would be required to attend school for seven years and would possibly need to spend an additional year to prepare for the second round of the judicial exam with no guarantee that they would pass it and be qualified to practice law after such an enormous investment of time, effort, and resources. In addition, there was no participation by the judiciary or the legal profession in the formulation of this proposal. It should come as no great surprise then that the Supreme Court expressed its opposition to any proposal to reform the education of the legal profession without the input of legal professionals. The proposal was not implemented.

D. Reform Possibilities under the Roh Moo-Hyun Administration

President Roh came into office in February 2003. On August 22, 2003, the president and the chief justice agreed to proceed with joint efforts to review and reform almost all aspects of the national justice system, legal education and the judicial exam. The Supreme Court Committee on Judicial Reform was thus established on October 28, 2003. It was a great opportunity to introduce sweeping changes and reforms with the blessing of the heads of the two branches of government. After fourteen months of debate and public hearings, the committee recommended a number of far-reaching reform proposals to President Roh in December 2004, including a plan for American-style three-year graduate law schools to be launched in 2008, and for the current judicial exam to be phased out by 2013.

On January 18, 2005, President Roh launched a new Presidential Committee on Judicial Reform, a special follow-up body to work on the concrete implementation steps for specific judicial reform proposals that had been recommended to him. The committee was co-chaired by the prime minister and a senior practitioner, and composed of the ministers of the following ministries: Education and Human Resources Development, Justice, National Defense, Government Administration and Home Affairs, Labor, Planning and Budget, Government Legislation, and Court Administration. It also included the head of the Office for Government Policy Coordination, the Senior Secretary to the President for Civil Affairs, and eight other civilian members, including this author.

In addition to the establishment of professional graduate law schools, many other matters were proposed, including promotion of greater citizen participation in the administration of justice (mainly via a jury system), redefining the functions and organization of the Supreme Court, restructuring the system of recruitment and appointment of judges, substantial reform of criminal procedures, and expansion of judicial services. Before the presidential committee votes for any implementing measures for the final adoption, they are subject to review by the Planning and Implementation Board of the Presidential Committee as well as a working committee composed of vice ministers of the above ministries and a number of civilian members.

Unfortunately, a discussion of the Presidential Committee on May 16, 2005 regarding the establishment of a small number of graduate law schools was disappointing. Primary concern was entirely focused on the total number of enrolled students and how many and which universities would be selected.

Introduction of American-style law schools would mean a historical revolution for the Korean legal profession. The traditional way of producing legal professionals, which was to rely exclusively on the national judicial exam, will be shifted to a new way based mainly on a newly introduced American-style legal education system. It was hoped therefore that discussion would center around or touch upon how to offer a high-quality legal education at the new law schools. At the moment it looks like a tug of war between law professors and the bar association over the number of enrolled students as well as the number of newly licensed law schools, although these numbers would be determined by the Ministry of Education and Human Resources Development.

Conclusion

Japanese expansion in the nineteenth century replaced the Korean monarchy with a colonial administration and protectorate. Just as the central theme for Korea in the last century was decolonization and the emergence of a new nation-state, so the theme for Korea in the twentieth century may have been the rise of constitutionalism, a system of separation of powers, and checks and balances through a presidential system. The legal profession in Korea played an important role in this process, especially since liberation from Japan in 1945, but there is still a long way to go. Over the past six decades, Korea has achieved many things: reemergence of an independent judiciary, active judicial review by the Constitutional Court, improved corporate governance, and human rights protection by law, among other things. Korea is one of the few countries in the vast Asian continent where the court system works as it should. Generally, the court processes are fair, predictable, and speedily managed.

Most of the problems in legal education and the legal profession can be traced directly or indirectly to the excessive competition of the judicial exam that has distorted legal education as a whole. Until Korea changes the standards by which students are conferred entrance into the legal profession, it is unrealistic to expect them to stop cramming for the exam and adopt a more intellectual approach to the study of law. As long as the number of candidates allowed to pass remains too low to meet the social demand for legal services, access to the law will remain a privilege of the few. This does not mean that the standards for selecting legal professionals should be lowered, or that the judicial exam should be completely eliminated, but it does mean that we must find more meaningful and efficient ways to assess the potential of candidates for the bar.

Systemic reform of the legal education system is also desperately needed if Korea is to produce capable legal professionals who are able to function in the global environment. The curricula at Korean law schools cannot remain aloof from the practical aspects of legal practice if we expect to hold the attention of our students. Law schools must provide practical training in addition to theoretical grounding. However long the legal education period, the most important issue is what to teach and how to teach it. Law professors and the JRTI have identified subjects to be added, such as newly emerging fields of law, comparative law, legal tradition, and languages. In terms of methodology, many law professors are in favor of the Socratic method of teaching and case-based exam questions. Yet currently, classroom discussions, if they occur at all, focus on finding the "correct" answer, and exam questions usually ask students to provide the only true answer as if they were judges. Legal education remains focused on producing "jureaucrats" who will deal with disputes, rather than on the many other roles for lawyers that society requires.

An American-style law school with a three-year graduate law program could provide an excellent structural framework for a more integrated and comprehensive curriculum. However, it will not win the support of students or their parents unless the judicial exam system is reformed as well.

Continued resistance by the Korean bar to any increase in the number of successful exam candidates or changes in the legal education system may hinder efforts at reform, but younger attorneys who did not serve as judges and prosecutors prior to becoming private attorneys represent a new trend of specialization and professionalism that may cause a divergence of interest between judges, prosecutors, and attorneys. Young lawyers and graduate students with educational experience abroad are bringing new ideas and direction to many areas of legal practice and scholarship. As Korean society grows more open and democratic, the demand for legal services will grow as citizens seek to use law to solve their disputes and problems. The market for legal services will inevitably open to meet this demand, serving to spread the rule of law to all of Korea's citizens.

Works Cited

Chosun Ilbo. [Chosun daily newspaper]. 2001. 26 October.

Korean Bar Association. 2002. *The Roster of Attorneys.* 25 May. Seoul: KBA.

Law Times. 2000. Hanguk beopjoin daegwan [A general survey of legal professionals in Korea]. 31 August.

West, James M. 1991. *Education of the legal profession in Korea.* Seoul: International Legal Studies, Korea University.

Two

Legal Profession and Legal Culture during Korea's Transition to Democracy and a Market Economy

JaeWon Kim*

Introduction

Korea[1] has a long history and rich cultural heritage,[2] but it was the Korean War and post-war economic development that chiefly drew the attention of the Western world to the country known as "the Land of Morning Calm." The 1950–1953

---

*Dean, Professor of Law, and Director of the Institute for Legal Studies at Dong-A University College of Law, Busan, South Korea. He has served as Associate Dean, Director of the Law Library, Legal Education Subcommittee Member of the Presidential Commission on Education Reform, and Director of the Korean Association of Law & Society.

I dedicate this chapter to the late Dr. James M. West, whose ideas and writings laid the foundations of the chapter. The initial version of this chapter was presented at the Harvard Law School Conference on the Legal Profession in East Asia in 1998. I am grateful to Anne-Marie Slaughter and David B. Wilkins for their insights and suggestions, and most especially to William P. Alford for hosting the conference and for supporting the publication of this volume. I am greatly indebted to John K. M. Ohnesorge and Geraldine Chin for their constructive criticisms and invaluable help for improving this chapter. An earlier version of this chapter was published in 2 *Asian-Pacific Law & Policy Journal* 45 (2001). I am deeply grateful to the *Journal* editors, especially Maria Estanislao, for their excellent suggestions. Errors are mine alone.

1. Positioned between two big neighbors, China and Japan, Korea has been perceived as a small country by outsiders as well as by Koreans themselves. Although its population density is high, Korea is, in fact, not small. The total size of Korea is about the same as that of Great Britain, and the population is about 67 million. The kingdoms in the Korean peninsula were reunited by the Koryo dynasty in 936 A.D., but during the temporary occupation (1945–1948) of Korea by the United States and the USSR for the disarming of the Japanese imperial armed forces, the nation was divided as the Republic of Korea (South Korea) and the Democratic People's Republic of Korea (North Korea) and has since remained so. North Korea covers slightly more than half of the total land, but its population is much smaller than South Korea, which is about 46 million. In this chapter, the term "Korea" is used interchangeably with "South Korea."

2. Korea is one of the oldest nations in the world and has nurtured unique customs and a distinctive way of life (see generally Osgood 1998).

war caused an enormous loss of human life[3] as well as property damage. Major cities, including the capital city of Seoul, industrial plants, and rail transportation systems were practically destroyed (Nahm 1996, 400). In the shambles left by the war, Koreans worked very hard to rebuild their nation, and the subsequent economic accomplishments have been truly remarkable. After three decades of progress, one of the poorest countries in the world was transformed into the world's twelfth largest trading nation.[4] Being praised as "the miracle on the Han River,"[5] the economic development of Korea became a model for many other developing countries (Amsden 1989, 3).

While undergoing a condensed industrial revolution, Korea also experienced social and political turmoil. Its story of economic success has often been overshadowed by a dictatorship[6] and widespread human rights violations.[7] Political democratization in South Korea, especially during the late 1980s, began to improve human rights conditions substantially and finally displaced the military regime in 1994. When Korea proudly joined the "rich man's club," i.e., the Organization for Economic Cooperation and Development (OECD), in 1996, the future of "Korea, Inc." seemed ever promising.[8]

Unfortunately, it did not take long to prove that the Champagne corks had been popped prematurely. In late 1997, the miracle-makers had to face an unprecedented economic disaster that wiped out years of hard-earned economic progress almost overnight. The government of South Korea had to request an International Monetary Fund (IMF) bailout to avoid bankruptcy resulting from a shortage of foreign currency (Yoo 1997). The Korean public was shocked by the news because it was not just a matter of financial problems. The bailout request "left, among other things, a deep scar on the Korean public's pride" (Lee 1997). Experts from all walks of life strove to find out what had gone wrong.

Many economists blamed the crisis on the long-standing governmental policy focused on sponsoring a handful of ultra-large business groups, the *chaebol*.[9] They have also pointed out a lack of transparency as a major factor responsible

---

3. Some 774,000 Korean civilians were killed and about 388,000 were listed as missing. Some 225,000 South Korean soldiers and 294,000 North Korean soldiers were killed. About 900,000 Chinese soldiers and 33,629 American soldiers were reported to have been killed (Nahm 1996, 400).

4. South Korea's gross national product (GNP) increased from US$2 billion in 1962 to US$276 billion in 1992. The GNP per capita also grew from US$87 to US$6,749 in the same period (see Choi 1996, 13).

5. This phrase was used to invoke images of "the Miracle on the Rhine."

6. See generally Sohn (1989).

7. See Ogle (1990).

8. See *Korea Times* (1996).

9. The *chaebol* are family-owned and family-managed large business groups, such as Samsung, Hyundai, and Lucky-Gold Star (LG) (see Kim 1997, 51).

for the economic crisis.[10] Other critics raised questions regarding the rule of law and the malfunctioning of Korea's legal profession. They argued that Koreans would have suffered less tragic consequences if their legal profession had functioned to help the nation combat widespread corruption, enhance transparency in business transactions, and maintain rational processes of decision-making.[11] This is the very point with which the present chapter is concerned. The basic proposition of this chapter is that the Korean legal profession, in general, has failed to play the role that could have been appropriately expected by society during Korea's transition to democracy and a market economy. The passive role or nonparticipation by lawyers might have been considered excusable during Korea's past. However, a changed environment demanded the positive and active participation of lawyers in Korean society.

In recent years, some significant changes have been observed in the Korean legal profession. A major characteristic of such changes is the introduction of competition into the domestic legal market. Although over-generalized, all of the current changes seem to be closely related to and affected by two factors. One factor is the substantial increase in the annual quota of new lawyers; the other is the globalization of the legal profession and the impending opening of the legal services market. Nevertheless, it seems that the current legal system, as well as the legal profession, persistently resists incorporating such changes.

This chapter presents a socio-legal study of the Korean legal profession. In it, I examine how and why the profession functioned or malfunctioned in the Korean socio-cultural context. I thus begin by providing an overview of the Korean legal profession. Next, I try to provide a practical description of different branches of the profession, notably judges, public prosecutors, private attorneys, and law professors. Following this Part, I critically examine legal education and the professional training system in Korea, as well as unfulfilled plans for reform. In this regard, I argue that most of the basic problems of the Korean legal profession today have a significant bearing on the legal education process. Finally, I consider the implications of the malfunctioning of the profession and suggest reform measures.

I. The Reality of the Korean Legal Profession: An Overview

There are two distinctive features of the contemporary Korean legal profession. One is the small size of the lawyer population; the other is the profession's homogeneous composition. With respect to the size of the profession, in 2002 there were approximately 8,600 licensed lawyers, including 1,700 judges, 1,300

10. See Overholt (1998).

11. See, e.g., West (1998a).

prosecutors, and 5,600 practicing attorneys.[12] This is small considering Korea's economic scale and population of 46 million. More striking is that even this tiny number of lawyers has only been achieved through substantial increases in very recent years.[13] The small size of the profession adds to its prestige and makes lawyers the most privileged class in Korean society (Lewis 1997, 55).

Scarcity, however, has had profoundly negative ramifications, not only for the Korean legal system, but also for the lawyers themselves. Judges and prosecutors have had to handle a high number of cases,[14] and this heavy burden has been a leading factor in the increasing number of those who retire from judicial office to enter private practice.[15] The shortage of lawyers also distorts the roles and functions of lawyers and has denied ordinary citizens access to the judicial system.[16] The role of practicing attorneys has long been confined to litigation before civil or criminal courts. Lawyers have felt little pressure to expand their services because demand in these areas was sufficient to guarantee a lucrative income.[17]

---

12. For statistics, see the Ministry of Court Administration (2002), and the Korean Bar Association website at http://www.koreanbar.or.kr. As in most other countries, doctors and lawyers are two of the most privileged professions in Korea. It is therefore noteworthy to compare the size of the medical profession to that of the legal profession. In the year 2000, the number of Korean doctors was over 70,000. See the website of the Korean Medical Association at http://www.kma.org.

13. The extremely small legal profession is a result of a tightly restricted annual quota for producing new lawyers. From 1949 to 1980, a total of 1,902 candidates passed the National Judicial Service Examination (judicial exam), which is an average of about 59 per year. In 1981, the annual quota was substantially increased to 300 per year (see Yoon 1990, 114–15). In 1992, the total number of private lawyers (not including judges or prosecutors) was 2,450, and it reached 5,000 in 2002. This means that during that ten-year period, the total population of private lawyers doubled (see J. Lee 2002).

14. According to a report of the Korean Institute of Criminology, a judge in a district court had to decide sixteen cases per day on average, while a prosecutor had to handle fewer than seven cases per day (see S. Kim 1999, 185).

15. The number of judges who have resigned from office has dramatically increased in recent years. In 1998, eighty judges left office, which was 5.4 percent of all judges. The reason for retirement, however, is not always related to the heavy workload. The increasing number of new lawyers tends to make the legal market more competitive and produce less income for each lawyer. Under these circumstances, judges and prosecutors are eager to open their law offices as early as possible after retiring from government, to garner clients (see Ha 1999).

16. See generally D.K. Yoon (1996).

17. Until recently, a litigant who could not afford to retain a lawyer had no choice but to receive legal assistance from a certified judicial scrivener because lawyers generally did not prepare documents for clients who acted for themselves in a court proceeding. One of the services provided by certified judicial scriveners is to prepare documents to present to a court or prosecutor's office (Certified Judicial Scriveners Act, Law No. 5180, December 12, 1996, Article 2 (Duties), as amended as Law No. 5453, December 13, 1997). Due to the substantial increase of lawyers, it is reported that some lawyers have begun to take on such work.

Along with a shortage of lawyers, another distinctive characteristic of the Korean legal profession is its homogeneous composition. A unified system of legal training is primarily responsible for that composition. Those who aspire to be lawyers must first pass the judicial exam and attend the Judicial Research and Training Institute (JRTI). Only those examinees who successfully pass the judicial exam obtain the privilege of entering the JRTI, which is the country's most elite institution. The JRTI is supervised by the Supreme Court, and its full-time faculty is composed of judges and prosecutors only. Over a two-year period, its training courses focus on developing litigation skills.[18] At the JRTI, all trainees are treated as functionaries of the government.[19] They not only enjoy official status but also receive a salary from the government. All Korean lawyers, whether judges, prosecutors, or practicing attorneys, thus receive the same professional training in the same institution. Undergoing a single unified training course has built a military-like hierarchy among Korean lawyers. This kind of hierarchy seems to have been reinforced by the Confucian tradition in which seniority carries great privileges (Yoon 1990, 29). In many contexts, lawyers are expected to respect the judgment of senior lawyers regardless of merit.[20]

It is also interesting to note the particular terminology describing "lawyer" in Korean. Most lawyers, including judges and prosecutors, do not like to be called *bopyulga* or "lawyer," but instead strongly prefer to be called *bopjoin,* which literally means "judicial officer." The conscious choice or preference of the term is not necessarily related to their perception of the profession's social function or role. It rather reflects a sense of superiority in the mind of the lawyers: they are the high-ranking officials who are superior to other government employees, and they are the elite who passed the most competitive exam in the nation. Since there are many people who did not pass the exam but who engage in legal work that in other countries is usually done by lawyers,[21] this elite mentality allows Korean lawyers to distinguish themselves from such "inferior" law-related professionals.[22]

---

18. Since 1996, the JRTI has adopted some features of a graduate school and offered new elective courses on nontraditional legal subjects, such as WTO law and intellectual property—some of which have been taught by practicing attorneys (see K. Yoon 1996).

19. Before 1983, all graduates from the JRTI were appointed either as a judge or a prosecutor, but due to the increasing annual quota, the number of graduates who directly enter private practice has been dramatically growing.

20. See Han (2000, 367).

21. In addition to non-lawyers holding jobs that have a specific professional title such as certified judicial scrivener, tax attorney, patent attorney, and labor affairs consultant, there are numerous companies which hire law graduates who have not qualified as lawyers to handle legal work that is usually done by in-house legal counsel in the United States.

22. In this regard, even law professors are often excluded from the notion of *bopyulga* or lawyer.

   The traditional dominance of one school in training legal professionals is another problematic feature of the Korean legal system which contributes to the homogenous composition of the legal profession. Among ninety-two universities that confer undergraduate law degrees, only one university, Seoul National University (SNU), has swept the judicial exams. Although the number has gradually decreased since 1981 when the annual quota of successful bar candidates more than doubled, graduates of Korea's most prestigious university still make up 43 percent of those who pass the exam.[23] Not only is the sheer number an issue, but SNU graduates fill a largely disproportionate share of major positions in the court hierarchy.[24]

   In addition to the common training received by legal professionals, the predominance of the alumni of this single university seems to produce a strong esprit de corps among the majority of Korea's lawyers. Although social and legal norms require judges, prosecutors, and practicing attorneys to play their respective roles in distinct domains, subconsciously they treat each other as old friends who attended the same school.[25] All of these circumstances indicate that hierarchy and cordial personal relationships are key factors in the Korean legal circle. Convincing arguments or technical legal skills thus seldom play a major role in legal practice (Yoon 2000, 395). Heavy reliance on personal connections has undoubtedly contributed to the underdevelopment of legal practice, and the propagation of unethical practices within the Korean legal community as well (West 1991, 80).

   With respect to its homogeneous composition, it is quite interesting to observe the rapid increase in the number of women in the Korean bar. As in many other countries, the legal profession in Korea has long been a gentleman's club.[26] The proportion of female lawyers, however, has dramatically increased since 1981. Before 1981, at best, one woman passed the exam each year. The proportion of women passing the exam jumped to 10.8 percent in 1994 and then to 17.2 percent in 1999 when 122 women passed (Kim 1998). In 2001, 173 women passed the nation's most competitive exam, representing 17.5 percent of all successful candidates (Chang 2002). The dramatic increase of women in the bar can

---

23. In 1998, the percentage of SNU graduates among those who passed the judicial exam fell below 50 percent (42.4 percent or 297 out of 700) for the first time. The statistics show that SNU graduates were 55.8 percent in 1995, 50.2 percent in 1996, and 54.3 percent of passers in 1997. In the 1998 exam, the graduates from Korea University (21 percent) took second place, and those from Yonsei (8 percent) took third (see Kim 1998). Among the 991 passers in 2001, 398 (40 percent) were SNU graduates (see Choi 2001).

24. SNU graduates made up 83 percent of all senior judges at the high courts in recent years (see Kang 2002).

25. Judges, prosecutors, and practicing attorneys are together referred to as *bopjo samryun*, meaning "the judicial three-wheeler." Widespread use of this term also demonstrates well the cohesiveness of the profession.

26. In the United States, for example, the proportion of female lawyers was less than 5 percent until the 1970s (see Abel 1989, 90). But female enrollment at U.S. law schools reached 49 percent of total enrollment in 2001 (American Bar Association 2002).

be attributed to the substantial increase in the annual quota for new lawyers. Ironically, widespread gender discrimination has also helped to diversify the legal community. The reason for this is that while gender ideology in Korean society remains intact, the gender-blind exam system, together with a seniority-based promotion system, has made the legal profession more attractive to career-oriented women than many other lines of endeavor (Lewis 1997, 54).

It is too early to speculate whether increased gender diversity in the Korean legal profession will affect its traditionally male-dominated and conservative culture. Female lawyers have already begun to organize themselves to conduct systematic research on legal issues related to women, while also responding to the practices of gender discrimination (Kang 1999). The increase in female lawyers has provided Korean women with greater opportunities to retain legal counsel of their choice and to be better represented, especially in family law matters. Having provided a broad overview of the Korean legal profession, the next Part of this chapter will consider in detail the different roles within it.

II. The Legal Profession in Contemporary Korea: In Action

A. Judges and the Courts

To realize the rule of law, a basic precondition in any country is an impartial, competent, and independent judiciary. For decades, the military and authoritarian regimes in South Korea have often interfered in the decisions of judges, especially when politically sensitive matters were adjudicated.[27] The impartiality and independence of the judicial branch has been impaired, particularly as a result of pressure from the Korean Central Intelligence Agency (KCIA) and from military intelligence organs.[28] With political democratization, the judiciary has gradually gained independence from such outside influence. It still has a long way to go, however, to overcome undue influence from inside, which is manifested as judicial cronyism (Yoon 2000, 404).

Despite denial by the judiciary of cronyism (Lee 2001), the public widely believes that the practice of judicial cronyism exists and that it is quite damaging to a fair trial.[29] The practice, known as *junkwanyewu* in Korean, consists of

---

27. See Judge Kim Jong-Hun's opinion published on page one of *Bopjong Shinmun* (Law and Politics News) and reprinted in Chong (1996, 234–35).

28. One of the most notorious cases is the so-called *inhyukdang* (People's Revolution Party) case. On April 9, 1975, eight men were executed at dawn after the Supreme Court, just twenty hours before, denied their petition for nullifying the death penalty. The Presidential Truth Commission on Suspicious Deaths confirmed that the KCIA tortured the defendants to obtain false confessions. The Korean Bar Association, calling this case a "judicial killing," urged an official apology from the Supreme Court (see Ahn 2002).

29. A survey shows that only 11.2 percent of the respondents denied the existence of such a practice (see S. Kim 1999, 147).

affording preferential treatment during litigation to recently retired judges.[30] This preferential treatment is made possible by the unusual guild mentality (Yoon 2000, 395) produced by the unified training and the homogeneous composition of the legal profession, as outlined above. Such preferential treatment clearly implies a lack of impartiality, but the Korean legal profession has long accepted this unethical practice nonetheless. Because of the perception of a high probability of a favorable outcome, former judges can charge fees significantly above normal rates and, thus, make a considerable sum in a short time after retirement (Chamyoyondae 1996, 154–55). Those who can afford to retain recently retired judges as their counsel enjoy a high probability of winning their cases (Yoon 2000, 397–98). This cronyism makes it a custom for judges to help former colleagues in this way. Undoubtedly, this practice substantially undermines the public's trust in the judiciary,[31] reflected in the popular phrase *yujon-mujei mujonyujei*, which means "innocence for the rich, guilt for the poor" (Han 2000, 367).

With respect to the status and function of judges, it might be worthwhile to examine the Korean judiciary from a comparative perspective. In the common law world, as John Merryman notes (1994, 34), the legal tradition was originally created and developed by judges through reasoning in individual cases. From Coke and Mansfield to Marshall and Holmes, many great names of the common law tradition are those of judges. In the civil law world, by contrast, the great names are not those of judges but of legislators (Justinian, Napoleon) or of legal scholars (Gaius, Mancini, Pothier, Savigny) (34). This reflects the traditional view that the function of a civil law judge is to be mechanical and essentially uncreative, resembling a civil servant. The image is that of "an operator of a machine designed by legislators and scholars" (36–37). Because the Korean legal system follows the civil law model, the status and function of a judge are similar to those of a civil servant in many ways. Like his counterpart in an administrative agency, a judge's career follows the promotion system of a highly structured bureaucracy. After first sitting as a junior judge in the lowest ranking court, he or she will rise in the judiciary step by step, based on a combination of seniority and ability.

Even taking into account this fact, the bureaucratization of the Korean judiciary seems to go too far (Yang 1995a, 591–93). A judge's career must trace ten official promotional steps, which, in fact, contain sixteen discrete levels (Chamyoyondae 1996, 29). Any judge who fails to rise to the next position in the hierarchy within a reasonable time is expected to respect tradition within the judicial branch by resigning (Chong 1996, 297). Judges, like all Korean

---

30. In a survey conducted by a Korean newspaper, forty-five out of one hundred practicing attorneys attested that they had experience with such preferential treatment in cases they handled (Kwon and Park 1999).

31. Many Koreans seem to believe that "the first case never loses," which is a rumor circulated around courthouses. The rumor says that when a former judge takes his or her first case after leaving judicial office, the colleagues at the office always help the new attorney win the case.

lawyers, are classified both by the year they passed the judicial exam and the year they entered the JRTI. In the judicial and prosecutorial branches, if anyone who passed the exam or entered the JRTI later is promoted to a higher rank, those who were passed over earlier are expected to leave office.

In comparison to the excessive number of promotional stages, the concentration of power and authority over the appointment process in the hands of one person—the chief justice of the Supreme Court—presents a greater problem (Chong 1996, 287). The chief justice hires and promotes all judges, except for justices of the Supreme Court. Although the chief justice is required to obtain consent from the Supreme Court Justices' Council before making appointments,[32] this council in practice hardly exercises effective screening authority (252). This type of power concentration, in combination with the promotion system, reinforces Korean judges' civil servant mentality, thus undermining the independence of the judiciary.

Regarding the career system, an interesting practice shows the disparity in social position between Korean lawyers and other civil servants. In comparison to a public official who has passed the higher civil service exam, a judge or prosecutor who has passed the judicial exam is not only better paid, but also enjoys substantial privileges within the government hierarchy. It is a long-standing practice that a junior judge or prosecutor starts his or her career at a civil service ranking two levels higher than that of a counterpart in an administrative agency (Yang 1995b, 16). For such an official to rise to a position two levels higher takes an average of twenty years in an administrative department.

A powerful government commission in charge of planning and budgets once proposed lowering the starting level of judges and prosecutors to a position equivalent to those of higher civil servants (Lee 1999). The commission publicized this inequality in order to cut inflated spending on the salaries of judges and prosecutors, and, not surprisingly, both the judicial branch and prosecutors were quick to respond. They argued that the commission erred because the functions of judges and prosecutors are inherently different from those of civil servants. Opponents of the commission's proposal are quite right in arguing that the role or function of a judge is quite different from that of a civil servant, but one might disagree with the proposition that the role of a judge is much more complicated and valuable than that of a public official in an administrative position, especially in light of Korean history.[33]

A simple question one might ask is whether a Korean judge is more like a French or an American judge. A cursory glance at the career system would indicate that a Korean judge is more like a French judge. In reality, however, this is

---

32. The Court Organization Act (*bopwonchojikbop*), Law No. 3992, December 4, 1987, Article 41(3), as amended as Law No. 6408, January 29, 2001.

33. It is commonly believed that the rapid economic growth in South Korea was largely orchestrated by powerful bureaucrats, notably those of the Economic Planning Board (see Haggard and Moon 1993, 67).

not so. There is a strong conviction among the Korean public that the role of the judge should be distinguished from the mechanical role of a civil servant, although this conviction is contrary to that of the civil law tradition.[34] Many Koreans seem to believe that a judge must be not only a legal expert, but also a person of wisdom and integrity (Jacobs 1985, 41–47). They tend to regard an equitable decision as much better than one based on the strict application of law. Confucian influence on Korean culture[35] also seems to deeply affect this kind of perception or tendency.

Korean judges are frequently expected to render a less severe judgment by taking into account specific mitigating circumstances (*chongsang chamjak*).[36] Under a well-established practice, a trial attorney finishes his or her closing argument with the saying "Have mercy, your Honor!" From a comparative perspective, the public image of the Korean judge shares many common features with an English court of equity. Korean judges are expected to render Solomonic decisions reflecting contextualized justice and the wisdom of the ages (Yoon 1990, 116). This public image and expectation has been both a blessing and a burden to judges. They are much more respected and much better treated than their counterparts in other branches of the government, and they enjoy more discretionary power than other public officials (Chong 1996, 314). At the same time, however, they are expected to live up to much higher moral standards.[37] A typical judge is, therefore, a hybrid of the civil law and common law judge. The institutional environment of the Korean judiciary resembles that of a typical civil law judge, but the role of the judge in the public eye is more like that of a common law judge.

The judiciary does not, however, seem to meet the public's expectations. As mentioned earlier, a tiny number of judges are struggling to handle a rapidly growing number of cases (J.O. Kim 2000). Under this structural limitation, a thorough review of a case in a Korean courtroom is nothing but a utopian goal. A judge usually allocates less than five minutes to review a case (Chamyoyondae 1996, 166). While judges complain about their overload, many litigants see the

---

34. As Merryman points out, the anti-judicial ideology of the European revolutions reinforced the tradition in which the judge has never been conceived of as playing a very creative part (1994, 37).

35. There has been a widely circulated misunderstanding that due to the Confucian influence, law and legal institutions have been historically insignificant in Korea. No doubt Confucian teachings stressed moral example, but at the same time Korea has had well-developed legal institutions from at least the mid-Koryo dynasty years. The teachings of the neo-Confucian thinkers in thirteenth century Korea also should not be undervalued in this regard (see Yang 1989; Kim 1991; C. Lee 2002, 431–58).

36. See Shaw (1996, 26–27).

37. There was considerable public outrage when a lawyer's list of bribery revealed that many judges had regularly accepted "a token of lawyer's gratitude." It is often reported that some Koreans give and take money or financial benefit as a token of gratitude (*chonjee*), in the fields of business and government. Nevertheless, because the public expects higher ethical standard from judges, the scandal caused six judges to resign (see Cho 1999).

current system as depriving them of their basic right to present their case and be heard for a reasonably sufficient amount of time (166). In addition to the rushed trial, the lack of experienced judges also damages the public's trust in the judiciary. A substantial majority of judges retire from office and enter private practice when they are in their forties (Chong 1996, 283). Because of this, a majority of judges are under the age of forty. Without seasoned and experienced decision-makers, it is quite natural for the judiciary to lose the public's trust and thus fail to play a pivotal role in a complex society like contemporary Korea.

In addition to hiring more full-time judges, some also suggest that the judiciary should appoint part-time judges for certain categories of cases (Chong 1996, 325–26). But many others, including the judiciary, reject this proposal, arguing that it is prohibited by the Korean constitution, as well as by relevant laws such as the Court Organization Act. The relevant constitutional provision vests all Koreans with the fundamental right to be tried by judges who are licensed under the law.[38] The intention or spirit of this provision is well understood in so far as it seeks to guarantee a just and competent trial by independent and qualified judges. Critics, however, argue that amending the relevant laws to allow involvement by appropriate part-time judges would not necessarily contradict this spirit. Such measures would help reduce the burden on judges and thus allow them to pay more attention to each case.[39]

B. The Prosecution

A glimpse of the architecture of a prosecutor's building may be a good starting point to understand the reality of Korean public prosecutors today. In most countries, courts are symbols of the highest authority. Because of this, the court building itself is usually majestic in appearance, and Korean court buildings are no exception. They are not only tall and massive, but they are also designed to convey the highest sense of dignity. Although the effectiveness of such symbolism is debatable, the motive is understandable. An interesting sight in Korea, however, is a prosecutor's building. They are as big and dignified as those of the courts, and are located next to court buildings. The location and the appearance are not simply matters of architecture or style; they illustrate the relationship between the Korean judiciary and the prosecution. Korean prosecutors do not think of their judicial role or function as subordinate to that of the judge. This mentality is not only incompatible with the adversarial system, which the

---

38. Article 27 of the constitution provides that it is a fundamental right of all Korean citizens to have a trial by judges qualified under the constitution and the statutes. A relevant statute, the Court Organization Act, Article 42(2), specifies that qualified judges are only those who passed the judicial examination and completed the Judicial Research and Training Institute program.

39. For example, law professors, who typically are not certified lawyers, might be able to handle some types of cases, if the relevant laws were amended.

Korean legal system presupposes, but also tends to increase the possibility of abuse of prosecutorial powers.[40]

Korean prosecutors monopolize prosecutorial powers under the Criminal Procedure Act.[41] They also exercise a wide range of discretionary power through indictments.[42] In the past, they have abused their high level of public power to please power-holders (Han 2000, 369–70). Political neutrality among prosecutors may seem to be a utopian ideal, but partisan bias in law enforcement is not only vicious and morally reprehensible but also undermines public trust in the legal system as a whole (West 1998b). This is, however, what has happened in Korean society. For example, prosecutors have indicted many political dissenters on charges of violating the National Security Law (NSL),[43] which is designed to protect South Korea from the threat of North Korea. Prosecutors, in cooperation with the police and intelligence agencies such as the KCIA, have indicted more than 12,000 people since 1964 for violating the NSL (Suh et al. 1998) and have themselves committed serious human rights abuses through the application of harsh extrajudicial punishment.[44] Critics thus argue that the NSL has functioned as a legal tool for maintaining authoritarian regimes in South Korea for half a century (Cho 1997, 127).

The misuse of prosecutorial power is further complicated in contemporary Korean society by the reluctance of prosecutors to exercise their powers in certain instances. It has been a real challenge in many countries, including Korea, to make laws enforceable against high officials. A major reason that the Korean public feels a distrust and suspicion of the prosecution results from the so-called prosecutorial sanctuary (*sungeuk*) (Han 1998, 264). Despite repeated official denials, many Koreans believe, from past patterns of prosecution, that some areas are beyond the reach of prosecutors. For example, it is widely believed that prosecutors are unable to bring an incumbent president to justice. The 1996 trials and convictions of two former Korean presidents attracted worldwide attention,[45] but a sitting president, as well as his family members and close aides, seems to enjoy a kind of sanctuary. In a political structure like Korea's, where extensive powers are vested in the president,[46] the inability of the law to reach wrongdoing by these powerful individuals is especially harmful to achieving the rule of law.

---

40. See generally Han (2000, 363–70).

41. The Criminal Procedure Act (*hyungsasosongbop*), Law No. 341, September 23, 1953, Article 246, as amended as Law No. 5454, December 13, 1997.

42. Ibid. Article 247.

43. The National Security Law (*kukgaboanbop*), Law No. 3318, December 31, 1980, as amended as Law No. 5291, January 13, 1997.

44. See generally Park (1989).

45. Despite the popularity of these prosecutions in Korea, however, critics see the two cases as motivated by revenge or political opportunism. For details, see an excellent analysis of the dramatic criminal trial by James West (1997).

46. The Korean constitution vests a president with more power than the United States constitution does (see C. Kim 2000, 1035).

The de facto existence of the "sanctuary" is a necessary consequence of the Korean prosecution's dependency on political power-holders. A member of the president's party is often pleased to find that the prosecution overlooks his or her party's illegal election activities, while members of the opposition party are regularly charged with and convicted of unlawful campaign activities and illegal spending (C. Kim 2000, 1035). In order for the nation's highest prosecutor, the attorney general, to be insulated from political influence, the Prosecution Act was amended in 1988, when the pro-democracy party controlled the National Assembly. The amendment guarantees the tenure of the attorney general, the "commander"[47] of all Korean prosecutors, for two years (Article 12(3)) and also prohibits consecutive appointments. By guaranteeing tenure, the legislators intended to have an able and impartial attorney general who could fulfill a just prosecutorial mission without fear of removal by the president. In reality, however, the new provision has so far served to secure the office for those demonstrating loyalty to the president and his party, even though they fail to meet the public's expectations.

In addition, other legislation has been proposed to cut the political ties between the prosecution and the ruling party, as it has been the established practice in Korea for top prosecutors faithful to the president or his party to be appointed to prestigious public offices or recruited by the president's party after retirement. The 1997 amendment to the Prosecution Act provided that an attorney general shall not be appointed to any public office for two years following retirement (Article 12(4)). It also restricted his or her participation in any political party (Article 12(5)).

Although this legislation appeared to be of questionable constitutional validity, the public in general, as well as a majority of legal scholars, supported the amendments (Han 1998, 267; *Dong-A Ilbo* 1997). Proponents argued that such measures were reasonably necessary in unique situations where prosecutorial powers had been employed to maintain undemocratic governments and to insulate power-holders from criticism.[48] In January 1997, however, nine high-ranking prosecutors, including the attorney general, challenged the constitutionality of the amendment.[49] The Constitutional Court, ruling with unprecedented speed, agreed with the applicants, finding the measures to be unconstitutional restrictions on the freedom to choose one's occupation guaranteed by Article 15 of the constitution.[50] This ruling demonstrates that Korean society still has a long way to go before the office of the prosecutor achieves full independence.

---

47. The Prosecution Act (*kumchalchongbop*), Law No. 3882, December 31, 1986, Article 7, as amended as Law No. 5430, December 13, 1997, Article 7(1) provides that public prosecutors shall obey any order of a superior with respect to prosecutorial matters. The undemocratic nature of this provision has long been severely criticized (see Han 2000, 271–74).

48. See Han (1998, 265–67).

49. See Nam (1997).

50. The Constitutional Court Ruling, July 16, 1997. 97 *Hon Ma* 26.

In Korea, where public prosecutors retain sole and ultimate authority for the investigation and prosecution of all crimes, it has been a very serious problem that the prosecutors are often politically biased. In this regard, leading non-governmental organizations (NGOs) have proposed various measures to secure the political neutrality of the prosecutorial authority. Among them, the most heated controversy has been the proposal to establish an independent counsel system. The public and the principal opposition party strongly endorsed such proposals (Han 2000, 371). However, although the president's party itself put forth a draft independent counsel act before it controlled the presidency, it subsequently rejected such a proposal (Shin 2002).

C. Lawyers and the Bar

In most countries, lawyers constitute a unique profession, subject to two quite opposite public images: one good, the other evil.[51] This contrast seems especially severe in contemporary Korea. In the eyes of the Korean people, lawyers are the champions of human rights and the personification of self-sacrifice,[52] while at the same time they are seen as a class of lawfully licensed thieves (*Hankyorech Shinmun* 1998). Many people are, of course, well aware of the fact that lawyers of the former kind are rare, but this image in Korean society has been so strong that it has frequently compensated for the negative image of the majority of lawyers (W. Park 1995, 56).

The Attorney-at-Law Act obligates attorneys to protect fundamental human rights and to ensure the realization of social justice.[53] Because the law itself identifies the protection of human rights as the foremost duty of a lawyer, the widely used term *inkwon byunhosa* (human rights lawyer) has a redundant ring in Korean. The term, however, has a special meaning in contemporary Korean society, where it is used to identify a group of lawyers who have fought against past military-authoritarian regimes. The lawyers fought not only for the fundamental rights and freedom of their clients, but also against governmental authorities that denied the very basic principles of democracy.[54]

As far back as the 1930s, one can find Korean lawyers who challenged Japanese colonial rule to protect the fundamental rights and freedoms of their fellow citizens. Those activities could perhaps be best characterized, however, as political acts supporting the national liberation movement.[55] In the 1960s, after a military coup led to the creation of an authoritarian state, Koreans witnessed the appearance of another group of heroic lawyers. Among them, Lee Byung-Rin

---

51. See Sarat and Scheingold (1998, 3).

52. See Park (1998a).

53. The Attorney-at-Law Act (*byunhosabop*), Law No. 3594, December 31, 1982, Article 1(1), as amended as Law No. 6207, January 28, 2000.

54. See W. Park (1995).

55. Kim Byung-Ro, Lee In and Huh Heon were the most notable lawyers who utilized their licenses for the purpose of the national liberation movement. For details, see W. Park (1995, 57–64).

was most prominent. His enthusiastic efforts to protect the civil liberties of those arrested for anti-government activities provided a role model for his fellow lawyers. In addition to his personal striving for human rights, Lee was the first lawyer who had a clear vision for the Korean Bar Association, stressing its pivotal role and function. Serving as president of the Korean Bar Association as well as of the Seoul Bar Association, he rebuilt these organizations to fight against the military dictatorship. Emphasizing the principle of the rule of law, he made the bar a pioneer promoter of the independence of the judiciary and of democracy (W. Park 1995, 67–76).

In December 1972, the Park Chung-Hee regime, through an illegally manipulated process of constitutional amendment, enacted a new constitution, called the Yushin (revitalizing) Constitution.[56] The Yushin Constitution era did not mark the birth of another constitution in Korea; rather, it meant the death of constitutionalism for the nation. The new supreme law of the land enhanced the president's powers to the point that Park Chung-Hee "lawfully" obtained unrestricted power to rule by emergency decree. It thus opened the era of "rule by decree," not by law. Under the Yushin Constitution, the Korean head of state was legally able to do whatever he wished, while the National Assembly became a rubber stamp. The press was gagged, and the political opposition, as well as student and labor groups and the church, were put under surveillance by the KCIA.

From the very beginning the Yushin Constitution provoked a storm of protest. To block a campaign for a million signatures demanding a return to a democratic constitution, Park issued his first emergency decree in January 1974. Although the decree provided that criticizing the Yushin Constitution was a felony punishable by up to fifteen years in prison, it was insufficient to suppress the opposition.[57] Among numerous protests against the anti-democratic regime, the so-called *minchung hakyon* (National League of Democratic College Students) incident in 1974 was one of the most famous.[58] The KCIA investigated 1,204 students on, among others, charges of joining illegal organizations and violating the emergency decree and the National Security Law. Eventually, 253 students were brought to trial before an emergency military court. Human rights lawyers volunteered to represent the defendants. However the military court, which did not fully guarantee procedural safeguards, sentenced the defendants to severe sentences, including death.[59]

---

56. In October 1972, the Park Chung-Hee regime unlawfully suspended parts of the constitution, declared martial law, and dissolved the National Assembly. Park then proposed a new Yushin Constitution, which was approved by a national referendum in December 1972. Shortly thereafter, Park was elected by an electoral college to a six-year term of presidential office with no limits on re-election (see Rees 1988, 156–57).

57. See Ogle (1990, 67–68).

58. See Korean Catholic Human Rights Committee (2001).

59. The military court sentenced seven defendants to death, seven to life imprisonment, twelve to twenty years' imprisonment, and six defendants to fifteen years' imprisonment (see Han 1984, 10–12).

Sometimes, defense attorneys themselves were arrested for their zealous advocacy. During the trial of Kim Jae-Kyu, a KCIA director who was charged with the "rebellious" killing of President Park Chung-Hee in 1979, his defense attorney expressed sympathy for his client and was arrested and sentenced to ten years in prison by the military judges.[60] This should not have come as a surprise, however, since the judges and the public could hardly distinguish permission from praise. In a country such as Korea, which lacks a tradition of liberalism, allowing a practice is not considered to be different from endorsing such a practice.[61] Therefore, defending the rights of anti-government activists was naturally regarded as evidence that the lawyers themselves favored, or at least sympathized with, the cause of the defendants, which was at that time illegal.

Unfortunately, the bravely provided legal assistance could not have obtained justice for the defendants. Since the military court as well as the applicable rules did not treat the defendants justly, the lawyers' efforts, however enthusiastic, were doomed to achieve little, if anything. During the Yushin period, there was a widely accepted notion that the more a human rights lawyer advocated zealously, the more likely his client was to receive a heavy sentence. Nevertheless, what the lawyers did was not futile. Their activities kept alive the cherished ideal of lawyers as guardians of human rights and inscribed a positive image of the lawyer in the public eye. Those activities "put a human face on the lawyer" (Sarat and Scheingold 1998, 3). Despite the fact that the lawyers were unable to provide their clients with the legal assistance to which they were entitled under the law, both their clients and the general public fully appreciated their efforts. The defendants were comforted by the legal elite, who firmly supported their cause and strongly denounced the charges against the defendants, and the public viewed the lawyers' efforts as part of the Confucian tradition of "the learned man taking moral responsibility."

The limited ability of individual lawyers to combat unlawful actions by the authorities was so clear that activist lawyers widely recognized the need for joint efforts, but it took a decade to see the birth of such an organization. In May 1986, twenty-eight lawyers founded an association called the Lawyer's Association for the Realization of Justice (*jeongbyophoe*) (Park 1998b, 23–24). The founding of this association was the outcome of a joint effort between the first and the second generations of human rights lawyers. Those of the first generation were the senior lawyers who had been individually practicing "cause lawyering"* since the early 1970s,[62]

---

60. See *News Maker* (2000).

61. See generally Sandel (1984).

*Ed. note: As Benjamin Liebman explains later in this volume, "Sarat, Scheingold, and Ellmann define public interest law and cause lawyering to refer to lawyers' work that is directed at altering some aspect of the social, economic and political status quo (Ellmann 1998, 349; Sarat and Scheingold 1998, 3)." (Liebman, in this volume). Professor Kim also uses the term this way.

62. Leading figures of the first generation of human rights lawyers were Lee Byong-Lin, Han Sung-Heon, Lee Don-Myong, Cho Jun-Hee, Hwang In-Chul, and Hong Sung-Woo, among others.

while those of the second generation were mostly young lawyers who became licensed to practice during the 1980s. The cooperation of these two groups, particularly in some major cases, led to the formation of an organization for human rights work. Among those seminal cases, it is worthwhile mentioning a series of civil suits seeking compensation from the government for flood damage.

The flood damage cases arose out of disastrous flooding that occurred in the Mangwon-dong area of Seoul in September 1984.[63] The flood damaged about 17,000 houses, and the estimated number of victims was around 80,000 people. Although a torrential, localized downpour caused the flooding, residents of the area claimed that mismanagement of floodgates by the local authorities was the direct cause of the damage. The extraordinary feature of this litigation was the large number of plaintiffs, as well as the enormous amount of damages sought. Following victories by 80 plaintiffs, approximately 20,000 additional flood victims filed suit against the local government. It was unprecedented in Korean history for so many people to bring suit at the same time against the government. Because Korea had no collective litigation procedure such as the class action procedure in the United States, handling all the suits was technically very difficult, if not impossible. The victories of the plaintiffs in these cases, which took seven years to litigate, significantly influenced Korean attitudes toward litigation, as well as toward the legal system. In other words, the social impact of the outcome far outweighed the actual monetary compensation to the plaintiffs. Many citizens, especially the politically underrepresented and economically disadvantaged, had strongly believed that they could not prevail in legal action against the government. The outcome of this litigation changed that belief.

Behind the unprecedented litigation was a lawyer named Cho Young-Rae. Cho, who had been a human rights activist himself, played a leading role in successfully organizing the litigation.[64] When cancer caused his sudden death, Cho was working to launch a public interest law movement. As Cho Young-Rae was one of the most creative, enthusiastic and respected lawyers of his time, cause lawyering in Korea suffered a heavy loss with his premature death.

In the early 1980s, the Chun Doo-Hwan regime doubled the annual quota of new lawyers. The hidden motive of the dramatic increase was known: he wished to reduce the prestige of lawyers and thus weaken the Korean Bar Association, which was then one of the most powerful organizations checking the misuse of governmental power. Ironically, a substantial portion of the new lawyers produced by the authoritarian regime became a major force of human rights lawyers, later forming and joining Lawyers for Democratic Society (*minbyun*). Minbyun was founded by fifty-one lawyers in May 1988. The birth of the group marked the beginning of a new era in the systematic activities of lawyers in Korea. Although Jeongbyophoe, formed two years earlier (see above), already

---

63. See *Bop Kwa Sahoe* (1991).

64. See W. Park (1995, 87–88).

existed, it operated as an underground organization due to harsh suppression by the authoritarian regime. Minbyun was thus the first official organization dedicated to cause lawyering in Korea. In addition to representing workers in labor disputes, Minbyun lawyers vigorously pursued lawyers' ideals, including campaigning for the release of prisoners of conscience and for the abolition of undemocratic laws such as the National Security Law. Leading Minbyun members also played significant roles in expanding the positive functions of lawyers in contemporary Korean society.

For example, Kim Chang-Kuk, as chairman of an active NGO called People's Solidarity for Participatory Democracy (PSPD) (*chamyoyondae*), has substantially contributed to the enhancement of justice in Korean society. Kim was nominated for the position of head of the National Human Rights Commission.[65] Another Minbyun member and a leading figure of the third generation of human rights lawyers, Cho Yong-Whan, has actively sought international remedies for human rights violations by the Korean government. He also played a major role in establishing the National Human Rights Commission in 2001.

Minbyun member Park Won-Soon volunteered to serve as secretary-general of the PSPD. As the first Korean lawyer working full-time for an NGO, Park provided an admirable role model for lawyers in Korean society.[66] During the general elections in 2000, Park organized numerous NGOs to fight against political corruption. Under his leadership, an allied NGO launched a negative campaign against corrupt or undemocratic politicians, which received unprecedented support from the Korean public (Lee 2000). The activities of these heroic human rights lawyers culminated in Roh Moo-Hyun's victory in the 2002 presidential election. President Roh is not only the first lawyer to hold the position in Korean history, but is also, not surprisingly, an heir of Korean cause lawyering.

Unlike the lawyers described above, the majority of Korean lawyers, unfortunately, have been plagued by negative publicity. Clients often express dissatisfaction with unreasonably high fees and poor quality service.[67] Another frequently criticized problem is the widespread practice of hiring brokers[68] and paying them high referral fees (Yoon 2000, 398–400). In addition, the practice of contingent fees has been regarded as the ugliest face of the legal profession (Han 1998, 248). In Korea, where the rate of arrest and detention before trial is extremely high, lawyers have long utilized contingent fee arrangements for the service of obtaining the release of a client on bail. At one point, such criminal defense work became the most lucrative business of lawyers. Public dissatisfaction with this unethical practice, however, finally boiled over in 1995 when the

---

65. See Oh (2001).

66. See Park (1998a, 4–6).

67. According to a survey of client complaints against the members of the Seoul Bar Association, 60 percent of complaints were about high fees and 37 percent about the quality of service (see Chamyoyondae 1996, 92).

68. Of one hundred lawyers, ninety-three responded that most Korean lawyers used brokers, especially to obtain criminal law cases (see Kwon and Park 1999).

Korean Bar Association reluctantly announced that it would prohibit contingency fee arrangements in criminal cases (E. Park 1995). Nevertheless, the prevailing practice of using contingency fees in most cases, including domestic matters, continues to be regulated ineffectively. The most frequent justification for contingent fees is that they enable people who could not otherwise afford a lawyer to engage the services of a lawyer.[69] But in Korea, most lawyers working on a contingent fee basis receive a substantial retainer regardless of the outcome of the litigation.

The persistent problems of poor quality service face a new challenge. Due to its small and exclusive character, the differentiation of the Korean bar has been very slow; the scarcity of practicing lawyers has made it practically impossible to specialize in a particular area of law. Until recently, most attorneys considered themselves capable of handling any legal matter whatsoever, even when a total lack of understanding of underlying technical matters might, in other countries, cast doubt on the lawyer's capacity to provide competent advice or representation.

The relatively rapid increase of the legal population in recent years, however, began to affect the landscape of the Korean bar significantly. Because of intensified competition within the profession, many lawyers established or joined law firms.[70] The proliferation of law firms in Korea is also attributable to the success of Kim & Chang, a Seoul-based law firm, which pioneered the expansion of traditional legal practice in Korea into corporate and transnational spheres.[71] The impending opening of the legal services market also seems to have pressured Korean lawyers to develop more sophisticated legal services.

Despite these developments, there exist chronic problems in legal practice by Korean law firms, especially in the area of corporate law, which raise some serious questions about legal ethics. One of them is the conflict-of-interest problem. Many firms have a tendency to shrug off conflicts of interest, either concurrent or successive, without full disclosure to prospective clients. In the past, such unethical practices were frequently justified and tolerated by the reality that the number of competent law firms was so small given the demand for their services. However, in December 1998, the disciplinary committee of the Korean Bar Association, until then inactive and lenient, took sanctions against a managing partner of a major law firm for malpractice based on conflicts of interest.[72]

D. Legal Academia

Korean legal scholarship has been greatly influenced by the so-called legal science approach developed primarily by German legal scholars of the middle and

---

69. See Gillers (1992, 112).

70. In October 2002 there were 233 law firms in South Korea (see *Korean Bar Association News* 2002). In May 2004 there were 258 firms (KBA website).

71. See JaeWon Kim (2000, 421–24).

72. See Kim (1999, 136–37).

late nineteenth century (Merryman 1994, 61). Although many of Korea's modern legal norms and institutions are of German origin, it was the Japanese colonizers who brought them to Korean soil. It is therefore quite natural to observe a dependency of Korean legal scholarship on that of the Japanese. In this regard, it is particularly noteworthy to examine the politics of language in Korea. After liberation from Japan in 1945, the first generation of Korean legal scholars used Japanese virtually as if it were a mother tongue. The majority of the first generation legal textbooks were therefore no more than Korean translations of Japanese law books. However, antagonism against, and a sense of superiority over, the Japanese led Korean scholars to conceal the contributions of Japanese scholarship to the greatest extent possible. They struggled to establish a direct link between their theoretical work and the original German sources, but due to the difficulty of obtaining the German materials, and more fundamentally due to a poor command of German, most of the German writings they cited were nothing more than double-translations of Japanese texts.

The second generation of Korean legal scholars, under the guidance of the first generation, went abroad for advanced legal study which was then unavailable at home. Some went to Japan, but the majority of graduate law students or scholar-aspirants were eager to go to Germany. They sincerely hoped to reach the original fount of legal science and thus to bypass Japanese scholarship. This preference for Germany continued among young legal scholars and researchers until very recently. Considering the fact that Korean education, as well as its political system, has been manifestly shaped by American influence since 1945,[73] the predominantly German influence on contemporary Korean legal scholarship seems quite odd.[74] Familiarity with German legal science through easy access to Japanese scholarship is a major reason for such strong ties. Another reason may be the generous financial assistance available from the German government, which has provided state-supported, tuition-free education, while foreign law students find it extremely difficult to obtain financial assistance to meet expensive tuition costs in the United States.[75]

Compared to most other countries, there exists little interaction in Korea between university law faculties and the realm of legal practice. Few professors are qualified as attorneys, although the number has been growing recently, and even if they were qualified, there are legal restrictions on consulting activities permitted by law professors. Judges, prosecutors and practicing lawyers seldom

---

73. See generally Ahn (1997).

74. Since many Korean educators and scholars have received some education in the United States, many critics express their concern that the pedagogy as well as the contents of Korean education is too Americanized. In the area of legal studies, however, only a minority have studied in the United States, although the number has grown since the early 1990s.

75. The Korean government and various educational foundations have supported Korean students studying abroad. But those studying law have had few chances to receive such financial help, because the government policy stressing rapid economic development has favored those who pursue areas such as engineering, economics, and management.

lecture in the universities,[76] although they do teach in the JRTI or oversee apprentices. The academic and practical spheres are thus segregated to a considerable extent,[77] yet in light of the nature of law, which is very practical, both scholars and practitioners would benefit if this segregation were brought to an end as quickly as possible.

A final target of criticism is the overly formalistic approach toward legal scholarship and teaching that has long dominated Korean academic circles.[78] There are a growing number of functionalists who focus less on doctrinal exegesis and more on the policy goals and interests expressed in statutory norms and sociological studies. In this regard, the Korean Law and Society Association (*bop kwa sahoe liron hakwhoe*), led by Kun Yang,[79] played a pivotal role. The members of this group, well aware of the limits of legal formalism, substantially contributed to the improvement of legal scholarship in Korea. While organizing symposiums and publishing *Bop Kwa Sahoe* (the Korean Journal of Law & Society), the association also provided blueprints for reforming the judicial system and various proposals for enacting or amending laws.

The problems examined in this Part are closely related to the system of legal education and professional training in Korea. Having examined problems within the Korean legal profession, I will now discuss the system that educates and produces Korean lawyers.

III. Legal Education and Professional Training

Since the quality of legal services is closely related to the system of legal education, most countries, including Korea, have shown a strong interest in improving legal education. There have been numerous debates over reforming Korean legal education,[80] and such debates, along with criticisms of the current educational system, have produced various reform proposals. Most reform proposals stressed practice-oriented curricula, more diversified elective courses, and

---

76. Korean judges and prosecutors are discouraged from engaging in outside activities including teaching law in universities. Universities usually allow practicing attorneys to teach only procedural law such as civil and criminal procedure.

77. In this respect, the first congress for Korean law professors held in October 1998 in Seoul marked an epochal event in Korean history. Though not many legal practitioners actually turned out, the occasion was a good trial to bridge the gap between academia and the legal practice world.

78. See West (1991, 45).

79. See Yang (1994).

80. As early as 1955, Yu Chin-Oh, who drafted the original constitution of the Republic of Korea, proposed a reform of the law school education system. The Korean Law Professors Association held a nationwide conference in 1967 on legal education and the judicial exam (see Park 1978, n1).

extending the length of study.[81] Those proposals met strong opposition, however, from the bar and the judiciary (Roh 1995) and eventually failed. A lack of
concern and support from the general public has also been cited as another reason for the failure (Chamyoyondae 1996, 6). Because most participants in the
debates were legal scholars, the reformist agenda never succeeded in getting the
attention of the public or the government.

Every system or institution has some purpose or goal, yet Korean legal education has historically lacked a clear purpose. Educating lawyers may be
regarded as a major goal of legal education. The standard curriculum of a typical Korean law faculty, which requires civil and criminal procedure in addition
to various substantive law courses, seems oriented toward such a goal. Nevertheless, the reality is quite different from the appearance. There are some ninety
universities that award the degree of Bachelor of Law, but approximately 80 percent of these faculties have never produced a graduate who passed the judicial
exam and became a lawyer. At most law faculties, then, legal education can
hardly be regarded as being aimed toward training lawyers.[82] Rather, it seems
aimed at providing advanced civic education.

Confusion over the goal of legal education in Korea has been complicated by
the judicial exam. The passage rate of the exam has been so low (less than 3 percent) as to render legal education institutionally disconnected from the training
and licensing of lawyers.[83] Furthermore, regulations governing the judicial
exam require no educational background of any kind, quite contrary to the system for licensing medical doctors. Without graduating from an accredited medical school, one could not hope to be licensed as a doctor in Korea, because one
would be prohibited by law from sitting for the medical exam. However, Korean
law places no educational requirements whatsoever on those who wish to compete for a lawyer's license on the odd pretext of "equality before the law." Despite
no educational requirement, a great number of students aiming to become
lawyers in fact enter Korea's undergraduate colleges of law or university law
departments. However, in a system where the only way to become a lawyer is to
pass the judicial exam, the impact of a law that does not require legal education
to take the exam has been very detrimental. Since it is not institutionally incorporated into the system of producing lawyers, Korean legal education has had
difficulty identifying its proper role.

The fact that the judicial exam system rewards rote memorization has also
been criticized by many legal academics.[84] In any system of legal education,
memorization of some doctrinal material, rules, and procedures is essential.
The extreme emphasis in Korea on the judicial exam, however, has substantially
discouraged students from focusing on the professional knowledge and skills

---

81. See generally Hankukbophakkyosuhoe (1992).

82. See Yang (1995b, 13–14).

83. See Lewis (1997, 55).

84. See West (1991, 27) and Yang (1995b, 15).

that a society expects from its legal profession. Under these circumstances, it is not surprising that the education offered by law faculties resembles, and in some way competes with, the numerous judicial exam cram schools which constitute a large and lucrative industry in Korea (J. Y. Kim 2000).

Viewed in a social context, the judicial exam represents only the last in a series of hyper-competitive exams, which determine who will be admitted to the best universities and the most prestigious career tracks.[85] There also exists a basic historical continuity with the Confucian tradition of recruiting higher officials through state-administered exams.[86] In 1315, when the Chinese revived their Confucian exam system, they were aware that exams were not very reliable indicators of the capability of aspirants to the civil service. They adopted the system, however, to serve "as a corrective to what otherwise would be a system of advancement through open bribery" (Dardess 1983).

Despite modernization of the content, the Korean judicial exam is basically in the tradition of a Confucian civil service exam of the kind imported from China by the Koryo dynasty (936–1392) and systematically administered through the end of the Choson dynasty (1391–1910). Like the old Chinese exams, the Korean judicial exam has effectively served its function of selecting lawyer-aspirants: the process of selecting future judges, prosecutors, and private attorneys has not been tainted by bribery or the advantages of family ties. The exam has also earned a reputation as a fair and objective test, capable of distinguishing aspirants with sufficient legal knowledge from those without.

Despite its contributions, however, the exam system also has its limits. Sole reliance on a single exam has proven insufficient for selecting the innovative lawyers necessary in the age of a global economy, the information revolution, and the acceleration of political democratization at home.

IV. Judicial Reform in Korea: Aspirations and Frustrations

The Kim Young-Sam administration, inaugurated in 1993 as the first civilian government since the 1961 military coup of Park Chung-Hee, exhibited a strong interest in legal reform as part of its general reform program. New momentum for reform arose in early 1995 when the Presidential Commission on the Promotion of Globalization (PCPG) announced an ambitious plan to combat corruption and to make the infrastructure of Korean society compatible with a "global" standard (Kwon 1996, 11). As a part of the reform package, the PCPG proposed a concrete plan of judicial reform, which, unlike similar earlier proposals, gained enormous public attention due to the changed environment within and beyond Korea (*Chosun Ilbo* Legal Research Team 1995).

---

85. See West (1991, 20).

86. For useful insights on the traditional role of state exams in China, many of which apply also to Korea, see Elman (1991).

The contents of the PCPG proposal, as well as subsequent developments, are worthy of close examination because the proposal addresses nearly all of the shortcomings of the Korean legal system and legal profession and because it has served as the foundation for ongoing reform measures, especially regarding legal education.

What the PCPG proposed was revolutionary in light of the history of the Korean legal profession: it intended to completely remake the roles and functions of the legal profession to reflect the perspective of the consumer, not of the supplier (Kwon 1996, 129). The PCPG perceived that the severe entrance barrier to the legal profession, and therefore the reinforcement of the Korean Bar Association's monopoly, had served only the interests of the legal profession, while erecting barriers to the public's access to the judicial system. Its proposal to remedy this was to increase substantially the number of lawyers. Thus, the PCPG intended to generate competition in the legal market and thereby produce better-quality legal services.[87] Of all the judicial reforms proposed, the plan for reforming legal education aroused the most heated controversy (PCPG 1995, 541–43). The proposal called for the replacement of undergraduate legal studies with a three-year graduate course modeled after the American legal education system. Opponents of the proposal were quick to denounce it for aping a foreign institution (*Korea Times* 1995). Simply applying the label "American-style law school" allowed the critics to gain substantial support from nationalistic public opinion. Given Korea's tragic modern history, it is no surprise that nationalism is a potent force among many citizens. Hurt by such emotional tactics, proponents of the proposal tried hard to salvage their plan (Moon 1995). In order to differentiate theirs from the American model, the PCPG invented a rather odd name, *jonmunbopkadaehakwon* (professional graduate school of law) (PCPG 1995, 29). Despite the name change, one could hardly deny that the critics were correct in calling the proposal an imitation of the American system of legal education.

This proposal was closely linked to a proposal that would change the judicial exam to make it more like bar exams administered in the United States. In the course of changing the character of the judicial exam and improving legal education, it appeared likely that the JRTI would be abolished. The PCPG argued that the current exam and the monopoly of the JRTI should be replaced with a new system. To justify the adoption of the new law school system, it advocated a basic shift from "selection through examination" to "cultivation or training through education" (Kwon 1996, 49). Eventual Korean reunification was also given as a reason for increasing the number of lawyers. It was argued that the South Korean bar should prepare to supply lawyers to the North Korean region once the two are reunited.

The reformers maintained that Korea needed the new legal education system, first, because undergraduate legal studies were insufficient to deal with the

---

87. See generally PCPG (1995).

complex legal problems of contemporary Korean society. Before studying law, one needs to learn more about how a society works, and to be a competent lawyer, one should study various law-related subjects, argued the PCPG. At the same time, premature concentration on legal studies was also cited as a problem. The existing curriculum for law majors began with one year of "general education," usually including required courses in Korean language and composition, history, economics, a foreign language (usually English), and a few electives. Even before beginning the second year, however, many serious lawyer-aspirants start to prepare for the judicial exam, restricting their studies to only those topics tested on the exam. Courses which students consider unhelpful for passing the exam are typically not selected or not attended. Considering the fact that most students are between eighteen and twenty years old upon admission to an undergraduate law program, it was argued that this early narrowing of focus has led to an unbalanced education (West 1991, 28–31).

Second, the reformers challenged the existing system of legal education as greatly deficient in producing specialists such as patent attorneys or international lawyers (Kwon 1996, 28). The normal route for entry to the Korean bar was an undergraduate concentration in law. Under these circumstances, it was very difficult for someone with a university education in natural science or engineering, or experience in industry, to become a lawyer (Yang 1995b, 15).

Not surprisingly, the legal establishment, including the Supreme Court and the Korean Bar Association, opposed these proposals (Roh 1995). First, the judiciary and the bar argued that law professors were incapable of producing lawyers through the proposed graduate law school system. They raised the issue of balancing theoretical knowledge with practical experience in legal education. The debate is not, of course, unique to Korea; even in the United States, where law schools are professional schools, judges and practicing lawyers often complain that law schools teach students to think like law professors, not like lawyers.[88] The argument in Korea, however, has another dimension, which is the bar's perceived superiority over members of legal academia. Since the majority of law professors have not passed the judicial exam, those who passed—"the lawyers"—have a strong tendency to ignore the scholarship of legal academics regarding the "real" operation of the legal system (Kwon 1996, 13).

Second, the legal establishment, which has consistently resisted any attempt to increase the number of people passing the judicial exam, argued that the adoption of the American system of legal education would automatically result in an enormous number of new lawyers, as happened in the United States. They maintained that the too-many-lawyers situation would produce many "ambulance chasers" and thus do more harm to Korean society than would the scarcity of lawyers (Im 1995).

In the face of the unexpectedly strong opposition from the legal establishment, the proposal for the graduate law school system suffered a setback. The PCPG and

---

88. See Edwards (1992).

its proponents had no alternative but to either withdraw or modify their proposal; otherwise, they thought, their legal education proposal could endanger their entire legal reform agenda. The PCPG, therefore, reluctantly modified its original proposal and announced that the issue of legal education would be separated from the general legal reform agenda, which would instead be addressed under the government's wider education reform agenda (PCPG 1995, 70).

Satisfied with defeating the graduate law school plan, the Supreme Court and the bar agreed with the PCPG on an increased annual quota for new lawyers. They agreed to an increase in the quota from three hundred in 1995 to five hundred in 1996, with one hundred more added each year until the quota reached one thousand.[89] By this concession, the Supreme Court maintained its control over the unified legal training provided by the JRTI. The bar, although not completely happy with the concession, was pleased to have prevented adoption of the graduate law school system.

President Kim Dae-Jung, elected in 1997, expressed deep concern over the issue of judicial reform. The administration revived the proposal for reform of the legal education system, and the Presidential Commission on Education Reform (*saekyoyookkongdongchewiwonhoe*) reopened the issue of adopting a graduate law school system. Based on the proposals of the former administration's PCPG, the new commission proposed changing the legal education system to a graduate-level system (Cho and Moon 1998). One noticeable difference between the new proposal and that of the PCPG was the proposal to adopt a dual system. Unlike the previous administration's proposal, which allowed only a graduate-level legal education, the new one would allow each educational institution to choose either to establish a new graduate law school or to maintain its current undergraduate legal education. In addition to this option, it proposed that any institution that met the requirements of accreditation would be allowed to open a new law school. Being well aware of the PCPG's intent to limit the total number of new law schools, which invited significant opposition from educators, the new proposal aimed to please school administrators and teachers. The proposal stated that those who graduated from a new law school would enjoy the privilege of waiving the first part of the judicial exam.

The new proposal, however, met an almost identical response from the bar and the judiciary (Ku 1999). Although the final report of the Presidential Commission on Education Reform was published, and the Department of Education announced that the graduate law school system would commence in 2003 (Park 2000), the proposal was not implemented. Due to the strong opposition from the legal establishment, no legislation was enacted to realize the proposal. Despite intense battles, the basic framework for legal education and the way Korean lawyers are produced remained untouched, and prospects for reform

---

89. In 2000, 801 people passed the exam. In 2001, the total number of successful candidates was 991 (see J. Lee 2002, 49).

were still uncertain.[90] Neither the lame-duck government nor the legislature had the power to implement any reform proposals. However, almost the same legal reform agenda reappeared after the new president, Roh Moo-Hyun, was inaugurated in early 2003.

The Roh administration had a new plan to change the legal education system from the undergraduate to the graduate level. One major development, which was quite surprising to many observers, is that this time, the Supreme Court endorsed such reform—in fact, the committee was formed under the Supreme Court.*

Conclusion

Law is deeply rooted in culture. Law responds, within cultural limits, to the specific demands of a given society in a given time and place. Discourse on any legal system therefore would be insufficient without examining the culture's legal tradition, which is much more than a set of rules of law. It relates the legal system to the culture of which it is a partial expression. Under Confucian culture, which stresses respect for hierarchical order and harmonious personal relationships, the homogeneous composition of the Korean legal profession has reinforced judicial cronyism, thus propagating unethical practices. Judicial cronyism and misuse of prosecutorial powers have lowered the Korean public's trust in the legal system as a whole.[91] The extremely small legal professional population has also been responsible for blocking access to judicial services by resisting moves to increase the number of new entrants to the legal profession.

---

90. Interestingly, comparable steps are being taken in Japan. Japan decided to adopt the American-style law school system, and began to implement it in April 2004. Although there exist some differences between the two countries' plans, the influence of the powerful neighbor state will sooner or later affect decisions made by Korea.

*Ed. note: In late 2004, the Presidential Commission on Judicial Reform, under the Supreme Court, announced a plan for American-style three-year graduate law schools to be launched in 2008, and for the current judicial exam to be phased out by 2013. The number passing the exam would be decreased annually from 2008 until 2013. It has been reported that in the beginning, approximately 1,200 to 1,300 people would pass the judicial exam, which is close to the average number of current passers. In April 2005, there were indications that the actual enrollment numbers would be determined by the Ministry of Education and Human Resources Development. The plan called for ten universities to open law schools, with each one allowed to accept 150 students per year. The Ministry of Education and Human Resources Development planned to decide by the end of 2006 which colleges and universities would be selected.

91. In discussing Korean prosecutors, I have been very critical about the misuse of prosecutorial power. After finishing the manuscript of this chapter, however, there occurred a remarkable development: the appointment, in 2003, of Kang Kum-Sil as head of the Ministry of Justice was shocking news to many Koreans. As a progressive female lawyer, who also served as a vice president of Minbyun, Minister Kang began making substantial progress toward achieving the independence of the prosecutor's office. Unfortunately, President Roh replaced her in 2004.

On the other hand, human rights lawyers in Korea have set a good model for cause lawyering and have consolidated the tradition of "the learned man taking moral responsibility."

For the last decade, social changes significantly affected the Korean legal profession. Political democratization, deregulation of economic activities, and intensified global competition have demanded a more responsive legal system, as well as better lawyers. The relatively rapid growth of the legal population in recent years has produced competition in the Korean legal market, which has generated better services. As the national economy has become more internationalized, the emergence of international corporate law firms has been another positive development toward the provision of sophisticated legal services. Accelerated democratization of Korean society naturally demands a more positive role for the legal profession. Legislative and administrative processes, which only a decade ago were essentially authoritarian, are facing demands that they be more responsive to civil society. The worldwide phenomenon of the "information revolution" is giving rise to expectations of a more active and creative role for the Korean legal profession as well. Today, lawyers find themselves being called upon to discharge several novel roles such as lobbying for new legislation affecting frontier technologies and educating bureaucrats on initiatives for international harmonization of laws and regulations.

To meet these challenges, Korea urgently needs to replace the defective legal culture and system with ones compatible with the changed environment. As a start, it should implement the proposed reform measures in the area of legal education. Without an increased lawyer population, a more sophisticated training program, and reinforcement of legal ethics, the legal profession will not be able to meet the demands of Korean society in the twenty-first century.

Works Cited

Abel, Richard L. 1989. *American lawyers.* New York: Oxford University Press.

Ahn, Kyong-Whan. 1997. The influence of American constitutionalism on South Korea. 22 *Southern Illinois Law Journal* 71.

Ahn, Seok-Bae. 2002. Dasibonun Inhyukdang sakun [Reconsidering the Inhyukdang case]. *Chosun Ilbo* [Chosun daily newspaper]. 17 September.

American Bar Association. 2002. *First year enrollment in ABA approved law schools 1947–2002 (percentage of women).* See report on the ABA website, Legal Education section, at http://www.abanet.org/legaled/statistics/femstats .html.

Amsden, Alice H. 1989. *Asia's next giant: South Korea and late industrialization.* New York: Oxford University Press.

Bop Kwa Sahoe [Korean journal of law and society]. 1991. Case Report. 4 *Bop Kwa Sahoe* 107.

Chamyoyondae [People's Solidarity for Participatory Democracy]. 1996. *Kukminul wihan sabopkehuk* [Judicial reform for people]. Justice Watch Center. Seoul: Parkyongyulchulphansa.

Chang, Se-Hoon. 2002. Sasi hapkeuk tongge [Statistics of the judicial exam]. *Korea Daily News.* 30 December.

Cho, Ho-Yun and Young-Doo Moon. 1998. Bophakjeonmundae hakwon doipnoran [Revival of law school controversies]. *Kyonghyang Shinmun* [Metropolitan daily newspaper]. 7 July.

Cho, Kuk. 1997. Tension between the National Security Law and constitutionalism in South Korea: Security for what? 15 *Boston University International Law Journal* 125.

Cho, Won-Pyo. 1999. Daebopwon, tchukgap pansa sapyo suri [Supreme Court censures scandalous judges]. *Dong-A Ilbo* [Dong-A daily newspaper]. 20 February.

Choi, Yeo-Kyong. 2001. Sasi hapkeukja daehak pyunjung whanhwa [Easing off the disparity in passing rate among major schools]. *Korea Daily News.* 31 December.

Choi, Young-Hwan. 1996. The path to modernization: 1961–1992. In *Korea at the turning point: Innovation-based strategies for development,* eds. L. M. Branscomb and Y. H. Choi. Westport, CT: Praeger.

Chong, Jong-Sup. 1996. *Heonbop yonku (2)* [A study on constitutional law, II]. Seoul: Chulhakkwahyunsilsa.

Chosun Ilbo Legal Research Team. 1995. Sabop kehuk [Judicial reform]. *Chosun Ilbo.* 26 February.

Dardess, John W. 1983. *Confucianism and autocracy: Professional elites in the founding of Ming Dynasty.* Berkeley: University of California Press.

Dong-A Ilbo. 1997. Editorial. Kumchalchongjang ui honbopsowon [On the constitutional challenge by the attorney general]. 23 January.

Edwards, Harry T. 1992. The growing distinction between legal education and the legal profession. 91 *Michigan Law Review* 34.

Elman, Benjamin. 1991. Political, social and cultural reproduction via Civil Service Examination in late Imperial China. *Journal of Asian Studies* 50:7.

Gillers, Stephen. 1992. *Regulation of lawyers: Problems of law and ethics*, 3rd ed. Boston: Little, Brown.

Ha, Tae-Won. 1999. Hundulrinon bopwon [Crisis of the bench]. *Dong-A Ilbo*. 8 February.

Haggard, Stephan and Chung-In Moon. 1993. The state, politics, and economic development in postwar South Korea. In *State and society in contemporary Korea*, ed. H. Koo. Ithaca, NY: Cornell University Press.

Han, In-Sup. 1998. *Hankuk hyungsabop kwa bop ui jeebae* [Korean criminal law and the rule of law]. Seoul: Hanul Akademi.

———. 2000. A dilemma of public prosecution of political corruption. In *Recent transformations in Korean law and society*, ed. D. K. Yoon. Seoul: Seoul National University Press.

Han, Sung-Heon. 1984. *Yushin chaeje wha minjuhwaundong* [The Yushin regime and the democratization movement]. Seoul: Samminsa.

Hankukbophakkyosuhoe [The Korean Association of Law Professors], ed. 1992. *Bophakkyoyook kwa bopjosilmu* [Legal education and legal practice]. Seoul: Kyoyookkwahaksa.

Hankyorech Shinmun [Korean people's daily newspaper]. 1998. Editorial. Bopjobiri chukgyul kegi daeoya [An opportunity to clean judicial corruption]. 23 February.

Im, Chae-Jung. 1995. Bopyulmunwha saesidae [New era of legal culture]. *Dong-A Ilbo*. 26 April.

Jacobs, Norman. 1985. *The Korean road to modernization and development*. Urbana: University of Illinois Press.

Kang, Sun-Im. 1999. Namyeochabyeulkumgibop ui munjeom [The problems of the sex discrimination act]. *Korea Daily News*. 30 June.

Kang, Sung-Man. 2002. Seouldae kongwhakuk [SNU Republic]. *Hankyorech Shinmun*. 10 January.

Kim, Chul-Soo. 2000. *Honbophakgeron* [An introduction to constitutional law], 12th ed. Seoul: Parkyongsa.

Kim, Eun-Mee. 1997. *Big business, strong state: Collusion and conflict in South Korean development, 1960–1990*. Albany, NY: State University of New York Press.

Kim, JaeWon. 1991. Law, politics and social transformation in Korea. Unpublished paper, on file with Washington College of Law, The American University.

———. 2000. Transnational legal practices. In *Recent transformations in Korean law and society,* ed. D. K. Yoon. Seoul: Seoul National University Press.

Kim, Jang-Yul. 2000. Kosichon Sanchek [Bar exam prep town]. *Korea Daily News.* 9 October.

Kim, Jeong-Oh. 2000. The changing landscape of civil litigation. In *Recent transformations in Korean law and society,* ed. D. K. Yoon. Seoul: Seoul National University.

Kim, Jin-Won. 1999. *Law firm.* Seoul: Tduindol.

Kim, Sung-Eun. 1999. *Corruption in legal circles and its control.* Seoul: Hankukhyongsajeongchekyonguwon [Korea Institute of Criminology].

Kim, Sung-Soo. 1998. Sasi hapkeuk 700 myung balyuo [700 candidates pass the judicial exam]. *Korea Daily News.* 28 November.

Korea Times. 1995. Seoul judges oppose law school system. 15 July.

———. 1996. Editorial. OECD entry ratification. 28 November.

Korean Bar Association News. 2002. Statistics. 21 October.

Korean Catholic Human Rights Committee. 2001. *Sabop salin* [Judicial killings]. Seoul: Hakminsa.

Ku, Bon-Young. 1999. Hakge-bopjoge law school doip lonran [Controversies over new law school system]. *Korea Daily News.* 13 September.

Kwon, Jae-Hyun and Jung-Hun Park. 1999. Byunhosa 33%, pankumsaeke chonji jungeuk itda [33% of lawyers respond, they give some money to judges and prosecutors]. *Dong-A Ilbo.* 21 January.

Kwon, Oh-Sung. 1996. *Sabopdo servisda* [Judicial work is also a service]. Seoul: Miraemedia.

Lee, Chulwoo. 2002. Talking about Korean legal culture. In *Korean politics: Striving for democracy and unification,* ed. and publisher Korean National Commission for UNESCO. Seoul: Hollym International Corp.

Lee, Jung-Eun. 2001. Bopjoke junkwanyewu munje upda [Judge says no preferential treatment]. *Dong-A Ilbo.* 23 June.

———. 2002. Byunhosa "hareuhan sijeol" katda [Lawyer's "good old days" gone]. *Dong-A Ilbo.* 29 March.

Lee, Soo-Hyung. 1999. Kowhikongmuwon gikkupchabyul lonran [Controversies over discrimination among high-ranking officials]. *Dong-A Ilbo.* 19 March.

Lee, Soo-Jeong. 2000. Civic group leads fight for participatory democracy. *Korea Times.* 22 February.

Lee, Sung-Yul. 1997. IMF bailout hurts Korean pride. *Korea Herald.* 25 November.

Lewis, Linda. S. 1997. Female employment and elite occupations in Korea: The case of "Her Honor" the judge. *Korean Studies* 21. Hawai'i: University of Hawai'i Press and The Center of Korean Studies at University of Hawai'i.

Merryman, John Henry. 1994. *The civil law tradition: An introduction to the legal systems of Western Europe and Latin America,* 2nd ed. Stanford, CA: Stanford University Press.

Ministry of Court Administration, ed. 2002. *Sabopyongam* [The judicial year-book]. Seoul: Ministry of Court Administration.

Moon, Ho-Young. 1995. Sabopbunun law school suyong hara, Lee chongri chokgu [Prime minister urges the judiciary to accept law school proposal]. *Korea Daily News.* 6 October.

Nahm, Andrew C. 1996. *Korea: Tradition & transformation: A history of the Korean people,* 2nd ed. Elizabeth, NJ: Hollym International Corp.

Nam, In-Soo. 1997. Controversy surrounds prosecutors' petitions. *Korea Herald.* 25 January.

News Maker. 2000. Interview with lawyer Kang Sin-Ok. 8 June.

Ogle, George E. 1990. *South Korea: Dissent within the economic miracle.* Washington, DC: International Labor Rights Education and Research Fund.

Oh, Poong-Yun. 2001. Kim Chang-Kuk byunhosa kukkainkwonwiwonjang nae-jeong [Lawyer Kim Chang-Kuk nominated as new head of NHRC]. *Korea Daily News.* 2 August.

Osgood, Cornelius. 1998. *The Koreans and their culture.* New York: Ronald Press Company.

Overholt, William. 1998. A dangerous, decisive year. *Newsweek* (the Pacific edition). 9 November.

Park, Eun-Ho. 1995. Byunhyop byunhosa sungkongbosu kumji [KBA to ban contingent fee]. *Korea Daily News.* 15 April.

Park, Hong-Ki. 2000. Bop-uihak jeonmun dahakwon doip [Professional law school and medical school system]. *Korea Daily News.* 23 October.

Park, Kiljun. 1978. Problems concerning the reform of legal education in Korea. 6 *Korean Journal of Comparative Law* 56.

Park, Won-Soon. 1989. *Kukkaboan bop yonku* [A study of national security law]. Seoul: Yoksabipyongsa.

———. 1995. Hankuk inkwon byunronsa siron [A short history of Korean human rights advocacy]. In *Mujeda ranun mal hanmadi* [A single word proclaiming "not guilty"], ed. Committee for Commemorating Hwang In-Chul. [Compiled in memory of attorney Hwang.] Seoul: Moonhakkwa-jisungsa.

————. 1998a. A camel passing through the eye of a needle. *Youndae* [Solidarity]. September.

————. 1998b. Ohkongwhakuk hubangi ui inkwon byunhosa [Human rights lawyers during the latter half of the Fifth Republic]. In *Minbyun Baekseo* [Lawyers for a Democratic Society white paper], 23–24. Seoul: Minbyun.

PCPG. See Presidential Commission on the Promotion of Globalization.

Presidential Commission on the Promotion of Globalization (PCPG). 1995. *Bopyulservice mit bopyulkyoyookui sekewha* [Globalization of legal service and legal education]. Seoul: PCPG.

Rees, David. 1988. *A short history of modern Korea.* Port Erin: Ham.

Roh, Ju-Suk. 1995. Daebop jeonmun bopkwadaehakwon bandae [Supreme Court opposes law school proposal]. *Korea Daily News.* 10 October.

Sandel, Michael, ed. 1984. *Liberalism and its critics.* New York: New York University Press.

Sarat, Austin and Stuart Scheingold, eds. 1998. *Cause lawyering: Political commitment and professional responsibilities.* New York: Oxford University Press.

Shaw, William R. 1996. Social and intellectual aspects of traditional Korean law, 1931–1996. University of California at Berkeley Korea Research Monograph No. 2. Reproduced in *Korean law in the global economy,* ed. S. H. Song. 1996. Seoul: Bak Young Sa.

Shin, Yong-Bae. 2002. Rival parties on collision course over alleged secret money deal with North. *Korea Herald.* 30 September.

Sohn, Hak-Kyu. 1989. *Authoritarianism and opposition in South Korea.* New York: Routledge.

Suh, Young-Ah and Chang-Hee Kim, et al. 1998. Kukkaboan bop bansegi [Fifty years of the national security law]. *News Plus.* 3 December.

West, James M. 1991. *Education of the legal profession in Korea.* Seoul: International Legal Studies, Korea University.

————. 1997. Martial lawlessness: The legal aftermath of Kiwangju. 6 *Pacific Rim Law & Policy Journal* 85.

————. 1998a. Fluxlog: Transparency. *Korea Herald.* 10 August. Reprinted in James M. West, *A critical discourse on Korean law and economy.* 2002. Busan, Korea: Hanguel.

————. 1998b. Fluxlog: Prosecutors and politics (II). *Korea Herald.* 14 September. Reprinted in James M. West, *A critical discourse on Korean law and economy.* 2002. Busan, Korea: Hanguel.

Yang, Kun. 1989. Law and society studies in Korea: Beyond the Hahm theses. 23 *Law & Society Review* 891.

————. 1994. Bop kwa sahoe liron yonkuhoe ui eoje wa neil [The past and future of the Research Group for Law and Society]. 9 *Bop Kwa Sahoe* 305.

————. 1995a. *Heonbop yonku* [A study of constitutional law]. Seoul: Bopmunsa.

————. 1995b. *Sabopkehuk eejebuteo* [Let's restart judicial reform]. Seoul: Hyohyungchulphansa.

Yoo, Cheong-Mo. 1997. Seoul to seek IMF loans. *Korea Herald.* 22 November.

Yoon, Dae-Kyu. 1990. *Law and political authority in South Korea.* Boulder, CO: Westview Press.

————. 1996. Recent judicial reform on access to justice in South Korea. In *Yearbook Law & Legal Practice in East Asia,* eds. A. J. de Roo and R. W. Jagtenberg. Vol. 2. The Hague: Kluwer Law International.

————. 2000. Unfair and irregular practices in the Korean legal profession. In *Recent transformations in Korean law and society,* ed. D. K. Yoon. Seoul: Seoul National University.

Yoon, Kihong. 1996. Sabopyonsuwon ilde kehuk [Big changes in JRTI]. *Bopyul Shinmun* [Law times]. 20 May.

THREE

International Strategies and Local Transformations: Preliminary Observations of the Position of Law in the Field of State Power in Asia: South Korea

YVES DEZALAY* AND BRYANT G. GARTH**

Introduction

Internationalization is unquestionably changing the role of law and lawyers in Asian countries, but our tools for understanding these changes are not well developed. Most of the available literature tends to be one-sided, indeed often promotional. This tendency is understandable. There is an ongoing global competition involving what kind of state—more generally, what rules of the game for government and the economy—will be recognized as legitimate. It is fought in diplomatic activities, in academic and professional circles, in the World Bank, and in the media—consider the accounts of "crony capitalism."[1] In such a competition, we can expect partisans of one side or another to mobilize all available resources.[2] As scholars, however, we must seek to avoid one-sided accounts and

*Director of Research for the Centre national de la recherché scientifique (CNRS) located at the Centre de sociologie Européenne, which is attached to the Collège de France and the Maison des sciences de l'homme in Paris.

**Formerly the director of the American Bar Foundation; from 2005, dean of Southwestern Law School.

We appreciate the helpful comments of Professor Alford, who has shared his insights and helped us appreciate some factors that complicate what we took from our interviews and readings, and of Kim Seong-Hyun, whose insights also led us to rethink some of our conclusions. Their helpfulness and corrections underscore the need to emphasize the tentative nature of our findings.

1. Robert Wade's discussion (1996) of the battle over what organization of the state accounted for the "East Asian economic miracle" illustrates these wars. Michael Lewis' polemic (1998) against Asian capitalism provides one of many examples of the new version.

2. The continuing competition is evident in the way that the United States and Japan responded to the Asian crisis. According to the *Wall Street Journal*, the Japanese sought to create a large Asian fund to help with the financial crisis in the region. "The sum was immense

try to understand this global competition, which relates very closely to the changing position of lawyers and law in particular national settings.[3]

We have begun research on these issues in Asia, but our Asian research is not far enough along to allow the detailed analysis that we would like to be able to offer. Instead, therefore, we will highlight what we believe are some limitations of current research strategies, suggest some other ways of studying the changing position of law and lawyers, drawing mainly on our Latin American research, and then try to apply this kind of analysis very preliminarily to the situation in South Korea. We know that our observations about Korea will require more detail and refinement, but we offer them here in order to raise some issues that are normally left unexamined.

The promotionalism in the literature on lawyers and the "rule of law" in Asia is evident in efforts to ascertain how far Asian countries have come toward attaining the status of a society based on the modern rule of law—which generally means a U.S.-style rule of law.[4] This is true also of research that looks for indicators of the growing importance of law or lawyers—proliferating corporate law firms, more human rights and environmental organizations, projects for the reform of legal education according to the U.S. model of graduate education. The problem is not that individuals seek to promote such political programs, but rather that the promotional dimension tends to distort scholarly research. They hide their promotionalism behind neutral definitions of progress identified with the rule of law. The one-sidedness inherent in this promotional literature also slips easily into a basic dichotomy, which tends to organize the relatively sparse social science literature about the law in Asia (and elsewhere).

The major distinction found in that literature is between the rule of law on one side, and *guanxi* or personal relations on the other—in other terms, the *Rechtsstaat* versus patrimonial state.[5] Daniel Lev, for example, while rejecting

---

[$100 billion], but Mr. [Robert] Rubin [U.S. Secretary of the Treasury, 1995–1999] and Mr. [Lawrence] Summers [U.S. Deputy Secretary of the Treasury, 1995–1999; Secretary of the Treasury, 1999–2001; president of Harvard University, 2001–2006] feared the fund would offer big loans with less-stringent conditions than the IMF's and would threaten U.S. economic supremacy. Treasury officials worked the corridors of the Hong Kong Convention Center and the city's private dining rooms to slow the Japanese plan's momentum." Ultimately, the United States succeeded in killing the Japanese role and therefore "Americanized" the crisis (Wessel and Davis 1998).

3. This approach is developed in *The Internationalization of Palace Wars: Lawyers, Economists, and the Contest to Transform Latin American States* (Dezalay and Garth 2002b). It focuses on Latin America, but the analysis is generally of processes of import and export. We also develop this approach in chapters in our edited volume, *Global Prescriptions: The Production, Exportation, and Importation of a New Legal Orthodoxy* (2002a).

4. This tone is evident in work sponsored by the Asian Development Bank (Pistor and Wellons 1999).

5. Carol Jones' article (1994) on Weber versus Confucius is a good example of this dichotomy. For a nice account of the inadequacy of the dichotomy in China, see Michelson (2003).

simple cultural explanations in an important body of work concerning Indonesia and Malaysia, still tends to explain the law's marginality by contrasting the rule of law versus the patrimonial state.[6] Lev produces important analyses of the indeterminacy of the position of law, but he sees that position as the result of a continuing struggle between two incompatible institutions. The same general dichotomies are also seen in the literature lamenting the decline in the position of lawyers in India,[7] examining the position of lawyers in Korea[8] or Taiwan,[9] or, in another form, in debates about a distinctive "Asian model" of human rights.[10] The literature that juxtaposes the rule of law with patrimonialism or corruption in Latin America is also consistent with this approach.

While much of this literature is quite subtle, the formation of the research problem as "how well the rule of law is doing" has certain implications. Whether or not translated directly into promotional literature, it can serve as a weapon in local political struggles. Those who take the position in favor of practices considered to promote the rule of law *against* certain groups—perhaps identified as corrupt—are necessarily involved in local "palace wars" for power and legitimacy. When scholars criticize legal education in Korea, for example, those criticisms—however valid by criteria that now command a wide consensus— serve as part of battles about the legitimacy of a certain kind of Korean state (in comparison especially to a more U.S.-style state apparatus). There is no easy way out of this political problem. Writings that are limited to such seemingly discrete and neutral subjects as corporate law, courts, the legal profession, or legal education, cannot avoid the larger questions of the politics of law and the politics of the state.

Politics is inseparable from law, and vice versa—which is not the same as saying that only politics matters. The questions of who becomes a lawyer and what serves to legitimate the position of law and lawyers in Korea, for example, are important aspects of an international competition involving the United States and Japan (and, to a lesser extent, others, including China and continental Europe). The stakes of this competition are the mode of reproduction of the state and the reproduction of the field of power. Questions about the legitimacy of power—and therefore the position of law—are necessarily implicated in this competition.

Instead of trying to erect a boundary between something labeled "the legal profession" and these larger "political" issues, therefore, it is preferable to use the law and lawyers as a unique point of entry into the larger political issues and

---

6. See, e.g., Lev (1998).

7. See, e.g., Baxi (1987).

8. See James West's well-informed critique in *Education of the Legal Profession in Korea* (West 1991).

9. See the detailed and useful empirical work in Winn (1994) and Winn and Yeh (1995).

10. Examples from the debates around the 1993 Vienna United Nations World Conference on Human Rights include Kausikan (1993) and Neier (1993).

competitions. This point of entry facilitates access to the field of state power, and it also facilitates access to questions of internationalization. Indeed, the law works especially well for understanding and tracking international factors promoting domestic change since, even in Asia, lawyers have long served as compradors between east and west. Not surprisingly, they can be found today as agents in the new "symbolic imperialism," constructing themselves as both importers of ideas and approaches from abroad and as defenders of particular national practices. We can thus use them to study internationalization and state transformations.

I.   A Research Strategy

Since our approach is somewhat unusual, we will take a few pages to describe it. Using the law as a point of entry, our approach is both structural and historical. We try to focus on the field of state power, exploring its earlier historical construction and how it has changed. In doing so, we try to take into account sites that have been involved in producing expertises and know-how that, in addition to law, contribute to reproducing and transforming the state. We therefore seek to examine also the world of academic disciplines and, in particular, economics. This general approach has much in common with the research being produced by new generations of economists, political scientists, and sociologists, who now emphasize the path-dependent nature of economic and political institutions, and with studies by anthropologists who have long emphasized the "pre-capitalist" legacies found in modern capitalism. Most of such research, however, pays little attention to the social study of law.

Another major characteristic of our approach is that we emphasize the simultaneous study of the national and international. To do so, we focus on "international strategies" used by national actors in their own palace wars. That is to say, one way of gaining power and prestige locally is to draw on international connections and expertises. Such international strategies have always existed, but the possibilities have multiplied with the growth of international commerce and exchange in recent decades. A key to this approach is the recognition that, since careers are still essentially local, international strategies are above all local strategies, even when they result in considerable investment in the construction of international institutions (out of domestic materials). Expertises and know-how produced abroad, especially in the United States in the period after World War II, are used to gain local power, leading also to the investment of those transnational expertises into local contexts. Depending on the local contexts, therefore, the importation of the internationally legitimated expertise—human rights, corporate law, liberal economics—can succeed in transforming the field of state power. Our research, in other words, seeks to see how international strategies feed into local palace wars and contribute (in widely varying degrees) to reshaping the rules of governance of the state and the economy—and therefore also to the transformation and reproduction of the state.

At the same time, palace wars in dominant countries—especially but not only in the United States—also involve similar international strategies and foreign investment. The battles in the United States and in institutions like the World Bank over how to account for the so-called East Asian economic miracle in the first instance, and then for the apparent economic collapse in the second, are also domestic struggles about who and whose expertise is best suited to govern the state and the economy in the United States (and in Japan). Debates between economist Jeffrey Sachs and Robert Rubin may focus on Asia—and may be quite crucial in shaping the fate of Asia—but they are also about who has the best expertise for determining who and what policies the United States should follow in relation to the international economy.

In order to study the position of law in Asia, and to go beyond the dichotomy of *guanxi* versus the rule of law, however expressed, it is important to take into account the different points of departure, as well as different trends which are in some sense converging. The role of international strategies in national settings depends greatly on the details of the national landscape. Our approach in Latin America has been to focus on three historical "moments." Preliminary research suggests that this kind of approach can also serve as a starting point for the study of the transformations that are taking place in Asian contexts.[11]

The first moment for analysis is the legacy of colonial struggles, which provides a conceptual starting point (although obviously not something that can be fixed precisely). The second moment, beginning in the 1930s and 1940s and continuing roughly into the 1970s, was the period of the so-called developmental state—a term coined by Chalmers Johnson with respect to Japan but also applied to Latin America.[12] In Asia, as in Latin America, this period was characterized by the use of an import substitution strategy and a strong state.[13] The developmental states were also "authoritarian states" in Asia.[14] The focus on economic expertise, the role of the state bureaucracy, and close relations between the state and business, tended to marginalize law and lawyers. In India, in fact, the link of the legal profession to the British tradition (in which the law was essentially outside of the welfare state) made it even easier to reduce the role

---

11. For present purposes, we have drawn mainly on secondary literature concerning four particular countries: Indonesia, Korea, Taiwan, and India. We also draw briefly on our research to date in Malaysia and Singapore. Even to study those countries requires that we also take into account regional relationships and divisions of labor. We thus have tried to focus some attention also on the role of Japan and China as influences competing against the United States, and on the position of places such as Singapore and Hong Kong, which tend to complement other economies.

12. See, e.g., Johnson (1995).

13. For Korea and Taiwan, cf. Fields (1995) and Wade (1990); for India, contrasted with China, see Rosen (1992); for Taiwan, see Haggard and Pang (1994); for Indonesia, see Hill (1994).

14. See, e.g., Hill (1994); Cumings (1997); Winn and Yeh (1995). For a discussion of the strong assertions of executive power in India, see generally Evans (1995).

and prestige of the legal profession.[15] Despite more or less ambitious efforts, in various countries, in support of law and development,[16] it appears that the position of law did not improve during this period.

The third moment or period is that associated with the end of the Cold War in the 1980s and especially the 1990s. It corresponds to the new wave of internationalization and the recent transformation of states toward more open economies and reduced state involvement in the economy. The multiple debt crises and the flourishing of the human rights movement are associated with this moment. Internationalization provided new opportunities and openings for law and the legal profession. Relatively marginal groups in the legal field could use international strategies to build or regain (in a very different way) their influence and power in the state and economy. The development or considerable expansion of corporate law firms is obviously part of this story, as is the development of public interest groups organized especially around the protection of human rights, the environment, and, increasingly, anti-corruption issues.[17]

II.   Latin American Patterns[18]

The general framework is not meant to suggest that the pattern is the same everywhere. It is meant to justify an analytical approach. In Latin America, there is a relatively common historical legacy that provides some unifying patterns, discussed below, but there are some very significant distinctions as well. To begin with the similarities, we found that, among the four countries that we studied—Argentina, Brazil, Chile, and Mexico—there was an almost "classic" historical pattern.

In this classic pattern, most evident in Brazil and Chile, the law graduates who governed tended to come from the old Latin American families—sometimes called the "traditional oligarchy." The position of the law was thus closely linked to the leading families, who used the law to legitimate their positions of leadership. There was relatively little investment in the autonomy of the courts or legal scholarship, even though elite legal careers often required study in Paris, Coimbra, Madrid, or Rome. Members of the elite, occupying several positions simultaneously in courts, faculties of law, business, journalism, and politics, operated almost above the law, ensuring social peace less through the law than through personal and familial relations. The ruling elite was accessible to some new entrants admitted to the relatively small faculties of law, but the openings

---

15. See generally Baxi (1987) and Galanter (1989).

16. For India, cf. Galanter (1968–69) and Rowe (1968–69); for Indonesia, cf. Lev (1972); for Korea, see Murphy (1965).

17. For India, see Baxi (1987); Bhagwati (1985); Cassels (1989); Moog (1998); Mullick (1997); Susman (1994). For Indonesia, see Lev (1998). For Korea, see Ahn (1994); E. Lee (1998); S. Lee (1998); Yoon (1998). For Taiwan, see Shih (1998) and Winn and Yeh (1995).

18. Much more detail is in Dezalay and Garth (2002b).

were relatively limited. Consequently, the system was quite conservative and resistant to change. The law and law graduates were important to social peace and the reproduction of the state, but the law itself was not of much importance in business or the state.

The Great Depression was one of a number of historical challenges to this elite. The challenge in the 1930s was both a social one—by outsiders of the ruling group—and a challenge grounded in new learning and new expertise. In particular, economics had been gaining prestige, and the worldwide depression increased the demand for that expertise in the state. During the period after World War II, economists gained further prominence by taking the lead in promoting "development," identified with a strategy of import substitution and strong central governments. A new generation of law graduates joined economists, sociologists and others in the many state institutions expanded or created around that time. As economics and other disciplines became more professionalized, especially with the help of U.S. foundations and foreign aid, law became more discredited and identified with the past. Efforts in Chile and Brazil to promote "law and development" were seen as failures by both domestic and foreign promoters—undermined even by the legal establishment. Law appeared to be too conservative, too formal, and even too local (Gardner 1981).

Ambitious and well-connected students increasingly invested in other careers and expertises. In particular, economists—subsidized to study abroad, especially in the United States—became oriented toward an international market of ideas which the United States was beginning to dominate (in economics, deposing Cambridge, England). Not surprisingly, economists trained in the United States returned to use the best economics and their connections with the "best" economists in their local palace wars. Economics gained power in the construction of the developmental state, but in the 1960s and 1970s the best economics was increasingly defined by an attack on the developmental state as wasteful and inflationary. In the period of the 1960s, however, these insurgent economists were still mostly outside the governments, which at that time were still focused on Keynesian and developmentalist economic policies.

The third moment in Latin America is associated with the move from developmental states to neo-liberal states. The discredit of locally oriented, generalist law, which began in the 1930s; the leftward pull of the student movement; and the investment of the United States in fortifying military leaders with training and an anti-communist disposition, helped create the conditions for military coups in Argentina, Brazil, and Chile. The coups were supported by the old legal elite, nervous about populist and leftist tactics. The new military governments, however, typically built their legitimacy not on a return to the status quo of the old legal elite but rather on the ideas of the new generation of economists educated in the United States. The "Chicago Boys" in Chile, who gained power after Pinochet's coup in 1973, are only the best-known examples of a phenomenon seen strongly in all four countries. Economists were quite important to the military government in Argentina after 1976 and in Brazil after 1966, and recent Mexican governments have been dominated by U.S.-trained economists.

The debt crisis of the 1980s particularly enhanced the local positions of cosmopolitan economists connected to the United States and the international financial institutions. Increasingly, in fact, the sons and daughters of the old governing elite took a cue from the prestige of the new economists and studied economics themselves. In some respects, under different forms and with a different legitimating discourse, they stepped into positions formerly occupied by the old gentlemen-lawyers. While thus maintaining the continuity of the old elite, the process of using the imported expertise that helped them gain power also changed the rules of the game. The developmental states were largely dismantled.

The law in Latin America, which was discredited both as a career and in terms of its centrality to the legitimacy of the state in the developmental and neo-liberal periods, has begun to "come back," also in a very different package. One pillar of this new form of law was built through a human rights movement that did not arise in law, but became oriented to law largely through transnational influences—especially the philanthropic foundations and human rights organizations dominated by the U.S. Another pillar arose through the provision of legal services to multinational businesses operating in Latin America, and also to the economists who have led the governments. The neo-liberal policies brought considerable new foreign investment. Family-dominated law firms—historically very small and, with a few exceptions with foreign clients, focused on litigation—have expanded greatly and, in many cases, even become organized more along the lines of U.S. firms, even if with a strong family component remaining. They serve the new privatized companies as well as the multinationals that do business in their countries.

The economists still central in Latin American governments, in addition, have begun to focus more attention on building legal legitimacy for their policies and practices. The debt crisis and economic liberalization led by economists in the governments of generals thus provided new opportunities for law graduates in the public and private sectors. The new generation of lawyers has begun to use these opportunities to gain local power. In the process, they have also begun to reorient law and the legal profession to become more technically proficient and more oriented toward U.S. and international legal norms and practices (which are heavily influenced by the U.S.). Where gentlemen-lawyer-generalists a generation ago cherished their connections to the continental civil law tradition, the new generation typically requires an advanced law degree from the United States.

Lawyers' roles and prestige are thus changing again in response to this dramatic reorientation. Consistent with the new embeddedness in the international market of legal expertise, there is a focus on the courts and on legal education, with U.S. ideas very prominent in the debates. U.S.-style alternative dispute resolution, for example, has been enacted into Argentine law. Nevertheless, close attention to local situations suggests that a convergence in the discourses of reform does not necessarily produce much actual investment in the autonomy of the law.

The law continues to play a very different role in these countries than it does in the United States, even if legal legitimacy is much more important to the state and economy than it was prior to or during the military regimes. There are new roles for lawyers, and the legal profession is relatively more open, but the law still owes much to the family position of those who study it and move into elite careers. Indeed, the "return of law" means that, while access to elite positions is more open than in the past, once again children of the elite families are using their advantages—now including the ability to study abroad—to find key places in the field of state power and in serving the privatized economy.

This classic pattern, of course, overlooks many significant differences. One purpose of our research is to discover the specific ways that transnational phenomena interact with the fields of political and economic power found in individual countries. As we have emphasized, the position of any legal institution can only be understood in relation to the specific history of the construction of its state. There is more of a tendency in Brazil (at least in some regions) and Chile to invest in the "transnational ideal" that comes especially from the United States—independent courts with a relatively strong national political role—than there is in Argentina or Mexico, although there are also formidable obstacles in Brazil and Chile.

Mexico has had a divided elite since the Mexican Revolution of 1910, and this has particularly hindered investment in the law and legal institutions. One group went from leadership of the revolution to leadership of the state, while the targets of the revolution stayed in business and the private sphere, and there has been very little crossover even in subsequent generations. Neither the elite that typically went into the state sector, nor the opposing elite that went into the business sector, for example, produced ambitious law graduates with incentives to pursue careers in the judiciary. Those in the judiciary occupied a very subordinate position—oriented above all to the PRI (the Institutional Revolutionary Party), Mexico's longtime ruling party. One result of internationalization in Mexico has been to break down the barriers between the two sides of Mexico's divided elite, with potentially major social impacts. Descendants from the old elite have used the new legal expertise that has emerged through the debt crisis and the human rights movement to gain access to political power. Since Mexico had a very different political and legal landscape than Brazil and Chile when this new period of internationalization accelerated, international strategies have led to a major variation on the classic pattern.

In Argentina, the intense political fighting that accelerated with Juan Peron in the 1940s promoted a pattern that involved the periodic purging of not only the courts, but also the state and even the faculties of law. There was virtually no cumulative professional investment in the state, especially through law but even, in comparison to Brazil, Chile, or Mexico, in economics. The risks of investment in the state were too high. One result in the Argentinean state was that law played a role completely subservient to politics. Lawyers stayed away and instead built a well-remunerated legal elite outside the state—exemplified by family law firms serving as go-betweens for the state, foreign investors, foreign institutions, and foreign expertises. Again starting with a very different legal and political landscape, the institutional legacy of the international strategies over the past two decades in Argentina has differed from that found in the other countries. The tendency, even with the proliferation of international strategies through the debt crisis and the human rights movement, has been to create and fortify entities around—but rarely in—the state, including law firms and also major think tanks. As in Mexico, but for somewhat different reasons, obstacles barring the way to increased legal autonomy in Argentina continue to be very profound.

The impact of international strategies, therefore, depends greatly on the relative starting points for each country at the time of the intensification of the production and exportation of the new expertises. Differences also relate to the degree of the country's embeddedness in the international marketplace of ideas. Argentine professionals in the 1970s and earlier, interestingly, were more embedded in the international arena than those of Chile or Brazil, with Mexico's professionals divided. Those from the private professional elite in Mexico were very international, while the public elite maintained a nationalism that tended to deny the worth of foreign learning, especially that from the United States.

The stories in Latin America have some resonance with what we know about experiences in at least parts of Asia. In India, at one relative extreme, British colonialism and the independence movement produced what could be seen in retrospect as a lawyer's paradise.[19] Lawyers who had served traditionally as compradors between the colonists and the colonized were very active, as in Latin America, in the independence movement, and they moved likewise to the center of the state after independence. Similarly, although to a much lesser extent, it appears that in Indonesia, while the numbers were quite small, lawyers were important in the move to independence from the Dutch, were subsequently portrayed as the reactionary enemy by Soekarno's* leftist government in the early 1960s, and then held a rather marginal position in the army-led regime of Soeharto that took power in 1967–1968.[20] The theme of a rise and fall of the legal profession can also be applied to Malaysia and Singapore, with important variations.

In a number of important countries of Asia, however, we start with a very different position of law in the field of state power, which necessarily produces an alternative history over the periods that have been our focus. In Japan, for example, the very different starting points meant that, by World War II, there had already been a strong reaction against legalization, on behalf of traditional values that a certain sector of the elite sought to promote—and use to maintain

---

19. See, e.g., Cohn (1996); Paul (1991); Baxi (1987); Gandhi (1982).

*Ed. note: See Professor Lev's chapter in this volume.

20. See, e.g., Lev (1972 and 1976) and Rahardjo (1994).

their own position in the field of power.[21] In order to suggest in more detail one possible pattern in Asia, we can draw on a set of thirty interviews conducted in South Korea.

III. Preliminary Observations on the Position of Law and Lawyers in South Korea

Our interviews in Korea were mainly of Korean-Americans and Koreans who studied or otherwise spent substantial time in the United States. The two groups, not surprisingly, were fairly easy to locate and to contact from our positions as researchers. Koreans who have studied abroad are very privileged in Korea, and they also can play a double game not available to most Koreans. By definition, indeed, they are not representative of a society that is highly segmented and hierarchical. At the same time, however, our focus on the law provides an almost opposite bias. Lawyers in Korea, as we shall see, are both central and marginal, serving as what can be called a "scholastic elite." They play mainly a symbolic role in the field of power in Korea, both politically and economically, at least to date. Histories and analyses of Korean society therefore tend to emphasize mainly the role of the giant family conglomerates termed *chaebol*, the major political leaders, and the bureaucratic elite (Cumings 1997; Woo 1991). Judges and lawyers tend at best to merit a footnote, usually a disparaging one, for their inability to resist authoritarian state power. Lawyers were not central to the Korean developmental state.[22]

The individuals who were the source of most of our information balance the bias away from power because their position within the legal field is closest to the field of power. The advantage of a detour from a typical Korean trajectory to the United States—which in Korea, as elsewhere, including Latin America, has become the source of credentials increasingly as important as international currency—is that it allows many of them to cross over boundaries and avoid the segmentation that limits others' possibilities. In the terms of Bruce Cumings, who we consider the leading historian of modern Korea, they can play a double game of "interest" as well as "virtue."[23] Virtue, as we shall see, has historically placed strong limits on the activities of Korean lawyers. Our boundary-crossers, in particular, can move closer to business.

---

21. See Haley (1991).

22. Cf. Kim (1991).

23. Cumings organizes the beginning of his 1997 book around the themes of virtue and interest. Virtue is used to refer to the more traditional authority in Korea. In his words, "In addition to the filial virtues, the practical glue holding the system together was education, the paradigmatic figure being the 'true gentleman,' the virtuous and learned scholar-official who was equally adept at poetry and statecraft" (Cumings 1997, 59). The chapter on modernization and westernization, referring to the period 1860–1904, is entitled "the interests" to refer to more material forms of legitimacy.

Also, these individuals—more frequently than elsewhere in the Korean legal field—are at the same time *héritiers*, coming from prominent families in business or professional circles. Since the rules of entry into the United States (and other places abroad) are somewhat different than the rules of scholastic selection that operate domestically, those with greater social capital tend to have advantages—linguistic skill, economic resources, connections abroad, knowledge of foreign opportunities and their relative value—in gaining access to foreign study.

It is important to take our necessarily biased position, and that of our informants, into account, and we seek to do so in the following pages. The principal limitation is that we do not have much primary information specific to the actors in and around the Korean state or the families that control the *chaebol*. We can make some assumptions about these actors on the basis of secondary information and what we do *not* see in our interviews with lawyers, but we need to do more research in these domains of power. Nevertheless, the exceptional nature of the source group we focus on can be used to reveal certain structural rules that illuminate the place of law in Korea. What allows the individuals to go around the rules can reveal the structural logic of the rules themselves. Their strategy is a variation of that logic determined largely by social or family capital. Finally, the examination of their strategies serves not only to reveal the logic of rules, which could be described as an anthropological quest for the keys to a particular social structure, but it also enables us to suggest that exceptions to the rules make it possible for the rigid local system to work. The system in the end is not so rigidly meritocratic, since it can be by-passed by using an international strategy. Rigidity can be overcome through detours that allow boundaries to be crossed and categories to be mixed and blurred.

A.   Law as "Ornamental Confucianism"

There is an apparent paradox in the structure of the Korean legal profession. Lawyers present themselves as the most prestigious professional group. Parents all over Korea are described as pushing their children to pass the difficult exams necessary to gain access to the prestigious law faculty of Seoul National University (SNU), and then later to pass the difficult bar exam to become above all a judge, but also a prosecutor or lawyer. To make it into the legal profession is to gain extraordinary occupational prestige and ultimately access also to wealth, since the very limited size of the profession provides monopoly profits to practitioners. At the same time, however, testimony was also unanimous that this prestigious social group has relatively little, if any, actual power except for guild issues—fighting to preserve lawyers' monopoly power.

There are a number of lawyers active in politics, and legal careers in the provincial areas outside of Seoul do provide a kind of status that can translate into local and then national political power. We would like to know more about the careers that track into politics, but our interviews also showed patterns that reinforce trajectories that avoid political activity. With respect to economic

power, moreover, the major family business groups, the *chaebol,* have historically had little reason to use lawyers except for the most menial of tasks. They
did not need lawyers for their relations with the state, since the major business
leaders dealt directly and personally with state representatives. The law graduates that they hired to serve in-house typically had not passed the bar exam, rel-
egating them to relatively inferior status within the legal profession. The *chaebol*
might have needed lawyers for transactions abroad, but in that case they would
not have called upon Korean lawyers to provide the help. At home, the key relations were with the other *chaebol* and the state, limiting the need for professionals whose expertise was in the law.

The typical legal career, moreover, has long followed a path that moves outside of political or economic power. The career of a "lawyer" followed a very
particular pattern, leading from judge or prosecutor ultimately to private litigator, with very little crossover—except as described above—toward positions of
power in the state or the economy, either as intermediary or as principal. From
this perspective, the worlds of prestige and of power were thus not only separate, but also operated through almost reverse logic and hierarchies. Put simply,
the more prestige, the less power, and vice versa.

As suggested by leading scholars of Asian capitalism, the construction of
Korea as a republic and later "Korea, Inc.," required a borrowing, reinvention,
and even perversion of whole sets of institutions built in pre-capitalistic periods
of Korean history.[24] Among the interrelated sources for this borrowing were the
traditions of a scholastic hierarchy, family hierarchy, patrimonialism, and Confucianism.

Korea was rebuilt in part through a re-tooling of Confucianism, which was
in effect a total transformation. Korea historically was supposedly the most
Confucian of societies. Historical accounts suggest that social stability was
maintained in large part by the multiplicity of roles occupied by Confucian
scholars. They were not only scholars, but also statesmen, landowners, and even
judges. The new Korean order, in contrast, depended on a very strict division of
the various roles and the knowledge that goes with each. The earlier system of
scholars was sufficiently meritocratic to allow some social advancement, but
many, if not most, of the scholars were the sons of scholars. In the new system,
built on the social destruction wrought by Japanese colonialism and the Korean
War, the scholastic system became much less connected to the reproduction of
family capital.

These transformations have produced different hierarchies within the different state scholastic groups. There are rigid distinctions, for example, between
the state bureaucracy, law, political science, and economics. It is very difficult to
pass from one of the hierarchies to another, in part because each hierarchy does
not occupy the same position. They are themselves arranged in other, rather
rigid, hierarchies. The closer one comes to the center of symbolic prestige, the

24. See, e.g., Hamilton and Biggart (1988) and Greenhalgh (1994).

stricter the border lines between the groups and the more difficult the task of reproduction of family capital. That is to say, the relatively newer scholastic knowledge imported largely from the United States—political science and economics—permit more diversification than is permitted for law. It is possible to be a scholar, politician, and bureaucrat in these domains. But in the field of law, it has been almost impossible to combine the roles or cross the boundaries. Indeed, as suggested above, there was a general progression for the few who made it to this privileged position. They began as judges (from the top of the group) or prosecutors and then moved only later, if at all, into private practice.

There is also a strong contrast between the thousands of Ph.D.s in Korea and the hundreds of lawyers, which relates also to familial reproduction. The strategy of going abroad for a Ph.D. permits families to more easily reproduce their social positions, while the strict system of exams for legal training and certification are relatively disconnected from familial reproduction. It is simply too difficult to gain a legal credential in comparison with those credentials that are not so wedded to the traditional Korean hierarchy. This is not to deny the advantages that flow to families with the ability and commitment to get the best possible private education for their children. They certainly increase the chances that their children will be able to enter the legal profession. But the structural position of the law keeps it relatively disconnected from the major sources of wealth and power.

B. Constructing the Law as a Scholastic Meritocracy

The starting point for understanding this position is the fundamental historical illegitimacy of the law—at least the dominant law imposed on Korea by colonial Japan late in the nineteenth century, and the leading law school (now SNU), then designated as the Imperial University. In contrast to most of the Western world, the law in Korea did not have the legitimacy that comes from the history of its concepts, doctrines, and institutions.[25] Instead, it was imposed by the Japanese after they had borrowed it from the European continent, and the lawyers who prospered under Japanese rule further disqualified the law by their collaboration with the Japanese.

Drawing also on the Japanese system, but carried to an extreme in Korea, the law was embedded in a scholastic meritocracy that goes way beyond the exam to enter the Judicial Research and Training Institute (JRTI)—the very difficult bar exam that now has become generous enough for perhaps 2 percent of applicants to pass. A scholastic meritocracy began with exams to get into the most prestigious high schools, including a famous high school (Kyunggi) in Seoul that fed SNU. Students from all over Korea studied diligently for the prize of getting into the leading high school. There they studied for the prize of passing the exam to get into SNU, and those with the very best scores almost unfailingly

---

25. Professor Alford points out that there was also a more indigenous tradition in law that might have provided a better pedigree—even if not a pedigree akin to that found in Europe. The law that was produced, and dominated Korea, however, was that imposed by the Japanese.

chose to study with the law faculty—reportedly whether or not they had any interest in the subject at all. Passing the bar exam, which some graduates would take every year for more than fifteen years, still hoping for the status of lawyer, permitted entrance to the JRTI.

Even there, the hierarchization continued. Grades determined who would be allowed to become judges—the top of the hierarchy. And relatively early in Korea's post-war history, top grades on an exam determined who, from among the (usually) "K-S" graduates (from Kyunggi-SNU) who passed the bar exam, would be selected to apply to Harvard Law School, thus placing them at the top of the top. Through the same logic that made the top of the hierarchy depend on graduation from SNU, the international degree necessary for the top status had to be from Harvard.

It is easy to say that the bar exam tests only rote memorization skills and an ability to take tests (supported by the huge number of Koreans who pass the New York bar exam after a year in the United States), but it nonetheless represents a relatively egalitarian competition. As noted above, it is not completely disconnected from social capital.[26] Parents often must hire tutors to give their children any possibility of winning the competition, and they must have enough resources to make the investment in private schools and tutoring for their promising children. There are also advantages that come from the ability to purchase housing in a district with an elite private school. Still, this kind of test and relative openness ensures the political legitimacy of the process and those who go through it. Only those who pass the most rigorous and open tests are entitled to attain the elite status of judge, prosecutor, or lawyer. This borrowing and transformation of a Confucian pattern successfully legitimated law and lawyers in Korea.

This political gain in the legitimacy of the legal scholastic elite, however, comes at tremendous professional cost. The costs can be seen by considering another apparent paradox. The law program at SNU and at other faculties of law as well, have been hotbeds of student political activism. Intense political activity is fueled and exacerbated by students who are typically displaced from their origins, anxious about their status and about passing the bar exam, and suddenly presented with more time, since the actual curriculum is reportedly not that demanding. This activism is quite reminiscent of the law schools in Latin America. But little political activism has followed the law school experience in Korea. For the most part, the products of the system working in the bar, the judiciary, and the prosecutors' office were silent during military regimes that

---

26. We cannot provide data on the social composition of those who gain admission, but our informants were adamant and tended to emphasize openness. It is true, of course, that women were long discouraged from going to law school, and the advantages of family resources for school clearly exist. In any event, what is important is that the tests have appeared to be fair enough to legitimate the law and were constructed in such a way as to make it difficult to reproduce family capital in law.

opposed everything they stood for in the law. Again, there is a powerful explanation for this paradox, evident in the stories of many of the student activists.

The scholastic selection system can in this respect be seen as a remarkably efficient disciplinary mechanism—in the sense used by Foucault. The preparation
for the bar exam—as law studies proceed—consumes the students' energy and
time. As many former activists testified, it was necessary to choose between the
streets and the prospect of passing the bar exam. Too much of a commitment to
political activism would preclude capturing the ultimate fruits of the system.[27]
Further, because of the prestige of those who pass the exam, and the fact that
everyone has an opportunity to pass the exam, it is relatively easy to rationalize
intense preparation in order to gain the opportunity to change the system from
within—turning revolutionaries into reformers. And finally, the bar exam creates both winners and losers. Those who fail the exam are disqualified by many
as scholastic failures. They cannot challenge the scholastic system without being
regarded as complaining about their own inability to succeed.

Looked at from the perspective of the small minority who make it through
the eye of this very tiny needle, it is also relatively easy to buy them off with high
prestige—and the high compensation that scarcity produces. The same is true,
relatively speaking, for those who pass the civil service exam and join the bureaucracy—one level below those who succeed in the bar exam, but also frequently
coming from studying under the law faculty of SNU (which has varied in its
treatment of those studying for civil service). The vast majority of people in all
these hierarchal scholastic sectors, in short, are disqualified as "failures" in a
process that is repeated over and over. As a result, there is a hierarchy made up
of, at the top, those who go through the JRTI, followed by SNU law graduates,
then SNU graduates in other fields, with law professors falling below those who
pass the bar exam. They too are organized in their own strict hierarchy of law
professors, with SNU law faculty at the top.[28] The system maintains itself in part
by disqualifying criticism of those who occupy better positions: they are justified
in holding their positions due to better performance on the relevant exams.

C. The Price of Virtue

There are of course many social advantages that come from the respect that is
afforded those who are at the top of this meritocratic elite.[29] A basic problem of
the virtuous scholastic elite, however, is that they cannot easily reproduce them-

---

27. Professor Alford suggests that the increased opportunities to pass the bar exam today further quell activism, as perhaps fewer give up hope.

28. There are also a number of so-called legal scriveners who can provide services to individuals that require some legal expertise. Many reportedly are individuals who have degrees
from the faculties of law and have served in such positions as members of the bureaucracy.

29. We were told that those who pass the bar exam are immediately contacted by marriage
brokers who propose alliances between the young lawyers or judges and daughters of individuals with family resources.

selves. The exam system simply poses too many obstacles. This problem is important because a common characteristic of the legal profession around the world—essential in maintaining its position in the field of power—is that, when relatively successful, it succeeds in reproducing family capital. Children can build on the practices and contacts of their parents. Korea's exceptionalism in this respect is quite striking, especially in a society where businesses were built around family relationships. Not surprisingly, therefore, this relative meritocracy in the legal profession tends to create its own exceptions in order to have some way to escape from the rigid Korean rules. One of the advantages to elite families of the escape of studying abroad, as discussed below, is that it mitigates the harshness of the meritocratic domestic selection system. It allows advantaged individuals to gain reputable credentials and careers connected to power without having to survive the nearly impossible domestic competitions.

The second aspect of this disempowerment of the powerful elite in Korea, in addition to the inability to reproduce family capital in law, is that the first victims of the myth of the virtuous scholastic lawyers are the lawyers themselves.[30] In particular, the pattern for most of those who make it into the judiciary is to stay there for a relatively long period, despite pay much lower than what could be earned as a practicing lawyer in litigation. Within the bureaucracy, similarly, the pattern is to continue to serve in the bureaucracy, despite wages lower even than those in the judiciary, until it is time to retire into a comfortable position in the private sector or in a state-owned business (akin to Japanese *amakudari*). Interestingly, this system is the reverse of the English one, and, to a lesser extent, the one in the United States, according to which lawyers build up earnings in the private sector—when their children are young—before taking a pay cut and joining the bench. The internalization and institutionalization of this virtue can also be found in the role of the judges and prosecutors as relatively independent but strongly insistent on their nonpolitical role—promoting a positivism subservient to political power.

The traditional position of legal professionals in Korea, therefore, provides a remarkable contrast to that seen in Latin America. Lawyers have higher prestige in Korea, but they are not connected to power and cannot even reproduce their own relatively prestigious position through their families. They have great legitimacy and respect, but they are for the most part kept—including by themselves—in a very confined space in the political and economic system. The action is simply elsewhere.

In this respect, the developmental state in Korea is similar to that in Latin America in that lawyers are not central players. But the reasons are very different. The legal profession in the classic Latin American pattern represents the embodiment of an old elite that resisted new ideas associated with economic development. In Korea, as noted above, this moment in Korean history simply proceeds with lawyers and the law left aside.

---

30. As suggested by Pierre Bourdieu. See, e.g., Bourdieu and Wacquant (1992).

D.   The Paradox of Internationalizing Pseudo-Confucianism

International strategies in the legal profession play an ambiguous role in Korea. On the one hand, the very top Korean graduates in law and elsewhere are exported to complete their education and credentialing. We encountered several examples of individuals who were number one at SNU, number one at the JRTI, and then went on to get a J.D. at Harvard Law School. Harvard, as many people testified, is the crowning of the scholastic competition. The ambiguity of the Harvard strategy, however, comes from the fact that Harvard (and other U.S. law schools as well) does not operate by exactly the same rules as the Korean meritocracy. It is not that the rules for admission to Harvard are illegitimate, but they are different. Professional achievements that are not valued as highly in Korea as in the United States, not to mention the ability to speak English and to finance a Harvard education, can also play a role, as can personal contacts.

It is possible, therefore, to go around the strict Korean meritocracy and still get to Harvard (or another top U.S. law school).[31] There are also many Korean-Americans who complete their entire educational careers in the United States before going to Korea. The new layer of selection for the Korean elite—above all Harvard and to a lesser extent other U.S. law schools—thus operates according to a very different logic than that found within Korea. It both fits the Korean meritocracy and blurs the distinctions. As a result, we find a number of ambiguous characters on the Korean scene. The hierarchy is still quite evident, perhaps even more so with an international dimension assimilated into the rankings, but it is no longer so closely connected to the pseudo-Confucianism and segmentation that defines law in Korea. International strategies in the legal profession—as with the disciplines around the law—have the potential to disturb the traditional hierarchies that strictly limit the place of lawyers and the law.

E.   Scholastic Hierarchies and Double Agents Fighting Fire with Fire

The internationally oriented law firm, for example, in many respects goes against the standard career patterns associated with Korean lawyers. In order to break the prison of virtue, it was necessary that the founders of successful law firms had resources not available to most Korean lawyers. Almost all of the founders of the most successful Seoul law firms were among the relatively few lawyers who came from families with significant social capital. It could be that the family capital led these individuals to go to the United States in the first place, or it could be that it allowed them to capitalize on their investment when they returned to Korea by diversifying their portfolio of capital. In either case,

---

31. We do not mean to imply that Harvard *should* fall in line with the Korean system. Harvard and other law schools must apply their own criteria to identify what they consider to be the best students for their particular school. The point is that in Korea, as elsewhere, international strategies can blur or circumvent rigid career patterns and hierarchies and in doing so lead to national changes.

the result was that they stepped out of the mold in order to serve the new group of international investors in Korea. In order to do so, they did not stay long in the judiciary. They instead became professional entrepreneurs and brokers for foreign business. They were able in this manner to forge new career trajectories that provided a shortcut to wealth and access to major actors in the Korean economy—at least foreign actors, if not yet the *chaebol.*

These individuals moved across boundaries to pursue routes that were not available to others. There are many examples of the unusual mobility of this group. A general counsel could move to business, or a licensed lawyer could decide to teach at SNU. Others crossed boundaries by going into politics, by combining economics and the law, or even by moving from one specialty to another as a law professor. For those practicing law, there was an emphasis on expanding or broadening the range of legal services. They used their connections and the availability of this international strategy to redefine professional practice and professional careers in Korea—among other things, moving closer to economic and political power.

These individuals have also been better able to control the reproduction of their family capital, perhaps even having businesses on the side or positions in real estate. In addition, because of their reputations and successes as innovators, they were able to attract people who want to follow their lead. Their international reputations also gave them credibility when they recommended individuals for study in the United States. Ambitious young lawyers saw the attraction of shortcuts to wealth and also to potentially greater influence than normally afforded lawyers, and they therefore would try to follow the successful innovators.

One way to see the role of these boundary-crossers is to note the remarkable pattern of responses to questions about career trajectories. Among these well-connected pioneers and their firms, we find a succession of firsts—first lawyer in government, first to advise Korean business, first to send Korean lawyers abroad, first to recruit CPAs, first lawyer to teach at SNU. There is also a group of similar pioneers who have used human rights activity to move into the world of nongovernmental organizations (NGOs) and into political careers. These individuals generally have pioneered in pushing the boundaries of the law and legal practice.

At the same time as these individuals, akin to *heresiarchs* (a term from Bourdieu, describing well-connected individuals who use their social capital to follow heterodox careers), pioneer in transforming the legal profession in Korea, they also serve as foot soldiers on behalf of American law. They take their credentials and their ties with the United States and seek to reinvest them in Korea—trying to not only upgrade their own legal careers in a new pattern, but also to make U.S.-style law more relevant to business and the state generally. In this respect the pioneers are assisted by another ambiguous group—Korean-Americans, some of whom pass the bar in the U.S. but not in Korea. Korean-Americans have relatively limited possibilities in Korea. They lack access to court as a matter of law, and as a practical matter they lack access to the large business groups or to the government—unless they have family connections. They represent in many respects a second-class group both in Korea and in the United States. The same is perhaps true of other pioneers who have taken U.S. or other law degrees to Korea. This latter group also has grown substantially in number—playing this international experience as an alternative career strategy commenced in the U.S. or elsewhere in the legal core. These individuals have to work in the shadow of official Korean lawyers, and they tend to maintain a low profile because of their relatively marginal position. But this relative invisibility allows them also to serve as a mass army serving the legal entrepreneurs. This army helps provide the requisite learning and expertise necessary to turn the pioneer law firms into better imitations of U.S. law firms.

At the same time, the cosmopolitan strategies of the *heresiarchs* tend to disqualify the traditional legal elite trained in and limited to Korean institutions. What was once the crème-de-la-crème begins to appear parochial and out-of-date. The Supreme Court today may still be comprised mainly of individuals who cannot speak English and are not at home among U.S. lawyers and judges, but the law faculties at SNU and the JRTI, to take two leading examples, contain prominent individuals close to the United States and even to Harvard. They are showing signs of replacing the group that was trained domestically, or in Japan or Germany, the two main competitors for legal expertise in Korea. In the current situation, therefore, the criteria of *national* competence are changing, and part of the change is a general devalorizing of the career track that emphasized service in the judiciary or prosecutor's office. More profit and prestige are beginning to come from the private sector, in particular by joining internationally oriented law firms. By highlighting these processes of change, we do not mean to suggest that the changes are definitive or inevitable. Since our point of entry into the law and the legal profession in Korea was through the individuals whose careers we highlight, we cannot at this stage assess the extent to which the more traditional trajectories still dominate. What is clear is that these processes are underway, and they are having some impact.

Indeed, boundary-crossers—forming alliances with, for example, law professors—have helped increase the number of those who pass the bar exam substantially, from only three hundred in 1994 to five hundred in 1995, and to one thousand in the year 2000. The increase in numbers has increased the competition among litigators, causing the incomes of young lawyers to come under some pressure, and it has correspondingly bolstered the position of the one sector capable of absorbing new lawyers—law firms oriented toward international business. The business law firms are thriving. Lawyers are leaving the judiciary and prosecutor's offices more quickly. For a variety of reasons, therefore, traditional lawyers are declining in relative status. The rewards of the traditional virtuous path within the legal profession are declining. The more permissive standards to pass the bar exam also may begin to open more opportunities for prominent lawyers to move their children into the legal profession.

While there is a new trajectory for boundary-crossers, it is not true that the civic virtue that traditionally characterized Korean lawyers has been exchanged for a new role in Korean economic and political life. While more difficult to demonstrate at this point, it appears that civic virtue in Korea is increasingly maintained by true believers, those whom Bourdieu has termed *oblats*. The general characteristics of these individuals are that they have provincial backgrounds and no family access to wealth or power. They have passed the bar exam, but they have no other resources to bring to their careers. Relatively few of these provincial individuals who have passed the bar exam have gone to the United States, and those who have tend to be law professors rather than practitioners. These individuals for various reasons have much less ability to diversify in their careers, except within the confines of their own scholarship. They do not cross the boundaries. They are the additional proof—the counter-examples—that without the right combination of family capital and meritocratic achievement, law professors in Korea and even a growing portion of the expanded group of lawyers will be stuck in the middle range of the meritocracy. Among other limitations, they are—as noted before—victims of the beliefs they are supposed to transmit. The best examples are the professors who only teach, taking seriously what they teach or what they were taught. Rather than challenging the fundamentals of the system that confines them to their particular statuses, they tend to support the system by calling for more virtue, less corruption, and more access to the rewards of the legal profession.

These individuals are caught in a double bind, since some people who have better scholastic standing are among those taking advantage of new and more flexible career opportunities. As a result, the true believers among law graduates in Korea tend to occupy variations on traditional positions. Because of this army of true believers, the boundary-crossers still have to take the traditional scholastic position seriously. One result is that true believers tend to cut their political ties to the groups from which they came. An important example of this phenomenon is the relationship between lawyers (and law professors) and the labor movement. At the beginning in the 1980s, there were very close ties between the student and labor movements, but now the "social movements" in Korea are defined and structured with little connection to labor. As with corporate law, the ideals of the NGOs are imported, expressed in concepts that have particular meaning on U.S. campuses and among U.S. philanthropic organizations. Their insistence on a divorce from politics is consistent with the historical position of the law in Korea, however, and allows organizations to exist in a space divorced not only from labor and subordinated groups, but also—with few exceptions—from government and politics.

A prominent and typical example is the Citizens' Coalition for Economic Justice, which occupies this in-between space through a moral and scientific strategy. This quite prominent Korean NGO is staffed by Korean professionals, including a number of economists now prominent in the government, and it focuses on issues of social equity, the environment, and corruption. It operates on the model of the "international NGO," strengthened by visits that its leaders have made to prominent activist organizations in the United States. The international model—and set of connections—serves as an inspiration and also provides legitimacy in Korea, but the role of lawyers in the Citizens' Coalition is still mainly to bear moral witness. In this manner, it serves to reproduce the model of virtue characteristic of the traditional scholastic elite.

Similarly, although also not easy to document at this point, the rank and file lawyers of even the corporate law firms do not appear ready to move into positions as key advisors to major businesses or the state. While more of them have moved from the traditional career pattern of judiciary or prosecutor to private practice, their practices in nontraditional positions are still not so different from those who continue to follow the tried and true path, which has the promise of relatively high social status, moral authority, and a payoff when the judge or prosecutor converts to a private practice before his or her former colleagues do.

Preliminary Conclusions

International strategies within the legal profession in Korea as in Latin America are transforming the position of law in the field of state power, and also changing the field of state power. Coming from very different starting points than their Latin American counterparts who were long connected to the governing elite, the Korean importers of law and legal practices from the United States have begun to make places for the law and lawyers in major transactions involving the state and the economy, even involving the *chaebol*. Mobilizing on behalf of corporate law, the environment, or anti-corruption, they combine with other professionals with a similar orientation—and advisors from the World Bank, the IMF, and the United States—to challenge what is now called "crony capitalism" but was earlier termed the "East Asian miracle"—characterized by close relationships between the state and the major *chaebol*. Leading lawyers are very visible in these campaigns.

At the same time, however, the scholastic virtue that brought legitimacy to the law in Korea remains quite important in shaping the possibilities for most of those who make it through the bar exam or to teaching positions in major law schools. True believers who still make up most of the entrants into the legal profession are not so willing or able to embrace fundamentally different roles, whether as lawyers, judges, prosecutors, politicians, economic actors, or professors. The pioneers following international strategies within the legal profession, connected especially to the United States—above all, Harvard—have created new legal roles and broken traditional boundaries. They are shifting the hierarchies to an important extent. At the same time, however, they may also take some of the pressure off of the rigidly meritocratic system—thus helping to preserve it in some form.

The financial crisis of the late 1990s provided an opportunity to develop a larger cadre of lawyers in corporate law firms and in the ranks of the social movements which are capable of playing nontraditional legal roles. But unlike the situation in Latin America, where lawyers also took advantage of opportunities to use a new imported knowledge that could compete with (and complement) economics and political science—and also family relationships—in the management of social conflicts and the legitimation of the new role of the state, the legal profession in Korea started with a huge disadvantage. Those who sought to reproduce social capital through international strategies typically invested in disciplines that were not as difficult to enter as law. As a result, there are many more well-connected, foreign-trained economists and political scientists, for example, than there are lawyers. It is interesting that Korean corporate law firms have even hired some of them to provide the high-profile services to businesses that lawyers are unaccustomed to providing in Korea.

The role of the legal profession in Korea is changing, and the practice of law—as with other disciplines—has become internationalized into the U.S.-dominated market of expertise. But the position of law in the field of state power is still relatively weak, which also helps to account for the prestige of lawyers. To return to the dichotomy that we sought to challenge at the outset, the transformations in the legal profession and the position of law do not necessarily mean that the more traditional forms of reproducing the field of state power have been replaced. International strategies are breaking down traditional boundaries and changing the rules of the game, but any changes will be constructed on a Korean landscape with a particular history of law and legitimacy.

Works Cited

Ahn, Kyong-Whan. 1994. The role of the bar and changes in the lawyer's role: Korea's dilemma. In *Law and technology in the Pacific community*, ed. P. S. C. Lewis. Boulder: Westview Press.

Baxi, Upendra. 1987. On the shame of not being an activist: Thoughts on judicial activism. In *The role of the judiciary in plural societies*, eds. N. Tiruchelvam and R. Coomaraswamy. New York: St. Martin's Press.

Bhagwati, Prafullachandra Natvarlal. 1985. Judicial activism and public interest litigation. 23 *Columbia Journal of Transnational Law* 561.

Bourdieu, Pierre and Loic Wacquant. 1992. *An introduction to reflexive sociology.* Chicago: University of Chicago Press.

Cassels, Jamie. 1989. Judicial activism and public interest litigation in India: Attempting the impossible. 37 *American Journal of Comparative Law* 495.

Cohn, Bernard. 1996. *Colonialism and its forms of knowledge: The British in India.* Princeton: Princeton University Press.

Cumings, Bruce. 1997. *Korea's place in the sun: A modern history.* New York: W.W. Norton.

Dezalay, Yves and Bryant G. Garth. 2002a. *Global prescriptions: The production, exportation and importation of a new legal orthodoxy.* Ann Arbor: University of Michigan Press.

———. 2002b. *The internationalization of palace wars: Lawyers, economists, and the contest to transform Latin American states.* Chicago: University of Chicago Press.

Evans, Peter. 1995. *Embedded autonomy: States and industrial transformation.* Princeton: Princeton University Press.

Fields, Karl. 1995. *Enterprise and the state of Korea and Taiwan.* Ithaca: Cornell University Press.

Galanter, Marc. 1968–69. The study of the Indian legal profession. 3 *Law & Society Review* 201.

———. 1989. *Law and society in modern India.* Delhi: Oxford University Press.

Gandhi, Jogindra Singh. 1982. *Lawyers and touts: A study in the sociology of the legal profession.* Delhi: Hindustan Publishing Company.

Gardner, James. 1981. *Legal imperialism.* Madison: University of Wisconsin Press.

Greenhalgh, Susan. 1994. De-orientalizing the Chinese family firm. *American Ethnologist* 21:766.

Haggard, Stephen and Chien-Kuo Pang. 1994. The transition to export-led growth in Taiwan. In *The role of the state in Taiwan's development*, eds. J. Aberback, D. Dollar, and K. Sokoloff. Armonk, NY: M.E. Sharpe.

Haley, John. 1991. *Authority without power: Law and the Japanese paradox.* New York: Oxford University Press.

Hamilton, Gary and Nicole W. Biggart. 1988. Market, culture, and authority: A comparative analysis of management and organization in the Far East. *American Journal of Sociology* 94 Supp: S52.

Hill, Hal, ed. 1994. *Indonesia's new order: The dynamics of socio-economic transformation.* Honolulu: University of Hawai'i Press.

Johnson, Chalmers. 1995. *Japan, who governs? The rise of the developmental state.* New York: Norton.

Jones, Carol. 1994. Capitalism, globalization and the rule of law: An alternative trajectory of legal change in China. 3 *Social and Legal Studies* 195–221.

Kausikan, Bilahari. 1993. Asia's different standard. *Foreign Policy* (Fall): 24.

Kim, JaeWon. 1991. Critical legal studies: A comparative application to the Korean society and jurisprudence. Unpublished paper, on file with J. W. Kim (see Chapter 2 in this volume).

Lee, Eun-Young. 1998. A proposal of citizen principles to ban corruption. Unpublished paper, on file with B. Garth.

Lee, Su-Hoon. 1998. Popular movements in contemporary South Korea. In *Reinventing Han,* ed. N. Eder. Armonk, NY: M.E. Sharpe.

Lev, Daniel. 1972. Judicial institutions and legal culture in Indonesia. In *Culture and politics in Indonesia*, ed. C. Holt. Ithaca: Cornell University Press.

———. 1976. The origins of the Indonesian advocacy. *Indonesia* 22:135.

———. 1998. Lawyers' causes in Indonesia and Malaysia. In *Cause lawyering: Political commitments and professional responsibilities*, eds. A. Sarat and S. Scheingold. New York: Oxford University Press.

Lewis, Michael. 1998. The real Asian miracle: The world's biggest going-out-of-business sale. *New York Times Magazine.* 31 May.

Michelson, Ethan. 2003. Old wine in a new bottle: Lawyers, clients and *guanxi* in the Chinese legal system. Unpublished paper, on file with B. Garth.

Moog, Robert. 1998. Institutional politics of India's Supreme Court. Paper presented to annual meeting of the Law and Society Association. Unpublished paper, on file with B. Garth.

Mullick, Sanjay Jose. 1997. Power game in India: Environmental clearance and the Enron project. 16 *Stanford Environmental Law Journal* 256.

Murphy, Jay. 1965. *Legal education in a developing nation: The Korean experience.* Seoul: Korea Law Research Institute.

Neier, Aryeh. 1993. Asia's unacceptable standard. *Foreign Policy* (Fall): 42.

Paul, John J. 1991. *The legal profession in colonial South India.* Bombay: Oxford University Press.

Pistor, Katharina and Philip A. Wellons. 1999. *The role of law and legal institutions in Asian economic development 1960–1995: Final comparative report.* New York: Oxford University Press (revised text).

Rahardjo, Satjijpto. 1994. Between two worlds: Modern state and traditional society in Indonesia. 28 *Law & Society Review* 493.

Rosen, George. 1992. *Western economists and Eastern societies: Agents of change in South Asia 1950–1970.* Baltimore: Johns Hopkins.

Rowe, Peter. 1968–69. Indian lawyers and political modernization: Observations in four towns. 3 *Law & Society Review* 219.

Shih, Wen-Chen. 1998. The legalization of a transforming society: The Taiwan experience. Paper for annual meeting of the Law and Society Association. Unpublished paper, on file with B. Garth.

Susman, Susan. 1994. Distant voices in the courts of India: Transformation of standing in public interest litigation. 13 *Wisconsin International Law Journal* 57.

Wade, Robert. 1990. *Governing the market.* Princeton: Princeton University Press.

———. 1996. Japan, the World Bank, and the art of paradigm maintenance: The East Asian miracle in political perspective. *New Left Review* 217:3–36.

Wessel, David and Bob Davis. 1998. How global crisis grew despite efforts of a crack U.S. team. *Wall Street Journal.* 24 September.

West, James. 1991. *Education of the legal profession in Korea.* Seoul: International Legal Studies, Korea University.

Winn, Jane Kaufman. 1994. Relational practices and the marginalization of law: Informal financial practices of small businesses in Taiwan. 28 *Law & Society Review* 193.

——— and Tang-chi Yeh. 1995. Advocating democracy: The role of lawyers in Taiwan's transformation. 20 *Law & Social Inquiry* 561.

Woo, Jung-En. 1991. *Race to the swift: State and finance in Korean industrialization.* New York: Columbia University Press.

Yoon, Dae-Kyu. 1998. Current reform efforts in legal education and the delivery of legal services in Korea. Paper for Bangkok Conference on Legal Services for Unrepresented Groups. Unpublished paper, on file with B. Garth.

FOUR

The Politics of Judicial Reform in Japan: The Rule of Law at Last?

Setsuo Miyazawa[*]

Introduction

Reform of the judicial system and legal profession in Japan has finally begun in earnest. In April 2004, sixty-eight new graduate professional law schools began their first academic year. In 2006, a new national bar examination debuted. The background to these significant events sheds light on the process of, and prospects for, further judicial reform in Japan.

This chapter will examine the history, process, and current status of the reform of the system for producing legal professionals in Japan, including reform of the bar examination, legal education and training, and the development of graduate professional law schools. It will discuss the various interests involved, including different parts of the government, the legal community, and academia.

Part I discusses the recent history of attempts to reform the bar examination, the parties involved in the discussions, and the debates around legal education and training in the 1990s. Part II briefly examines administrative reform and the problems with transparency and accountability. Part III discusses specific proposals for judicial reform that came up in the mid- and late 1990s, and Part IV briefly examines the legal aid system and ideas for its reform. Parts V, VI, and VII examine in detail the Justice System Reform Council, some of its recommendations, and problems with the implementation of these proposals. Parts VIII and IX examine the JSRC's recommendations on the issue of so-called American-style law schools and legal education and training programs more generally, the politics behind the debates about these issues, the implementation of this set of proposals, and prospects for the future.

*Vice President of Omiya Law School; LL.B., LL.M., and S.J.D., Hokkaido University; M.A., M.Phil., and Ph.D. in sociology, Yale University.

Earlier versions of this chapter were presented at Harvard Law School, the University of California at Berkeley, and at a symposium sponsored by the Japan Foundation. I wish to thank for their editorial assistance Andrew Beaten, Dimitrios Angelis, Geraldine Chin and the editorial board of the *Asian-Pacific Law & Policy Journal* which published an earlier version of this chapter in 2001. I also wish to express my gratitude for the extreme patience of Professor William P. Alford, the editor of this book.

In June 2001, the Justice System Reform Council or JSRC (*shihō seido kaikaku shingikai*), established by the Cabinet of Prime Minister Keizō Obuchi in 1999, released a report recommending far-reaching changes to the justice system in Japan.[1] An examination of the history culminating in the release of this report and the subsequent process of implementation provides an interesting case study of the politics of judicial reform in Japan. The cast of players involved in judicial reform has spread from legal professionals (judges, prosecutors, and attorneys) to major actors in the larger political process, namely the Liberal Democratic Party or LDP (*jiyū minshutō*), which is the ruling conservative party, and the Japan Federation of Economic Organizations (*keizai dantai rengōkai* or *keidanren,* hereafter Keidanren), which is one of the most influential organizations representing business interests.[2]

The issue of judicial reform has been a political issue in Japan for many years now. Reform of the national bar examination (*shihō shiken*), which is required for admission to the Japanese bar, has long been a controversial issue. To appreciate fully the significance of the recent developments relating to judicial reform, it is helpful to start with an historical account of the preceding reform of the national bar examination, because it entailed a different kind of political process in which the major players were limited to the three organizations within the legal profession (*hōsō*): the Japan Federation of Bar Associations or JFBA (*Nihon bengoshi rengōkai,* also known as *Nichibenren*), the Ministry of Justice (*hōmushō*), and the Supreme Court (*saikō saibansho*).

I. Earlier Reform of the National Bar Examination

A. The Initial Movement to Reform the National Bar Examination

The Japanese bar has long been able to maintain a monopoly over the provision of legal services because of the extraordinarily high entry barrier to the legal profession in the form of the extremely competitive national bar exam.[3] In 1990, only about 500 of the more than 20,000 candidates actually passed the exam. While the number of successful candidates has gradually risen since then, the number of practicing attorneys was still only 16,369 as of October 29, 1998.[4]

---

1. See Shihō Seido Kaikaku Shingikai (2001).

2. Keidanren merged with another economic organization, the Japan Federation of Employers' Associations (*nikkeiren*) and became the Japan Business Federation (*Nippon keidanren*) in May 2002. For further discussion of Keidanren and Nikkeiren, see Schwartz (1991, 32).

3. For the situation until the early 1980s, see generally Rokumoto (1988).

4. See the JFBA website at http://www.nichibenren.or.jp. Figures for 1998 are used here because the recent movement for comprehensive judicial reform started that year, as will be explained later in this chapter. Also see Shihō Seido Kaikaku Shingikai (2001).

The Japanese bar is definitely the smallest per capita among developed countries.[5]

This situation started to change in the late 1980s when the Ministry of Justice proposed an increase in the number of candidates who successfully passed the bar exam in order to make it easier for younger lawyers to enter the legal profession. After passing the exam, candidates at that time spent two years as judicial trainees (*shihō shushusei*) at the Legal Training and Research Institute or LTRI (*shihō kenshūjo*), with salaries paid by the government, after which they could become a judge, prosecutor, or attorney.

When the ministry proposed an increase in the number of successful candidates, there was strong suspicion that its real motivation was to alleviate the problem of trying to recruit sufficient trainees to fill prosecutorial positions. Because prosecutors are career bureaucrats in the ministry, it is advantageous to enter the ministry as early as possible in order to reach higher positions within its hierarchy. The ministry may also have wanted to compete against other government agencies that recruit employees immediately after they complete their undergraduate education.

One way to address this issue was to reform the bar exam to make it easier for candidates to pass before they finished their undergraduate legal education, so that the ministry could recruit them before they were eligible to apply to other agencies.[6] The Supreme Court supported the ministry's proposals. It is relevant to note that like the prosecutor's office in Japan, the judiciary is a career bureaucracy.[7] Unlike countries such as the United States where judges are appointed or elected from among experienced lawyers, a successful exam candidate can commence a career as an assistant judge (*hanjiho*) directly after completing the two-year LTRI traineeship.

The JFBA immediately opposed this initiative of the Ministry of Justice, arguing that an increase in the number of successful candidates would reduce the quality of lawyers in Japan. However, the ministry cleverly presented its initiative in terms of a broader perspective based on the need both to produce lawyers who can cope with the increasing complexity and internationalization of Japanese society and to expand public access to lawyers.[8] Thus, in 1987, the

---

5. Japan had 14.8 lawyers per 100,000 people in 2001, including judges, prosecutors, and practicing attorneys, compared to 54.7 in France in 1999, 141.4 in Germany in 2000, 168.8 in the United Kingdom in 2000, and 352.1 in the United States in 2000.

6. As discussed below, candidates for the national bar exam do not have to complete their undergraduate legal education before applying to take the exam. Other than the difficult task of passing the exam, there are no prerequisites for admission to the Japanese bar, except that candidates must have completed so-called general education in the first two years of undergraduate education or have passed a qualifying exam to test general knowledge if they have not entered a college.

7. For the status of Japanese judges, see generally Miyazawa (1994); Ramseyer and Rasmusen (2003).

8. For instance, see the statement by the head of the Personnel Department of the Ministry of Justice, in Hōmu Daijin Kanbō (1987).

ministry succeeded in setting the agenda. It formed the Informal Committee on Fundamental Problems of the Legal Profession (*hōsō kihon mondai kondankai*), which consisted of twelve members: two retired judges, a retired prosecutor, a former president of the JFBA, a former bureaucrat, two businesspeople, and five academics. After a report from this committee generally supported its initiative, the ministry convened the Three-Party Committee on the Legal Profession (*hōsō sansha kyōgikai*) in 1988, which consisted of representatives from the ministry, the Supreme Court, and the JFBA. The Ministry of Justice managed to obtain an agreement in the twenty-second session of this committee in 1990, and the National Bar Examination Act was amended in 1991.[9] As a result, the number of those passing the exam increased from approximately five hundred to roughly six hundred in 1991, and to seven hundred in 1993.[10]

These three groups within the legal profession also agreed to certain numerical targets to be achieved by 1995, designed to weed out those who had failed the bar exam repeatedly. So it was that at least 30 percent of those passing in 1995 were candidates who had taken the exam within the last three years, and more than 60 percent were those who had taken it within the last five years. These targets were intended to stabilize trends so that more than 40 percent of candidates passing after 1995 would be those who had taken the exam within the last three years, and that more than 75 percent of successful candidates after 1995 would be those who had taken the exam within the last five years. A clause was attached in case these numerical targets were not reached, creating a system known as "three years and you're out." Under this system, the first five hundred candidates were to pass based on their exam scores, but the next two hundred would be chosen from among only those who had taken the exam within the past one to three years.

B. The JFBA Outvoted

It became apparent in 1994 that these numerical targets would not be reached in 1995. Since the JFBA opposed the "three years and you're out" system as discriminatory when it was first proposed, the JFBA leadership attempted to prevent its implementation by agreeing to a further increase in the annual number of successful candidates. The JFBA leadership sought to maintain its negotiating position by agreeing to an increase in the annual number of passers to one thousand on the condition that the number of judges and prosecutors would also be increased, that the legal aid system would be expanded, and that free defense counsel would be provided to pre-trial detainees. A further important condition was the JFBA's insistence that the existing training system, with its two-year salary, be maintained. The board of the JFBA adopted this proposal on October 12, 1994.

---

9. For data presented during this process, see Hōmu Daijin Kanbō (1991).

10. For the situation of the bar at that time, see generally Ōta and Rokumoto (1993).

However, the media immediately criticized the JFBA proposal as an attempt to nullify the existing agreement. Moreover, a group quickly formed within the JFBA to oppose the board's decision. Its counterproposal was more conservative. These lawyers proposed to maintain the number of exam-passers at seven hundred and to examine the need to increase the number only after observing expansion of the judicial system as a whole. They succeeded in collecting enough proxies to force the leadership to call a special general meeting on December 21, 1994. To prevent an overt split in the JFBA, the leadership agreed to reduce the annual number of passers from one thousand to eight hundred, while nominally saving their original position by stipulating various conditions of agreement.

The JFBA leadership started negotiations with the Ministry of Justice and the Supreme Court in April 1995. In spite of the above-mentioned decision to limit the increase in the number to eight hundred, they came close to agreeing to one thousand as the annual number of successful candidates. The remaining issue was whether the two-year training system with salaries paid by the government would be maintained. The Supreme Court and the Ministry of Justice apparently did not want to negotiate with the Ministry of Finance (*ōkurashō*) to increase the capacity of the LTRI with the resultant budget increase necessary for more trainee salaries under the then-austere budgetary policy of the government. Instead, the Supreme Court sought simply to shorten the training period in order to accommodate one thousand trainees with the same budget and facilities.

The JFBA rejected the proposal to shorten the training period. It held another special general meeting on November 2, 1995 and formally registered its opposition. As a result, negotiations among the three parties within the legal profession collapsed. The Three-Party Committee to manage the national bar exam met on December 11, 1995. The JFBA was overruled in its discussions, and the "three years and you're out" system was implemented starting with the 1996 exam.[11]

C. Discussion by the Legal Profession of the Bar Examination and Training System

While the government was working on these reforms, the legal profession also organized to discuss fundamental reforms in the examination and training of legal professionals. In 1991, the three principal groups within the legal profession established the Committee on the System of Training of Legal Professionals and Related Matters (*hōsō yōsei seido to kaikaku kyōgikai*) (the Reform Committee), based on an agreement reached in 1990. In addition to four judges, five prosecutors, and six attorneys, the committee also included seven

---

11. For a story of the developments between 1988 and 1997 from the perspective of an attorney who served on the Three-Party Committee, see generally Iwai (1998).

law professors, a journalist, a businessperson, and the president of a national consumer organization. The JFBA expected the outside members to support it, but the result was the opposite. The outside members strongly criticized the JFBA's unwillingness to increase the number of successful candidates and rejected the JFBA's proposals. Contrary to seeing the JFBA's proposals as concessions, the outside members interpreted proposals to increase the number of judges and prosecutors, to expand the legal aid system, and to provide free legal counsel to pre-indictment criminal detainees as an attempt by the JFBA to prevent an increase in the number of exam-passers.

The Reform Committee issued its opinion in November 1995. It agreed only on the need to increase the number of successful candidates in order to increase the number of lawyers. The majority proposed 1,500 as an intermediate target as a step toward a larger increase in the number of lawyers. The majority also recommended further reducing the length of practical training by the LTRI coupled with strengthening continuing education for already-qualified lawyers. The JFBA's proposal to limit the increase to 1,000 and to introduce the other reforms above was presented as a minority opinion. The committee also required the three groups within the legal profession to start discussions to achieve fundamental reform of the bar exam and the system of training lawyers (Hōsō Yōsei Seido to Kaikaku Kyōgikai 1996).

D.   Decisions by the Three-Party Committee

Following the opinion of the Reform Committee, the Three-Party Committee again started work, in July 1997, and reached an agreement in October 1997. It decided to increase the annual number of successful exam-takers to 800 in 1998 and to 1,000 in 1999. The length of training at the LTRI was to be reduced to one and a half years in 1999. The majority, which consisted of the Ministry of Justice and the Supreme Court, presented an intermediate goal of increasing the annual number of successful candidates to 1,500 in the future, and the three parties agreed to discuss it again in 2002. In 1998, 812 candidates passed the exam.

Since the two-year joint training period was first introduced as a post-war reform meant to equalize the social status of practicing attorneys with that of judges and prosecutors, the length of training at the LTRI has been as controversial as the number passing the national bar exam. This time, the proposal by the Supreme Court and the Ministry of Justice was simple: reduce the training from two years to one and a half years. Knowing that it could not prevent this reduction, the JFBA leadership proposed providing supplementary training, as attorney-trainees (*kenshū bengoshi*), to those who had completed the one and a half year program at the LTRI. This proposal was remarkable, because it was the first attempt by the JFBA to take part directly in the professional training of future lawyers. However, the proposal was opposed not only by the Ministry of Justice and the Supreme Court, which did not want the involvement of the JFBA, but also by many attorneys who wanted to keep the two-year paid traineeship. The result was a simple reduction of the training period from two years to one and a half years starting in 1999.[12]

In sum, the Ministry of Justice, which dominated the reform process until early 1998, managed, with the Supreme Court, to limit reform to the number of successful candidates and to the length of practical training. They were able to avoid other issues that required changes to their respective groups, such as increasing the number of judges and prosecutors and strengthening the legal aid system, even though scholars and the media often argued that such additional reforms were necessary.

E.   The Role of the JFBA

During this reform process, the JFBA was constantly kept on the defensive. It made no positive proposals of its own until it offered its counterproposal of introducing attorney-trainees, a proposal that ultimately failed. As the JFBA was pressed against the wall, it desperately attempted to find a way to re-align its battle plan and to shape its own future.

To understand the JFBA's position, it is useful to examine its history. The Japanese bar has always been a highly regulated profession, although important aspects of enforcement are delegated to the bar associations themselves. Examples of regulation include the following: until October 2000, advertisement was virtually prohibited;[13] until April 2002, attorneys could not have more than one law office (Practicing Attorney Law, Article 20);[14] it published a fee schedule that could be used as a guideline; attorneys were required to obtain permission from the local bar association if they wanted to join a corporate legal department (Article 30);[15] and attorneys were prohibited from becoming government employees (Article 30).[16] Moreover, the small size of the profession inevitably

---

12. For a discussion of this process from the perspective of the deputy secretary-general of the JFBA, see generally Mizuno (1998).

13. See Nihon Bengoshi Rengōkai (1990). This prohibition was lifted in October 2000, and advertising is now possible in principle. See *Jiyū to Seigi* (2001).

14. This prohibition was moderated in June 2001 when the Practicing Attorney Law was amended to allow incorporation of law offices effective April 2002. Incorporated law offices may open branch offices under certain conditions. For the purposes of this chapter, the term "attorney" refers to a lawyer engaged in the private practice of law. For the text of the amended Practicing Attorney Law (Law No. 205 of 1949), see http://www.nichibenren.or.jp /en/about/pdf/practicing_attorney_law.pdf at the JFBA website.

15. An amendment of this requirement was proposed in 2003 and passed; only a report to the local bar association is now required.

16. Practicing attorneys may not even become full-time faculty members of public universities. This prohibition has slightly been relaxed since November 2000; those who are registered as attorneys may now be employed by government agencies with fixed terms of employment, but are prohibited from acting as attorneys while so employed. An amendment of this restriction is also likely to be proposed in which attorneys employed by government agencies will be allowed to act as attorneys.

produced a highly skewed geographical distribution of private attorneys.[17] In 1996, for instance, while Tokyo had 7,336 attorneys for a population of 11,772,000 (one attorney per 1,600 people) (Watanabe et al. 1997, 131), Shimane Prefecture had only 22 attorneys for a population of 770,000 (one attorney per 35,000 people) (Yonemoto 1995, 115, 116). Many attorneys justified these regulations, the extreme difficulty of the bar exam, and the very small number of private attorneys by referring to the need for attorneys to maintain a commitment to human rights and social justice as required by Article 1 of the Practicing Attorney Law.[18]

Fortunately, however, some signs of internal change in the bar indicated an increasing willingness of a growing number of attorneys to increase their number gradually and to begin to push for deregulation of their practice. An increasingly larger number of attorneys and even some bar association committees started to re-examine these regulations and problems, and some of them tried to present a more flexible and expansive view of lawyering. An early example of this was an ambitious book edited by Kōji Miyakawa and other attorneys (Miyakawa et al. 1992). Miyakawa later became the chair of the editorial committee of *Jiyū to Seigi* (Liberty and Justice), the monthly journal of the JFBA. In 1996, he turned it into an open forum for exchanging different views about the future of attorneys in Japan by publishing a series of articles under the series title *Perspectives on Attorneys for the New Century* (*Atarashii seiki e no bengoshi-zō*). The contributors to this series included several academics, including this author, and the articles published in this series were later published as a book (Nihon Bengoshi Rengōkai 1997).

Several local bar associations, bar committees, and private groups of attorneys also presented their views and visions. One example by a bar association committee was a book edited by the Tokyo Bar Association's Special Committee on Measures for the Problems of the Judicial System (Tokyo Bengoshikai 1996). Another example of participation by a private group was a book by attorneys and scholars, including this author, published in November 1998 (Miyazawa and Kumagai 1998). Although there was still strong opposition to any proposal for increasing their number or reducing their regulation, JFBA leaders were clearly moving in that direction by 1998. One of the problems was that the internal decision-making process was still extremely slow.

It is noteworthy that however dramatic the entire process of reform of the national bar exam and practical training might appear to many attorneys, it still largely took place within a fairly closed circle, mainly consisting of the groups within the legal profession: judges, prosecutors, and practicing attorneys. In contrast, developments in more recent years radically departed from this pattern.

---

17. For an economic analysis of the Japanese bar as a failed cartel, see generally Ramseyer (1986).

18. Article 1 states that a practicing attorney is entrusted with a mission to protect fundamental human rights and to realize social justice.

The LDP and Keidanren joined the scene, and the JFBA needed to find strategies to cope with these more powerful political players who could directly influence the legislative process and who could introduce radical changes through their own initiatives.

II.   Deregulation, Transparency, and Legal Accountability

As background for the LDP and Keidanren's 1998 proposals for comprehensive judicial reform, a brief examination of the politics of administrative reform in Japan is required.

A.   The Politics of Administrative Reform

Administrative reform has been a dominant theme in Japanese politics since the early 1960s.[19] It gained momentum under Prime Minister Yasuhiro Nakasone (1981–1987). At that time, the national debt was accumulating rapidly, and Nakasone wanted to reduce the costs of government. Deregulation quickly became the central issue with regard to administrative reform. The Ad Hoc Advisory Council for the Promotion of Administrative Reform (*rinji gyōsei kaikaku suishin shingikai*) was formed in 1987, and another Ad Hoc Council came into existence in 1990. In the meantime, the Structural Impediments Initiative talks between the United States and Japan began in 1989, and a Policy Action Reform Proposal, which included more than two hundred items, was presented to the Japanese government in 1990. This proposal included reforms for strengthening the Anti-Monopoly Law and the consumer protection administration as well as many other reforms that the Japanese public had sought for years. In 1991, the Ad Hoc Council submitted a report calling for, among other things, the enactment of an administrative procedure act.

In other words, the politics of deregulation did not simply try to reduce government intervention. It also created a political opportunity to re-examine many aspects of the post-war political and economic structure, particularly the role of the administrative bureaucracy. Various legal reform movements that had been advanced since the end of the war were finally in a position to realize their long-advocated ideas, at least to a degree.

B.   Examples of Administrative Reform in the 1990s

During the 1990s, law reform took the form largely of administrative reform. For example, in 1993, the Commercial Code was amended to strengthen shareholder rights. The effect of this amendment was that a shareholder derivative action was defined to include a suit seeking a non-monetary result wherein losing board members paid damages to the company and not to shareholder plaintiffs. The

---

19. For a concise description of the history of administrative reform until 1991, see Abe et al. (1994).

filing fee was fixed at ¥8,200. This instigated a sudden increase of such actions, so that although only 31 cases were filed between 1950 and 1993, some 145 new cases were filed in 1994 (Hayakawa 1996, 247–48).[20] Another example of legal reform was the implementation of the Administrative Procedure Act in 1994. Government agencies are now required to provide reasons when they reject applications for licenses and permits or make decisions unfavorable to private parties. Government agencies are also prohibited from conducting administrative guidance (*gyōsei shido*)[21] in areas outside their jurisdiction and from mistreating a private party that has refused to comply with administrative guidance (Duck 1996). In 1995, the Products Liability Act was implemented, introducing the concept of strict liability (Young 1996). On January 1, 1998, the new Code of Civil Procedure was implemented, strengthening the judicial power to order parties to produce documents (Taniguchi 1997). In May 1999, the Freedom of Information Act was enacted, allowing any person to apply to the head of an administrative agency for disclosure of documents that were made or acquired by its members for use at the agency.

The above examples were all results of political compromise and were far from what legal reformers had originally envisioned. Nevertheless, they increased, albeit slightly, the transparency of governmental decision-making and opportunities for the public to seek accountability from government agencies and private corporations. Proposals by the LDP, Keidanren, and other organizations for judicial reform, however, have gone far beyond these specific pieces of legislation. They have sought to change the judicial system and legal profession in its entirety. Details of these proposals are discussed below.

III. Judicial Reform on the National Agenda

The past number of years have seen a series of reform proposals on the judicial system and legal profession presented by major players in Japanese politics—the government's Administrative Reform Committee (*gyōsei kaikaku iinkai*), the LDP, and Keidanren. They have all taken the same basic perspective. The

---

20. The Osaka District Court on September 20, 2000 ordered a former president and other executives at Daiwa Bank to pay the bank ¥82.9 billion (roughly US$775 million) in compensation for massive losses incurred by the bank stemming from unauthorized securities trading conducted at its New York branch over an eleven-year period from 1984. This case triggered lobbying by Keidanren and other business organizations to amend the Commercial Code to impose limitations on the amounts of compensation. The Commercial Code was amended in October 2001, and the amendment became effective in May 2002. The amount of damages was limited to a level equivalent to six years of remuneration for representative directors (*daihyō torisimariyaku*), four years for other board members, and two years for external board members. The reductions must be approved by a two-thirds majority at a shareholders meeting or by a board meeting, and a board decision for reduction can be nullified if opposed by 3 percent or more of shareholders with voting rights.

21. On administrative guidance, see Upham (1987, 166–204); Haley (1991, 139–68).

argument is that because deregulation will reduce government intervention in many aspects of life, the public should be given better access to the judicial system and legal profession to ensure their protection.

A. Proposals for Reform: The Government, Keidanren, and the LDP

The Administrative Reform Committee, established by the government in 1994, presented its final opinion to the prime minister on December 12, 1997 (Gyō-sei Kaikaku Iinkai 1998). In addition to deregulation, the report also recommended that public access to government information should be radically expanded, consumer protection strengthened, anti-monopoly laws more stringently enforced, and product liability laws adopted. The logic behind these proposals was that the legal protection of individuals must be expanded if regulation was to be reduced. Based on these recommendations, the Cabinet adopted a three-year plan to promote deregulation on March 31, 1998 (Kaguki Kettei 1998). Two main proposals of comprehensive judicial reform soon followed it, one by Keidanren, the other by the LDP, as will be discussed below.

Furthermore, two government committees also published reports in 1998 on judicial and legal reform, including a proposal to strengthen legal aid. The Research Committee on Business Law (*kigyō hōsei kenkyūkai*) of the Ministry of International Trade and Industry[22] or MITI (*tsūsanshō*), long considered the champion of business interests, published a report on June 1, 1998 that urged allowing private legal actions against unfair trade practices, and strengthening the legal aid system. The MITI Deliberative Committee on Industrial Structure (*sangyo kōzō shingikai*) published a report on July 1, 1998 proposing comprehensive reform of the judicial system to ensure business compliance with the legal rules of a market economy. The strengthening of legal aid was again included in these recommendations. The LDP Special Research Committee on the Judicial System (*shihō seido tokubetsu chōsakai*) published a report on June 15, 1998, proposing comprehensive reform of the judicial system and legal profession in Japan, including a proposal to strengthen legal aid. Keidanren also recommended similar reforms in early June 1998. Among all these recommendations, the most important were those by the LDP and Keidanren.

1. Keidanren's Proposal

Keidanren adopted its *Opinions on the Reform of the Justice System* (*Shihō seido kaikaku ni tsuite no iken*)[23] at its board meeting in May 1998. This proposal indicated that as Japan changes from an economy and society dependent upon state administration to a society with a free and fair market, companies and individuals will be required to behave according to the principles of self-responsibility (*jiko sekinin*) and transparency (*tōmeisei*). Therefore, strengthening the judicial

---

22. In 2001 MITI became METI, the Ministry of Economy, Trade and Industry.

23. On file with this author.

system as a fundamental part of the infrastructure of the economy and society was an immediate priority. The proposal also noted that the judicial infrastructure did not possess personnel and institutional capabilities that could be effectively used by the public and by companies. Thus, it recommended a series of reforms including the following:

First, the number of judges should be increased. Second, judges should be appointed from the ranks of practicing attorneys. Third, non-attorney corporate legal staff should be allowed to represent their own companies in litigation and provide legal services to related companies. Fourth, while legal education has been historically provided in Japan by undergraduate nonprofessional law faculties, graduate professional law schools should be established. Fifth, members of the Diet (the Japanese parliament), their policy assistants (*seisaku hisho*), and corporate legal staff should be allowed to practice as private attorneys without undertaking judicial traineeships once they pass the national bar exam. Sixth, Keidanren recommended that considering the concentration of attorneys in large cities, the monopoly of legal services by attorneys should be abolished in order to increase the legal representation of residents in rural areas. Therefore, judicial scriveners (*shihō shoshi*), who are authorized only to prepare legal documents, and patent agents (*benrishi*), who are authorized to represent clients only in patent proceedings, should be allowed to handle some routine legal matters. Finally, it recommended that multidisciplinary partnerships between attorneys and other law-related occupations be allowed.

2. The LDP's Proposal

The LDP Special Research Committee on the Judicial System held a series of sessions beginning on June 12, 1997. It invited a wide variety of organizations and individuals to present their views, including Keidanren, the JFBA, and several prominent law professors. The above-mentioned Keidanren proposal was actually prepared in this context. The LDP published its report *Firm Guidelines for the Judicial System of the Twenty-first Century* (*21-seiki no shihō no tashikana shishin*) on June 16, 1998 (Jiyū Minshutō 1998). The report stated that transparent rules and self-responsibility must be realized while maintaining the traditional national virtue of harmony (*wa*) and that the judicial system must be strengthened as a basis for transforming Japanese society into a society based on the principle of self-responsibility. It also stated that in such a society, legal specialists should participate in many aspects of civic life and economic activities and that the judicial system should take appropriate measures to respond to crime.

The LDP report further recommended a series of reforms that included the following: First, it recommended the strengthening of both the quality and quantity of the legal profession and a consideration of the introduction of graduate law schools. Second, it proposed an examination of the possibility of recruiting judges from among practicing attorneys and an examination of the prospect of continuing education for the legal profession. Third, the report recognized the importance and urgency of strengthening the civil legal aid system and recommended an examination of the criminal defense system from a broader perspective, including the defense of suspects.[24] Fourth, it recommended consideration of the possibility of allowing attorneys to open more than one office, to incorporate law firms, and to form multidisciplinary partnerships. Fifth, it proposed an examination of public participation in the justice system such as introducing a jury and lay judges. Sixth, it recommended that discussion on the judicial system should be widened beyond the three parties within the legal profession and that the LDP's responsibility to discuss it in the Diet should be fulfilled. Finally, it recommended an examination of the budget of the courts and the Ministry of Justice, an increase in the use of alternative dispute resolution (ADR), and an examination of judicial review of administrative agencies.

The LDP's recommendations had a more conservative "law and order" tone than Keidanren's, but the two sets of recommendations widely overlapped. Comprehensive reform of the entire judicial system suddenly became a top priority in national politics. In the interest of strengthening the legal aid system, it is significant that the LDP committee also clearly recommended the expansion of civil legal aid.

3. The 21st Century Institute's Proposal

On December 22, 1998, the 21st Century Public Policy Institute (*21-seiki seisaku kenkyūjo*), a think tank established with funds from Keidanren, published its recommendations, *Toward the Revitalization of the Japanese Civil Justice System* (*Minji shihō kasseika ni mukete*), which focused on civil disputes. Although the institute still recognized the court as the last resort for resolving civil disputes, it clearly recommended a shift in focus from the courts to alternative dispute resolution and proposed creating a comprehensive ADR system called the Citizen's Court. The main function of the Citizen's Court would be to provide a forum and professional legal assistance for autonomous negotiation. Adjudication might also be available, if necessary, but that would not be its main function. Providers of legal assistance would not be limited to attorneys. Retired judges, foreign attorneys, judicial scriveners, patent agents, administrative scriveners (*gyōsei shoshi*), non-attorney corporate legal staff, retired employees of financial institutions, and even medical doctors and engineers would be allowed to provide assistance. Eventually, a comprehensive legal services profession would be formed, and the Ministry of Justice would supervise it for the sake of consumers. This proposal was clearly an expanded version of Keidanren's proposal to reduce the legally protected monopoly of legal services by attorneys. This image of the new legal services profession appears to be strikingly similar to the situation of judicial scriveners because as non-attorneys, they would be placed under the supervision of the Ministry of Justice, unlike practicing attorneys who remain independent from the government, subject instead to bar discipline.

---

24. The present system does not provide free counsel to suspects before indictment.

B.   The Reasons behind the Reform Proposals

Given these groundbreaking reports, one might wonder what has been happening to Japanese legal culture, which some scholars, particularly conservative ones, have viewed as controlling the attitudes and behavior of the majority of Japanese people. Why did conservative groups like Keidanren and the LDP want to expand the role of law, the judicial system, and the Japanese legal profession?

As long as business could rely on government agencies to promote its interests, business tried hard to keep the judicial system and legal profession small and to limit the chances for ordinary people to use law to protect their interests. With a prolonged and severe economic recession, however, the cost of maintaining the bureaucracy became prohibitive, and the increasing globalization of the Japanese economy made the existing system terribly uncompetitive. Therefore, a reduction of the government bureaucracy and the need to obtain independence from it—in other words, administrative reform—became a main concern of business. Working together with the LDP, business groups led by Keidanren accordingly succeeded in generating the 1997 final report of the Administrative Reform Committee that called for significant administrative reform.

It is likely that business groups learned about the use of law as an alternative to bureaucracy through their international activities, particularly in the United States. In looking at the Japanese system in a comparative context, they may have realized how the present system is small, costly, and inefficient. In particular, Keidanren's proposal to allow not only judicial scriveners and patent agents but also non-attorney corporate legal staff to represent parties in litigation reflects its concern with efficiency in handling legal matters. Because business groups must have realized that Japanese judges who joined the judicial bureaucracy immediately after finishing the LTRI do not understand contemporary business practices, Keidanren proposed that judges be recruited mainly from among experienced practicing attorneys. To promote this type of reform proposal to the public, however, business groups and conservatives needed other elements in the package that would satisfy the needs of ordinary people. This may explain the inclusion in the proposal of a call for the strengthening of legal aid.

Whether this hypothetical explanation is correct or not, it is clear that business groups and, to a lesser extent, LDP politicians were indicating that people needed greater access to the law. If so, it appears that they were trying to create a new orthodoxy in Japanese society. In this context, what is described as Japanese legal culture should probably be considered an invention by the elite of earlier times that has become less useful under present circumstances.[25]

It should be noted here that the private bar has lost its noble position as the sole supporter of legal aid among major organizations in Japan. Moreover, whereas the bar has no direct access to the legislative process, the conservative elite does. Whether the reform would be based ultimately on a proposal from

---

25. For this perspective, see generally Upham (1998).

the bar or from these conservatives, an expanded legal aid system would certainly require a larger number of attorneys to provide legal services. Thus, the bar needed to be ready to expand in number or otherwise adjust itself in order to meet the needs of an expanded legal aid system.[26]

IV. Discussions on Legal Aid

The Ministry of Justice and the Japan Legal Aid Association formed a joint study group on legal aid in 1988, and were later joined by the JFBA. This study group had met fifty times by June 1994. In June 1993, the Executive Committee of the Judiciary Committee of the House of Representatives (*shūgiin*), the lower and more powerful of the two houses in Japan's legislature, issued a statement to the effect that the Ministry of Justice should engage in systematic research for the further development of legal aid in Japan. In response, the ministry formed the Research Committee on the Legal Aid System (*hōritsu fujo seido kenkyūkai*) in October 1994, including members from the Supreme Court, the JFBA, the Japan Legal Aid Association, and academia. Unfortunately, the ministry immediately excluded criminal legal aid at the pre-indictment stage from the scope of this committee despite the JFBA's insistence that it be included. Nevertheless, it is fair to say that the creation of this committee in itself was due to the efforts of the Legal Aid Association and the JFBA.

A. Report of the Research Committee on the Legal Aid System

The committee published its final report on March 23, 1998 (Hōritsu Fujo Seido Kenkyūkai 1998, 209). Although the report did not go so far as to recognize each individual's right to receive legal aid per se, it did assert that legal aid would substantively guarantee the people's constitutional right to have access to the courts[27] and would be compatible with the spirit (*shushi*) of the people's rights to a wholesome and cultured life,[28] respect as individuals, the pursuit of happiness,[29] and equality under the law.[30] It declared that a legal aid system could be based on both the ideal of the rule of law and the ideal of a welfare state, so that the state would be responsible for, among other things, establishing such a

---

26. For a pertinent article written by attorneys, see generally Kodera and Kamei (1997).

27. "No person shall be denied the right of access to the courts." The Constitution of Japan, 1946, Article 32.

28. "All people shall have the right to maintain the minimum standards of wholesome and cultured living." Ibid., Article 25.

29. "All of the people shall be respected as individuals. Their right to life, liberty, and the pursuit of happiness shall, to the extent that it does not interfere with the public welfare, be the supreme consideration in legislation and in other governmental affairs." Ibid., Article 13.

30. "All of the people are equal under the law and there shall be no discrimination in political, economic or social relations because of race, creed, sex, social status or family origin." Ibid., Article 14.

system by legislation and bearing an appropriate financial burden. This was the first time in Japanese history that a government committee recognized the state's responsibility for providing legal aid to indigent people.

At the same time, the legal aid report also recognized the responsibility of private attorneys to participate actively in legal aid in light of their required commitment to the public interest (Practicing Attorney Law, Article 1) and their monopoly on legal services (Article 72). It did not specify whether the bar should continue to share the financial burden for legal aid with the state in the future or whether the bar's financial responsibility should be reduced. Some attorneys expressed concern about this ambiguity (Kodera and Kamei 1997, 55–56).

B. Implementation of the Legal Aid Report

Following the release of the legal aid report, the Ministry of Justice prepared a bill to reform the civil legal aid system which was passed as the Civil Legal Aid Law (*minji hōritsu fujohō*) in April 2000. In anticipation of the establishment of a new public interest corporation (*kōeki hōjin*), which would be required to be more clearly separated from the bar, the Japan Legal Aid Association radically changed the size and composition of its board of directors in April 2000. The number of vice presidents was reduced to 2, down from a maximum of 8, and the number of board members was reduced to 20–25 members, down from a maximum of 100 members. The proportion of attorneys was also reduced to 50 percent of the board. Thus, as of April 1, 2000, there were 12 attorneys on the board (including its president, 2 vice presidents, and an executive board member) and 9 non-attorney board members (3 non-attorney board members were added shortly afterwards).

The Ministry of Justice submitted a budgetary request to the Ministry of Finance to increase the government contribution to the legal aid system from ¥584 million (approximately US$5.1 million)[31] for fiscal year 1999 to ¥2.2 billion (approximately US$20.4 million)[32] for fiscal year 2000. Compared to other developed countries, this amount was still very small. Nevertheless, the increase was welcome. The Justice System Reform Council, established in late July 1999, decided at its second meeting on September 2, 1999 to present a proposal to radically expand the national budget for legal aid in an effort to support the initiative of the Ministry of Justice.

The Civil Legal Aid Law came into effect in October 2000. The Ministry of Justice designated the Japan Legal Aid Association as the sole public interest organization to administer civil legal aid for the whole country. Prior to this law, unlike most legal aid systems in developed countries, the Japanese legal aid system consisted of interest-free loans of attorney's fees to indigents, with repayment required at the conclusion of a case. Although the new law continued to

---

31. This is calculated at the 1999 exchange rate of approximately 114 Japanese *yen* to one U.S. dollar (¥114:US$1).

32. At the 2000 exchange rate of approximately ¥108:US$1.

require recipients to pay into the fund in principle, this change clearly marked the beginning of a new era of civil legal aid in Japan. At the same time that this new era was ushered in, radical changes to the legal profession were debated which would increase the number of attorneys and therefore the capacity to provide legal aid services and increase access to justice.

V.   The Justice System Reform Council

A.   Background on the Establishment of the JSRC: Keidanren, the LDP, and JFBA

The JSRC was established in response to requests for reform of the judicial system. As discussed above, business groups led by Keidanren spearheaded the movement from administrative reform to judicial reform. When Keidanren strongly lobbies for something, the LDP often responds positively. That is precisely what happened when Keidanren presented its proposal for judicial reform in May 1998. In addition to Keidanren and the LDP, a wide range of groups and individuals presented their views on judicial reform. The media responded positively, promoting the idea that the judicial system and legal profession should be more easily accessible and that the bureaucratic nature of the judiciary should change. Liberal reformers also joined the debate, recognizing an opportunity to introduce fundamental changes to the judiciary for the first time in Japanese history. Even the JFBA began to explore possibilities to seize this opportunity to realize its long-standing goals of abolishing the bureaucratic judiciary and replacing it with judges mainly recruited from experienced attorneys, under the slogan "a unified legal profession" (*hōsō ichigen*). As if to test the waters, the JFBA leadership made a remarkable decision to invite representatives of Keidanren and the LDP to its Seventeenth Biennial Judicial Symposium on November 6, 1998, held to discuss the reform of judicial appointments.

   The culmination of this movement was the decision of the late Prime Minister Keizō Obuchi to establish the JSRC. Unlike many earlier committees on the judicial system, the JSRC was to be established under the prime minister's Cabinet, rather than under the Ministry of Justice, because the JSRC would have to discuss matters managed or controlled by the ministry. In fact, many reformers, particularly businesspeople and some scholars, argued unsuccessfully that active members of the three primary groups within the legal profession should not even be included on the committee.

B.   The Role and Composition of the JSRC

The law establishing the JSRC was enacted by the Diet on June 2, 1999.[33] Article 2 of this law, relating to the mandate of the JSRC, went through an interesting

---

33. The Law Concerning the Establishment of the Justice System Reform Council (*shihō kaikaku shingikai secchihō*) (Law No. 68).

process of amendment. The original bill as proposed by the bureaucracy simply stated that the JSRC should clarify the role of the judicial system in Japanese society in the twenty-first century and should investigate and deliberate about basic policies necessary for the reform of the judicial system and the improvement of its foundations. This did not specify what kinds of reforms were expected. After much maneuvering by politicians and bureaucrats, the Diet inserted a clause that clarified the general direction of the expected reform. This clause specified that the reform should include policies to make the judicial system more accessible to the public, allow public participation in the judicial system, and enrich and strengthen the legal profession.

Both houses of the Diet attached special resolutions to the law. The House of Representative's resolution provided that the JSRC discuss such important matters as the unification of the legal profession,[34] the enhancement of both the quantity and quality of the legal profession, public participation in the judicial system, and the relationship between human rights and criminal justice. The House of Councillors (*sangiin*), the less powerful upper house, resolved that the JSRC pay particular attention to the protection of fundamental human rights, to the realization of the constitutional ideal of the rule of law, and particularly to the perspective of the public as users of the judicial system. As a piece of legislation in Japan, this was nothing short of remarkable. The JSRC was mandated to present its final report to the prime minister in two years.

Thus, the selection of the thirteen members of the JSRC became a critical issue. Eventually, the following were selected: three law professors, three senior members of the legal profession (each representing one of the principal groups in the legal profession), two businesspeople (one each representing Keidanren and the Tokyo Chamber of Commerce), the president of the Federation of Private Universities, a professor of accounting, the president of a major foundation (the Nippon Foundation), and one representative each from the largest labor organization (the National Confederation of Private-Sector Trade Unions or *rengō*) and a consumer organization (the Federation of Housewives or *shufuren*).

The three law professors were Kōji Satō of Kinki University Law School and Kyoto University, a constitutional scholar heavily involved in administrative reform; Morio Takeshita, a civil procedure scholar who had formerly been at Hitotsubashi University prior to becoming the president of Surugadai University; and Masahito Inouye, a criminal procedure scholar at the University of Tokyo who was widely known for work that had provided the theoretical underpinning for legislation legalizing wiretapping for criminal investigations. Satō argued that the rule of law had failed to materialize in Japan, that administrative reform was the first step to the realization of that ideal, and that judicial reform would complete the transformation of Japanese society so that autonomous individuals would be able to design their own society through

---

34. By unification, it meant the abolition of career judicial officers and the appointment of experienced attorneys as judges.

their participation in legislative and judicial processes (Satō 1999, 54–58). Satō was also known for his proposal to introduce law schools as the best way to assure the quality of lawyers, whose numbers would inevitably increase in order to improve public access to justice. The other two law professors, Takeshita and Inouye, were not known for their views on judicial reform and were widely expected to hold more traditional views.

The most well-known person of the three senior members from the legal profession was Kōhei Nakabō, an Osaka attorney and former JFBA president who had played a significant role in recovering money from debtors of a government corporation.[35] Although many people who did not want to introduce real reforms opposed his inclusion in the JSRC, the government apparently had no other choice than to select him as a representative of attorneys. At the age of seventy, he declared that he would work on judicial reform full-time and that he would not take the narrow perspective of representing only the interests of the bar. Instead, he would aspire to take a much broader perspective and reflect the concerns of ordinary users.

The two other senior lawyers were Kōzō Fujita, the former head of a high court, and Toshihiro Mizuhara, the former head of a high prosecutor's office. Their views on judicial reform were unknown, but they were widely expected to hold more traditional views. The views on reform of the two academics from outside the legal field, Yasuhiko Torii, an economist and president of Keio University, and Keiko Kitamura, an accounting professor and dean at Chuo University, were not apparent at the time of their appointment.

The four members representing users of the judicial system, namely business, labor, and consumers, were also relative unknowns; they were Masaru Yamamoto, Hiroji Ishii, Tsuyoshi Takagi, and Hatsuko Yoshioka. Although each of these groups had more prominent and eloquent representatives widely

---

35. When the bubble economy collapsed and banks were unable to recover their losses from loans to housing loan companies (*jūsen*), the government bailed out those banks by giving them tax money of ¥685 billion (approximately US$5.7 billion). In return, the government acquired those bad debts and established a special corporation to recover as much money as possible from those debtors who were able to pay. Because those debtors included purported members of organized crime and exposing their hidden assets would be extremely difficult, a person with enormous courage and integrity was needed to head the special corporation. The government asked Nakabō to take the job and he agreed.

In the first two years and seven months of its establishment, this corporation, the Housing Loan Bad Debts Management System, Inc. (*kabushiki-gaisha jūtaku kinyū saiken kanri kikō or jūkan*), succeeded in recovering an astonishing ¥1.55 trillion (approximately US$12.8 billion). Nakabō assembled a group of attorneys and used a wide array of legal instruments in this work (Nakabō 1999). He sued former executives of those housing loan companies for their individual responsibility in the failure of their companies. He even sued Sumitomo Bank for its role in misleading a housing loan company into lending money to a losing project, while requiring the loan company to open and keep an account in return for its service of introducing customers. Nakabō openly criticized the judicial system for its failure in handling these and other financial issues. He became an undeniable national hero.

known for their views, those people were not appointed. The final person, Ayako Sono, was a foundation head and a writer who was a ubiquitous figure in government committees and known for her realistic views on human nature, barbed comments, and criticism of the JFBA.[36]

In this group of thirteen members, only Satō and Nakabō were clear reformers, but their styles differed, as could be expected from their respective backgrounds. The views of the other members were more or less unknown. If Satō and Nakabō managed to form an alliance and sway a majority of members, the JSRC could actually deliver a comprehensive reform package as directed by the special resolutions of the Diet. If they failed, the present system, which had remained virtually unchanged since the Meiji era, would continue.

C. The JSRC's Secretariat and Initial Meetings

Although the JSRC was established under the Cabinet, which includes all the ministries, the Ministry of Justice managed to control its secretariat. At its first meeting, on July 27, 1999, the secretariat had sixteen members. Its head, the secretary-general, was a prosecutor from the Ministry of Justice. The Ministry of Justice had six more members in the secretariat, including a former lower court judge who had been transferred to the ministry. The Supreme Court sent another lower court judge, while the JFBA sent two attorneys. The remaining members included three from the Ministry of Finance and one each from the Ministry of Education (*monbushō*), MITI, and the Ministry of Construction (*kensetsushō*). No academics were included. Because the JSRC members worked on a part-time basis, the members of the secretariat were the only people who would be working full-time on judicial reform. The secretariat was expected to prepare a list of issues to be discussed and to present materials and drafts to the JSRC. As is always the case on government committees, the relationship between the JSRC and its secretariat was another key element in determining what would be accomplished.

When the JSRC held its initial meeting, the first issue was the selection of the chairperson. The secretary-general immediately proposed selecting the chairperson, but Nakabō argued that it was nonsensical to do so without knowing each member's views. Thus, every member was virtually forced to express some commitment to reform, although several members expressed reservations about wholesale reform, stating that they should carefully examine whether the proposed reforms suited the Japanese system. After that, Nakabō nominated Satō to serve as the chairperson, denying the secretariat the opportunity formally to nominate Satō.

---

36. For instance, in an article in *Nihon Keizai Shimbun*, September 5, 1992, Sono wrote that the JFBA looked like a pressure group. The reason for this, she argued, was that the JFBA intruded into the freedom of thought and expression by opposing local ordinances that restricted the use of loudspeakers in public places even though many individual members of the bar supported such restrictions.

The next issue was the extent to which deliberations should be open to the public. The JSRC quickly agreed to publish minutes in both printed form and via the Internet, but could not reach agreement on whether to allow observers to attend meetings. Nakabō, who favored opening deliberations to the public, and Sono, who opposed it, engaged in a confrontational exchange. When the JSRC held its second meeting on September 2, 1999, representatives of the three groups within the legal profession were allowed to observe deliberations, but the media was still excluded. The lack of media coverage threatened seriously to hinder the public's ability to present their views in a timely fashion, but the media was finally allowed to observe deliberations through a closed-circuit television.

In any event, there was no guarantee that the JSRC would actually present a comprehensive reform proposal. Therefore, to ensure reform, it was important that the public constantly remind the members of why the JSRC was formed. It was also important that the public obtain information regarding its activities. For this purpose, a group of scholars, including myself, started a monthly journal, the *Gekkan Shihō Kaikaku* (Journal of Judicial Reform) on October 5, 1999.

VI.   The Final Report of the Justice System Reform Council

A.   The Historical and Political Context of the Report

Historically, the Japanese legal system has largely been a tool of the government, used to govern its citizens. The legal system has rarely played a significant role as a method for citizens to challenge the government or big business or to solve disputes among themselves. Hence, JSRC chair Satō wrote, just before his appointment to the council, that Japan, even after World War II, has been characterized by "rule by law," rather than "rule of law" (Satō 1999). A combination of factors suddenly made business groups and conservative politicians interested in judicial reforms that could potentially facilitate the rule of law in Japan. From mid-1998 to mid-1999, Japan was clearly in the midst of a rare opportunity to introduce some tangible reforms to promote the rule of law.

It was also possible, however, that the LDP and Keidanren would stop their drive for judicial reform once they had satisfied their immediate goals, without attempting further reforms that would improve ordinary people's access to justice. The only group in Japan that had previously claimed to be the champion of the ordinary people was the bar. The bar, however, had been extremely reluctant to reform itself in relation to a vital issue, namely increasing the number of lawyers. It was evident that the bar would largely be excluded from the politics of judicial reform, unless it quickly, radically, and publicly changed its position on this issue.

In the meantime, the groups that controlled the system, namely the Supreme Court and the Ministry of Justice, were working hard to influence the JSRC. They virtually controlled the JSRC's secretariat. A large number of attorneys and law professors also wanted to maintain the present system of legal education. Their opposition would inevitably result in serving the interests of the Supreme Court and the Ministry of Justice as well as those of the cram schools.

Therefore, much depended on the battle within and around the JSRC.

B.   Issues Raised by the Justice System Reform Council

An important development occurred when the JSRC met on November 9, 1999. Each member except Satō, the chair, and Sono, the author, individually presented a list of issues to be discussed. There was, reportedly, a broad consensus on the need to discuss the possibilities for changing the system of judicial appointments. Since the war, new judges have predominantly been installed immediately upon their completion of training at the LTRI. The proposed system would recruit a wider variety of more experienced lawyers to the judiciary. Other issues considered included the introduction of jury trials or lay judges (the *saiban-in* system), a radical increase in the number of lawyers, and a radical expansion of the legal aid system. There was even a suggestion that legal aid be provided to the criminally accused at the pre-indictment stage. This was a promising sign.

The JSRC formally published its self-selected agenda on December 21, 1999.[37] Those advocating for fundamental reforms had to express their views quickly, publicly, and loudly to prevent backpedaling by the JSRC under various pressures. That is what I did from mid-1999 to mid-2001, particularly through writing in nearly every issue of *Gekkan Shihō Kaikaku*.

In the meantime, the leadership of the JFBA worked hard to persuade the rank and file members of the JFBA to accept self-reforms, particularly an increase in the number of attorneys. The JFBA leadership finally succeeded in passing a resolution at an extraordinary general meeting on November 1, 2000 that the JFBA "will endeavor to secure the number [of legal professionals] the public needs while maintaining their quality." This meeting lasted more than eight hours, and there were many moments when fistfights nearly erupted—all televised. Nonetheless, this resolution cleared the way for the JFBA to maintain its reform proposals on other issues, such as judicial appointments, public participation in the administration of justice, and publicly funded criminal defense lawyers in the pre-indictment stage, as well as making it possible for the JFBA to engage directly in the discussion on the reform of legal education, particularly the introduction of graduate professional law schools.[38]

---

37. *The Points at Issue in the Justice Reform* (*Ronten seiri*). See more at the website of the Prime Minister of Japan at http://www.kantei.go.jp/foreign/policy/sihou/singikai/991221_e.html.

38. For the debate over the reform of the bar itself just before this meeting, see *Gekkan Shihō Kaikaku* (2000).

C. From the Final Report of the JSRC: Reform of the Justice System

The Justice System Reform Council presented its final report[39] to Prime Minister Junichiro Koizumi on June 12, 2001. The council proclaimed its lofty mission at the beginning of the report:

> [T]his Council has determined that the fundamental task for reform of the justice system is to define clearly what we must do to transform both the spirit of the law and the rule of law into the flesh and blood of this country, so that they become 'the shape of our country' and what is necessary to realize, in the true sense, respect for individuals . . . and popular sovereignty . . . , on which the Constitution of Japan is based. (Miyazawa 2002e, 5)

Among its many recommendations, the JSRC proposed the following. In the area of civil justice, it proposed reducing the average length of litigation by half; allowing the winning party to recover part of their attorney's fees from the losing party under certain conditions; and strengthening civil legal aid. In the area of criminal justice, the JSRC proposed providing free defense counsel from the investigation stage, in contrast to the existing system that provides free defense counsel only after indictment; and making certain decisions by the Prosecution Review Board (*kensatsu shinsakai*) binding, instead of the existing system in which they are only advisory.[40] In the area of public participation in the administration of justice, the JSRC recommended the introduction of lay judges (*saiban-in*) in certain serious criminal cases. They would be randomly selected on a case-by-case basis to decide both fact and law with professional judges, and the defendant would be allowed to appeal their decisions.

In the area of legal education and the production of legal professionals, the JSRC recommended establishing graduate professional law schools in 2004, a new national bar exam, an increase in the number of those passing the exam to 1,500 people per year by 2004 and 3,000 by 2010, and an increase in the total population of active legal professionals (judges, prosecutors, and attorneys) to approximately 50,000 by 2018 (see Part VIII D below).

In the area of reform of the legal profession, the JSRC recommended abolishing or loosening several regulations over private attorneys and the provision of legal services, including permitting judicial scriveners (*shihō shoshi*) to represent parties in summary courts (*kan'i saibansho*).[41] In relation to the judiciary, it proposed the appointment of more judges from among practicing attorneys and an "in principle" requirement that every assistant judge should obtain practical

---

39. See Shihō Seido Kaikaku Shingikai (2001) for an official English translation of the report. The council disbanded after the presentation of the final report.

40. For this author's view on the recommendations regarding criminal justice, see Miyazawa (2002e).

41. Japan has two kinds of courts of first instance: district courts (*chihō saibansho*) and summary courts. Summary courts handle civil cases worth up to ¥900,000 or criminal cases punishable by a fine. District courts handle larger or more serious cases.

experience outside the court. It also recommended the establishment of an advisory organization to oversee the appointment of lower court judges by the Supreme Court and the establishment of clearer standards and more transparent procedures for the internal evaluation of judges.

Among these and other proposed changes, the reform of legal education and the production of more lawyers were priorities, because the JSRC considered the production of vastly more better-educated legal professionals to be the basis for its entire reform agenda. Therefore, the JSRC urged the concerned agencies (*kankei kikan*) to set the standards for accrediting graduate law schools as soon as possible.

VII. Domination of the Implementation Process by Judicial Bureaucrats

A. The Preparation Office, Promotion Office, and Promotion Secretariat

The process for implementing the recommendations of the JSRC was initiated by the establishment of the Office for the Preparation of the Promotion of Justice System Reform (*shihō seido kaikaku suishin junbishitsu*) (the Preparation Office) under the Cabinet.[42] The main function of the Preparation Office was to draft the Law on the Promotion of Justice System Reform (*shihō seido kaikaku suishinhō*) (the Promotion Law) and to prepare for the establishment of the Office for the Promotion of Justice System Reform (*shihō seido kaikaku suishin honbu*) (the Promotion Office) that would be headed by the prime minister.

The establishment of the Preparation Office marked the return of a legislative process dominated by the Ministry of Justice. A prosecutor was appointed to head the Preparation Office. The office had approximately thirty members including several who were temporarily assigned from various government agencies and the JFBA, but the majority were prosecutors and judges. In other words, the implementation of the reforms was largely placed in the hands of judicial bureaucrats who themselves were the main targets of the proposed reforms.

The Preparation Office did not limit its activities to the drafting of the Promotion Law and the preparation of the Promotion Office. Although the Promotion Office was to become the main agency for designing the details of the reforms, the Preparation Office proceeded to start discussions about substantive policy matters with various government agencies and outside organizations that were involved with each reform item. Furthermore, the office took the position that it was not required to open its policy-making process to the media

---

42. For developments between June and December 2000, see Miyazawa (2002d, 5); Ozaki (2002).

and the public, because its process should be the same as that of any other Japanese government agency.

Through all this, the Preparation Office succeeded in obtaining a higher status and more power than existing government agencies that were more directly related to the particular issues involved.

The Promotion Law became effective in November 2001. The law stipulated that the government was responsible for drawing up a plan to promote judicial system reform and to take whatever legal, financial, and other measures necessary to implement concrete policies within the three-year period during which the Promotion Law remained effective. The committees on legal affairs (*hōmu iinkai*) in both houses of the Diet had attached a resolution to the bill before its passage that specifically required all meetings of the relevant committees be open to the public.

The Promotion Office was formed on December 1, 2001, pursuant to the Promotion Law. The prime minister became its head, and all cabinet members became members, with the justice minister and the chief cabinet secretary (*kanbō chōkan*) as the vice heads. It was not anticipated that the prime minister and other ministers could actually design the details of the plan for reform. The real work was to be carried out by the Promotion Secretariat (*jimukyoku*), established as the successor of the Preparation Office. The new secretariat had some fifty members. The secretary-general (*jimu kyokuchō*) was a typical example of judges in Japan who transfer to the Ministry of Justice as prosecutors in the middle of their judicial careers.[43] He had served as the director of the bureaus in charge of government litigation (*shōmukyoku*) and of civil justice (*minjikyoku*) in the Ministry of Justice before taking this new assignment. As secretary-general, the majority of members under him were prosecutors and judges who were temporarily assigned to the secretariat. Many observers suspected that a secretariat largely staffed by mainstream prosecutors and judges would not be inclined to implement vigorously the JSRC recommendations.

B.   The Promotion Advisory Board and the Consultation Groups

The Promotion Office Advisory Board (*komon kaigi*) was established to aid the Promotion Office. It had eight very prominent members including Professor Satō as the chair, as he was of the JSRC; the president of Keidanren; the chief editorial writer of *Nihon Keizai Shimbun*; the president of Rengō; the president of the University of Tokyo; the president of Waseda University, who had been a law professor; the president of Tsudajuku University; and a news commentator. Becoming chair of this board was the highest official position Professor Satō attained in the implementation process, though he did go on to be a member of the law school committee of one of the accrediting organizations. Since the prime minister was expected to attend some of its meetings, it was widely expected that Professor Satō would try to oversee the Promotion Secretariat through the Promotion Advisory Board.

---

43. For discussion of this type of judicial bureaucrat, see Miyazawa (1994, 269–71).

The implementation process started in earnest in January 2002 when ten consultation groups of experts (*kentōkai*) were formed under the Promotion Secretariat, one for each of the following areas: labor disputes; access to the justice system; ADR; arbitration; administrative litigation; public participation in the administration of justice (the *saiban-in* system) and criminal affairs; the public criminal defense system; internationalization; legal training (education and training of legal professionals); and the system for the legal profession (lawyers, public prosecutors, and judges). A group on intellectual property litigation was added in October 2002. Each consultation group had eleven members. The Consultation Group on Legal Training (*hōsō yōsei kentōkai*) included Professor Shigeaki Tanaka of Kyoto University Faculty of Law, the chair; Professor Inouye,[44] a JSRC member; Professor Daniel Foote, the first North American to join the University of Tokyo law faculty; another law professor from Chuo University; a judge; a prosecutor; an attorney; an in-house counsel of a pharmaceutical company; a former legal department head of the Japanese subsidiary of Apple; the head of the National Institute for Academic Degrees; and a member of a research institute affiliated with the Ministry of Health, Labor and Welfare (*rōdōshō*). Only Professor Foote and the attorney were known for their strong commitment to the ideals presented by the JSRC. The other members were considered either moderate or conservative.

The Promotion Secretariat took the position that these consultation groups were only advisory and that the secretariat was responsible for drawing up policy details. Furthermore, different consultation groups adopted different policies regarding public access to their meetings. All the groups allowed the media to observe their meetings. However, only six groups initially decided to publish their minutes on the website of the prime minister's office, and four decided to publish only summaries of minutes.[45]

From the perspective that seeks to promote the rule of law, the most important area remaining that would make government agencies legally accountable was the reform of administrative litigation. Precisely because this was an area where government agencies resisted reform, the JSRC's final report merely outlined issues to be examined. Much depended on the Consultation Group on Administrative Litigation.[46] The group included four law professors, a judge, a

---

44. Professor Inouye also became the chairperson of the consultation group on the *saiban-in* system and criminal affairs and of the consultation group on the publicly funded criminal defense system. He also became a member of the law school committee on one of the accrediting organizations along with Professors Satō, Tanaka, and Foote.

45. The latter four included the consultation group on administrative litigation, on *saiban-in* and criminal affairs, on a public criminal defense system, and on the system for the legal profession. Furthermore, five groups, including the group on legal training, initially decided not to identify the authors of specific statements in minutes or summaries. Most groups became more open following criticism of their opacity.

46. For reports on the administrative litigation group, see Hiroshi Saitō's column in the bimonthly *Kausa*.

prosecutor, a practicing attorney, a bureaucrat from an administrative agency, a member of a think tank, an officer of a labor organization, and an academic from outside law. The chairperson was a retired professor in administrative law from the University of Tokyo. At an early meeting, there was a debate about the proper role of the Promotion Secretariat and the chairperson, because the secretariat hastily tried to prepare a summary of opinions from the Promotion Office that did not really reflect the full range of opinions of that office, and the chairperson appeared to have allowed the secretariat to do this. The Promotion Secretariat took a more careful approach after a strong protest from some members. However, there was always a strong temptation for the secretariat to manipulate the course of deliberation because of the very nature of the issues.

A similar problem may have existed in the Consultation Group on the System for the Legal Profession that was in charge of reform for judges, public prosecutors, and attorneys.[47] With regard to the reform of the judiciary, the JSRC proposed, among other things, the creation of a system that would let assistant judges acquire experience working as other legal professionals do (this came into effect in April 2005); the creation of organizations that would evaluate judicial candidates and present opinions on them to the Supreme Court; the introduction of a more transparent system for the evaluation of incumbent judges; and the introduction of a system that would let administration of the lower courts reflect public opinion. Although the JSRC did not go so far as to abolish the system of assistant judges in favor of one that would appoint experienced attorneys as judges, the proposed reforms certainly had to influence the way the General Secretariat of the Supreme Court controls courts and judges. The General Secretariat of the Supreme Court would certainly have wanted to minimize the reform in this context, and the Promotion Secretariat may have shared such a desire.

Still another consultation group that was in charge of highly contentious issues was the consultation group on public participation in the administration of justice, the *saiban-in* system, and criminal affairs. As described earlier, the JSRC recommended introducing the idea of a panel of professional judges and lay judges that would jointly decide relatively serious criminal cases. The composition of this panel became a major issue both inside[48] and outside the consultation group. While conservatives proposed making the number of lay judges smaller than the number of judges, progressives proposed making the number of lay judges far larger than the number of judges.[49] Again the Supreme Court took the more conservative position, and the Promotion Secretariat likely shared that view. In May 2004 a *saiban-in* law was enacted.

---

47. For reports on the legal profession group, see Ken'ichi Baba's column in the bimonthly *Kausa*.

48. For reports on this group's work, see Akira Gotō's column in *Kausa*.

49. For instance, Kōichi Yaguchi, a former chief justice of the Supreme Court and member of the People's Forum (see Part VII D below), proposed, among other things, to form panels with one judge and eleven lay judges in *Yomiuri Shimbun* (November 13, 2002).

C. Politicization of the Implementation Process

Another complication that had not existed during the term of the JSRC was the aggressive involvement of LDP politicians. The continuous control of the government by the LDP since 1955, except the period between 1993 and 1996, had led to the development of a policy-making system that allowed intervention by LDP politicians at the stage between the preparation of a policy by respective government agencies and the final adoption of the policy by the Cabinet. The central forum for this political intervention was the LDP Policy Affairs Research Council (*seimu chōsakai*), which was divided into several divisions, each of which roughly corresponded with a ministry. LDP politicians representing the constituents of respective ministries, or concerned pressure groups, commonly called *zoku* (tribes), tried to exert their influence to promote, block, or modify proposed policies affecting their respective constituencies.[50] Among these divisions, the Special Research Council on the Judicial System (*shihō seido chōsakai*) had jurisdiction over judicial reform; its Subcommittee on the System of Training of Legal Professionals, Legal Education, and Qualifying Examination (*hōsō yōsei, hōgaku kyōiku oyobi shikaku shiken no arikata ni kansuru shō iinkai*) started to meet in March 2002.

These developments alerted progressive reformers. It was apparent that it would be far more difficult for the public to follow and provide timely criticisms on the developments in the Promotion Secretariat and the consultation groups than those in the JSRC. Therefore, the same group of scholars who had published *Gekkan Shihō Kaikaku* in October 1999[51] started a new bimonthly, *Kausa* (Cause) in May 2002, supplemented with an e-mail magazine.[52]

Furthermore, a wide range of groups and individuals, including all the members of the Promotion Advisory Board, some of the former members of the JSRC, and a large number of leading members of business, labor, and consumer organizations formed the National Council on Judicial Reform (*kokumin shihō kaigi*) in April 2002. It held a symposium on May 29, 2002, and Prime Minister Koizumi attended and expressed his commitment to judicial reform.[53]

Individual reformers also expressed their views in the media. In June and July 2002, for instance, Kōhei Nakabō, the most progressive member of the JSRC, wrote op-ed articles in the *Asahi* and *Yomiuri* newspapers warning against the deterioration of judicial reform in the hands of judicial bureaucrats (Nakabō 2002a and 2002b), while I wrote an op-ed article on law schools (Miyazawa 2002c). Those who resisted reform, of course also publicly expressed their views

---

50. For discussion of the Policy Affairs Research Council and *zoku* politicians, see Schwartz (1991, 23–25).

51. This monthly magazine folded in September 2001.

52. This author was a member of the editorial board and wrote for *Kausa*, which folded in March 2004.

53. For the activities of the National Council on Judicial Reform, see the regular column on the council by Katsuhiko Iimuro, a journalist, in *Kausa*.

and lobbied the politicians heavily. Indeed, they had a tremendous advantage in terms of their access to LDP politicians. The entire process of judicial reform thus became extremely politicized.

D. An Advisory Board Member Speaks Out

As explained above, the fundamental problem in the implementation process was that it was ultimately in the hands of judicial bureaucrats who staffed the Promotion Secretariat. The only official organization that might have been able to control it was the Promotion Advisory Board chaired by Professor Satō, the JSRC chair. However, action by the board focused on issues not directly related to the issues discussed above. The board presented an appeal to the prime minister and the public on July 5, 2002 that was entitled *Toward a Transparent and Open Society Where Each and Every National Will Shine* (*Kokumin hitori hitori ga kagayaku tōmei de hirakareta shakai o mezashite*).[54] Although it covered several items, the media paid most attention to a specific proposal that appropriate measures be taken so that any case filed in a court would be decided on within two years of filing. This proposal appeared to be simplistic but actually meant much more from the perspective of Professor Satō. He explained in a long interview in *Asahi Shimbun* (November 13, 2002) that such a target was necessary in order to require all the players to introduce a wide range of reforms that would reduce the delays in court proceedings without causing a decline in the quality of justice by merely hastily handling cases. He mentioned, for instance, the need to introduce discovery in both civil and criminal proceedings, to make the process of criminal investigation more transparent, and to establish a publicly funded criminal defense system. An increase in the number of judges, and reform of the education and training of lawyers would also be necessary in order to produce a radically larger number of better-educated legal professionals.

The secretary-general of the Supreme Court criticized this proposal by stating that while there was a need to recognize the public's opinion, the courts would be hard-pressed to complete cases within two years (*Asahi Shimbun,* November 8, 2002). The Promotion Advisory Board, however, seemed to have succeeded in mobilizing the support of the prime minister. The media reported that the Promotion Office was preparing a bill to impose the duty to endeavor (*doryoku suru*) to complete a trial within two years on all involved in litigation, including not only judges but also prosecutors, plaintiffs, and defendants (*Asahi Shimbun,* November 10, 2002). Professor Satō seemed to be planning to use this law to force judicial bureaucrats to implement more faithfully the recommendation of the JSRC.

In the interview for *Asahi Shimbun,* Professor Satō said that he wanted to urge the judiciary, the Ministry of Justice, and the bar to make up their minds to

---

54. For the full text in Japanese, see http://www.kantei.go.jp/jp/singi/sihou/komon/dai5 /5gijisidai.html at the website of the Prime Minister of Japan.

adopt reform, and expressed his expectation that the debate on reform would proceed with more intensity. He acknowledged the possibility that simply speeding up litigation could result in mere hastiness would ignore the rights of litigants. He insisted, however, that speedy litigation and complete litigation need not contradict each other and added that as an absolute condition for speedy and complete litigation, Japan needed a legal profession better in quality and larger in numbers. He also mentioned, among other things, the need for pre-trial discovery, expansion of the ADR program to screen out cases that do not require formal litigation, and a simplified style of decision-writing for civil cases, as well as the need for expanded discovery, increased transparency in interrogation, and the introduction of criminal defense lawyers paid for by public funds. He expressed his concern about the preliminary exam for the new national bar exam and concluded the interview with a pointed statement that the whole reform would ultimately depend on the leadership of the prime minister.

Additional pressure came from prominent members of the business community, labor, academia, the legal profession, and the media, which formed the People's Forum on Judicial Reform (*shihō kaikaku kokumin kaigi*) as a watchdog and pressure group seeking faithful implementation of the proposals of the JSRC. Kōichi Yaguchi, a former chief justice of the Supreme Court, was a member, and proposed the progressive version of the *saiban-in* system mentioned above in note 49. The forum presented a set of recommendations that basically supported the effort by Professor Satō.[55]

VIII.   The Issue of Graduate Professional Law Schools

One of the most important and controversial issues raised in the course of the JSRC deliberations was the movement to introduce graduate professional law schools and to modify the role of the LTRI. This was an issue that had been discussed in Japan for some time, but it only became a major policy issue after 1999. A discussion of the politics surrounding the debate over this issue also illustrates the importance of public awareness regarding developments in the JSRC, given the concerted effort by some to influence the JSRC to maintain the status quo.

A.   The Context of Proposals on Legal Education and Training: The Existing System

In Japan, law was traditionally taught at undergraduate nonprofessional law schools (Taniguchi 1994, 298–302). No other academic institutions provided comprehensive academic legal education. However, a law degree has never been required to sit for the national bar exam. Even after successful candidates

---

55. Takao Suami of Waseda University, a participant in the conference on which this volume is based, was the secretary-general of the People's Forum.

passed the bar exam, the required schooling provided at the LTRI consisted of only practical training. In other words, there has been no required academic legal education directly connected to the training of future lawyers. Therefore, several legal academics, including this author, proposed the introduction of graduate professional law schools (hereafter, "law schools") in Japan as early as the 1980s.[56] At that time, the idea did not receive serious attention, mostly because the discussion was limited to a closed circle of the legal profession and law professors.

In 1999, however, the establishment of law schools suddenly became a major policy issue, both in relation to proposals for judicial reform and to university education reform in general. JSRC chairperson Satō was a leading proponent of law schools. Both Keidanren and the LDP mentioned the idea in their reform proposals in 1998. Among advocates of university reform, the Deliberative Council on Universities (*daigaku shingikai*) of the Ministry of Education presented its recommendations on October 26, 1998, and recommended that it examine the possibility of law schools as part of its larger recommendation to strengthen graduate education.

Under the existing system, completion of a four-year undergraduate legal education is not a prerequisite for the bar exam. Passing the six-subject exam[57] is the only requirement for admission to the LTRI. Given the extreme competitiveness of the bar exam, most candidates simply go to private cram schools immediately after entering college and, in some cases, even before entering college. Most of those who pass the exam in such a manner lack any significant intellectual background outside law or any meaningful social experience. Even their legal backgrounds are limited and shallow, because they learn only the patterns of questions and answers in the limited range of subjects included on the exam. Their legal knowledge lacks a foundation in broader and, more importantly, critical reflection about the law, the judicial system, and the legal profession.

Nor does the eighteen-month stint at the LTRI—consisting of three months of classes at the beginning of the traineeship and three months at the end with a twelve-month traineeship in local courts, prosecutors' offices, and law firms sandwiched in between—provide adequate academic and practical legal training. A six-month period in the classroom is too short to compensate for what most trainees fail to acquire before passing the exam. Moreover, the principal teachers at the LTRI are carefully selected mainstream judges who teach only orthodox legal doctrine and practice skills.

This system of practical training, along with the system that appoints assistant judges immediately upon completion of their LTRI program, and administrative control over judges throughout their careers are the main institutional

---

56. For an eloquent argument by an eminent law professor that Japan has no professional legal education and that the LTRI cannot be seen as a professional law school, see generally Tanaka (1982, 251–55).

57. The exam tests the following areas: constitutional law, civil law, commercial law, criminal law, civil procedure, and criminal procedure.

bases of the extreme legal positivism and passivity of most judges in Japan. I have argued for years that the system of practical training under the LTRI needs to be replaced with a decentralized method of professional legal education in universities, where faculty members, who enjoy both academic freedom and independence from the judiciary, present a wide range of different views to future lawyers.[58]

The LTRI experience is also deficient with respect to work placement. Although most of the trainees eventually become practicing attorneys, they spend only three months in law offices during their eighteen-month apprenticeships. I believe that such brief and shallow apprenticeships can never guarantee quality lawyers to the public.[59]

B.   Proposals for Reform: Academia and the Ministry of Education

As part of the broader reform of university education in Japan, the Ministry of Education formed the Conference of Cooperating Scholars on Research Regarding Methods of Legal Education (*hōgaku kyōiku no arikata ni kansuru chōsa kyōryokusha kenkyū kaigi*), consisting of fifteen law professors from seven national and six private university law faculties. Kyoto University and Osaka University law faculties held symposia on this issue in July 1999, and the University of Tokyo and Kobe University law faculties held symposia in September 20 1999. Okayama and Hitotsubashi law faculties soon followed.

During this time, there were many proposals for reforming the legal education and training system. I put forward the following proposal.[60] First, because most undergraduate law faculties teach both law and political science, law programs should be turned into liberal arts programs combining political science and social science approaches to the study of law and reducing technical and doctrinal courses. This would be comparable to undergraduate legal studies programs in the United States, such as the Legal Studies Program at the University of California at Berkeley. Second, three-year law schools should be established to provide professional legal education as a prerequisite to taking the national bar exam, and their clinical programs should be used as resources for legal aid. Third, law schools should admit students from a broad range of undergraduate educational backgrounds as well as a sizable number of older students with work experience. Finally, the LTRI should be abolished and practical training should be provided by the bar itself, as in the Canadian model.[61] I

---

58. For this author's view on reform of the judicial system and the legal profession in 1998, see Miyazawa and Kumagai (1998, 9–13).

59. For this author's view in 1999, see, for instance, Miyazawa (1999a, 11). See also Miyazawa (1999b, 9–13). For a comprehensive history of the role of legal education in Japan, see Miyazawa and Ōtsuka (2000).

60. For this author's view in late 1999, see Miyazawa (2000).

61. For more elaborate proposals following the United States model, see generally Yanagida (1998, 111; 1999, 72; 2000).

was fully aware, however, that radical proposals such as this were not likely to be adopted soon because undergraduate legal education was so well-entrenched in the Japanese educational system, on the one hand, and because the Supreme Court and many private attorneys would strongly resist immediate abolition of the LTRI, on the other.

Less-radical proposals led the debate. For instance, Professor Tanaka of Kyoto University, who became a member of the consultation group on legal training, presented an influential model (see Tanaka 1999, 53). He proposed that the senior (fourth) year in undergraduate law programs be combined with a two-year graduate program to create a three-year professional law school model. He also proposed that these three-year professional law schools provide education not only for those intending to become lawyers in a narrow sense (judges, prosecutors, and practicing attorneys) but also for those planning to take the civil service examination or to join corporate legal departments without taking the national bar exam. Tanaka further proposed that the LTRI should provide at least one year of practical training during the first few years after the introduction of graduate professional law schools in Japan. However, if the number of trainees increased beyond a level that was manageable for the LTRI to train, it should be abolished or supplemented by additional training institutes.

The University of Tokyo Faculty of Law presented a slightly modified version of Tanaka's proposal. It proposed a special program in the third and fourth year of the undergraduate law curriculum for those interested in professional legal careers that would be a prerequisite for entrance into two-year professional law schools. The Kobe University Faculty of Law, where this author was teaching at the time, proposed a three-year graduate program that would admit graduates of both law and non-law undergraduate faculties, with a condition that non-law graduates take a one-year immersion program before actually beginning the graduate professional program.

The initial number of students in an entering class at a graduate professional law school in the above-mentioned proposals varied from 2,000 to 4,000. All proposals assumed that the national bar exam would become a purely qualifying exam without a predetermined quota and that 70 to 80 percent of law school graduates would pass.

C. The Debate over Graduate Professional Law Schools

Strong opposition to the introduction of law schools was anticipated from the Supreme Court, many members of the bar, and many law professors. The Supreme Court's opposition was easy to understand. It would lose its monopoly on professional legal education if law schools were established. Moreover, it would lose control over judicial ideology if universities became the primary purveyors of theoretical legal education for those people intending to become lawyers.

Within the bar, the Second (*daini*) Tokyo Bar Association, one of the three bar associations in Tokyo, presented its own proposal on October 12, 1999 (Kawabata 1999). It proposed the introduction of two-year graduate professional law schools that admitted graduates of both law and non-law undergraduate faculties. It also proposed to abolish the LTRI and to replace it with a system of two years of practical training as trainee-attorneys (*kenshū bengoshi*) under authorized supervising attorneys, a system similar to that existing, inter alia, in Ontario, Canada and Queensland, Australia.

Many members of the bar, however, opposed this idea because they viewed training at the LTRI as a symbol of the post-war movement to equalize the social status of attorneys with that of judges and prosecutors. Arguably, the other side of that achievement has been that the training of future attorneys was firmly placed in the hands of mainstream judicial bureaucrats. Additionally, the programs designed for training attorneys have always been a minor part of the post-war system. Furthermore, the Ministry of Justice and the Supreme Court had already shortened the traineeship from two years to one and a half years.

Nevertheless, many attorneys wanted to maintain the post-war system of practical training at the LTRI. One of their main reasons was that the bar exam, which does not even require candidates to have an undergraduate legal education, is, along with Korea's, probably the most open exam to qualify lawyers in the world.[62] Requiring candidates to finish law school before taking the exam would destroy its egalitarian character.

Opponents of legal education reform did not mention, however, that only 3 percent of candidates pass the exam and that most spend much time and money in cram schools and attempt to pass several times before ultimately failing. They did not mention that even those few who eventually pass have done little other than cram for the exam, without enriching themselves either through broader study or practical experience.

Finally, many law professors opposed the idea of establishing law schools. One obvious reason was that a clear hierarchy in institutional reputation would emerge between universities with law schools and those without them. Those professors who opposed the idea of law schools were better disposed toward moderate proposals that would preserve undergraduate law faculties,[63] but they still wanted to prevent the introduction of law schools if possible.

Various other reasons for opposing graduate-level education were also mentioned, including the following. Some argued that the Ministry of Education would control accreditation of law schools and impose its policies on the curriculum. Doctrinal scholars could thus expand their control over legal education, and, under their legal positivism, theoretical, interdisciplinary, and comparative scholars would be excluded from law schools. Others argued that a large number of practitioners might be hired as full-time faculty members, and they would undermine the quality of legal scholarship in Japan. Critics also argued that law schools could not train scholars alone, and, because Japanese

---

62. The requirements to sit for the judicial examination in Korea are discussed in JaeWon Kim's chapter in this volume.

63. See, for instance, how Professor Tanaka's proposal is treated by a leading opponent, Michiatsu Kainō (1999, 3).

private universities heavily rely on student tuition, most of them cannot afford to open the more resource-intensive law schools. In terms of social prestige, private graduate law schools might well fall behind national universities. Others argued that most American law schools are trade schools without much interest in professional ethics, and law schools in Japan would become more like them. Finally, some maintained that undergraduate legal education should not be abolished because of its historic role in educating government officials and business executives and because it produces a large number of legally trained citizens.

What these opponents failed to mention is that university legal education has largely become irrelevant both for those who want to become lawyers and for those who do not. On the one hand, those who want to become lawyers simply go to cram schools immediately after entering, or even before entering, undergraduate law faculties. Passing the exam is everything; what is achieved in schools or in society is viewed as irrelevant. Although law faculties constantly introduce new courses or otherwise revise their curricula, their students do not pay much attention to courses other than those subjects that are included on the bar exam. (This is why the admissions officers of American law schools are often surprised by the low grade-point averages of Japanese attorneys who apply to their LL.M. programs.[64]) On the other hand, those students who go to undergraduate law schools without having a clear idea about their future, other than the notion that law will give them a wider range of options than other fields, are required to take a large number of highly technical or sophisticated courses even though they are not really interested in them or able to understand them. For the most part, they are quite relieved when they graduate, because they no longer need to study the law.

While law professors failed to take any measures to remedy these problems, cram schools rapidly extended their tentacles, and some infiltrated university campuses. A few law faculties even invited the cram schools to hold courses on their campuses in order to increase the number of their students who pass the exam; some universities even gave credit for such courses. I criticized this trend as the death knell blow to university legal education in the first issue of *Gekkan Shihō Kaikaku*, without naming the law faculties. Ironically, in the same issue, a cram school placed an advertisement proudly disclosing those law faculties and

---

64. While teaching at an American law school in 1997, this author was visited by a group of Japanese law students who had just passed the national bar exam. Because they had passed the exam before finishing their undergraduate legal education, they visited some American law schools to use their time before graduation productively. When asked which professors they liked the best at their universities, the students could not answer because they had spent most of their time in cram schools. Some of them asked me to recommend English-language books on Japanese law. The author informed them that their universities have excellent libraries, but they apparently did not know how to find books. Such is the caliber of the current bar-passers in Japan, praised by the media as the brightest stars to lead Japan into the twenty-first century. University legal education resulted in almost nothing to them.

encouraging others to join its network in anticipation of the introduction of the new law schools.

D.   From the Final Report of the JSRC: Reform of the Bar Exam and Legal Education and Training

The JSRC's recommendation to establish graduate professional law schools in 2004 called for standard law school programs requiring three years of study, and shortened programs requiring only two years of study for students who already have acquired a high level of legal knowledge. As mentioned above, the proposal for a new bar exam called for an increase in passers to 1,500 people per year by 2004 and 3,000 by 2010. This is in contrast to the approximately 990 people who passed in 2000 and the 1,183 people who passed in 2002, a passage rate of 2.85 percent—the lowest in five years.

There were, however, various problems with the details of these proposals. First, undergraduate law faculties might remain in some revised form even after the introduction of graduate professional law schools. Therefore, universities with an undergraduate law faculty might be tempted to create a graduate law school consisting of a two-year program and fill it with its own undergraduate law students, unless some clear guidelines were introduced to prevent this scenario.

The JSRC proposed the introduction of an aptitude test for admission, similar to the Law School Admission Test (LSAT) required for admission to most U.S. law schools. In addition, it also mentioned the possibility of introducing a preliminary exam on legal knowledge for students applying to the two-year program. If such an exam were introduced in the form of a single national exam, undergraduate law students might simply go to cram schools to prepare without learning much in universities, just as they have with the current bar exam.

Although graduation from a graduate law school would be the main qualification to sit for the national bar exam, the JSRC also mentioned the need to create a "bypass," whereby those who cannot afford to go to a law school or those who have already acquired practical legal experience would be allowed to take the exam without satisfying the law school requirement. This raised questions about whether it would be possible to introduce such a bypass without creating a general disincentive to attend a graduate law school, and what methods should be used to screen people allowed to sit for the bar exam without attending law school.

Finally, although the JSRC proposed to create new graduate law schools as "professional schools," it also proposed that practical apprenticeship (*jitsumu shushu*) be maintained. But if the LTRI were maintained as part of the process, there would be a risk of it becoming a bottleneck artificially limiting the number of people who could pass the bar exam and attend the LTRI.

There were details surrounding the JSRC's recommendations which remained undecided. Much depended on the legislative and bureaucratic agency process that began shortly after the final report was released.

E. Implementation of the JSRC's Recommendation to Establish Law Schools: The Ministry of Education and the Preparation Office

Since the JSRC recommended that new law schools be established as part of the university system covered by the Law on School Education (*gakkō kyōikuhō*), the Ministry of Education assigned the matter to its Central Education Council (*chūō kyōiku shingikai*). The ministry's Subcouncil on Universities (*daigaku bunkakai*) established the Committee on Graduate Professional Law Schools (*hōka daigakuin bukai*) on June 15, 2001, only three days after the presentation of the JSRC's final report.

The committee included sixteen highly prominent members. Professor Satō, the head of the JSRC, became its chairperson. Seven law professors were appointed to the committee, including the president of Waseda University; one professor each from Nagoya University, Kobe University, Chuo University, and Tohoku University; Professor Inouye of the University of Tokyo, a member of the JSRC; and Professor Foote of the University of Tokyo. Two other academics on the committee were the president of Hitotsubashi University, an economist; and a professor from the National Institution of Academic Degrees, a specialist in higher education. Members were also included from the Ministry of Justice, the judiciary, and the JFBA. Three members were appointed to represent end-users of legal services, including a vice president of Rengō, who was also a JSRC member; a legal commentator from *Nihon Keizai Shimbun,* the top financial newspaper; and the head of the legal department of Toyota. Every member was very knowledgeable about the issues. Meetings of the committee were open to the media, and its minutes were published on the website of the Ministry of Education.[65]

The establishment of the new system for the production of legal professionals included four main issues: standards for the chartering of new graduate law schools; a system of and standards for their accreditation; a new bar exam; and a new apprenticeship system. Since the first two items related to the establishment of new law schools, while the latter two issues related to stages after graduation, one might expect that the committee quickly took charge of the first two issues, especially given the highly sophisticated membership of the committee.

The reality was far different. At its first meeting on August 31, 2001, the committee decided to limit its jurisdiction to the chartering standards, much simpler and more abstract than the accreditation standards. It even announced that the Preparation Office should decide the details of the legal education standards for chartering, believing that office more appropriate for the task. In doing so, the committee referred the more substantive question of the content of the new legal education system to the closed process dominated by judicial bureaucrats.

---

65. See the website of the Ministry of Education, Culture, Sports, Science and Technology (MEXT) at http://www.mext.go.jp.

Many observers believed that the surprising self-restraint of the distinguished Committee on Graduate Professional Law Schools was an indication that the Ministry of Education lost to the Ministry of Justice in the power struggle behind the scenes, and that this result reflected the generally higher status of and stronger support for the Ministry of Justice among the ruling LDP members.

It is interesting to note that the Preparation Office did not actually examine the content of the new legal education system by itself. The substance of the work was delegated to a private group of law professors headed by Professor Tanaka from Kyoto University who was the chair of the consultation group on legal training. The Ministry of Education originally formed the group at the request of the JSRC in 2000. The membership of this group and its relationship with various government agencies changed over time, but the group maintained its status as a private group. Its policy-making process was never open to the media or the public, except when it chose to present or publish its proposals. The significant, even decisive, role of such a private group is characteristic of the policy-making process in Japan.

IX.   The Politics of Reforming Legal Education and Training

Reform of the system for the education and training of legal professionals was the top priority of the Promotion Secretariat because the JSRC deemed it the basis of the entire judicial reform agenda. New laws and regulations were enacted in the fall of 2002 in order to establish the new law schools in April 2004.[66] The political process relating to this issue had reached a conclusion in August 2002 ahead of all the other reform issues. As stated above, this reform included four main items: standards for chartering new law schools; the system and standards for accreditation of chartered law schools; a new bar exam; and a new system of apprenticeship. The main points of each item of the Promotion Secretariat's plan are summarized below.[67]

A.   Standards for Chartering New Graduate Law Schools

The Central Education Council presented three related reports to the education minister on August 5, 2002. The first report, entitled *On the Construction of a New System to Secure the Quality of Universities* (*Daigaku no shitsu no hoshō ni kansuru aratana shisutemu no kōchiku ni tsuite*), proposed the introduction of a mandatory accreditation system under which a serious violation of accreditation standards could result in revocation of a school's charter. The second report, entitled *On the Training of Higher Professionals at Graduate*

---

66. The Japanese academic year starts in April and ends in March, with summer, winter, and spring recesses interspersed.

67. For the situation in April 2002, see Miyazawa (2002a, 31–36). For developments in the relevant committees, including the Promotion Advisory Board, see this author's regular columns in the bimonthly *Kausa.*

Schools (*Daigakuin ni okeru kōdo senmon shokugyōjin yōsei ni tsuite*), proposed the introduction of graduate professional schools (beyond just law schools) that would issue degrees. The third report, entitled *On Chartering Standards and Other Matters Concerning Graduate Professional Law Schools* (*Hōkā daigakuin no secchi kijun to ni tsuite*), recommended specific standards for chartering new law schools along with detailed notes.[68] The reforms recommended by the first and second reports provide a general institutional foundation on which the chartering of new law schools will be carried out. The third report contained several key points about law schools.

First, it proposed that a standard law school program should require a student to complete three years of study with a minimum of ninety-three credits. Those who had already acquired basic knowledge in law might be allowed to shorten their length of study by up to one year. The possibility of this two-year shortened course was a compromise the JSRC made with the existing undergraduate law faculties. The JSRC carefully noted, however, that those eligible to apply for a shortened course would not be limited to graduates of undergraduate law faculties, while also implying that graduates of undergraduate law faculties should not be automatically judged eligible to undertake the shortened course.

Second, it stated that, in order to secure diversity in the student body, measures should be taken to ensure that entering classes contain both mature students (*shakaijin*) and graduates of undergraduate programs other than law. In admissions decisions, each law school would be required to adopt a clear admissions policy, taking into consideration academic record, extracurricular activities, and activities after graduating from an undergraduate program, as well as an entrance exam. All candidates would be required to take a uniform aptitude test, with each law school administering its own exam to those seeking to shorten their duration of study.

Third, the minimum number of full-time faculty members of each graduate law school was set at twelve, with a faculty-to-student ratio of better than one-to-fifteen. Full-time faculty members could not be counted as full-time faculty members at another graduate school or at an undergraduate program in the same school, although for ten years this would be waived for up to one-third of the full-time faculty members. A minimum of 20 percent of full-time faculty members should come from law practice, each with a minimum of five years experience. As many as two-thirds of those practitioner faculty members would be allowed to teach as little as six credits a year, far fewer than regular faculty members, in the hope that they would stay linked to practice.

Fourth, education in legal theory was to be the central part of the curriculum, although an introduction to practice was also to be provided, and an emphasis placed on the bridging of theory and practice. Instruction was to be conducted in small classes via an intensive and multi-directional interactive method. A strict policy would be adopted in academic evaluation and in decisions regarding

68. For the full text in Japanese, see the website of MEXT at http://www.mext.go.jp.

graduation. And, fifth, accreditation was to be conducted by an accrediting organization that included professors, legal practitioners, and users of legal services.

The most substantive hurdles for chartering appeared to be the minimum faculty-to-student ratio and the minimum proportion of practitioners among full-time faculty members. As long as a law school could satisfy these numerical standards and present a coherent curriculum, it would be difficult for the Ministry of Education to reject an application to establish a graduate law school. In fact, this is the present policy of the ministry with regard to private universities.

One of the points that attracted much criticism was the requirement of ninety-three credits for a three-year standard program. Many observers were concerned that this would be too onerous given the intensive nature of graduate law school education. Contrasts were made to the normal workload at U.S. law schools which typically require fewer than ninety credits for J.D. students.[69] However, the model curriculum that was prepared by the team of law professors led by Professor Tanaka recommended it, and the Committee on Graduate Professional Law Schools adopted it.

One of the points that was most disappointing to progressive reformers was that the standards did not require that a graduate law school be independent from an existing undergraduate law faculty. At present, most graduate programs in law are simply appended to an undergraduate law faculty, so that the same faculty members decide matters in both graduate and undergraduate programs. In the new system, an undergraduate law faculty would have a vested interest in sending as many graduates as possible to its new law school; this could pose a serious conflict of interest. While the report on law schools by the Central Education Council emphasized the need for the relative autonomy of graduate law schools, it failed to require these new schools to be institutionally independent.

In any event, it is clear that chartering standards will be simple and abstract, and the chartering procedure will not be too intrusive. Therefore, universities that intend to establish a graduate law school will likely pay more attention to accreditation standards, which are more detailed than the chartering standards.

B.   System and Standards of Accreditation

1. System of Accreditation

Originally, the JSRC proposed requiring every graduate law school to undergo accreditation before the graduation of the first entering class of its two-year curriculum, and that only graduates of accredited law schools be allowed to take the new national bar exam. The Central Education Council presented an interim report in April 2002 proposing a general structure for the accreditation of new law schools. Following the general policy of deregulation, the council proposed that the government not be directly involved in the accreditation process, but

---

69. For instance, the J.D. program of the Boalt Hall School of Law of the University of California, Berkeley, requires eighty-five credits.

rather be involved only in certifying accrediting organizations. It was expected that more than one accrediting organization would be established (which has turned out to be the case), that some would apply higher accreditation standards, and that therefore competition would ensue among law schools as some would seek accreditation by the more prestigious accrediting organizations.

The Ministry of Justice and, hence, the Promotion Secretariat disagreed with the Ministry of Education. The secretariat made a counterproposal for a single accrediting organization; they argued that accreditation pertinent to the right to sit for the national bar exam should be more closely controlled by the government in order to avoid the confusion that would be created by multiple accrediting organizations. Many observers believed that the Ministry of Justice should establish or certify such an organization and control the number of law schools and candidates for the national bar exam, and, hence, the number of new legal professionals.

A majority of LDP politicians involved in judicial reform did not agree with this counterproposal. They argued that the government's involvement would be excessive, and would violate the general policy of deregulation. However, the justice affairs tribe (*hōmu-zoku*) politicians fought back. They argued that since the Ministry of Justice had jurisdiction over such issues, it should actively participate in the accreditation of law schools.

A compromise was struck when the LDP Special Research Council on the Judicial System completed its report entitled *In Search of Ideals of the New System of Training Legal Professionals* (*Aratana hōsō yōsei seido no risō o motomete*) on July 26, 2002.[70] There were several main points in this report. First, it argued that a law school must be accredited by an organization that has been certified by the minister in charge of this matter (*shumu daijin*). More than one accrediting organization should be certified, and there should be fair competition among them. Second, the justice minister should present general opinions to the education minister regarding changes in chartering standards, and maintenance and improvement of the quality of the law schools. Third, the education minister should set certification standards and conduct certification of accrediting organizations either jointly or after consultation with the justice minister. Fourth, if the education minister finds conditions that violate the law's requirements at a chartered school, he or she should take measures against the school, including providing advice and, if need be, revoking its charter and closing the school.

Some uncertainties still remained. Who would be the *shumu daijin* who certifies accrediting organizations? Should it be the justice minister instead of the education minister? How would the justice minister exercise the power to present opinions to the education minister?

---

70. For the full text in Japanese, see the website of the LDP at http://www.jimin.jp.

2. Standards for Accreditation

The standards for accreditation were less politically controversial. They were prepared by the private group of scholars led by Professor Tanaka. The six accreditation standards incorporated the main points of the chartering standards plus several other issues: First, law schools must take measures to ensure fairness, openness, and diversity in admissions decisions. Law schools must adopt a proper method to ensure fairness in admissions by comprehensive consideration of an aptitude test such as the U.S. LSAT, other entrance exams, academic records in undergraduate faculties and other programs, and extracurricular activities. For the time being, law schools should endeavor to fill more than 30 percent of the entering class with graduates of non-law undergraduate faculties or mature students. When the combined proportion of such students is less than 20 percent, the accrediting organization should hear an explanation and judge whether the school satisfies the requirement of fairness, openness, and diversity.

Second, law schools must make fair and proper judgments in admitting students to a course of study shorter than the norm.

Third, law schools must offer courses in the following areas: public law (constitutional and administrative law); private law (civil law, commercial law, and civil procedure); criminal law (substance and procedure); basic practical skills (*jitsumu kiso*) (including basic professional skills, professional responsibility, and other matters); theories of law (*kiso hōgaku*) and related disciplines (*rinsetsu kamoku*); and, advanced (*tenkai*) and cutting-edge (*sentan*) courses such as intellectual property.

Fourth, law schools must take measures regarding class size. The standard size of a class in basic law (public law, private law, and criminal law) should be 50 and not exceed 80.

Fifth, law schools must strictly evaluate student performance.

Sixth, a minimum of 93 credits should be required to complete a standard course, while a minimum of 63 credits should be required to complete a shortened course. Students should not be allowed to register for more than 36 credits a year, except for the final year when 44 may be taken. For a standard three-year program, the following are minimum requirements: 10 credits in public law; 32 in private law; 12 in criminal law; 5 in basic practice skills (this requirement would be raised to 9 credits around 2011); and 34 in other areas (including 4 credits in legal theory and other disciplines). For a student taking the two-year program, the minimum credits for public law, private law, and criminal law should be 24.

A number of criticisms were raised in relation to these standards. First, the ceiling of 116 credits in three years was considered too high, assuming professional legal education requires student preparation outside the classroom. Second, the minimum requirement of 54 credits in public law, private law, and criminal law merely reflects traditional undergraduate legal education and was considered too restrictive for graduate law schools that hope to develop creative curricula. Third, the minimum requirement of 5 credits in basic practice skills was considered too conservative.

The third point requires an additional explanation. Courses in basic practical skills were supposed to include legal research and writing; simulations in interviewing, counseling, mediation, and trial advocacy; an externship; legal counseling of real clients; the judicially developed theory on the distribution of the burden of proof in civil litigation (*yōken jujitsu ron*); and the judicially developed method of fact-finding.[71] Hence, students could easily use up 5 credits or more covering these topics thoroughly.

Many observers believed that the requirement of a mere 5 credits for basic practice skills reflected a general reluctance among members of Professor Tanaka's group to increase the number of practice-oriented courses offered and, hence, to hire a larger number of practitioners as faculty members. Another observation was that the Ministry of Justice and the judiciary did not welcome an increase in practice-oriented courses at law schools because they did not want to reduce the role of the LTRI.

Interestingly, however, a representative from the judiciary once suggested at a meeting of the Consultation Group on Legal Training that the LTRI might consider abolishing the six months of coursework at the beginning of the apprenticeship period once 9 credits of practice skills were required at all law schools. If the initial classwork were abolished, the LTRI would stop functioning as a bottleneck and the bar exam could become a qualifying exam without an artificial quota. If the above-mentioned statement was sincere, those law professors who had set a very conservative requirement in practice-oriented courses foreclosed an excellent opportunity to change the exam to fit the ideal presented by the JSRC. In fact, when the representative from the judiciary mentioned the possible abolition of the LTRI's initial coursework, a member of the consultation group who was a professor at a major law faculty responded that the requirement should not be raised to 9 credits too soon lest the success of the law school experiment be jeopardized.

C. The Debate over the New National Bar Examination

The design of the new national bar exam became the most politically contentious issue in the debate over the reform of the system of education and training of legal professionals. The central subject of the debate was not the new bar exam itself, but the preliminary exam for those who wished to take the new bar exam without going to law school.

The Ministry of Justice initiated the debate. On the one hand, the JSRC proposed an exception to the requirement of a degree from a law school to sit for the exam for those who cannot afford to go to a law school or for those who do

---

71. The last subject has occupied a central place at the LTRI. Since new graduate professional law schools are expected to take over some functions provided by the LTRI and, hence, to reduce its role as the largest road block to efforts to increase bar passage, this subject needs to be an essential part of law school curricula.

not need to go to a law school because of their practical experience in law-related jobs. However, the Ministry of Justice argued that such limitations were impossible to design in early February 2002, soon after the start of the Consultation Group on Legal Training. Several members of the Committee on Graduate Professional Law Schools of the Central Education Council also criticized the Ministry of Justice's position, as did members of the Promotion Office Advisory Board. Yet the Ministry of Justice and the Promotion Secretariat argued that their proposal would not violate the JSRC's ideal or its proposal because candidates' financial conditions and practical backgrounds could still be examined in the preliminary exam, which could be designed to test whether candidates had the same level of legal knowledge as did law school graduates. Many observers believed that the Ministry of Justice and the Promotion Secretariat took such a position because they wanted to maintain the importance of the bar exam itself and with it, the power of the ministry. The Consultation Group on Legal Training never published a formal report on this issue. It simply stopped discussion on it after April 2002, leading many observers to believe that the ministry prevailed in this debate.

The most vocal *hōmu-zoku* politicians of the LDP Special Research Council on the Judicial System wanted to go further. In late June 2002, six such politicians proposed that the best policy would be to continue the present national bar exam and not require a law degree to take it. Alternatively, they proposed to make the bar exam via the preliminary exam the main route to qualify as a legal professional in Japan. These *hōmu-zoku* politicians were lobbied and supported by a group called Judicial Reform Forum (*shihō kaikaku*). This was a group of fifteen scholars, businesspeople, and journalists committed to promoting radical deregulation of Japanese society. Their proposals on judicial reform included, among other things, an increase in the number of legal professionals to more than 90,000 by 2011, instead of the 50,000 proposed by the JSRC, and allowing non-attorneys to provide legal services to consumers.[72] They argued that Japan should rapidly increase the number of legal professionals by simply allowing more people to pass the national bar exam. They criticized the movement to introduce graduate professional law schools as a desperate effort by universities to regain ground lost in their competition with cram schools. They also argued that most universities were trying to establish a graduate law school mainly as a device to improve the status of their existing undergraduate law faculties. Many observers believed that their opposition to graduate law schools reflected the interest of the owner of one of the largest cram schools who had belonged to this forum.

The *hōmu-zoku* politicians seemed to be winning the debate in early July 2002. The situation changed, however, when Kōmeitō, one of the two coalition partners of the LDP, opposed them. Kōmeitō-affiliated politicians argued that new graduate law schools would not survive if the preliminary exam became a key route for becoming a legal professional. Kōmeitō is related to the Soka

---

72. Their proposals for judicial reform are presented in Fukui and Kawamoto (2001).

Gakkai Buddhist sect that has Soka University as an affiliated institution, and many observers believed that while Kōmeitō's opposition to the LDP proposal was faithful to the JSRC proposal, it also reflected the interest of Sōka University, which was considering establishing a law school.

The third partner in the coalition, the Liberal Party (*jiyūtō*), supported the LDP, and the following compromise agreement was made on July 26, 2002 among the three coalition members. First, graduate law schools should become the core of the new system of training of legal professionals. Second, the new bar exam and the preliminary exam should be designed in light of this ideal. Third, there should be limitations on who would be allowed to take the preliminary exam. Fourth, the preliminary exam should not interfere with the primary process of training legal professionals via graduate law schools. It should be designed to test whether candidates have the same abilities as graduates of the new law schools. Fifth, in the national bar exam, those who take it from law schools and those from the preliminary exam should be judged by the same standard. Sixth, the way the preliminary exam is conducted should be re-examined in light of the ideal that law schools be the core of training legal professionals, with an eye toward taking account of developments once the law schools have been launched. The last point was LDP's concession to Kōmeitō.

It should be noted that while the new national bar exam was introduced in 2006 for the first students to graduate from the new two-year programs of law schools, the present bar exam will be maintained until 2010 in the interest of those already committed to the present exam. This means that the preliminary exam route will not come into effect until then, so those who want to make the new law schools the main route to the bar exam still have several more years to persuade the public and policy-makers. To do so, it will be necessary for universities to make their new law schools truly independent from their undergraduate law faculties and to introduce totally new curricula and teaching methods, or critics will say that the law schools are merely devices to save undergraduate law faculties that have been losing in the competition against cram schools (Miyazawa 2002b).

A more immediate problem is whether the route through the present exam will be gradually narrowed in the five-year transition after 2006. The JSRC proposed that the number of people who pass the present exam should be increased to 1,500 in 2004. If this number remains fixed through the five-year transition period, and the total number who pass either the present or the new exam is increased only gradually to reach 3,000 in 2011, while at the same time many more law schools are established, then only a small number of graduates of the new law schools will be allowed to pass the new exam. The new exam would become fairly competitive, and new law schools would be in serious jeopardy even before the introduction of the preliminary exam because many prospective lawyers would opt not to go to graduate law schools. Much will, therefore, depend on the implementation of the present and new bar exams by the new National Bar Examination Administration Committee. While the present exam committee consists of only three members, with one each from the

Ministry of Justice, the judiciary, and the JFBA, the JSRC proposed to expand it to include law professors and public members. Such an expanded committee might not be as easily dominated by the Ministry of Justice and the judiciary, as is the case under the present system. Still uncertainty remains, and those who want to firmly establish law schools as the dominant route for becoming legal professionals in Japan will have to focus their efforts on the implementation of the present and new bar exams in the immediate future.

In contrast, the content of the new national bar exam did not become a major political issue. As decided by the Consultation Group on Legal Training, its main points are the following: it will include multiple-choice questions in public law, private law, and criminal law, and essay questions in the same three areas, and an elective. The exam committee will determine whether professional ethics or responsibility should be included. A wide range of electives will be adopted upon consultation with the new committee.[73] The content of the preliminary exam also failed to attract much political attention. The exam is likely to cover the six main codes (constitutional law, civil law, civil procedure, criminal law, criminal procedure, and commercial law), administrative law, general knowledge, and subjects related to basic legal practice skills; it will include multiple-choice questions, essay questions, and oral questions.

D.   The New Apprenticeship System

Final plans for the new apprenticeship system await resolution of four main issues. One is the length of the apprenticeship. While bar-passers are now obligated to spend eighteen months at the LTRI, a consensus appears to be forming to shorten that to twelve months, considering that two or three years will have been already spent in law school. Another issue is financial support for trainees. Under the present system, trainees are full-time government employees and receive government salaries. The Ministry of Finance has already expressed concern about this under the new system, with at least triple the number of trainees. The JFBA still argues that salaries should be paid, but a consensus seems to be emerging that would replace the present system with some form of student loan. A third issue is whether the initial coursework at the LTRI at the beginning of the apprenticeship period should be abolished. And finally, there is the question of whether the number of people allowed to pass the bar exam will continue to rise after reaching 3,000 in 2011.

E.   Issues Raised by Major Universities Regarding Law School Proposals

Whether law schools will become the main route to becoming a legal professional in Japan will depend on how they are designed. Universities will face dif-

---

73. The exam would be administered in May, which is roughly two months after university graduation. This would be a clear improvement from the present exam, which is held five months into an academic year, making those who are taking the exam unable to attend classes.

ficulties if they fail to establish law schools that admit a wide range of students and that adopt new educational content and teaching methods commensurate with their status as professional schools. If the law schools fail to rapidly expand courses in basic practice skills, the LTRI will remain a bottleneck against changing the national bar exam into a purely qualifying exam. And if universities establish law schools merely as devices to maintain or improve the status of their undergraduate law faculties, they will not be able to refute the criticism by the Judicial Reform Forum and others who argue that expanding the bypass obviates the need for candidates to have a graduate legal education.

Unfortunately, there is an imminent danger of such a scenario. This is illustrated by the plan that was presented by the most prestigious undergraduate law faculty in Japan, the Faculty of Law of the University of Tokyo (Tōdai). It published its plan entitled *On the Outline of the Reform* (*Kaikaku no kosshian ni tsuite*) on January 24, 2002.[74] As at most universities in Japan, the undergraduate Faculty of Law and the Graduate School of Law at Tōdai are inseparable: the latter is built on top of the former and the same faculty members teach at both. The unified Tōdai Law Faculty wants to maintain this basic structure.

Under the plan, the size of the entering class of the undergraduate Faculty of Law will be reduced from 590 to 400. This reduction is natural because more faculty members will be concentrating on the graduate program. The size of the entering class of the master's program in the Graduate School of Law will be expanded from approximately 143 to 420, divided into three courses. The largest course of study will be called the Legal Professionals Training Course (*hōsō yōsei senkō*). In other words, Tōdai is proposing that a new law school curriculum be established merely as part of the existing graduate program in law that is appended to an undergraduate law faculty. As part of this proposal, approximately 200 spaces will be kept for the two-year program, while only approximately 100 spaces will be allocated for the three-year program.

The second-largest course of study will be called the Public Policy Course (*kōkyō seisaku senkō*). This course will be designed for those who wish to enter government agencies upon graduation, and for continuing education of government employees. It will admit 100 students each year. The smallest course of study will be called the Basic Legal and Political Studies Course (*kiso hōsei senkō*). This course, which will admit 20 students each year, will be for those who are interested in academic careers. A doctoral program will be maintained on top of this program.

Many observers interpreted this plan to mean that graduates of the undergraduate Tōdai Law Faculty who apply to the Legal Professionals Training Course would almost always be admitted to the two-year shortened program. There is an obvious possibility of conflict of interest with this plan. Faculty

---

74. For the full text in Japanese, see the newsletter at the website of the University of Tokyo Faculty of Law and Graduate Schools for Law and Politics at http://www.j.u-tokyo .ac.jp/about/news/list/08.html. For a comprehensive criticism of this plan, see Miyazawa (2002f, 102).

members will have to balance the desire to send their undergraduate students to their own graduate law school with the requirement that they maintain fairness, openness, and diversity in the admissions decisions.

The Tōdai Law Faculty, then, seems to have designed its graduate law school as a device to maintain the status of its undergraduate program. Applicants to its undergraduate program are likely to believe that they will have a tremendous advantage in obtaining admission to its graduate law school. In fact, a prominent faculty member wrote in December 2001 that the status of undergraduate law faculties would be undermined if more than 25 percent of the new graduate law school students are selected from outside undergraduate law schools (Nishida 2001).

Waseda University intends to follow a different plan that is more consistent with the ideal of the JSRC. Waseda has decided to establish its new graduate law school as a freestanding graduate program that will be institutionally separate from its undergraduate law faculty and its existing graduate program in law. It is planning to admit 300 students each year without specifying the number in the standard and shortened programs. Those who want to shorten their study will be evaluated only after they are admitted to the school. It has also established a research institute to examine the possibility of introducing a live-client clinical program, with a grant from the Ministry of Education. Although there is no student practice rule in Japan that allows law students to represent clients in litigation, the institute is now exploring various possibilities for student practice.

While several smaller universities are taking approaches similar to that of Waseda,[75] larger universities tend to emulate the Tōdai plan. Furthermore, there is still strong opposition from faculty members even at universities like Waseda who want to adopt a more conservative approach like Tōdai's. These conservative universities and faculty members do not seem to understand that the future of their law schools could be limited unless they quickly change their plans to better fit the ideal presented by the JSRC. Opponents of the mandatory graduate law school education idea may use these conservative proposals as a justification for their demand that the bypass route to the national bar exam be larger than the law school route.

F.   Legislation to Establish Graduate Professional Law Schools

After the political process mainly led by LDP politicians described above, on October 18, 2002 the Cabinet approved the establishment of graduate

---

75. Probably the most radical model is a law school in Omiya, a suburb of Tokyo, established by a local private educational corporation (*gakkō hōjin*), Satoe Gakuen, in collaboration with the Second Tokyo Bar Association. Although Satoe Gakuen already had an undergraduate law faculty, its law school is freestanding and totally separate from its existing undergraduate law faculty. It has only a three-year standard program; approximately half of its full-time faculty members will be recruited from among practicing attorneys, mostly from the Second Tokyo Bar Association; and live-client clinics will be established. This author was an adviser to Satoe Gakuen, and is vice president of Omiya Law School.

professional law schools in 2004 and immediately presented legislation to the Diet designed to accomplish this. The House of Representatives and the House of Councillors both passed it in November 2002.

As part of the legislation, an amendment to the Law on School Education was passed with two main features. One was the introduction of the concept of professional schools as a new category of graduate programs at Japanese universities, with law schools as a prime example. The other was the introduction of the concept of accreditation. The education minister will certify accreditation organizations, and more than one accreditation organization can exist for each field. Universities and colleges will be required to achieve periodic re-accreditation. If an institution fails to receive re-accreditation, the education minister may advise the institution to take proper measures for improvement and ultimately may order the closing of the institution.

The introduction of the new law school system also entailed the passage of a law concerning coordination between law schools and the national bar exam. Although this law stipulates the purpose of law schools and the responsibility of the government in the implementation of the new system of legal education, including financial matters, the provisions regarding the role of the justice minister vis-à-vis the education minister in chartering and accreditation are more important. As the LDP council plan proposed (see Part IX B above), the justice minister may present opinions to the education minister regarding chartering standards and accreditation organizations, and may request that the education minister take measures against a law school; and the education minister may seek consultation with the justice minister.

Another law that was amended is the Law on the National Bar Examination. As mentioned above, the new bar exam was introduced in 2006, the present exam will remain until 2010, and candidates may take either one until then. In 2011, the present bar exam will be abolished, and the preliminary exam will be introduced. The preliminary exam is to test if the candidates' ability is equal to that of new law school graduates. Those who pass the preliminary exam may take the new bar exam without graduating from a law school. Candidates may take the new bar exam up to three times within five years of graduating a law school or passing the preliminary exam.

Still another law that was amended is the Law on Courts (*saibanshohō*). The amendment reduced the length of the judicial traineeship to one year for those who pass the new national bar exam, and to one year and four months for those who pass the present national bar exam. Both houses of the Diet attached special resolutions to these amendments and the new law. The resolution of the Legal Affairs Committee is noteworthy.[76] It emphasized the importance of training legal professionals through a process instead of a single exam; the need to provide financial assistance to private accreditation organizations; the need to recognize the exceptional nature of the preliminary exam; the need to expand

---

76. On file with this author.

financial assistance to students (including utilization of funds from the private sector); and the need to subsidize the establishment of graduate law schools throughout the country. This resolution was obviously the result of lobbying by those who want to build strong law schools and so minimize the impact of the preliminary exam.

Pursuant to the legislation above, the Ministry of Education set accreditation standards in March 2003. Seventy-two applications for accreditation were received by the ministry and sixty-eight schools were accredited, comprising a total of 5,590 students.

The most crucial issue for the successful development of graduate law schools, and the new system for training legal professionals based on them, is the administration of the new national bar exam and the preliminary exam. If the new bar exam is administered as a competitive exam with a limited quota, or if the preliminary exam passes a large number of candidates who simply do not want to go to law school, the schools will have no future. The amended and new laws regarding law schools do not have any provisions on how these two exams should be administered. Universities that have or are planning to establish a graduate law school on top of their undergraduate law faculties would be wise to change their plans so that opponents of the graduate law school idea will lose their justification for maintaining a highly competitive bar exam or introducing a large bypass to the law school route. Reformers who want more idealistic law schools will have to continue their fight.

Sixty-eight new law schools opened in 2004, but the distance between the ideal presented by the JSRC and the reality may be quite substantial. Much will depend on the continuing effort of those who want to move closer to the JSRC's ideal. However, given that the JSRC deemed that reform of the system for producing legal professionals (and, hence, the production of many more better-educated legal professionals) would provide the basis for making the judicial system and the law more accessible and useful to the public, the new law schools mark a significant departure from the previous system and an important step toward further reform of the entire judicial system in Japan.

Conclusion

The political process since the presentation of the JSRC's recommendations to the prime minister in June 2001 abundantly indicates how difficult it is to overcome the hurdles of policy-making and a legislative process that is dominated by bureaucrats who are themselves targets of reform proposals. It is unclear how effective efforts to put pressure on the judicial bureaucrats who are handling the implementation of the JSRC proposals were or will continue to be. It is also unclear whether these efforts will actually result in new laws that will make it easier for ordinary people to challenge the government. This is, after all, what the rule of law means. The process is still moving forward, although the pace has been slow and compromises will continue to be inevitable on many points.

The final result is not likely to be exactly what the JSRC recommended. Nevertheless, the result will be significantly different from what was the Japanese justice system. It is still too early to tell the extent to which the rule of law will be realized in Japan.

I have written in the Introduction of this chapter that an "examination of the history culminating in the release of this report and the subsequent process of implementation provide an interesting case study of the politics of judicial reform in Japan." What does this story of an ongoing political process tell us about Japanese politics? At least three general points may be made.

First, the process until the presentation of the final report by the Justice System Reform Council appears to indicate that when a major group in the power elite of Japanese society[77] engages in serious self-examination of the status quo under a prolonged crisis, politically astute reformers can seize the opportunity to create a situation in which they can pursue at least a partial realization of reform of a system that existed in Japan at least since the end of World War II. A new political orthodoxy that recognizes the use of law as a legitimate way of solving problems among the people, and seeking accountability of government agencies, seems to be forming.

Second, the legislative process after the presentation of the final report of the JSRC appears to indicate that once the legislative process begins to implement the details of reform, bureaucrats, politicians, and groups who have vested interests in the system have an ample opportunity to chip away at and minimize reform. This possibility is particularly strong when the concerned bureaucrats themselves are targets of reform. Those who want to maintain the original reform ideas must be extremely capable in mobilizing the political capital necessary to counter such a backlash.

And third, the leadership of the prime minister counts greatly in the politics of implementing the reforms—politics which are as complex as the judicial reforms themselves. The Justice System Reform Council needed the support of the late Prime Minister Keizō Obuchi to become firmly established. Any success of the progressive pressure on the proposed reforms by Professor Satō and the People's Forum depended on the commitment and popularity of Prime Minister Koizumi. Although political scientists tend to emphasize the need for constraints on the exercise of power by prime minister in Japan,[78] a prime minister appears to be able to make a real and positive difference when serious doubt is cast on the status quo.

Thus, the ongoing politics of judicial reform can help us improve our understanding of Japanese politics in general and our appreciation of the changing role of law in Japanese society.

---

77. For a discussion of the power elite in Japan, see Miyazawa with Ōtsuka (2000).

78. See, for instance, Richardson (1997).

Works Cited

Abe, Hiroshi, Muneyuki Shindo, and Sadafumi Kawato. 1994. *The government and politics of Japan.* Translated by James W. White. N.p.

Duck, Ken. 1996. Now that the fog has lifted: The impact of Japan's administrative procedures law on the regulation of industry and market governance. 19 *Fordham International Law Journal* 1686.

Fukui, Hideo and Akira Kawamoto, eds. 2001. *Shihō o sukue: Shōhisha hon'i no sābisu e* [Save justice: Toward consumer-centered services]. Tokyo: Tōyō Keizai Shinpōsha.

Gekkan Shihō Kaikaku. [Journal of judicial reform]. 2000. Tokushū: Tobe! Bengoshi! [Symposium: Attorneys! Jump!]. 13 *Gekkan Shihō Kaikaku* 8.

Gyōsei Kaikaku Iinkai. 1998. Gyōsei kaikaku iinkai saishu iken [Final opinions of the Administrative Reform Committee]. 49 *Jiyū to Seigi* [Liberty and justice, the monthly journal of the JFBA] 2:170.

Haley, John Owen. 1991. *Authority without power: Law and the Japanese paradox.* New York: Oxford University Press.

Hayakawa, Masaru. 1996. Shareholders in Japan. In *Japan: Economic success and legal system,* ed. H. Baum. New York: Walter de Gruyter.

Hōmu Daijin Kanbō [Ministry of Justice], ed. 1987. Jinjika [Personnel Department] *Shihō shiken kaikaku o kangaeru: Kihon shiryōshū* [A study on reform of the national bar examination: A collection of basic information]. Tokyo: Yūhikaku.

———. 1991. Shihō Hōsei Chōsabu [Department of Research on the Judicial and Legal System]. *Hōsō yōsei seido kaikaku: Shihō shiken wa kō kawaru* [Reform of the training of legal professionals: The national bar examination will change this way]. Tokyo: Yūhikaku.

Hōritsu Fujo Seido Kenkyūkai [Research Committee on the Legal Aid System]. 1998. Hōkokusho [Report]. 49 *Jiyū to Seigi* 5:193.

Hōsō Yōsei Seido to Kaikaku Kyōgikai [Committee on the System of Training of Legal Professionals and Related Matters]. 1996. Opinion. 1084 *Jurisuto* [Jurist].

Iwai, Shigekazu. 1998. Shihō shiken hōsō yōsei seido kaikaku no keii to gaiyō [Process and outline of reform of the national bar examination and the training of lawyers]. 49 *Jiyū to Seigi* 1:88.

Jiyū Minshutō, Shihō Seido Tokubetsu Chōsakai Hōkoku [Liberal Democratic Party, Special Research Committee on the Judicial System]. 1998. 21-seiki no shihō no tashikana shishin [Firm guidelines for the judicial system of the twenty-first century]. 49 *Jiyū to Seigi* 8:197.

———. 2001. Tokushū 1: Kōkoku jiyūka to bengoshi gyōmu [Symposium 1: Liberalization of advertisement and practice of attorneys]. 52 *Jiyū to Seigi* 7:22.

Kakugi Kettei [Cabinet meeting decision]. 1998. Kisei kanwa suishin sankanen keikaku—shō [Three-year plan for promoting deregulation—A summary]. 49 *Jiyū to Seigi* 5:178.

Kainō, Michiatsu. 1999. Shihō kaikaku to rō sukurū kōsō [Judicial reform and law schools]. 71 *Hōritsu Jihō* [Current law journal] 8:1.

Kawabata, Yoshiharu. 1999. Daini Tokyo Bengoshikai no hōka daigakuin teigen [Second Tokyo Bar Association's proposals on graduate professional law schools]. 3 *Gekkan Shihō Kaikaku* 55.

Kodera, Kazuya and Tokiko Kamei. 1997. Hōritsu enjo rippō to bengoshi bengoshikai no aratana kadai [Legal aid legislation and new tasks for attorneys and bar associations]. 48 *Jiyū to Seigi* 9:52.

Miyakawa, Kōji, Minoru Koyama, Kōhei Nasu, and Hideaki Kubori. 1992. *Henkaku no naka no bengoshi* [Attorneys in reform]. Tokyo: Yūhikaku.

Miyazawa, Setsuo. 1994. Administrative control of Japanese judges. In *Law and technology in the Pacific community,* ed. P. S. C. Lewis. Boulder: Westview Press.

———. 1999a. Hōka daigakuin ni kitai [Hoping for the realization of graduate professional law schools in Japan]. *Yomiuri Shimbun* [Yomiuri newspaper]. 10 August.

———. 1999b. Hōka daigakuin rongi no kasseika to tōmeika no tameni [For more active and transparent discussion on graduate professional law schools]. 1 *Gekkan Shihō Kaikaku* 9.

———. 2000. Hōsō ichigensei ka no hōsō yōsei seido [The training of lawyers under the united legal profession]. In *21-seiki bengoshi ron* [Lawyers in the twenty-first century], ed. Nihon Bengoshi Rengōkai [JFBA]. Tokyo: Yūhikaku.

———. 2002a. Hōka daigakuin gutaika no saishu dankai o mae ni shite [Facing the final stage of giving shape to graduate professional law schools]. *Hōritsu Jihō Zōkan: Shihō Kaikaku 2002* [Current law journal, special issue: Judicial reform 2002] 31–36.

———. 2002b. Hōka daigakuin no mei-un o kimeru no wa daigaku jishin no torikumida [Actions of universities themselves will determine the fate of law schools]. 74 *Hōritsu Jihō* 11:1.

———. 2002c. Hōka daigakuin risō wasureruna [Never forget the ideal of law schools]. *Yomiuri Shimbun.* 16 May.

———. 2002d. Saikin no hōka daigakuin kentō katei no mondaiten to kongo no kadai [Problems of the recent process of examination of graduate professional law schools and the issues in the future]. 74 *Hōritsu Jihō* 1:56.

———. 2002e. Summary and comments on recommendations of the Japanese Justice System Reform Council. In *The Japanese adversary system in context: Controversies and comparisons,* eds. M. M. Feeley and S. Miyazawa. New York: Palgrave Macmillan.

————. 2002f. Tōdai rō sukurū kōsō ni igi ari [Objection to the University of Tokyo's plan for a law school]. *Ronza* (April): 102.

Miyazawa, Setsuo and Naoyuki Kumagai, eds. 1998. *21-seiki shihō e no teigen* [Proposals for the judicial system of the twenty-first century]. Tokyo: Nihon Hyōronsha.

Miyazawa, Setsuo and Hiroshi Ōtsuka. 2000. Legal education and the reproduction of the elite in Japan. 1 *Asian-Pacific Law & Policy Journal* 1. An electronic copy can be seen at http://www.hawaii.edu/aplpj/pdfs/02-miyazawa.pdf. Reprinted in shorter form in *Global prescriptions: The production, exploration, and importation of a new legal orthodoxy*, eds. Y. Dezalay and B. G. Garth. 2002. Ann Arbor: University of Michigan Press.

Mizuno, Kunio. 1998. Hōsō sansha kyōgikai no keii to sansha gōi no gaiyō [Process of the Three-Party Committee on the Legal Profession and an outline of the agreement]. 1998. 49 *Jiyū to Seigi* 1:1.

Nakabō, Kōhei. 1999. *Jūkan kikō saiken kaishū no tatakai: Shihō no rinen to shuhō o motte* [The struggle for bad debts collection: Guided by the principles and methodologies of Japan's judicial system]. Tokyo: Daiyamondosha.

————. 2002a. Shihō kaikaku kokumin no te ni torimodosaneba [We must get back judicial reform to the hands of the people]. *Asahi Shimbun*. 28 June.

————. 2002b. Shihō kaikaku no genten wasureruna [Never forget the starting point of judicial reform]. *Yomiuri Shimbun*. 18 July.

Nihon Bengoshi Rengōkai [Japan Federation of Bar Associations]. 1990. Code of Ethics for Practicing Attorneys (Adopted on 2 March 1990 at the Extraordinary General Meeting) [English version]. Tokyo: JFBA. See the JFBA website at http://www.nichibenren.or.jp/en/about/pdf/cepa_1990.pdf.

————. 1997. Henshū Iinkai [Editorial Committee]. *Atarashii seiki e no bengoshi-zō* [Perspectives on attorneys for the new century]. Tokyo: JFBA.

Nishida, Noriyuki. 2001. Hōka daigakuin kōsō no yukue [Trends in the planning of law schools]. 255 *Hōgaku Kyōshitsu* [Law class].

Ōta, Shōzō and Kahei Rokumoto. 1993. Issues of the lawyer population: Japan. 25 *Case Western Reserve Journal of International Law* 2:315.

Ozaki, Junri. 2002. Shihō seido kaikaku suishinhō no shingi to futai ketsugi [Deliberation on the law on the promotion of judicial system reform and its attached resolution]. *Hōritsu Jihō Zōkan: Shihō Kaikaku 2002* 48.

Ramseyer, J. Mark. 1986. Lawyers, foreign lawyers, and lawyer-substitutes: The market for regulation in Japan. 27 *Harvard International Law Journal* 499.

Ramseyer, J. Mark and Eric B. Rasmusen. 2003. *Measuring judicial independence: The political economy of judging in Japan*. Chicago: University of Chicago Press.

Richardson, Bradley. 1997. *Japanese democracy: Power, coordination, and performance*. New Haven: Yale University Press.

Rokumoto, Kahei. 1988. On the way to full professionalization. In *Lawyers in society: Civil law world,* eds. R. L. Abel and P. S. C. Lewis. Berkeley: University of California Press.

Satō, Kōji. 1999. Jiyū no hō chitsujo [Legal order for liberty]. In *Kenpō gojūnen no tenbō* [The prospect of the constitutional law at its fiftieth anniversary], eds. K. Satō, M. Shiyake, and M. Ōishi. Tokyo: Yūhikaku.

Schwartz, Frank J. 1991. *Advice and consent: The politics of consultation in Japan.* Cambridge: Program on U.S.-Japan Relations, Harvard University.

Shihō Seido Kaikaku Shingikai [Justice System Reform Council]. 2001. *Recommendations of the Justice System Reform Council—For a justice system to support Japan in the 21st century.* Official English translation at the website of the Prime Minister of Japan at http://www.kantei.go.jp/foreign/judiciary/2001/0612report.html.

Tanaka, Hideo. 1982. *Hābādo Rō Sukurū* [Harvard Law School]. Tokyo: Nihon Hyōronsha.

Tanaka, Shigeaki. 1999. Hōsō yōsei seido kaikaku to daigaku no hōgaku kyōiku [Reform of the legal system of training of the legal profession and university legal education]. In *Kyoto daigaku hōgakubu hyakushūnen kinen ronbunshū* [Papers commemorating the centenary of Kyoto University Faculty of Law], ed. Kyoto Daigaku Hōgakubu. Tokyo: Yūhikaku.

Taniguchi, Yasuhei. 1994. Legal education in Japan. In *Law and technology in the Pacific community,* ed. P. S. C. Lewis. Boulder: Westview Press.

———. 1997. The 1966 Code of Civil Procedure of Japan: A procedure for the coming century? 45 *American Journal of Comparative Law* 767.

Tokyo Bengoshikai Shihō Mondai Tokubetsu Iinkai [Tokyo Bar Association Special Committee on Measures for the Problems of the Judicial System]. 1996. *21-seiki no shihō* [Visions of the judicial system in the twenty-first century]. Tokyo: Tokyo Bengoshikai.

21-seiki Seisaku Kenkyūjo [The 21st Century Public Policy Institute]. 1998. *Minji shihō kasseika ni mukete* [Towards the revitalization of the Japanese civil justice system]. 22 December. Tokyo: The 21st Century Public Policy Institute.

Upham, Frank K. 1987. *Law and social change in postwar Japan.* Cambridge: Harvard University Press.

———. 1998. Weak legal consciousness as invented tradition. In *Mirror of Modernity: Invented traditions of modern Japan,* ed. S. Vlastos. Berkeley: University of California Press.

Watanabe, Yasuo, Setsuo Miyazawa, Shigeo Kisa, Seizaburō Yoshino, and Tetsuo Satō. 1997. *Tekisutobukku gendai shihō* [Textbook on the contemporary judicial system]. 3rd ed. Tokyo: Nihon Hyōronsha.

Yanagida, Yukio. 1998. *Nihon no atarashii hōsō yōsei (1) (2)* [A new system of the training of the legal profession in Japan]. *Jurisuto.* Part I: 1 February; Part II: 15 February.

―――. 1999. Rō sukurū hōshiki no kōsō ni tsuite [On the proposal of a system of graduate professional legal education]. *Jurisuto.* 15 July.

―――. 2000. A new paradigm of legal training and education. 1 *Asian-Pacific Law & Policy Journal* 1. An electronic copy may be seen at http://www.hawaii .edu/aplpj/pdfs/01-yanagida.pdf.

Yonemoto, Kazuhiro. 1995. The Shimane Bar Association: All twenty-one members strong. Translated by Daniel H. Foote. *Law in Japan: An Annual* 115.

Young, Nancy L. 1996. Japan's new product liability law: Increased protection for consumers. Comment. 18 *Loyola Journal of International & Comparative Law* 767.

FIVE

The Turn Toward Law: The Emergence of Corporate Law Firms in Contemporary Japan

Ryo Hamano*

Introduction

In this chapter, I focus on the emergence of corporate law firms in contemporary Japan and the context in which it is happening. First, I review briefly the development of corporate law firms. I then look at this development in the wider context of modern Japanese history, particularly that of the marginality of lawyers in Japan. Lastly, I suggest that the recent growth of corporate law firms can be understood in the context of a widening legal domain[1] in Japan, driven by structural changes in the Japanese economy.

As is well known, Japan has developed a highly industrialized society without much reliance on lawyers[2] and courts (Kawashima 1963; Upham 1987;

*Professor of Sociology of Law at the Faculty of Law and Politics, Rikkyō University, Tokyo, Japan.

This chapter expands upon and brings current two articles previously published in the *Rikkyō Hōgaku* (Hamano 1996 and 1998). The Rikkyō Hōgakkai's permission for reproduction in revised form from these essays is gratefully acknowledged. I thank the participants at the Harvard Law School Conference on the Legal Profession in East Asia for their helpful comments and discussions. I also thank Darryl E. Flaherty, Japan Foundation Research Fellow, and Geraldine Chin, Research Assistant at East Asian Legal Studies, Harvard Law School for their valuable suggestions. Finally, I would like to express my special thanks to Professor William Alford, who has read and commented on the whole text. Of course, I take sole responsibility for errors remaining.

1. In this chapter, the term "legal domain" is used generally to represent the field and area of thought, activity, and interest over which the legal profession has control, influence, and rights. For more specific and distinctive uses of this and similar terms, see Haley (1991, 14–15 and 1998, 20–39) and Dezalay and Garth (1997). See also Bourdieu (1987).

2. In this chapter, the term "lawyer" is used to designate attorney-at-law (*bengoshi*), judge, or public prosecutor. In Japan, there are various other separately licensed professions which can be categorized as quasi-lawyers (see Ramseyer 1986, 519–20; Ōta and Rokumoto 1993, 315; Henderson 1997, 29–40; Ramseyer and Nakazato 1998, 10–12).

Tanase 1990; Haley 1991 and 1998; Henderson 1997; Wollschläger 1997).[3] Japanese lawyers in private practice have played a comparatively limited role in business and the economy.[4] Historically, attorneys considered drafting legal documents and providing legal advice for businesses less important than litigation in general. Big businesses in Japan tended to rely on extralegal measures and administrative guidance instead of lawyers and courts for dispute resolution. Administrative bureaucrats and technocrats, rather than legal practitioners, and judges were major players in ordering the economy.

Recently, however, major changes have occurred. As I will show, the commercial practice of lawyers, especially in Tokyo and Osaka, has expanded. Some practitioners have begun to specialize in new business law areas, such as major business transactions, intellectual property, antitrust law, mergers and acquisitions, and international legal matters. Several corporate law firms of considerable size have emerged in Tokyo and Osaka. In addition, business leaders have come to realize that the "catch-up" strategy and related systems of a "developmental state" in the post-war period are no longer effective. They have begun to attack over-regulation by the bureaucracy. In this context, business leaders have called for reform of the judicial system to make it suitable for a deregulated and globalized economy.

Legal scholars and lawyers in Japan now argue that Japanese society is in the process of "legalization" (hōka). There is discussion about what roles lawyers and courts can and should play, and what kind of social order Japan should seek.[5] They do not refer to legalization as the development of an American-style litigious society. Rather, they mean more frequent use of legal institutions, especially courts and lawyers in private practice, as a mechanism of dispute resolution and social ordering. This is in contrast to past reliance on extralegal measures such as reciprocity-based, long-term relations, third-party intervention in the context of a close-knit community, and administrative guidance.

While the legalization process in Japan in this sense is generally considered to have begun in the 1960s (Rokumoto 1971 and Tanaka 1996, 1–2), the process has accelerated since the 1980s. One of the main factors is, of course, the internationalization of the Japanese economy, which propelled not only the development of corporate legal practice but also major reforms of laws and legal institutions, culminating in the movement toward judicial reform in the 1990s. Thus, practicing attorneys have faced waves of change and reform. These

---

3. I must note that Professor Mark Ramseyer, based upon an analytical framework using the "rational-choice" model, has presented exceptional and thought-provoking challenges to the conventional accounts of and assumptions on law in Japanese society (see, for example, Ramseyer 1990, 1991 and 1996; Ramseyer and Nakazato 1998).

4. For a general account of practicing attorneys in Japan, see Rokumoto (1988); Ōta and Rokumoto (1993); Ramseyer (1986); Henderson (1997); Haley (1998, 50–58); Ramseyer and Nakazato (1998, 6–16).

5. See, e.g., Tanase (1991 and 1995); Tanaka (1996); Hamano (1997a and 1997b); Hirowatari (1997).

include opening the legal market for foreign lawyers in 1987 (Wohl, Chemtob, and Fukushima 1989; Henderson 1997, 65–67; Ramseyer and Nakazato 1998, 15–16), the reform of the national bar examination in 1991 (Ōta and Roku-moto 1993, 331–32) and in 1998, as well as the enactment of the new Code of Civil Procedure in 1996. Attorneys have also been active.

In 1990, the Japan Federation of Bar Associations or JFBA (*Nihon bengoshi rengōkai,* also known as *Nichibenren*) declared that it considered judicial reform to be one of its long-term objectives in order to widen a traditionally limited legal domain (Nihon Bengoshi Rengōkai (hereafter, NBR) 1990). All the local bar associations have introduced a voluntary pro bono representation scheme for criminal suspects based on the idea of the "duty solicitor" scheme in England and Wales (NBR 1992; Marushima 1996; Takenouchi 1998). Some local bar associations have also introduced new arbitration systems for civil disputes, designed to provide easy access to justice for ordinary citizens.[6]

The bar has pushed ahead with reform and expansion of legal aid. A research committee that included representatives of the JFBA, the Supreme Court, the Legal Aid Association, and legal scholars presented a report to the minister of justice in March 1998 calling for a major change in the legal aid system (Hōritsu Fujo Seido Kenkyūkai 1998). The Civil Legal Aid Act was passed by the government and came into effect in 2000.

The government established the Justice System Reform Council or JSRC (*shihō seido kaikaku shingikai*) in 1999, which held deliberations for two years in order to consider fundamental measures necessary for judicial reform. A final report was issued in June 2001 which made far-reaching recommendations in the area of justice system reform (Shihō Seido Kaikaku Shingikai 2001). In response to this report, the Cabinet established the Office for Promotion of Justice System Reform in December 2001, which held its first meeting in January 2002.[7]

The recent expansion of corporate legal practice and its implications must be understood within the wider context of society and economy. Japanese lawyers have gained power and prestige in the process of legalization. They have also confronted a transformation of their identity and of their role in society, which has produced not only new opportunities, but also tensions and conflicts within the bar.

---

6. See, e.g., Daini Tokyo Bengoshikai (1997).

7. The first meeting of the Advisory Board of the Office for Promotion of Justice System Reform is mentioned on the website of the Prime Minister of Japan, at http://www.kantei .go.jp/foreign/koizumiphoto/2002/01/18sihou_e.html.

I.   Recent Developments in the Practice of Corporate Law

A.   Private Practice in Tokyo

Tokyo is the center of the Japanese economy. Most big businesses have their head offices in Tokyo. Major financial institutions, manufacturers, and service corporations from abroad also have branch offices in Tokyo. The recent trend toward the expansion of corporate legal practice in Japan can be identified best in Tokyo. After a brief overview of private practice in Tokyo generally, I will look at the commercial practice of lawyers in that metropolis.

There were about 9,100 practicing attorneys in Tokyo in 2002.[8] They constituted a little less than half of all the attorneys in Japan. It is well known that the Japanese practicing bar is very small (Figure 5.1), and the distribution of this small number of lawyers is far from even (Figure 5.2). Tokyo and Osaka attract about 60 percent of all the lawyers. Additionally, law practices in Japan are generally small. In 1990, 56 percent of attorneys in Japan were solo practitioners. Another 9 percent were solo practitioners with one or more associates. (The percentage of solo practices is relatively low in Tokyo—42 percent in 1990—compared with other areas). Collective professional practices are not as developed in Japan as in other industrialized countries. Management of law offices under the rubric of partnership is uncommon. Of the attorneys in Tokyo, only 11 percent were in partnerships in 1990. The practice of office sharing is more common than partnership among collective practices in Tokyo. Of lawyers operating collectively in 1990, 66 percent shared offices and 32 percent were in partnerships (NBR 1991, 14, 18).

The form and size of law practices in Tokyo is an exception in Japan. There are a considerable number of large law firms in Tokyo that have formed partnerships, and some are internationally known. Some of these firms expanded rapidly in the 1980s and 1990s, and the largest now contains more than two hundred lawyers.[9] Tokyo also differs from other regions in Japan in the work and clientele of its attorneys, as (scarce) empirical data show. With respect to civil matters, lawyers in Tokyo handled more preventive work (legal advice, counseling, drafting contracts, and other legal documents) than in other regions. As for clientele, lawyers in Tokyo served more large corporations than their counterparts elsewhere in Japan (NBR 1991, 39, 44).

---

8. The membership figures in October 2002 for the three bar associations in Tokyo (Tokyo Bengoshikai, Daiichi Tokyo Bengoshikai, and Daini Tokyo Bengoshikai), including foreign special members, were, respectively, 4,317, 2,365, and 2,463, according to the membership directory of the Japan Federation of Bar Associations.

9. See Part I C of this chapter.

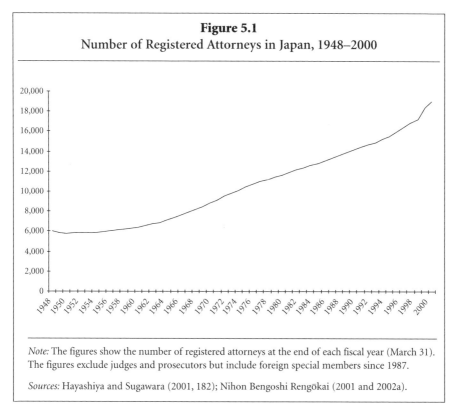

Figure 5.1
Number of Registered Attorneys in Japan, 1948–2000

Note: The figures show the number of registered attorneys at the end of each fiscal year (March 31). The figures exclude judges and prosecutors but include foreign special members since 1987.

Sources: Hayashiya and Sugawara (2001, 182); Nihon Bengoshi Rengōkai (2001 and 2002a).

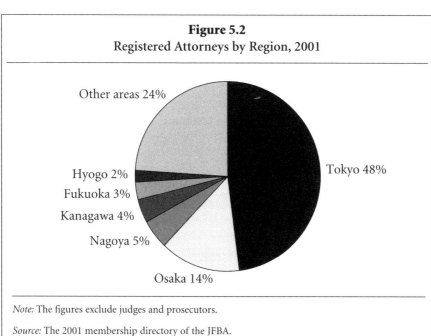

Figure 5.2
Registered Attorneys by Region, 2001

Other areas 24%

Hyogo 2%

Fukuoka 3%

Kanagawa 4%

Nagoya 5%

Osaka 14%

Tokyo 48%

Note: The figures exclude judges and prosecutors.

Source: The 2001 membership directory of the JFBA.

B.   The Practice of Corporate Law in Tokyo

In 1988, this author mailed a survey to a random sample of attorneys in private practice in Tokyo.[10] The survey was designed to elicit data about the respondent's practice (for example, the number of attorneys in the firm), the handling of corporate legal matters, and prospects and hopes for future commercial practice. The questionnaire was sent to a sample of 500 practitioners. The response rate was 37 percent or 185 attorneys.[11] Based on the results of this survey and other empirical data available, I will look at the state of the practice of lawyers in Tokyo in the 1980s and their handling of commercial law in particular as a prelude to a discussion of their practice today.

If we look at civil legal practice in general (which includes practice not only for business corporations but also for private individuals), matters at court (i.e., litigation and formal dispute resolution) decreased slightly in the 1980s. On the other hand, work related to non-contentious matters and out-of-court settlement negotiations increased slightly (Table 5.1 and Figure 5.3). In the 1980s, attorneys in Tokyo enjoyed economic prosperity. Empirical data show that their gross revenue and net income increased considerably. The average net income of attorneys in Tokyo increased from ¥7.6 million in 1980 to ¥17.9 million in 1989 (NBR 1991, 78). After discounting for inflation, the real increase was by 98 percent. This growth may have been due to the rapid rise in land prices and the volume of real property transactions and disputes. Rationalization, through the use of personal computers and other office equipment, is cited (86) as another cause. The increase of non-contentious matters, especially in the areas of corporate law and international legal work, may also have contributed to the rise in the average revenue.

Although traditional legal work—such as cases concerning real property and debt collection, for individuals and small businesses—still accounted for more than half of all cases at hand, the relative importance of large corporations as clientele of Tokyo attorneys grew (Table 5.2 and Figure 5.4). In 1989, 43 percent of the clientele were still individuals in terms of the number of cases, but the percentage of large corporations (25 percent) was catching up with that of small corporations (29 percent). Tokyo was conspicuous in this respect, yet matters related to large corporations occupied a growing share of lawyers' clientele in all regions in the 1980s (NBR 1991, 44).

What did attorneys do for these businesses? In the 1988 survey, I asked respondents about their commercial practice, including work for small family enterprises. Some of the findings are as follows. In the questionnaire, I asked the respondents to identify the three categories of work that occupied most of their time in October 1988. Real property litigation, debt collection litigation, and preventive legal work were named, respectively, by 40 to 50 percent of the

---

10. For a detailed analysis of the results of the survey, see Hamano (1991 and 1993–94).

11. A comparison between the respondents and a different random sample from the same population assured the representativeness of the sample.

Table 5.1

Types of Civil Cases: Average Number and Percentage per Attorney (Tokyo)

Year	Non-dispute	Tribunal	Court	Out-of-court settlement	Total
1980	3.3	1.3	22	4.5	31
	10.4%	4.2%	71.1%	14.3%	100%
1988	3.8	1.1	13	5	23
	16.7%	4.8%	56.5%	21.9%	100%

Note: "Tribunal" means disputes brought before a public agency for dispute resolution, such as a tax tribunal. "Court" means disputes brought before a regular court including mediation and lawsuits. "Out-of-court settlement" means disputes handled without intervention of the court or other kinds of public agencies for dispute resolution.

Sources: Nihon Bengoshi Rengōkai (1988a, 60); unpublished data from the JFBA's survey in 1990.

Figure 5.3

Types of Civil Cases: Average Percentage per Attorney (Tokyo)

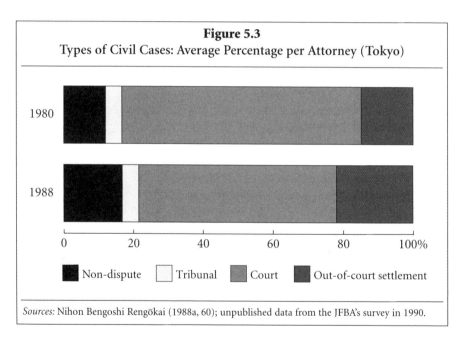

Sources: Nihon Bengoshi Rengōkai (1988a, 60); unpublished data from the JFBA's survey in 1990.

respondents. While Japanese attorneys tend to involve themselves in preventive legal practice less routinely than their American counterparts, the survey showed that the situation was changing at least for practitioners in Tokyo. I also asked about expectations for future work. The respondents identified the three categories that they would like to handle chiefly five years ahead. While nearly 30 percent of the respondents intended to concentrate on real property litigation and 30 percent on debt collection litigation, 30 percent of respondents also

Table 5.2

Types of Clients in Civil Cases: Average Percentage per Attorney (Tokyo)

	Individual	Small- or medium-sized company	Large company	Government agency	Other organizations	Total
1980	44.6%	30.6%	17.9%	1.4%	5.5%	100%
1989	42.5%	29.2%	24.5%	1.3%	2.5%	100%

Source: Nihon Bengoshi Rengōkai (1991, 44).

Figure 5.4

Types of Clients in Civil Cases: Average Percentage per Attorney (Tokyo)

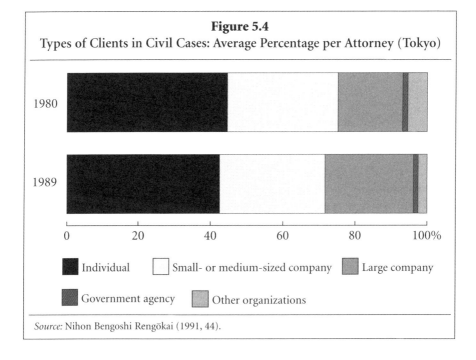

Source: Nihon Bengoshi Rengōkai (1991, 44).

showed a preference for company law and anti-monopoly law work. Complicated legal counseling was another category that a third of the respondents preferred as a future field. This suggests that in Tokyo there are a considerable number of legal practitioners who are interested in a business law specialty, a new phenomenon in Japan.

In the 1990s, the Japanese economy confronted its worst recession in fifty years. Land prices dropped drastically and the number of real property transactions also fell off severely. In retrospect, 1988 was the height of the so-called bubble economy. Evidence suggests that the average income of lawyers dropped considerably after the bubble burst; however, there is no reliable data set to estimate the impact of the recession upon legal practice in general.[12] One can speculate that the recession in the 1990s created opportunities in practice areas such as debt collection, bankruptcy, and mergers and acquisitions, yet lawyers in Tokyo no longer enjoyed the kind of prosperity they did in the late 1980s. However, there is no indication that corporate legal practice in Tokyo declined. Rather, as I show below, large firms in Tokyo constantly grew in size, apparently responding to the development of the corporate law market.

C. The Emergence of Large Law Firms

In spite of the tendency toward a focus on corporate practice in Tokyo, I must hastily point out that the general pattern of practice changed little. Many lawyers in Tokyo continued to practice in very small units. The average size of practice was still small (i.e., 1.8 lawyers per firm).[13] In 1998, 73 percent of firms were solo practices, containing 40 percent of all practitioners (Okada and Takahata 1998, 50). The majority of attorneys remained in solo practice or in an office-sharing arrangement.

However, statistical data identifies the growth of larger firms in Tokyo clearly. What is noted firstly is that the proportion of firms containing one or two attorneys declined: from 87 percent of all firms (containing 64 percent of all practitioners) in 1985 to 85 percent of all firms (containing 54 percent of all practitioners) in 1998 (Tables 5.3 and 5.4 and Figure 5.5). On the other hand, the proportion of firms containing five or more attorneys increased from 4 percent of all firms (containing 19 percent of all practitioners) in 1985 to 5.4 percent of all firms (containing 29 percent of all practitioners) in 1998 (Tables 5.3 and 5.4).

Among the firms containing five or more attorneys, a different pattern of growth can be identified. Between 1985 and 1990, the number of firms with ten or more attorneys increased more rapidly than any other category of law firm (by 38 percent). During that period, the number of firms containing six to nine attorneys increased very slightly (by 3.6 percent). Between 1990 and 1998, however, the medium-sized firm with five to nine attorneys increased in number remarkably (by 48 percent), although the rate of increase in the number of large firms with ten or more attorneys was still high (by 55 percent) (Table 5.4). It might be that the larger firms could take advantage of the expanding legal market more readily than smaller ones. Small firms with four or fewer attorneys also increased in number between 1985 and 1998, but their rate of growth was considerably lower than that of firms with ten or more lawyers (Table 5.4). To sum up, although the firms with five or more lawyers were still in the great minority (5.4 percent of all firms, containing 29 percent of all practitioners), their proportion increased fairly rapidly.

---

12. Daini Tokyo Bengoshikai (1996, 68–69, 71) presents a preliminary analysis of trends in the incomes of lawyers.

13. Okada and Takahata (1998, 50) reported that in May 1998, there were 7,786 lawyers practicing in 4,309 law firms in Tokyo.

Table 5.3

Attorneys: Distribution by Size of Law Firm (Tokyo), 1985, 1990, 1998

	Size of firm (number of attorneys)				
	1–2	3–4	5–9	10+	Total
1985	3,728*	997	702	411	5,838*
	64%	17%	12%	7%	100%
1990	3,898	1,179	705	668	6,450
	60.4%	18.3%	10.9%	10.4%	100%
1998	4,193	1,344	1,053	1,196	7,786
	53.9%	17.3%	13.5%	15.4%	100%
1985–1990	+170	+182	+3	+257	+612
increase	4.6%	18.3%	0.4%	62.5%	10.5%
1990–1998	+295	+165	+348	+528	+1,336
increase	7.6%	14%	49.4%	79%	20.7%

Note: Asterisked figures are estimates.

Sources: Nihon Bengoshi Rengōkai (1988b, 59–61 and 1990b); Tanase (1987, 21); Okada and Takahata (1998, 50).

Table 5.4

Firms: Distribution by Size of Law Firm (Tokyo), 1985, 1990, 1998

	Size of firm (number of attorneys)				
	1–2	3–4	5–9	10+	Total
1985	3,055*	302	110	29	3,496*
	87.4%	8.6%	3.1%	0.8%	100%
1990	3,378	355	114	40	3,887
	86.9%	9.1%	2.9%	1%	100%
1998	3,672	406	169	62	4,309
	85.2%	9.4%	3.9%	1.4%	100%
1985–1990	+323	+53	+4	+11	+391
increase	10.6%	17.5%	3.6%	37.9%	11.2%
1990–1998	+294	+51	+55	+22	+422
increase	8.7%	14.4%	48.2%	55%	10.9%

Note: Asterisked figures are estimates.

Sources: Nihon Bengoshi Rengōkai (1988b, 59–61 and 1990b); Tanase (1987, 21); Okada and Takahata (1998, 50).

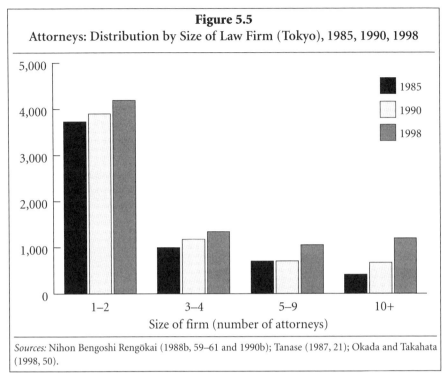

Figure 5.5
Attorneys: Distribution by Size of Law Firm (Tokyo), 1985, 1990, 1998

Sources: Nihon Bengoshi Rengōkai (1988b, 59–61 and 1990b); Tanase (1987, 21); Okada and Takahata (1998, 50).

Secondly, it should be noted that the largest firms continued to grow in size in the 1980s and 1990s. In 1998, the largest firm, Nishimura Sōgō,[14] had sixty-three attorneys, followed by two firms with sixty-two attorneys each: Nagashima & Ohno[15] and Mori Sōgō[16] (Table 5.5).

The emergence of large firms is also evident in Osaka, the second focus of the economy in Japan. In Osaka, the largest firm, Oh-Ebashi,[17] consisted of twenty-

14. Nishimura Sōgō had 110 attorneys in November 2001. In 2004 it merged with Tokiwa Sōgō Law Offices. The merged firm, called Nishimura & Partners, had 190 attorneys in May 2005. See the website at http://www.jurists.co.jp/en/.

15. Nagashima & Ohno merged with Tsunematsu Yanase & Sekine in 2000. The amalgamated firm, called the Law Offices of Nagashima Ohno & Tsunematsu, was staffed with 139 attorneys in June 2002. See the firm's website at http://www.noandt.com, which states that NO&T was "the first law firm in Japan to surpass the 100-lawyer milestone." As of June 2005 the firm had 206 attorneys.

16. Mori Sōgō had only four lawyers in 1970, ten in the early 1980s, thirty-six in 1992 (Kubori 1993, 370–73), sixty-two in 1998, and ninety-two in 2002, when it merged with Hamada & Matsumoto, with forty-two attorneys. At the time the firm changed its name to Mori Hamada & Matsumoto. See the website http://www.mhmjapan.com. In July 2005 it merged with Max Law Offices (but retained the MHM name), which brought the total number of attorneys to around two hundred.

17. Oh-Ebashi LPC & Partners had thirty-eight attorneys in 2002. In 2005 it had sixty-four, including fourteen in a Tokyo office opened in 2002. See Oh-Ebashi's website at http://www.ohebashi.com.

Table 5.5

Size and Location of the Ten Largest Law Firms, 1998

	Firm	Location	Number of attorneys
1.	Nishimura Sōgō	Tokyo	63
2.	Nagashima & Ohno	Tokyo	62
3.	Mori Sōgō	Tokyo	62
4.	Anderson & Mori	Tokyo	50
5.	Asahi	Tokyo	48
6.	Mitsui & Yasuda	Tokyo	36
7.	TMI Sōgō	Tokyo	33
8.	Mastuo Sōgō	Tokyo	29
9.	Iwata Gōdō	Tokyo	28
10.	Oh-Ebashi	Osaka	27

Source: Niwayama and Yamagishi (1998, 35).

seven attorneys in 1998, and the second-largest firm had twenty-five attorneys (Table 5.5). Between 1985 and 1998, the number of firms with ten or more lawyers increased by 375 percent in Osaka, from four to nineteen, while in Tokyo, it increased by 114 percent, from twenty-nine to sixty-two. Among the twenty largest law firms in Japan in 1998, eighteen firms were located in Tokyo, and two were in Osaka (Niwayama and Yamagishi 1998, 35). The emergence of large firms in Tokyo and Osaka indicates the growth of corporate practice in Japan.

I must emphasize that not all of the large firms specialize in corporate law. Some large firms are known for their specialty in representing labor unions and workers in labor disputes. It was estimated that four of the twenty largest law firms in Japan in 1998 developed from firms specializing in representation on behalf of workers and labor unions in labor disputes (*rōdō-jiken jimusho*) (Niwayama and Yamagishi 1998, 35). Anecdotal evidence suggests that some large firms commit themselves more or less to politically leftist ideals, for example, socialism or communism. These firms may provide legal services mainly for small companies, labor unions, and private individuals. They may also be active in pro bono work. In addition, there are not as many corporate law firms in Japan, in the strict sense of the word, as can be found on Wall Street or in London. Typically, medium-sized firms have a mix of business and individual clients, although empirical data is lacking.

With the above reservations, the growth of large law firms is mainly due to the development of corporate law practice in Japan. Most of the largest firms are active in international legal matters, corporate law, intellectual property, anti-monopoly law and so on. The three largest firms in 2002, Nagashima Ohno

& Tsunematsu, Nishimura Sōgō (now Nishimura & Partners), and Mori Sōgō (now Mori Hamada & Matsumoto), are well-known corporate law firms founded by Japanese partners. In fact, the great majority of the twenty largest firms in Japan specialize in corporate law. These firms are a new species and are performing an important role in the globalizing Japanese economy.

D. Globalization of the Economy and the Recent Growth of Large Firms

Business lawyers are not a new phenomenon in Japanese history. But the recent growth of large firms indicates the coming of a new era. It is true that these firms are not as large as the biggest American law firms. However, they are distinguished by the rapidity of their growth as demonstrated above.

To understand this rapid growth of the limited number of large firms properly, one should first see the traditional pattern of underdevelopment of law firms in Japan and its reasons. In *Gendai Shakai to Bengoshi* (Modern Society and Lawyers), Takao Tanase presented a theoretical explanation for the small size of Japanese law firms (Tanase 1987, 91–118). According to Tanase, law firms in Japan were under constant pressure, which kept them small and underspecialized. Corporate law practice generally requires highly specialized legal skills, which in turn leads to the development of large law firms with specialized divisions. The increase of complicated legal needs, arising from various kinds of business transactions and government regulations, is one of the most important factors facilitating the growth of corporate law firms in Japan.[18] However, although more than a few lawsuits against big corporations played an important role in social change in Japan (Upham 1987), the risks of litigation and other legal disputes that a company faced in Japan were generally so limited that the need for corporate attorneys with sophisticated skills was also confined and as a result, underdeveloped. The informal and consensual nature of government regulation (Upham 1987 and Haley 1991) served to counter challenges by formal legal means. Litigation between Japanese companies, especially between large leading companies, was also uncommon. Extralegal measures, such as business negotiations without relying on lawyers, were comparatively effective. Administrative bureaucrats tended to play principal roles in resolving major conflicts in business and society (Upham 1987, 124–204).

Japanese consumers were less litigious than their American counterparts. Even a small law firm or a solo practice was, therefore, able to meet the limited and simple needs of a corporation. They could easily cope with routine legal work at a comparatively low cost. At the same time, Japanese companies, especially large corporations, had their own in-house legal staffs. Although the great majority of their employees were not practicing lawyers (*bengoshi*), they drew on much experience and expertise and provided necessary services for the companies.

---

18. Galanter and Palay (1991) showed that competition among associates within a firm was another factor ("growth engine") facilitating the rapid growth of big law firms in the U.S.

In addition to these factors, the number of new entrants into the legal profession was so limited, as is discussed below, that private practitioners enjoyed little competition. They, therefore, had little incentive to enlarge and specialize their practice. Rather, they found great interest in providing general legal services instead of specialized ones, because general practice, as far as viable, was able to attract and maintain a wide variety of clientele, and specialization into a narrow field was risky for solo or small-sized practitioners. As long as they could obtain sufficient lucrative work, it was quite natural that they did not dare to innovate their practice significantly.[19]

In spite of such general conditions surrounding Japanese lawyers, there existed some enterprisingly spirited members of the profession who were involved in specialized corporate work. Some of them established their own law firms under the rubric of a partnership in the 1960s and 1970s. These and a few firms established by foreign attorneys[20] were exceptions handling mainly corporate legal work. Most of them specialized in international and foreign law matters. Since the 1980s, when the Japanese economy started its internationalization more thoroughly than ever, these firms took advantage of their pioneering positions and succeeded in recruiting many young attorneys which resulted in the quick growth of the firms' size. Some firms also amalgamated into larger firms by merger.

The rapid growth of large firms in the 1980s and 1990s, and of medium-sized firms in the 1990s, as demonstrated above, corresponds to the increase in corporate legal needs. Most of the new legal needs arose in the area of corporate law and especially in international matters. Since 1987, several major foreign international law firms have set up branch offices in Japan under the 1986 Special Measures Law Concerning the Handling of Legal Business by Foreign Lawyers (the Foreign Lawyers Law).[21] This is another example of the expansion of the corporate legal market in Tokyo. Major international law firms from New

---

19. The factors I point out in the text, including the underdevelopment of law firms, are only parts of a larger configuration and general pattern of socio-legal ordering in the Japanese economy.

20. Under the Allied occupation, the Practicing Attorney Law of 1949 (*bengoshihō*) was enacted with a special provision allowing foreign attorneys to practice in Japan without passing the national bar exam if they could demonstrate that they possessed "an adequate knowledge of the laws in Japan." A few American attorneys who obtained licenses under the provision established law firms in Japan, which are known as *jun-kaiin jimusho* (quasi-member firms) (see Henderson 1997, 64–65).

21. In 1986, the Foreign Lawyers Law was enacted to allow registered foreign lawyers (*gaikokuhō jimu bengoshi*) to practice in Japan. For an account of the new system, see Wohl, Chemtob, and Fukushima (1989). Under this law, about 30 foreign lawyers were practicing in April 1988 (Hamano 1994b, 49), 87 in June 1998, and 188 in April 2002 (NBR 1998b and 2002b). There were 236 registered foreign lawyers as of April 2005. The increase since the late 1990s is remarkable.

York, London, and Los Angeles opened branch offices.[22] Empirical evidence shows that the new system affected, to a certain extent, the domestic approach to the provision of international legal services (Hamano 1989 and 1993–94). The Foreign Lawyers Law was amended in the 1990s under pressure from abroad for a more open legal market. Foreign lawyers in Japan are now constructing a network of international legal services with Japanese lawyers, especially in large corporate law firms.

Furthermore, management considerations of economies of scale may also be factors in the growth of large law firms. In 1988, several partners of such firms in Tokyo emphasized two points to me during interviews: the importance of economies of scale in office management and the necessity of constantly recruiting young associates while increasing the number of partners and associates (Hamano 1994a, 68). In light of the inner dynamics of large firms that drive constant growth, the increase of new entrants into the legal profession, due to the reform of the national bar exam, will bring about the sustained growth of large firms to a certain extent.

E. The Development of Corporate Legal Departments

Corporate legal departments in Japan began to develop in the 1960s.[23] Mainly adapting to the internationalization of the Japanese economy, but partly responding to the increase of domestic legal disputes, the legal sections of Japan's major companies have grown significantly since the late 1970s and early 1980s. Most large corporations now have an in-house legal department staffed mainly with non-lawyer legal specialists. For example, in the late 1990s Fujitsu, one of the leading computer manufacturers in Japan, had a legal and intellectual property department with nearly 250 employees (Shinohara 1998). The development of in-house legal sections has continued hand-in-hand with the growth of corporate legal practice by outside counsel. However, most small companies, which constitute the vast majority of Japanese corporations, do not have their own legal departments.

Corporate legal departments in Japan are distinctive because they largely consist of non-lawyers. Although the majority have a legal degree, most have not qualified as *bengoshi*. These employees are trained mainly on the job. Some of them have also studied law abroad, and a few of them have even acquired a legal qualification in a foreign jurisdiction. In the mid-1990s, only about sixty qualified

---

22. Based on interviews with twelve foreign attorneys and eleven Japanese attorneys, whose specialty is in the area of foreign law, I identified the strategies of foreign law firms opening branch offices in Tokyo; see Hamano (1989, 168–69). In the 1990s, as the economy faced great difficulties, business conditions for foreign lawyers in Japan changed. They may have had new business opportunities or they may have lost some clients.

23. For the characteristics of corporate legal departments in Japanese businesses, see Kojima (1981, 179–218 and 1986); Keiei Hōyūkai (1986); Degawa (1986); Keiei Hōyūkai and Shōji Hōmu Kenkyūkai (1996); Ōta and Rokumoto (1993, 327–28); and the chapter by Professors Kitagawa and Nottage in this volume.

lawyers were employed in corporate legal sections (Daini Tokyo Bengoshikai 1996, 54). Non-lawyer legal staff have been common in large corporations since the pre-war period. Non-lawyer graduates of undergraduate law programs worked in various sections and provided legal services for a single company. Even before the development of in-house legal departments, companies hired non-lawyer graduates of law faculties for their legal knowledge. The non-lawyer employees also carried out non-legal work, and the degree of specialization regarding legal affairs within a company was limited. The underdevelopment of the legal section of the Japanese company until recent years cannot be properly understood unless one takes into consideration the marginality of the legal domain vis-à-vis the economy. Even after corporate legal needs increased, the supply of qualified lawyers was chronically limited. Therefore, the system of corporate legal sections composed of legal staff who had not qualified as *bengoshi* developed.

Non-lawyer corporate legal staff are in a sense functional substitutes for *bengoshi*, especially in major business enterprises. One can speculate that their technical knowledge and experience is generally at the same level as that of specialist attorneys. Some observe that they lack the variety of perspectives and practical knowledge of litigation that would derive from legal practice. They may also lack the institutional independence that attorneys enjoy in principle. Members of corporate legal staff are salaried workers within the lifelong employment system. They probably cannot avoid being integrated into personal networks and administrative bureaucracies that exist throughout the Japanese economy any more than an ordinary Japanese businessperson. These propositions remain to be tested by empirical data. In the process of the legalization of the economy, corporate legal staff may partly compete and partly cooperate with *bengoshi* in private practice.

II.   Marginality of Lawyers in Society and the Economy

In this Part, an overview of the position of Japanese lawyers will be provided from an historical perspective in order to show the context of the recent development of corporate legal practice.

A.   Models of the Role of Practicing Attorneys

Following the Meiji Restoration of 1868, when Japan opened itself to the West after more than two hundred years of isolation, the new government tried at any cost to transplant the western legal system (Takayanagi 1963; Noda 1976, 41–62; Rahn 1990, 58–129; Haley 1991, 67–82). New legal institutions such as courts were created, and judges and public prosecutors were selected. The need for lawyers was also recognized, and finally, the Practicing Attorney Law of 1893 was enacted to regulate private practitioners.[24]

---

24. For details of the pre-history of Japanese attorneys and the development of the institution of the legal advocate in the early years of the Meiji era, see Okudaira (1914); Hattori (1963, 111–28); Koga (1970); Ōno (1970); Noda (1976, 145–46); Takikawa (1984); Haley (1991, 100); Henderson (1997, 41–46).

From the beginning, practicing lawyers were considered to have a lower social status than both public prosecutors[25] and judges, who were government officials or state bureaucrats enjoying high social prestige and great influence (Rokumoto 1988, 160–61; Ōta and Rokumoto 1993, 316; Henderson 1997, 43–44). In the process of modernization before the Second World War, especially in commerce and industry, private attorneys played a limited and peripheral role in comparison to administrative bureaucrats (Koga 1970, 29–48). Contrary to their counterparts in the United States, Japanese lawyers in private practice were not widely used by large corporations. Most of the clientele of Japanese attorneys were probably small companies and individuals.[26] In criminal defense activities and advocacy for the poor and the oppressed, most Japanese legal practitioners prided themselves on their role as defenders of legal rights for social or political minorities against the bureaucratic state of Imperial Japan. There was considerable antagonism between judicial bureaucrats (i.e., judges and public prosecutors) and private practitioners (Ōno 1970, 32, 36–66).[27]

Despite the reform just after the end of the Second World War, which gave the bar the capacity for autonomous self-government for the first time in Japanese history, the antagonism between the two branches of the Japanese legal profession persisted (Henderson 1997, 57). Private practitioners tended to identify themselves as lawyers of the "opposition camp," opposed to the judges and public prosecutors who were the lawyers of the "ruling camp" (Rokumoto 1988, 161–62; Ōta and Rokumoto 1993, 317). Practitioners and leaders of bar associations idealized this role of opposition against government, although the model was substantially ideological. The daily practice of attorneys may have focused on mainly civil litigation for ordinary businesses and individuals, which had little to do with protest and defense against the powerful.

In spite of the persistence of traditional ideas about lawyers, a new conception emerged, which is, in some respects, contrary to the above-mentioned model (Miyakawa 1992, 4–14). Under the influence of the new constitution of 1946 and Anglo-American legal ideas such as the "rule of law," younger generations of lawyers looked to American or English lawyers as their model. In addition, some

---

25. For public prosecutors and criminal procedures in Japan, see Nagashima (1963); Noda (1976, 149–51); Tanaka (1996, 556–57); Haley (1991, 121–38); Oda (1992, 99, 398–403).

26. Reliable data on Japanese corporate legal practice in the pre-war period is scarce. A few renowned attorneys were retained or employed by major corporations. For example, Yoshimichi Hara was retained by the House of Furukawa, one of the leading *zaibatsu* (pre-war conglomerates) (see Mitani 1980, 214n1, relying upon Hara's autobiography). Hara gave legal advice to Ōji Seishi and Mitsui Gomei as well (Hara 1935, 241, 242). Another famous lawyer, Chū Egi, was a legal adviser to Mitsui Bussan (242). However, these lawyers may have been the exceptions. Most Japanese attorneys probably worked mainly for individuals and small companies (see Hamano 2001). Further analyses based upon historical sources are required.

27. Hattori (1963, 145–46) pointed out that active cooperation between judges and advocates was lacking in the administration of justice before the war.

of the leading legal scholars and lawyers advocated the value of legal practice based upon the ideal of the "legal profession" (Ishimura 1969 and Ishii 1970).[28] Under this new model of the legal profession, a private attorney is considered to be an officer of the court, and he or she is thus a colleague of judges and public prosecutors. Since around 1970, this model, which is often called the "profession model," has become very influential among lawyers opposing the traditional opposition camp model (Miyakawa 1992, 5–6).

Needless to say, this profession model could easily be used to defend an attorney's self-interest—for example, to oppose liberalizing the regulation of commercial advertising by lawyers.[29] Since early in the 1980s, a third model has been presented, which mainly considers legal practitioners as providers of legal services promoting private rights and interests without emphasizing the ideal of public service (Tanase 1987 and 1996; Nasu 1992).[30] Although the third model seems to be supported by only a minority of Japanese lawyers, it has contributed to the demystification of the profession and triggered opportunities to reconsider the values and virtues of professionalism.[31]

Since the end of the Second World War, Japanese attorneys have gained prestige and consolidated their political and social influence to a considerable extent. However, they are basically still contained within traditional political and social structures. The institutional framework that partitions the legal domain defines the position of Japanese lawyers. The next Part will briefly elaborate on the context in which Japanese attorneys are located.

B. Marginality of Lawyers

In "Law, Lawyers and Social Capital: 'Rule of Law' versus Relational Capitalism," Yves Dezalay and Bryant Garth (1997) examined the peripheral role of Japanese lawyers in business and society. They interpreted the marginality of lawyers[32] through a theoretical framework that regarded marginality not as a timeless feature, but as a socially and historically constructed structure. They did not deny the existence of cultural traits or traces, but emphasized the contingent nature of the processes forming and constructing the structures in which lawyers and other protagonists compete, compromise, or cooperate with

---

28. See also Rokumoto (1974).

29. See Tanase (1987, 119–22) and Miyakawa (1992, 7).

30. See also Miyakawa (1992, 8–9).

31. See, e.g., Miyakawa et al. (1992–93); Yoshikawa (1997); Hamano (1997a); Tanaka (1997).

32. In "Relational Practices and the Marginalization of Law," Jane Kaufman Winn (1994) used persuasively the concept of "marginalization of law" to analyze the functioning of law in Taiwan. As Upham's (1994) comment on his review of Winn's article shows, there seems to be a similarity between Taiwan and Japan in the marginality of the role of law in ordering society. For a comment on the differences between the two legal cultures, see Winn (1994, 203). To identify the similarities and differences, further studies with detailed comparative analysis remain to be done.

each other in their struggle for power. Dezalay and Garth presented a fresh interpretation of the "marked segmentation of the legal field—which strongly limits the autonomy of law in the field of power" (Dezalay and Garth 1997, 128). They described this as a structural weakness and convincingly showed that there was containment of Japanese lawyers and "subordination of legal practitioners and the justice system to a technocratic and paternalist ideology" in the field of power (131).[33]

While I agree basically with Dezalay and Garth's interpretation of the formation of structures in the field of power in Japan,[34] I would like to emphasize the significance of the effects of the post-war reform, which have comparatively weakened the subordination of lawyers and the judicial system to bureaucrats and technocrats. The impact of defeat and the post-war Allied occupation was so great that various ideas from Anglo-American law came into Japan and spread rapidly and extensively. This occurred at the expense of traditional legal concepts, which had been mainly based upon continental European law (Tanaka 1976, 249–52; Haley 1991, 105–6; Oda 1992, 31–34; Haley 1998, 61–62, 71, 103–4). Above all, the idea of the "rule of law" was appealing and influential as a new legal value among young lawyers and law professors. The emergence of the new model of attorneys as a member of the legal profession instead of the traditional model of lawyers in the opposition camp is a good example. The new constitution of 1946 vests courts with the power to determine the constitutionality of any law, and the courts lie outside the jurisdiction of the Ministry of Justice (Noda 1976, 119–24). Thus, until the 1960s, the judiciary was not as restrained in cases involving political issues as they were during the pre-war period. Liberal opinions were expressed by a considerable number of judges in the lower courts and a few judges on the Supreme Court (Abe 1995, 315).

---

33. Dezalay and Garth, relying on works by Haley (1991) and others, attribute the formation of the present structure of the legal field in Japan to the legal controls and containment of attorneys in the 1930s pursued by the political elite. At that time, they say, a compromise might have been struck between the elite of the bar and the bureaucrats (Dezalay and Garth 1997, 129–30). They also explain the results of the reform just after the end of the Second World War, which "concretized" the segmentation of the legal field (130). Although their explanation is illuminating, it seems to me that their theoretical perspective underestimates cultural factors and historical legacies since pre-modern times (cf. Rokumoto 1986 and Wollschläger 1997). Further detailed and empirical studies are yet to be done (see also note 34 below).

34. Their thesis remains to be examined by historical studies based upon firsthand material. See, for example, Wollschläger (1997, especially 102n40, 131–33) for his critical comments on Haley's conclusion (1978) that institutional incapacities, especially deficiencies of the court system, were responsible for the sudden decrease in civil litigation in Japan in the 1930s. Wollschläger suggests that the institutional incapacity, if it ever existed at all, should be interpreted as an additional cause in the fundamental historical trends of the low rate of civil litigation per population, which can be traced back to the Tokugawa period. Wollschläger (1997, 131) also notes that the civil litigation wave since the early years of the Meiji period until around 1890 was caused by the Matsukata finance crisis and concludes that it was only an accidental and exceptional event.

However, in the early 1970s, responding to a political campaign against purported socialist or communist judges by the then-ruling Liberal Democratic Party (LDP), the Japanese judicial elite made every effort to minimize intervention in political matters (Abe 1995, 314–18). That was really a turning point in the history of the Japanese judicial branch in the post-war period. The process of widening the legal domain was slowed down in a tense political climate. Since then, the judiciary has come to pay more deference to decision-making by the political branches of government (Abe 1995, 318–19).[35] As Masaki Abe analyzed correctly, this judicial turn to self-restraint means avoidance of politics in order to preserve and reinforce the organizational autonomy of judicial power (316–17).[36] In Dezalay and Garth's terminology, it appears that a bargain was tacitly struck between the judicial elite and the political elite in order to reestablish and confirm "the boundary that separated the world of law and that of the technocracy" (Dezalay and Garth 1997, 129). This resulted both in self-restraint leaning toward conservatism by judges and powerful bureaucratic control of lower court judges by the General Secretariat of the Supreme Court (Ramseyer and Rosenbluth 1993; Miyazawa 1994b, 191–219 and 1994a; Abe 1995). However, as Dezalay and Garth (1997, 131) suggest, "the relationship among law, business, and the state is not necessarily stable."

The legal domain in Japan has expanded gradually until recently. In order to show the present state of Japanese lawyers in transition, I will focus on the mechanisms for controlling the number of lawyers and recent attempts for institutional reform. The population of lawyers is one of the basic conditions upon which the legal domain is constructed. In Japan, lawyers have been constantly limited in number, which is rather exceptional in industrial societies. Government committees, bar associations, legal scholars, and the mass media have taken up the issue of the lawyer population, and, as a result, not only were minor reforms realized, but also some major changes. A brief look at this issue will show that behind the political process of reform lie forceful economic factors which are simultaneously pushing the development of corporate legal practice in Japan.

C. Mechanisms Controlling the Number of Lawyers

One of the distinguishing characteristics determining the number of fully qualified lawyers is an artificial control at the level of qualification. The great majority of new entrants into the Japanese legal profession each year consist of graduates of the Legal Training and Research Institute or LTRI (*shihō kenshūjo*), who are admitted to the LTRI if they pass the national bar exam.[37] In effect, the

---

35. See also Miyazawa (1994a) and Haley (1995).

36. See also Haley (1995, 10–12). But cf. Miyazawa (1994a, 277–80).

37. For an account of the institutional mechanisms for recruiting and educating lawyers including training at the Legal Training and Research Institute, see Ramseyer (1986); Rokumoto (1988, 165–66, 174–77); Haley (1991, 106–11); Ōta and Rokumoto (1993, 318–20); Henderson (1997, 55–57); Haley (1998, 40–46); Ramseyer and Nakazato (1998, 6–9).

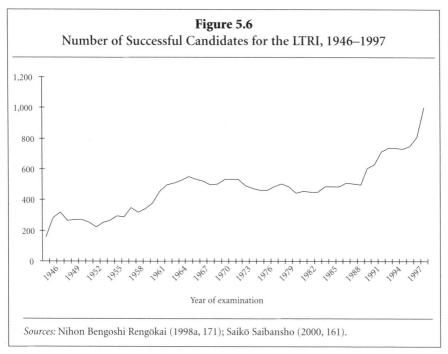

Figure 5.6

Number of Successful Candidates for the LTRI, 1946–1997

Year of examination

Sources: Nihon Bengoshi Rengōkai (1998a, 171); Saikō Saibansho (2000, 161).

number of successful candidates for the institute is the primary determinant of how many newly qualified lawyers are available for the legal profession (upon completion of the LTRI's eighteen-month course). From the middle of the 1960s until the beginning of the 1990s, the number of successful candidates for the institute was maintained continuously at around 500 each year (Figure 5.6). From 1991, the number of applicants who passed the national bar exam gradually increased and finally reached 1,000 in 1999 (Shihō Seido Kaikaku Shingikai 2001), resulting in a slight and gradual increase in the number of fully qualified lawyers. Because the number of judges and public prosecutors was fixed at a very low level, the result was a slight and gradual increase in the number of practicing attorneys (Figure 5.1).[38] If we compare this with other highly developed countries, the situation in Japan seems quite unusual. In many western countries, the recent rapid increase of law graduates resulted in a growing number of lawyers, especially of private practitioners.

By contrast, in Japan, the dramatic increase in law program graduates since the 1960s (Hōmu Daijin Kanbō 1991, 121) has not resulted in a corresponding increase in the number of lawyers. In the late 1980s, the total number of graduates from undergraduate law faculties per year was estimated to be around

---

38. Japan had 2,949 judges (including summary court judges) and 2,223 public prosecutors (including assistant public prosecutors) in 1999. The number of judges was 2,139 in 1949, 2,475 in 1964, and 2,747 in 1980. The number of public prosecutors was 1,667 in 1949, 1,829 in 1964, and 2,092 in 1980 (see Saikō Saibansho 2000, 157. See also Haley 1991, 96–111).

37,000,[39] but only about 500 successfully passed the national bar exam required to enter the LTRI. The number of applicants for entrance into the LTRI is quite large. Every year more than 20,000 (e.g., 27,112 in 1997) apply, but the acceptance rate has been kept at about 3 percent since the late 1960s (Hōmu Daijin Kanbō 1991, 64; Hori 1998, 80; Ramseyer and Nakazato 1998, 7). Some believe the national bar exam is extremely and unreasonably difficult, and that as a result, many young law students who may otherwise become good lawyers avoid even applying and instead choose other promising careers. As early as 1963, Justice Hattori (1963, 141–43), who went on to become chief justice of the Supreme Court, noted that "the legal profession as a whole does not necessarily recruit the most promising graduates of the law departments."

Why is the acceptance rate kept at such a low level? This is a question often raised by foreign observers. It is difficult to convincingly explain the low number of lawyers to people who have no knowledge of the cultural and institutional basis of the Japanese legal system.[40] Various factors, cultural and institutional, are intertwined. They have much to do with the "enigma" of how Japan can cope without many lawyers in a highly industrialized society. Although this should be analyzed in the wider context of Japanese society, I can present here a rather simple explanation by narrowing my focus to the institutional mechanisms that determine the number of lawyers.

In order to qualify as a lawyer (which not only *bengoshi* but also judges and prosecutors had to do), one had to pass the national bar exam and enter the LTRI, although section five of the Practicing Attorney Law of 1949 provides several exceptions. From 1965 until 1990, the number of successful candidates for the LTRI was around 500 each year, which corresponded to the seating capacity of the hall at the institute (Nihon Hōritsuka Kyōkai 1982, 67–70, 97–99; Ōta and Rokumoto 1993, 320). The capacity of the institute was a de facto ceiling. Some leading legal scholars argued for an increase in the number of admitted students but failed.[41]

---

39. See Hōmu Daijin Kanbō (1991, 120), which shows that the total capacity for faculty of law students per grade or year was about 37,000 in the late 1980s. The dropout rate was negligible. The capacity is prescribed formally by university regulations and rules; however, each university often admits more students within a certain limit. This implies that the real number of students is larger. However, I must also note that some of the law faculties of Japanese universities include students who are not majoring in law.

40. Haley (1991, 110–11) finds difficulties in "explaining the causal factors behind the government restrictions" on the number of people admitted to the LTRI, and he presents a few tentative explanations, while Ramseyer and Nakazato (1998, 6) simply say the "dearth of lawyers results from government policy."

41. One of the advocates for increasing the number of lawyers was Akira Mikazuki, Emeritus Professor of Law at the University of Tokyo. In 1987, the Ministry of Justice appointed him as a member of the Informal Committee on Fundamental Problems of the Legal Profession (*hōsō kihon mondai kondankai*) to discuss the lawyer population problem. Later, he was appointed minister of justice.

To increase the number of lawyers, it would be necessary to expand the capacity of the LTRI and to reform its basic scheme of education and training, which would mean an increase in funds allocated from the national budget. In this respect, one should note that the judicial apprentices of the institute receive salaries from the government. The JFBA, which is not only the professional lawyers association at a national level but also a powerful pressure group, has been guaranteed an opportunity to participate in the decision-making process for major institutional reform concerning judicial matters. Formally, the JFBA has either consistently opposed, or shown no interest in, an increase in the number of lawyers. Until the late 1980s, the other two major players, namely the General Secretariat of the Supreme Court and the Ministry of Justice, were also inactive in increasing the number of lawyers, despite their heavy caseloads and backlogs.

The opposition and passivity by the JFBA can be easily understood. Most attorneys may have wanted to protect vested interests in the current system by sticking to a Malthusian strategy that they believed would benefit solo and small-sized practitioners, the vast majority of attorneys. But why have the judicial bureaucrats of the General Secretariat of the Supreme Court and the Ministry of Justice not done more to increase the number of judges and public prosecutors? Without empirical studies, one can only offer a hypothesis. The relatively weak position of the judicial administration in the political process, especially vis-à-vis the Ministry of Finance, may have much to do with the inaction by the General Secretariat of the Supreme Court and the Ministry of Justice. However, it is too early to conclude that the Ministry of Finance was in control. I suggest that the elite judges at the General Secretariat of the Supreme Court who managed the judicial system may have been satisfied with the present number of judges and public prosecutors as long as an adequate number of promising young recruits continued to be found.

Setsuo Miyazawa (1994a, 279) goes further. In "Administrative Control of Japanese Judges," he concludes that

> the reduction of the size and authority of the Japanese judiciary can be understood as a rational behavior from the perspective of elite judges. An expanded judiciary will make it more difficult for them to control other judges and increase chances for the public to challenge the government. Elite judges seem to find satisfaction in their role as a rear guard of the status quo of the government.

Dan Fenno Henderson (1997, 56) simply comments that "the real reason for the small bar is that, once a member, lawyers also prefer a small bar and the bureaucracy has no incentive to implement a rule-of-law."

From a wider perspective, neither the major political parties nor the mass media launched a campaign to increase the number of lawyers until recently. The administrative bureaucracy also remained silent, which was natural because more lawyers might threaten their power and influence. In this sense, the extremely low passage rate of the national bar exam can be understood as reflecting a partly consensual national policy.

In summary, the national bar exam and the education and training system of the LTRI have been the institutional mechanisms determining the number and the pace of the increase of practicing attorneys (Figures 5.1, 5.6, and 5.7). These two mechanisms are embedded within political processes in a broad sense. The mechanisms for controlling the number of lawyers are centralized and well managed as demonstrated above.[42]

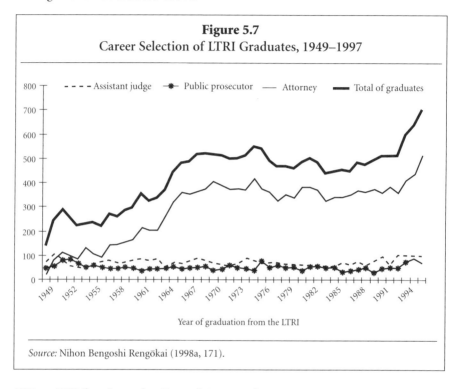

Figure 5.7
Career Selection of LTRI Graduates, 1949–1997

Year of graduation from the LTRI

Source: Nihon Bengoshi Rengōkai (1998a, 171).

III. Widening the Legal Domain

The situation has changed remarkably since the late 1980s. Just after the introduction of the Foreign Lawyers Law of 1986, which allowed branch offices of foreign law firms to operate under limited conditions, the Ministry of Justice began campaigning for reform of the national bar exam. In 1987, the ministry formed an ad hoc panel, the Informal Committee on Fundamental Problems of the Legal Profession for the purpose of reviewing the national bar exam (Hōmu

---

42. Ramseyer (1986, 530) describes the mechanisms to determine the number of new lawyers in Japan as a "bureaucratic control" over admissions ("the Ministries of Justice and Finance effectively determine the number of new lawyers by determining the number of places in the Legal Training and Research Institute") (see also his footnote at 126). I would like to emphasize that the "control," if one may use this term, is better understood in the context of Japanese informal and consensual decision-making processes. My explanation in the text might be helpful to show one aspect of those processes.

Daijin Kanbō 1987). The panel was composed of thirteen members and held ten sessions over about a year. The final report of the panel was published in March 1988. Based upon the report, the Ministry of Justice in April 1988 published a tentative plan for reform of the national bar exam. One of the major proposals of the plan was to increase the annual number of entrants into the LTRI to 700 (Hōmu Daijin Kanbō 1991, 10; Ōta and Rokumoto 1993, 331–32). The ministry's major objective seemed to be the recruitment of young and smart law students, especially those seeking to become public prosecutors. The Ministry of Justice had faced a chronic shortage of public prosecutors for many years (Hōmu Daijin Kanbō 1987, 68).

In addition, the General Secretariat of the Supreme Court and some influential members of the bar, including senior partners of large law firms specializing in international business matters, were also concerned about the shortage of young lawyers. Due to the rapid expansion of the international legal market in Japan, many of the young attorneys were absorbed into that market in the 1980s. Some major firms succeeded in recruiting bright qualified graduates from the LTRI who might otherwise have started their careers as judges. Still, the shortage of new attorneys was evident for senior partners of large law firms in Tokyo.

As a result of the shortage, the elite members of the bar, the bench, and the Ministry of Justice seemed to share an interest in increasing the number of new entrants into the profession. In addition, the elite members of the bar, especially some of those on the executive committees, apparently thought it was time to consider the lawyer population problem not only from the viewpoint of corporate legal practice but also from the perspective of general legal services and access to justice.[43]

The environment surrounding the legal profession has changed distinctly since that time. Rapid internationalization of the economy in the 1980s made it evident that the justice system had to become more effective and accessible and that the national bar exam had to be reformed in order to attract many talented people who would otherwise take lucrative corporate jobs. The business elite and the mass media began to criticize the conservative attitudes of the Japanese legal profession, particularly the bar, toward the issue of increasing the lawyer population.[44]

In 1990, the JFBA, the Supreme Court, and the Ministry of Justice negotiated an agreement to raise the annual number of students admitted to the LTRI to 700 as a first step toward reform (Hōmu Daijin Kanbō 1991, 12, 34–35). In the next stage, the Supreme Court and the Ministry of Justice proposed to raise the number of entrants to 1,000 per year within a few years and to 1,500 in the near

---

43. Information from my interview of a partner in an international law firm in Tokyo in 1987 (unpublished transcript, July 16, 1987, on file with this author). See also Higuchi (1987, 37–38); Zadankai (1987, 6–7) (comments by Masao Ōno).

44. See, e.g., Keizai Dōyūkai (1994); Suzuki (1995); Miyake (1995).

future (Mura 1995).[45] Initially the JFBA proposed a raise to only 800 per year. However, it finally agreed to an increase that accommodated approximately 1,000 entrants per year starting in 1999 with the condition that the number of judges and public prosecutors be increased at the same time (NBR 1995, 97–101; Mura 1995 and 1996, 39–41). From 1999 to 2003, the annual number of successful candidates for the LTRI rose from around 1,000 to 1,170, with 1,500 planned for 2004 (Shihō Seido Kaikaku Shingikai 2001).[46]

The issue of the population of lawyers cannot be understood properly without taking into consideration the wider political and economic context. First, one of the leading industrial associations, the Japan Association of Corporate Executives or JACE (*keizai dōyūkai*) recommended in 1994 that the capacity of the judiciary should be expanded to cover unmet legal needs (Keizai Dōyūkai 1994). JACE diagnosed the present condition of the Japanese judiciary and the legal system in general as one of "serious malaise." This announcement was remarkable; the business elite had rarely shown much interest in the judiciary and lawyers. This change in attitude was a prelude to a new era. Not long after the announcement, in December 1994, the government established the Administrative Reform Committee (*gyōsei kaikaku iinkai*), which had a subcommission for deregulation (*kisei kanwa shō-iinkai*). One of the major issues on the agenda of the subcommission was an increase in the population of lawyers. The subcommission criticized the monopoly practices by Japanese attorneys.[47] In December 1995, the Administrative Reform Committee published a report recommending a substantial increase in the number of lawyers, judges, and public prosecutors (Gyōsei Kaikaku Iinkai 1996).[48] In addition, the government targeted a substantial increase in the population of lawyers as a necessary measure for deregulating the Japanese economy. On March 29, 1996, the Cabinet decided to revise the program for promoting deregulation of the Japanese economy. A substantial increase in the number of lawyers, including judges and public prosecutors, was offered as a specific measure for deregulation (Kakugi Kettei 1996). On March 28, 1997, the Cabinet again decided to revise the program in order to enlarge the specific measures for deregulation with respect to providing legal services (Kakugi Kettei 1997). In 1998, the Japan Federation of

---

45. Seemingly anticipating the policy change, a new building for the LTRI was built at Wakō, Saitama with a hall that seats more than 1,000 students.

46. In order to raise the number of entrants to the LTRI, a shorter course of training was proposed by the Ministry of Justice and the Supreme Court. At first, the bar was very critical of the proposal. However, the JFBA finally decided at an extraordinary general meeting on October 16, 1997 to support the proposal for shortening the term of training from two years to one and a half years (see NBR 1997). In 1998, the Diet passed an amendment to the Courts Law (*saibanshohō*) to shorten the term of training to one and a half years. With the new bar exam of 2006, there are suggestions that the training period may be further reduced to one year.

47. See Suzuki (1995, 176–78).

48. For critical comments on the report of the Administrative Reform Committee, see, for example, Odanaka (1997).

Economic Organizations (*keizai dantai rengōkai* or *keidanren*) published *Opinions on Reform of the Justice System* (Keizai Dantai Rengōkai 1998). In the same year, the ruling LDP's Special Committee made public a report on the judicial system (Jiyū Minshutō 1998). It proposed to establish a deliberative council to discuss fundamental reform of the judicial system.

Second, the bureaucracy in Japan has faced major transformation since the early 1990s. The authority of the bureaucrats has been under constant attack following the collapse of the bubble economy of the late 1980s. The legitimacy of the authority and power of the bureaucrats, especially those of the Ministry of Finance, was shaken. As John O. Haley shows in *Authority without Power* (1991, 139–68), the frequent or almost constant resort to informal enforcement of rules by administrations in Japan can be explained by two factors: the predominance of promotional as opposed to regulatory policies, and the weakness of formal law enforcement. A main objective of past administrations was to promote the growth of industries and to coordinate conflicts of business interests through informal measures rather than legal coercion. Recent economic conditions have undermined a consensus for the so-called catch-up industrial policy that has enjoyed long-standing support in post-war Japan. Promotional policies are gradually losing ground to regulatory policies. At the same time, economic conditions have influenced trends toward the institutionalization of formalized administrative procedures and more coercive powers for law enforcement. As a result, the system of "consensual governance" (Haley 1991) has been in a period of transition.

The LDP-led coalition government established the Justice System Reform Council or JSRC (*shihō seido kaikaku shingikai*) under the Cabinet in July 1999. The statutory mission of the council was to "consider fundamental measures necessary for judicial reform and judicial infrastructure arrangement by defining the role of the Japanese administration of justice in the twenty-first century" (Article 2 of the Law Concerning the Establishment of the JSRC). The agenda of the council included major increases in the lawyer population, reform of the legal education and training system, public participation in the judicial system, reform of the appointment and promotion system of judges, and deregulation of legal services. The establishment of the JSRC marked a new phase in the widening of the legal domain.[49] The final report, issued in June 2001 (Shihō Seido Kaikaku Shingikai 2001), and the implementation of its recommendations, has necessarily made a substantial impact on the judicial system and legal profession. The final report recommended that the number of successful candidates for the LTRI each year be increased with the aim of reaching 1,500 in 2004

---

49. Business interests and neo-liberal ideology played a major role in the establishment of the Justice System Reform Council. However, values of democratic liberalism also contributed substantially to the deliberations of the council. Progressive attorneys and legal academics exerted considerable influence, directly or indirectly, on the deliberations. A representative of consumer interests participated in the deliberations as a member of the council. The JSRC was a focal point where various interests and ideologies confronted one another.

and 3,000 in about 2010. The total number of lawyers, including judges and public prosecutors, is expected to reach 50,000 in 2018 (compared to the total of 20,730 lawyers in 1999).

The business and political elite may have come to realize that the segmentation and marginalization of the legal domain is weakening the bases of their very power and rule, such as the sustained growth of the Japanese economy. The end of rapid growth of the economy and Japan's increasing involvement in the global economy is transforming the structure of the field of law and power. Reforms promoting a considerable increase in the lawyer population are a significant step toward widening the domain of the law and lawyers in Japan. This step is considered necessary for a more internationalized and deregulated economy.[50]

Conclusion

Generally speaking, the Japanese economy has drawn its strength from an indigenous ordering mechanism based on relationalism and informality. The normal functioning of the economy is achieved with relatively little input from attorneys and law firms. The recent growth of corporate demand for lawyers does not necessarily mean the fundamental transformation of the pattern of socio-legal ordering in the economy. The litigation risk which companies face every day remains comparatively low. The limiting factors of the supply side have reinforced the basic pattern of the ordering of the Japanese economy. Informal and relational mechanisms are widespread and even penetrate formal organizations. Reciprocity between the parties in long-term and continuing relationships still plays an important role, even between businesses and government agencies. As long as this pattern of informal, extralegal ordering of the economy remains rational and politically viable, it will survive and continue to determine the functioning of legal institutions.

There exists, therefore, a kind of built-in reinforcing mechanism ordering the Japanese economy. This mechanism tends to eliminate seeds of new patterns of ordering and to obstruct the development of new patterns that might threaten the traditional socio-legal order of the economy, one based on reciprocity between corporations and marginality of legal institutions, including lawyers.[51] This sort of inertia is culturally influenced and systemically rooted; therefore, socio-legal ordering can change itself only little by little. Formal legal institutions are unable to respond to the new circumstances quickly.[52] Still,

---

50. I do not expect that the basic structure of the "public law regime" of Japan as compared to the "private law regime" of the West—see Haley (1991, 10–11)—will transform itself, but private initiative in law enforcement will be stronger if the legal domain becomes wider. This will also mean a greater role for lawyers in private practice.

51. For the concept of complementarity and interconnectedness of economic institutions, see Aoki (1994; 1995, 18–25, 191–221).

52. For the concept of institutional inertia, see Aoki (1994, 22, 31). See also Ramseyer and Rosenbluth (1995, especially 160–66) analyzing pre-war Japanese politics and showing convincingly significant aspects of institutional inertia.

Japan seems to be at a crossroads now, where reform of its economic and legal institutions is understood to be necessary to make the socio-legal order of its economy more legalistic and formal.[53] In this respect, forthcoming judicial reforms are fundamentally important.

The globalization of the world economy and a deepening of the interdependence among major economies require the so-called harmonization of economic institutions among the major industrial societies to a certain extent. The Japanese economy cannot escape this trend. It is true that what is most important is the degree of harmonization and the way it happens, but nonetheless, major institutional reforms have been taking place rather rapidly in several areas and these are important also. In addition to the reform of the national bar exam and the enactment of the Foreign Lawyers Law mentioned above, I point to the enactment of the Administrative Procedure Act of 1993, the amendment of the Commercial Code in 1993[54] to give shareholders economic incentives to file a derivative action (i.e., a liability suit on behalf of and for the benefit of the company against directors engaged in activities which are illegal or against the interests of the company and that have caused damages), and the enactment of the Products Liability Act in 1994.[55] The Fair Trade Commission is enforcing the Anti-Monopoly Law and Regulations more strictly and severely against businesses engaged in illegal actions. Financial regulatory reforms in recent years have been so far-reaching that a new rules-based system seems to be emerging. These reforms in the 1990s culminated with the establishment of the Justice System Reform Council. The forthcoming judicial reforms will lead to a stronger legalization of the Japanese economy. Of course, the point is how legal and in what way it will be, and that is a matter for future research.

In "Retail Convergence: The Structural Impediments Initiative and the Regulation of the Japanese Retail Industry," Frank Upham (1996) showed that the globalization of the economy has not changed the degree of Japanese legal informality.[56] However, recent movement toward legal and judicial reform is already notable, because members of the Japanese business elite and leading politicians have committed themselves to the reform, using the rhetoric of the "rule of law." The bar has also taken the offensive since 1990 when the JFBA

---

53. The basic pattern of relationships among Japanese companies may be transformed, to some extent, in the near future. See, for example, Murakami and Rohlen (1992, 100–105).

54. See West (1994) and Milhaupt (1996, 55–57).

55. See Nottage and Wada (1999, 331–44).

56. Focusing on the issue of the regulation of the Japanese retail industry, Upham (1996) analyzes the impact of the Structural Impediments Initiative on the Japanese legal system. He concludes, "the fundamental legal nature of Japanese economic regulation has not changed. The legal informality that allowed the privatization of the process in the 1980s remains throughout Japanese government activity and even within retailing regulation." But Milhaupt (1996) and Milhaupt and Miller (1997), analyzing corporate governance and the financial market, emphasize the changing aspects toward more legalized ordering in the recent Japanese political economy.

declared that it would pursue judicial reform. Conflicts within the bar regarding the nature of reforms have continued. Issues include the size of the lawyer population in Japan, limits on the deregulation of restrictive legal practices, reform of the legal education and training system, and changes in the system of recruiting judges, to mention a few.[57] However, the bar's commitment to reform is now firmly established.

The implementation of the final report of the Justice System Reform Council will facilitate and accelerate the process of widening the legal domain and might transform the present set of relationships among private business, government, and law. Although the final report of the JSRC did not recommend abandoning the quota system for new entrants into the legal profession, it clearly proposed a considerable and fairly rapid increase in the number of new entrants. There will be an increase in the number of judges and public prosecutors as well. The report also called for a drastic overhaul of legal education, proposing the introduction of American-style law schools at the graduate level. The review and deliberations of the JSRC, which continued for two years, seem to have contributed to a shift in dominant legal ideology. "From ex ante co-ordinations by administrative discretion to ex post monitors by rule-bound judiciary" was a leading idea of the final report. The impact of judicial reform on the Japanese economy may be widespread. However, the point is how and to what extent the indigenous socio-legal ordering or "law in action" will be transformed. A widening of the legal domain does not necessarily mean a fundamental change in the traditional pattern of social organizations and interpersonal and corporate relationships.

Against the background of a changing economy and polity, major actors are now competing and struggling in the field of law and power. The results of this struggle may bring about the construction of a new structure, but it might result in the co-opting of the forces for change. On the one hand, economic forces and political interests will drive the struggle powerfully. On the other hand, the traditional pattern of social ordering and government will still continue to shape the process and results of the struggle to a considerable extent.

As changing legal landscapes in the West during the last few decades suggest, a rapid increase in the lawyer population will result in a distinctive growth of corporate law firms, which should necessarily facilitate division and stratification of the legal profession. Large corporate law firms may occupy a smaller but more powerful, influential, and prestigious "hemisphere" (Heinz and Laumann 1982), as is often the case in the West. Corporate lawyers may play a major role in ordering the Japanese economy, competing and cooperating with administrative bureaucrats. However, the competition and cooperation is not limited or localized, but interconnects with the wider context of politics, economy, and society. An emerging structure might still be within reach of the traditional fundamental pattern. A challenging and significant task facing sociologists of law will be to identify the results and consequences of the widening of the legal domain.

---

57. See, e.g., NBR (1998a).

Works Cited

Abe, Masaki. 1995. The internal control of a bureaucratic judiciary: The case of Japan. 23 *International Journal of the Sociology of Law* 303.

Aoki, Masahiko. 1994. The Japanese firm as a system of attributes: A survey and research agenda. In *The Japanese firm: The sources of competitive strength,* eds. M. Aoki and R. Dore. Oxford: Oxford University Press.

———. 1995. *Keizai shisutemu no shinka to tagensei* [Evolution and variety of economic systems]. Tokyo: Tōyō Keizai Shinpōsha.

Bourdieu, Pierre. 1987. The force of law: Toward a sociology of the juridical field. Translated by Richard Terdiman. 38 *Hastings Law Journal* 805.

Daini Tokyo Bengoshikai, Shihō Kaikaku Suishin Niben Honbu [Second Tokyo Bar Association, head office for promoting judicial system reform]. 1996. *Shimin no tame no shihō e* [Toward a justice responsible to citizens]. Tokyo: Daini Tokyo Bengoshikai.

———. 1997. *Bengoshikai chūsai no genjō to tenbō* [The present state of and prospects for arbitration established by the Bar]. Tokyo: Hanrei Taimuzusha.

Degawa, Kazuo. 1986. *Kigyō hōmu no kōzō to tenkai* [Structure and development of corporate legal practice]. Tokyo: Hōrei Sōgō Shuppan.

Dezalay, Yves and Bryant G. Garth. 1997. Law, lawyers and social capital: "Rule of law" versus relational capitalism. 6 *Social and Legal Studies* 1:109.

Galanter, Mark and Thomas Palay. 1991. *Tournament of lawyers: The transformation of the big law firm.* Chicago: University of Chicago Press.

Gyōsei Kaikaku Iinkai [Administrative Reform Committee]. 1996. Kisei kanwa no sokushin ni kansuru iken—shō [Opinions on the promotion of deregulation—a summary]. 47 *Jiyū to Seigi* [Liberty and justice, the monthly journal of the JFBA] 2:134.

Haley, John Owen. 1978. The myth of the reluctant litigant. *Journal of Japanese Studies* 4 (2): 350.

———. 1991. *Authority without power: Law and the Japanese paradox.* New York: Oxford University Press.

———. 1995. Judicial independence in Japan revisited. *Law in Japan: An Annual* 1.

———. 1998. *The spirit of Japanese law.* Athens: University of Georgia Press.

Hamano, Ryo. 1989. Gaikokuhō jimu bengoshi seido no dōnyū to sono inpakuto [Japan's new foreign lawyers law and its impact]. *Hōshakaigaku* [Sociology of law] 41:168.

———. 1991. Tokyo no bengoshi ni yoru kigyō kankei hōmu shori no genjō [The present state of handling of corporate legal matters by attorneys in Tokyo]. *Hōshakaigaku* 43:155.

————. 1993–94. Bengoshi ni yoru kigyō hōmu no shori (1)-(12) [Attorneys and their handling of corporate legal matters]. *NBL* [New business law] 530: 6–17; 532:35–41; 533:35–39; 537:36–41; 539:38–41; 542:43–47; 550:60–71; 552:61–65; 555:42–49; 557:47–51; 558:61–66; 559:52–57.

————. 1994a. Bengoshi ni yoru kigyō hōmu no shori (7) [Attorneys and their handling of corporate legal matters]. *NBL* 550:60–71.

————. 1994b. Bengoshi ni yoru kigyō hōmu no shori (10) [Attorneys and their handling of corporate legal matters]. *NBL* 557:47–51.

————. 1996. Lawyers in Tokyo and their work for businesses. *Rikkyō Hōgaku* [Rikkyō journal of law and politics] 43:218.

————. 1997a. Hōka shakai ni okeru bengoshi yakuwari ron [The role of lawyers in a legalized society]. In *Atarashii seiki e no bengoshi-zō* [Perspectives on attorneys for the new century], ed. Nihon Bengoshi Rengōkai Henshū Iinkai [JFBA Editorial Committee]. Tokyo: Yūhikaku.

————. 1997b. Nihon no keizai shakai no hōka [Legalization in the Japanese economy]. *Rikkyō Hōgaku* 48:53.

————. 1998. Japanese lawyers in transition. *Rikkyō Hōgaku* 49:306.

————. 2001. Keizai funsō no hōteki shori [Legal resolution of business disputes]. In *Meiji, Taishō, machi no hōso* [A town practitioner in the Meiji and Taishō era], ed. Y. Kawaguchi. Tokyo: Hōsei Daigaku Shuppankyoku.

Hara, Yoshimichi. 1935. Ah, Hanai kun [A farewell to Mr. Hanai]. In *Hanai Takuzō zenden (ge-kan)* [Biography of Hanai Takuzō, vol. 2], ed. G. Ōki. Tokyo: Hanai Takuzō Zenden Hensanjo [Editorial committee of the biography of Takuzō Hanai].

Hattori, Takaaki. 1963. The legal profession in Japan: Its historical development and present state. In *Law in Japan: The legal order in a changing society*, ed. A. von Mehren. Cambridge, MA: Harvard University Press.

Hayashiya, Reiji and Ikuo Sugawara, eds. 2001. *Detamukku minji soshō (dai 2-han)* [Data book: Civil litigation, 2nd edition]. Tokyo: Yūhikaku.

Heinz, John P. and Edward D. Laumann. 1982. *Chicago lawyers: The social structure of the Bar*. New York: Russell Sage Foundation and American Bar Foundation.

Henderson, Dan Fenno. 1997. The role of lawyers in Japan. In *Japan: Economic success and legal system*, ed. H. Baum. New York: Walter de Gruyter.

Higuchi, Shunji. 1987. Hōsō jinkō to shihō shiken kaikaku [Lawyer population and reform of the national bar examination]. 892 *Jurisuto* [Jurist] 37.

Hirowatari, Seigo. 1997. Nihon shakai no hōka [Legalization in Japanese society]. In *Gendai hōgaku no shisō to hōhō* [Ideas and methods of modern jurisprudence], eds. M. Iwamura, et al. Tokyo: Iwanami Shoten.

Hōmu Daijin Kanbō, ed. 1987. Jinjika [Personnel Department]. *Shihō shiken kaikaku o kangaeru: Kihon shiryōshū* [A study on reform of the national bar examination: A collection of basic information]. Tokyo: Yūhikaku.

———. 1991. Shihō Hōsei Chōsabu [Department of Research on the Judicial and Legal System]. *Hōsō yōsei seido kaikaku: Shihō shiken wa kō kawaru* [Reform of the training of legal professionals: The national bar examination will change this way]. Tokyo: Yūhikaku.

Hori, Tsuguaki. 1998. Heisei 9-nendo shihō shiken dai 2-ji shiken no kekka ni tsuite [On the results of the second stage of the National Legal Examination in the year of 1997]. 1132 *Jurisuto* 69.

Hōritsu Fujo Seido Kenkyūkai [Research Committee on the Legal Aid System]. 1998. Hōkokusho [Report]. 1137 *Jurisuto* 56.

Ishii, Seiichi, ed. 1970. *Bengoshi no shimei, rinri* [Lawyers' tasks and ethics]. Tokyo: Nihon Hyōronsha.

Ishimura, Zensuke. 1969. *Gendai no purofesshon* [Professions today]. Tokyo: Shiseido.

Jiyū Minshutō [Liberal Democratic Party]. 1998. *Shihō seido tokubetsu iinkai hōkoku* [Report by the Special Committee on the Judicial System]. 49 *Jiyū to Seigi* 8:94.

Kakugi Kettei [Cabinet meeting decision]. 1996. Kisei kanwa suishin keikaku no kaitei ni tsuite—shō [On the revision of the plan for promoting deregulation—a summary]. 47 *Jiyū to Seigi* 6:179–81.

———. 1997. Kisei kanwa suishin keikaku no sai-kaitei ni tsuite—shō [On the second revision of the plan for promoting deregulation—a summary]. 48 *Jiyū to Seigi* 5:155.

Kawashima, Takeyoshi. 1963. Dispute resolution in contemporary Japan. In *Law in Japan: The legal order in a changing society*, ed. A. von Mehren. Cambridge, MA: Harvard University Press.

Keiei Hōyūkai [Association of Japanese Corporate Legal Departments], ed. 1986. Kaisha hōmubu [The corporate legal department]. *NBL* 16 (special issue).

Keiei Hōyūkai and Shōji Hōmu Kenkyūkai [Association of Japanese Corporate Legal Departments and the Commercial Law Center, Inc]. 1996. *Kaisha hōmubu* [The corporate legal department]. Tokyo: Shōji Hōmu Kenkyūkai.

Keizai Dantai Rengōkai (Keidanren) [Japan Federation of Economic Organizations]. 1998. Shihō seido kaikaku ni tsuite no iken [Opinions on the reform of the justice system]. *NBL* 642:4.

Keizai Dōyūkai [Japan Association of Corporate Executives]. 1994. *Gendai Nihon shakai no byōri to shohō* [Japan's social malaise and its remedies]. Tokyo: Keizai Dōyūkai.

Koga, Masayoshi. 1970. Nihon bengoshi-shi no kihonteki shomondai [Basic issues in the history of Japanese lawyers]. In *Bengoshi no gyōmu, keiei* [Lawyers' practice and management], ed. M. Koga. Tokyo: Nihon Hyōronsha.

Kojima, Takeshi. 1981. *Bengoshi* [Practicing attorney]. Tokyo: Gakuyō Shobo.

———. 1986. Seijuku-ki o mukaeta kigyō hōmubu no kadai to tenbō [Problems and prospects of the corporate legal department in maturity]. *NBL* 16:6.

Kubori, Hideaki. 1993. Kyōdō hōritsu jimusho no keiei [Management of law firms]. In *Henkaku no naka no bengoshi (ge)* [Attorneys in reform, vol. 2], eds. K. Miyakawa, M. Koyama, K. Nasu, and H. Kubori. Tokyo: Yūhikaku.

Marushima, Shunsuke. 1996. Higisha kokusen bengo seido no jitsugen ni mukatte [Toward establishing state subsidized legal advice and representation for criminal suspects]. 47 *Jiyū to Seigi* 12:24.

Milhaupt, Curtis J. 1996. A relational theory of Japanese corporate governance: Contract, culture, and the rule of law. 37 *Harvard International Law Journal* 3.

Milhaupt, Curtis J. and Geoffrey P. Miller. 1997. Cooperation, conflict, and convergence in Japanese finance: Evidence from the "*Jūsen*" problem. 29 *Law & Policy in International Business* 1.

Mitani, Taichirō. 1980. *Kindai Nihon no shihōken to seitō* [The judicial branch and political parties in modern Japan]. Tokyo: Hanawa Shobo.

Miyakawa, Kōji. 1992. Asu no bengoshi [Tomorrow's lawyers]. In *Henkaku no naka no bengoshi (jō)* [Attorneys in reform, vol. 1], eds. K. Miyakawa, M. Koyama, K. Nasu, and H. Kubori. Tokyo: Yūhikaku.

Miyakawa, Kōji, Minoru Koyama, Kōhei Nasu, and Hideaki Kubori, eds. 1992–93. *Henkaku no naka no bengoshi (jō), (ge)* [Attorneys in reform, vol. 1 and 2]. Tokyo: Yūhikaku.

Miyake, Shingo. 1995. *Bengoshi girudo* [Lawyers' guild]. Tokyo: Shinzansha.

Miyazawa, Setsuo. 1994a. Administrative control of Japanese judges. In *Law and technology in the Pacific community*, ed. P. S. C. Lewis. Boulder: Westview Press.

———. 1994b. *Hō katei no riaritī* [Realities of the legal process]. Tokyo: Shinzansha.

Mura, Kazuo. 1995. Shihō shiken kaikaku mondai no genjō to kongo no kadai [The present state and problems of the reform of the national bar examination]. 46 *Jiyū to Seigi* 9:115.

———. 1996. Kaikaku kyōgikai iknensho to kongo no shihō kaikaku [The Reform Committee's opinions and the prospects for judicial reform]. 1084 *Jurisuto* 8.

Murakami, Yasusuke and Thomas P. Rohlen. 1992. Social-exchange aspects of the Japanese economy: Culture, efficiency, and change. In *The political economy of Japan: Cultural and social dynamics*, eds. S. Kumon and H. Rosovsky. Palo Alto: Stanford University Press.

Nagashima, Atsushi. 1963. The accused and society: The administration of criminal justice in Japan. In *Law in Japan: The legal order in a changing society*, ed. A. von Mehren. Cambridge, MA: Harvard University Press.

Nasu, Kōhei. 1992. Bengoshi shoku o meguru jiyū to tōsei [Freedom and control concerning lawyers]. In *Henkaku no naka no bengoshi (jō)* [Attorneys in reform, vol. 1], eds. K. Miyakawa, M. Koyama, K. Nasu, and H. Kubori. Tokyo: Yūhikaku.

Nihon Bengoshi Rengōkai [Japan Federation of Bar Associations], ed. 1988a. Bengoshi Gyōmu Taisaku Iinkai [Committee on Legal Practice Reform]. *Nihon no hōritsu jimusho* [Law firms in Japan]. Tokyo: Gyōsei.

———. 1988b. Hōritsu jimusho kyōdōka no genjō to kadai: Hōkoku to shiryō [The present state and issues of partnership and office sharing: Report and materials]. 39 *Jiyū to Seigi* 13.

———. 1990a. Dai 41-kai teiki sōkai hōkoku [Report of the 41st general meeting]. 41 *Jiyū to Seigi* 8:114.

———, ed. 1990b. Kaiin meibo [Membership directory (of the JFBA)]. Tokyo: Nihon Bengoshi Rengōkai [JFBA].

———, ed. 1991. Nihon no hōritsu jimusho, '90 [Japanese law firms in 1990]. 42 *Jiyū to Seigi* 13.

———. 1992. [Article on pro bono representation ("duty solicitor") for criminal suspects]. 43 *Jiyū to Seigi* 2:12.

———. 1995. Rinji sōkai hōkoku [Report of an extraordinary general meeting]. 46 *Jiyū to Seigi* 12:97.

———. 1997. Rinji sōkai hōkoku. 48 *Jiyū to Seigi* 12:207.

———. 1998a. 2010-nen e no shihō kaikaku [Judicial reform toward 2010]. 49 *Jiyū to Seigi* 4:155.

———. 1998b. Kaiinsū [Number of JFBA members]. 49 *Jiyū to Seigi* 8:227.

———. 2001. Kaiinsū. 52 *Jiyū to Seigi* 4:184.

———. 2002a. Kaiinsū. 53 *Jiyū to Seigi* 6:156.

———. 2002b. Kaiinsū. 53 *Jiyū to Seigi* 7:154.

Nihon Hōritsuka Kyōkai [Japan Lawyers Association], ed. 1982. *Shihō shiken; sono genjō to kadai* [The present state and problems of the national bar examination]. Tokyo: Gyōsei.

Niwayama, Shōichirō and Kazuhiko Yamagishi. 1998. Nihon ni okeru kyōdai hōritsu jimusho no kanōsei [A possibility of mega-law firms in Japan]. 49 *Jiyū to Seigi* 11:34.

Noda, Yoshiyuki. 1976. *Introduction to Japanese law*. Translated and edited by A. H. Angelo. Tokyo: University of Tokyo Press.

Nottage, Luke and Yoshitaka Wada. 1999. Japan's new product liability ADR centers: Bureaucratic industry, or consumer informalism? 65 *Hōsei Kenkyū* [Journal of law and politics of Kyushu University] 3–4:295.

Oda, Hiroshi. 1992. *Japanese law*. London: Butterworths.

Odanaka, Toshiki. 1997. Gendai bengoshi-ron no kansei [Pitfalls of the recent discussions on lawyers]. In *Atarashii seiki e no bengoshi-zō* [Perspectives on attorneys for the new century], ed. Nihon Bengoshi Rengōkai Henshū Iinkai [JFBA Editorial Committee]. Tokyo: Yūhikaku.

Okada, Yasuo and Mitsuru Takahata. 1998. Hōmu hōjin kōsō no genjō to tenbō [Incorporation of law firm: The present state and future]. 49 *Jiyū to Seigi* 11:48.

Okudaira, Shōkō. 1914. *Nihon bengoshi-shi* [A history of the Japanese lawyer]. Tokyo: Gannandō Shoten.

Ōno, Masao. 1970. Shokugyō to shite no bengoshi oyobi bengoshi dantai no rekishi [A history of lawyers as a profession and of professional associations]. In *Bengoshi no dantai* [Lawyers' associations], ed. M. Ōno. Tokyo: Nihon Hyōronsha.

Ōta, Shōzō and Kahei Rokumoto. 1993. Issues of the lawyer population: Japan. 25 *Case Western Reserve Journal of International Law* 315.

Rahn, Guntram. 1990. *Rechtdenken und Rechtsauffassung in Japan* [Legal theory and legal ideas in Japan]. München: C.H. Beck.

Ramseyer, J. Mark. 1986. Lawyers, foreign lawyers, and lawyer-substitutes: The market for regulation in Japan. 27 *Harvard International Law Journal* 499.

———. 1990. *Hō to keizaigaku* [Law and economics]. Tokyo: Kōbundō.

———. 1991. Legal rules in repeated deals: Banking in the shadow of defection in Japan. 20 *Journal of Legal Studies* 91.

———. 1996. *Odd markets in Japanese history: Law and economic growth*. Cambridge, UK: Cambridge University Press.

Ramseyer, J. Mark and Frances McCall Rosenbluth. 1993. *Japan's political marketplace*. Cambridge, MA: Harvard University Press.

———. 1995. *The politics of oligarchy: Institutional choice in Imperial Japan*. Cambridge, UK: Cambridge University Press.

Ramseyer, J. Mark and Minoru Nakazato. 1998. *Japanese law: An economic approach*. Chicago: University of Chicago Press.

Rokumoto, Kahei. 1971. *Minji funsō no hōteki kaiketsu* [Legal resolution of civil disputes]. Tokyo: Iwanami Shoten.

————. 1974. Bengoshi to hō [Lawyers and the law]. In *Hōshakaigaku*, ed. T. Ushiomi. Tokyo: Tokyo Daigaku Shuppankai.

————. 1986. Nihonjin no hō ishiki-ron saiho [The debate on legal consciousness of the Japanese revisited]. In *Hō to hōkatei* [Law and the legal process], eds. R. Mochizuki, Y. Higuchi, and T. Andō. Tokyo: Sōbunsha.

————. 1988. The present state of Japanese practicing attorneys: On the way to full professionalization? In *Lawyers in society: The civil law world*, eds. R. L. Abel and P. S. C. Lewis. Berkeley: University of California Press.

Saikō Saibansho [Supreme Court of Japan]. 2000. 21-seiki no shihō seido o kangaeru [A study on the judicial system of the 21st century]. 51 *Jiyū to Seigi* 1:161.

Shihō Seido Kaikaku Shingikai [Justice System Reform Council]. 2001. *Recommendations of the Justice System Reform Council—For a justice system to support Japan in the 21st century*. Official English translation at the website of the Prime Minister of Japan at http://www.kantei.go.jp/foreign/judiciary/2001/0612report.html.

Shinohara, Shunji. 1998. Kigyō hōmu to bengoshi [Corporate legal practice and practicing attorneys]. 49 *Jiyū to Seigi* 3:14.

Suzuki, Yoshio. 1995. *Nihon no shihō koko ga mondai* [Problems of the administration of justice in Japan]. Tokyo: Tōyō Keizai Shinpōsha.

Takayanagi, Kenzō. 1963. A century of innovation: The development of Japanese law, 1868–1961. In *Law in Japan: The legal order in a changing society*, ed. A. von Mehren. Cambridge, MA: Harvard University Press.

Takenouchi, Akira. 1998. Tōban bengoshi seido no tōtatsuten to kadai [The present state and problems of the duty attorney scheme]. 49 *Jiyū to Seigi* 2:24.

Takikawa, Masajirō. 1984. *Kujishi, Kujiyado no kenkyū* [A study on Kujishi and Kujiyado (inns of court and their managers in the Tokugawa period)]. Tokyo: Akasaka Shoin.

Tanaka, Hideo, ed. 1976. *The Japanese legal system: Introductory cases and materials*. Assisted by Malcolm D. H. Smith. Tokyo: University of Tokyo Press.

Tanaka, Shigeaki. 1996. *Gendai shakai to saiban* [Modern society and adjudication]. Tokyo: Kōbundō.

————. 1997. Kiro ni tatsu bengoshi [Lawyers at a crossroads]. In *Atarashii seiki e no bengoshi-zō* [Perspectives on attorneys for the new century], ed. Nihon Bengoshi Rengōkai Henshū Iinkai. Tokyo: Yūhikaku.

Tanase, Takao. 1987. *Gendai shakai to bengoshi* [Modern society and lawyers]. Tokyo: Nihon Hyōronsha.

————. 1990. The management of disputes: Automobile accident compensation in Japan. 24 *Law & Society Review* 651.

————. 1991. Hōka shakai to saiban [Legalized society and adjudication]. 971 *Jurisuto* 68.

————. 1995. Katari to shite no hō enyo [The application of law as discourse]. 111 *Minshōhō Zasshi* [Journal of civil and commercial laws] 4–5:131; 6:1.

————. 1996. Bengoshi rinri no gensetsu bunseki [The discourse analysis of lawyers' ethics]. 68 *Hōritsu Jihō* [Journal of law] 1:52; 2:47; 3:72; 4:55.

Upham, Frank K. 1987. *Law and social change in postwar Japan.* Cambridge, MA: Harvard University Press.

————. 1994. Comment: Speculations on legal informality: On Winn's "relational practices and the marginalization of law." 28 *Law & Society Review* 233.

————. 1996. Retail convergence: The structural impediments initiative and the regulation of the Japanese retail industry. In *National diversity and global capitalism*, eds. S. Berger and R. Dore. Ithaca: Cornell University Press.

West, Mark D. 1994. The pricing of shareholder derivative actions in Japan and the United States. 88 *Northwestern University Law Review* 1436.

Winn, Jane Kaufman. 1994. Relational practices and the marginalization of law: Informal financial practices of small businesses in Taiwan. 28 *Law & Society Review* 193.

Wohl, Richard H., Stuart M. Chemtob, and Glen S. Fukushima, eds. 1989. *Practice by foreign lawyers in Japan.* Chicago: American Bar Association.

Wollschläger, Christian. 1997. Historical trends of civil litigation in Japan, Arizona, Sweden, and Germany: Japanese legal culture in the light of statistics. In *Japan: Economic success and legal system*, ed. H. Baum. New York: Walter de Gruyter.

Yoshikawa, Seiichi. 1997. Kisei kanwa to purofesshonarizumu [Deregulation and professionalism]. In *Atarashii seiki e no bengoshi-zō* [Perspectives on attorneys for the new century], ed. Nihon Bengoshi Rengōkai Henshū Iinkai. Tokyo: Yūhikaku.

Zadankai [Roundtable]. 1987. Hōsō yōsei no arikata to shihō shiken seido [The legal education and training system and the national bar examination]. 892 *Jurisuto* 6.

Six

Globalization of Japanese Corporations and the Development of Corporate Legal Departments: Problems and Prospects

Toshimitsu Kitagawa* and Luke Nottage**

Introduction

An inordinate amount has been written in English about practicing attorneys (*bengoshi*) in Japan. Much of this is concerned with the scope of practice permitted for foreign lawyers in Japan.[1] Most of these studies come from the United States (Baum and Nottage 1998). This interest reflects the fact that the largest multinational law firms, at least until developments in the United Kingdom in the 1990s, have been based in the United States. But it also says much

*Professor of Law, Kansai University; Attorney, Oh-Ebashi LPC & Partners, Osaka; LL.M. (Harvard, 1971); LL.B. (Kyushu, 1962). Formerly corporate legal counsel at Toshiba Corporation and Professor of Transnational Law at Kyushu University Law Faculty.

**Senior Lecturer, University of Sydney Faculty of Law; founding Co-Director of the Australian Network for Japanese Law; B.C.A. (Victoria University of Wellington, 1989); LL.B. (VUW, 1990); LL.M. (Kyoto, 1993); Ph.D. (VUW, 2002). Formerly Associate Professor of Transnational Law, Kyushu University.

This is a greatly expanded and updated version of a paper presented at the Conference on the Legal Profession in East Asia, held at Harvard Law School, December 11–14, 1998. For helpful ideas and information, we thank the conference participants, and also Kent Anderson (Australian National University), Tom Ginsburg (University of Illinois), Shigenobu Kato (former Consul-General of Japan, Sydney), Brett Williams (Sydney University), Leon Wolff (University of New South Wales), and others identified in footnotes. All conclusions and any errors remain our own.

As this chapter was going to press, results of a survey conducted in 2005 were published (Keiei Hōyūkai and Shōji Hōmu Kenkyūkai 2006). These largely confirm the characteristics and trends identified in this chapter based on previous survey data. A paper by Luke Nottage highlighting these points is forthcoming via http://www.ssrn.com.

1. Foreign lawyers must qualify with the Ministry of Justice in order to practice law in Japan, under the registered foreign lawyer (*gaikokuhō jimu bengoshi* or *gaiben*) system introduced in 1987 and progressively liberalized (Law No. 66 of 1986, the Special Measures Law Concerning the Handling of Legal Business by Foreign Lawyers). See, e.g., *Law in Japan: An Annual* (1988); Coulter (1995, 431–61) (discussing 1994 amendments only); Choy (1998) (discussing 1998 amendments); Comrie-Taylor (1997); Pardieck (1996); Zaki (2002). See also note 109 below.

about the central role of practicing attorneys in the legal system, and in popular consciousness, in the United States.[2]

For over thirty years, however, commentators such as Dan Henderson have been urging studies into a range of legal professionals in Japan, not just *bengoshi* (Henderson 1965; 1973; 1997, 27; Hattori, Henderson and Reich n.d., §2.09).[3] This is important in practice, for instance when considering to whom to turn for assistance when joining the growing wave of investment into Japan from abroad (Nottage 2002b, 16–18)[4] or when dealing with investors in (or, more common recently, "disinvestors" from) Japan.[5]

It is also important from a theoretical perspective. At a minimum, it helps to avoid making inapposite comparisons between the legal profession in Japan and the United States.[6] Thus, Henderson advocates searching for functional equivalents to American lawyers within Japan. To *bengoshi* he adds tax agents (*zeirishi*), patent agents (*benrishi*), judicial scriveners (*shihō shoshi*, handling mainly property and corporate registry work), certified public accountants (*kōnin kaikeishi*), administrative scriveners (*gyōsei shoshi*, dealing with administrative agencies), notaries (*kōshōnin*, maintaining their own registries of authenticated documents), public registry clerks, and "house counsel" (*kigyō hōmuin*—we will term them "corporate legal staff" in this chapter).[7]

However, a functional or "problem-oriented" approach to comparative study does not resolve the issue of defining the problem, nor of why one is making comparisons (Gessner 1995; Nottage 2001a). Those going beyond a mere critique of inapposite comparisons, and driven by the conviction that expanding the number and roles of *bengoshi* is an essential step in Japan's modernization or

---

2. See generally Macaulay (1993).

3. See also Ramseyer (1986, 500).

4. Cf. generally Henderson (1973) and Yanagida (2000, ch. 2).

5. Cases of Japanese investments unwinding in New Zealand, for example, include Yoshimoto v. Canterbury Golf International Ltd. (2001) 1 N.Z.L.R. 523; MacAlister & Anor v. Ishizuka & Anor (June 18, 1998, Court of Appeal, C.A. 254/97, Richardson P., Thomas & Keith JJ.); Fukumoto v. Rudd Watts & Stone (September 15, 1995, High Court, Christchurch, C.P. 47/95, Holland J.); Multiply Ltd. v. Old Mill Farm Ltd. & Ors; Millbrook Country Club Ltd. v. Multiply Ltd & Anor (1995) 7 N.Z.C.L.C. 260,746; and Mitsui & Co (NZ) Ltd v. Commissioner of Inland Revenue (1995) 17 N.Z.T.C. 12,112. Courts in the U.S. have also had to rule on arguments that communications from staff in legal departments of Japanese corporations should be protected from discovery obligations because of the functional equivalence of in-house counsel. See, e.g., Honeywell v. Minolta, 1990 U.S. Dist. Lexis 5954; with discussion in Marin (1998, 1558–1605). See also Yoshida (1997, 209).

6. Henderson (1997) (opening by quoting Lee Iacocca's quip: "[The Japanese have] got about as many lawyers as we've got sumo wrestlers"). See also Miller (1987, 201).

7. In addition to around 19,000 *bengoshi*, in December 2001 there were 65,831 tax attorneys, 35,423 administrative scriveners, 17,162 judicial scriveners, and 4,776 patent attorneys. See the website of the Japan Federation of Bar Associations at http://www.nichibenren.or.jp/en /about/system.html.

in promoting liberal rights-based democracy,[8] not surprisingly see the approach of Henderson and others as going too far. To put such arguments in proper context, this chapter adds to a still very sparse literature in English by presenting detailed and up-to-date information on the development of Japanese corporate legal departments, especially over the 1990s, including information on their work, concerns, and interactions with other professionals such as *bengoshi*.[9]

It also casts light on a theoretical puzzle related to modernization or the promotion of liberal democracy, namely why the corporate sector in Japan appears to have played a pivotal role in promoting whole-scale civil justice reforms from the end of the 1990s. The received wisdom is that Japan has been governed since the 1950s by an "iron triangle" of conservative Liberal Democratic Party (LDP) politicians, bureaucrats, and corporate elites. Commentators have differed as to whether the power of Japanese bureaucrats has been predominant (Johnson 1982)[10] or whether it has been exercised in the shadow of the clear policy preferences of their political masters in the LDP (at least until its temporary fall from power in 1993) (Ramseyer and Rosenbluth 1995), and some have emphasized the particular relative strength of Japan's corporate sector.[11] Most agree, however, that these elites have not wanted to allow Japan's judicial system to develop in idiosyncratic and unpredictable ways.[12]

It therefore seems very odd for its corporate leaders from the late 1990s to have actively encouraged reforms to bolster the judicial system, including considerable increases in the number of *bengoshi* and the scope of legal services which can be offered by other legal professionals. As sketched in Part III below, many recommendations from business circles in 1998 and 2000 were incorporated into the final report of the blue-ribbon Justice System Reform Council (*shihō seido kaikaku shingikai*) presented to Prime Minister Koizumi on June 12, 2001.[13] This oddity also runs counter to tendencies in many other industrialized

---

8. See, respectively, e.g., Ōta and Rokumoto (1993, 315–32); Miyazawa (1997, 101–115). Cf. also Rokumoto (2001, 545–60); Miyazawa (2001, 89).

9. In addition to the above-mentioned, see Stevens (1978, 34) (based on data through to the early 1980s and focusing primarily on legal departments in Japanese affiliates in the United States); Yoneda (1995a, 113).

10. Also in this tradition, see, e.g., Gao (1997). Upham (1987) is usually read as stressing the power of "bureaucratic informalism." See, e.g., Matsuura (1989). See also Ginsburg (2001). But see Upham (1997, 396).

11. See, e.g., Schaede (2000); Tilton (1996); Callon (1995); Mito (1998, 147). Cf. also Nottage (2001e) (emphasizing "industry informalism," as well as "government formalism," and bureaucratic informalism).

12. See, e.g., Ramseyer (1996, 721); Ramseyer and Rasmusen (1997, 259; 1999 and 2000) (arguing that Japanese judges' careers tend to suffer if they rule against LDP party preferences, at least in some areas); Upham (1987) (suggesting that bureaucratic informalism was used to divert burgeoning cases away from court adjudication).

13. See McKenna (2001, 123 and generally); McAlinn (2002a and 2002b); Miyazawa (in this volume).

democracies in recent years, not just in the U.S. (often an exception in legal developments viewed from a global perspective),[14] but also for example in Australia, where the corporate sector has pushed strongly for limiting access to the courts.

Examining the development of Japan's corporate legal departments over the 1990s suggests that there has been a paradigm shift in governance in Japan, apparent also in other areas ranging from corporate governance to public law.[15] Maintaining the received wisdom, this can be conceived as a relative gain in influence for corporate elites vis-à-vis bureaucrats and even politicians. But it could also mean that the "iron triangle" has become more malleable, with other influential interest groups being formed or suddenly finding traction, especially from bases within Japan (although able to use strategically ongoing foreign pressure (*gaiatsu*)).[16] This might be explained simply by changes in a limited number of fairly tangible parameters, such as the LDP's dramatic fall from power in 1993 and resultant changes in public law.[17] But it may also implicate factors which are more difficult to describe quantitatively: the independent power of new ideas, a relatively autonomous and steady evolution of legal norms (through, after all, a sophisticated judicial system), and even chance occurrences at particular historical junctures.

Reassessing ways of analyzing Japanese law and society in the 1990s and into this decade, in turn, may lead to revisiting the received wisdom regarding other periods of Japan's post-war history.[18] It should certainly help provide better assessments of its future, questioning for example the idea that Japanese law has simply become "Americanized."[19] It can also offer new data and perspectives for the much broader debate about ongoing tensions between globalization of economic or legal relations and local circumstances or variety.[20]

---

14. See Galanter (1999).

15. See, e.g., Nottage (2001b); Shishido (2001); Uga (2002); Muroi (2002); Amyx (2002). See generally Noble (1998); Ginsburg (2002).

16. See, e.g., Abe (1995).

17. Cf. Cox et al. (2000). See also McKean and Scheiner (2000).

18. See, e.g., Sasaki-Uemura (2001) (arguing that the significance of the 1960 protests against the U.S.-Japan Security Treaty lay in the efforts of diverse groups of politically conscious actors attempting to reshape Japan's body politic, rather than international diplomacy); S. K. Vogel (2001) (arguing that consumer groups in Japan have repeatedly advocated policies at odds with their economic self-interest, leading scholars to mischaracterize their role in politics and to misinterpret more broadly Japan's post-war political economy); Richardson (1997) (arguing that Japanese political life has been extremely fragmented and discordant at all levels: in the bureaucracy, legislatures, parties, interest groups, and in business and industry).

19. Cf. Kelemen and Sibbitt (2002, 269) and the special issue of *Law in Japan: An Annual* (2001).

20. See generally, e.g., Wiener (1999); Twining (2000); Nayyar (2002); Dezalay and Garth (2002a and 2002b); Potter (2001).

Part I of this chapter therefore begins with an overview of the development of Japanese corporate legal departments over the 1970s and 1980s, led primarily by their expansion into overseas markets. This sets the stage for a detailed analysis of trends over the 1990s presented in Part II. This focuses on comprehensive survey data mainly from 1995, incorporating comparisons with the situation in 1990 and showing an already dramatically changing situation, and with 2000 showing a consolidation of many of these tendencies. Accelerating globalization and deregulation of the Japanese economy,[21] combined with a deepening recession, created growing challenges not only for larger corporations focused on exports or investing outside Japan. Legal issues involving product liability, competition law, shareholder derivative suits, or (increasingly) insolvencies, became "domesticated"—significantly heightening the risks involved in doing business for a much broader range of firms. Declining and even negative economic growth also restricted their room to maneuver: to trade their way through legal problems or to further boost in-house legal staff to protect themselves against legal risks and actively use the legal system to pursue economic gain.

Growing concerns of corporate legal staff also started to get through more readily to top management, as the positions of legal departments improved within their organizations, especially over the first half of the 1990s. When a banking crisis struck Japan in 1998, the Japanese government did not bail out even large financial institutions, and foreign corporations rapidly expanded their involvement (Milhaupt 2001). It became clear to Japanese corporate leaders that their corporations would need to look after themselves, even more than hitherto. Reorienting Japanese law and society through a more functional legal system therefore became a central policy recommendation by a range of corporate interest groups, although many challenges remain for Japanese corporate legal departments, as explained in Part III.

I. Globalization of Japanese Corporations and Strengthening of their Legal Departments since the 1970s

Japanese corporations' rapid expansion of business activities into the global market, since the 1970s in particular, has been well charted by economists and organizational theorists.[22] The consequent strengthening of their legal departments and legal staff, however, has been less studied.[23] Based on data prior to the early 1980s, Setsuo Miyazawa examined the development of the legal departments of the affiliates of Japanese corporations in the United States. He argued that until the 1970s, business considerations may have played a major role in disputes involving Japanese corporations, thus diminishing their need

---

21. See generally, e.g., Gibney (1998) and Tilton and Carlile (1998).

22. See, e.g., Tsurumi (1976) and Roger (1989).

23. But see Kitagawa (1994a, 41).

for highly developed legal expertise (Stevens 1978, 35). This began to change throughout the 1970s, however, as they expanded their activities into new markets, encountering new business and legal environments, and as legal disputes emerged, primarily in the United States.

Miyazawa developed the interesting hypothesis that the legal departments in these affiliates would become more or less professionalized, especially in the sense of hiring in-house American lawyers, depending on the type of business in question and the type of disputes or claims to which that business tended to be subjected. For manufacturers subjected more often to product liability claims, for instance, he argued that most of the response needs to be met or directed in the foreign jurisdiction in which the accident occurred, forcing affiliates of Japanese corporations to hire more foreign lawyers to staff their legal departments. By contrast, in the case of traders more subject to antitrust claims, requiring relatively more investigation and a tactical response at the level of parent firms back in Japan, their affiliates abroad would not professionalize their legal departments as much.

Miyazawa's data supports these propositions, and it accords with our personal experience. We would add that another major category of disputes requiring a response more at the level of affiliates, rather than of parent firms in Japan, was related to labor law issues.[24] These disputes escalated in the 1980s as Japanese firms invested in manufacturing facilities abroad, especially in the United States.[25] Assisted by an appreciating yen, this investment abroad was driven in part by attempts to minimize antitrust or international trade law issues, such as dumping, and more generally to help Japan's leaders (both in business and government) diffuse trade tension, given its burgeoning trade surpluses.

In the 1990s, as the downturn in Japan's economy forced some corporations to liquidate these investments, other constellations of disputes and issues emerged, which also tended to require a response at the level of the foreign affiliate rather than the parent firm.[26] In addition, after a liberalization of foreign exchange transactions and corporate bond issuance from the early 1980s, Japanese corporations expanded their use of foreign-qualified lawyers and in-house counsel to plan for and obtain corporate finance overseas (Nagashima and Zaloom 2002, 4), as well as to resolve consequent disputes. Overall, transnational transactions embroiling Japanese corporations and their affiliates expanded from the world of "goods" (trade) to include the world of "money" (investment) and "personnel" (investment management). A parallel development was their expansion into the world of "technology" (intellectual property rights and related services).[27]

---

24. See generally Kitagawa (1997, 951).

25. In the U.S., for instance, civil rights claims were often brought for alleged discrimination with respect to locally hired staff. Cf. generally Efron (1999).

26. See, e.g., the cases listed above at note 5.

27. See generally Kitagawa (1995).

Miyazawa's thesis also can be developed by focusing on the processes by which legal departments *within* Japan were strengthened. This occurred directly by having to deal with international legal disputes in areas like antitrust. It also occurred more indirectly through at least having to supervise or follow the conduct of major litigation by foreign affiliates and legal departments or lawyers abroad. This trend was reinforced by the fact that such litigation was often very protracted. Claims or litigation could be brought for years in a variety of fora— some more political than legal, but always requiring careful legal responses. An example is the decade of strife, from 1968 to 1978, stemming from repeated allegations that Japanese television sets were being dumped into the United States. This can be characterized as an example of "multiple legal harassment" (Kitagawa 1999). Another example from the mid-1980s, involving a less drawn-out but equally complex dispute resolution process, centered on semiconductors. Such harassment represents an important factor behind the strengthening of legal departments in parent corporations back in Japan.

Another factor encouraging the development of new legal expertise, and the consolidation of the role of legal departments within Japanese corporations, was their role in planning transactions, even those primarily involving foreign affiliates and foreign law. Much of the law involved can be transplanted across jurisdictional boundaries. An example is contract law, despite significant variation in rules and even key organizational principles between the common law (even its United States variant) and Japanese law (following continental European traditions) (Nottage 1997a and 1997b). And as contract law developed in Japan along with other new areas such as intellectual property and product liability law, corporate legal departments gained deeper and broader experience in these fields and their role thus developed as well.

Trends in these areas of law were supported by their accelerating "domestication" in the 1990s. Partly, this occurred directly in response to calls for "global standards" and for the creation of a "level (regulatory) playing field" for international trade and investment (e.g., under the Structural Impediments Initiative (S.I.I.) in the early 1990s (Saxonhouse 1991) and more recently under multilateral negotiations and rules). Partly, it occurred because of domestic developments. These, in turn, could be indirectly influenced by a range of developments overseas, often from a contingent and shifting pattern of interest groups.[28] This adds another, more complex dimension to the globalization of the legal environment for Japanese corporations at the end of the 1990s.

These developments also can be traced from a slightly different perspective.[29] Corporate legal departments in Japan grew in the 1970s and 1980s in an era of managed trade policy. This period was characterized by industry promotion strategies domestically and voluntary external trade arrangements, along

---

28. For an analysis of the transplanting of Japanese product liability law, see Nottage (2001e).

29. See generally Kitagawa (1994c).

with unilateral retaliatory action and bilateral dispute settlement.[30] In the 1990s, they have developed as industry-based negotiations and "results-oriented" trade policy and have now given way to "rule-oriented" trade policy in the shadow of new multilateral rules, such as the General Agreement on Trade in Services of the World Trade Organization.[31] Specifically in relation to access to Japanese markets, issues of non-tariff barriers gave way to market-share target policies, with all the problems involved in defining and enforcing these targets (epitomized by the Semiconductors Accord),[32] to growing rejection of administrative leadership in these matters and to deregulatory initiatives underpinned by the new multilateral regime. Closely tied to these latter trends were stricter enforcement of intellectual property rights and antitrust law and the enactment of new product liability legislation in 1994.[33] Less directly related, but nonetheless aimed at creating a new framework facilitating redefined relationships, were the enactment of amendments to the Code of Civil Procedure (in effect from January 1, 1998) and changes to corporate law and patterns of corporate governance.[34]

Together, these developments amounted to increasingly strict legal requirements going to the heart of corporate management and the conduct of business. Combined with more long-standing elaboration of pollution and environmental regulation and of consumer law (to a lesser extent, but with a rise in consumer consciousness), this reconfiguration of key parameters of the legal environment also meant a significant increase in the scale and severity of legal risk in the 1990s. So much so that many Japanese corporations realized that their very existence could be threatened, especially in the protracted economic downturn over the latter half of the 1990s. At the same time, complex legal problems continued to emerge from new types of business transactions (leasing, franchising, mergers and acquisitions, electronic commerce, etc.). These offered new opportunities, but they also brought risks.

The structures and roles of Japan's corporate legal departments were further fortified by all of this. By the end of the 1990s, they were increasingly concerned about limits to their freedom to maneuver to meet these new responsibilities, limits set for instance by the limited accessibility of practicing attorneys. Nonetheless, these developments had already brought noticeable and wide-ranging improvements in the structure of legal departments and their roles

---

30. See, e.g., Case (1999).

31. See, e.g., Sano (1999); Loeb and Behnam (1999); Southwick (2000); Nottage (2002c).

32. See also, e.g., Kaufman (1994) and Gantz (1999).

33. Law No. 85 of 1994. See translation in Nottage and Wada (1998, 40); Nottage (2004). On intellectual property rights in Japan in recent years, see, e.g., Takenaka (2000). On antitrust, see generally Haley (2001) (emphasizing somewhat surprising convergence with developments in Germany, including important educational effects over recent decades).

34. See generally Ōta (2001); Taniguchi (1997); Satō (2000).

within Japanese corporations, especially evident over the first half of the 1990s. This can be seen from large-scale surveys that have been undertaken every five years since 1965.

In 1976, commenting on the third survey, Takeshi Kojima observed that legal departments were "in substance very weak, to say nothing of the form they take, compared to American corporations." In 1981, however, he saw them as "strengthening their influence, and establishing their own existence as permanent institutions." By 1986, he thought they seemed to "have reached a mature stage" (Kojima 1976; 1981; 1986). In fact, this conclusion may have been premature. The following year, Toshiba Machinery Corporation got into serious trouble for exporting products in breach of COCOM[35] rules, exacerbating U.S.-Japan trade friction.[36] To avoid further incidents, Japan's Ministry of International Trade and Industry (MITI) strongly urged Japanese corporations to further strengthen their legal departments. This strengthening seems to have borne fruit through the early 1990s, as we can see from the surveys undertaken in 1990 and 1995 jointly by the Business Management-Related Law Association (*keiei hōyūkāi*), an association of legal department staff or executives doing law-related work within corporations, and the Japanese Association of Business Law, Inc. (*shōji hōmu kenkyūkai*),* a for-profit incorporated body promoting business law more generally, funded by corporate memberships and revenue from seminars and publications. As Kojima (1996) noted astutely in introducing a panel discussion on the results of the 1995 survey:

> While until some point, following internationalization, international legal departments have tended to lead the way and raised the level of specialization of legal departments, at this stage domestic and international legal departments have become an inseparable whole; instead, they have had to move forward together from a unified starting point, and at least a partial merging of both has become apparent.

II. Japanese Corporate Legal Staff and Legal Departments in the 1990s

This latest tendency, and the more long-standing strengthening of the structure and roles of legal departments in Japanese corporations described above, can be seen from the results reported in the 1995 survey (including comparisons with 1990 survey results when applicable and relevant), reinforced with some results from the 2000 survey.

---

35. The Coordinating Committee for Multilateral Export Controls, which had seventeen member countries when it officially disbanded in 1994. Created in 1949 by the U.S., some NATO countries, and Japan, it controlled the export of items deemed security concerns.

36. See Kitagawa (1994c).

*Ed. note: *Keiei hōyūkai* is also known as the Association of Japanese Corporate Legal Departments, and *shōji hōmu kenkyūkai* is also known as the Commercial Law Center, Inc.

The 1995 survey was undertaken in September and October 1995, when Japan's economic slowdown had become painfully apparent even to the most optimistic. Questionnaires were sent to 3,487 corporations and were completed by 992 (a 28.4 percent response rate). In the 1990 survey, only 547 responses were received from 2,682 corporations (20.4 percent). The increase in corporations surveyed, and the improved response rate, already indicate a heightened interest in corporate legal affairs in the first half of the 1990s. This interest was largely maintained according to the 2000 survey, implemented from June 30 to August 31, 2000, and sent to 5,077 corporations, of which 1,183 (23.8 percent) responded.

In the 1995 survey, only 49 respondents were very small corporations, with capital of ¥500 million or less; 499 were small or medium-sized corporations, with capital of between ¥500 million and ¥10 billion: a total of 548 or 55.9 percent. Larger corporations made up 433 respondents (44.1 percent): 365 with capital of between ¥10 billion and ¥100 billion and 68 very large corporations with more than ¥100 billion. The sizable proportion of small or medium-sized corporations and their absolute numbers (299 of 547 in 1990; 548 of 992 in 1995; 672 of 1,183 in 2000) mean that the results give an indication of the role of legal departments and their staff across a broad range of Japanese corporations.[37] The largest individual category of respondents in the 1995 survey consisted of manufacturers of goods such as machinery, electronic goods, and vehicles (240 or 24.2 percent), but respondents within the generic category of services amounted to 195 or 19.7 percent (excluding financial services: another 66 or 6.7 percent), while traders made up 137 or 13.8 percent of total respondents (Keiei Hōyūkai and Shōji Hōmu Kenkyūkai 1996 (hereafter, "1995 Survey"), 40–41). These proportions were largely unchanged from the 1990 survey and remained similar in the 2000 survey (Keiei Hōyūkai and Shōji Hōmu Kenkyūkai 2001 (hereafter, "2000 Survey")).

A.   Legal Staff and the Structure of "Legal Departments"

In 1993, Shōzō Ōta and Kahei Rokumoto noted from 1990 survey data that the total number of employees in charge of legal matters was 2,439, an average of 5.2 per corporation. They also noted that on average there were 9.4 employees of all types in corporate units dealing with legal affairs. While this implied that total employees of all types amounted to 4,408 individuals, they estimated that the relevant number was probably 2,500 to 3,000, as total employees could include mostly (but not exclusively) those with neither legal training nor operational responsibilities (Ōta and Rokumoto 1993, 328). Henderson argued that

---

37. Cf. Kono (1997, 73) (asserting that the results of the 1990 survey "apply mainly to major Japanese corporations"). Note also that the Commercial Code was amended in 1990 to increase minimum required capital in stock corporations (*kabushiki-gaisha*) to ¥10 million and to ¥3 million in limited liability (close) corporations (*yūgen-gaisha*). This may contribute to the low number (49) of very small corporations in the 1995 survey.

"probably including only the 3,000 *kigyō hōmu-in* (and not the larger core of other law-trained management) seriously understates these Japanese functional counterparts of U.S. 'corporate house counsel'" (1997, 36n26). In any case, he argued that by 1995 (when he was writing), the number would probably be higher than the estimate.

Indeed, in the narrowly defined category of those responsible for legal matters (corresponding to figures of 2,844 in 1990 and 7,571 in 2000), respondents to the 1995 survey reported 6,051 such legal staff within their organizations.[38] Some 43.9 percent of respondents said this was an increase compared to 1990; 12.2 percent reported a decrease. Two-thirds (66.2 percent) of financial services providers reported increases, no doubt reflecting a more complicated regulatory and business environment.[39] In a majority of corporations with capital exceeding ¥10 billion and those with a legal unit, legal staff had also increased, suggesting more weight being placed on legal work. The proportion of those *shedding* staff also is positively related to corporation size; but this appears due to a generic factor, namely, restructuring (*risutora*) due to the economic recession hitting larger companies harder. While overall, 55.8 percent of companies reported restructuring, with a third saying this involved "personnel adjustments," 79.4 percent of the largest 68 companies had restructured by 1995 (1995 Survey, 46, 65–66). Similar patterns emerged for 2000: staff increased by 948, although this came from only 36.4 percent of the respondent corporations (2000 Survey, 58–9).

Of the 992 respondents to the 1995 survey, 233 corporations (23.5 percent) reported a department (*bu*) specializing in legal affairs, and 230 (23.2 percent) reported a smaller section (*ka*): a total of 46.7 percent. Another 42.9 percent reported no specialized in-house unit at all, but the presence of staff dealing with legal affairs, with about a quarter of them (8.9 percent of all respondents) dealing with only legal affairs and most (34 percent) dealing with a combination of legal and other affairs. The remaining 9.7 percent, 96 companies, still had neither legal units, nor legal staff; instead, they referred legal matters to *bengoshi* or other outside legal professionals. In the 1990 survey, only 42.2 percent of respondents reported having legal units, so at first glance it seems that the proportion had increased by 4.5 percentage points by 1995. In fact, however, the increase was by 9.5, since corporations with no legal staff had been excluded from the 1990 survey. In the 2000 survey, 616 respondents (52.1 percent) had specialist legal units, with 82.7 percent concentrated in one part of the corporation (compared to 80.2 percent in 1995, and 72.8 percent in 1990).

As in previous surveys, in 1995 the presence of legal units and legal staff was highly correlated with the increasing size of corporations. Accordingly, since

---

38. These figures are deduced from the reported total numbers of respondents multiplied by the averages given (1995 Survey, 45; 2000 Survey, 56).

39. See generally Hall (1998, 128; 1999); Katayama and Makov (1998, 128); McAlinn (1998, 3); Wiley (1999).

respondents in services and trade tend to be smaller than manufacturing and especially financial corporations, the former two categories tended to have both more respondents reporting no legal staff and more reporting specialist legal units even when they did have legal staff.

Respondents with legal departments mostly called them *hōmu-bu* (60.9 percent), or *hōmu-shitsu* (subdepartments) (21.9 percent) if units were smaller than departments (*bu*) but larger than sections (*ka*). Only 1.3 percent called them *hōki-bu* (legal and regulations department), compared to 8 percent using this sort of expression among respondents in the 1990 survey. This suggests not only increasing acceptance of the term *hōmu* (legal affairs), which may also indicate or contribute to a growing sense of a shared profession among corporate executives in Japanese corporations. More tentatively, perhaps it indicates awareness of ongoing deregulatory initiatives in Japan since 1990. Further consolidation in these respects was apparent in the 2000 survey. Around 30 percent (albeit of 579 corporations responding) called these *hōmu-bu*, while 13 percent called them *hōmu-ka*; another 11 percent called them *hōmu-shitsu*, 19 percent called them *hōmu-gurūpu*, and 10 percent called the units by other names. Only 2 percent used the term *hōki* (2000 Survey, 49–50).

A striking trend revealed by the 1995 survey was the accelerating rate at which legal units have been established since the mid-1960s, according to the 463 respondents who reported having separate units. In the decade between 1965 and 1974, 60 reported establishing such units (13 percent); between 1975 and 1984, 80 did (17.3 percent); in just five years between 1985 and 1989, 103 did (22.2 percent); and, between 1990 and 1995, 155 did (33.5 percent). Of these last 155 corporations, 107 did not have any units specializing in legal matters at all prior to 1989 (1995 Survey, 43–44). A similar growth pattern emerged from the 2000 survey for these periods, but the number establishing separate units leveled off at around 150 corporations between 1995 and 2000 (2000 Survey, 53).

The 1995 survey also revealed how the legal units were created. Four relevant categories could be distinguished from the responses:

(1) Of the 463 corporations with legal units, 70.2 percent had retained the same form since inception, either since incorporation (7.3 percent of the total) or when later established (62.9 percent).

(2) Of the remaining 29.4 percent that had undertaken some internal transformation, about half (15.6 percent of the total) were departments that had evolved from a section specializing in legal affairs (albeit, perhaps, with other titles); the reverse course, of a department specializing in legal affairs being merged with other units and reverting to a section, was rare (3.9 percent).

(3) Moreover, as one route to evolving into a specialist legal section, or possibly proceeding directly to departmental status, 5.4 percent (out of the 29.4 percent of those undergoing internal transformation) had been

created by merging many sub-units within the corporation that had dealt with legal matters.[40]

(4) Finally, "other" internal transformations were reported as making up 4.5 percent of the total.

These four main categories can be contrasted with those developed by Kenichi Yoneda from interviews of around 60 legal staff in 20 corporations, conducted from 1991 to 1994 and summarized in interim reports in 1995 (Yoneda 1995a and 1995b). The first category he distinguishes, said to be typical, is a group that has handled legal issues and has been spun off as a legal unit separate from or within the general affairs department (*sōmu-bu*). Assuming the "group" he mentions is not a formal unit within the organization, this can be subsumed into number (1) above.[41] Similarly is a second common category he identifies: a legal group within an international affairs department (*kokusai-bu*), which had handled international contracts and so on, has been set up as a distinct unit. In these two categories, he suggests that while the staff involved have developed skills in handling legal affairs, their work tends to remain limited to what it was formerly, since there are other groups specializing in legal work in other parts of the organization (e.g., within the same general affairs department or in a unit dealing with intellectual property matters).

Yoneda contrasts a third category, a legal unit that is suddenly created out of staff in formerly non-legal units, often with no particular background or skills in legal matters. They must develop experience through attracting legal work from wherever they can, case by case. Some instances of this arguably will be subsumed by number (1) above as well. Finally, he distinguishes the category of a legal department or section created by gathering together staff in various units which had handled legal matters, corresponding to (3). He suggests that the challenge for these new units is that the staff tends to remain focused on servicing the needs of their former colleagues, although bringing together a range of legal specialists into one overarching unit creating the potential for developing its capability as such. Yoneda goes on to argue that these differing patterns are related to various strategies adopted then by legal staff to attract and deal

---

40. An example of this is Toshiba Corporation. Originally, there was a section dealing with domestic legal matters entitled *bunsho-ka* within the general affairs department (*sōmu-bu*) and another section within the international affairs department (*kokusai-bu*) which dealt with international licensing matters (mainly contract, since purely intellectual property matters were dealt with by a specialist patent division). An international legal group developed within the former section, and in around 1982, it merged with the latter section, forming the international legal and licensing department. In 1990, this merged with the remnant of the *bunsho-ka*, leaving just one *hōmu-bu* (legal department) covering both domestic and international legal matters. This extended coverage, incidentally, also illustrates Takeshi Kojima's point, and ours above (Part I), about the accelerating domestication of international matters into the 1990s.

41. If it already constituted a section within that department and is transformed into a legal department, it is subsumed by (2).

with work. Unfortunately, the categories used in the 1995 survey and its aggregate data do not permit these hypotheses to be tested, but some of his ideas will be touched on below (especially in Part II C).[42]

Related data in the 1995 survey showed that those respondents without legal units assigned staff dealing with legal matters overwhelmingly to the general affairs department (84.5 percent); and that, overall, 66.6 percent of the 888 respondents with legal units were (at least nominally) within the jurisdiction of that sort of department. Corporations dealing with services generally had an even higher proportion (82.5 percent); but financial services providers had a lower proportion (46.2 percent), with many such companies (23.1 percent) instead putting them under planning (*keikaku*), investigations (*chōsa*), and/or public relations (*kōhō*) departments. Overall, the tendency was much more pronounced when the unit was a legal section (75.5 percent) rather than a legal department (only 25.3 percent). Some 27.9 percent of departments instead were responsible directly to the president, and 12 percent were fully independent, while only 8.2 percent came under the planning department (1995 Survey, 44). Hence, the higher ratio of specialist legal departments to legal sections compared to the 1990 survey suggested increasing status within the corporation, a trend reinforced by the 2000 survey. In 2000, the average number of staff rose slightly to 6.4 (81.9 percent male, again with about half in the managerial track). Interestingly, 34 out of 1,008 respondents reported a total of only 61 foreign legal staff members (2000 Survey, 56).

Growing status could also be seen from the 1995 survey in that on average, legal departments in 1995 had 11.7 staff specializing in legal affairs, while legal sections had 5.9 such staff. Overall, this gave an average of 6.1 staff per legal unit, compared to 5.2 staff in the 1990 survey. The proportion of male staff declined to 80.9 percent in 1995, from 84.6 percent in 1990, and overall almost half (43.5 percent) were in the managerial track (*kanrishoku*). Staff size was also correlated with company size. In 1995, the 68 largest companies (almost of all of which had legal units and all with specialized legal staff) had 19.6 staff on average. Traders constituted the category with the highest average (6.9), but the variance was large: the average was dragged up by 8.6 percent of traders (especially Japan's famous general trading companies, like Mitsui & Co. Ltd.) having departments with over 20 staff, although 22.4 percent of (much smaller) traders had only one legal specialist (1995 Survey, 45).

Further, 80.2 percent of legal staff were concentrated within one unit, compared to 72.8 percent in 1990. Such attempts to increase efficiency and strengthen the provision of legal services were particularly noticeable in financial services providers: 52.3 percent had concentrated staff in 1995, compared to 31.3 percent in 1990. On the other hand, as corporations become bigger, this proportion declined. Instead, they allocated legal staff to a variety of units: in corporations with more than ¥100 billion in capital, 39.7 percent did this in

---

42. Cf. also Yoneda (2001).

1995. Perhaps this comes from having optimized efficiency gains from concentration, such that additional legal staff can be allocated directly to other units to increase efficiency and provide further legal services more directly "on site." A seemingly related trend was for larger corporations to divide up their specialist legal units. While 67.7 percent of the respondents overall did not do this, only 23.5 percent did not amongst the largest corporations (with capital of more than ¥100 billion). Overall, the most common division was by area of law (16.6 percent) or by national versus international (13 percent) (1995 Survey, 49).

One risk in dividing up legal departments, or in allocating legal staff to other units, is that the focus on providing *legal* services may be lost, even in the largest corporations.[43] This seems quite real in that, overall, legal staff in business units remained formally part of a legal unit only in 7.6 percent of the corporations and under its direct control in only 3.8 percent. This tendency is particularly strong in financial and other service providers. In Japan's rapidly changing regulatory environment nowadays, it would seem very important that these corporations avoid legal problems, and then deal with those which arise, using true legal specialists associated with others rather than subsumed within business units. Indeed, as shown in other respects in the 2000 survey, the continued strengthening of legal units within financial institutions was seen in the latter half of the 1990s, driven by concerns about heightened expectations from shareholders and other stakeholders in those corporations.

On the other hand, it is understandable that financial services providers seem to want generalists in their legal personnel. In part, this may be because the changing environment creates new markets and opportunities for new financial services, but exploiting these within a legal framework requires a broad-based understanding of the practical operations of financial markets. Also, as described below, these corporations tended to be the larger ones, with many branches necessitating quick decision-making on the spot. For such corporations, it may be most efficient to have legally trained personnel on the ground level able to address legal issues as they arise there, but also able to carry out other tasks when called upon to do so.

The preference for generalists was apparent in the 1995 survey in that only 17.6 percent of legal staff in financial services providers had dealt exclusively with legal matters since joining (1995 Survey, 47–48). The remaining legal staff had experience working in other areas (mainly business departments, or personnel, information, or general affairs departments). This compares with 33.7 percent on average, and almost half of legal staff in corporations engaged in trading activities, with no experience working in non-legal positions and who therefore had concentrated exclusively on legal matters. In the 2000 survey, the average across all sectors of staff having no experience outside legal affairs dropped from 33.7 percent to 26.7 percent. However, the proportion remained over 30 percent for corporations with capital over ¥10 billion, which also prefer training specialists (2000 Survey, 58, 60).

---

43. Cf. generally Kitagawa (1994b).

The valuing of generalists was evident, secondly, from responses to questions as to how corporations train legal staff. Respondents in 1995 overall, including trader respondents, were evenly split on training generalists compared to specialists. Larger corporations and manufacturers (like Toshiba) tended to prefer training specialists. By contrast, twice as many financial services providers preferred training generalists rather than specialists (1995 Survey, 50).

Correspondingly, and thirdly, financial services providers in 1995 had a below-average proportion of managerial-track veterans with more than ten years' experience in legal affairs (14.2 percent compared to 38.1 percent), as well as non-managerial track (*ippanshoku*) veterans (18.5 percent compared to 30.6 percent). Traders had an above-average proportion in the managerial track (51 percent) (1995 Survey, 48–49).

Fourthly, reflecting the fact that overall, 62.3 percent of legal staff were graduates of undergraduate law programs (down from 68 percent in 1990), overall 20.6 percent of the corporations with legal staff reported no law graduates. By contrast, the proportion was 24.6 percent for financial services providers and 31 percent for traders (1995 Survey, 47).

Fifthly, in 1995 financial services providers had a higher than average (6.5 percent) proportion of utilizing formal education by sending staff to universities and so on, as researchers or teaching staff or even just to study (23.1 percent).[44] That method probably offered a much more generalist education than sending staff to outside seminars (78.5 percent compared to the average of 91.8 percent). The other primary methods of education for legal staff were (1) in-house study groups (32.7 percent), (2) in-house seminars with invited *bengoshi* lecturers (16 percent), and (3) distance learning (15.2 percent) (1995 Survey, 50–51). Method (1) and especially method (3) probably entailed more generalist education of legal staff, as did a new method listed in the 2000 Survey "on-the-job training" (used by 77.3 percent of its respondents) (2000 Survey, 60).

Finally, employing *bengoshi* as legal staff—hiring a specialist from the start—was a strategy for some manufacturers in the 1995 survey (2 percent), but not at all for financial services providers or traders. Similarly, 13 percent of manufacturers favored hiring legal staff in mid-career (perhaps already with considerable

---

44. A much-heralded reform in the early 1990s in Japanese national universities was the development of postgraduate law degrees for *shakaijin* (literally, "people of society"), namely those who had joined the workforce after completing their undergraduate education. The aim was to provide courses focused on more practical topics, alongside the more traditional academic courses for students planning careers as legal academics. Unfortunately, momentum petered out, probably because the courses were taught largely by the same set of law professors with very little experience of legal practice and not much more in policy-making. (Hopefully, that lesson will not be lost on the universities that have established postgraduate law schools, as mentioned in Part III below.) Interestingly, the 2000 survey confirmed a noticeable preference for sending legal staff for training at overseas universities (10.9 percent of all respondents, or 51.7 percent of the largest corporations), rather than at Japanese universities (5.4 percent or 29.9 percent); and many more legal staff had attended foreign universities (often for postgraduate studies, presumably) than had completed postgraduate degrees at Japanese universities (2000 Survey, 60; and Table 6.1 below).

experience in legal practice) and putting him or her to work immediately, but only 9.2 percent of financial services providers preferred this.

Generally, nonetheless, there was a slight increase in the number of staff hired in mid-career: 181 individuals in 115 corporations (13 percent) in 1995, compared to 169 people in 89 corporations (16.3 percent) in 1990. The small increase probably reflected general cautiousness in hiring during the economic recession. More noteworthy was the tripling in the number of *bengoshi* employed as full-time legal staff: 21 in 16 corporations (1.8 percent) in 1995, compared to just 7 in 6 corporations (1.1 percent) in 1990. Even more dramatic was the rise in the number of those qualified as lawyers in overseas jurisdictions: 97 in 59 corporations (6.6 percent) in 1995, 29 in 17 corporations (3.1 percent) in 1990. Most were probably Japanese who had gone abroad: in 1995, 286 legal staff in 110 corporations (12.4 percent) had studied abroad (compared to 159 in 68 corporations in 1990), while 275 in 111 corporations (12.5 percent) had been posted abroad (191 in 74 corporations). In addition, 11 corporations (1.2 percent) employed a total of 13 patent attorneys in 1995, and 7 (0.8 percent) employed 8 judicial scriveners (1995 Survey, 46).

In the 1995 survey, while only 1 percent of respondents "definitely" wanted to hire *bengoshi* and lawyers qualified abroad, 17.7 percent and 12.5 percent respectively wanted to do so "if possible." On the other hand, 64.6 percent still said they did not need *bengoshi,* while 55 percent remarked that they did not need staff qualified abroad. Nonetheless, heightening specialist knowledge by employing legal professionals continued over the latter half of the 1990s.[45] The 2000 survey showed the following transformations:

Table 6.1
Qualifications of Legal Staff in Corporations

Legal staff	2000 1,008 respondents			1995 888 respondents		
	Number of corps.	%	Number of staff	Number of corps.	%	Number of staff
Hired mid-term	290	28.8	491	115	13.0	181
Completed postgraduate education in a Japanese university	131	13.0	181	80	9.0	111
Studied abroad	129	12.8	401	111	12.5	275
Qualified as a foreign lawyer	75	7.4	163	59	6.6	97
Passed Japan's national bar exam	28	2.7	37†	16	1.8	21
Qualified as a judicial scrivener	15	1.5	21	7	0.8	8
Qualified as a patent attorney	13	1.3	14	11	1.2	13

Source: 2000 Survey, 57.
†With 30 later qualified as *bengoshi.*

45. See, e.g., *Nikkei Weekly* (1997).

The most prominent change was the increase in lateral hiring of those with experience as legal staff in other corporations (with 18.4 percent of respondents planning more of this, compared to 12.8 percent adopting this policy in 1995). However, 2.3 percent of respondents also expressed a distinct interest in directly hiring *bengoshi* or foreign-qualified lawyers, building on steady increases in such hires.

The rise in the number of, and interest in hiring, legal professionals in corporations within Japan is only gradual and is starting from a very small base; a marked contrast remains with the preponderance of qualified lawyers as in-house counsel in U.S. corporations.[46] Nonetheless, the trend is underpinned by a number of factors. In response to the globalization of Japanese corporations' activities since the 1970s, sketched above (Part I), Japanese corporations began both to professionalize their legal departments in subsidiaries or affiliates abroad and to send staff from parent corporations to study law abroad before returning to Japan to work on those cases from that end. In the 1990s, along with accelerating "domestication" of areas of law such as product liability, important areas of the regulatory environment were also changing within Japan—or at least the possibility of many changes had become much more real, as for example in the field of financial services.[47]

Some legal principles and techniques, for instance in the field of contracts, also proved readily transportable from abroad. Employing Japanese who had studied these and other areas of law, gaining professional qualifications abroad, was cheaper than employing *bengoshi*, who were older, with more human capital invested from the years needed to pass the still tremendously more difficult (than in the U.S., for example) bar examination in Japan (*shihō shiken*), and now belonged to a pseudo-cartel able to charge quite high fees.[48] Such relative economies probably constitute the primary reason for the relatively strong growth of foreign-trained Japanese lawyers within Japanese corporations in recent years, even if more hiring of *bengoshi* is also a noticeable development.

A second reason for preferring Japanese who qualified as lawyers abroad, rather than in Japan, may be more directly related to their being younger on average. This may allow them to fit in better with personnel strategies based on hiring recent university graduates and training them in a corporation's ethos, linked to the promise of lifelong employment and promotion linked to seniority.[49] Granted, this pattern of employment has never really applied to lower-tier

---

46. Cf. Miyazawa (1986).

47. See, e.g., Nottage (2001e); *The Lawyer* (2001) ("About a decade ago, many of the Japanese [financial] institutions did the bulk of their work in-house, using external lawyers as and when they were needed. But the concept of bringing a number of fully qualified *bengoshi* in-house to provide advice on transactions is new, and is one that is gaining steam, particularly as private practice conducts its own personal [*sic*] wars.").

48. See Ramseyer (1986). But see also text below.

49. Cf. also Miyazawa (1986, 106).

corporations. Even in larger corporations, at least until recently, there has also been a reluctance to extend its privileges to foreigners, and some of the Japanese who qualified overseas may be considered too "foreign" for the liking of some of the more conservative employers. Arguably, too, lifetime employment seems to have emerged in the post-war period as a result of exceptionally tight labor market conditions, (Foote 1996; Nottage 2001b) so it is not surprising that it is coming under increasing strain as unemployment reached record highs and Japan's economic recession dragged into the late 1990s. Nonetheless, this system remains entrenched in the largest corporations, and most of these retain the financial muscle to hire—and retain long-term—more of the highly trained legal staff needed to deal with increasingly complex and risky legal environments.

Another more problematic consideration can be suggested, however. Japanese corporations may prefer to hire Japanese who have qualified abroad, rather than *bengoshi,* because it allows them to obtain specialized legal advice without the strictures of professional ethics imposed on *bengoshi* even when employed by corporations.[50]

Nonetheless, the emerging trend to hire more highly trained legal professionals appears to be underpinned by the broader structural changes affecting legal staff and legal departments in Japanese corporations, discussed above. In turn, these are related to changes in the nature of the work done by legal staff, discussed next (Part II B), and the reconstruction of legal departments' relations both with other departments (Part II C 1) and with the legal profession in Japan as well as abroad (Part II C 2).

B. The Work of Legal Staff and Legal Departments

Let us turn then to the work of these "legal departments" (henceforth used generically to comprise departments or *bu,* sections or *ka,* and so on). When asked to list their five most important types of work in the 1995 survey, legal departments stressed domestic contract-related work (87.6 percent), domestic general legal advice (64.4 percent), domestic corporate affairs such as corporate finance and shareholders' meetings (59.9 percent), administration of directors' meetings (47.1 percent), managing litigation both domestically and internationally (52.7 percent), preserving documentation domestically (38.7 percent), and international contract-related work (33.4 percent) (1995 Survey, 51–53). These areas were also the most important in the 1990 survey; but the relative importance of contract-related work and of general legal advice had increased, as it continued to do over the latter half of the 1990s. In the 2000 survey, domestic contract-related work was mentioned as the most important category by 88.3 percent of the respondents and international contracts by 36.7 percent. General domestic legal advice was mentioned by 69.5 percent and international

---

50. Cf. Miyazawa (1986, 149) (arguing that the professional ethics of U.S. attorneys was one obstacle to the professionalization of legal departments of Japanese subsidiaries in the U.S.).

legal advice by 15 percent (up from 12.3 percent in 1995). Corporate reorganizations (including mergers and acquisitions) also increased, from 11.8 percent in 1995 to a total of 16.3 percent in 2000 (2000 Survey, 63).

By sector, a noteworthy exception again consisted of financial services providers, who in 1995 reported well-below-average importance for contract-related work both domestically (61.5 percent) and, especially, internationally (7.7 percent). One explanation advanced by the editors of the 1995 survey report was that financial transactions became more routinized (1995 Survey, 53). This may be related to the tendency mentioned above (Part II A) for financial services providers to retain less-specialized legal staff: specialists are less needed. But routinization as an explanation needs to be explored further. After all, international contract-related work was only a quarter of the average across all sectors (7.7 percent compared to 33.4 percent), whereas domestic contract-related work was much less noticeably below average (61.5 percent compared to 87.6 percent). Yet one would have expected the domestic side to involve more routinized transactions than the international side. Perhaps domestic financial markets and products were changing more rapidly than those internationally. Alternatively, perhaps international transactions were indeed less routinized at the level of contract negotiation and drafting, creating more contract-related work, but international financial services contracts disputes were resolved more informally than domestic disputes, meaning relatively less contract-related work. Such issues await further comparative research.[51]

Incidentally, the greater importance of domestic as opposed to international legal work (especially that related to contracts and general legal advice) does not mean that Japan is more litigious or legal-minded in these areas than other jurisdictions. The simple explanation for this, most probably, was that most corporations responding to the 1995 survey were primarily focused on domestic markets, rather than international markets.[52] As some Japanese commentators noted already in the 1960s, Japanese corporations' increased preparedness in addressing issues of contract law and practice was boosted by increasing exposure to international markets (Hoshino 1972; Kawashima 1974). Similarly, as mentioned above (Part I), more general legal expertise was developed through the 1970s and 1980s following exposure to labor law, product liability, and antitrust issues, primarily abroad. And Japan's civil litigation rate remains significantly below that of other industrialized economies. Yet there has been an exponential increase since the early 1970s, indicating an important structural change in the myriad of factors which arguably influence overall litigation rates (Wollschläger 1997; Nottage and Wollschläger 1996).[53] As well as macro-economic trends and demographics,

---

51. They were the topic of an international conference held on March 21–23, 1999 at the Law Center for European and International Cooperation in Cologne (see Horn and Norton 2000).

52. This was clarified in the 2000 survey.

53. See also Goodman (2001).

these include more micro-level issues, such as institutional barriers to litigation preventing suits being brought, comparative certainty of result promoting out-of-court settlement and more ingrained "cultural" factors which may affect the entire dispute emergence and transformation process.[54] Breaking down trends in disputes and litigation by area suggests that dispute resolution in Japanese law and society continued to experience significant changes throughout the 1990s.

Legal departments in Japanese corporations are well aware of this. For the first half of the 1990s, 38.8 percent of respondents in the 1995 survey reported an increase in disputes domestically, compared to 17.5 percent reporting an increase in international disputes (1995 Survey, 55).[55] For the latter half of the 1990s, an even larger 50.8 percent reported an increase in disputes domestically and 19.9 percent internationally (2000 Survey, 69).[56] Moreover, in the 1995 survey, 60.1 percent thought that domestic disputes would increase, whereas 35.3 percent thought that international disputes would increase (55–56).[57] In the 2000 survey, the proportion expecting a further increase in domestic disputes had grown to 74.2 percent (indeed, 80.2 percent amongst financial services providers) and international disputes to 46.7 percent. Main growth areas expected for domestic disputing were again business contracting (*torihiki keiyaku*), consumer issues, intellectual property (arguably also reflecting Japan's growing e-commerce market), and insolvencies (70–71).[58] Thus, although the strengthening of Japanese corporate legal departments was initially prompted by international exposure, increasingly it seems driven by domestic developments.

---

54. Cf. generally Ramseyer (1988).

55. However, 32.1 percent gave no answer when asked about the trend in international disputes, compared to just 5.9 percent when asked about domestic disputes. The former may have included some corporations which in fact had an increase in disputes, but were unwilling to risk disclosing this even when results are reported in aggregate and anonymously. This would mean that there had been a greater increase in international disputes than reported. Alternatively, though, it may have been that many legal departments simply did not handle any international matters, e.g., because their corporations focused on domestic markets, or they did have international disputes but did not know enough about them all to pick any trend: for example, because many minor ones are handled by subsidiaries overseas without the need for reporting back to Japan.

56. Again, around a third gave no answer (33.6 percent). However, the question in this survey asked to "respond for domestic transactions only, if no international transactions." The report editors therefore argue that non-responses regarding international disputes should be taken as indicating that the corporation had no international dealings and that on this basis, 22.2 percent of manufacturers, 43.9 percent of traders, 55.4 percent of financial services providers, and 47.8 percent of service providers appear to fall into that category.

57. Again, 15.8 percent gave no answer to this question when asked about international disputes, whereas 4.3 percent gave no answer for domestic disputes. This continued difference suggests that the alternative explanations given above are plausible.

58. "Insolvencies" was a new category for expected disputes added in the 2000 survey. For an excellent summary of the data on burgeoning insolvencies in Japan and consequent changes in its laws, see Anderson (2001). On electronic commerce legislation, see, e.g., Kakinuki (2000).

1. Legal Department Involvement in Disputes or Litigation

Asked to select the three most important categories of disputes, domestically and internationally, respondents to the 1995 and 2000 surveys reported as follows:

Table 6.2
Most Important Categories of Disputes
PERCENTAGES

Category	Domestic		International	
	1995	2000	1995	2000
Business contracts	71.8	68.1	39.7	35.4
Intellectual property	35.2	36.3	26.6	23.5
Consumer-related	29.1	32.5	7.1	5.9
Labor	21.7	19.4	4.8	4.3
Antitrust	10.6	8.3	4.9	4.0
Corporate law	10.0	5.9	3.9	3.5
Pollution and environment	9.8	5.0	1.9	0.8
Tax	4.4	2.4	6.3	4.0
International trade and investment	1.4	0.7	7.2	4.4
Insolvencies	–	50.0	–	6.3
Other	8.1	5.8	5.6	2.4
No response	10.8	2.5	46.4	33.5

Source: 1995 Survey, 56; 2000 Survey, 70–71.

Comparing the importance of the various categories in domestic as opposed to international disputes may point the way to some rough comparisons between Japanese and foreign law, although to do this more convincingly we would need more data and more precise questioning.[59]

Business contracts, as opposed to consumer contracts (most probably captured within the consumer-related category), were the most important both domestically (71.8 percent) and internationally (39.7 percent). This is consistent with other empirical studies demonstrating the importance of contract both within Japan and between Japanese and New Zealand corporations (Nottage 1997c, 59; 1997d, 482; 1998a, 611). Next in importance was intellectual property-related disputes, again both domestically (35.2 percent) and internationally (26.6 percent), and particularly so for large manufacturers. The lesser

---

59. It is also particularly rough in that, again, far more respondents to the 1995 survey gave no answer in the case of international disputes (46.4 percent) than did in the case of domestic disputes (10.8 percent). For the 2000 survey, the 33.5 percent non-response rate regarding current international disputes represented 396 corporations—almost the same number as those who did not respond regarding expected changes in international disputing—reinforcing the 2000 survey editors' view that this number, or about a third of the corporations, did not have any international dealings.

importance domestically, relative to contracts, may suggest that intellectual property law and practice in Japan is still less developed or inadequately enforced, compared to other major jurisdictions. This would be so despite many improvements since the late 1980s, arguably in Japan's national interest given its transformation into a major technological innovator.[60] The greater importance of tax matter disputes internationally (6.3 percent), as opposed to domestically (4.4 percent), may reflect a greater unwillingness for Japanese corporations to take on government authorities.[61] On the other hand, perhaps suggesting that measures gradually strengthening enforcement in Japan are bearing fruit,[62] antitrust disputes were more important domestically (10.6 percent) than internationally (4.9 percent). And while international trade and investment (*tsushōhō*) disputes were overwhelmingly less important domestically (1.4 percent) than internationally (7.2 percent), this is to be expected given that such law usually only becomes relevant when local manufacturers or affected parties complain about the activities of Japanese exporters or their overseas subsidiaries. Pollution and environmental disputes were relatively more important domestically (9.8 percent) than internationally (1.9 percent), as were consumer-related disputes (29.1 percent versus 7.1 percent); labor law-related disputes (21.7 percent versus 4.8 percent); and, to a lesser extent, corporate law-related disputes (10 percent versus 3.9 percent).

Before concluding that these areas of law are much more important in Japan, however, we should realize that some areas of law may only be relevant (or proportionately much more so) domestically, e.g., corporate law in the case of Japanese corporations with no corporate presence overseas, labor law for corporations with no employees based or hired overseas, or environmental law for corporations with no factories overseas. Similarly, although Japanese corporations may have subsidiaries or dealers overseas to sell products to consumers abroad, the latter initially may wish to claim directly against the Japanese corporation (e.g., because the dealer is less solvent or under a manufacturer's warranty), but give up more readily than Japanese consumers because of the impracticalities of pursuing such claims internationally. Hopefully, future surveys will add questions to elicit data along these lines, so we can further expand the field for comparative studies of Japanese law beyond the black-letter rules in legislation and case law (Nottage 1997a and 1997b). Already, however, we

---

60. Cf. generally Heath (1997, 331). See also Nottage (1998b).

61. However, tax litigation—as well as tax planning—seems to have become more popular in recent years in Japan. In 2001, for example, *bengoshi* and tax attorneys set up a professional association called the Tax Litigation Society (*sozei soshō gakkai*). See *International Tax Review* (2002). Cf. generally Murai (1980, 47).

62. Cf. generally Haley (1995). See also Haley (1998b; 2001); Fry (2001); Lightbourne (2001). In addition, of course, it may be more difficult for foreign antitrust authorities to pursue claims extraterritorially against purely domestic Japanese corporations, although such claims are an emerging global phenomenon. See, e.g., Brill and Carlson (1999) and Warner (1999).

begin to perceive what legal matters are important nowadays for Japanese corporations and also what areas of law are particularly topical.

The 1995 survey also added some more specific questions to identify these. Asked what new issues legal departments had addressed over the previous five years, 71 percent responded "product liability," related to an expanded interest in consumer issues since the late 1980s (doubtless underscoring the importance of consumer-related disputes, just mentioned) (Nottage 1997a and 1997b); 43.2 percent responded "shareholder derivative suits," a major challenge to corporate governance and affairs in Japan over the 1990s;[63] 44.3 percent responded "abiding by antitrust law"; 27.3 percent responded "securing a risk management system"; 9.9 percent responded "restructuring," implying labor issues;[64] and 7.4 percent responded "pollution and environmental issues." Rankings were generally similar in the 2000 survey, although the percentages varied, partly because of more choices offered (1995 Survey, 62). In 2000, the top-ranking issue was the Y2K problem (40.7 percent), followed by product liability (36.6 percent), antitrust (27.8 percent), corporate ethics and compliance programs (26.5 percent), risk management (23.7 percent), management reforms (board system, etc., 16.6 percent), shareholder derivative suits (13.4 percent), sexual harassment (12.5 percent),[65] and pollution and environmental issues (6.9 percent) (2000 Survey, 85).

The large majority stressing product liability issues, especially in the 1995 survey, varied according to sector. This is understandable given the scope of application of additional strict liability legislation, in force since July 1, 1995. The proportion was particularly high for manufacturers (84.1 percent), usually caught by Article 2(3) Paragraph 1 of the Product Liability Law of 1994, and traders (81 percent), who may be importers or certain "own-branders" deemed manufacturers under Paragraphs 2 or 3, or who may be sued by consumers under other law (primarily in tort under Article 709 of the Civil Code) and thus want to seek indemnification from manufacturers (1995 Survey, 62).[66] Similarly, in the 2000 survey, these categories of respondents had higher than average percentages (47.6 percent and 47.1 percent, respectively) (2000 Survey, 85). Overall, the proportion was particularly high for larger companies (80.2 percent for corporations with capital between ¥10 billion and ¥100 billion).

Similarly, while overall 71.7 percent of corporations in 1995 had established some sort of intra-firm structure to deal with product liability issues, 79.9 percent of manufacturers and 87.9 percent of traders had done so, whereas only 53.8 percent of financial services providers and 38.1 percent of other services

---

63. See generally West (2001b) and Utsumi (2001).

64. See generally Yamakawa (2001).

65. On sexual harassment, see generally Parker and Wolff (2000) and Yamakawa (1999).

66. For a detailed commentary on the product liability law, see generally Nottage and Kato (2000).

providers had done so.[67] Moreover, while overall, 32.7 percent of corporations had established a specialist unit or team to address product liability issues, 44.8 percent of manufacturers had done so. Of the latter, 22 percent had units made up of between ten and fifteen staff. But 18 percent of these reported no staff assigned full-time to the unit, while those that did mostly assigned only between one to three full-time staff. Further, only 45.3 percent responded to a question asking how many were legal staff, and the majority of these respondents answered that there were only one or two of them (1995 Survey, 63). The strategy preferred by manufacturers therefore seems to be to create a structure that brings together (or can quickly bring together) a range of personnel dealing with legal, management, technology, quality assurance, and other issues. This is understandable, for the most common type of defects giving rise to uncertainties which can result in persistent and major claims—design defects— calls for a broad-based balancing test, while until the legislation is amplified by an accumulation of case law, the only practical solution for Japanese manufacturers is to combine legal, business, and technological expertise to try profitably to produce safe products.[68]

By contrast, 11.2 percent of traders in 1995 reported dealing with product liability issues "mainly through the legal department," compared to just 5.6 percent of corporations overall who did so; and 47.2 percent of the former reported that the "legal department dealt with product liability issues in collaboration with other departments," compared to 33.4 percent of corporations overall. This reflects the more limited and more "legal" aspects of product liability legislation applicable to traders, especially negotiations with suppliers as to indemnification if defects give rise to claims, and perhaps adding warnings (even though the ultimate responsibility for warning defects lies with "manufacturers" under the Product Liability Law).

Such sectoral differences are also apparent from questions inquiring specifically into the impact of the new Product Liability Law per se. When asked in 1995 how legal departments dealt with product liability issues before the law came into effect, 34.6 percent overall reported that they dealt with product liability claims or suits, compared to 44.2 percent for manufacturers and 39.7 percent for traders. Incidentally, when asked how they dealt with product liability issues after enactment, the proportion overall actually fell to 25.6 percent (1995 Survey, 63–64). This does not mean that the Product Liability Law has been

---

67. With limited possible exceptions, mostly still to be resolved by future litigation (e.g., as to defects in software), the product liability law only applies to movable products, not services. In practice, however, service providers are affected by the law because it is often unclear whether a defect in the product was the cause of an accident (e.g., a gas heater) or a concomitant service (e.g., installation thereof) (see also Nottage and Wada 1998, especially 60–61).

68. Hence Kitagawa's repeated urgings for Japanese corporations not only to improve product safety activities through organizational initiatives, education, and so on, but also to do so by the development of corporation- or industry-based guidelines (see, e.g., Kitagawa 1997).

ineffective.[69] On the contrary, other results from this survey indicate that manufacturers have become much more conscious of product liability issues and accordingly have adopted countermeasures to improve product safety. This is in addition to the above-mentioned establishment of specialist units to deal with product liability issues, which was undoubtedly driven primarily by the widespread debate since the early 1990s leading to enactment of the Product Liability Law in 1994.[70] Specifically, whereas 53.6 percent undertook instruction in product liability issues beforehand, 68.9 percent did so afterwards (even 55 percent of financial services providers, presumably because many act as general business advisors to Japanese firms—particularly in a recessionary economy—and may have volunteered this sort of information, or more directly because some of them were insurance corporations offering damage insurance).

Further, while beforehand only 28.5 percent of respondents overall undertook investigations into risk analysis/countermeasures (quality assurance, warning labeling, etc.) for their own products, this rose to 37.4 percent after the Product Liability Law came into effect (again with a higher proportion, 40.6 percent, for manufacturers). And while 35.1 percent entered into or maintained product liability insurance coverage beforehand, 39.1 percent did so afterwards (42.7 percent for manufacturers) (1995 Survey, 63–64). Considering that the 1995 survey was done only a few months after the Product Liability Law came into effect in July 1995, and allowing for the high likelihood of more countermeasures already being taken prior to and upon passage in June 1994, this indicates that the Product Liability Law has had some important effects on Japanese corporations.[71] This conclusion is supported by a range of empirical studies done at the time and later, and the continued importance of product liability issues in the work of corporate legal departments, reported in the 2000 survey.[72]

Another major area of work, particularly in the first half of the 1990s, evidenced by 43.2 percent overall in the 1995 survey, was shareholder derivative litigation. This was particularly true for financial services providers (69.2 percent), which continue to face strong criticism for poor management during the bubble years of the late 1980s and for shady dealings with financial regulators through to the 1990s.[73] Unfortunately, however, legal departments of financial services providers did not seem to be adopting more than average, as of 1995, positive measures to address derivative suits and their underlying causes: reviewing minutes and operating records of directors' meetings (25.5 percent of respondents overall), regularly educating or informing directors about these

69. Cf. generally the negative prognoses of Bernstein and Fanning (1996, 45); Marcuse (1996).

70. See generally Nottage (2001e).

71. Cf. Melchinger (1997).

72. Summarized in Nottage and Wada (1998, Part II); Nottage and Kato (2000); Nottage (2000c). See also Rothenberg (2000); Easton (2000); Kelemen and Sibbitt (2002).

73. On the latter, see, e.g., Fitzgibbon (1991).

issues (14.1 percent overall), or even educating or informing them on demand (23.2 percent overall). Instead, they stood out as more likely to adopt the more reactive measures: entering into or maintaining insurance (partly or totally at the corporation's expense) for claims based on directors' negligence (40.2 percent overall, but 49.2 percent for financial services providers) and collaborating with other departments to deal with suits when brought by shareholders against the corporation (44 percent versus 56.9 percent).

Again, we get a sense of the relatively weaker position of legal departments or staff among financial services providers. More generally, moreover, we should note that 17.5 percent of legal departments in corporations overall still did not undertake any special measures at all. Only 6.8 percent reported that the corporation was prepared actively to get involved in shareholders' suits "in specified cases," i.e., presumably when they appear very strong and in the corporation's clear interest to pursue liability against wayward directors (1995 Survey, 64–65). This could be read as indicating that shareholders' derivative actions, and their implications for corporate governance, still had not brought about major change in Japan. Arguably, only small improvements in this pattern were evident from the 2000 survey. However, that survey was done before the judgment in the Daiwa Bank case where the Osaka District Court awarded a record ¥83 billion against directors, sending shock waves throughout the corporate sector.[74]

Also potentially impinging on the corporate governance field, however, has been another important area of work for legal departments in recent years: abiding by antitrust law. Naturally, this was particularly important for larger corporations, in the 1995 survey: 75 percent of the largest (with capital of ¥100 billion or more), and 59.2 percent for large corporations (¥10–100 billion), compared to 44.3 percent overall. Manufacturers again stood out, with 52.1 percent reporting this as an important recent area of work. They were affected by increased enforcement of regulations regarding cartels and collusive bidding practices (*dangō*)[75] and greater concern about unfair practices as the recessionary environment caused corporations even within broad corporate groups (*keiretsu*) to review long-standing business relationships.[76] Also prominent were financial

---

74. See generally Yamada (2002).

75. Manufacturers also have to grapple with the implications of the abolition of numerous areas where cartels had been explicitly permitted, following a 1997 amendment to the anti-monopoly law. Problems with *dangō* arise particularly in government procurement, exacerbating trade friction. See generally Toyama (1987); Grier (1995). For the historical origins of cartels in Japan, see, e.g., Gao (2001). For an example of *dangō* coming to light, see *Asahi* (1998b) (JFTC investigation of collusive tendering for supply of garbage incinerators to local authorities).

76. See, e.g., *Asahi* (1998a) (Nissan orders a new gearbox from a major supplier hitherto firmly within the Toyota manufacturing *keiretsu*). One example was the concern that larger corporations would abuse their dominant position, using the enactment of the product liability law as a pretext, to squeeze their suppliers. In addition, the interaction between

institutions, 47.7 percent of whose legal departments stressed antitrust law. In response to the changing regulatory environment, and poor sectoral and economy-wide performance, the financial sector has been one area where tie-ups—often adopting innovative forms—have continued to increase rapidly, frequently involving foreign firms.[77]

Merger and acquisition activity in this sector could be expected to spill over into others, whereas in the 1995 survey, respondents overall reported mainly (52.1 percent) "no change" regarding mergers and acquisitions work, with 10.5 percent each reporting an increase or a decrease (and 25 percent of the largest corporations reporting a decrease) (1995 Survey, 62). A very important change from the late 1990s is the rapidly growing foreign direct investment into Japan, especially in the services sector (Nottage 2002b; Lebrun 2001). In the 2000 survey, 24.9 percent of respondents (47.1 percent of the largest corporations) expected a further increase in merger and acquisition activity in Japan over 2001–2005, with hardly anyone (only 3.1 percent) expecting a decline (2000 Survey, 83). Other responses confirm significant transformations or challenges to the corporate governance regime which caught the imagination within and outside Japan from the 1950s through to the early 1990s.[78]

Finally, recall that 27.3 percent of respondents to the 1995 survey stressed "securing a risk management system" as an important area of legal work in the previous five years. This becomes readily understandable given that each of the above-mentioned areas requires stronger and more effective intra-organizational controls.[79] A related development was that more legal departments (23.7 percent compared to 13.2 percent in 1990) reported "proposing activity plans,

---

antitrust law and civil law became a hot topic over the 1990s, highlighted by prominent litigation in the cosmetics sector. There is considerable empirical evidence that these cases brought about significant changes in corporate mentality (see Visser't Hooft 2002; Taylor 2001). On unwinding in *keiretsu* relationships, especially horizontal ones centered on banks, see, e.g., Nottage (2001b); Shishido (2000). More generally on *keiretsu*, see, e.g., Ahmadjian and Lincoln (2001); Miwa and Ramseyer (2000).

77. For an excellent overview, see Sibbitt (1998).

78. For example, restructuring of the corporation was reported by 69.5 percent of the respondents to the 2000 survey (82.8 percent of the largest), compared to 55.8 percent in 1995. Of these, 20 percent of financial services providers reported "employee adjustments," close to the average of 26.5 percent, whereas in 1995 only 15.9 percent of restructuring financial institutions had restructured staff, compared to 29.8 percent of all respondents reporting restructuring. Secondly, 55.1 percent of the respondents to the 2000 survey reported implementing management reforms over the previous five years, mostly (56.1 percent) by reducing the number of board members (to an average of 12.1, from 19.8 in 1995). Thirdly, 17.8 percent of the respondents to the 2000 survey had implemented stock repurchases, while 30.9 percent had investigated the possibility. More importantly, 18.2 percent had issued stock options, while 30.8 percent had investigated this (2000 Survey, 80–85). On the significance of some of these changes for corporate governance, see further Nottage (2001b and 2001d).

79. See West (2001b) and Utsumi (2001). Stressing the importance of this coordinated approach, see also Kitagawa (1996).

norms of conduct, structural reform" in response to "major risks," identified this time as "insider trading" (the only one identified in both 1990 and 1995), "antitrust law violations," and "shareholder derivative suits." Similarly, the proportion of legal departments reporting that they could give advice or guidance on their own initiative to other departments increased from 76.8 percent to 82.7 percent. And, perhaps even more significantly, the proportion that said they "could not" do this at all declined from 17.9 percent to 8.9 percent (1995 Survey, 61). Consistently with these trends, in the 2000 survey, 34.1 percent of respondents reported introducing a corporate compliance program (with legal departments playing a pivotal role for 54.6 percent of these—50.8 percent also playing such a role regarding internal rules) and 23.8 percent reported legal departments "actively" providing advice at their own initiative to company officers and other departments (2000 Survey, 78–79). These tendencies also reflect the growing status and role of legal departments and legal staff in Japanese corporations generally, mentioned above in Part II A.

On the other hand, it is difficult to determine yet the impact of this trend on the resolution of disputes by legal departments. First, 46.5 percent of legal departments in the 1995 survey left the approach to resolving disputes "in principle to the judgment of the front-line (department in question)," reserving to themselves only "important cases." This proportion rose to 69.7 percent for financial services providers. The survey editors suggested that this may be because the powers of each branch or business department in such situations are clearly spelled out (1995 Survey, 57). However, combined with other trends within financial services providers (see Part II A above), this tendency can be seen as a more problematic under-valuing of legal expertise in Japanese financial institutions. Indeed, in the 2000 survey, the gap had closed significantly: 47.7 percent of respondents overall still left the approach to disputes "in principle to the front-line," but 52.5 percent of financial institutions did so by that stage (2000 Survey, 71–71).[80] Overall, moreover, fully 84.3 percent of the respondents in 1995 (and still 79.3 percent in 2000) admitted that they did not spell out criteria for differentiating the "importance" of cases, the prerequisite for referral to legal departments. Only 25.6 percent of the respondents in 1995 (18.7 percent in 2000) required business departments to discuss disputes with legal departments as soon as they arose, regardless of their importance. And only 19.1 percent in 1995 (23.2 percent in 2000) adopted the strategy of having legal departments in principle deal with disputes, but leaving "minor ones to the judgment of the front-line (i.e., the department in question)."

A more indirect reflection of the legal department's status may lie in its relation to outside legal professionals, particularly lawyers. Associating with

---

80. Domestically, 45.9 percent of respondent corporations "conducted cases under the guidance of lawyers, with the legal department providing support," while 27 percent (a small rise over 1995) reported "conducting litigation jointly." Internationally, the proportions were 23.7 percent and 8 percent respectively, although 25.3 percent gave no answer in addition to the 37.3 percent reporting "no experience in international litigation."

professionals with respected expertise and high social status like *bengoshi* may advance the status of a legal department and its staff, but this may vary (to the extent also that this becomes obvious to others) depending on its degree of relative independence and leadership in those dealings. In domestic litigation, 46.1 percent of 1995 respondent corporations "conducted cases under the guidance of lawyers, with the legal department providing support," while only 23.1 percent reported "conducting litigation jointly." The latter proportion rose to 27.9 percent among the largest corporations and was the case for the majority of corporations with specialist legal departments. The latter, therefore, may have the most reflected status from their dealings with *bengoshi*.

Asked about the division of labor in international litigation, similar trends were apparent, but 47.8 percent in 1995 gave no answer, and where there were specialist legal departments, the majority of these instead preferred still to "conduct litigation under the guidance of lawyers, with the legal department providing support" (1995 Survey, 59–60). The latter tendency probably does not detract from the legal departments' reflected gain in status from such dealings, however, because others within the corporation as a whole no doubt would understand this to be a sensible policy given the extent of extra expertise needed to resolve international disputes, as opposed to domestic ones. Similar tendencies were apparent in the 2000 survey, which also asked whether respondents had no experience of domestic litigation (11.1 percent) or international litigation (37.3 percent) (2000 Survey, 76).

An interesting further question, arising if this "reflected social status" hypothesis has some validity, is how to interpret the fact that in the 1995 survey, 35.9 percent of legal departments reported conferring with Japanese lawyers specializing in international matters (*shōgai bengoshi*), rather than lawyers in the jurisdiction overseas with which the dispute is connected (28 percent) or foreign lawyers in Japan (14.1 percent) (1995 Survey, 59). Perhaps this is related to the nature of the dispute, with the former being retained for the (presumably more frequent) disputes which do not or probably will not result in litigation, especially in the jurisdiction overseas. Only in the latter case will it usually make more sense to deal directly with foreign lawyers either in that jurisdiction or in Japan (e.g., if language is a concern). Yet it could be related also to a preference for legal departments to deal with *bengoshi*, who are perhaps perceived as the higher status professional, at least in Japanese society. The plausibility of this depends in part on whether relations between legal departments and *bengoshi* are still driven by more traditional, "social" relationships, or whether they are becoming more commercially driven. This issue is discussed below in Part II C in the context of overall relations between legal departments and lawyers.

Let us return to what actually happens to disputes generally within Japanese corporations, as indicating the contemporary roles and status of legal departments. When asked to rank the most common means to resolve domestic disputes, the overwhelmingly popular first choice given in the 1995 survey was to attempt to resolve them through direct negotiation with the outside party or parties (86 percent); only 5.1 percent "gave up asserting rights," while only 4.1 percent sought "settlement within litigation" (*soshōjō no wakai*) and only 2.7 percent sought a court judgment. Arguably, the first choice correlates roughly to the first stage of dispute resolution. When asked about the most common second choice of resolving disputes, which can be roughly correlated to a second stage if we assume a significant proportion of disputes are resolved through direct negotiation, most respondents sought settlement within litigation (34.6 percent) or gave up asserting rights (32 percent). The proportion seeking judgment rose to 15.3 percent and formal, mainly court-annexed "conciliation" (*chōtei*), became significant (11.3 percent). When asked about their third choice, only 12.3 percent gave up, conciliation remained quite popular (12.7 percent), but so did settlement within litigation (28.2 percent), and most popular was taking the dispute through to judgment (39.9 percent) (1995 Survey, 57). The popularity of these last two preferences, involving formal court procedures, is understandable if we conceive this as a third stage of at least some disputes.

Trends were generally similar for the resolution of international disputes. An even more popular first choice was direct negotiation (88.1 percent). As second choice, giving up was more common (34.8 percent) than settling within litigation (29.9 percent), and pursuing the dispute to judgment was somewhat less common (11.6 percent) than for domestic disputes. This is understandable given the greater costs of pursuing a dispute, even "in the shadow of the law," in an international context. A more striking difference is the preference that emerges, as a second choice or perhaps as a second stage of dispute resolution, for arbitration (8.5 percent) rather than conciliation (4.8 percent). This relative preference was also apparent for the third choice (9.8 percent versus 9.3 percent, but 11.4 percent versus 7.6 percent in the 1990 survey) and was the opposite for domestic disputes (1995 Survey, 58). This indicates that although it remains true that dispute resolution by arbitral proceedings is uncommon in domestic disputes, that is not necessarily so nowadays in international disputes.[81] Otherwise, there is a somewhat more pronounced tendency to pursue disputes through to judgment (38.7 percent, but 43.1 percent in 1990), rather than settling (22 percent, and 22.1 percent in 1990), compared to domestic disputes.

---

81. Japanese corporations still do not use much the services of the Japan Commercial Arbitration Association, with its head office in Tokyo (website at http://www.jcaa.or.jp/e/) (see generally Nottage 2002c). However, a review of arbitral awards and appeals or enforcement proceedings through local courts, reported even in English in well-known publications such as the Yearbooks of Commercial Arbitration, shows that Japanese corporations have been quite frequent users of arbitration (Nottage 1999, F1 Appendix A. See also Nottage 2000b). Future research should examine possible differences in the use of arbitration among different types of Japanese corporations, using for example this set of data and other cases reported on legal databases such as LexisNexis.

These patterns appear to have been largely maintained over the latter half of the 1990s. Responses regarding the three most frequent dispute resolution methods, reported for 2000 and (in italics) for 1995, were as follows:

Table 6.3(a)
Domestic Dispute Resolution Methods
2000, *1995*
PERCENTAGES

Dispute resolution method	Giving up rights	Negotiation between parties	Mediation	Arbitration	Settlement during trial	Judgment etc.
1st	4.9	83.2	1.4	0.3	5.7	4.5
(most frequent)	*6.2*	*85.5*	*1.1*	*0.2*	*3.6*	*3.4*
2nd	26.0	8.9	11.4	1.6	31.9	20.2
	31.4	*8.9*	*10.9*	*1.3*	*31.1*	*16.6*
3rd	14.9	5.0	12.0	3.5	29.2	35.4
	12.4	*3.8*	*11.6*	*3.2*	*31.3*	*37.7*
Total	36.0	93.8	18.5	3.9	50.7	35.4
	39.8	*95.0*	*17.3*	*3.3*	*48.7*	*37.7*

Table 6.3(b)
International Dispute Resolution Methods
2000, *1995*
PERCENTAGES

Dispute resolution method	Giving up rights	Negotiation between parties	Mediation	Arbitration	Settlement during trial	Judgment etc.
1st	4.9	84.1	0.2	1.8	6.5	2.5
(most frequent)	*5.8*	*84.8*	*0.0*	*1.4*	*5.1*	*2.9*
2nd	39.6	7.6	5.9	12.2	21.5	13.2
	41.9	*9.7*	*5.4*	*11.4*	*21.9*	*9.7*
3rd	15.3	6.4	6.4	20.7	30.5	20.7
	17.5	*3.4*	*6.2*	*21.5*	*32.2*	*19.2*
Total	38.7	92.2	7.2	19.5	34.9	20.8
	41.4	*92.8*	*6.3*	*18.3*	*33.5*	*17.6*

Source for Tables 6.3(a) and (b): 2000 Survey, 72. These percentages do not correspond precisely to those given in the text above, even when comparing 1995 survey data, because the percentages are for a different set of respondents and exclude those who did not answer this part of the survey (344 respondents regarding their situation domestically in 1995, leaving 839 corporations; 768 for international disputes in 1995, leaving only 415 corporations).

The totals of each of these tables suggests a slight shift (for both domestic and international disputes) away from giving up and negotiating a resolution, toward more arbitration, conciliation, settlement during litigation, and taking a case to final judgment (2000 Survey, 73n3).[82] A possible explanation is that Japan's deepening recession over the latter half of the 1990s left Japanese corporations less willing and able to accept losses which could be recouped for more structured dispute resolution procedures.

As a result of such patterns, corporations reported an average of 12.4 pending domestic suits in the 1995 survey. However, this was heavily influenced by financial services providers, which reported an average of 195.4 cases pending, not surprising given the nature of their business and the economic climate at that time. Even adjusting for reporting more cases than in the previous survey and forming a smaller proportion of respondents, overall there was a noticeable increase in average suits pending compared to 1990 (3 cases) and 1986 (2.7) (1995 Survey, 58). In the 2000 survey, the average dropped back to 3.9 suits (2000 Survey, 74),[83] probably because financial institutions had less incentive to pursue bad loans, due for example to various government interventions to clean up that problem at a macro-economic level after the banking crisis of 1998. Another feature of the 2000 survey was an increase in valid responses, from 73.7 percent in 1995 to 88.4 percent in 2000, which the authors interpret as indicating a declining "allergy" toward litigation (2000 Survey, 74).[84]

The 1995 and 2000 surveys asked corporations to list the top three categories of domestic suits and elicited the following responses:

---

82. Considering the 833 respondents who answered in 2000 about the situation domestically both five years and one year previously, concerning the first and second most frequent dispute resolution mechanisms, the decline in giving up (dropping from 32.8 percent to 27.3 percent) and increase in taking the dispute through to judgment (rising from 17.2 percent to 21.1 percent) were statistically significant.

83. Of 1,046 valid responses, 47.5 percent indicated no suits pending; 38.8 percent had 1 to 5 suits; 7 percent had 6 to 10 pending suits. Therefore, 93.3 percent involved up to 10 suits pending on average, compared to just 68.8 percent in 1995.

84. Previously, a common reason for not disclosing the existence of pending suits was that this was a "trade secret."

Table 6.4
Most Important Categories of Domestic Suits
PERCENTAGES

Category	1995	2000
Business contracts	56.8	57.4
Intellectual property	21.7	22.6
Labor	21.7	18.4
Consumer-related	17.0	15.5
Insolvencies	n.a.	13.1
Pollution and environmental	11.1	8.6
Corporate law	3.7	2.7
Antitrust	2.7	5.8
Tax	1.2	1.5
International trade and investment	1.0	0.2
Other	14.6	14.0
No response	3.2	2.2

Source: 1995 Survey, 58–59; 2000 Survey, 74–75.

Most respondents to the 1995 survey said that the *suits* involved business contracts: 56.8 percent. This was somewhat less than the proportion which reported *disputes* involving such contracts (71.8 percent; see Table 6.2 above). Similarly, 21.7 percent listed intellectual property *suits* as among the three most prevalent, compared to 35.2 percent listing intellectual property *disputes* (Table 6.2). We can infer a greater tendency to resolve these categories of disputes before final judgment, probably to maintain long-term business relationships, although we should not forget that judgments and associated litigation proceedings in these categories remain quite important.

A similar point can be made regarding the new category in 2000 of insolvency *suits* (13.1 percent), compared to insolvency *disputes* (50 percent), although the main reason for not pursuing litigation in this area is of course that debtors are often "judgment proof."

By contrast, the proportion listing labor *litigation* in the 1995 survey was equal to that listing labor *disputes* generally (21.7 percent), while pollution and environment-related *suits* (11.1 percent) were slightly greater than such *disputes* generally (9.8 percent). There was also a significantly lower proportion of consumer-related *suits* (17 percent) than *disputes* generally (29.1 percent), probably reflecting more the well-known barriers consumers face when claiming against "repeat-player" businesses.[85] The proportion of company law-related *suits* (3.7 percent) was even lower than corporate law *disputes* (10 percent), although this

---

85. Such barriers constituted one reason for the interest by the Economic Planning Agency, in charge of consumer policy in Japan in the 1990s, in developing alternative dispute resolution mechanisms for consumer contract disputes, in parallel with proposed legislation to govern the contract negotiation process and consumer contract terms.

may be rising because shareholder derivative litigation has increased steadily, and in an increasingly high-profile manner, since the reduction of required court fees in 1993 (Nottage 2001b).

Despite an upward trend in average suits pending, and especially the greater significance of litigation and disputes in particular areas, the legal department's role remained quite circumscribed in electing the appropriate dispute resolution method even in "important" cases. In the 1995 survey, only 3.5 percent of respondent corporations "left this virtually to the judgment of the head of the legal department." Instead, 55.7 percent left the decision to the board of directors or others (1995 Survey, 60).[86] Even less of a role for the legal department can be inferred for corporations which left the decision to it "in collaboration with the responsible department" (39.5 percent), usually meaning a joint decision is required. The latter tendency, in particular, suggests persistent relative structural inertia in Japanese corporate decision-making,[87] even though they face a business environment which is gradually becoming more legalized. There was little change in this respect according to the 2000 survey. Further, only 4 percent of respondents had rules or a manual dealing with the selection of appropriate dispute resolution procedures for various types of disputes, although 11.5 percent of the largest corporations did (2000 Survey, 73, 77). This is probably changing as Japanese individual and corporate citizens become increasingly aware of the various options for resolving civil disputes and measures are taken to make them more viable pursuant to the Justice System Reform Council recommendations of 2001.[88]

2. Legal Departments and Transactional Work

If legal department involvement remains potentially problematic even at the stage of resolving disputes, we might expect even greater obstacles at the stage of planning transactions. Only 3.3 percent of legal departments in the 1995 survey (and 2.4 percent in the 2000 survey) were involved in all projects—involved in discussions, advising, and directing. More surprising is that only 19.6 percent of respondent corporations had their legal departments check all contracts. Instead, 50.7 percent had them check only "important" or "specific" (i.e., particular) contracts; 14 percent did not get involved in project planning at all, except for contractual matters, and 56.4 percent got involved in "specific" projects (1995 Survey, 53). Similar percentages reported in 2000 were, respectively: 20 percent, 55.1 percent, 6.8 percent (although considerably lower than 14 percent for non-involvement in 1995), and 56.3 percent (2000 Survey, 64). Selective involvement, depending on scale and complexity, generally makes sense, and it is not

---

86. One practical problem still, even in the case of very large Japanese corporations, is a requirement for board approval (*ringi*) to bring a counterclaim, even once sued. That can make this common tactical response very difficult.

87. Cf. generally Kashiwagi and Zaloom (1996, 89).

88. See generally McKenna (2001, 123); McAlinn (2002a and 2002b); Miyazawa, in this volume.

surprising that this tendency was stronger in larger corporations. However, 71.7 percent of the 1995 respondents, especially smaller companies, did not have express provisions establishing the basis for legal department involvement in these matters. Further, when asked what criteria determined "importance" or "specificity," 67.6 percent answered that this depended on the judgment of the person responsible for the project or contract overall, probably indicating a more subjective decision and almost invariably a final decision by non-legal staff. On the other hand, 26.9 percent responded that it depended on the amount involved in the project or contract and 24.3 percent on whether or not it was "a set type of contract (approved by the legal department)." Similar patterns remain apparent from the 2000 survey: percentages in 2000 were, respectively: 65.4 percent, 67.8 percent, 35.2 percent, and 17.2 percent (2000 Survey, 64).

The most common way for a legal departments' judgments or views to be expressed was for legal staff to participate in meetings dealing with the project in question (60.7 percent in the 1995 survey, 55.3 percent in 2000). This was closely followed by a requirement for a manager in the legal department to affix his (rarely, her) seal on the formal decision-ratifying document or *ringisho*.[89] The *ringi* approval process, still common in Japanese corporations and now quite familiar to corporations and even courts overseas,[90] involves a written proposal from a department being circulated for approval to various other departments (often defined strictly by written internal rules, especially in larger corporations) (Hahn 1984). It includes, and usually accumulates, varying degrees of background information on the project or contract and is often preceded by informal prior discussions between the originator(s) and those whose approval is formally required (Kashiwagi and Zaloom 1996). Hence, inclusion in the *ringi* approval process provides considerable opportunity for legal department involvement. Far less involvement is implied where the legal

---

89. In the 2000 survey, this occurred in 43 percent of the respondents, but further multi-answer possibilities were added implying possibly growing means for active integration of legal departments in project planning. For example, "giving opinions in other documentary form (such as by fax or e-mail)" was mentioned by 48.4 percent of respondents and "advice by telephone or in person" by 41.2 percent (2000 Survey, 65). In follow-up interviews of corporate legal staff conducted in May 2000 by one of the authors for a project comparing the impact of intellectual property on legal affairs mainly in larger Japanese corporations (see http://juria.law.kyushu-u.ac.jp/~itlepp/index-e.html), several interviewees stressed that e-mail made it much easier especially for younger staff in other departments to get access to legal information and advice from legal departments. This was said to be particularly helpful when they suspected non-legal department superiors may be mistaken about legal ramifications, yet might have been embarrassed to raise this possibility in a face-to-face encounter with often older legal department staff.

90. See, e.g., Pacrim Forest Products (N.Z.) Ltd. v. Mitsui & Co. Ltd. & Anor (unreported, C.P. 16/96, High Court of New Zealand at Christchurch, Hansen J., judgment of December 7, 1997). In this case, the Mitsui parent company and its Australian subsidiary argued successfully that a contract was not concluded at the stage alleged by Pacrim after explaining carefully to the court the internal procedures which had to be undertaken before reaching that decision (arguably known to Pacrim, due to previous experience).

department manager (or assigned legal staff member) is required merely to sign or affix a seal to the project plan or the contract form (16.2 percent of respondents in the 1995 survey, and 14.8 percent in 2000) or to formally attend a board meeting (10 percent and 8.2 percent respectively).

Specifically in relation to transaction planning in contracting, when asked when they got involved, legal departments responded to the 1995 survey that this remains primarily at the stage of preparing draft contract documents (51 percent) and to a lesser extent, of checking contract documents (25.9 percent). There was minimal involvement at the overall planning stage (4.6 percent) and little in contract negotiations (12.9 percent). The latter proportion increased slightly for manufacturers (14.9 percent) and declined for traders (6.3 percent), reflecting more variety in contractual relations; otherwise, the patterns were quite stable across sectors and varied little from results given in the 1990 survey. In the 2000 survey, respondents were instead asked to give the top two ways in which legal departments became involved in contract planning. Contract drafting rose to 71.8 percent and contract checking to 45.2 percent. Involvement in contract negotiations was mentioned by 37 percent, but involvement in the planning stage still by only 13.7 percent (2000 Survey, 67–68). When the 1995 survey asked the slightly different question of how they actually participated in contract negotiations, 22.7 percent responded that they "did not participate" (i.e., presumably, they either did not attend despite being entitled to or they did not voice an opinion). However, a total of 76.3 percent (64.5 percent in 2000, but only 57.9 percent among financial institutions) did so always, or when important, or upon request. When legal departments were not involved, 75.9 percent were not assigned responsibility for any dispute which might arise, compared to 70.2 percent in 1990. Surprisingly, 17.2 percent (14.5 percent in 2000) were assigned responsibility, so perhaps they did get involved in contract negotiations even though they were not formally supposed to do so.

The roles and influence of the legal department in these various processes can be further strengthened by its drawing on the expertise (and social status) of outside legal professionals, although this may be less so than after disputes have arisen[91] because those professionals may be less visible at the planning or transactional stage. When making their views known within the corporation, only 6 percent of legal departments reported in the 1995 survey that they "almost never discussed" the matter with their *komon bengoshi* (lawyers retained on an ongoing basis for a fixed periodical fee, in exchange for advice on demand unless this advice exceeded an agreed limit) (1995 Survey, 77).[92] Over three-quarters of corporations (77.4 percent) did so "depending on the circumstances," with this proportion steadily increasing for larger corporations, and 14.2 percent "almost always discussed" the matter. Correspondingly, 45.1

---

91. Cf. Part II B 1 above.

92. For "a day in the life" of a *komon bengoshi*, giving a good sense of the personal relationship strongly underpinning the professional one, even recently, see generally *Law in Japan: An Annual* (1995).

percent of respondents reported "having domestic contracts checked" to be high in their list of the three main categories of work for which lawyers were retained (45.1 percent), although "strategic legal advice domestically"—presumably overlapping with project development—still constituted a very low proportion (5.6 percent). Further, in the 2000 survey, 75.6 percent of respondents reported obtaining opinion letters from *bengoshi* (not just *komon bengoshi*) and 51.6 percent of these (65.8 percent of the subset of financial institutions) thought this practice had increased over the previous five years. The most important objectives were "to increase the persuasiveness of the legal department's decision or judgment" (74.3 percent of the 75.6 percent) and "to prepare for litigation" (55.6 percent, and 67.1 percent of financial institutions) (2000 Survey, 67).

A litmus test for the role of legal departments, however, remains whether they can insist on a project or contract being changed or abandoned if they think it should be. Almost unchanged from 1990, 83.4 percent of the 1995 survey respondents said that they could only give advice to that effect, but that ultimately it was up to the department in charge of the relevant deal. Only 9.7 percent reported that they could get the deal changed or stopped. Moreover, this proportion was higher for the legal departments in the smallest corporations (12.2 percent) as well as smaller ones (11.6 percent). Thus, this may be simply a function of their role also in advising in the business aspects of the deal, rather than a reflection of the importance of their judgment as to legal risk. Consistent with this trend, the larger corporations or those with specialist legal departments reported that their advice was more often "generally taken on board." Overall, 49.4 percent reported this was so, with 44.4 percent "unable to say," and only 4.5 percent saying that "their role was almost always limited to giving advice" (with the implication that it had very little or no impact) (1995 Survey, 54).

This was an area in which significant differences appeared in the 2000 survey, probably reflecting the growing popularity of the corporate compliance schemes mentioned above.[93] The proportion of respondents saying non-legal departments ultimately decided whether to proceed with the original project declined to 69.4 percent, and the legal department advice given in this situation was more often "generally listened to" (66 percent). While only 5.4 percent stated outright they could get the project halted or changed, another 23.8 percent said they could "depending on the circumstances."

In sum, even if the legal departments' ability to formally alter or put a stop to a deal remains circumscribed, they play an important role at earlier stages or in the more run-of-the-mill cases. In both respects, their roles are greater in larger corporations, and there seems to have been some steady improvements over the latter half of the 1990s.

---

93. See above, particularly on risk management and on e-mail; 2000 Survey, 66.

3. Legal Departments and Legal Information Management

By contrast, the role of legal departments' management of legal information within corporations increased in much more visible form from the first half of the 1990s. This trend appears to have continued or even accelerated, fuelled for example by amendments to the Code of Civil Procedure (in effect from January 1, 1998), increasing the scope of discovery obligations.[94] Japanese office equipment manufacturers like Ricoh positioned themselves to take advantage of this by, for instance, introducing online storage systems (*Asia Pulse* 1998). In the 1995 survey, progress in information technology in Japanese corporate legal departments was not striking, but at least in the largest corporations it appears to have improved rapidly since then, in line with the reinvigoration of information technology generally in Japan since the mid-1990s.[95] In the 2000 survey, for example, 28.6 percent of the respondents (42.5 percent, for the largest corporations) reported "standardization of contract and other documentation, for provision over a corporate intranet" and 22.2 percent (52.9 percent), "developing an intranet manual of standard legal problems." An intranet was also used by 41.5 percent of the 71.5 percent respondents who had a system for accumulating and sharing legal information (2000 Survey, 108–9).

More mundanely, 61.2 percent of respondents to the 1995 survey and 77.8 percent of those in the 2000 survey reported company rules on the preservation or destruction of legal documents, compared to 55.1 percent in 1990. This proportion increased in 1995 to 65.2 percent for corporations having a department or section dealing specifically with legal matters (56 percent in 1990), and to 73.5 percent for the largest corporations. More generally, 57.8 percent of all corporations in 1995 had rules on organizing and managing "legal information." The most common involved company rules on internal information (49 percent). Also common were company rules concerning trade secrets (26.7 percent), followed by company rules on other types of information (10.1 percent). These patterns were maintained or strengthened in responses to the 2000 survey (2000 Survey, 106–7).[96] In 1990, only 8.4 percent reported rules on trade secrets. The much higher proportions in 1995 and 2000 reflect major amendments to the Unfair Competition Prevention Act in 1991.[97]

This amendment, along with the other "hot" new topics for the 1990s mentioned above (Part II A), help explain why almost half of respondents to the 1995 survey (45.5 percent) reported having in-house training on legal matters,

---

94. See generally Mochizuki (1999).

95. See 1995 Survey, 61. Cf. Nottage (1998b, Part II B and 2000a, 17–19); Ibusuki and Nottage (2002).

96. In addition, rules on insider information were reported in 66.4 percent of the respondents (and 79.4 percent of public corporation respondents), compared to 49 percent in the 1995 survey. Describing significant changes in Japan's securities regulation over the 1990s, see Kelemen and Sibbitt (2002, 303–315).

97. See, e.g., Svetz (1992).

compared to just 28 percent in 1990. The proportion was even higher for finan-cial services providers (60.6 percent). The survey editors suggested that this reflects the fact that much of the work of their staff involves or touches on legal matters, with such training being integrated into these corporations' management systems and linked to staff evaluations and promotions. These ten-dencies were reinforced in the 2000 survey (1995 Survey, 84; 2000 Survey, 109).[98]

Overall, the focus of the training was quite consistent. For corporate officers, almost always for listed corporations (83.1 percent of which organized train-ing), the focus was on corporations and securities law (22.4 percent), followed by antitrust law and product liability. For newly employed corporate employees, the focus was on basic legal knowledge (34.4 percent): contracts, followed by general private and commercial law. For mid-career employees, the focus was on practical areas such as contracts, taking security interests, and managing credit. For managers, the focus was mostly on antitrust and product liability (1995 Survey, 84). No data was collected on who led this training, but personal experience suggests that it is primarily led by legal staff themselves, rather than sending corporate staff to outside seminars (for the overwhelmingly most pop-ular method for training legal staff, see Part II A above) or inviting legal profes-sionals to give seminars or lectures.[99] As well as increasing the quantity and quality of information flowing through the organization, which then has to be managed, this helps heighten the visibility of legal staff in a legal specialist capacity and hence, no doubt, their status and self-esteem.

Similarly, 9.1 percent of the corporations regularly issued internal newslet-ters or bulletins on legal matters and 10 percent did so intermittently, compared to a total of just 11.2 percent in 1990. Again, this tendency was stronger for financial services providers (36.4 percent). It was also so especially for corpora-tions with specialist legal departments or sections and for the largest corpora-tions (51.5 percent). While accepting that this can be due to the latter having relatively more spare time to engage in this activity, the survey editors argued that this was also an efficient strategy in big corporations. They also noted that this serves to communicate their existence within the corporation, related to our point about heightening status and self-esteem, and added that it also appears to provide an opportunity for legal departments to bring together and study legal information and knowledge (1995 Survey, 84).

Consistent with this trend, in 1995 over half of the corporations drafted in-house manuals on legal matters (57.5 percent), compared to 23.4 percent in

---

98. In-house training was reported by 54.7 percent of the respondents (73.3 percent among financial institutions). Exceptional emphasis was placed on training regarding contract issues among traders (41.5 percent, compared to 20 percent over all respondents); general civil and commercial law amongst financial institutions (36.5 percent, versus under 20 percent); and, antitrust among manufacturers (12 percent, versus 3 to 5 percent).

99. The low incidence of inviting lawyers as lecturers can be inferred also from the fact that only 3.6 percent of the corporations reported this as one of the top three categories of work for which *bengoshi* were retained (1995 Survey, 84).

1990. This increase was prominent not only among financial services providers (53 percent versus 21.9 percent), but particularly among manufacturers (62.8 percent versus 21.9 percent). For the latter, heightened interest in product liability and safety issues no doubt forms an important reason for this.[100] However, the most popular topic for them was antitrust (54.7 percent), also so (not surprisingly) for the very largest companies (71.9 percent) and no doubt reflecting the "hotness" of this topic generally (see Part II B above). Overall, antitrust (47.5 percent), "contract drafting, etc." (43.7 percent), and "shares and shareholders' meetings" topics (25.8 percent) were most popular for inclusion in increasingly widespread in-house manuals (1995 Survey, 85). This pattern was further consolidated in responses to the 2000 survey: for example, manuals were brought together by 58.5 percent of respondents, especially by financial institutions (71.3 percent). One noteworthy change is that "credit management and debt collection" (35.1 percent) displaced corporate issues (30.5 percent) in popularity for coverage in such manuals overall (2000 Survey, 110–11).

C. Reconstructing Relations

These trends in legal information management, together with legal departments' involvement in transaction planning and dispute resolution, reinforce the steady expansion in their comparative status and roles, sensed also from structural developments mentioned above (Part II A). This is so within corporations, in relation to other departments, and in legal departments' dealings with outside legal professionals, particularly *bengoshi*.

1. Legal Departments and Other Departments

The relationship between a corporation's legal department and its other departments depends greatly on what the other department in question is, and its field of activity. When asked about their relationship with departments dealing with intellectual property rights, for instance, fully 30.7 percent of the respondents to the 1995 survey indicated that only legal departments were responsible for these. Another 7.9 percent adopted a positive attitude, in that there was continuous discussion between the two departments (7.9 percent), but a similar proportion maintained a more closed or defensive attitude, reporting no relationship (7.6 percent). This left about half (51 percent) reporting a relationship whereby discussions took place if the intellectual property department had call for advice. With other departments, such as labor relations or public relations, this latter sort of relationship was even more common (80.5 percent and 76.7 percent respectively), and overall, it increased along with company size. Exceptionally, 23.1 percent of legal department respondents reported "no relationship" with departments dealing with tax matters. Also, 15.5 percent had no relationship with quality management departments, although legal departments retained more positive relationships

---

100. See also some other survey results summarized in Nottage and Wada (1998); Nottage and Kato (2000).

with consumer relations departments, especially within manufacturing corporations (1995 Survey, 66–68).

Partially overlapping with these patterns, relationships between legal and other departments also depend on what sort of work is in question. Categories of work which were clearly dealt with mainly by legal departments include work related to "shares/bonds/shareholders' meetings (domestic)"; "litigation management (domestic, international)"; "legal advice (domestic)," excluding "labor law" and "tax law"; "intellectual property rights (domestic)"; and "documentation (domestic)," although this was so particularly for "checking documentation for outside use." Work which was less distinctly, but still noticeably, dealt with mainly by legal departments included "managing foreign lawyers" and "studying local laws" (1995 Survey, 89). This reflects the resilience of "international corporate legal departments" (*kokusai hōmubu*) and more generally the contribution of legal departments to the globalization of Japanese corporations, albeit often in association with other departments.

Categories of work dealt with mainly by other departments included work related to "contracts (international)" except for "checking contracts" (i.e., only the planning, proposing and negotiating stages of contracting); "investment and joint venture business (domestic and international)" except for "study of the relevant legal rules"; "management of credit owed and taking of security (domestic and international)"; and "legal advice (international)," except for "studying local laws" and "general legal advice." This last category, however, probably included many corporations which did not have much international business. Once the high proportion of those giving "no answer" (25 percent) is excluded, the relative unimportance of legal compared to other departments dissipates considerably (1995 Survey, 92). Further, although other departments were mainly responsible for most international contract work, nonetheless this does not exclude the possibility of legal departments playing significant roles in contracting, either at the "checking" stage or within even circumscribed scope for participation at early stages. When asked to select categories of work in which legal departments played a "central role," a third of the corporations chose "international contract-related" work. A third also chose "international legal advice" work. The responses for all categories in the 1995 survey, revealing a pattern little-changed from 1990, were as follows:

Table 6.5

Areas of Work in which Legal Departments Played a Central Role

Area of work	Percentage
Stocks, debentures, shareholders' meetings	55.6
Directors' meetings	45.6
Subsidiaries and affiliates (domestic and international)	19.7
Contract (domestic)	68.8
Contract (international)	33.0
Investment, joint venture (domestic and international)	10.6
Management of credit and security interests	19.0
Litigation management (domestic and international)	78.4
General legal advice (domestic)	78.4
General legal advice (international)	33.1
Intellectual property	29.6
Documentation	41.2
Other (domestic)	2.2

Source: 1995 Survey, 93.

Overall, legal departments seemed quite confident about their relationships with other departments. Almost three-quarters thought they were meeting the latter's expectations and needs, even if not completely satisfactorily (72.4 percent); and 7.1 percent, that they were offering satisfactory legal services. Only 19.1 percent considered that their services were unsatisfactory (76 percent of them being from corporations without specialist legal departments) (1995 Survey, 70). Steady growth in self-confidence emerged from the 2000 survey: in that survey, 72.7 percent thought they were meeting expectations and 10 percent (26.4 percent of the largest corporations) thought their legal services were satisfactory; 15.7 percent thought they were unsatisfactory (2000 Survey, 89).

Legal departments in 1995 described their roles within their organizations as follows: two-thirds (66.8 percent) responded to occasional requests from other departments for "preventive legal advice" (*yōbō hōmuteki na sōdan*) and another 21.8 percent did so on a regular basis. Another increasing tendency since 1990 was for legal departments to be asked for legal judgments when important management decisions are being made (56.5 percent), with 8.4 percent reporting that this happened on a regular basis. Less common, but still important, was for them to be consulted only when a problem arose (42.1 percent). This represented a large increase compared to the 1990 survey, especially for the largest corporations (27.9 percent compared to 2.4 percent in 1990) (1995 Survey, 70). However, this response appears to be largely due to not making it clear in the 1990 survey that multiple responses were permitted, for the largest corporations in particular tend to have fully functional specialist legal departments which play an important role (e.g., through participation in discussions or via the *ringi* process) in planning transactions to avoid disputes. Thus, this response should not be seen as indicating a decline in the role of legal departments. On the contrary, combined with the other responses, it can be said that by 1995, the role of legal departments had become more of an accepted part of the organizational culture of Japanese corporations.

This interpretation is supported by the legal departments' views on how they were perceived by other departments. Over the first half of the 1990s, almost half (44 percent) thought that they had come to be seen as "important to a degree," and another 28 percent as "important." The remaining quarter (25.9 percent) saw no change. As a result, two-thirds of legal departments (65.1 percent) thought they had come to be seen as "important to a degree," and another 19.1 percent as "important" (41.5 percent for the largest corporations). Only 14.8 percent thought they were not seen as important by the other departments, a decline since 1990 (1995 Survey, 69).[101] And, also in 1995, looking forward over the next five years, 42.9 percent predicted that instead they would come to be seen as "important" and another 38.9 percent, as "important to a degree." In the 2000 survey, respondents confirmed mostly that over 1996–2000 legal departments had become important (34.6 percent) or important to a degree (34.6 percent), expecting this trend to intensify over 2001–2005.[102] It would be helpful to survey other departments to see if their perceptions of legal departments correlate with the latter's views on those perceptions; but other departments' perceptions in any case may be influenced by the legal departments' views on this matter.

Asked to select the two factors deemed most important for legal departments to gain the trust of others within the organization, 74.7 percent of respondents to the 1995 survey stressed legal expertise. About half (51 percent) chose "awareness of business reality." This is arguably related to "creativity in producing alternative plans" (41.9 percent), impliedly incorporating legal judgment, rather than pure "business sense" (only selected by 3.3 percent of respondents). "Ability to join contract negotiations, etc." was chosen by 11.1 percent, an increase of three percentage points since 1990. A similar increase was recorded for "good human relations with other departments" (16.7 percent) (1995 Survey, 71). While at first this strategy may seem contrary to building up specialist legal expertise, it could be understandable if legal departments have already achieved that and a secure role within the organization, or may do so in the

---

101. This decline arguably is more significant than a decline also in the proportion who see other departments as perceiving legal departments as "important." The latter tendency may not be necessarily related to a declining role, but rather an indication of legal departments being accepted in a new role gradually built up over the years.

102. Further, 51 percent predicted they would become more important, 31.2 percent more important to a degree (2000 Survey, 88–9).

near future. In the 2000 survey, similar results were recorded and growing self-confidence can be inferred from 26.9 percent selecting "explanations in easily understandable language" as a new prerequisite to gaining trust from other departments (2000 Survey, 89).[103]

2. Legal Departments and the Legal Profession

As mentioned in Part I above, legal departments in Japanese corporations—especially the larger ones—began developing expertise in the 1970s to meet new types of work accompanying the globalization of their organizations' activities. In turn, new types of work brought a redefinition of their roles within their organizations, and we can see that this trend continued through the 1990s. Legal departments, like their corporations as a whole, therefore have been directly exposed to outside change.

Resultant transformations, however, have also been influenced by legal departments' interactions with legal professionals. Within Japan, *bengoshi* have been particularly important, since the other lawyer-substitutes (such as patent or tax attorneys) still tend to be retained directly by other departments as required. This can strengthen the role of legal departments, both in dealing with their work and in repositioning themselves within their organizations, as alluded to already above. But tensions can emerge, because although *bengoshi* retain high social status and certainly have expertise in certain areas, as a profession—and even as individuals or specific firms—they have tended to be less responsive to external changes due to the interposition of a regulatory framework and associated traditions.[104] Hence, the transformation of legal departments' relations with *bengoshi* throughout the 1990s tended to be slower and less obvious than the changes apparent in legal departments' role within their organizations. Nonetheless, some changes are apparent, both in corporations' retainer relations with *bengoshi* as individuals or firms and more generally in the form of pressure on the legal profession to adapt to new conditions. At both levels, these are underpinned by the globalization of economic relations.

According to the 1995 survey, most Japanese corporations engaged 3.3 *komon bengoshi* on average, with most having had just one (37.4 percent) and almost three-quarters having had up to three. Similar figures were reported for the number and variance of law firms retained on a regular basis (*komon bengoshi jimusho*). Most of their work involved civil matters (68.8 percent) and corporate law (43.6 percent). International matters (20.1 percent), intellectual property rights (16.8 percent), labor law (16.2 percent) and so on formed less of their work, but became more important as the size of respondent corporations and specialization of their legal departments increased. In addition,

---

103. "Plain language" creates a particular challenge for legal education, where little emphasis is placed on learning to write simply (cf., e.g., Butt 2002). On the contrary, students are still expected to learn a traditional, stylized form of legal writing.

104. This is also a tentative conclusion from the empirical study mentioned above, which also compared intellectual property usage in legal practice by *bengoshi*.

on average, Japanese corporations engaged 3.6 *bengoshi* on an individual and case-by-case basis; again, mostly just one (43.9 percent), with three-quarters engaging up to 3. Reflecting their greater specialization, these lawyers' work involved a lesser proportion of civil matters (43.9 percent), followed by international work (32.8 percent), intellectual property rights-related matters (25.4 percent), and then company law matters (18.4 percent) (1995 Survey, 73–74). There was little change in these patterns in the 2000 survey, although the average number of non-*komon bengoshi* dropped from 3.6 to 2.6, probably because of pressures to rationalize costs during the deepening recession over the latter half of the 1990s (2000 Survey, 95–6).

Overall, both types of *bengoshi* were retained primarily for litigation and dispute resolution (70.5 percent in 1995, 77.9 percent in 2000), even excluding the more mundane debt collection and taking of security (55.1 percent, 51.1 percent), followed by advice about, and attendance at, shareholders' meetings (48.3 percent, 43.4 percent) (1995 Survey, 77).[105] *Bengoshi* were also retained, as mentioned above, to check domestic contracts (45.1 percent, 36.1 percent), check international contracts and legal documents (19.2 percent, 17.8 percent), and draft the latter (7.4 percent, 6.8 percent). While these proportions and rankings have not changed much since 1990, 53.9 percent of respondents in 1995 reported an increase in the use of *bengoshi,* especially among financial services providers (69.7 percent) but also in larger companies; 39.1 percent reported no change, and only 3.3 percent reported a decline (1995 Survey, 75). In 2000, an even larger proportion (58.9 percent) perceived an increase in *bengoshi* use over the previous five years (2000 Survey, 96).

Increased use can help strengthen and boost the profile of legal departments. However, like the type of work and the relative leadership role in such cases (see above), this depends on who within the organization actually

---

105. *Bengoshi* often have been invited to attend shareholders' general meetings (*sōkai*) of listed corporations to try to decrease the possibility of blackmailers (*sōkaiya*) (often with links to rightists or gangs) attending to try to disrupt or prolong them unnecessarily. The main strategy adopted even in recent years, however, has been for corporate managers simply to pay off blackmailers. This practice is contrary to the Commercial Code (as amended in 1981), however, and may decline since shareholder derivative suit filing fees were reduced in 1993 and thus suits increased (see generally Hayakawa 1997, 237). Whether this will increase outside *bengoshi* involvement in shareholder meeting-related work, on balance, is less clear. West (1999) presents empirical evidence that Japanese firms with short meetings tend to have better stock price performance and suggests that this is due to three factors: (1) less disclosure of negative information, (2) signaling to investors that the corporation is in good financial health, and (3) signaling that management control is strong. Rather than using *sōkaiya* to achieve such short meetings and better stock prices, however, Japanese corporations surely could use more *bengoshi*. Dealing with gangsters also entails more risk than dealing with one's lawyers, presumably, so this alternative should be particularly attractive to more conservative Japanese corporations or their shareholders (who become particularly important, in West's analysis, because they should be the ones most interested in stock price performance).

engages the *bengoshi*. Overall, 57 percent of corporations in 1995 (59.2 percent in 2000) reported that only legal departments were primarily responsible for engaging *bengoshi*, whereas 36 percent (33.6 percent) reported other departments played this role (1995 Survey, 74–75). It is unclear how often the latter did so, however. Generally, it seems that legal departments stand to benefit most from increased use of *bengoshi*.

Interestingly, the ratio of corporations engaging *bengoshi* only through legal departments, compared to other departments having (some) primary responsibility for this as well, declined as corporation size increased. This should not necessarily be interpreted as unfavorable to legal departments. Rather, it will become increasingly efficient for larger corporations to have front-line departments calling directly on *bengoshi*, and there may still be a background advisory role for legal departments (e.g., in vetting *bengoshi* for suitability on the first occasion they are retained by the corporation or giving a "third opinion" if necessary). Those legal departments may already have achieved such specialization and improved status within the larger corporations that they do not derive any additional status from monopolizing access to and primary responsibility for managing their *bengoshi*. These aspects need to be examined on a case-by-case basis, however. Financial services providers, for instance, constituted the sector reporting the highest proportion of other departments allowing (some) primary responsibility for engaging *bengoshi* (56.1 percent in the 1995 survey), and these corporations also engaged the most *bengoshi* on average (28.7 lawyers, 25.8 firms). Allowing this (delegating responsibility to branch managers and so on) is no doubt an efficient strategy. And these corporations' legal departments may retain some residual role, having achieved secure status within the organization. But the latter should not be taken for granted, in the light of the structural features sketched above (Part II A).

Another question put to respondents concerned the type of information legal departments thought they needed regarding *bengoshi*. Almost all wanted to know about areas of specialization (84.1 percent in the 1995 survey, 88.3 percent in the 2000 survey), 69.5 percent (76 percent) wanted to know their practical experience in terms of cases they had dealt with and so on; and 22.8 percent (26.7 percent) wanted to know what corporations they advised as *komon bengoshi*. This sort of information remains hard to come by, given continued restrictions on advertising by *bengoshi*, despite some recent liberalization (Miyazawa, in this volume). A third of the respondents in 1995 (35.5 percent) wanted to know about their fees, but (as mentioned below) this does not mean that Japanese corporations were relatively unconcerned about the cost of *bengoshi* services. Rather, it partly reflects the fact that *bengoshi* are still retained primarily for domestic litigation-related work, as just mentioned, and the fees for such work are basically set by bar associations and are well known.[106] Further, almost half of respondents to the 2000 survey (49.8 percent) mentioned remuneration as

---

106. See generally Henderson (1997, 61–63). But see text below (1997 newspaper survey).

one of the three things they most wanted to know about *bengoshi* (2000 Survey, 99). This growing concern probably reflects both the ongoing recession afflicting Japanese corporations, the steady increase in *bengoshi* numbers even over the latter half of the 1990s, and heightened expectations regarding legal services in light of various reform initiatives such as those of the Justice System Reform Council. It helps explain efforts particularly by the largest Japanese law firms to rapidly expand their practices through mergers (Zaki 2002; Nagashima and Zaloom 2002).

Otherwise, these patterns were largely unchanged from 1990. A noticeable difference lies in the increasing proportion of corporations with written retainer agreements with their *komon bengoshi:* 53.7 percent in 1995 and 61.6 percent in 2000, following an increase of 10 percentage points between 1990 and 1995 (and the 1995 figure is almost double the proportion that had these in 1986). This may suggest a more formal type of relationship being demanded by corporations, rather than a diffuse one based more on trust and social norms. On the other hand, this trend may have been initiated, or at least maintained in the 1990s, on the part of *bengoshi,* less willing in that economic climate to risk leaving informal their often lucrative *komon bengoshi* retainers. This interpretation may explain the fact that only 26.5 percent of the largest corporations in 1995 reported having written retainer agreements. Their *komon bengoshi* may be less concerned about the financial viability of such corporations, compared to the smaller corporations they advise.

Whoever initiated it, the above provides some indication of the increasing formalization of the relationship between *bengoshi* and their corporate clients. What corporations reportedly would like more of when engaging *bengoshi* nowadays may also indicate a more hard-nosed, commercially minded approach, driven by more than just harsher economic conditions in Japan in the 1990s. At first glance, another result provides some support for this view: 17.9 percent of the respondents to the 1995 survey (22.1 percent in 2000) reported terminating relationships with their *komon bengoshi,* whom (as we have seen) provide less specialist advice than *bengoshi* retained on a case-by-case basis, compared to 11.2 percent in 1990. Yet the predominant reason given for this, a distinct increase over 1990, was that the *komon bengoshi* "had become elderly" (39.9 percent, compared to 29.5 percent in 1990). Indeed, only 5.1 percent stated that termination was due to "a problem in trust," which represented a decrease from 13.1 percent in 1990, and only 7.9 percent said it was due to "lack of ability" (8.2 percent in 1990). Further, about one-fifth paid former *komon bengoshi* a lump-sum amount upon terminating the relationship (17.4 percent did so always, 1.7 percent did so occasionally) (1995 Survey, 78). In the 2000 survey, the main reason for terminating *komon bengoshi* relationships was still their "old age," but the percentage was lower (29.5 percent), while "reducing *bengoshi* fees" was mentioned by 13.8 percent of respondents. Further, only 6.1 percent made a one-time payment upon terminating the relationship (2000 Survey, 100).

Those corporations without written retainer relationships, which may provide for this sort of lump-sum payment, may pay *komon bengoshi* ex gratia or with little regard to the formal legal prescription in these circumstances.[107] The attitude appears to be simply to let *komon bengoshi* relations die from attrition, as the older ones retire or become clearly too old. Nonetheless, the fact that this process is accelerating suggests that this type of retainer is being superseded by retaining more specialized *bengoshi* on a case-by-case basis. Particularly in a socio-legal system which has been supportive of long-term relationships, this represents a potentially significant metamorphosis.[108]

This change may have been prompted by increasing exposure to foreign lawyers following the enactment of legislation in 1987 (with several subsequent amendments) allowing registered foreign lawyers in Japan to advise primarily on the law of their home jurisdiction (see note 1 above). In 1995, 206 corporations (20.8 percent) reported having used foreign-trained lawyers, with the proportion rising to 32.2 percent for large corporations (¥10 billion–¥100 billion) and 43.6 percent for the largest ones. Almost all of these lawyers are retained on a time charge basis, indeed like many local *bengoshi* (even some advising on international matters). Certainly, to our knowledge, no foreign lawyer has a *komon bengoshi* relationship with a Japanese corporation. Incidentally, 26.2 percent of corporations engaging foreign lawyers were reportedly "satisfied" with them, 63.1 percent "couldn't say, either way," while 6.8 percent (14 corporations) were "unsatisfied." The "unsatisfied" proportion rose to 13.8 percent among the largest corporations (1995 Survey, 80). No doubt this reflects the high standards achieved by their legal departments and corresponding needs and expectations regarding their outside lawyers. Similar satisfaction was expressed in the 2000 survey, despite considerable liberalization of the regime for foreign lawyers and a considerable increase in their numbers from the end of the 1990s, no doubt related also to double the proportion of respondents (43.1 percent) having used them (2000 Survey, 103).[109]

---

107. In other types of long-term contractual relationships, such as distributorships and franchises, Japanese case law had developed a supportive framework that in effect requires some sort of compensation upon termination, even without express provision in a written contract (see generally Taylor 1993). But Japanese courts probably would be much less willing to develop this line of reasoning to assist *komon bengoshi*.

108. See generally Yanagida (2000, ch. 3); Haley (1998a, 876–918). Cf. Nagashima and Zaloom (2002).

109. In March 2000, around 130 foreign lawyers (*gaikokuhō jimu bengoshi* or *gaiben*) were registered; in May 2002, 186 were registered (Nottage 2002a). In April 2005, 236 were registered. This increase has been accompanied by an increase in joint ventures (*kyōdō jigyō*), permitted since a 1994 revision to the Foreign Lawyers Law (see note 1 above). The Foreign Lawyers Association of Japan has long been critical of this system (*The Lawyer* 2001). However, it should be noted that Singapore only allowed such a system from 2000 (*International Financial Law Review* 2001b). In Japan, for most visitors and clients, a joint venture is almost indistinguishable from a single firm comprising both *gaiben* and *bengoshi*. In 2001, Freshfields in Tokyo estimated that over 100 *bengoshi* were engaged in joint ventures

Not surprisingly, larger corporations were also the greatest users of lawyers from outside Japan and had the highest standards and expectations in their dealings with them (1995 Survey, 78–80). Overall, 44.4 percent of all corporations in the 1995 survey (43.7 percent in 2000) reported having used such lawyers, an increase from 40.4 percent in 1990. Around half (52 percent in 1995, 49.7 percent in 2000) also reported increased use over the previous five years, compared to 38.2 percent in 1995 (40.8 percent in 2000) reporting no change. This trend is very similar to responses about increased use of *bengoshi* in Japan, but the work involved is probably quite different. In particular, over the last decade, foreign lawyers have probably been retained less for transactional and planning work than for litigation and dispute resolution. The collapse of the bubble economy in Japan constricted the room to maneuver for Japanese corporations, often forcing them to liquidate investments and pursue associated claims overseas.[110]

Asked how lawyers abroad came to be engaged, around half in the 1995 survey (and a total of 50.3 percent in the 2000 survey) reported this as resulting from a referral by a "Japanese *bengoshi*," 44.3 percent from those specializing in international matters (*shōgai bengoshi*), and 6.4 percent from others. Around a quarter (25.9 percent in 1995, 20.1 percent in 2000) had a referral from "a lawyer overseas." Many of these corporations may have been embroiled in overseas litigation or projects in the past and then engaged other lawyers at the recommendation of those old acquaintances; "multiple legal harassment" may be the driving factor in this process (see Part I above). Or, they may have engaged foreign lawyers in multinational law firms in one jurisdiction, who recommended their firm for work involving another foreign jurisdiction.[111] Another 14.3 percent of the respondents in 1995 (but only 6.6 percent in 2000) retained their existing foreign lawyers through "access via their own corporate records,"

(*International Financial Law Review* 2001a). In 2002, foreign law firms which had established joint ventures in Tokyo included: (1) Freshfields (with *bengoshi* Naoki Kinami replacing in 2002 the veteran *gaiben* Charles Stevens as head of the joint venture) (*The Lawyer* 2002a); (2) Baker & McKenzie; (3) White & Case; (4) Morrison & Foerster; (5) Jones Day; (6) Simmons & Simmons (*International Financial Law Review* 2002); (7) Orrick, Herrington & Sutcliffe (through Mr. Kaoru Haraguchi, previously in a joint venture with Allen & Overy) (*Business Wire* 2001); (8) Haarmann Hemmelrath; (9) Dorsey & Whitney (*The Lawyer* 2002b). Successful experiments with such joint ventures likely will increase pressure to liberalize further the regime (cf. Zaki 2002).

110. See, e.g., in New Zealand, Multiply Ltd. v. Old Mill Farm Ltd. (1995) 7 N.Z.C.L.C. 260 (a Japanese partnership invested in a luxury golf resort complex and fell out with the venture partner from Hong Kong, who sued for minority oppression). Another major case, which settled in the high court in Auckland just before the main trial in 1996, involved a claim by a Japanese investor against a major New Zealand law firm for alleged negligent advice when making the investment initially in 1990.

111. This category may also include referrals from a *gaikokuhō jimu bengoshi*. This was not a possibility offered in the survey, unfortunately, but it is already significant and likely to become more so.

also suggesting past engagement with that foreign system (or perhaps more fleeting contacts with those lawyers, e.g., at business conferences). Another 10.2 percent (6.4 percent in 2000) relied on introductions from "associations or institutions." Probably, these were mainly Japanese business organizations, but some reported cases in foreign jurisdictions reveal that Japanese parties have sought an introduction from a local reputable association.[112] All these routes tend to suggest increasingly hard-nosed, considered judgments in retaining foreign lawyers, looking to their expertise and experience. Some 20.5 percent (16.8 percent in 2000) instead relied on "introductions from other corporations," possibly indicating judgments based more on personal history and diffuse relations. The latter tendency had been strong among Japanese corporations when retaining their *bengoshi* within Japan.[113]

Previous dealings with foreign lawyers, especially dating back to the days when Japanese corporate legal departments' relative position within their organizations was less secure, may help explain the fact that 51.1 percent of the respondents to the 1995 survey still reported retaining foreign lawyers not just through legal, but also other departments, and only 28.2 percent retained them solely through their legal departments. Although this ratio was similar to that of responses on how *bengoshi* were retained (see above), we might have expected a more dominant role for legal departments given the extra complexity of international dealings. However, the proportion of respondents reporting retainers by departments other than legal departments increased for larger corporations, so again this may be an efficient strategy that does not detrimentally affect the position of legal departments in such organizations.

Having retained foreign lawyers, only 6.4 percent of respondent corporations in 1995 (7 percent in 2000) "left everything" to them, but 65 percent (71.6 percent in 2000) "left many matters to them, due to unawareness of local circumstances." Only a fifth used them "simply as advisors" (21.8 percent in 1995, 16.4 percent in 2000), indicating a more active role for corporate legal departments in particular. The latter proportion increased as corporations increased in size. Overall, this pattern was not dissimilar from the reported "division of roles between lawyers" (generically) and legal departments, for litigation, mentioned above. A difference is that there, the subset of corporations having specialist legal departments reported them more often "supporting lawyers, who play the leading role" rather than pursuing cases "jointly"; but for both this subset and that of the larger corporations, there is a tendency to use foreign lawyers more "simply as advisers," suggesting a shared role. No doubt, the latter trend arises because the question posed is about the use of lawyers overall. That is, not only for litigation—where it usually is much more necessary to rely on local advice—

---

112. See, e.g., Tak & Co. Inc. v. AEL Corporation Ltd. (1995) 5 NZBLC 103,887. The plaintiff, a Fukuoka-based corporation, obtained an introduction from the New Zealand Angus Association for a local lawyer who sued (very successfully) a New Zealand exporter of live cattle for fraudulent breach of contract.

113. Most *bengoshi* are still introduced by personal acquaintances.

but also for transactional work, where legal departments can provide more input through experience in other jurisdictions which may be readily "transplantable," and the pressures of time and other practical issues (communications, etc.) may be less.

Finally, when it comes to remunerating foreign lawyers, 55.2 percent of respondents in 1995 spent up to ¥10 million in the previous year, 10 percent spent ¥10–30 million, 4.5 percent spent ¥30–50 million, 3.9 percent spent ¥50–100 million, and 6.4 percent spent over ¥100 million (about US$0.7 million) per annum (1995 Survey, 80).[114] A difference reported in the 2000 survey was the greater proportion (a total of 15.3 percent, compared to 10.3 percent in 1995) paying foreign lawyers fees of more than ¥50 million. Although allowance should be made for higher communication costs, and remaining differences may stem from different types of work (litigation tending to cost more than transactional advice), these figures seem somewhat higher than the proportion for fees spent on *bengoshi* within Japan.[115] Overall, Japanese corporations reported fees charged by lawyers in Europe and the United States as "too high" (52.5 percent in 1995, 50.5 percent in 2000). Only 1.4 percent (0.4 percent in 2000) found them "cheap," while 30.9 percent (35 percent in 2000) found them "appropriate." However, while 55.7 percent of the respondents in 1995 (54 percent in 2000) had no experience of negotiating for a reduction in fees charged by these lawyers, a third had such experience (34.4 percent in 1995, 34.3 percent in 2000), and the latter proportion increased to 41.2 percent for corporations having specialist legal departments, 62.3 percent for the largest corporations. This reinforces the general impression of the professional, commercially minded retaining of lawyers overseas, especially by larger corporations. This, and other experiences and expanded dealings with foreign lawyers, in turn may be increasingly influencing Japanese corporations' dealings with *bengoshi* within Japan (Nagashima and Zaloom 2002).

The fees charged by *bengoshi* also represent a persistent complaint by Japanese corporations. In a 1997 survey conducted by Japan's leading financial newspaper, the *Nihon Keizai Shimbun*, 34.9 percent of respondent corporations said *bengoshi* charged high fees on an unclear basis (Choy 1998). The main problem perceived at that stage, however, was more the lack of clarity than the high level of fees. A difference tends to arise when engaging *bengoshi* as opposed to foreign lawyers (including *gaikokuhō jimu bengoshi*). The latter state clearly the basis of their retainer (almost invariably a time charge), they are very reluctant to estimate a total fee for a job, and they have no compunction about presenting a fee generated (increasingly by computer software) based on the time charge plus

114. One-fifth of respondents gave no answer to this question. Perhaps some of them spent high amounts in fees and did not want to reveal this because it was potentially commercially sensitive information with which they did not even trust the survey organizers.

115. Proportions for *bengoshi* in the 1995 survey were, respectively, 55.9 percent, 14 percent, 4.2 percent, 4.3 percent, and 2.9 percent. In the 2000 survey they were 51.1 percent, 16.1 percent, 6.1 percent, 3.6 percent, and 4.1 percent (2000 Survey, 97).

disbursements. Consequently, as this 1997 newspaper survey showed, there is considerable discussion about the fee when the bill eventually arrives.

By contrast, *bengoshi* tend to commit to doing a job beforehand for an estimated sum, and only rarely come back to the client saying they want more (e.g., because the job took longer than expected). Perhaps this is because the nature of *bengoshi* work is more predictable, but there is also an element of pride involved for the *bengoshi:* he or she wants to be seen as driven by more than just money. Some may see this as duplicitous, and others say they still can make more than an adequate living because of the limited number of *bengoshi* permitted to practice in Japan. This element of honor linked with high social status is an old one. Samurai also used to be subject to it, as a proverb shows ("*bushi wa kuwanedo, taka yōji*").[116] In any event, even if the basis is less clearly spelled out, this makes fees charged by *bengoshi* seem quite reasonable, compared to those charged by foreign lawyers, with much less negotiation after the bill is presented. Overall, however, they may still seem high to many Japanese businesspeople, because there is still some general reluctance to pay highly for services and intangibles rather than goods.

On the other hand, a third of respondents to the 1997 newspaper survey also complained that *bengoshi* worked too slowly (32 percent), lacked business experience (32.6 percent), or were unable to properly handle large or international cases. Overall, 25 percent were dissatisfied with *bengoshi* and 16 percent had some complaints. Similar complaints were voiced by a total of 79 percent of respondents to the 1995 survey. This attitude contributed considerable lateral pressure to reform key aspects of the civil justice system: the number of those permitted to pass the national bar exam and the scope of practice of foreign lawyers (nowadays, mainly *gaikokuhō jimu bengoshi*). These issues had long been determined almost exclusively by the triumvirate of the Japan Federation of Bar Associations or JFBA (*Nihon bengoshi rengōkai,* also known as *Nichibenren*), the Ministry of Justice (particularly interested in public prosecutors), and the General Secretariat of the Supreme Court (administering the courts). The JFBA was very reluctant to allow liberalization, because it appeared certain to lose its tasty share of an existing pie with no guarantee of the pie being increased (as more lawyers uncover latent legal needs). The other two players stood to benefit from more people passing the bar exam, by gaining more personnel, but did not (especially the secretariat) want to risk being seen as "politicking" by pushing for this and the higher budget it implied. Yet they appeared quite happy to let others, such as organized business interests, push this for them, especially in the climate of the late 1990s, as explained further in Part III below.[117]

Thus, it is significant that in the 1995 survey, 34.5 percent of corporations favored further liberalization regarding foreign lawyers' activities, while only

---

116. "A Samurai warrior, even when he has eaten little, will hold his toothpick high" (glorying in poverty).

117. See Nottage (1998b) and Miyazawa, in this volume.

18.9 percent favored the status quo, with 33 percent undecided (1995 Survey, 81). In 2000, the proportion favoring "liberalization in principle" rose further to 44.2 percent, while those favoring the status quo dropped to 18.9 percent (2000 Survey, 103). Such pressure for liberalization helps explain the progressive expansion in scope of legal practice permitted to foreign lawyers in Japan throughout the 1990s.[118] In addition, 43.3 percent of the respondents in 1995 favored increasing the number allowed to pass the bar exam because "if the number of *bengoshi* increase, competition will become more severe and the quality of legal services will improve," while another 27.8 percent responded that "if the population of the legal profession (*hōsō*) grows, it will become easier to engage *bengoshi* and civil justice will become closer to hand." Further, 28 percent said that an increase would mean "young and able students would pass, linked to the strengthening of the world of the legal profession generally, civil justice and so on," and 25.2 percent thought "an increase in those passing would make it easier for legal departments to hire them, resulting in a strengthening of legal departments." Thus, they perceived liberalization in this respect as both increasing access to high-quality legal services from *bengoshi,* perhaps helping resolve pressing legal problems in a rapidly changing environment; and leading to more ready incorporation of *bengoshi* into their organizations, perhaps a longer-term structural change. Few respondents were critical of liberalization; for instance, only 17.2 percent responded that "an increase in *bengoshi* would lead to a litigious society and an increase in social costs" (1995 Survey, 81).

On balance, pressure for liberalization in this respect helps explain the steady increase in the number passing the bar exam, from around 500 in 1990, to around 750 in 1998, to 1,000 in 1999, to 1,500 agreed to "for the medium-term"[119] (Hamano, in this volume). Further pressure, underscoring the Justice System Reform Council's strong recommendation to reach 1,500 per annum by 2004 and 3,000 per annum by 2010, is also apparent from the 2000 survey. Responses regarding the effects on corporate legal departments from growth in the legal profession, as then being discussed, were as follows:

---

118. See the authors mentioned in note 1 above.

119. See generally Hamano (1998, 325). See also Miyazawa, in this volume.

Table 6.6
Opinions Regarding the Effects of Judicial Reform Measures to Increase the Number Who Pass the Bar Examination

Response	Percentage
A more diverse legal profession will grow and professional specialization will increase, so corporate needs will be even better met.	55.5
Competition will become more severe and the quality of legal services will improve.	51.0
It will be become easier to employ them in corporations, thus connecting to strengthening of corporate legal departments.	31.0
Expansion of law firms will proceed, become easier for corporations to use.	21.6
Social cost increases will result from the need to react legalistically to core litigation and stricter transactions.	21.2
More professionals will lower quality, so more stress will be involved when retaining lawyers or using the legal system.	18.3
Considering the current circumstances and legal profession, increasing numbers will not have all that much effect on corporate legal departments.	13.4
The numbers of those with qualifications as legal professionals will grow in the executive, universities, corporations and so on, so the disposal of problems through legal means will proceed.	13.2
Other	1.1
No answer	6.5

Source: 2000 Survey, 104–5.

Further, the 2000 survey indicated that corporate legal departments were keenly aware that the legal environment is shaped not only by the "legal profession" in the traditional sense (*bengoshi,* judges, and prosecutors). These were the responses about the possibility of expanding the scope for others to give legal advice, through legal consultations and the like, as part of deregulatory measures:

Table 6.7

Opinions Regarding the Deregulation of Legal Services

Response	Percentage
This should be permitted for judicial scriveners, tax attorneys, and other neighboring professions.	46.3
This should be restricted to *bengoshi* only, as at present.	19.4
This should be permitted for corporate legal staff, etc.	15.6
No regulation is particularly necessary.	9.0
Other	1.4
No answer	8.3

Source: 2000 Survey, 104–5.

Thus, changing relations between legal departments and their legal professionals, related to steady improvement in their roles in relation to other departments and to the broader environment, have an impact back onto civil justice reform as an aspect of that environment. Underpinning all levels of this process is the globalization of economic relations. New trends in retainer relationships stem from the new types of tasks which legal departments must undertake for their increasingly globalized organizations. New types of retainers also become possible (such as introduction and expansion of the registered foreign lawyer system), and changes are encouraged in the regulatory environment, through outside pressure (*gaiatsu*) in the context of bilateral and multilateral (WTO) trade negotiations. *Gaiatsu* is not necessarily the definitive factor; change also comes from within. But it remains an important influence.

III.   Japanese Corporate Legal Departments into the Twenty-first Century

What, then, of the future of legal departments in Japan's corporations? Despite the "debacle at Seattle" stalling further liberalization under WTO auspices, the globalization of economic relations seems set to continue, although this does not necessarily entail any simple globalization of political relations or of law itself (Nottage 1999).[120] Many important structural changes are well underway within Japan, too. If the economic recession continues for a few more years, this may actually prove a blessing in disguise, especially for the legal system. It could maintain economic and political pressure both to cement changes thus far and to encourage others. In this environment, the structures, roles, and relations of legal departments and legal staff in Japanese corporations should continue to be strengthened.

---

120. Cf. Nottage (1998b); see also Nottage (2001e and 2000d).

This sort of awareness emerged even from the 1995 survey. The majority of legal departments responding to open questions as to their future (230 corporations) thought that their role would be seen to be more and more important. In sharp contrast to 1990 survey results, the majority thought that top management now realized the importance of legal departments, to a degree. Few pointed to a greater awareness of their role within their organization as a future issue (1995 Survey, 104). These patterns were reinforced by an even higher proportion of responses (30 percent, representing 356 corporations) in the 2000 survey, emphasizing transformations in the corporate environment (including restructuring and legislative changes), "the globalization of corporate activities, needs relating to compliance, [and] the expansion of legal risk" (2000 Survey, 122).

In both surveys, respondents were very concerned with the need to strengthen their departments by engaging, retaining, and training good staff. Some reiterated that this could involve employing those in mid-career (a trend that emerged over the second half of the 1990s) and those qualified as *bengoshi* or other legal professionals, as well as strengthening relations with the latter. Yet legal departments were also conscious of the difficulties this entails given the economic climate, particularly in hiring professionals like *bengoshi,* with so much sunk costs in developing their human capital (passing the still-difficult bar exam, followed by another eighteen months of training), and a fee structure that reflects this, at least to some degree.

We can expect more hiring of Japanese returning with legal qualifications from overseas law schools and especially those who have gone on to pass a foreign bar exam and gain some practical experience in law firms abroad. Their skills are still not fully transplantable, however. Therefore, the hiring of more legal professionals qualified in Japan is also foreseeable, at least in the bigger corporations that can most afford them. However, a paradox exists in that those larger corporations may least benefit from hiring or strengthening relations with *bengoshi* and others, in terms of strengthening corporate legal departments' roles within their organizations, because those departments are already most secure within the larger corporations. Further, the costs involved in this remain high at present. In the 2000 survey, only 1.7 percent "certainly wanted to employ" *bengoshi,* 8.9 percent "would like to, if possible," while 21.9 percent "would investigate this if there were applicants." Only 7.8 percent "encouraged" staff to pass the bar exam. Proportions were even less regarding foreign lawyers, probably because the short-term costs of securing them were even more difficult to justify given Japan's economic predicament (2000 Survey, 93).

A shift toward significantly more "in-house counsel" in Japanese corporations, especially qualified *bengoshi,* therefore seems conceivable only over the medium- to long-term. Indeed, already in 1995 and especially in 2000, respondents were concerned about the slimming down of legal departments as a result of the recession, and we can expect this more in corporations in which their role and structure is weakest. Perhaps the group of primary concern in this respect remains financial institutions, especially the smaller ones, despite some notable improvements over the latter half of the 1990s.

On the other hand, for several years there have been calls to allow legal department staff to represent their corporations in some litigation, such as cases involving up to ¥5 million (1995 Survey, 82; 2000 Survey, 125). Such proposals may be voiced more since the new small claims procedures under the amended Code of Civil Procedure, for summary courts, came into effect. They most probably originate from financial services providers, and thus may provide a new avenue for strengthening their legal staff and legal departments. However, while this sort of proposal was discussed among corporate executives and their associations for many years, it was done very discreetly, since it directly challenges the monopoly awarded to *bengoshi* of representation in any court.

Nonetheless, continued pressure for reform of Japan's market for legal services became more openly exerted by the corporate sector and its political allies from around 1998. Failures of banks and one of Japan's "Big Four" securities firms, Yamaichi, destroyed the implicit guarantee of full-scale government bailouts and derailed the "convoy" system whereby financial markets were allowed to develop only at the pace of the slowest financial institution.[121] The crisis in Asian financial markets further undermined confidence in the competence of government authorities to regulate ex ante, and underlined the power of economic globalization. It became more widely appreciated that Japan's "big bang" deregulation of financial markets, launched in 1997, was the only way forward to address moral hazard and other structural problems in this sector in Japan. More generally, even the LDP-led government realized that deregulation was needed to address deep-rooted problems in other sectors of the economy, particularly utilities (such as telecommunications) which could create bottlenecks for economic growth.[122] Wide-ranging deregulation programs, proclaimed by Japanese governments since the 1980s, suddenly seemed more likely to be implemented. Leaders of Japan's corporate world realized that they would have to have a more functional legal system to navigate their way through this brave new world and to protect themselves from more complex legal risks.

By the 2000 survey, corporate legal staff reported as follows regarding the two ends they wanted most from judicial reform:

---

121. See generally Hoshi (2002) and Hoshi and Kashyap (2000, 129).

122. See, e.g., Kawabata (2001) and Cowling (2001).

Table 6.8

Desired Outcomes of Judicial Reform by Corporate Legal Staff

Outcome	Percentage
Increased speed of court proceedings.	83.9
Improved means of resolving disputes out of court.	30.2
A litigation system able to cope with more specialized arguments.	25.5
Rights of representation in suits, for experienced corporate legal staff.	18.2
A judicial system easy to use also for international disputes.	11.8
Introduction of a system for appointing judges from *bengoshi*.	8.9
Other	0.8
No answer	4.6

Source: 2000 Survey, 103.

Asked for specific suggestions regarding Japan's court system, most added that they wanted a faster system, especially via more judges and adoption of more concentrated trials. The next most frequent recommendation was to address judges' lack of understanding of practical realities, even by introducing a jury or "lay assessor" system (2000 Survey, 103).

Many of these concerns and suggestions were echoed in various reports presented in 1998 and 2000 by groups supportive of business interests. For example, two reports were presented by MITI-sponsored deliberative bodies in mid-1998. Such suggestions were consolidated during the deliberations of the Justice System Reform Council from mid-1999 to mid-2001, and contained in the latter's final report presented to the prime minister in June 2001.

Another body, Keidanren (the Japan Federation of Economic Organizations), mainly made up of larger corporations, approved at its May 1998 board meeting a report entitled *Opinions on the Reform of the Justice System* (*Shihō seido kaikaku ni tsuite no iken*),[123] emphasizing Japan's transformation into an open market society and promoting comprehensive reforms such as:

(1) increasing the number of judges and appointing them from the ranks of *bengoshi;*

(2) allowing non-*bengoshi* corporate staff to represent their own corporations in litigation and provide legal services to related companies;

(3) allowing practice as *bengoshi* by corporate legal staff, parliamentarians, and their policy assistants (*seisaku hisho*) without undertaking training at the Legal Training and Research Institute after passing the national bar exam;

---

123. See Miyazawa (2001, 99–100) and in this volume.

(4) allowing judicial scriveners and patent attorneys to represent clients in certain court proceedings;
(5) allowing multidisciplinary partnerships between *bengoshi* and such other legal professionals; and
(6) establishing postgraduate professional law schools.

In a report dated June 16, 1998, a committee of the LDP also reviewed issues for Japan's civil justice system created by an increasingly complex, information-based, and global society, with transparent rules and self-responsibility, and in an atmosphere of deregulation. Although the only specific recommendation was an increase in funding for Japan's court system, it did raise challenges for the legal profession and called for further study.[124]

More hard-hitting and specific was a report dated December 22, 1998 from the 21st Century Public Policy Institute (*21-seiki seisaku kenkyūjo*), affiliated with Keidanren. From similar premises, it proposed:

(1) various concrete measures to strengthen the existing court system;
(2) establishment of new "citizens' courts" in which parties could argue their case and negotiate directly with each other, assisted by a range of "professionals" (*bengoshi,* foreign lawyers, former judges, doctors, patent attorneys, etc.) and "practitioners" (former corporate legal department staff, bankers, etc.);
(3) liberalization of legal consultation and other services; and
(4) establishment of a broader-based "Council for Reform of the Administration of Justice," to promote ongoing reform of civil justice beyond that proposed by the trinity of judges, *bengoshi,* and the Ministry of Justice (prosecutors). (21-seiki Seisaku Kenkyūjo 1998.)

Legislation creating the Justice System Reform Council (JSRC) was soon enacted in June 1999. The council included not only three senior members of the legal profession, each representing one part of the trinity, but also two businesspeople, representing Keidanren and the Tokyo Chamber of Commerce; three law professors; the president of the Federation of Private Universities; a (female) professor in accounting; a (female) writer; one representative from a labor organization, the National Confederation of Private-Sector Trade Unions (*rengō*); and one from a consumer organization, the Federation of Housewives (*shufuren*) (Miyazawa 2001, 107). It soon became apparent that at least some of the measures to strengthen existing courts had a considerable chance of being implemented.

In relation to (2) and (3) above, however, the institute's report had recommended a drastic amendment of Article 72 of the Practicing Attorney Law (*bengoshihō*). Specifically, non-*bengoshi* would also be permitted to provide legal services out of court (with the report noting that bank and insurance company staff already do this to a degree), and the *bengoshi* monopoly on representation in court would be restricted to the High Court and Supreme Court. Amendment

---

124. See also Nottage (1998b, Part II C).

of Article 30 was also proposed, abolishing the restrictions on *bengoshi* working as civil servants, and abolishing the need for *bengoshi* to get specific dispensation to undertake nonprofessional work while remaining a practicing attorney. Although perhaps rather optimistically, in view of the other challenges remaining for Japanese corporate legal departments, outlined in this chapter, the institute argued that amendment of Article 30 would "facilitate having attorneys work as corporate lawyers to check corporate activities from the standpoint of strictly observing laws and social rules" (21-seiki Seisaku Kenkyūjo 1998).

In April 2000, a private study group including prominent business leaders proposed a wide-ranging set of changes, including increasing the scope of legal practice permitted to non-*bengoshi* and increasing the number passing the bar exam by an extra 1,000 individuals each year through to 2010. Similarly, in May 2000, the LDP proposed increasing the number of *bengoshi,* judges, and prosecutors to 90,000 within ten to twenty years. A report was also presented the same month by the Corporate Legal System Study Group for Research on Economic Activity and the Judicial System, established by the Ministry of Economy, Trade and Industry (METI, the successor to MITI, since a central government reshuffle in January 2001).[125] Comprising more professors and lawyers, but also representatives from large companies and the 21st Century Public Policy Institute, the group similarly recommended increases in *bengoshi* numbers (without suggesting any specific figures), liberalization of the scope of practice of other legal professionals, relaxation of the prohibition of foreign lawyers hiring *bengoshi* or forming ongoing cost-sharing partnerships with them, and other measures.

Most importantly, on June 12, 2001, the Justice System Reform Council presented a final report to the prime minister. It recommended extensive changes to the civil justice system, roughly paralleling those suggested in the 21st Century Public Policy Institute report, as follows:

(1) *Strengthening the existing court system*: reducing delays by half for contested first-instance cases, especially in more complex areas (medical misadventure, labor, and intellectual property cases); expanding small claims jurisdictions; enhancing execution of civil judgments; reducing court filing fees; simplifying rules for claiming other (non-lawyer) litigation costs; allowing more scope for a winning party to claim reasonable lawyers' fees from the losing party (presently only possible in tort claims); expecting a growth in litigation cost (first-party) insurance; and further expanding the civil legal aid budget.

(2) *Expanding alternative dispute resolution*: coordinating ADR (in and out of courts); expanding training; enacting a basic law on ADR and new

---

125. See the May 9, 2000 *Report of Corporate Legal System Study Group (kigyō hōsei kenkyūkai) for Research on Economic Activity and the Judicial System* at the website of the Ministry of Economy, Trade and Industry at http://www.meti.go.jp/english/report/data /gCorpConte.html. See also Nottage (2002a).

legislation on arbitration; and rethinking the scope of Article 72 of the Practicing Attorney Law (especially for corporate legal staff).

(3) *Liberalizing legal consultation services*: expanding the number who pass the (revamped) bar exam to 1,500 per annum by 2004 and 3,000 per annum by around 2010; establishing postgraduate law schools in universities to help meet this goal; liberalizing Article 30 of the Practicing Attorney Law, so that ex post notification of non-lawyer work is needed rather than ex ante permission; replacing local bar association minimum fee requirements with heightened duties to disclose individual fees to clients; further expanding information disclosure and advertising (permitted in principle since 2000) regarding law firm services; further encouraging law firms to incorporate and establish branches (now allowed since 2002), and possibly to form multidisciplinary practices; relaxing the scope of "joint enterprises" permitted since 1994 between foreign lawyers and *bengoshi;* considering the recognition as *bengoshi* of certain corporate legal staff (at least those who have passed the bar exam but have not yet undertaken the state-supported legal training courses); reviewing and then clarifying the ability of such staff and other "quasi-legal professionals" to provide legal advice, still restricted under Article 72; and allowing certain rights of representation in courts to such professionals (including patent attorneys, but not yet corporate legal staff). (Shihō Seido Kaikaku Shingikai 2001.)[126]

Many of these recommendations have already been implemented, and others most likely will be in the next few years. Many recommendations remained short on details, fudged issues, or were much less reformist than they appeared at first blush (noticeably, for example, the decision to add postgraduate law schools but retain undergraduate law programs).[127] Further amendment of Article 72; may be met with stiff opposition from *bengoshi,* but the tide has

---

126. Certain rights were specifically recommended for judicial scriveners, tax attorneys, and patent attorneys (cf. generally Rousso 2001) (legislation implementing this recommendation now in effect since April 2002). The possibility was also left open to reconsider rights of representation for administrative scriveners, consultants on social insurance and labor (*shakai hoken rōmushi*), real estate and building appraisers, or other specialists, "if it becomes clear in the future that their expertise is necessary in lawsuits and that their performance is suitable" (Shihō Seido Kaikaku Shingikai 2001, Chapter III, Part 3 (7)).

127. Nottage (2002d and 2001c). Results from the 2000 survey (at 105) accord with the author's repeated criticisms that Japan's new law school system, implemented in April 2004, was also—at least in original formulations—too narrowly focused on training legal professionals in a narrow sense, in better black-letter law analysis (see also Fujikura 2001). By contrast, 62.3 percent of respondents wanted the law schools to foster a legal profession "with flexible ideas, wide-ranging common sense and education, and imagination"; 52.7 percent wanted one "with a further deepening of practical experience in corporations, etc."; 30.1 percent wanted one "with an international sense and language ability"; and, 28.3 percent wanted one "with variety, having knowledge of numerous specialist areas outside the law, in human and social sciences, natural sciences, etc." A "legal profession familiar with knowledge of specialist legal areas" was mentioned by 30.1 percent of the respondents.

clearly turned against conservative factions within the JFBA (Miyazawa, in this volume; Nakabō 2001 and 2002; Nagashima and Zaloom 2002).

Amendment of Article 30 (to allow *bengoshi* to hold positions in the public sector or to work in the private sector) came quickly, in 2003, because it was attractive even to the legal profession.[128] After all, working solely in a law firm will likely become increasingly problematic financially. For many years, despite the strong control over entry into the profession, *bengoshi* incomes overall have not been very high compared to other similarly trained professionals (e.g., doctors) (Ramseyer and Nakazato 1998). As the economic recession in Japan drags on, moreover, there will be continued pressure from the corporate sector to keep lawyers' fees low. This situation will be exacerbated by already agreed upon increases in the number permitted to pass the bar exam, even before the Justice System Reform Council's 2001 final report,[129] and especially given its specific recommendations for further increases over the next decade. Working even part-time in a corporate legal department may provide attractions especially for newly qualified *bengoshi,* particularly in the case of larger corporations which still provide generous insurance policies and other benefits.

From the corporations' perspective, hiring on a part-time basis may also be attractive, particularly given Japan's current situation. More generally, expanding in-house *bengoshi* in part as a result of amending Article 30 would allow corporations to deal more effectively with corporate governance issues. As we

---

128. In a JFBA meeting on July 22, 2002, the following matters were discussed: (1) to replace the current permit system (under Article 30) with a new system allowing attorneys to assume a public post or a governmental position, or to engage in business activities with notification to the JFBA; (2) to reform the disciplinary system to promote its transparency and effectiveness; (3) to delete the attorney fees clause from the matters to be stipulated in articles of association of the JFBA; (4) to add "other laws" into the provisory clause of Article 72 of the law to narrow its scope of application; (5) to give a legal professional license to prosecutors who were non-lawyer assistant prosecutors (*fuku-kenji*) and who were specially promoted to prosecutors through internal examination (*tokunin-kenji*); and, (6) to exempt a person with experience in law-related work such as corporate legal affairs from judicial apprenticeship. Further, the group discussed three more issues in early 2003: (1) to utilize persons with experience as a summary court judge or assistant prosecutor; (2) to promote transparency in the management of bar associations; and, (3) to clarify the scope of Article 72. Amendments to allow joint enterprises between *gaiben* and *bengoshi,* and to enact item (1) (immediately above) were in place in 2004.

129. Further, as pointed out to us some years ago by Mr. Hidetomo Ueda (Fukuoka Prefecture Bar Association), the changeover from a two-year to eighteen-month Legal Training and Research Institute training period meant that in the year 2000, a total of about 1,800 newly qualified professionals (800 in April, 1,000 in October) were suddenly looking for employment. In 2006, the period will become twelve months for new exam takers. Hitherto, many graduates have become *bengoshi,* but the market became tighter from 2000. It will grow even tighter now, since the number of those passing the bar exam rose in 2004 to 1,500 per annum; over the rest of this decade the number is expected to rise to at least 3,000 per annum. It is expected that 1,600 will be allowed to pass the bar in 2006.

have seen (Part II B 1 above), corporations (and their legal departments) are already busy with derivative suits, and attention is also being paid to more preventive action and risk management. But there appear to be limits since inhouse education is still quite modest, and outside *bengoshi* are brought in primarily to prepare for and manage shareholder meetings (Part II C 2). More in-house *bengoshi*—preferably on a full-time, but even on a part-time, basis— would strengthen efforts to create sounder corporate governance within Japanese corporations and the corporate sector more generally. This is so especially given the continued lack of impact of the statutory auditor (*kansayaku*) regime, and other barriers that still exist to derivative litigation.[130]

All of the above reports, many stemming from pro-business circles, were premised on some significant new dimensions to the socio-economic environment in Japan over the 1990s. This environment also reflected or implied some major changes to the legal environment. In both the 1995 and 2000 surveys, corporate legal departments saw the changes as another major future challenge, underpinning their views as to the increasing importance they play within their organizations. Generally, they relate this to globalization of corporate activities. Consistent with their experiences in the early 1990s (Part II B above), legal departments stress the increasingly strict requirements of Japan's legal environment created by developments in antitrust law, intellectual property rights and enforcement, and product liability. Many of these areas have also been developed in a global context, but they are increasingly domesticated, affecting much more of Japan's corporate sector.

As mentioned at the outset (Part I), these areas of law also have a corporation-wide impact, both in terms of the issues raised and the potential severity of sanction in the event of breach. Hence, even in 1995, respondents talked of the need to nurture a "legal mind," heightening normative standards throughout the organization (such as improving corporate governance). The 2000 survey confirms strong interest in developing and applying corporate compliance programs. Within these strictures, legal departments also will have to retain their understanding of how deals are put together. They must continue to develop their capacity to present alternative proposals and to work proactively with colleagues in other departments, avoiding disputes rather than (like many *bengoshi* even today) letting these form the main focus of their work (Kitagawa 1996).

Developments over the last few decades and particularly in the 1990s, in parallel with globalization of Japanese corporate activities generally and the unfolding of socio-legal pressures domestically, provide grounds for some confidence that legal departments in Japanese corporations will meet these new expectations into the twenty-first century.

---

130. See generally Kawashima and Sakurai (1997); West (2001b); Miyazawa, in this volume.

Conclusion

This chapter has sought to fill a gaping void in Western-language literature on legal professionals in Japan, dominated by writing about *bengoshi*. Part I related the emergence of effective corporate legal staff in Japanese corporations to the expansion in their trade and investment overseas over the 1970s and the 1980s; but also sketched a retrenchment in this expansion over the 1990s, combined with burgeoning legal risks domestically. This interaction between globalization and localization offers new material to test hotly debated theories about "legal transplants." It runs against Pierre Legrand's view that the very fact of transplanting legal institutions and ideas across borders always transforms them into something radically different (Legrand 2001). It also counters directly Alan Watson's argument that transplants are effective regardless of underlying socio-economic circumstances and, indirectly, his weaker-form thesis that frequent borrowings arise from interactions between lawyers and legal academics.[131] On the other hand, it gainsays some of the more extreme claims for globalization made by Lawrence Friedman.[132]

Part II further illustrated some of these tensions, presenting detailed data on corporate legal departments' structures, work, and relations within their organizations and with outside professionals. Overall, it suggested growing commonalities with counterparts elsewhere, yet significant divergences which seem likely to diminish only slowly over the next few decades, for example in terms of hiring staff qualified as *bengoshi* or as lawyers outside Japan. As that example shows, there is still no outright Americanization of Japanese corporate legal departments, and their resilience in turn affects chances of Japanese law firms merging or otherwise developing along U.S. lines.[133] Indeed, it seems that Japanese corporate legal staff increasingly work effectively as "policemen" within their corporations, whereas a study in the late 1990s of in-house counsel in the U.S. concluded that the latter predominantly identified their role as

---

131. Cf., e.g., Watson (2001). In his voluminous writings, admittedly mostly focused on examples dating back to Roman law and its later revival in Europe, Watson has never referred to lawyers or other legal specialists within corporations who must therefore develop an identity as corporate employees.

132. See, e.g., Friedman (2001).

133. Cf. Nagashima and Zaloom (2002, 6): "much . . . demand for legal advice might have been met by Japanese corporate legal departments. Indeed, these departments continue to grow. But they themselves have become consumers rather than providers of advice, limiting their role to coordinating the provision of it by outside counsel to their business departments," with the following comment attributed to a U.S. lawyer in Tokyo as to why there has not been more merger activity among Japanese law firms: "It's true to say that there aren't many *bengoshi*, but there's certainly plenty of lawyers. Some of the trading houses have very large in-house legal teams. These lawyers may not be *bengoshi* but many of them have studied in the U.S. and qualified in New York or California. They're certainly capable of doing— and have done—major transactions" (*International Financial Law Review* 2001a).

"businessmen."[134] This suggests conflicting trends, which may be resulting now in convergence, but might ultimately lead to divergence with Japan becoming *more* legalistic than the U.S.[135] These must remain only tentative hypotheses, however, demanding comparative empirical studies focused on corporate legal departments in a variety of countries, to complement the disproportionately extensive studies comparing lawyers around the world.[136]

Part III argued further that the rapidly growing significance of Japanese corporate legal staff over the first half of the 1990s, consolidated over the latter half despite growing economic constraints on providing effective legal services within their corporations, appears to have driven corporate leaders from 1998 on to risk vigorously promoting wide-ranging reforms in Japan's judicial system. This counterintuitive development suggests a reappraisal of the role of Japan's corporate sector vis-à-vis its bureaucrats and politicians, although this reform process clearly involves other interest groups such as activist *bengoshi* and various citizens' organizations, requiring a broadening of the debate to include proposals for criminal justice reform or expansion of civil legal aid.[137] This not only underlines the need to rethink "who governs" Japan.[138] It also points to the need for comparative studies, again, for example into whether organized business interests were also key players in promoting widespread improvements in civil justice in other countries in recent years, such as in the United Kingdom.[139]

In sum, closer examination of Japan's corporate legal departments is important not only for a range of practical purposes. It also leads to rich implications for a better theoretical understanding of Japanese law in a contemporary socio-economic context, past and future, and of parallel or divergent tendencies in other modern industrialized democracies in an era of evolving forms of globalization.

---

134. Cf., e.g., Nelson and Neilson (2000, 457). Readers of that article would not have been surprised by subsequent revelations of widespread corporate excesses in the U.S., epitomized by the Enron collapse (see generally, e.g., Tomasic 2002). The backlash to that, however, may result in in-house corporate counsel (re)emphasizing their "policing" role.

135. Cf. also D. Vogel (2001) (suggesting that European regulatory style, at least in some areas, was becoming more "American" than the U.S. over recent years); Upham (2001) (arguing that Japan may be *more* faithful to the rule of law than the United States).

136. For an exhaustive review, see Nottage (1993). Also see, e.g., Barcelo and Cramton (1999); Flood (2002).

137. Miyazawa (1986, 101–3) (suggesting that pro-business associations advocating expansion of legal aid was a compromise to other interests). See also S. K. Vogel (1999) (on consumer groups); Richardson (1997) (on more widespread fragmentation in Japanese politics).

138. Cf. Johnson (1995).

139. Cf. generally Woolf (1997).

Permissions

Permission has been granted to Professor Nottage by RoutledgeCurzon for use of some text and tables from his 2004 book *Product Safety and Liability Law in Japan: From Minamata to Mad Cows*: pages 192–196, including Table 4.9 and notes 20 and 21, were altered slightly and used in this chapter.

Works Cited

1995 Survey. See Keiei Hōyūkai and Shōji Hōmu Kenkyūkai (1996), below.

2000 Survey. See Keiei Hōyūkai and Shōji Hōmu Kenkyūkai (2001), below.

Abe, Masaki. 1995. Foreign pressure and legal innovation in contemporary Japan: The case of the Administrative Procedure Act. Paper presented at the Annual Meeting of the ISA Research Committee on Sociology of Law, "Legal Culture: Encounters and Transformations," 1–4 August 1995, Japan Section Meeting II. The University of Tokyo, Sanjo Conference Hall, Tokyo, Japan.

Ahmadjian, Christina L. and James R. Lincoln. 2001. *Keiretsu*, governance, and learning: Case studies in change from the Japanese automotive industry. *Organization Science* 12 (6): 683.

Amyx, Jennifer. 2002. A new face for Japanese finance? Assessing the impact of recent reforms. Shibusawa Seminar on Japanese Studies, 23 June. Aomori, Japan. Unpublished paper, on file with L. Nottage.

Anderson, Kent. 2001. Small business reorganizations: An examination of Japan's Civil Rehabilitation Act considering U.S. policy implications and foreign creditors' practical interests. 75 *American Bankruptcy Law Journal* 3:355.

Asahi Shimbun. [Asahi newspaper]. 1998a. Nissan, Toyotakei kara buhin chōtatsu [Nissan gets parts from a Toyota *keiretsu* supplier]. 31 October.

————. 1998b. Ōgata shōkyakuro nyūsatsu, ōte 5-sha chūshin ni dangō 18-nen [Eighteen years of collusive bidding for garbage incinerators]. 29 October. *Asia Pulse.* 1998. Japan's Ricoh moves into online document storage service. AAP Newsfeed. 13 May.

Barcelo, John J. and Roger C. Cramton, eds. 1999. *Lawyers' practice and ideals: A comparative view.* The Hague: Kluwer.

Baum, Harald and Luke Nottage. 1998. *Japanese business law in western languages: An annotated selective bibliography.* Littleton, CO: Fred B. Rothman.

Bernstein, Anita and Paul Fanning. 1996. "Weightier than a mountain": Duty, hierarchy, and the consumer in Japan. 29 *Vanderbilt Journal of Transnational Law* 45.

Brill, Charles A. and Brian A. Carlson. 1999. U.S. and Japanese anti-monopoly policy and the extraterritorial enforcement of competition laws. 33 *The International Lawyer* 1:75.

Business Wire. 2001. Orrick continues expansion of its international securitization practice. 10 September.

Butt, Peter. 2002. The assumptions behind plain legal language. 32 *Hong Kong Law Journal* 32:173–176.

Callon, Scott. 1995. *Divided sun: MITI and the breakdown of Japanese high-tech industrial policy, 1975–1993.* Palo Alto: Stanford University Press.

Case, Kristin Leigh. 1999. An overview of fifteen years of United States-Japanese economic relations. 16 *Arizona Journal of International & Comparative Law* 1:11.

Choy, Jon. 1998. Tokyo loosens the leash on foreign lawyers. *JEI Report (Japan Economic Institute of America)* 19:1.

Comrie-Taylor, Jason. 1997. The "appropriate" role for foreign trainees in Japan. 15 *UCLA Pacific Basin Law Journal* 2:323.

Cooper, Matthew. 2001. The role of positive comity in U.S. antitrust enforcement against Japanese firms: A mixed review. 10 *Pacific Rim Law & Policy Journal* 2:383.

Coulter, Linda. 1995. Japan's *Gaiben* law: Economic protectionism or cultural perfectionism? 17 *Houston Journal of International Law* 431.

Cowling, Paul. 2001. The *Kanagawan* wave of change: Pressures for fundamental reform of Japanese telecommunications. 59 *University of Toronto Faculty of Law Review* 2:117.

Cox, Gary W., Frances M. Rosenbluth, and Michael F. Thies. 2000. Electoral rules, career ambitions, and party structure: Comparing factions in Japan's Upper and Lower Houses. *American Journal of Political Science* 44 (1): 115.

Dezalay, Yves and Bryant G. Garth. 2002a. *Global prescriptions: The production, exportation, and importation of a new legal orthodoxy.* Ann Arbor: University of Michigan Press.

———. 2002b. *The internationalization of palace wars: Lawyers, economists, and the contest to transform Latin American states.* The Chicago Series in Law and Society. Chicago: University of Chicago Press.

Easton, Susan H. 2000. The path for Japan? An examination of product liability laws in the United States, the United Kingdom, and Japan. 23 *Boston College International & Comparative Law Review* 2:311.

Efron, Jacqueline M. 1999. The transnational application of sexual harassment laws: A cultural barrier in Japan. 20 *University of Pennsylvania Journal of International Economic Law* 1:133.

Fitzgibbon, John E. 1991. *Deceitful practices: Nomura securities and the Japanese invasion of Wall Street.* New York: Carol Publications Group.

Flood, John. 2002. Barristers. In *Legal systems of the world: A political, social and cultural encyclopedia,* ed. H. Kritzer. Santa Barbara: ABC-CLIO.

Foote, Daniel H. 1996. Judicial creation of norms in Japanese labor law: Activism in the service of—stability? 43 *UCLA Law Review* 635.

Friedman, Lawrence M. 2001. Erewhon: The coming global legal order. 37 *Stanford Journal of International Law* 2:347.

Fry, James D. 2001. Struggling to teeth: Japan's antitrust enforcement regime. 32 *Law & Policy in International Business* 4:825.

Fujikura, Koichiro. 2001. Reform of legal education in Japan: The creation of law schools without a professional sense of mission. 75 *Tulane Law Review* 4:941.

Galanter, Marc. 1999. Makers of tort law. 49 *DePaul Law Review* 2:559.

———. 2000. The conniving claimant: Changing images of misuse of legal remedies. 50 *DePaul Law Review* 2:647.

Gantz, David A. 1999. Lessons from the United States-Japan semiconductor dispute. 16 *Arizona Journal of International & Comparative Law* 1:91.

Gao, Bai. 1997. *Economic ideology and Japanese industrial policy: Developmentalism from 1931 to 1965.* Cambridge, UK: Cambridge University Press.

———. 2001. The state and the associational order of the economy: The institutionalization of cartels and trade associations in 1931–45 Japan. *Sociological Forum* 16 (3): 409.

Gessner, Johannes. 1995. *Praesumptio similitudinis?* A critique of comparative law. Paper presented at the Annual Meeting of the RSCL (International Sociological Association), Meetings Supplement 2, 41. University of Tokyo, Japan.

Gibney, Frank. 1998. *Unlocking the bureaucrat's kingdom: Deregulation and the Japanese economy.* Washington, DC: Brookings Institute Press.

Ginsburg, Tom. 2001. Dismantling the "developmental state"? Administrative procedure reform in Japan and Korea. 49 *American Journal of Comparative Law* 4:585.

———. 2002. Japanese legal reform in historical perspective. Paper presented at the Conference of the American Society for Legal History, 7–8 November 2002. San Diego, California.

Goodman, Carl F. 2001. The somewhat less reluctant litigant: Japan's changing view towards civil litigation. 32 *Law & Policy in International Business* 4:769.

Grier, Jean Heilman. 1995. U.S.-Japan government procurement agreements. 14 *Wisconsin International Law Journal* 1.

Hahn, Elliott J. 1984. *Japanese business law and the legal system.* Westport, CT: Quorum.

Haley, John Owen. 1995. Competition and trade policy: Antitrust enforcement. Do differences matter? 4 *Pacific Rim Law & Policy Journal* 303.

———. 1998a. Error, irony, and convergence: A comparative study of the origins and development of competition policy in postwar Germany and Japan. In *Festschrift für Wolfgang Fikentscher zum 70. Geburtstag* [Commemorative essays for Wolfgang Fikentscher on his 70th birthday], eds. B. Grossfeld, R. Sack, T. Mollers, J. Drexl, and A. Heinemann. Munich: C.H. Beck. Tübingen: Mohr Siebeck.

———. 1998b. *The spirit of Japanese law.* London: University of Georgia Press.

———. 2001. *Antitrust in Germany and Japan: The first fifty years, 1947–1998.* Asian Law Series, no. 16. Seattle: University of Washington Press.

Hall, Maximilian. 1998. Financial reform in Japan: "Big Bang." *Journal of International Banking Law* 128.

———. 1999. Japan's Big Bang: The likely winners and losers. 14 *Journal of International Banking Law* 7:204.

Hamano, Ryo. 1998. Japanese lawyers in transition. *Rikkyō Hōgaku* [Rikkyō journal of law and politics] 49:325.

Hattori, Takaaki, Dan Henderson, and Pauline Reich. N.d. *Civil procedure in Japan.* Dobbs Ferry, NY: Transnational Juris Publications, loose-leaf.

Hayakawa, Masaru. 1997. Shareholders in Japan: Conduct, legal rights, and their enforcement. In *Japan: Economic success and legal system*, ed. H. Baum. New York: Walter de Gruyter.

Heath, Christopher. 1997. Bureaucracy and the protection of national interests in Japan: Exemplified for intellectual property and competition law. In *Japan: Economic success and legal system,* ed. H. Baum. New York: Walter de Gruyter.

Henderson, Dan Fenno. 1965. *Conciliation and Japanese law: Tokugawa and modern.* 2 vols. Seattle: University of Washington Press.

———. 1973. *Foreign enterprises in Japan: Laws and policies.* Tokyo: Tuttle.

———. 1997. The role of lawyers in Japan. In *Japan: Economic success and legal system,* ed. H. Baum. New York: Walter de Gruyter.

Horn, Norbert and Joseph Jude Norton. 2000. *Non-judicial dispute settlement in international financial transactions.* Studies in Transnational Economic Law, vol. 13. Boston: Kluwer Law International.

Hoshi, Takeo. 2002. The convoy system for insolvent banks: How it originally worked and why it failed in the 1990s. *Japan and the World Economy* 14 (2): 155.

Hoshi, Takeo and Anil K. Kashyap. 2000. The Japanese banking crisis: Where did it come from and how will it end? *NBER Macroeconomics Annual 1999* 14:129.

Hoshino, Eiichi. 1972. The contemporary contract. Translated by John Owen Haley. *Law in Japan: An Annual* 1.

Ibusuki, Makato and Luke Nottage. 2002. Intellectual property and transformations in legal practice and education in Japan and Australia. 4 *University of Technology Sydney Law Review* 31.

International Financial Law Review. 2001a. Foreign firms aim to be big in Japan. 20 *IFLR* 6:64–68.

———. 2001b. Jury still out on Singapore joint ventures. 20 *IFLR* 9:78–82.

———. 2002. Global firms battle tough in Japanese market. 21 *IFLR* 6:69–73.

International Tax Review. 2002. Asia shows stability in turbulent times. 20 *IFLR* (6): 11.

Johnson, Chalmers. 1982. *MITI and the Japanese miracle.* Palo Alto: Stanford University Press.

———. 1995. *Japan, who governs?: The rise of the developmental state.* 1st ed. New York: Norton.

———, Laura D'Andrea Tyson, John Zysman, and Berkeley Roundtable on the International Economy. 1989. *Politics and productivity: The real story of why Japan works.* Cambridge, MA: Ballinger.

Kakinuki, John Goto Yasuyoshi. 2000. Electronic commerce law: Japan. *Asia Business Law Review* 30:33.

Kashiwagi, Noboru and Anthony Zaloom. 1996. Contract law and the Japanese negotiating process. In *Doing business in Japan*, ed. G. McAlinn. Singapore: Butterworths.

Katayama, Tatsu and Richard Makov. 1998. Deregulation of financial markets in Japan. *Journal of International Banking Law* 128.

Kaufman, Charles S. 1994. The U.S.-Japan Semiconductor Agreement: Chipping away at free trade. 12 *UCLA Pacific Basin Law Journal* 329.

Kawabata, Eiji. 2001. Sanction power, jurisdiction, and economic policy-making: Explaining contemporary telecommunications policy in Japan. *Governance* 14 (4): 399.

Kawashima, Shiro and Susumu Sakurai. 1997. Shareholder derivative litigation in Japan: Law, practice, and suggested reforms. 33 *Stanford Journal of International Law* 9.

Kawashima, Takeyoshi. 1974. The legal consciousness of contract in Japan. Translated by Charles Stevens. *Law in Japan: An Annual* 1:1.

Keiei Hōyūkai and Shōji Hōmu Kenkyūkai [Business Management-Related Law Association and Japanese Association of Business Law, Inc.], eds. 1996. Kaisha hōmubu: Daishichiji jittai chōsa no bunseki hōkoku [Corporate legal departments: Analytical report on the seventh empirical survey]. *Bessatsu NBL* [New business law] 38. Tokyo: Shōji Hōmu Kenkyūkai. [Ed. note: Keiei Hōyūkai is also known as the Association of Japanese Corporate Legal Departments, and Shōji Hōmu Kenkyūkai is also known as the Commercial Law Center, Inc.]

————, eds. 2001. Kaisha hōmubu: Daihachiji jittai chōsa no bunseki hōkoku [Corporate legal departments: Analytical report on the eighth empirical survey]. *Bessatsu NBL* 63. Tokyo: Shōji Hōmu Kenkyūkai.

————, eds. 2006. Kaisha hōmubu: Daikyui jittai chōsa no bunseki hōkoku [Corporate legal departments: Analytical report on the ninth empirical survey]. *Bessatsu NBL* 113. Tokyo: Shōji Hōmu Kenkyūkai.

Kelemen, R. Daniel and Eric C. Sibbitt. 2002. The Americanization of Japanese law. 23 *University of Pennsylvania Journal of International Economic Law* 269.

Kitagawa, Toshimitsu. 1994a. Kigyō hōmu no rekishiteki hatten (sengo) [The post-war historical development of legal departments]. *Hōgaku Kyōshitsu* [Law class] 41.

————. 1994b. Kigyō no naka de no supesharisuto [Legal specialists within corporations]. *Hōgaku Seminā* [Law seminar] 238.

————. 1994c. *Nichi-bei bijinesu funsō* [Japan-U.S. business disputes]. Tokyo: NHK Shupppansha.

————. 1995. *Kokusai hōmu nyūmon* [Introduction to international legal affairs]. Tokyo: Nihon Keizai Shimbunsha.

————. 1996. *Risuku manējimento to keiei hōmu* [Risk management and legal aspects of management]. Tokyo: Kōdansha.

————. 1997. Seizōbutsu sekininhō no moto ni okeru seihin anzen gaidorain: No kōchiku no kokoromi [An attempt at constructing product safety guidelines under the products liability law: Product safety guideline]. *Hōsei Kenkyū* [Journal of law and politics of Kyushu University] 63:951.

————. 1999. Dispute resolution on semiconductors: United States v. Japan. 16 *Arizona Journal of International & Comparative Law* 1:143.

Kojima, Takeshi. 1976. Kaisha hōmubu: Kadai to kaiketsu shishin [Corporate legal departments: Issues and guidelines to resolving them]. In *Bessatsu NBL* 2, eds. Keiei Hōyūkai and Shōji Hōmu Kenkyūkai. Tokyo: Shōji Hōmu Kenkyūkai.

————. 1981. Kaisha hōmubu no risō to genjitsu [Corporate legal departments: Ideal and reality]. In *Bessatsu NBL* 8, eds. Keiei Hōyūkai and Shōji Hōmu Kenkyūkai. Tokyo: Shōji Hōmu Kenkyūkai.

————. 1986. Seijukuki o mukaeta kigyō hōmu no kadai to tenbō [Issues and prospects for corporate legal departments having attained a mature phase]. In *Bessatsu NBL* 16, eds. Keiei Hōyūkai and Shōji Hōmu Kenkyūkai. Tokyo: Shōji Hōmu Kenkyūkai.

————. 1996. Hōmubu: Sono soshiki to katsudō [Legal departments: Organization and activities]. In *Bessatsu NBL* 38, eds. Keiei Hōyūkai and Shōji Hōmu Kenkyūkai. Tokyo: Shōji Hōmu Kenkyūkai.

Kono, Toshi. 1997. Judges and mediators in Japan: The administration as motionless mediator. In *Japan: Economic success and the legal system*, ed. H. Baum. New York: Walter de Gruyter.

Law in Japan: An Annual. 1988; 1995; 2001.

The Lawyer. 2001. East side story. 23 April.

————. 2002a. Freshfields appoints *bengoshi* to top spot. 8 September.

————. 2002b. Japan bar penalizes foreign joint ventures. 25 September.

Lebrun, Laurie N. 2001. Recent amendments to the Commercial Code of Japan: Impact on mergers & acquisitions. 32 *Law & Policy in International Business* 4:811.

Legrand, Pierre. 2001. What "legal transplants"? In *Adapting legal cultures*, eds. D. Nelken and J. Feest. Oxford: Hart.

Lightbourne, Muriel. 2001. FTC, MITI and recent trends in Japanese competition law. *Patent World* 132:20.

Loeb, Hamilton Dayanim Behnam. 1999. Unilateralism in international trade relations: The recent United States-Japan experience and privatization of unilateralism? 16 *Arizona Journal of International & Comparative Law* 1:77.

Macaulay, Stewart. 1993. The future of American lawyers. Paper presented at the Kobe International Seminar on the Role of Lawyers in Contemporary Societies, 9–11 August 1993. Kobe University, Kobe, Japan.

Marcuse, Andrew. 1996. Why Japan's new Products Liability Law isn't. 5 *Pacific Rim Law & Policy Journal* 365.

Marin, Jason S. 1998. Invoking the U.S. attorney-client privilege: Japanese corporate quasi-lawyers deserve protection in U.S. courts, too. 21 *Fordham International Law Journal* 4:1558.

Matsuura, Yoshiharu. 1989. Law and bureaucracy in modern Japan. 41 *Stanford Law Review* 6.

McAlinn, Gerald. 1998. Financial reform in Japan: The "big bang." 22 *Asia Business Law Review* 3.

———. 2002a. Law reform in Japan: Building infrastructure for the twenty-first century. Part I. 35 *Asia Business Law Review* 3.

———. 2002b. Law reform in Japan: Building infrastructure for the twenty-first century. Part II. 36 *Asia Business Law Review* 3.

McKean, Margaret A. and Ethan Scheiner. 2000. Japan's new electoral system: *La plus ça change. Electoral Studies* 19 (4): 447.

McKenna, Sabrine Shizue. 2001. Proposal for judicial reform in Japan: An overview. 2 *Asian-Pacific Law & Policy Journal* 2:123.

Melchinger, Glenn Theodore. 1997. For the collective benefit: Why Japan's new strict Product Liability Law is "strictly business." 19 *University of Hawaii Law Review* 2:879.

Milhaupt, Curtis J. 2001. Creative norm destruction: The evolution of non-legal rules in Japanese corporate governance. 149 *University of Pennsylvania Law Review* 6:2083.

Miller, Richard. 1987. Apples vs. Persimmons: Let's stop drawing inappropriate comparisons between the legal profession in Japan and the United States. 17 *Victoria University of Wellington Law Review* 201.

Mito, T. 1998. Business-government relations in Japan: MITI and the petroleum industry during the high economic growth era. *Research Bulletin of the International Student Center of Kyushu University* 9:147.

Miwa, Yoshiro and J. Mark Ramseyer. 2000. Rethinking relationship-specific investments: Subcontracting in the Japanese automobile industry. 98 *Michigan Law Review* 8:2636.

Miyazawa, Setsuo. 1986. Legal departments of Japanese corporations in the United States: A study on organizational adaptation to multiple environments. 20 *Kobe University Law Review* 97.

———. 1997. For the liberal transformation of Japanese legal culture: A review of the recent scholarship and practice. *Zeitschrift für Japanisches Recht* [Japanese law journal] 4:101.

———. 2001. The politics of judicial reform in Japan: The rule of law at last? 2 *Asian-Pacific Law & Policy Journal* 2. See http://www.hawaii.edu/aplpj/pdfs/v2-19-Miyazawa.pdf at the website of the *Journal*.

Mochizuki, Toshiro M. 1999. Baby step or giant leap?: Parties' expanded access to documentary evidence under the new Japanese Code of Civil Procedure. 40 *Harvard International Law Journal* 1:285.

Murai, Tadashi. 1980. *Japanische mentalität und Japanisches steuerrecht* [Japanese mentality and Japanese tax law]. *Kansai University Review of Law & Politics* 47.

Muroi, Takashi. 2002. Nihon no jūmin tōhyō [Local referenda in Japan]. Paper presented at the Japanese Law Colloquium, 21–23 July 2002. Sydney, Australia.

Nagashima, Yasuharu and E. Anthony Zaloom. 2002. The rise of the large Japanese business law firm and its prospects for the future. Paper presented at the Conference on Law in Japan: A Turning Point, 23–24 August 2002. University of Washington, Seattle, Washington.

Nakabō, Kōhei. 2001. Judicial reform and the state of Japan's attorney system: A discussion of attorney reform issues and the future of the judiciary. 10 *Pacific Rim Law & Policy Journal* 3:623.

————. 2002. Judicial reform and the state of Japan's attorney system: A discussion of attorney reform issues and the future of the judiciary (Pt. 2). 11 *Pacific Rim Law & Policy Journal* 1:147.

Nayyar, Deepak. 2002. *Governing globalization: Issues and institutions.* Unu/ Wider Studies in Development Economics. Oxford: Oxford University Press.

Nelson, Robert and Laura Beth Neilson. 2000. Cops, counsel, and entrepreneurs: Constructing the role of inside counsel in large corporations. *Law & Society Review* 34:457.

Nikkei Weekly. 1997. More corporations focusing on in-house legal staffs. 17 November.

Noble, Gregory W. 1998. *Collective action in East Asia: How ruling parties shape industrial policy.* Cornell Studies in Political Economy. Ithaca: Cornell University Press.

Nottage, Luke. 1993. Keeping lawyers in comparative and social science perspective: The issue of foreign lawyers in Japan. Paper presented at the Kobe International Seminar on the Role of Lawyers in Contemporary Societies, 9–11 August 1993. Kobe University, Kobe, Japan.

————. 1997a. Contract law and practice in Japan: An antipodean perspective. In *Japan: Economic success and legal system,* ed. H. Baum. New York: Walter de Gruyter.

————. 1997b. Contract law and practice in Japan: An antipodean perspective—revisited. *Hikakuhō Zasshi* [Comparative law review of the Institute of Comparative Law in Japan] (Chuo University) 31:55.

————. 1997c. Economic dislocation in New Zealand and Japan: A preliminary empirical study. 26 *Victoria University of Wellington Law Review* 59.

————. 1997d. Planning and renegotiating long-term contracts in New Zealand and Japan: An interim report on an empirical research project. *New Zealand Law Review* 482.

————. 1998a. Bargaining in the shadow of the law and the law in the light of bargaining: Contract planning and renegotiation in the U.S., New Zealand, and Japan. In *Changing legal cultures II: Interaction of legal cultures,* eds. J. Feest and V. Gessner. Onati: Onati International Institute for Sociology of Law.

————. 1998b. Cyberspace and the future of law, legal education and practice in Japan. *Web Journal of Current Legal Issues* 5. See http://webjcli.ncl.ac .uk/1998/issue5/nottage5.html.

————. 1999. Educating transnational commercial lawyers for the 21st century: Preparing for the Vis Arbitral Moot in 2000 and beyond (part 1). 66 *Hōsei Kenkyū* 1: F1.

————. 2000a. Jōhō gijutsu (IT) to hōritsu jitsumu no hensen [Information technology (IT) and transformations in legal practice]. *Kyūshū Hōgakkai Kaihō* [Kyushu law association newsletter] 17.

————. 2000b. Practical and theoretical implications of the *lex mercatoria* for Japan: Central's empirical study on the use of transnational law. 4 *Vindabona Journal of International Commercial Law and Arbitration* 2:132.

————. 2000c. The present and future of product liability dispute resolution in Japan. 27 *William Mitchell Law Review* 1:215.

————. 2000d. The vicissitudes of transnational commercial arbitration and the *lex mercatoria*: A view from the periphery. *Arbitration International* 16 (1): 53.

————. 2001a. *Convergence, divergence and the middle way in unifying or harmonizing private law.* EUI Working Paper in Law No. 2001/01. See http://hdl.handle.net/1814/165 at the website of the European University Institute.

————. 2001b. Japanese corporate governance at a crossroads: Variation in "varieties of capitalism." 27 *The North Carolina Journal of International Law & Commercial Regulation* 2:255.

————. 2001c. Reformist conservatism and failures of imagination in Japanese legal education. 2 *Asian-Pacific Law & Policy Journal* 2. See http://www.hawaii.edu/aplpj/pdfs/v2-16-Nottage.pdf at the website of the *Journal*.

————. 2001d. Stakeholders in Japanese corporate governance. *New Zealand Law Journal* 35.

————. 2001e. The still-birth and re-birth of product liability in Japan. In *Adapting legal cultures*, eds. D. Nelken and J. Feest. Oxford: Hart.

————. 2002a. Form, substance and neo-proceduralism in comparative private law: Law in books and law in action in New Zealand, England, the United States of America, and Japan. Ph.D. dissertation, Victoria University of Wellington.

————. 2002b. Investing in Japan today. *CCH Asiawatch Newsletter* 49:16.

————. 2002c. Japan and the WTO game. *CCH Asiawatch Newsletter* 47:1.

————. 2002d. Japan's impending reform of the administration of Justice: Far from final. *CCH Asiawatch Newsletter* 48:7.

————. 2004. Product Safety and Liability Law in Japan: From Minamata to Mad Cows. London: RoutledgeCurzon.

Nottage, Luke and Masanobu Kato. 2000. Product liability. In *Japan business law guide* (loose-leaf), ed. V. Taylor. North Ryde: CCH.

Nottage, Luke and Yoshitaka Wada. 1998. Japan's new product liability WTO centers: Bureaucratic, industry, or consumer informalism? *Zeitschrift für Japanisches Recht* 6:40.

Nottage, Luke and Christian Wollschläger. 1996. What do courts do? *New Zealand Law Journal* 369.

Ōta, Shōzō. 2001. Reform of civil procedure in Japan. 49 *American Journal of Comparative Law* 4:561.

Ōta, Shōzō and Kahei Rokumoto. 1993. Issues of the lawyer population: Japan. 25 *Case Western Reserve Journal of International Law* 2:315.

Pardieck, Andrew. 1996. Foreign legal consultants: The changing role of the lawyer in a global economy. 3 *Indiana Journal of Global Legal Studies* 457.

Parker, Christine and Leon Wolff. 2000. Sexual harassment and the corporation in Australia and Japan: The potential for corporate governance of human rights. 28 *Federal Law Review* 3:509.

Potter, Pitman B. 2001. *The Chinese legal system: Globalization and local legal culture.* New York: RoutledgeCurzon.

Ramseyer, J. Mark. 1986. Lawyers, foreign lawyers, and lawyer substitutes: The market for regulation in Japan. 27 *Harvard International Law Journal* 500.

————. 1988. Reluctant litigant revisited: Rationality and disputes in Japan. *Journal of Japanese Studies* 14:111.

————. 1996. The puzzling (in)dependence of the courts: A comparative approach. 23 *Journal of Legal Studies* 721.

Ramseyer, J. Mark and Minoru Nakazato. 1998. *Japanese law: An economic approach.* Chicago: University of Chicago Press.

Ramseyer, J. Mark and Eric Rasmusen. 1997. Judicial independence in a civil law regime: The evidence from Japan. *Journal of Law, Economics and Organizations* 13:259.

————. 1999. Why are Japanese judges so conservative in politically charged cases? Paper presented at the Annual Meeting of the Law and Society Association, 27–30 May 1999. Chicago, Illinois.

————. 2000. Skewed incentives: Paying for politics as a Japanese judge. 83 *Judicature* 4:190.

Ramseyer, J. Mark and Frances McCall Rosenbluth. 1995. *The politics of oligarchy: Institutional choice in Imperial Japan.* Cambridge, UK: Cambridge University Press.

Richardson, Bradley M. 1997. *Japanese democracy: Power, coordination, and performance.* New Haven, CT: Yale University Press.

Roger, Karl. 1989. *Japanese direct foreign investments: An annotated bibliography.* New York: Greenwood Press.

Rokumoto, Kahei. 2001. Law and culture in transition. 49 *American Journal of Comparative Law* 4:545.

Rothenberg, Phil. 2000. Japan's new product liability law: Achieving modest success. 31 *Law & Policy in International Business* 2:453.

Rousso, Lee. 2001. Japan's new patent attorney law breaches barrier between the "legal" and "quasi-legal" professions: Integrity of Japanese patent practice at risk. 10 *Pacific Rim Law & Policy Journal* 3:781.

Sano, Tad. 1999. Historical consequences of the trade relationship between Japan and the United States. 16 *Arizona Journal of International & Comparative Law* 1:29.

Sasaki-Uemura, Lesley. 2001. *Organizing the spontaneous: Citizen protest in postwar Japan.* Honolulu: University of Hawai'i Press.

Satō, Yasunobu. 2000. The 1998 civil procedure reform in Japan and its implications. *Civil Justice Quarterly* 19:224.

Saxonhouse, Gary R. 1991. Japan, S.I.I. and the international harmonization of domestic economic practices. 12 *Michigan Journal of International Law* 450.

Schaede, Ulrike. 2000. Cooperative capitalism: Self-regulation, trade association, and the antimonopoly law in Japan. Japan Business and Economics Series. Oxford: Oxford University Press.

Shihō Seido Kaikaku Shingikai [Justice System Reform Council]. 2001. *Recommendations of the Justice System Reform Council—For a justice system to support Japan in the 21st century.* Official English translation at the website of the

Prime Minister of Japan at http://www.kantei.go.jp/foreign/judiciary/2001/0612report.html.

Shishido, Zenichi. 2000. Japanese corporate governance: The hidden problems of corporate law and their solutions. 25 *Delaware Journal of Corporate Law* 2:189.

———. 2001. Reform in Japanese corporate law and corporate governance: Current changes in historical perspective. 49 *American Journal of Comparative Law* 4:653.

Sibbitt, Eric C. 1998. A brave new world for M&A of financial institutions in Japan: Big bang financial deregulation and the new environment for corporate combinations of financial institutions. *University of Pennsylvania Journal of International Economic Law* 4:965.

Southwick, James D. 2000. Addressing market access barriers in Japan through the WTO: A survey of typical Japan market access issues and the possibility to address them through WTO dispute resolution procedures. 31 *Law & Policy in International Business* 3:923.

Stevens, Charles. 1978. Multinational corporations and the legal profession: The role of the corporate legal department in Japan. In *Current legal aspects of doing business in Japan and East Asia*, ed. J. Haley. Chicago: American Bar Association.

Svetz, Holly Emrick. 1992. Japan's new trade secret law: We asked for it—Now what have we got? 26 *The George Washington Journal of International Law & Economics* 413.

Takenaka, Toshiko. 2000. Patent infringement damages in Japan and the United States: Will increased patent infringement damage awards revive the Japanese economy? 2 *Washington University Journal of Law & Policy* 309.

Taniguchi, Yasuhei. 1997. The 1996 code of civil procedure of Japan: A procedure for the coming century? 45 *American Journal of Comparative Law* 767.

Taylor, Veronica L. 1993. Continuing transactions and persistent myths: Contracts in contemporary Japan. 19 *Melbourne University Law Review* 352.

———. 2001. Re-regulating Japanese transactions. 3 *ICCLP* [International Center for Comparative Law and Politics] *Review* (University of Tokyo) 2:15.

Tilton, Mark. 1996. *Restrained trade: Cartels in Japan's basic materials industries.* Ithaca, NY: Cornell University Press.

Tilton, Mark and Lonny E. Carlile. 1998. *Is Japan really changing its ways?: Regulatory reform and the Japanese economy.* Washington, DC: Brookings Institution Press.

Tomasic, Roman. 2002. Corporate collapse, crime and governance—Enron, Andersen and beyond (United States/Australia). 14 *Australian Journal of Corporate Law* 2:183.

Toyama, Kōzō. 1987. Government procurement procedures in Japan. *The George Washington Journal of International Law and Economics* 91.

Tsurumi, Yoshi. 1976. *The Japanese are coming: A multinational interaction of firms and politics.* Cambridge, MA: Ballinger.

21-seiki Seisaku Kenkyūjo [The 21st Century Public Policy Institute]. 1998. *Minji shihō kasseika ni mukete* [Towards the revitalization of the Japanese civil justice system]. 22 December. Tokyo: The 21st Century Public Policy Institute.

Twining, William L. 2000. *Globalisation and legal theory.* London: Butterworths.

Uga, Katsuya. 2002. Development of the concepts of "transparency" and "accountability" in Japanese administrative law. Paper presented at the Conference on Law in Japan: A Turning Point, 23–24 August 2002. University of Washington, Seattle, Washington.

Upham, Frank. 1987. *Law and social change in post-war Japan.* Cambridge, MA: Harvard University Press.

———. 1997. Privatized regulation: Japanese regulatory style in comparative and international perspective. 20 *Fordham International Law Journal* 396.

———. 2001. Ideology, experience, and the rule of law in developing societies. Paper presented at the Conference on Change, Continuity and Context: Japanese Law in the Twenty-first Century, 6–7 April 2001. University of Michigan, Ann Arbor, Michigan.

Utsumi, Kenji. 2001. The Business Judgment Rule and shareholder derivative suits in Japan: A comparison with those in the United States. 14 *New York International Law Review* 1:129.

Visser't Hooft, Willem Maurits. 2002. *Japanese contract and anti-trust law: A sociological and comparative study.* London: RoutledgeCurzon.

Vogel, David. 2001. The new politics of risk regulation in Europe. Discussion paper of the London School of Economics, Centre for Analysis of Risk and Regulation.

Vogel, Steven K. 1999. When interests are not preferences—the cautionary tale of Japanese consumers. *Comparative Politics* 31 (2): 187.

————. 2001. The crisis of German and Japanese capitalism—stalled on the road to the liberal market model? *Comparative Political Studies* 34 (10): 1103.

Warner, Mark A. A. 1999. Restrictive trade practices and the extraterritorial application of U.S. antitrust and trade legislation. 19 *Northwestern Journal of International Law & Business* 2:330.

Watson, Alan. 2001. *Law out of context.* London: University of Georgia Press.

West, Mark D. 1999. Information, institutions, and extortion in Japan and the United States: Making sense of *sōkaiya* racketeers. 93 *Northwestern University Law Review* 3:767.

————. 2001. Why shareholders sue: The evidence from Japan. 30 *Journal of Legal Studies* 2 (part 1): 351.

Wiener, Jarrod. 1999. *Globalization and the harmonization of law.* London: Pinter.

Wiley, Jessica C. 1999. Will the "bang" mean "big" changes to Japanese financial laws? 22 *Hastings International & Comparative Law Review* 2:379.

Wollschläger, Christian. 1997. Historical trends of civil litigation in Japan, Arizona, Sweden and Germany: Japanese legal culture in the light of judicial statistics. In *Japan: Economic success and legal system,* ed. H. Baum. New York: Walter de Gruyter.

Woolf, Lord. 1997. Civil justice in the United Kingdom. 45 *American Journal of Comparative Law* 709.

Wright, Maurice M. 1999. Who governs Japan? Politicians and bureaucrats in the policy-making processes. 47 *Political Studies* 5:939.

Yamada, Tsuyoshi. 2002. The Daiwa bank case (1999). 15 *Columbia Journal of Asian Law* 2:193.

Yamakawa, Ryuichi. 1999. We've only just begun: The law of sexual harassment in Japan. 22 *Hastings International & Comparative Law Review* 3:523.

————. 2001. Labor law reform in Japan: A response to recent socio-economic changes. 49 *American Journal of Comparative Law* 4:627.

Yanagida, Yukio. 2000. *Law and investment in Japan: Cases and materials,* 2nd ed. Cambridge, MA: East Asian Legal Studies, Harvard Law School. Distributed by Harvard University Press.

Yoneda, Kenichi. 1995a. Developmental processes of corporate legal staffs in Japan: The pluralizing mechanism on legal practices within an organization. In *Annual Meeting of the RSCL (International Sociological Association).* University of Tokyo, Japan.

————. 1995b. Kigyō shoshiki to kigyō hōmu [Corporate organization and corporate legal practices]. *Kobe Hōgaku Zasshi* [Kobe law journal] 45:113.

————. 2001. Hōmu bumon no ruikei bunseki [Analysis by categories of legal departments]. In *Kaisha hōmubu: Daihachiji jittai chōsa no bunseki hōkoku* [Corporate legal departments: Analytical report on the eighth empirical survey]. *Bessatsu NBL* 63, eds. Keiei Hōyūkai and Shōji Hōmu Kenkyūkai. Tokyo: Shōji Hōmu Kenkyūkai.

Yoshida, Daisuke. 1997. The applicability of the attorney-client privilege to communications with foreign legal professionals. 66 *Fordham Law Review* 209.

Zaki, Saira. 2002. A rare chance for western firms to crack Japan's legal market is at hand: Radical, overnight change is unlikely, but fortress Japan is certain to open up at least a little. *The American Lawyer*. September.

SEVEN

Of Lawyers Lost and Found: Searching for Legal Professionalism in the People's Republic of China

WILLIAM P. ALFORD*

> *"I was impressed by the extent to which lawyers had penetrated the process,"* [Anthony Kronman] said. *"They are on their way to a very different system of adjudication."*
>
> —From Sara Leitch, "Law Dean Advises Chinese Law Reform,"
> *Yale Daily News,* September 16, 1998, page 1.

American scholars and policy-makers concerned with legal development in the People's Republic of China (PRC) share a deep faith in the value of China developing a legal profession that operates as we would like to think our own does. Indeed, this idea is so deeply ingrained that it is rarely broken out for critical examination, but instead is treated as an obvious good, the attainment of which is essentially a matter of time. Virtually all such observers seem to assume that lawyers, whether out of idealism or self-interest or some blend thereof, will prove to be a principal force leading the PRC toward the rule of law and a market economy, while some go so far as to treat the development of an indigenous legal profession as crucial to the promotion in China of a more liberal polity.

The hidden assumptions regarding the Chinese legal profession[1] found in both U.S. academic writing and policy papers warrant a scrutiny they have yet to receive here or abroad. Lurking not too far underneath the surface of such portrayals are further assumptions about the inexorability of convergence along a common path remarkably (surprise) similar to our own. Unexamined, such assumptions run the risk of leaving us with an impoverished understanding not only of the role that the emerging legal profession is playing in China, but also of both the complexity of legal development there more broadly and the limits of the idea of professionalism in law. This, in turn, may generate unwarranted

---

*Henry L. Stimson Professor of Law, Vice Dean for the Graduate Program and International Legal Studies, and Director of East Asian Legal Studies at Harvard Law School. An earlier version of this chapter was published in *East Asian Law and Development: Universal Norms and Local Culture,* eds. A. Rosett, L. Cheng, and M. Woo (RoutledgeCurzon, 2003).

1. For the purposes of this paper, I use the phrase "legal profession" in conjunction with the PRC advisedly—simply to refer to those Chinese citizens who have been certified by the state to engage in the practice of law.

expectations on our part as to the manner in which change may come in China while reinforcing the arguably inflated sense that too many of us in the American legal world have of our own profession's historic importance.

This chapter consists of three parts. After a brief discussion of the manner in which the PRC's legal profession has been portrayed, Part I endeavors to depict, in more balanced terms, its growth over the past twenty years and its current situation, drawing in part on a series of interviews this author conducted among Chinese practitioners between 1993 and 2000, as well as more conventional research sources. Part II then seeks to explain why scholars and policy-makers, particularly in the United States, have so misunderstood the development of the Chinese legal profession, suggesting that the problem may have as much to do with their appreciation of their own legal profession as with the difficulties of comprehending China's. The final Part of the chapter offers further thoughts regarding the challenges that we need to confront in thinking about the place of lawyers and legal development in the PRC.

I.   The Growth of the Chinese Legal Profession

American portrayals of Chinese legal development, whether for scholarly or more policy-oriented ends, have tended to take as a given the model of legality generally believed to be in effect in our country today. Only infrequently are its fundamental assumptions questioned or even scrutinized through balanced accounts of its historical development, careful consideration of the interplay of law with other norms and institutions in contemporary American society, or rigorous comparison with the experience of other nations. The result, all too often, is a faith that scrupulous adherence to what is presented as the American model will suffice to bring about major and desirable legal and perhaps political reform in China. These observers also tend to take an approach toward Chinese legal development that sometimes overly exalts modest steps made in emulation of the model or, more typically, bemoans China's failure better to appreciate and absorb the lessons we provide.[2]

Nowhere is this cast of mind more evident than in treatment of the legal profession. At its most pronounced, this leads scholars of considerable reputation to make what this chapter will argue are extravagant claims about the character and potential (at least in present circumstances) of the profession. Consider, for instance, the following assertion from *Dealing in Virtue*, a celebrated 1996 book by Bryant G. Garth, president of the American Bar Foundation (the

---

2. Faith in what can be accomplished through embracing the American model is not, of course, limited to China or to the legal profession. Consider, for example, Steven Calabresi's call for emulation of American constitutionalism ("the Federalist Constitution has proved to be a brilliant success, which unitary nation states and parliamentary democracies all over the world would do well to copy") or Reinier Kraakman and Henry Hansmann's declaration that, in corporate law, history has culminated in the American model (see, respectively, Calabresi 1998, 22; Hansmann and Kraakman 2000).

United States' pre-eminent center for socio-legal research), and Yves Dezalay, the leading disciple of Pierre Bourdieu in legal studies:

> Law may begin to rival Communism—perhaps more precisely, the legal profession may rival the Party—as the leading legitimating authority. Law may provide a kind of neutral ground between competing national elites. As we shall see, there is also evidence that the U.S. version of law and legal practice is of particular importance. (Dezalay and Garth 1996, 258)

Garth and Dezalay's views may be among the more fulsome, but they find echoes in the writings of some of our more astute and otherwise sober analysts of China as well as in the words of leaders of American legal education (such as those of Dean Kronman quoted at the beginning of this chapter), pillars of our bar and bench, and shapers of pertinent dimensions of American foreign policy. So it is, for example, that Jonathan Hecht of Yale, the author of an influential study on PRC criminal justice, assumes that the growing involvement of lawyers will perforce advance the rule of law and human rights (Hecht 1996). Or that Pei Minxin, who has taught at Princeton, posits that the legal system could be the "'backdoor' through which a gradual process of democratic transition could be introduced" and the Communist Party's power "contested and constrained" with China's "emerging professional legal community" potentially constituting "an autonomous social group capable of concerted political action" in the attainment of these goals (Pei 2000, 301–305). Or that Randall Peerenboom of UCLA suggests that whatever problems may now afflict the profession, at a minimum, the desire of competent attorneys to replace *guanxi* (roughly, "relationships") with legal substance is proving to be a significant factor in promoting the rule of law more broadly within China (Lawyers Committee 1998). Much the same positive reading of the development of the Chinese profession to date and considerable faith in its future prospects underlie the very considerable funding and energies that multilateral organizations (such as the World Bank and the Asian Development Bank),[3] foundations (most notably Ford) (McCutheon 2000), and governmental bodies (including the European Union, and the United States government via the State Department's rule-of-law initiative) have expended on it.[4] A similar sense of the profession informs the strategy of important human rights organizations, such as the Lawyers Committee for Human Rights, which has lauded the PRC bar and wrote of its potential "to play a vital role in encouraging more far-reaching reforms."[5] It is also echoed in much-trumpeted announcements by the American Bar Association and similar actors about their recently discovered PRC brethren (Stein 1999, 86).

---

3. I discuss efforts of multilateral organizations to promote legal development in China in Alford (2003).

4. See Alford (2000) for further discussion of the rule-of-law initiative and of governmental democracy promotion programs more generally.

5. See the preface in Lawyers Committee (1998).

So, what is wrong with this picture? How, I have been asked when venturing ideas of the type this chapter will discuss (especially in the halls of American legal academe or other such precincts), could one not share the aforementioned enthusiasm? Isn't this the very thing that those of us who have long toiled in the obscurity of Chinese legal studies have been waiting for and have something of an obligation to cultivate?

The answer, at least to the academic dimension of these questions, has three principal components. The first is that as a simple descriptive matter, the role of the profession, if not of legal development in China more generally, has been significantly overstated to date. The second is that the character of the Chinese legal profession has been badly misunderstood, with considerable consequences for the assessment of what it may (or may not) have done to foster a rule of law and liberalism more generally. The third is that while change of the type that many American and other observers desire may be possible over the long run, we lack an empirical foundation or even strong theoretical underpinnings for the tone of assurance that, consciously or otherwise, infuses such sentiments. The remainder of this Part will address these three issues.

It would certainly be erroneous to ignore either the exponential growth in the size of the Chinese legal profession over the past twenty-five years or the accompanying changes in its manner of organization, educational attainments, or relationship to officialdom, let alone the very substantial ways in which the Chinese legal system more generally has developed since the end of the Cultural Revolution in the mid-1970s. In little more than a generation, the Chinese bar has expanded from 3,000 members to some 150,000, with officials continuing to make noises about plans for China to have 300,000 lawyers by the year 2010 (Alford 1995, 21–39; author's interviews in Beijing in September 1997, August 1999, July 2000).[6] Whereas the operative legal framework in 1981 spoke of "state legal workers," the current governing national statute describes lawyers as professionals with duties to society as well as to the state (Zhonghua Renmin Gongheguo Lüshi Fa 1996). Nor, it is fair to say, are we dealing only with issues of size and nomenclature here, as the vast bulk, at least in urban areas, of China's law firms, all of which previously were under direct state ownership, are now organized as partnerships or collectives, and there is considerable evidence, at least at the anecdotal level, of lawyers wishing to shield their practice from intensive state scrutiny, if for no other reason than to avoid unlawful exactions.

Even as we recognize such changes in the Chinese profession, however, we would do well not to overstate the impact that they are making. Resort to law and lawyers remains very much the exception in Chinese affairs both large and small.

---

6. It is surprisingly difficult to determine the precise number of persons in China authorized at any given time to practice law. Sources differ—with some limited to active, full-time lawyers currently holding a license to practice and others also including part-time lawyers, retired lawyers, lawyers who have returned their licenses because they wished to work for foreign firms or because business was bad, lawyers whose licenses were revoked, and judges and prosecutors who passed the bar.

This is so, notwithstanding the inordinate publicity accorded such matters, particularly in the western media (where they have a bit of the dancing bear quality that also greets foreigners in China who manage to utter more than a few garbled phrases in Mandarin). Perhaps most tellingly, the Chinese Communist Party (CCP), which is not only the nation's leading repository of political power but which also continues to be its single most consequential actor economically and in many other respects, remains above the state's law, both as a formal and as a practical matter, as has been borne out all too painfully by those who have sought through the courts to cabin it (Alford 1993, 45–63),[7] even as the CCP remains intimately involved in the selection and oversight of judicial personnel (Lubman 1999). The same insulation from the state's law holds true for individual members, particularly those of consequence, who have been more likely to be called to task for corruption (whether in their governmental or CCP guises) via the CCP's internal disciplinary processes than through public positive law, save for those unlucky enough to be singled out for exemplary punishment (Luo 1996).

It is not only important cadres or others within the CCP, however, who have yet to acquire a taste for lawyers. Litigation in the PRC rose steadily during the 1990s before levelling off at approximately six million cases per annum (exclusive of actions to enforce judgments which, since 2004, have been added to the overall figures for litigation reported by the Supreme People's Court in its annual work report). But, even before we scrutinize the content of such cases, their number needs to be set in context. To a far greater extent than most outside observers appreciate, China remains fundamentally an administrative state, with administrative recourse (whether for routine civil matters or to address deviance, as through re-education through labor[8]) the norm, rather than the exception, and with respect to which lawyers essentially have a scant role representing clients. Beyond this, lawyers have had little, if any, part to play in vital avenues through which tens of millions of individuals routinely seek redress, including the letters and visits (*xinfang*) process,[9] extrajudicial mediation,[10] resort to rice roots legal workers (*falü gongzuozhe,* also referred to as *jiceng falü*

---

7. For a telling account of the shadowy involvement by the family of one of China's seniormost leaders in the management of a major joint venture, see Sender (2000).

8. China's police are authorized by the provisions on re-education through labor to sentence citizens to periods of up to three years in labor camp for deviant behavior that falls short of warranting criminal prosecution. Such confinement may be extended if the police deem the individual not to have made sufficient progress in redeeming himself. It is now possible for citizens to appeal such determinations to the courts, but there is little evidence of many having done so.

9. This process, which involves petitioning officials for discretionary relief in a manner reminiscent of imperial days and which is a more active channel for citizen grievances than the much-touted Administrative Litigation Law, has generally been ignored by legal scholars, foreign and Chinese. For a notable exception, see Minzner (2000).

10. The PRC has over one million neighborhood mediation committees, with over six million official mediators.

fuwuzhe) (see Professor Liebman's chapter in this volume), and other yet more informal processes. But we also need to scrutinize litigation itself; if we do, we can see that not more than approximately one out of every ten litigants appears to have been using legal counsel.[11] And, if we press our inquiry further, we may do well to question the simple equation that virtually all observers make between litigation and legality,[12] by asking precisely what it is that lawyers are doing even when present, given the near certainty of conviction in criminal cases (the area in which citizens are, by far, most likely to be represented by counsel),[13] the fact that the judiciary continues to be characterized by a relatively low level of legal training,[14] and the proliferation of accounts of lawyers and judges using litigation as a pretext for bribery.[15]

One might respond to criticisms regarding the frequency with which citizens use lawyers by suggesting that it does not necessarily diminish the core argument of those who have been relatively sanguine about the building of a legal profession in China and its implications, but instead shows simply that the process is more time-consuming than many assumed or perhaps that more resources ought to be devoted to the task than they had initially thought. But as the aforementioned account suggests, rather than presuming that the changes of recent years a fortiori have been a boon for the rule of law, we need more thoroughly to probe what is underway in China. That type of research, in part regarding illicit behavior (some of which may carry severe criminal sanctions, including the death penalty), is not easy to conduct—most especially in a society in which a number of important matters, particularly concerning the administration of criminal justice, remain off-limits, especially for foreigners. There is, however, a growing volume of articles to be found in the Chinese media regarding widespread corruption in legal processes (which lawyers are inclined to blame on judges and judges on lawyers), but questions of the role of the CCP in judicial processes—including the selection and promotion of judicial personnel—remain under-examined.

---

11. I discuss in detail the statistics for representation through the late 1990s in Alford (1998).

12. Typical of this is the writing of Pei (2000).

13. Conviction rates run between 98 and 99.5 percent, according to *Falü Nianjian* (Law Yearbook). In weighing this statistic, it helps to be mindful of a comparably high conviction rate in Japan (see Ramseyer and Rasmusen 1998) and of the fact that the overwhelming majority of criminal cases in the United States result in plea bargains. In the PRC, approximately 40 percent of criminal defendants are represented by counsel, although often they have little involvement in the all-important pre-trial stage.

14. Many are ex-soldiers, reassigned in the 1990s when it was determined that the army had too many people and the courts too few and that the requisite skill sets are somewhat comparable (He Weifang 1998). To be sure, the court system has made extensive efforts in recent years to provide on-the-job training.

15. As the noted social critic He Qinglian observed, "Among Chinese lawyers, there is a saying that 'to bring a litigation is to use one's connections' (*'da guansi jiu shi da guanxi'*)" (2000, 86). See also Ching (1998, 13). Also confirmed in this author's interviews in Beijing in July 2000.

My own interviews of scores of Chinese and foreign lawyers, judges, legal academics, and businesspeople working in Beijing, Shanghai, and other major cities suggest that the expansion of the Chinese bar has been accompanied by increasing corruption, with lawyers at times a conduit for, if not the instigators of, such behavior (Alford 1998). Indeed, although the list of questions I developed for these interviews did not specifically address corruption, each PRC lawyer interviewed brought up this topic him- or herself, with some expressing regret at what they described as the need to engage in such behavior in order to stay competitive and others boastful about what they claimed was their capacity to reach virtually any Chinese judge. My sampling, to be sure, makes no pretense of being broadly representative of the nation's bar as a whole. If anything, however, it drew disproportionately on urbanites with elite legal educations (whether obtained in China or abroad or both) whose predominantly business-oriented law practices and broader life experience generally involve a greater exposure to the sort of international norms typically lauded by those who vest considerable hope in China's developing a domestic counterpart to the bar in this country.[16]

Presumably, without minimizing such problems, some outside analysts may be tempted to view them as likely to abate substantially as increasingly professionalized lawyers (and others) with an interest in the cleaner administration of justice make their presence felt. That may happen, but then again, it may not—for reasons having to do with the degree to which the Chinese legal profession remains interwoven with the party/state. Western, and especially American, observers remain far too quick to read the Communist Party's ebbing enthusiasm for Marxist ideology and economics as encompassing either a concomitant receptivity to competing sources of authority or a naïve ignorance or obliviousness on the part of the CCP's leadership to the potential impact of forces set in motion by the policies of the reform era.[17] We need to guard against underestimating either the CCP's desire to retain power or the self-interest of those who are benefiting from the manner in which power is now held and exercised.[18]

---

16. Michelson's fine work, grounded in two larger-scale surveys of lawyers, also finds corruption to be a serious problem (2003).

17. For an example of such smugness about the naïveté of China's leaders (and a disturbing inattentiveness to the possible consequences of pointing this out on the op-ed page of the *New York Times*—which the PRC Embassy, no doubt, monitors) from an otherwise thoughtful writer, see Lewis (1998).

18. The pervasiveness of corruption is discussed in Hu Angang (2000). That volume, put together by one of China's most distinguished economists, estimates that some 16 to 17 percent of China's GDP (running well over 100 billion U.S. dollars) was lost annually to corruption and associated behavior in the late 1990s. See also Smith (2000); *Agence France-Presse* (2000) (indicating from official sources that more than 500,000 cases of corruption were investigated during the 1990s); Kynge (2000). The last article concerns the then-Minister of Justice of the PRC, Gao Changli, who was supposedly placed under house arrest for, inter alia, misuse of state resources after an investigation said to have been carried out by the CCP's central disciplinary authorities, rather than by the judiciary or a state administrative organ.

The party/state remains far more involved in the professional lives of lawyers than most foreign observers (perhaps blinded by what I have elsewhere described as the "tasselled loafers" phenomenon[19]) recognize or than Chinese attorneys, conscious of appearances, would wish to acknowledge.[20] Through the Ministry of Justice (MOJ) and its subnational counterparts, the party/state continues directly to have the authority to play an important role in determining such vital indicia of professional independence, as that term is understood in the West, as the size of the profession, admission, educational requirements, modes of organization, official fee schedules, and disciplinary proceedings, among others. Nor have the MOJ's much-vaunted efforts to assume a posture of macro (*hongguan*) oversight while leaving day-to-day governance to the bar associations done much to promote professional autonomy given the impact that, for example, the MOJ has had on the leadership ranks of the All-China Lawyers' Association (*quanguo lüshi xiehui*) and the lack of real interest in supporting calls that have arisen for malpractice measures that might make lawyers more subject to the discipline of the marketplace.[21]

The foregoing links have important implications for thinking about the independence of lawyers from the party/state, some such nexi having the potential for direct political influence and others constraining the bar in more subtle, but ultimately more consequential, ways. So it is, for example, that notwithstanding the tendency of most foreign observers to view the party/state as largely having written off direct ideological control, there are scores of regulatory measures governing law practice in Beijing that, inter alia, require law firms to form Communist Party cells and senior lawyers to provide junior colleagues with ideological, as well as practical, training. And so it was that the lawyers bureau of the Beijing municipal government, which oversees the annual renewal of lawyers' licenses, instructed attorneys not to represent individuals detained during the crackdown on the Falungong movement.

To heed the state's ongoing presence in the affairs of Chinese lawyers is not to suggest that the nature of its involvement is unchanged from the days when socialism was more than an adjective used to justify whatever economic measures the CCP might wish to promote. Senior partners interested in maximizing revenues may be none too keen to spend time in empty ideological exercises,

---

19. By this, I mean the tendency of some foreign observers to mistake appearances for substance (Alford 1995).

20. There is, to be sure, some quite sophisticated writing by PRC scholars about the situation of Chinese lawyers (see, for instance, Du and Li 1997; Zhang 1995).

21. To be sure, the Lawyers Law acknowledges the possibility of malpractice actions—but does not provide a mechanism for them. Interestingly, the criminal law has increasingly been invoked against lawyers' defrauding clients. (See, for instance, Xiehong District People's Court 2004.)

The All-China Lawyers' Association in the late 1990s prepared a report denouncing corruption and incompetence on the part of lawyers and suggesting that the number of people admitted annually to the bar be reduced. It is considered to have had little effect.

while warnings against representing the Falungong and other activists are, as one of the more outspoken members of Beijing's legal community put it, utterly superfluous. But before we break out the *maotai* (a Chinese liquor quaffed on special occasions) and celebrate the ways in which the profit motive may be sapping the ideological content of the party/state's efforts at political control, we need soberly to consider the possibility that it may be reinforcing the CCP's hold on power and impeding, rather than facilitating, movement toward the rule of law specifically and liberalism more generally.

There are undoubtedly exceptions, but it could be argued that at least some in the Chinese bar, and perhaps most especially elite business practitioners in the capital, have struck a Faustian bargain with the party/state, willingly accepting a good life materially and in terms of prestige and security in return for foregoing certain of the attributes (most notably, a considerable measure of independence from the state) generally associated with legal professionalism in liberal democratic states and for acquiescing in the role the CCP has accorded itself in Chinese political and legal life. This is perhaps most readily apparent in the array of corporatist alliances formed between the party/state and lawyers.[22] At their most extreme, this may include links between officialdom and law firms in which work is directed, foreign study opportunities promoted, authorizations for specialized tasks granted, and permits clients need doled out in return for pecuniary gain. We ought not, for instance, to be any more mesmerized by the proliferating forms of ownership of PRC law firms than we would be by those of industrial enterprises. In both cases, placards suggesting that a firm is non-state may still mask close financial and other ties to pertinent officials, while an ongoing designation as state-owned does not necessarily mean that we can rest assured that all proceeds are, at the end of the day, finding their way into state coffers.

But even if such practices are not as widespread as my interviewing would seem to suggest, there is the arguably more vexing dilemma presented by the ways in which lawyers benefit from the current distribution of power. This is neither to paint all PRC lawyers with a single brush[23] nor to ignore challenges that

---

22. A comparable point has been made with respect to the emerging business community in the PRC (see, for example, Pearson 1997; Wank 1996, 820). He Qinglian has expressed a good deal of disappointment with the ways in which businesspeople, lawyers, accountants, and the middle class more generally have exacerbated China's endemic problems (see He Qinglian 2000, 85–87 and generally). As Robert Bianchi's work of the 1980s on Egypt and Turkey suggests, we may want to guard against the pervasive assumption that the middle class will always be a force for liberalization (see Bianchi 1989).

23. There are, to be sure, isolated figures such as Zhang Sizi and Mo Shaoping on behalf of political dissidents, Guo Jianmei on behalf of abused women, and Wang Canfa on behalf of of pollution victims who have posed noteworthy challenges to the authorities. And, as previously indicated, my interviews have focused predominantly on business practitioners in Beijing for whom the stakes may be higher than for their provincial brethren engaged in more mundane areas of practice. Also, we ought not to allow our focus on the legal profession to overshadow the ways in which ordinary citizens may seek to avail themselves of the protections to which the law suggests they are entitled.

legal professionals may face worldwide. Rather it is to demand that those of us who consciously target China's lawyers as likely to be a major force in promoting greater liberality, confront such institutional factors and associated collective action problems (e.g., the disincentive, noted by many lawyers I interviewed, to eschew bribery if one wishes to retain clients). These factors surely present a daunting and very concrete set of challenges that noble visions of the place of legal professionals in other societies alone cannot will away.

II. Why Observers Misunderstand the Development of the Chinese Legal Profession

Why is it, then, that we are so inclined to see lawyers in the PRC as, in effect, junior colleagues—cut from the same cloth as their American brethren, but needing a bit more tailoring before their professional attire fits them as smartly as we like to think ours fits us (or at least once did)? The answer is, in some respects, quite obvious, while in others, appreciably less so. Ironically, the more obvious respects are those concerning the supposedly exotic Orient, while the less apparent are those much closer to home, linked to the ways in which we American lawyers and legal academics think of the very profession we seek to propagate.

There is no particular mystery to or instructive novelty about many of the difficulties that impede the conduct of research into topics such as the place of the legal profession in China. In this, as in many other areas, it is rarely easy to examine facets of Chinese life that might be politically sensitive because they touch directly on either the CCP's power or abuses thereof (as with corruption at high levels). Notwithstanding a movement toward greater transparency made in conjunction with various bilateral trade agreements and accession to the World Trade Organization (WTO), Chinese authorities, at least to the present, have continued to limit access to some potentially pertinent materials. Normative documents potentially of consequence may be limited to *neibu* or "internal circulation" (i.e., no foreigners need apply). An example is the Beijing municipality rule on the formation of party cells in law firms (e.g., all cells must have at least three CCP members).[24] On top of this, there are the endemic problems of working with official Chinese statistics—which in this area purport to tell precisely how many times lawyers negotiated international contracts, the value of such agreements (down to the last *renminbi*), drafted opinion letters, and provided other forms of legal guidance, but which differ between their public

---

24. Compliance with Article X of the General Agreement on Tariffs and Trade (concerning transparency) would seem to require far more extensive adjustment in Chinese rule-making and application processes than appears generally to be appreciated. For a thoughtful essay on the challenges posed by China's integration into the WTO, see Herzstein (2000, 63).

and internal versions and provide no information as to how many citizens were executed or sent to re-education through labor, with (or, more typically, without) the benefit of counsel (Alford 1998).[25]

There is little new or intriguing about such impediments to scholarly understanding. More interesting are the ways in which prominent figures in the scholarly and policy community in this country have read, or misread, the Chinese landscape. The point here is not that one expects that all who would venture to work with or write about China must possess the equivalent of an area studies background. So steep an entry price would deter many who may have contributions of value while privileging others whose vision may suffer constraints of their own, including insufficient disciplinary depth or comparative breadth. Rather, it is to decry the ignorance or arrogance of those who would deign to prescribe for another society without first taking the trouble to consider basic issues of historical experience, institutional structure, political power, and the like—to wit, the type of due diligence that we would demand of any foreign observer deigning to suggest ways in which our society might better itself.

In some instances, this may be a product of what Bruce Ackerman of Yale bemoaned in the *Harvard Law Review* as the relative lack of knowledge of the world beyond our borders demonstrated by American legal academics, at least in comparison with our brethren in political science (Ackerman 2000, 633). In other situations, it may result from the soothing sound of one's Chinese interlocutors invoking language that we, not always listening closely, may associate with liberal legality, as figures ranging from Jiang Zemin through members of the dissident community speak of ruling the country through law (*yi fa zhi guo*) (Xinhua News Agency 1997). In yet others, it may have to do with the desire of those outside China to disseminate values deeply cherished here or to use China as a staging ground to re-fight our ideological battles or otherwise vindicate signature theoretical positions in the manner Richard Madsen so artfully describes in more general terms in *China and the American Dream* (1995). And in yet others, it may be driven by a need to undertake "legal exportation projects" designed as much with an eye toward satisfying domestic American political concerns or economic interests as with the recipient country in mind, as arguably was the case with the Clinton administration's rule-of-law initiative for China.[26]

However interesting such concerns may be, ultimately they sound very much in the familiar comparativist's key of non- (area) specialists not knowing as much as they need to about something that is removed from their principal line of endeavor. There is, however, a more novel and engaging focus, whether from

---

25. The law yearbooks do indicate that approximately 200,000 people resided in such camps during the 1990s, but neither they nor other official sources I have found indicate how many citizens are annually committed or re-committed. Nor is this system a relic of the past, as some are inclined to suggest. Human rights groups believe that as many as 10,000 followers of the Falungong may have been consigned to re-education through labor camps in recent years.

26. I discuss the U.S. rule-of-law initiative in Alford (2000).

the vantage point of those wishing to probe more deeply into the reasons that the transplantation of foreign institutions into China is so problematic, or from the vantage point of those who are far more concerned with American legal thought than with anything Chinese. It is that the Chinese case can help us to see limitations of a fundamental nature in the non-China-related work of those who are seeking to foster the growth of an American-style legal profession in China.

The remainder of this Part supports this point with a consideration of the understanding of the legal profession portrayed in Dean Kronman's landmark book, *The Lost Lawyer* (1993). Kronman, to be sure, has not written about China specifically, but as the quote introducing this chapter illustrates, he did, in his role as the dean of Yale Law School (1994–2004) and as U.S. chair of a bilateral conference on legal education launched under the auspices of the State Department in conjunction with President Clinton's 1998 trip to the PRC, play a role both in disseminating American norms in China and in portraying China here (Leitch 1998). Perhaps even more importantly, whatever Kronman's direct involvement in things regarding China, the conception of the lawyer set forth in his book—which one commentator termed "a major document in the history of American law" and which has generally been treated as one of the most important books of its generation regarding the legal profession[27]—not only surely has made its influence felt in efforts to propagate American models of lawyering in China, but also exemplifies a central current in thinking in this country about what the legal profession should be.

At first blush, a book entitled *The Lost Lawyer: The Failing Ideals of the Legal Profession* might seem an odd source in a discussion of efforts to foster American notions of lawyering. But then again, Kronman clearly did not write his nearly 400-page book simply to mark the imminent passing of a golden age. Rather, very much in the manner of Confucian argumentation (even if not recognized as such), *The Lost Lawyer* is better understood as invoking the past in order both to make points about the deficiencies of the present and to suggest what a better future might be.

A complex book, to be sure, *The Lost Lawyer*'s central proposition is that over the course of the second half of the twentieth century, the legal profession in the United States has experienced a falling away from the ideal of the lawyer-statesman, with serious ramifications for our polity and society in general. To understand why this is, we need briefly to consider Kronman's vision of politics. For him, politics ought not to be construed only as the battling out of previously defined sets of interests, but instead as a potential act of fraternity in the course of which, through reasoned deliberation, interests can be developed, refined and either reconciled for the larger good or, if truly incommensurate, accommodated in as intelligent and fair a manner as reason permits.

---

27. The words are those of David Kornstein of the *New York Law Journal*, reproduced on the back cover of the paper edition of Kronman's book, along with lavish praise from Charles Fried, Robert Gordon, and other noted scholars of the legal profession. Even the book's critics treat it as a major work. For instance, see the insightful article by David B. Wilkins (1994).

The lawyer-statesman, Kronman argues, has a singular role to play in this all-important enterprise, so central to a sense of community, because the lawyer-statesman, by definition, "excels at the art of deliberation . . . [and] is a paragon of judgment" (Kronman 1993, 15). That means that even as he represents private interests vigorously, the lawyer-statesman is able to discern their impact on the public interest and to work with his clientele to define the former in a manner consistent with the latter, to the longer-term benefit of both interests. So, too, in public life, the lawyer-statesman is able to assist members of the polity to transcend parochialism and to realize their deeper interests as part of a larger community.

The attributes that make one a lawyer-statesman, contends Kronman, are "trait[s] of character" further cultivated through appropriate study to produce a prudence or "practical wisdom." In effect, says Kronman, in words that unwittingly echo the Confucian *Analects*, we should "look to him for leadership . . . [and] praise him for his virtue and not just his expertise" (1993, 16). That course of study, continues Kronman, in words that do not echo of the *Analects*, is rooted in the case method classically employed in American law schools. Through it, students, by virtue of being forced to imagine themselves as judges in exceptionally close appellate cases, learn not only to see issues from many sides, but also to cultivate the art of being simultaneously sympathetic and rigorous, and to understand that politics, and indeed life generally, prize the art of blending that which is ideal with that which is practical.

Alas, bemoans Kronman, forces in both the world of ideas and that of affairs, have over the past half-century increasingly militated against realization of the lawyer-statesman ideal. In the former regard, the legal academy has increasingly abandoned the very thing that set law apart from other disciplines—namely, the common law case method—in favor of what he describes as a belief in "scientific law reform" that may have begun at the end of the nineteenth century with Harvard Law School Dean Christopher Columbus Langdell and that may have grown further through the legal realists. Today, this belief finds expression in schools of thought as seemingly varied as Law and Economics on the one hand, and Critical Legal Studies on the other.

Whatever the virtues of economics or philosophy (or social science in general), they are, to his way of thinking, inferior to the law for the nurturing of the "practical wisdom" Kronman so prizes. This is because they stress an abstract and, in his mind, excessively ideological approach toward the resolution of problems that need to be understood in a more nuanced manner if one is to strike a prudential balance between the desirable and the attainable or between the general rule and individual circumstance. In effect, the growing reliance on these disciplines beyond the law has "encouraged lawyers to view themselves as 'social engineers' engaged in the structural design of institutions . . . focused on more abstract concerns . . . in contrast to the common lawyer of the past, who built by indirection and without a conscious plan in view" (Kronman 1993, 22).

Compounding this trend in the world of ideas has been a transformation in the nature of law jobs, whether at the bar or on the bench (or in the academy), which in an atmosphere of increasing commercialization and complexity have become almost too specific, in his view—as exemplified by their growing concern with technique and specialized knowledge that have dulled, rather than sharpened, the traits of character that, when properly honed, may yield the qualities of deliberation he so prizes.

But the seeming bleakness of parts of *The Lost Lawyer* notwithstanding, all is not despair, for why, otherwise, would Kronman have taken the trouble to write so substantial a book? We can indeed, he argues, recapture the ideal of the lawyer-statesman if we reshape our institutions accordingly (which presumably is how he would justify accepting the deanship of a law school known more for its commitment to social scientific and philosophical inquiry than to traditional doctrinal analysis) (Falk 1995).[28] And perhaps in China, which, as fortune would have it, has embarked in our lifetime on an epic effort of singular magnitude wholly to reconstruct itself legally, we have a critical role to play in helping to implement this ideal—which may also provide us with the opportunity, perhaps not easily available in our own society, to acquit ourselves as lawyer-statesmen of historic note.

Kronman's devotion to the ideal of the lawyer-statesman may in some respects seem excessive, but the general sentiment it expresses informs a good deal of both academic work and policy efforts concerning the development of a legal profession in China. We advocate the profession's further growth in China not so much to produce technicians (though there is, no doubt, some element of that desired by business and others who regularly need to deal with the PRC), but more so because we see lawyers as especially well-equipped to advance concerns that we value—such as the rule of law, devotion to a market economy, and even democratic government—be it through active propagation or simply the power of the example of their daily professional lives.

Ironically, however, some of the very same qualities that Kronman extols for the part they play in the nurturing of the lawyer-statesman bear a measure of responsibility for the misunderstanding of the Chinese profession reflected in Kronman's own observations and in both scholarly and policy circles more broadly. We can see this in Kronman's (repeated) statements, upon which he places great weight, of the nature and genesis of the habits of mind and traits of character that warrant our vesting leadership in the lawyer-statesman. The quality of practical wisdom and political fraternity that we (should) so cherish, Kronman tells us, are not primarily about "the structural design of institutions" of the type fostered through immersion in economics or philosophy and the capacity they promote to see things in broad, abstract, and perhaps ideological terms. Rather, they involve a more Solomonic interstitial, incremental balancing of potentially incommensurate ends that is imparted by the type of analysis and way of thinking that the case method fosters.

---

28. Of course, some have expressed skepticism about the depth of Yale Law School's commitment to social science (Tushnet 1991, 1515).

Structure, however, does matter. Kronman and virtually all others who would share what they take to be the ideals of liberal legal professionalism in the U.S. with China seem to be assuming that these ideas are so powerful that they will not only blossom in the PRC, but will also play a critical role in the liberalization of distinctly illiberal institutions there. As Dezalay and Garth put it at one point in a prognosis that, one suspects, echoes the thinking of many Americans engaged in legal transplantation, soon "the legal profession may rival" the Communist Party. As recounted in Part I of this chapter, the record so far suggests something quite different—namely, that it is the Communist Party, and China more generally, that are shaping the legal profession at least as much as the latter is shaping the former, judging both from the ways in which the PRC legal profession has assisted the party/state in legitimating its position[29] and, perhaps even more tellingly, from the role that lawyers appear to be having in exacerbating the corruption that so afflicts judicial and administrative life in China.[30]

That this is so ought not necessarily to be surprising if one were to realize that the qualities Kronman prizes would be better served were they informed by a greater appreciation of structure, not to mention a healthy dose of humility. The experience in China of Buddhism, Christianity, Marxism, and many other ideas possessed of a longer history, more innate power, and more effective proselytizing than legal professionalism, underscores the fact that we do not need to see context as static in order to appreciate the ways in which it shapes that which would shape it (Spence 1980). To take a more contemporary illustration that would seem obvious, but that has largely been ignored in considerations of the value of external cultivation of the legal profession, lawyers in the PRC function in an institutional setting quite different from that of our own society.[31] The Chinese bench has, at least in theory, been cast in a civil law frame (albeit quite different from that of liberal democratic states with a continental system), while

---

29. Many people concerned with China policy take considerable comfort in the fact that the PRC now often responds to criticisms of its rights record in the language of the law. While I, too, think it significant that the Chinese government has taken up this discourse (and happily acknowledge that there are serious Chinese scholars working on rights issues), we need also to take account of the ways in which the state (and some scholars) have used such rhetoric in a highly instrumental fashion to defend acts that would seem deeply problematic from the vantage point either of Chinese law or of international human rights, and to fend off foreign criticism. Consider, for example, the uses of law to justify the state's harsh crackdown on the Falungong movement. In that regard, see materials in Schechter (2000).

30. To note this is not to ignore the ways in which citizens have sought to hold the state to its own law—the "double-edged" phenomenon about which I first wrote in 1993 (Alford 1993). To the contrary, it is in part to point out the ways in which lawyers may be blunting, as well as facilitating, this phenomenon.

31. Kronman, to be sure, does acknowledge in passing that in some societies "there is no room . . . for civic friendship or the statesmen's art . . . because they [the statesmen] stand at the boundaries of political life and, if they lead anywhere at all, it can only be to revolution" (1993, 107). Judging from the nature of his involvement in and comments about the PRC, it would not seem that Kronman could fairly include the PRC in this category.

we promote a distinctly common law model of the profession, typically with lit-tle attention to how things function in civil law jurisdictions (He Weifang 1995). To put it mildly, PRC authorities have not yet come to prize independ-ence in any major dimension of social organization.[32] In addition, there are massive and immediate incentives for lawyers, among others, to accept a system arrested between plan and market, with many a bottleneck (and concomitant opportunities for rent-seeking), rather than to push for more thorough-going reform and accompanying competition (author's interviews in Beijing in Sep-tember 1997, August 1999, and July 2000).

But the failure of Kronman and others like him to engage in the type of inquiry that might elicit such an understanding raises broader questions, reach-ing beyond the PRC to our own society. For example, as a normative matter, how do we know that the values Kronman so strongly advocates are worthy of wider adoption, or even of retention here if, as our own society and bar have become more democratic, pluralistic and prosperous, each, along with the bench and the legal academy, has by Kronman's own account largely rejected them? More prac-tically, how do we know that the ideal Kronman sketches, centered around a call for a small legal-aristocratic leadership, is not so linked to the conditions (includ-ing a far more homogeneous elite) of the period within which Kronman suggests it flourished (i.e., this nation's first century) that even if desirable, it is unsustain-able, given the current structure of American life, economically, politically, and socially? And, to take but one more illustration, if we are so uncertain about the nexus between this ideal and the society from which it has emerged, how are we (or those whose lives it would shape) to determine its feasibility in another soci-ety that presumably differs in important respects from our own?

In one sense, Kronman's relative slighting of what he terms the structural in favor of practical wisdom seems odd, given that he earlier produced a book-length study of Weber's approach to law (Kronman 1983) and given that *The Lost Lawyer* describes itself as a work of philosophy and sociology that states quite explicitly that philosophical argument is the only remaining hope for recapturing the ideals embodied by the lawyer-statesman (Kronman 1993, 14). Yet, in another sense, it is very much of a piece with the great majority of Amer-ican writing about the sociology of the legal profession which, whether by lawyers, sociologists, or others, tends to present its theoretical findings as hav-ing universal validity, even if they emerge from work principally concerned with the United States.[33]

---

32. As Ken Lieberthal put it in 1995, "all nonofficial organizations exist only at the sufferance of the party" (Lieberthal 1995). This is not to denigrate the serious efforts, documented by Tony Saich, among others, of a growing number of citizens' groups to carve out space for themselves in the interstices (Saich 2000, 125).

33. This may be most obvious in the writing of Richard Posner. Although his writing on the legal profession is principally concerned with the experience of the United States, he treats the lessons he draws from this as having far broader application (Posner 1998b, 1. See also Posner 1998a, 1). I discuss Posner in Alford (2000).

This approach is taken in discussions of schools of thought as seemingly different as the functionalism of Talcott Parsons (1962); the professionalization project of Margali Sarfatti Larson (Larson 1977); the market-driven focus of scholars running the political gamut from Richard Abel (1988) to Richard Posner; and the knowledge-centered inquiry of Andrew Abbott (1988), David Trubek (1994, 407), Bryant Garth (Dezalay and Garth 1996), and others. It has produced a sociology of the profession that assumes a U.S.-specific backdrop of a weak executive, a highly independent bench, a strong profession largely distinct from the state but less so from commerce, and a vibrant civil society to such a degree that the theoretical guideposts emerging from it do not map comfortably even onto liberal democratic states with a civil law heritage, let alone societies such as the PRC.[34] Perhaps even more crucially because it takes our institutions so much as a given, such work, in the end, does not probe as thoroughly as it might into the relationship between the particular institutions of our society and the nature and role of our legal profession. As such, it is far less illuminating academically and far less empowering for those engaged in legal development than work that is of a more nuanced historical or richly comparative bent (Alford 2000).

III. The Challenge of Thinking about Lawyers in the PRC

Appearances to the contrary, the principal purpose of this chapter has not been to find fault with Anthony Kronman's much-celebrated work. Instead, it has been to utilize the phenomenon of Dean Kronman's hope of finding (or implanting) in China the ideals of legal professionalism that he believes we are losing here as a focal point for reflecting on what is assuredly the most concerted effort in world history to spawn a legal profession. For, as this brief concluding Part will endeavor to suggest, the Chinese experience raises difficult, but essential, questions not only about China, but about legal professionalism, legal academe, and the law more generally.

For all its use of the tools of sociology and philosophy, Kronman's book does not yield as much insight as at least this observer wishes it had into the broad implications of professionalism from the vantage point of either discipline as we turn to the Chinese case. From a sociological perspective, we need to know far more than we can glean from *The Lost Lawyer* (and most other writing

---

34. Interestingly, scholarly writing about the legal profession in Europe tends to be more self-conscious about the significance of institutional context, perhaps a reflection of the vicissitudes of the German legal profession over the past century or of the likelihood that those who write about societies other than the U.S. cannot help but be mindful of the American experience and the ways in which it differs from what they discern to be the case elsewhere (in a manner that does not have a direct counterpart for those whose principal focus is the American profession) (see, e.g., Rueschemeyer 1998; Ledford 1996; Halliday and Karpik 1997).

regarding the legal profession) about the interplay between ideas of professionalism and broader institutions and norms. If, for example, Robert Gordon is
correct in his provocative hypothesis (1983) that the patterns of American liberalism made themselves felt not only in tangible form, such as the manner in
which the late nineteenth century elite New York bar organized itself for the
practice of law, but also in the very ways in which those lawyers thought
through legal problems, what does this suggest for our consideration of lawyers
in the as yet decidedly illiberal PRC setting?

Or, to use Kronman's frame of analysis, what does it mean to speak of the
lawyer-statesman as possessing a singular capacity to formulate and articulate a
society's interests through politics in a setting in which the range of views that
might be given voice remains sharply constrained and in which behind the state
and its law lurks the CCP? Or if what Kronman describes as the qualities that
distinguish lawyers from other intellectuals in our society can only be cultivated
through the common law case method, what does that suggest about the
prospects for the bar in liberal democratic civil law states, let alone China? And
what are the implications of promotion of a legal profession for the access of
citizens, particularly among society's more vulnerable groups, to dispute resolution, especially if historically grounded alternatives to formal legal process
(such as mediation) are cut back as the bar and the state's law grow?

Nor are the questions we need to explore from a philosophical viewpoint any
easier. If we believe that the high ideals undergirding our profession are failing
here, what is the moral basis for our seeking to persuade the Chinese or anyone
else to adopt them? If we believe that the ideals of legal professionalism are
linked to or dependent upon the institutions and values of liberalism, does that
obligate us to push first or simultaneously for broader political change and, if
so, on what moral foundation? And if so sweeping a course is either inappropriate or impractical, what are the implications of our placing so great an emphasis on legal professionals, if not legal reform more generally, in the absence of
broader political change?

Lurking beneath many of these questions, both sociological and philosophical, are fundamental tensions in the nature of lawyering and the law (and, for
that matter, legal academe), at least in this society, that Kronman slights in his
hope of promoting the ideal of the lawyer-statesman and of which most American observers seem essentially oblivious as they seek to foster legal development in the PRC. Kronman, reflecting, one imagines, the pride that a great
many Americans who would export our legal institutions have had in at least
the ideals of our legal profession, clearly is taken with the sentiment expressed
in Tocqueville's statement that "it is at the bar or the bench that the American
aristocracy is found"—which he both quotes on the first page of his book and
affirms with the observation that "judging by the wealth and influence of
lawyers in contemporary America, one might conclude that his famous dictum
is as true today as when he uttered it a hundred and fifty years ago" (Kronman
1993, 1). Kronman, however, does not quote Tocqueville's accompanying
admonition—that although lawyers "value liberty, they generally rate legality as

far more precious; they are less afraid of tyranny than of arbitrariness, and provided that it is the law-giver himself who is responsible for taking away men's liberty, they are more or less content" (Tocqueville 1990 (1848), 266). This important dimension of Tocqueville's thinking is instead captured, if at all, in a fleeting acknowledgment well into *The Lost Lawyer* that "the observation that American lawyers tend to be conservative . . . [has] been made before most famously by Tocqueville" and Kronman's statement that our bar has tended to be "closely connected to the propertied class" and to have a disdain, coming from "above all, the discipline of legal reasoning . . . for the unruly proceedings of democratic assemblies" (Kronman 1993, 155).

American lawyers as a whole may (or may not) be conservative in the sense Kronman suggests, but that proposition, I would argue, fails adequately to convey the grave danger—regarding lawyers' potential to sacrifice liberty and embrace tyranny—against which Tocqueville sounded his warning both in the above-cited passage and in his further observation that a ruler "faced by an encroaching democracy" would do well to bring lawyers into his government, for "having entrusted to them a despotism taking its shape from violence, perhaps he might receive it back from their hands with features of justice and law" (Tocqueville 1990).

My point here is not to deny the good that lawyers can do. Our history and that of other nations contains many an admirable example of lawyers deeply dedicated to the promotion of liberty through law.[35] Rather, it is to urge that we not lose sight of Tocqueville's prescient observation regarding the profession's double-edged capacity, borne out in our history and with analogs elsewhere, to facilitate very different ends. One need not lapse into a relativism that would equate the U.S. and the PRC to observe that even as we take note of a 98–99.5 percent conviction rate in China in our discussion of the role of counsel there, we might also want to remain mindful as we consider the relevance for the profession here of the fact that some 90 percent of criminal cases in this country are resolved through plea bargaining (on which formal constitutionally oriented procedural protections cast at best a distant shadow). An awareness of the complex picture Tocqueville actually paints would seem to require that those who speak only of the profession's promise in China explain both why we would have reason to expect more of it there[36] and why the Chinese leadership, which

---

35. With respect to the United States, the work of the legal team in Brown v. Board of Education, the famed 1954 school desegregation case, comes readily to mind (see Kluger 1975). Examples of heroic lawyering abroad are discussed in a number of the essays in Sarat and Scheingold (1998).

36. It might also require that we take note of the observation of many Chinese lawyers I interviewed to the effect that American business lawyers in China present a more variegated picture than we might imagine. Even as my interviewees acknowledged that the expatriate bar may be introducing new norms of professionalism, they expressed considerable resentment that many foreign lawyers provide advice about local law in contravention of formal PRC legal requirements. For an account of one American lawyer's unwitting efforts to circumvent PRC requirements in order to work as a legal professional see Wonacott (2000).

is quite committed to maintaining its distinctly non-democratic hold on power, seems so intent on promoting the growth of the legal profession.[37] The recognition that law may be dual-edged should, in turn, prompt us to stay attentive (as Tocqueville also observed regarding the American experience) to the subtle and not always self-conscious ways in which lawyers and law may channel energies for political change into legal avenues, often to the fundamental preservation of the status quo and, not coincidentally, the enrichment of lawyers themselves. That may be one thing in a state that is essentially liberal democratic and quite another in a nation that remains highly authoritarian.[38]

The foregoing presents a stiff challenge to lawyers and others concerned with the legal profession and legal development in the PRC, particularly if we also seek to remain cognizant of the ways in which legalization may privilege some members of society and the impact it may have on less formal modes of dispute resolution and citizen redress. Dedicated to the good that lawyers and the law can do, we need to understand their pitfalls, even as we extol their potential. And, at least for those of us primarily situated in professional schools, we must not allow the allure presented by the opportunity to promote our ideals (or ourselves) to divert us from striving fairly to critique such endeavor. That may, in the end, pose a conundrum comparable in its complexity to the riddles posed by Laozi, Zhuangzi and other great ancient Daoist figures, but it would seem we owe no less to the Chinese and to ourselves.

---

37. As indicated earlier (see note 17 above), we should be wary of suggestions that authorities in the PRC are too naïve to understand the implications of their actions. This is not to deny that China's top leadership has relatively little direct experience with the institutions of liberal democracy. But nor is it to ignore the possibility that the CCP's top echelon may in desperation be tolerating changes that it appreciates present some risk to its tight grip on power or that there may even be some individuals of rank who would welcome a degree of liberalization, whether for reasons of philosophy or factionalism. Instead, it is to urge that those who portray foreign legal assistance as a Trojan horse demonstrate why they think they have a better understanding than China's ruling elite of how particular institutions may play out on Chinese soil, given the arduous political gauntlet through which those leaders have passed to reach and retain their present positions, their greater access to information about current Chinese circumstances, and the earnestness with which Beijing has dissected the experience of Eastern Europe and Taiwan over the past decade and a half.

38. For an account of the potential of foreign assistance to be used to legitimate problematic activity such as Beijing's crackdown on the Falungong, see Johnson (2000).

Works Cited

Abbott, Andrew. 1988. *The system of professions: An essay on the division of expert labor.* Chicago: University of Chicago Press.

Abel, Richard L. 1988. Comparative sociology of the legal profession. In *Lawyers in society: Comparative theories,* eds. R. L. Abel and P. S. C. Lewis. Berkeley: University of California Press.

Ackerman, Bruce. 2000. The new separation of powers. 113 *Harvard Law Review* 633.

Agence France-Presse. 2000. China handling 9,000 corruption cases. 11 December.

Alford, William P. 1993. Double-edged swords cut both ways: Law and legitimacy in the People's Republic of China. *Daedalus* 122 (2): 45–63.

———. 1995. Tasselled loafers for barefoot lawyers: Transformations and tensions in the world of Chinese lawyers. *China Quarterly* 141:22. Reprinted in *China's Legal Reforms,* ed. S.B. Lubman. 1996. New York: Oxford University Press.

———. 1998. Lawyers in China. Unpublished paper, on file with W. Alford.

———. 2000. Exporting the pursuit of happiness. 113 *Harvard Law Review* 1677.

———. 2003. The more law, the more . . . ? Measuring legal reform in the People's Republic of China. In *How far across the river? Chinese policy reform at the millennium,* eds. N. C. Hope, D. T. Yang, and M. Y. Li. Palo Alto: Stanford University Press.

Bianchi, Robert. 1989. *Unruly corporatism: Associational life in twentieth century Egypt.* New York: Oxford University Press.

Calabresi, Steven G. 1998. An agenda for constitutional reform. In *Constitutional stupidities, constitutional tragedies,* eds. W. N. Eskridge, Jr. and S. Levinson. New York: New York University Press.

Ching, Frank. 1998. Rough justice. *Far Eastern Economic Review.* 20 August.

Dezalay, Yves and Bryant G. Garth. 1996. *Dealing in virtue: International commercial arbitration and the construction of a transnational legal order.* Chicago: University of Chicago Press.

Du Gangjian and Li Xuan. 1997. *Zhongguo lüshi de dangdai mingyuan* [The contemporary fate of Chinese lawyers]. Beijing: Gaige Chubanshe.

Falk, Richard. 1995. Casting the spell: The New Haven School of International Law: Jurisprudence for a free society. 104 *Yale Law Journal* 1991.

Gordon, Robert W. 1983. Legal thought and legal practice in the age of American enterprise. In *Professions and professional ideology in America,* ed. G. L. Geison. Chapel Hill: University of North Carolina Press.

Halliday, Terence C. and Lucien Karpik. 1997. *Lawyers and the rise of western political liberalism.* New York: Oxford University Press.

Hansmann, Henry and Reinier Kraakman. 2000. The end of history for corporate law. 110 *Yale Law Journal* 3:387–440.

He Qinglian. 2000. Dangqian Zhongguo shehui jiegou yanbian de zongtixing fenxi [An overall analysis of the current change of China's social structure]. *Dangdai Zhongguo Yanjiu* [Modern China studies] 68 (3): 86.

He Weifang. 1995. Tongguo sifa shixian shehui zhengyi: Dui Zhongguo faguan xianzhuang de yige toushi [The realization of social justice through judicature: A look at the current situation of Chinese judges]. In *Zou xiang quanli de shidai: Zhongguo gongmin fazhan yanjiu* [Toward a time of rights: A perspective on the development of civil rights in China], ed. Xia Yong. Beijing: Zhongguo Zhengfa Daxue Chubanshe.

———. 1998. Fuzhuan junren jin fayuan [Retired soldiers in the courts]. *Nanfang Zhoumo* [Southern weekend]. 2 January.

Hecht, Jonathan. 1996. *Opening to reform? An analysis of China's revised criminal procedure law*. New York: Lawyers Committee for Human Rights.

Herzstein, Robert. 2000. Fitting China into the WTO: Can China function in a law governed trading system? *Harvard China Review* 2:63.

Hu Angang, ed. 2000. *Zhongguo: Tiaozhan fubai* [China fighting against corruption]. Hangzhou: Zhejiang Renmin Chubanshe.

Johnson, Ian. 2000. U.N. helps sponsor China conference on "evil cults." *Wall Street Journal*. 22 November.

Kluger, Richard. 1975. *Simple justice: The history of "Brown v. Board of Education" and Black America's struggle for equality*. New York: Knopf.

Kronman, Anthony T. 1983. *Max Weber*. Palo Alto: Stanford University Press.

———. 1993. *The lost lawyer: Failing ideals of the legal profession*. Cambridge, MA: Harvard University Press.

Kynge, James. 2000. "Personal conduct" costs Chinese minister his job. *Financial Times*. 5 December.

Larson, Margali Sarfatti. 1977. *The rise of professionalism: A sociological analysis*. Berkeley: University of California Press.

Lawyers Committee for Human Rights. 1998. *Lawyers in China: Obstacles to independence and the defense of rights*. New York: Lawyers Committee for Human Rights.

Ledford, Kenneth F. 1996. *From general estate to special interest: German lawyers 1878–1933*. New York: Cambridge University Press.

Leitch, Sara. 1998. Law dean advises Chinese law reform. *Yale Daily News*. 16 September.

Lewis, Anthony. 1998. The engine of law. *New York Times*. 6 July.

Lieberthal, Kenneth. 1995. *Governing China: From revolution through reform*. New York: W. W. Norton.

Lubman, Stanley B. 1999. *Bird in a cage: Legal reform in China after Mao.* Palo Alto: Stanford University Press.

Luo Bing. 1996. Mijian xielu zhonggong zuzhi fulan [Secret document exposes decay in Communist party organization]. *Cheng Ming (Zhengming)* [Contend] 225:6.

Madsen, Richard. 1995. *China and the American dream: A moral inquiry.* Berkeley: University of California Press.

McCutheon, Aubrey. 2000. Contributing to legal reform in China. In *Many roads to justice: The law-related work of Ford Foundation grantees around the world,* eds. M. McClymont and S. Golub. New York: Ford Foundation.

Michelson, Ethan. 2003. They talk the talk, but can they walk the walk? Obstacles to collective action among Chinese lawyers. Unpublished paper, on file with W. Alford.

Minzner, Carl. 2006. *Xinfang:* An alternative to formal Chinese legal institutions. 42 *Stanford Journal of International Law* 1.

Parsons, Talcott. 1962. The legal profession. In *Law and sociology,* ed. W. Evans. New York: Free Press of Glencoe.

Pearson, Margaret. 1997. *China's new business elite: The political consequences of economic reform.* Berkeley: University of California Press.

Pei Minxin. 2000. Political changes in post-Mao China: Progress and challenges. In *China's future: Constructive partner or emerging threat?,* eds. T. G. Carpenter and J. A. Dorn. New York: Lawyers Committee for Human Rights.

Posner, Richard. 1998a. Creating a legal framework for economic development. *World Bank Research Observer* 13:1.

———. 1998b. Professions. 40 *Arizona Law Review* 1.

Ramseyer, J. Mark and Eric Rasmusen. 1998. *Why the Japanese conviction rate is so high.* Discussion paper no. 240. John M. Olin Center for Law, Economics and Business, Harvard Law School, Cambridge, MA.

Rueschemeyer, Dietrich. 1988. Comparing legal professions: A state-centered approach. In *Lawyers in society: Comparative theories,* eds. R. L. Abel and P. S. C. Lewis. Berkeley: University of California Press.

Saich, Anthony. 2000. Negotiating the state: The development of social organizations in China. *China Quarterly* 161:125.

Sarat, Austin and Stuart Scheingold, eds. 1998. *Cause lawyering: Political commitments and professional responsibilities.* New York: Oxford University Press.

Schechter, Danny. 2000. *Falun Gong's challenge to China: Spiritual practice or "civil cult"?* New York: Akashic Books.

Sender, Henry. 2000. For Morgan Stanley, a Chinese headache. *Wall Street Journal.* 14 November.

Smith, Craig S. 2000. Graft in China flows freely, draining the treasury. *New York Times*. 1 October.

Spence, Jonathan D. 1980. *To change China: Western advisers in China 1620–1960*. New York: Penguin Books.

Stein, Robert A. 1999. Two billion reasons to cooperate. *American Bar Association Journal* 85 (February): 86.

Tocqueville, Alexis de. 1990 (originally 1848). *Democracy in America*. New York: Vintage Books.

Trubek, David, Yves Dezalay, Ruth Buchanan, and John Davis. 1994. The future of the legal profession: Global restructuring and the law: Studies in the internationalization of legal fields and the creation of transnational arenas. 44 *Case Western Reserve Law Review* 407.

Tushnet, Mark. 1991. Critical Legal Studies: A political history. 100 *Yale Law Journal* 1515.

Wank, David L. 1996. The institutional process of market clientelism: *Guanxi* and private business in a South China city. *China Quarterly* 147:820.

Wilkins, David B. 1994. Practical wisdom for practicing lawyers: Separating ideals from ideology in legal ethics. 108 *Harvard Law Review* 458.

Wonacott, Peter. 2000. As China opens the door, foreign lawyers are poised to rush in. *Wall Street Journal*. 15 November.

Xiehong District People's Court. 2004. Sichuan sheng Xiehong xian renmin fayuan xingshi panjueshu 138 hao [Criminal decision number 138 of the Xiehong District People's Court of Sichuan Province].

Xinhua News Agency. 1997. President tells legal profession to help promote reform. 27 January.

Zhang Zhimin. 1995. Dangdai Zhongguo de lüshi ye: Yi minquan wei jiben chidu [The legal profession in contemporary China: A civil rights perspective]. 9 *Bijiaofa Yanjiu* [Research on comparative law] 1.

Zhongguo Sifa Xingzheng Nianjian Bianji Bu [The editorial department of the China yearbook of administration]. 1999. *Zhongguo sifa xingzheng nianjian* [The China yearbook of judicial administration]. Beijing: Falü Chubanshe.

Zhonghua Renmin Gongheguo Lüshi Fa [People's Republic of China lawyers law]. 1996. Reprinted in *Zhonghua renmin gongheguo xin fagui huibian* [People's Republic of China collected new laws and regulations]. 1996 (2): 39. Beijing: Xinhua Shudian.

EIGHT

Lawyers, Legal Aid, and Legitimacy in China

BENJAMIN L. LIEBMAN*

Introduction

This chapter uses China's development of legal aid programs and pro bono requirements to highlight four broad questions regarding the role of lawyers and law in China. First, what distinguishes lawyers from others providing legal services in the Chinese legal system? In particular, are distinctions between lawyers and non-lawyers relevant in a legal system in which much legal work is performed by non-lawyers, most cases are litigated without counsel, and lawyers themselves are often poorly trained? Second, what are the boundaries of permissible activity by lawyers, and is China witnessing the development of cause lawyering? Third, to what degree are lawyers continuing to operate as, or be perceived as, state legal workers, and is the government succeeding in enlisting lawyers both in implementing state policies and in serving as checks on abuses in the legal system? Fourth, has the growth of legal aid programs and the legal profession taken sufficient notice of client interests?

The rapid recent development of legal aid programs and the legal profession in China precludes clear answers to these questions. Discussion of these questions is largely absent from Chinese writing on the legal profession and legal aid, as both lawyers and government officials responsible for lawyers rush to expand the legal profession and exploit new opportunities. Nevertheless, the development of the legal profession and legal aid programs provides insights into the evolution of law and lawyers. Indeed, many of the issues that this chapter discusses cannot be cabined into a discussion of legal aid programs alone. Chinese lawyers are working in a system that is increasingly tolerant of a range of activity by lawyers. This increased tolerance is at least in part the result of a central government commitment to a policy of increasing the profile of law in Chinese society—a policy that is manifest in the expansion of the legal profession and

*Associate Professor of Law and Director of the Center for Chinese Legal Studies, Columbia University School of Law; J.D., Harvard Law School, 1998.

This chapter was prepared for the December 1998 Conference on the Legal Profession in East Asia, held at Harvard Law School. It was revised during the first half of 1999, and reflects the author's understanding of the situation in China at that time.

legal aid programs, in the increasing attention legal disputes and issues are receiving from the Chinese press, and in government efforts to direct disputes into the formal legal system. Yet the increased number and availability of lawyers may also be shaping how the legal system develops. As law continues to increase in relevance, lawyers themselves may find their own roles altered in ways that are still difficult to predict.

Part I of this chapter provides a brief overview of China's recent development of legal aid programs and pro bono requirements, as well as a discussion of policies that lie behind China's recent attention to legal aid. Part II places China's development of legal aid programs in the context of both low rates of lawyer participation in litigation in China and the existence of well-established networks of non-lawyer legal workers who undertake work similar to that handled by lawyers. Part II argues that an absence of clear distinctions between lawyers and non-lawyers in China suggests that increasing the number of lawyers and the importance of legal aid work by lawyers may not necessarily be the best mechanism for meeting the legal needs of China's poor. The lack of such clear distinctions also demonstrates a need for further examination of what it means to be a lawyer in China.

Part III uses a discussion of one quasi-independent legal aid center to explore the limits and prerequisites to cause lawyering in China. Although the experiences of the center reflect the increasing willingness of lawyers and academics to criticize structural problems in the Chinese legal system publicly, lawyers advocating specific causes are generally well-connected members of the elite who are pursing goals consistent with those of the central government. Part IV examines government perceptions and uses of lawyers and suggests that the central government is increasingly aware of the role lawyers are playing in law implementation and in highlighting abuses by local governments. Part IV also argues that viewing the legal profession primarily in terms of its relationship to the state may be misguided, both because lawyers' interests may not conflict with those of the state and because there may be significant variety in state interests between local governments and the central government, and between the Ministry of Justice and other central government departments or entities.

Part V notes that the development of legal aid and the legal profession is taking place absent significant reflection on or discussion of client interests. This lack of attention to client interests may have its roots in a traditional lack of emphasis on individuals in the Chinese legal system, but the lack of attention to clients also reflects the degree to which both Chinese lawyers and the central government have been more concerned with expanding the number of and opportunities for lawyers than with the services lawyers provide to clients. The conclusion offers five observations on the development of the Chinese legal profession.

One larger question lurks behind much of the discussion in this chapter: why has the Chinese government, and the Ministry of Justice in particular, been so enthusiastic in supporting the development of both the legal profession and legal aid programs? Providing a clear answer to this question requires further research and is beyond the scope of this chapter. Nevertheless, certain themes do emerge from the questions examined herein.

First, China's embrace of lawyers and legal aid appears to result at least in part from China's desire to use lawyers and legal aid to help keep disputes off the street by steering disputes into the formal legal system, where such disputes can be better monitored. Expanding the availability of lawyers and legal aid is thus consistent with government efforts to maintain "social stability."

Second, the growth of the total number of lawyers, and government efforts to encourage lawyers to undertake a widening range of cases in which they challenge local authorities, are consistent with government efforts to use law, lawyers, and the press as checks on lawless behavior by local governments and people with local government ties. By encouraging lawyers to focus on local abuses, the central government may be addressing a prime threat to its own legitimacy (corruption and lawless behavior by local governments) and also preventing lawyers from turning their sights on the central government itself. Thus, the development of legal aid programs may be serving to maintain a degree of government control over both lawyers and local governments; indeed, lawyers and local governments may be serving as checks on each other. This focus on using lawyers as checks on local abuses may at least partially explain China's inattention to alternative strategies (and existing structures) that might more effectively address the legal needs of China's rural poor than will a reliance on lawyer-based legal aid programs.

Third, although the Chinese government does appear to be attempting to guide the development of the legal profession at least in part to serve the government's own aims, the government itself is not monolithic: there are significant differences in interests and opinions both within the central government and between the central government and regional and local governments. Indeed, it is difficult to pinpoint any government department or official who represents the views that I at times attribute to the central government.

This chapter does not attempt to examine these themes in detail. The chapter does, however, suggest that understanding the role and evolution of the Chinese legal profession requires further understanding of the complex relations among the central government, local governments, the legal profession, the courts, and the press. Deeper understanding of the significance of recent developments in China will also require placing China's experiences in a comparative context.

I. Legal Aid: Rapid Development

A. Background

I describe in detail elsewhere China's development of legal aid programs (Liebman 1999).[1] This Part of this chapter provides a brief summary of recent efforts in China to expand the provision of legal aid. "Legal aid" is loosely defined in China, encompassing work ranging from informal consultations to free and reduced-fee representation of the poor or powerless to legal advice government lawyers give struggling state-owned industries. The vast majority of legal aid work by lawyers consists of responses to legal inquiries, but lawyers also assist clients in mediation and, increasingly, represent the disadvantaged in court.

The growth of legal aid programs in China has occurred against the backdrop of a dramatic increase in the number of cases in China's courts and the rapid growth of the legal profession. Between 1995 and 1996, the number of cases brought in China's courts increased by 16 percent, continuing a trend that began in the 1980s. Between 1990 and 1996, the total number of first-instance cases brought in China's courts increased from 2,916,774 to 5,312,580. During the same period, the total number of civil disputes resolved by people's mediation committees (the traditional alternative to the court system) decreased from 7,409,222 to 5,802,230. Court cases do not necessarily result in formal adjudication: many cases in the courts are resolved by court-supervised mediation. Nevertheless, the percentage of cases brought in the courts that have been resolved through court-supervised mediation has also been steadily declining, from 65 percent in 1990 to 54 percent in 1996. In fact, in 1998, the number of first-instance disputes brought in the courts exceeded the number of disputes handled by mediation committees for the first time since the founding of the People's Republic in 1949 (Zhongguo Falü Nianjian Bianji Bu (ZFNBB) 1991, 933, 934, 956; ZFNBB 1997, 1055, 1056, 1074; ZFNBB 1999, 1021, 1041).

The number of lawyers has similarly increased at a dramatic rate, from a post-Cultural Revolution total of approximately 3,000 in 1979 to 40,000 in 1990 to more than 100,000 in 1996. Although the growth of the legal profession is a recent phenomenon, Chinese lawyers have long had obligations to serve society. China had just 2,500 full-time lawyers in 1957, for example, but regulations at the time required lawyers—all of whom were state employees—to provide free assistance in a range of cases. The effect of such regulations was likely limited, however, given both the small number of lawyers and the Chinese government's

---

1. Unless otherwise noted, material in this Part is based on this previous work. Additionally, much of the information in this chapter is based on interviews with Chinese lawyers and officials.

official disdain for litigation (Cohen 1966, 1201).[2] Similar regulations enacted after the Cultural Revolution and in place throughout the 1980s encouraged pro bono work and instructed lawyers to provide free legal services in a range of cases,[3] but the effect likewise appears to have been minimal.

In the late 1980s, as the number of lawyers continued to rise, the Chinese government began granting lawyers economic autonomy. Prior to 1988, all lawyers had been state employees and had worked largely for state-owned law firms; beginning in that year, the Ministry of Justice permitted lawyers to organize into cooperative law firms, financially autonomous from the government. In 1993, the Ministry of Justice permitted lawyers to form partnerships. By 1996, approximately one-third of China's lawyers were practicing outside of state firms.[4] In addition, even within state-run law firms many lawyers now have significant economic autonomy.

B. Government Policy

Although Chinese laws have long required that lawyers provide reduced-fee or free legal services to the poor, the Chinese term for legal aid, *falü yuanzhu*, was virtually unknown before 1993. Since then, the Ministry of Justice, which has jurisdiction over lawyers and law firms, has embarked on an ambitious program to develop a nationwide legal aid system. In June 1998, the Ministry of Justice reported that provincial or local justice bureaus had established 180 legal aid centers or offices, nearly quadrupling the number of centers that were in operation just one year earlier. The number of legal aid centers in operation is remarkable given that the first justice bureau legal aid centers were established in Guangzhou and Shanghai in 1995. The same Ministry of Justice report claimed that lawyers engaging in legal aid work—either in legal aid centers or on their own—had handled 70,677 cases and responded to more than 431,000 requests for legal information in 1997. These statistics are unverifiable, but they do suggest the importance that the Ministry of Justice is attaching to expanding

---

2. Formal legal aid programs were also likely at odds with Chinese communist ideology, which emphasized the existence of a classless society. As James Gordley has written in his discussion of legal aid in the Soviet Union, "Legal aid programs postulate an economic inequality so grave that comprehensive programs are needed"; the existence of such programs would "offend the belief that a classless society has been achieved" (1975, 82). As was the case in the Soviet Union (83), the entire Chinese legal system could have been viewed as a legal aid system.

3. In the criminal context, regulations in the first decade of the People's Republic stated that defendants had a right to hire a lawyer but made no provision for the appointment of counsel for indigent defendants. Beginning in 1979, Chinese laws instructed courts to appoint a "defender"—not necessarily a lawyer—to represent criminal defendants where courts deemed such representation to be necessary. In addition, certain classes of defendants— minors and the deaf or mute—were entitled to free representation.

4. However, the cooperative and partnership firms are largely concentrated in economically developed cities. In other areas of the country, the vast majority of lawyers continue to practice in state-run law firms. For example, in 1998 in Xinjiang, in western China, there were 1,567 lawyers and 200 law firms—but 156 of the law firms were state-run firms (Ma 1998).

legal aid programs. Chinese courts handled roughly 5.29 million cases in 1997 (Xinhua English Newswire 1999);[5] thus, the Ministry of Justice statistics suggest that legal aid lawyers were involved in between 1 and 2 percent of cases in China's courts in 1997.

A number of policies and goals appear to be responsible for the Ministry of Justice's embrace of legal aid. Expanding legal aid meshes with recent central government attempts to address income inequalities, even as the government continues to embrace economic reforms that have led to a widening gap between rich and poor. The growth of legal aid programs is consistent with efforts to boost the importance of law in Chinese society and in particular with efforts to pressure local governments to obey national laws. Ministry of Justice officials also view legal aid as a characteristic of most developed legal systems. Ministry officials thus believe that establishing a legal aid system is a prerequisite to China developing a mature legal system. Chinese advocates of legal aid further argue that establishing legal aid programs will assist China in rebutting western critiques of the Chinese legal system.

The development of legal aid programs has coincided with the implementation of China's Lawyers Law and revised Criminal Procedure Law, both enacted in 1996. The Lawyers Law imposes an affirmative obligation on lawyers to engage in legal aid work but provides no specifics as to the nature or amount of such work. The revised Criminal Procedure Law expands the class of defendants entitled to legal aid and states for the first time that in cases in which court appointment of a lawyer is discretionary, the court may consider a defendant's economic hardship in determining whether to appoint counsel. In addition, although the Ministry of Justice has permitted local justice bureaus to experiment in developing legal aid programs and has used such experiments as models for the expansion of legal aid elsewhere, the ministry has also issued a number of notices regarding legal aid. These notices instruct local justice bureaus to establish legal aid programs and provide rough guidelines about who is eligible for legal aid.[6] Numerous local and provincial governments have enacted their own more detailed regulations regarding legal aid.

---

5. The report stated that China's courts handled 5.41 million cases in 1998, a 2.31 percent increase over 1997.

6. Ministry of Justice notices function like regulations but are only binding on justice bureaus and those subject to the jurisdiction of justice bureaus—primarily lawyers and justice bureau officials. Such notices are not binding on other government actors, such as the courts or procuratorate. The Ministry of Justice initially proposed national regulations on legal aid but withdrew the regulations, apparently after running into opposition within the State Council. In early 1999, the Ministry of Justice renewed efforts to draft legal aid regulations that would be approved by the State Council. One legal aid lawyer commented that getting State Council approval of legal aid provisions or regulations had taken on added importance in the face of local government resistance to funding legal aid programs: with the passage of State Council regulations, the Ministry of Justice would be better positioned to compel local governments to spend money on legal aid.

China's efforts to expand the availability of legal aid have generally not distinguished between civil and criminal legal aid: the few full-time legal aid lawyers in China participate in both civil and criminal cases. However, with the exception of the legal aid center in Guangzhou, most centers in China initially focused on providing legal aid in civil cases.[7] Since the end of 1997, attention has shifted toward expanding legal aid for criminal defendants.[8] It appears, however, that many locales have been slow to reform their existing structures for providing legal aid to criminal defendants, whereby cases are often assigned to law firms with close ties to the local court. Although the roles legal aid lawyers are playing in criminal cases is a fascinating topic, this chapter focuses largely on the implications of China's development of civil legal aid, as this is the area in which China's initial efforts to establish legal aid programs were focused.

C. Ministry of Justice/Local Justice Bureau Programs

Local justice bureaus have experimented with a range of models for providing legal aid. In Guangzhou, the legal aid center has a staff of twelve full-time lawyers and operates a large office next door to the Guangzhou Intermediate Court and the Guangdong Provincial High Court. The Guangzhou center was established in 1995. More recently, a number of legal aid centers in other cities have followed this "Guangzhou Model," and the Ministry of Justice has explicitly encouraged other locales to follow Guangzhou's example of employing full-time legal aid lawyers.

Nevertheless, most of the programs established in China have relied on lawyers outside the local legal aid center to handle legal aid work. Thus, the legal aid center in Shanghai's Pudong District initially had only a single staff person

---

7. The precise reasons for this initial focus on civil legal aid are unclear. The relatively slow development of criminal legal aid programs appears to result at least in part from the fact that implementing such programs involves more coordination with the courts and the procuratorate than does implementing civil legal aid. In particular, justice bureaus and courts have differed over who is responsible for paying the costs of legal aid for criminal defendants. Prior to the 1996 revision of the Criminal Procedure Law, courts were responsible for paying for court-appointed counsel. At least some courts have seen the growth of justice bureau legal aid programs as an opportunity to shift the cost of such representation to the justice bureaus. In Guangzhou, where criminal cases have made up the bulk of cases undertaken by the local justice bureau's legal aid center, legal aid lawyers state that they have benefited from close relationships to the courts. In addition, some legal aid lawyers complain that the procuratorate has been slow to implement the 1996 Criminal Procedure Law, in particular new provisions regarding lawyers' access to their clients.

8. A legal aid lawyer I spoke with in April 1999 stated that government legal aid programs were increasingly focusing on criminal cases, often at the expense of civil legal aid. The lawyer indicated that he believed that civil legal aid work would increasingly be left to university-based programs and other legal aid programs outside the justice bureau system. Examining how this apparent shift in emphasis from civil to criminal cases by government legal aid programs relates to experiences elsewhere is an intriguing avenue of future comparative research.

and required local law firms both to send lawyers to work at the center on a rotating basis and to handle cases that the center accepted and assigned to them.[9] In Beijing, the legal aid center has an eight-person staff, including three lawyers, but the center's staff plays a largely administrative role. Each of Beijing's roughly 300[10] law firms is responsible for staffing the center for one week approximately every four years. Lawyers staffing the center respond to legal inquiries; if the center's administrative staff deems cases to be suitable for legal representation, the center then assigns cases to law firms on a rotating basis. However, law firms are also given the option of opting out of the program by making financial contributions to Beijing's legal aid fund, which is used to reimburse lawyers for expenses incurred in legal aid work. Statistics are not available on the number of law firms that have opted out of the program, but lawyers from a number of commercial firms state that their firms have decided to pay rather than participate.

Despite the Ministry of Justice's repeated endorsement of the Guangzhou system, it appears that only a dozen or so of China's legal aid centers rely on full-time legal aid workers. Most other legal aid centers have a small staff, or consist only of justice bureau employees, and assign work to local lawyers. Moreover, even those programs that employ full-time lawyers rely on lawyers outside the legal aid center to handle some cases.

D. University-Based "Nongovernment" Programs

In addition to the justice bureau programs, a number of law schools in China have established legal aid programs. In most cases, such programs consist of students answering general legal inquiries. However, both Wuhan University and Peking University have established legal aid centers where faculty, students, and staff lawyers all provide information and represent clients in litigation. Although based at universities and thus technically under the direction of the government, these programs consider themselves to be nongovernment legal aid providers, as they operate largely autonomously and have undertaken more controversial cases than the justice bureau legal aid programs.[11] The Wuhan University and Peking University centers are both funded by the Ford

---

9. The center's staff has since expanded, but the center still relies heavily on assigning work to law firms.

10. There were 270 law firms in July 1997; the number of law firms in Beijing has increased since then. A November 1998 report stated that representatives of 290 Beijing firms had attended a meeting of Beijing lawyers (Xinhua News Agency 1998c).

11. Like all universities in China, Wuhan University and Peking University are government institutions. Nevertheless, lawyers at both centers comment that there has been little oversight of their work either by university officials or by government officials outside the universities.

Foundation.[12] Ford also funds a third legal aid program, the Qianxi Women's Law Center, in Hebei Province's Qianxi County. The Qianxi center is run by the local branch of the All-China Women's Federation, a government body, but similarly operates largely independently of the local justice bureau.

The Wuhan University Center for the Protection of the Rights of Disadvantaged Citizens, established in 1992, was modern China's first legal aid center. The center maintains six departments: women's rights, administrative litigation, juvenile rights, environmental protection, elderly rights, and disabled people's rights.[13] The center relies on graduate and undergraduate students to respond to inquiries and handle initial client meetings. Graduate students, center staff, or faculty represent clients in cases pursued in court.

The Center for Women's Law Studies and Legal Services of Peking University differs from the Wuhan center in that it focuses only on cases relating to women's rights. Although the Peking University center has a smaller staff than the Wuhan University center, it similarly relies on a mixture of faculty, staff lawyers, and students (primarily graduate students) to handle cases. As discussed below, the center has also been more willing than any other center in China to undertake high-profile and complex cases.

E.   Pro Bono Requirements and Mandatory Financial Contributions

In addition to establishing legal aid centers and requiring lawyers either to work in the centers or to accept work that the centers assign to them, a number of local justice bureaus have imposed mandatory pro bono requirements on lawyers and have required lawyers to make financial contributions to support legal aid programs. Local authorities appear to have broad discretion to impose such requirements: although both the Lawyers Law and the Ministry of Justice's 1997 notice regarding legal aid state that lawyers shall undertake legal aid work, neither document specifies how much work lawyers should undertake.[14]

Most local regulations require lawyers to handle one or two legal aid cases per year, require lawyers to undertake any legal aid work that the local justice bureau or legal aid center assigns to them, or state that lawyers may not refuse legal aid cases that meet local eligibility requirements. Rates of compliance with

---

12. As of June 1998, the Peking University center was entirely funded by the Ford Foundation. The Wuhan University center relies on a number of other funding sources, including donations from domestic corporations.

13. Most cases relate to women's rights or elderly rights. As of early 1999, the environmental department was inactive.

14. The Lawyers Law, passed by the Standing Committee of the National People's Congress, replaced the 1980 Interim Regulations on Lawyers (Zhonghua Renmin Gongheguo Lüshi Fa 1996). Although the Lawyers Law has national effect, like many Chinese laws it provides few detailed provisions. The Lawyers Law thus establishes only a rough framework for the regulation of lawyers and the protection of lawyer rights. Details are left for future regulations, either from the State Council or from government ministries.

such requirements are unclear. Some locales rely on voluntary compliance by lawyers, but such efforts appear unsuccessful: in Guangzhou, for example, the fact that fewer than 10 percent of local lawyers have voluntarily undertaken legal aid cases has been cited as an argument for imposing mandatory pro bono requirements.[15]

Financial obligations of lawyers to support legal aid work also vary. Some cities require law firms to maintain legal aid funds to cover the costs of legal aid work that the firm undertakes, while other locales require that lawyers pay a percentage of their income to support a government legal aid fund. Such requirements have been justified as being part of lawyers' professional obligations, although lawyers complain that such requirements also reflect government unwillingness, or inability, to provide much-needed funds to support legal aid work.

II.   Legal Aid and the Role of Lawyers: Unnecessary Distinctions?

China's development of legal aid has progressed on the assumption that increasing access to lawyers is crucial to ensuring that individuals are able to use the legal system. This assumption stems partially from the view held by many advocates of an expanded legal aid system that a government-backed legal aid system is usually one aspect of developed legal systems and thus should become part of China's legal system. Although less explicitly stated, arguments in favor of legal aid also appear to be based on a presumption that increasing access to lawyers will redress power imbalances in Chinese society.

Yet the role lawyers, and in particular legal aid lawyers, play in China may also differ significantly from that of lawyers in western legal systems that are China's models for the construction of a legal aid system. First, most cases in China are litigated without the assistance of lawyers; there may be less need for *lawyers* to equalize imbalances of power and ensure access to the legal system if the adversaries of those in need are not represented by lawyers. Second, many Chinese lawyers are poorly trained, and China has an established system of non-lawyer legal services providers. Assumptions that lawyers are a crucial link in ensuring that the poor have access to the legal system may be out of place in

---

15. Low compliance rates in Guangzhou—where lawyers are relatively wealthy and where the local legal aid center has received widespread positive attention from the local and national media—may suggest that lawyers in other areas of the country may be even less likely to provide legal aid absent mandatory requirements. However, lawyers in economically developed cities such as Guangzhou may see legal aid work as having a high opportunity cost. Lawyers in the less-developed interior, and in particular those working on a fixed salary for state law firms, may actually be more willing to engage in pro bono work. Indeed, one Ministry of Justice official told me that in certain areas of China, all work by lawyers is legal aid work, because few people can afford to pay lawyers even the low officially set legal fees.

a system in which distinctions between lawyers and non-lawyers are nebulous and in which non-lawyers engage in extensive amounts of legal work.

Lawyers are involved in only a minority of cases brought in Chinese courts. In 1996, China's courts reported accepting 5,712,669 cases, while lawyers reported participating in 979,301 cases (ZFNBB 1997, 1055, 1074). Although the statistics come from two different sources,[16] and thus the ratio of lawyers participating in just 17 percent of cases is imprecise,[17] the statistics do demonstrate that the vast majority of litigants in China are not represented by lawyers. Available statistics provide only a rough breakdown of the types of cases that lawyers handle (separating cases into three categories, civil and economic, criminal, and administrative) and thus it is unclear whether the cases lawyers handle are concentrated in specific subject areas. Moreover, no statistics are available regarding how often one party is represented by an attorney when the other party is not. Nevertheless, that so many cases are being brought absent representation by lawyers suggests caution in assuming that lawyers are crucial to ensuring access to the legal system.

The fact that so many cases are brought without the assistance of lawyers does not mean that lawyers do not play important roles in cases in which they participate. Empirical evidence is sparse,[18] but Chinese lawyers and academics comment that litigants represented by lawyers are likely to fare better than those without representation.[19] Legal aid providers state that their clients either have little idea of how to navigate the legal system or do not believe that the system will be of any use to them. One legal aid provider argues that courts in urban areas look down upon poor litigants, especially migrant workers; the presence of lawyers may reduce the effect of such attitudes. Thus, lawyers are likely to play important roles in redressing power imbalances within the legal system and in encouraging the most marginalized members of Chinese society to use law to protect their interests. Power imbalances in China may be less between those who have money (and thus lawyers) and those who cannot afford lawyers, but rather more between those who have connections with courts and local governments and those who lack such connections. Nevertheless, lawyers can at

---

16. Statistics on the total number of cases are provided by the Supreme People's Court; statistics on cases handled by lawyers are from the Ministry of Justice.

17. The figure of 17 percent likely overstates the presence of lawyers, as it represents a rough calculation of the frequency of lawyer representation of a *single* party in a case.

18. A study of criminal cases in one province suggested that criminal defendants represented by lawyers were likely to receive lighter sentences than those not represented by lawyers (Zhang Geng 1998, 36). I am unaware of any similar research in the civil context.

19. There is no evidence, however, comparing the effect of representation by lawyers with representation by non-lawyers. In discussing the effect of legal representation, academics and lawyers generally compare those represented by lawyers with those who lack any representation. Representation by non-lawyers is discussed further below.

times be effective, either by providing their own connections to those with local influence[20] or by drawing attention to particular injustices.

The low rate of representation by lawyers reflects the small size of the Chinese bar relative to China's population and the concentration of lawyers in urban areas. That litigants are not represented by lawyers does not necessarily mean that litigants are not represented in court. Chinese laws impose few limits on the ability of non-lawyers to appear in court in civil matters, and even in criminal cases non-lawyers may, subject to certain limits, represent defendants (Liebman 1999).[21]

Moreover, although most Chinese lack easy access to lawyers, they may have access to China's network of basic-level legal service workers (*jiceng falü fuwuzhe*, also referred to in English as "rice roots legal workers"). China has more than 120,000 basic-level legal service workers working out of more than 35,000 basic-level legal services offices, often referred to as township or village legal services offices, mostly located in rural areas (Zhang Xiufu 1998). Approximately 4,000 of these workers are lawyers; the rest are non-lawyers who often have little legal training.

As Stanley Lubman notes, the Ministry of Justice intends for the township and village legal services offices to be quasi-independent organizations, responsible for their own finances and independent of any direct local government oversight (Lubman 1999, 281; Liu and Li 1995, 291). Yet while these basic-level legal services offices may be responsible for their own income, it appears unlikely that they have any significant autonomy. Government provisions and notices make clear that the offices are closely linked to local governments. The 1991 Provisions on Township and Village Legal Services Work state that the work of the township and village legal services offices includes, inter alia, engaging in civil, economic, and administrative litigation; serving as legal advisors and helping parties in non-litigation matters; mediation; creating legal documents; and assisting judicial assistants in legal education and propaganda work (Sifa Bu 1991, Article 3). Basic-level legal workers in such offices are to carry out their work under the leadership and supervision of local governments (Articles 4 and 12). Fees are to be set by the relevant department of the provincial government, but where no applicable fee regulations exist, basic-level legal workers are instructed to set fees in accordance with the corresponding fee regulations that apply to lawyers (Article 8). The provisions also expressly provide for basic-level

---

20. Of course, lawyers who use such connections to further their own and their clients' interests may also be contributing to the structural problems that weaken the effectiveness of Chinese courts. Yet the actions of such lawyers reflect the reality that lawyers are often ineffective absent such connections.

21. In the criminal context, there has been a gradual tightening of regulations on who can represent defendants in court. Thus, for example, while the 1979 Criminal Procedure Law stated that courts could appoint a "defender" to represent defendants who had not retained counsel, the 1996 revisions to the Criminal Procedure Law changed the word "defender" to "lawyer" (Liebman 1999).

legal workers to advise local governments in a variety of ways, including by providing legal advice regarding major government decisions and by assisting local governments in drafting legal documents (Article 16).

A 1997 Ministry of Justice notice regarding township and village legal services offices[22] emphasized the important role that basic-level legal workers play in transmitting the views of the rural population to local governments, helping local leaders make decisions in accordance with the law, uncovering illegal activities that harm peasants, providing legal services to township and village enterprises and the rural population (including providing legal aid to those who qualify), and assisting local governments in fighting crime and maintaining social stability. The notice also reported that 43 percent of townships and villages in China had established township or village legal services offices (Sifa Bu 1997).

There has been little scholarship in China on the role of basic-level legal service workers, but official statistics suggest that in many cases these service workers assume roles that would most likely be played by lawyers in other legal systems. In 1996, basic-level legal service workers reported representing parties in 491,700 civil cases, as well as in 1.1 million civil disputes that did not involve litigation (ZFNBB 1997, 1075). Additionally, although the majority of work they undertake appears to be providing information—"legal service workers reported providing legal consultations in more than 6,000,000 matters in 1996" (1997, 1075)—the number of cases resulting in litigation that they handle has been increasing in line with the general growth in litigation in China. The number of civil cases in which basic-level legal workers participated in 1996 was approximately triple the figure for 1990, when such workers represented litigants in 163,500 civil cases (ZFNBB 1991, 956).

In contrast, the number of civil cases handled by lawyers during the same period roughly doubled, from 333,206 in 1990 to 714,064 in 1996. The increase in the number of cases handled by basic-level legal workers is significant given that although the number of such workers increased during the six years—from 98,293 in 1990 to 113,612 in 1996—the rate of increase was far lower than that of lawyers: the number of lawyers in China rose from 38,769 in 1990 to 100,198 in 1996 (ZFNBB 1991, 955, 956; ZFNBB 1997, 1074, 1075).

China has pledged to continue to increase the number and training of basic-level legal workers. Nevertheless, the move to establish legal aid centers staffed by lawyers also reflects a desire to shift legal work to presumably better-trained legal professionals. Although this trend may reflect the maturation of the Chinese legal system and profession, viewed in the context of legal aid, it also highlights a number of issues relating to both the legal profession and efforts to meet the legal needs of China's poor.

First, the development of legal aid programs is not being coordinated with existing basic-level legal services structures. Chinese commentators and officials

---

22. The notice noted that there were reports of basic-level legal workers violating the law in numerous ways, including by charging excessive fees (Sifa Bu 1997).

repeatedly stress the need to boost the number of lawyers and legal aid programs in rural areas, but there has been little discussion of efforts to coordinate the work of legal aid centers—which are generally concentrated in urban areas—with the work of the basic-level legal offices.[23] The lack of coordination is striking given that the Ministry of Justice is responsible both for the development of legal aid programs and for overseeing basic-level legal service workers. Indeed, the only program that appears to be coordinating the work of basic-level legal offices and a legal aid center is the Qianxi County center. The program, based in the county seat, not only trains basic-level legal workers throughout the county in issues related to the protection of women's rights but also relies on the basic-level legal services offices to refer cases to the legal aid center. Yet the center is noteworthy in that it operates largely independently of the local justice bureau, despite the fact that the bureau is technically responsible for such offices. This lack of coordination may reflect both a lack of coordination within the Ministry of Justice and the fact that legal aid programs have to date been concentrated in urban areas, where basic-level legal workers play a much less important role than they do in the countryside.

The lack of emphasis on basic-level legal workers may also indicate uncertainty over their long-term role. Although China's legal press continues to emphasize the importance of basic-level legal offices, and China's deputy minister of justice has called for the number of these offices to be increased to 40,000 and for the number of basic-level legal workers to be increased to 150,000 by 2010 (Zhang Xiufu 1998, 4),[24] the little emphasis that Beijing-based officials and academics give to the basic-level legal worker system may reflect the view that the offices and workers are relics of a legal system that had few lawyers and in which all legal work was performed by state workers, either lawyers or non-lawyers. Nevertheless, at least some provincial governments have begun to emphasize the need to improve the quality of local legal services offices. In Jiangxi Province, for example, regulations issued in early 1998 called for basic-level legal workers to take part in training programs run by the provincial justice bureau and to pass an examination prior to being permitted to provide legal services. The regulations also called for increased scrutiny of any person representing parties in court (Sun 1998).

Second, the existence of tens of thousands of rural legal services offices demonstrates that the concept of providing legal assistance to the poor is not novel in China. Although Chinese writings on the need to develop a legal aid

---

23. Officials have, however, begun to use the term "legal aid" to describe work being done by the basic-level legal offices and workers (Zhang Xiufu 1998, 4). Although basic-level legal workers do charge for some of their services, it is unclear precisely how legal aid work by such workers is distinguished from their more ordinary work—which also largely serves China's rural poor.

24. Zhang has also called for increasing the legal training of such workers and for instituting an examination system for those seeking to become basic-level legal workers (Zhang Xiufu 1998, 4).

system with "special Chinese characteristics" do emphasize China's tradition of providing legal assistance to the poor, such writings present the idea of "legal aid" as something largely new and imported. Insofar as legal aid involves obtaining legal assistance from lawyers, it is new. Yet reliance on the view of legal aid as something novel for China may be limiting China's ability to draw on its own experiences in providing legal assistance to the poor via the basic-level legal services offices. The lack of attention to these offices may reflect the belief that such offices were better suited for an era in which most disputes were resolved via informal processes, most notably mediation.[25] The large number of cases that basic-level legal workers continue to litigate, however, demonstrates that closely identifying such workers with China's tradition of informal justice may be misguided. To the degree that the rise in litigation in China represents a shift toward more formal dispute resolution mechanisms, it may be mistaken to see lawyers as essential to that trend.

Third, China's development of a legal aid system suggests that the distinction in China between lawyers and non-lawyers is questionable. As Professor Alford discusses in his chapter of this volume, the majority of lawyers in China have received very little formal legal training. The percentage of lawyers who have received formal legal training is increasing,[26] but it appears that such lawyers are likely to be concentrated in major cities. In most areas of China, lawyers are not university-educated but rather have become lawyers after relatively short training courses or none at all. The education they receive may exceed that obtained by the basic-level legal workers, but the relatively low level of training required to become a lawyer also suggests that rather than perceiving a sharp divide between lawyers and non-lawyers, it is better to view Chinese professionals on a continuum ranging from basic-level legal service workers who have little formal training to lawyers with relatively little legal education to the

---

25. The vast majority of disputes in which basic-level legal workers participate are resolved via mediation. In 1996, such workers reported mediating 1,252,500 disputes (ZFNBB 1997, 1075).

26. Reports on the October 1998 bar exam (Xinhua News Agency 1998b) emphasized the fact that most people taking the exam had a formal legal education. For example, the Ministry of Justice reported that 60 to 70 percent of those who registered to take the exam had received legal training. However, legal training is rarely university training: the same report stated that "more than one-third of those registered in Beijing and Shanghai have completed four years of law education in colleges." The percentage of university-educated candidates is likely to be higher in Beijing and Shanghai than virtually anywhere else in the country, given the high concentration of universities in those cities. Thus, the statistics suggest that the total number of university-trained candidates is quite low. Viewed in historical context, the Chinese case is not unusual: as Mark Osiel points out, "As late as the beginning of World War I, not a single American state required attendance at a law school as a condition for legal practice" (1990, 2026).

relatively small number of well-trained, university-educated lawyers who are concentrated in major urban areas.[27]

Recognition of this continuum may be important as China continues to determine the appropriate roles lawyers play in the legal system and in legal aid programs. The fact that some Chinese lawyers may not be significantly better trained than basic-level legal workers suggests caution in assuming that most legal aid work should be performed by lawyers. The Ministry of Justice's recent emphasis on increasing the availability of lawyers to China's poor may reflect an imported view that there is certain work that should be done by lawyers alone. This view does not mesh with China's current experiences or conditions.[28] The Ministry of Justice's apparent belief that the role of non-lawyers in the legal system should be reduced and that representation by lawyers should be encouraged is reflected in press reports that have chastised the low quality of representation in certain cases. Such articles largely focus on cases in which parties have been represented by non-lawyers (Zhou and Li 1998 and Wei 1998).[29] Although in the long run making university-trained lawyers available to all clients may be preferable, in the short-term, assisting those in need of legal advice may be furthered by relying more on existing structures, in particular if lawyers are reluctant to perform legal aid work.

---

27. It is unclear just how well China's bar exam serves to separate well-trained candidates from those who lack training. The vast majority of those who take the exam fail: only 110,000 of the first 900,000 people who took the exam since it was introduced in 1986 passed (Xinhua News Agency 1998a). Some Chinese lawyers have commented that the rise in the number of people taking the bar is the result of a popular perception that becoming a lawyer is a route to wealth. Many people without legal training are apparently taking the bar exam on the off-chance they might pass. Statistics on the percentage of successful candidates who have attended university are not available. One report stated that those passing the 1998 exam were more educated than in previous years and that "college and university graduates . . . make up the majority of . . . people passing [the 1998] exam" (China Business Information Network 1998b). The bar exam has only recently become mandatory for anyone seeking to become a lawyer, and thus over time the distinction between lawyers and non-lawyers may come to be more significant.

28. As discussed below, the Ministry of Justice's concern with increasing the number of lawyers also likely reflects the ministry's desire to increase its own importance.

29. In one city in Shandong Province, authorities launched a crackdown on "black lawyers," i.e., people practicing without a license. Three unlicensed law firms and twenty-eight unlicensed practitioners were sanctioned; one of the individuals was referred to the local public security office for criminal investigation (Gao 1998). The Lawyers Law includes limited provisions regarding the unauthorized practice of law: Article 46 provides for penalties, including administrative detention of up to fifteen days, for non-lawyers who pretend to be lawyers and who provide legal services, and for non-lawyers who represent parties in court in order to gain economic benefit (Zhonghua Renmin Gongheguo Lüshi Fa 1996). Article 14 of the law states that only persons with licenses to practice law may represent parties for the purpose of obtaining economic benefits. These provisions suggest that non-lawyers *may* represent parties in court, provided such non-lawyers are not pretending to be lawyers and are not engaging in such representation for their *own* economic benefit (Qing 1997).

Ambiguity over what separates lawyers from other legal workers in China reflects not only uncertainty over the roles lawyers play within the Chinese legal system but also over what it means to be a lawyer in China. The Ministry of Justice appears to be moving toward an American model of what lawyers may and may not do without considering whether other models might be more or equally relevant. In the legal aid context, China is pushing for an increased role for lawyers just as many other developed and developing countries are recognizing the need to expand the use of non-lawyers in an effort to expand the rights of the poor.[30] Indeed, efforts to expand legal services in many developing countries in the 1970s and 1980s were designed "to undermine the lawyers' monopoly of knowledge of law" (Brandt 1988, 32);[31] China may be moving in the opposite direction.[32]

Although the number of people becoming lawyers is increasing rapidly, the role of lawyers within the system is also gaining in importance. Much of the discussion of alternative lawyering in the developing world has revolved around grass roots organizations and legal aid providers, often those openly opposing the existing political system (Brandt 1988, 31), and thus may not be applicable in China, where the government has only recently begun to permit nongovernment organizations of any kind. But China's increasing reliance on lawyers also appears to represent a shift toward increased use of the formal legal system and increased formality within that system.

Fourth, the emphasis on lawyers performing legal aid work and on increasing the number of full-time legal aid lawyers reflects a central government policy of increasing the number of lawyers, as well as the government's belief that a large legal profession is a mark of a developed legal system and that more lawyers are needed to handle the increase in legal disputes. Attempts to boost the number of lawyers may also stem from the Ministry of Justice's desire to maintain or enhance its own position at a time of government budget cuts. The policy of encouraging growth in the total number of lawyers also appears to result from the central government's desire to use lawyers to serve as checks on lawless behavior at the local level.

Yet this government policy of increasing the number of lawyers has been implemented absent significant reflection on the role of the legal profession— or even on what it means to have a legal profession. The policy of focusing on the total number of lawyers is at least partially responsible for a relative absence of discussion of professional norms and of lawyers' obligations to their clients. Indeed, to the degree that mandatory pro bono requirements reflect a belief that

---

30. For a discussion of the roles of non-lawyers in the United States, see Rhode (1996).

31. See Dias (1988, 64–66); Legal Resources Foundation (1992, 165); Association Peru Mujer (1992, 138); Rojas (1988, 241–43).

32. Government efforts to boost legal consciousness may be seen as consistent with efforts in other countries to empower people by providing legal knowledge. China is fundamentally different, however, in that the drive to increase legal knowledge comes from the government. Such efforts appear to be part of a larger government policy, discussed further below, of using law to enhance the legitimacy of the state.

lawyers, as lawyers, have certain obligations to society, the imposition of such obligations may be a rearguard attempt to impose some notion of professionalism on the Chinese bar. Such attempts, however, also reflect the possibility, discussed below, that government efforts to expand legal aid may be as much about maintaining a degree of control over the legal profession and enlisting lawyers in implementing national policies as they are about increasing access to justice for those in need.

China's focus on pro bono requirements reflects the rush to expand the legal profession without serious consideration of the role lawyers will play or of what separates lawyers from non-lawyers. Lawyers are viewed as essential to economic development, to meeting the needs of China's poor, and to pressing local governments to obey national laws. Yet under existing structures there appears to be little consideration of how lawyers will carry out these tasks. This lack of definition may permit lawyers to experiment. In some cases, most notably in class action litigation (Liebman 1998), this ability to experiment may be encouraging lawyers to undertake cases on behalf of the disadvantaged. The lack of a more defined government view of the role lawyers should play might also present the opportunity for lawyers themselves to begin to develop concepts of professionalism on their own—although there is no evidence of them doing so. Nevertheless, attention to increasing the number of legal aid centers and to expanding the size of the legal profession also reflects a government attitude that such expansion is more important (and more feasible) than addressing structural weaknesses that limit the usefulness of law in China.

III. University-Based Legal Aid: Cause Lawyering with Chinese Characteristics?

A small number of China's lawyers and legal aid centers are focusing their efforts on specific causes. Lawyers in Qianxi County specialize in meeting the legal needs of rural women. Legal aid centers at two universities—Peking University and Wuhan University—have undertaken cases, including class actions and suits against government authorities, which most government legal aid centers would likely avoid. The Peking University center is unique in its use of litigation to highlight broader problems that undermine the effectiveness of law in China: the center's work is premised on the belief that providing legal assistance in routine cases will, given the vast number of people in need in China, do little to address systemic problems.

This Part of the chapter provides a brief discussion of the Peking University center's work in particular and opportunities for cause lawyering[33] more

---

33. I use the term "cause lawyering" loosely. Sarat, Scheingold, and Ellmann define "public interest law" and "cause lawyering" to refer to lawyers' work that is "directed at altering some aspect of the social, economic and political status quo" (Ellmann 1998, 349; Sarat and Scheingold 1998, 3). The activities of the Peking University center, and of the academics discussed below, fit within this definition.

generally in China. The work of the Peking University center reflects the expanding boundaries within which Chinese lawyers are operating, but also suggests that lawyers pursuing specific causes tend to be well-connected members of China's elite who are pursuing goals consistent with those of the central government.

The Center for Women's Law Studies and Legal Services of Peking University, established in 1996, began by focusing on providing information and representing women in a range of what the center terms "ordinary" questions and cases (Guo 1997, 13). Recognizing that by handling such cases the center would be able to make only a small dent in the problems facing Chinese women, the center altered its focus. Beginning in 1997, the center concentrated on representing women in difficult and high-profile cases, with the explicit goal of raising awareness of problems in China's laws and in the enforcement of such laws. The center undertook a total of more than sixty cases through the end of 1997; the center characterized twelve of these cases as "major," "difficult," or representative of larger problems (13). Lawyers at the center see themselves as supplementing work done by government legal aid offices, which they perceive to be handling only routine, uncontroversial cases (14). Indeed, lawyers at the center point to the fact that they fail to obtain satisfactory outcomes in many of the cases they handle as evidence that they are taking cases that many other lawyers and legal aid centers avoid. Lawyers at the center are critical of the widespread practice of justice bureaus and legal aid centers publishing statistics that suggest legal aid workers have been successful in the majority of cases they handle; they say that such statistics demonstrate that most legal aid centers are taking easy cases, and that focusing on success ratios discourages lawyers from undertaking more difficult cases.[34]

Among the cases the Peking University center has handled have been a class action on behalf of eighty female migrant workers for back pay, cases on behalf of women forced into early retirement, a case on behalf of the family of a high school student who was raped by her school principal and then died during

---

34. The validity of such claims is unclear. Legal aid centers count both cases that have been successfully litigated and cases that have settled as cases in which they have been victorious. Yet it would be a mistake to discount the work of legal aid centers that handle such "routine" cases. Even simple cases can be extremely difficult to resolve in a system that has traditionally been inhospitable to individual litigants.

Just how legal aid lawyers are able to succeed is a fascinating question. For example, it is unclear to what degree legal aid lawyers who are successful are relying on the merits of their cases or are using connections and ex parte judicial contacts to advance their clients' interests. The mere fact of success on behalf of disadvantaged clients does not mean that the system is functioning effectively in such cases. Moreover, it appears that legal aid lawyers must struggle to win even in cases in which their clients have been egregiously wronged and clearly have the law on their side. It is likely far more difficult for legal aid lawyers to succeed in less clear-cut cases.

childbirth, and disputes between women and local officials responsible for carrying out China's one-child policy (Guo 1997, 14). Other lawyers and legal aid centers have taken on some similar high-profile cases and the Wuhan University center has undertaken a range of administrative cases in which it has represented individuals suing government entities. Nevertheless, the Peking University center undertakes such cases on a much more regular basis, and no other legal aid center in China appears to eschew routine cases in favor of impact-oriented litigation.

The Peking University center also appears unique in its attempts to link its experiences representing clients to broader calls for legal change. The center has sought press coverage to highlight cases it has undertaken—and also to apply pressure to judges hearing such cases. The center's written descriptions of its work aggressively criticize weaknesses in China's laws and legal system. For example, the center's 1997 annual report notes that cases it has handled raise questions regarding whether an individual's "right to live" can be protected in China and "whether the current judicial system works to protect the rights of ordinary people" (Meng 1997, 25–28). Discussing existing laws, lawyers from the center argue that China's substantive laws are insufficient to protect the basic rights of ordinary people and that laws are too vague. In particular, they criticize China's lack of sufficient punishment for perjury and argue that the Administrative Procedure Law fails "to encourage citizens to exercise their rights" (25–28). The 1997 report also states that the center's work is hampered by a general failure to implement laws, unchecked powers of courts and local officials, and government corruption and inefficiencies, which together result in violations of human rights (25–28). In cases in which the center has been unsuccessful, it often attributes its failures to corrupt and irresponsible judges.

The center's aggressive approach is striking in a system in which lawyers generally have been careful to avoid cases that could be viewed as political challenges to state authority. The center does appear to be working at the boundaries of what is permissible in China and has rejected some cases that might cause political difficulties. It is setting an example of just how far lawyers can go in using litigation and advocacy to press for change. At the same time, however, the center's work has been made possible by special conditions that suggest that it may be difficult for others to emulate its work. These conditions inform as much about the limits of cause lawyering in China today as do the cases the center has undertaken.

First, the center has been careful not to undertake cases that put it at odds with the central government or people with strong government connections. In most of the high-profile cases it has undertaken, its adversaries have been units of local governments or individuals with strong ties to local governments. In all of these cases, the center has alleged that such units or individuals have failed to follow national laws. Neither this nor any other legal aid center in China has represented political dissidents or has directly challenged the authority of provincial or national government officials. China's cause lawyers thus differ from cause lawyers elsewhere in Asia and the developing world whose identity has often been shaped by their opposition to the state (Ellmann 1998).[35] The Peking University center's legal arguments are straightforward: it argues that national laws must be followed. Thus, it is often pursuing goals that the central government says it shares, seeking to use litigation to rein in lawless behavior by local officials, government units, and individuals with government ties. The center couches its efforts in terms that are consistent with national policies, in particular in terms of protecting women and defending the rights of ordinary people.[36]

Second, the center benefits both from its location at Peking University and from ties to a number of people in government. It operates under the umbrella of China's leading law school, thus providing it with both prestige and a degree of protection that it would not possess were it operating wholly independently. Similarly, the center's "senior consultants" include a number of prominent government officials, including the vice chairwoman of the All-China Women's Federation, the former vice minister of the Ministry of Justice, a former vice president of the Supreme People's Court, and a member of the Standing Committee of the China People's Political Consultative Conference (Beijing Daxue Falü Xi n.d.).

The center's position at Peking University and its government ties demonstrate that lawyers at the center are very much part of China's elite. A number of its lawyers have come from government posts or from academia. Its success suggests that strong government connections may be essential for lawyers engaging in impact litigation or advocating structural changes. Indeed, the Wuhan University legal aid center similarly enjoys close ties with the Wuhan municipal government, and its location at one of China's leading law schools provides the center with both legitimacy and protection that might not otherwise be available to lawyers pursuing similar cases.

---

35. For example, as Daniel Lev describes, activist lawyers in both Indonesia and Malaysia have at times directly challenged the state (1998, 440). However, it is also important not to read too much into the fact that the Peking University and Wuhan University centers are not directly challenging the authority of the central government. In highlighting weaknesses in the legal system, the Peking University center is also advocating rule-of-law principles, as have cause lawyers elsewhere (432).

China's cause lawyers may be assuming roles somewhat akin to the roles Raymond Michalowski has observed in Cuba (1998, 523). Yet while Chinese lawyers have been careful to pursue goals and causes that do not bring them into conflict with the central government, they also appear to have significantly more leeway than do their Cuban counterparts. In particular, lawyers at the Peking University center are clearly using individual cases—whether on behalf of individuals or groups—to pursue broader goals and to effect system-wide changes. However, Chinese lawyers have been much less successful than their Cuban counterparts in strengthening the role of lawyers in the criminal defense context.

36. Chinese public interest lawyers are not unique in litigating where there is opportunity to litigate and in particular in focusing on socio-economic issues and not political or civil rights. As Ellmann comments, "To a very important extent, what human rights activists do is determined not by grand theory but by opportunity" (1998, 358).

Third, the Peking University center has also made effective use of ties to the legal and popular press. Lawyers at the center comment that they often delay seeking press coverage until they are convinced that, due to local protectionism or other factors, they have little other chance of swaying the court. In a number of cases, the center has sought and received extensive press coverage of its clients' hardships and predicaments. It is unclear whether such coverage has directly led to outcomes in favor of its clients. Nevertheless, its efforts demonstrate that ties to the press are an important weapon for lawyers in many cases in China today and in particular for lawyers pursing difficult or high-profile cases. Appeals to the press are now commonplace in litigation in China and lawyers, ranging from prosecutors to legal aid practitioners to commercial lawyers, acknowledge that a well-placed story in the press can often sway the outcome of a case. Effective use of the press appears to be increasingly noteworthy; although China lacks a strong tradition of using the courts and/or individual cases to bring legal change, there is a strong tradition of using the press both to disseminate policy and to highlight injustices.[37]

Fourth, the Peking University center has benefited both from foreign funding and from contacts with western scholars and lawyers.[38] Its use of terms such as "impact litigation" clearly stems from its western contacts, and its combination of scholarship, advocacy, and litigation almost certainly also results from its interactions with foreign lawyers and law students.[39] Indeed, to the degree that the work of the Peking University center resembles that of cause lawyers elsewhere in the world, such similarities likely result from it being funded by the Ford Foundation and having extensive western contacts.

The center's experiences demonstrate both the possibilities and the prerequisites for cause lawyering in China today. Lawyers must choose cases carefully, and the most successful lawyers are likely to be those with strong political ties. The center's unique position—at Peking University, with strong ties to people in national government, and backed by foreign funding—will be difficult to replicate in other areas of China.

Yet the Peking University center is not alone in pursuing high-profile cases or cases against adversaries with strong local political ties. Lawyers nationwide have begun to undertake class actions and some academics have undertaken cases on behalf of victims of particularly egregious wrongs. In these cases, challenges are often being brought against local governments or officials or people

---

37. The Peking University center has also received attention from the foreign press; the degree to which foreign press coverage may be useful is unclear.

38. The center's close foreign ties have also likely brought it scrutiny from the Chinese government. In June 1996, Hillary Clinton visited the center during President Clinton's visit to China. My research on its activities was completed prior to the Clinton visit. Prior to that date, the center had not come under direct criticism for its foreign ties.

39. A small number of American law students have spent time working at the center. In addition, others—including myself—have assisted in translating promotional materials for the center.

with strong ties to local governments.[40] But the center's work may be unique in highlighting the fact that the wrongs it seeks to redress are not simply the result of corrupt or incompetent local government officials but also stem from more general structural problems and weaknesses in China's legal system.

The center's efforts, although made possible by its contacts, also reflect the widening sphere of permissible activity in China. Lawyers are increasingly willing to challenge local authorities and to advocate changes in the legal system. The center is not alone in its frank discussion of problems in the Chinese legal system. Chinese legal academics are increasingly vocal in their calls for changes; such comments may be as effective as any single case in highlighting problems in the legal system. For example, one Beijing academic has called for a re-examination of the practice of assigning retired military personnel to serve as judges—despite their lack of legal training (He 1998). Other scholars have written articles criticizing the excessive use of force by police against criminal defendants (Cai 1998), arguing that the public's right to speak freely and ask questions of those in authority is crucial to ensuring that laws are enforced (Yan 1998).[41]

Like the Peking University center, lawyers and academics elsewhere in China who make such arguments are largely based at prominent institutions and thus are particularly attuned to the limits of permissible arguments. Pointed arguments criticizing existing structures and practices appear to be possible only insofar as they come from the elite; it remains unclear whether the increased willingness of lawyers to criticize aspects of the legal system, and of the press to publish such criticism, will expand to permit similar commentary from a broader range of individuals.

A more detailed examination of the role of such commentary, and the press more generally, is a topic for future research. Viewed in the context of both the development of legal aid programs and the efforts of the Peking University center, such commentary highlights two points regarding the development of legal aid and the legal system. First, like the work of the Peking University center, such commentary demonstrates the need to place criticism of the legal system in the context of government efforts to reform the system. Thus, for example, He Weifang's controversial criticism[42] of the practice of appointing soldiers to be judges is likely possible because it is couched in terms of raising the quality

---

40. I describe some such cases elsewhere. See Liebman (1998).

41. For English translations of additional examples of aggressive commentary from the same newspaper, see BBC (1998d) (discussing the application of the International Covenant on Economic, Social, and Cultural Rights to China, and criticizing certain aspects of the resettlement of communities as part of the Three Gorges Dam project) and BBC (1998c) (stating that "Many problems exist in the current system because the masses do not have the right to investigate"). The same newspaper has also written repeatedly of corruption and illegal behavior by local officials (BBC 1998k and 1998i).

42. He Weifang's article was criticized in a number of subsequent articles in other newspapers, and the paper that originally ran the essay was forced to issue an apology.

of judges, and Cai Dingjian's call for less abuse of criminal suspects is placed in the context of improving China's international human rights image. Second, both the Peking University center's work and the writings of legal commentators suggest growing attention to general problems that plague the Chinese legal system. Although the expansion of government legal aid programs is likely to help numerous individuals, it is unlikely to address many of these more general problems.

The roles being played by the Peking University center and academic commentators also demonstrate the degree to which challenges to government legitimacy may come less in the form of direct challenges to the central government and more via structural critiques. This is best seen by examining the role of the press in highlighting structural problems. The government is encouraging the press to report on local abuses and to serve as watchdogs on the legal system. But the government has also been quick to strike out at newspapers that have been too aggressive in reporting on corruption (BBC 1998b). At the end of 1998 and the beginning of 1999, for example, the central government closed one leading newspaper and publisher and issued warnings to a number of other magazines and newspapers; many of the targets of the crackdown had written widely about corruption and social and economic problems (Eckholm 1999). Thus, being too aggressive does not mean simply exposing corruption by leaders in Beijing—it means suggesting that local abuses reflect structural problems. Similarly, in public interest lawyering, challenges to the central government may come not so much from lawyers suing senior government figures as from lawyers arguing for structural reforms—to a degree, something that public interest lawyers and academic commentators are already doing. It remains to be seen whether such critiques are similarly perceived to be critiques of the central government and therefore whether more limits on lawyers are imposed.

A detailed examination of the parallels between the development of the legal profession and the development of the press is an intriguing topic for future research. The central government has encouraged the press to take a more active role in reporting on the development of—and abuses in—the legal system.[43] At the same time, the government has also taken steps to increase public access to the courts. In March 1999, the Supreme People's Court issued new rules regarding "open trials." The rules state that most trials must be open to the public, that courts must publicize cases in advance of trial, that verdicts must be announced in public, and that the failure of a court to conduct a trial in public will be grounds for a new trial. Exceptions to the open trial rules are made for cases involving "state secrets," "personal privacy," or juveniles (Xinhua News Agency

---

43. For example, in late 1998, National People's Congress chairperson Li Peng stated that "we should focus on positive reporting, giving greater publicity to examples about strict law enforcement and doing things according to law" and that "The media should also give play to their supervisory role by exposing serious cases of lawlessness so that the vast number of cadres and people can be educated by them" (BBC 1998j).

1999a). The government appears to expect that increased press and public supervision of the legal system will help curb some of the system's problems, and so, hopes to use the press and the public as checks on the system—much as it has attempted to use lawyers.

The increased ability of lawyers to bring high-profile cases, the increased attention of China's government-controlled press to such cases, and the heightened attention to legal issues more generally in the Chinese press all reflect the central government's recent efforts to increase the importance of law. This government policy of raising the profile of law and the legal system has both increased the ability of lawyers to use law to protect their clients' interests and has focused new attention on the role of lawyers within the legal system. The growth of legal aid programs and requirements is one manifestation of this renewed attention to lawyers and of efforts to use lawyers to implement government policies.[44]

IV.   Conflicting Aims? Legal Aid, Lawyers, and the State

The experiences of the Peking University center demonstrate that the evolving roles of lawyers, in particular legal aid and public interest lawyers, are in many ways shaped by lawyers' relationships to state actors. Nevertheless, lawyers' roles are not defined solely in terms of whether lawyers can challenge government authorities or espouse views different from those of the central government. This Part argues that the relationship of lawyers to the state is far more nuanced, reflecting at times contradictory attitudes of both lawyers and the central government. The evolution of legal aid programs reflects many of these competing impulses. The degree of control that the Ministry of Justice maintains over lawyers cannot be explained in political terms alone, but rather reflects political, economic, and bureaucratic interests. Indeed, the evolution of lawyers from state legal workers to moderately autonomous actors must be understood against the backdrop of bureaucratic restructuring, in particular recent efforts to reduce the size of the bureaucracy and make formerly state-dependent organizations and actors economically self-sufficient.

Although the efforts of university-based legal aid providers demonstrate the degree to which lawyers appear to possess increasing autonomy over the types of cases they undertake, the growth of government legal aid programs demonstrates that lawyers are being enlisted to serve central government goals and that the Ministry of Justice maintains a significant degree of control over the legal profession. Central government statements regarding lawyers have made

---

44. It is unclear whether the government's embrace of legal aid will make it easier for quasi-independent legal aid centers, such as those at Peking University and Wuhan University, to function. Both centers were established before the Ministry of Justice made legal aid a national policy. The Ministry of Justice's involvement, and in particular its desire to regulate all legal aid providers (and serve as the clearinghouse for all foreign contributions to support legal aid in China), may make it more difficult for quasi-independent legal aid centers to operate.

explicit the view that lawyers have an obligation to assist the government's efforts to rule the country "according to law." Thus, for example, the director of the Lawyers Department of the Ministry of Justice has written that lawyers play an important role in implementing the national strategy of ruling the country according to law. The same statement emphasized the important role lawyers play in supervising the implementation of law, ensuring laws are followed, and combating local protectionism (Duan 1998). The expansion of legal aid programs is consistent with such goals: increased use of lawyers and law to resolve disputes likely encourages greater compliance with law, especially at the local level. This explicit recognition of the important role lawyers play in combating local excesses mirrors the roles lawyers have begun to play on their own in public interest lawyering—whether acting via class actions or other high-profile litigation or carrying out legal aid work.

Government attempts to use the growing legal profession are not limited to requiring legal aid work. Lawyers advocating changes in the law are similarly responding to government requests for assistance. Government officials have written of the need to increase the role of lawyers in drafting laws and to take advantage of lawyers' experiences to recognize problems in existing laws. Such calls for greater involvement by lawyers parallel more general openness in law drafting: in 1998 China began, for the first time in nearly a decade, to publish drafts for public comment of some laws under consideration by the Standing Committee of the National People's Congress.[45] Calls for greater lawyer involvement appear to recognize that lawyers may have unique insights. Similarly, the Ministry of Justice has stated that one of the chief goals of developing the legal profession is to increase the number of legal advisors serving local and provincial governments, so as to ensure that such governments behave in accordance with the law (Duan 1998). Officials have called for greater lawyer involvement in the financial sector, so as to "further social stability" (Liu 1998). The Ministry of Justice has also called on lawyers to become more involved in major national projects and enterprise reform by providing legal opinions, drafting contracts, and participating in negotiations.

Efforts to enlist lawyers in furthering state policies—be they expanding access to the legal system for the poor or furthering reforms of the financial system—do appear to be sincere efforts to use lawyers to strengthen the legal system. Yet such policies may also be serving as methods for continuing state control of lawyers. One irony of the development of legal aid is that pro bono requirements have emerged just as the Chinese legal profession has begun to wean itself from direct state oversight. As noted above, legal aid programs and pro bono requirements emerged in the middle of the 1990s, at precisely the time that lawyers were beginning to see the fruits of economic autonomy. Legal

---

45. The government published a draft of the revised Land Management Law in the spring of 1998 (Xinhua English Newswire 1998).

aid requirements—both that lawyers undertake a certain volume of legal aid work and that lawyers contribute certain percentages of their income to legal aid programs—appear primarily to be attempts by the Ministry of Justice and local justice bureaus to take advantage of lawyers' new wealth. However, such requirements may also be allowing justice bureaus to continue to monitor the types of cases lawyers undertake.

The effect of such attempts may be limited, as the number of lawyers who are complying with mandatory pro bono requirements is unclear. But lawyers in some cities complain that such requirements are primarily attempts by local justice bureau officials to control lawyers. Indeed, in one Chinese city, lawyers complain that they are actually forbidden from engaging in pro bono work *absent* approval from the local justice bureau.[46] Some government officials argue that their involvement in monitoring legal aid work is essential to protecting clients' interests and ensuring that lawyers do their jobs well, but such oversight is also likely to weaken opportunities for lawyers to represent clients whose grievances are against government actors.[47]

China's development of a legal aid system cannot primarily be explained as an attempt to exert control over the legal profession. The Ministry of Justice also argues for the expansion of legal aid on moral grounds. Nevertheless, such moral exultations appear to stem mainly from the view that lawyers continue to owe obligations to the state, not from any view that lawyers as autonomous actors owe obligations to society more generally.[48]

The expansion of legal aid programs is not the only manifestation of the degree to which the Ministry of Justice continues to direct and control the legal profession. The Ministry of Justice's focus on expanding the number of lawyers likewise reflects a desire to direct the development of the legal profession. Rather than permitting the legal profession to develop on its own, in 1998, the Ministry of Justice called for the number of lawyers in China to reach 150,000 by the end of the century and to reach 250,000 to 300,000 by 2010 (Duan 1998), still its current projection. The ministry has set a target of two lawyers for every thousand people in China, which the ministry states is roughly equivalent to the ratio of lawyers in developed countries (Duan 1998). This focus on numbers

---

46. Lawyers at one firm complained to me that the local justice bureau implied that their licenses would not be renewed if the firm continued to take pro bono cases on its own.

47. To the degree local justice bureaus do supervise and monitor the types of cases lawyers handle, such efforts may be due less to ideology and more to bureaucratic interests. Lawyers at one Beijing law firm commented that they believe that, fearful of government reductions in the size of the bureaucracy, local justice bureau officials are attempting to demonstrate their continued usefulness. Monitoring legal aid work may be one means of doing so.

48. The expansion of pro bono requirements may also reflect a view that lawyers have certain obligations to society, but it is unclear whether government officials perceive a distinction between serving the state and serving society.

suggests that the development of the legal profession continues to be a government-directed effort. Thus, even as the profession itself is being permitted to operate with increasing autonomy, many indirect state controls remain.[49]

A number of rationales explain government efforts both to use lawyers to enhance the policy of ruling by law and to continue to exert control over the legal profession. As with the establishment of legal aid programs, the central government appears to be progressing on the assumption that a large legal profession and lawyer involvement in a wide range of activities is a characteristic of all mature legal systems and thus should be a part of China's continued legal development. Perhaps more importantly, lawyers are seen as potential checks on legal abuses by local governments and local courts. Much recent writing on lawyers in Ministry of Justice publications has attempted to portray lawyers as fighting corruption, in particular in the judiciary, or has portrayed lawyers as the victims of a corrupt judiciary.[50] The central government has begun to acknowledge massive problems in the legal system and in particular in the judiciary.[51] To the degree that the legal system is rotting, the Ministry of Justice is positioning lawyers to serve as cures for this rot.[52]

The central government's efforts to increase the role that the legal profession plays in day-to-day life in China—whether directly through expanding the availability of legal aid or indirectly by dramatically increasing the number of lawyers in China—is not the result of an out-of-date view of lawyers as state employees whose primary goal is to carry out work on behalf of the state.

---

49. The Communist Party also continues to play a role in regulating lawyers. Thus, for example, the secretary of Beijing's Communist Party Political-Legal Committee gave the opening address at an assembly of Beijing lawyers in late 1998 instructing lawyers to "establish a just, fair and honest image" (Xinhua News Agency 1998c).

50. For example, one report noted that the All-China Lawyers' Association had established a committee to protect lawyers' rights. The committee was established in the wake of a reported rise in attacks and abuses against lawyers (BBC 1998e).

51. In a September 1998 speech, Li Peng commented that "The violation of regulations in the [judicial] profession and neglect of work ethics by some officials in judicial departments are so serious that it has undermined judicial work and posed a threat to social stability" (China Business Information Network 1998a). In addition, the Supreme People's Court issued regulations designed to crack down on corruption among judicial personnel (BBC 1998f and Pomfret 1999). One report stated that "nearly 5,000 judges and procurators who violated laws and discipline have been solemnly investigated and punished" (BBC 1998g). Another report stated that officials attending a national conference on the courts were told that rural courts "must try to improve relations between local officials and citizens, while maintaining rural stability and promoting economic and social progress" (Xinhua News Agency 1998d).

52. As Professor Alford points out in his chapter in this volume, lawyers themselves are contributing to the corruption that is undermining the effectiveness of law in China. Thus, the Ministry of Justice's focus on corruption in the judiciary may be somewhat disingenuous.

Instead, the central government appears to be recognizing that its own interests are served by strengthening the importance of law,[53] and that lawyers can play—or are already playing—important roles in enforcing laws. Thus, although the development of legal aid programs stems in part from an attempt to assist people facing particular hardships, the development of legal aid is also the product of a government belief that channeling disputes and discontent into the legal system may head off broader challenges to state authority—a view evidenced by repeated references in Chinese legal aid literature to the valuable role legal aid plays in ensuring "social stability." This view may explain China's focus on expanding the number of legal aid programs and institutions at the expense of ensuring that legal aid work is being adequately performed.[54] Central government efforts to boost the role of lawyers and law may also reflect a view that building a legal system is the government's best mechanism for maintaining control over the nation and over itself.

Yet efforts to impose pro bono requirements and financial obligations also appear to be the result of economic and ideological rationales not directly linked to efforts to use lawyers to maintain control. Many lawyers have become financially successful; legal aid requirements serve to take advantage of some of this economic success. Moreover, such requirements are not merely efforts to tax lawyers, but also stem from the belief that lawyers should balance their economic success with moral obligations to serve those in need.

The development of legal aid programs also demonstrates that state and lawyer interests do not inevitably conflict. Lawyers are not outsiders: they remain integral parts of a state-dominated legal system and in many cases appear to perceive themselves as having obligations to the state. Legal aid and the expansion of the total number of lawyers cannot merely be explained as government efforts to continue to exert control over the legal profession,[55] or to use the legal profession to serve state interests, in part because many lawyers do not see themselves as pursuing goals at odds with those of the central government. Many legal aid

---

53. In one speech, Li Peng stated that "Administering the country according to law is in dialectical unity with adherence to party leadership and advocacy of the people's democracy" (BBC 1998h).

54. The lack of attention to the quality of legal services actually provided also reflects the fact that it is much easier for justice bureau officials to require legal aid work, or to assign such work to lawyers, than it is to monitor how such work is performed. Ministry of Justice and local justice bureau officials acknowledge the difficulties they face in monitoring legal aid work.

55. Questions of the degree to which legal aid may serve as a mechanism for exerting state control over lawyers are not unique to China: similar debates have occurred in the West (Cappelletti 1975, 29–30). But China differs from the countries that Cappelletti discusses, in that lawyers in China are not starting from a position of independence.

lawyers do appear to view themselves as having a responsibility to work to see that existing laws are enforced.[56] That legal aid lawyers view their roles in such a fashion suggests that representing the disadvantaged will not necessarily lead lawyers to pursue broader challenges to the legal or political system. Indeed, the attitudes of many legal aid lawyers—and in particular the view that they are helping to assist in the implementation of existing laws—suggests that developing even a quasi-independent bar requires changing the attitudes of lawyers as much as it requires loosening state regulation of the legal profession.[57]

Experiences to date demonstrate that, to a large degree, lawyers themselves are determining the roles they play. The central government has been remarkably permissive, allowing not only suits against local governments but also class actions, contingency fees, and in limited cases punitive damages. The growing diversity of roles lawyers are playing in contemporary China may at one level reflect a conscious decision by the central government to enhance the position of lawyers, but the actual roles lawyers are playing result from lawyers taking advantage of new opportunities. Lawyers themselves appear to be largely content with such enhanced economic opportunities and, with few exceptions, do not appear to be pressing for expanded ideological autonomy. Indeed, many lawyers have been extremely successful in the current system, taking advantage of legal and illegal opportunities; they may have little incentive to press for additional autonomy.

That lawyers are not autonomous from the legal system highlights an additional point: whether or not lawyers are state legal workers may be less significant than the actual relationship of lawyers to local governments in the areas in which lawyers practice. To the degree to which much lawless behavior in China stems from local governments, the key measure of lawyers' autonomy in the short-term may be their willingness to challenge local authorities. Central government efforts to boost the autonomy of the legal profession may be directed at permitting lawyers autonomy from local, not national, control.

Measuring autonomy in terms of lawyers' relationships to local authorities is consistent with government attempts to promote the role of lawyers and not that of basic-level legal workers. As basic-level legal workers remain linked to local governments, and lawyers are increasingly autonomous, the shift toward increased use of lawyers may suggest a shift toward legal representation by people not directly answerable to local governments. However, the shift toward increased use of lawyers may itself reflect the Ministry of Justice's view that lawyers are unlikely to pose a threat to central government authority. Indeed, just as the Peking University center has been successful in part because it has

---

56. This view is perhaps best demonstrated by the writings of legal aid lawyers whose work concentrates on representing criminal defendants and who argue that by helping defendants acknowledge their wrongs they have increased the efficiency of the criminal justice system. For a discussion of such views, see Liebman (1999).

57. Additionally, as Dietrich Rueschemeyer points out in his discussion of the Prussian Bar, state control over the bar does not necessarily lead to an unstable system (1997, 223).

pursued cases in line with central government policies, the limited financial autonomy lawyers enjoy when compared to basic-level legal workers may actually further government interests.

The chief challenge to the legitimacy of the central government comes from its inability to curb illegal behavior by local governments, not from direct challenges to the central government's authority by political dissidents. Being a state legal worker in China—whether a basic-level legal worker or a lawyer at a state firm—means being under the direct supervision of a local justice bureau and thus a local government. Freeing lawyers from direct state oversight—both formally, as in the Lawyers Law, and economically, as with the advent of private law firms, class actions, and contingency fees—may result in lawyers being more likely to insist on laws being followed and enforced by local officials. Expanding the number of basic-level legal workers might appear at an initial glance to be a less threatening path to expanding legal services for the poor than increasing the number of lawyers. Yet enhancing the role of basic-level legal workers may make little sense if a goal of increasing the availability of legal services is to make local governments more accountable.

The role the Ministry of Justice plays in regulating lawyers and the provision of legal services is perhaps not surprising given the long state dominance of the legal system and the fact that until 1996, all lawyers were formally classified as state legal workers. What is more surprising, given this historical backdrop, is the degree to which the Ministry of Justice has looked to foreign precedent and in particular the American experience. Reliance on the American example is manifest more in the overall size of the profession and in permissive attitudes toward class actions and contingency fees than in legal aid, where China has examined European models. Nevertheless, a comparison of China's development of legal aid with the origins of the American legal aid system, as described by Michael Grossberg, highlights two novel aspects of China's experience.

First, the development of legal aid in China has been almost wholly state-driven. In the U.S., efforts to defend the bar from state supervision and to protect the bar from interference from non-legal personnel marked the early years of the development of legal aid (Grossberg 1997, 307, 320). In contrast, in China, there has been virtually no lawyer-driven development of legal aid.[58] Extensive state involvement in the provision of legal aid is thus a consequence of the fact that the commitment to legal aid has largely emanated from the Ministry of Justice.[59] Second, whereas legal aid developed in the United States partially as an effort to police the lower reaches of the bar, in China, the Ministry of Justice is aiming at the opposite end of the spectrum: legal aid appears to be an attempt to take advantage of the financial success of many of China's law firms.

---

58. The only exceptions are the university-based programs.

59. The U.S. government was, of course, more involved in later efforts to develop legal aid programs through the Legal Services Corporation.

Unlike lawyers elsewhere, lawyers in China do not appear to be identifying common interests or ethical norms. In the legal aid context, this means that there is virtually no discussion—either written or in interviews—of the possibility that providing legal aid will enhance the image of the legal profession and thus promote the status of lawyers more generally. The development of legal aid programs and pro bono requirements as state policies impedes efforts to observe how lawyers perceive their obligations to society, as lawyers who are ordered to perform such work may view such work as stemming from their relationship to the state, not from their membership in a legal profession.[60] Indeed, although lawyers do not oppose mandatory pro bono work on ethical grounds, many lawyers I interviewed do resent the state's attempt to force them to perform work that the lawyers see as being part of the state's obligations to the poor. However, there has also been no significant debate in China regarding the value of mandatory pro bono work, perhaps a reflection both of lawyers' reluctance to challenge a prominent government policy and of a legal system in which, until recently, lawyers have all been state workers.

Heavy state involvement in the development of the legal profession may be inhibiting self-identification by lawyers, just as state involvement in legal aid may be limiting the degree to which lawyers perceive the expanded availability of legal services as being in their own interest. Lawyers in China appear to be in a unique position. Chinese lawyers have extensive economic autonomy, including the ability to pursue class actions and contingent-fee litigation—opportunities available to lawyers virtually nowhere other than in the United States. Chinese lawyers are also able to challenge some government actors directly—thus enjoying freedom of action not permissible in most other single-party states. At the same time, however, the involvement of the Ministry of Justice and local justice bureaus remains extensive.

China's experience reflects the need to be cautious of relying too heavily on labels classifying lawyers as independent or as state actors. For example, even if lawyers in China are enjoying a range of autonomy not previously possible, it may still be premature to declare that the Chinese bar is becoming independent. There is little evidence that most clients draw distinctions between lawyers and others working in the legal system, including judges, procurators, or basic-level legal workers. Additionally, economic autonomy is a significant development, and thus even if lawyers are not formally independent they are able to engage in a range of work that does not easily fit the mold of a state-dominated

---

60. Two qualifications are in order. First, some lawyers have explicitly taken on pro bono cases—in particular high-profile cases—in order to attract press coverage and thus obtain free advertising. Second, it may be premature to speak of self-identification in a system in which lawyers have only recently been permitted economic autonomy and in which many lawyers remain on the state payroll. To the degree to which lawyers are rushing to take advantage of new economic opportunities and are not concerned with more long-term issues, they are reflecting a more general trend in reform-era China.

profession. Even Chinese lawyers who continue to work at state firms appear to operate with a large degree of economic independence.[61]

This discussion of lawyers, legal aid, and the state highlights two broader themes regarding legal development in China. First, China continues to rely heavily on policy and political campaigns, not structural changes, to reform its legal system. Second, the development of the legal profession appears to be part of a conscious government effort to increase oversight over the legal system. Both themes suggest that, over time, changes in the Chinese legal system are as likely to alter the role lawyers play as lawyers are to alter the system.

Perhaps the most notable feature of China's recent development of legal aid to a western observer—aside from the dramatic growth in the number of legal aid programs—is the degree to which efforts to expand legal aid have taken on many of the aspects of a traditional government campaign. Arguments in favor of legal aid are placed in the context of efforts to fight rising inequalities, improve China's international image, and construct a market economy with special Chinese characteristics. Lawyers are entreated to serve the poor as part of their obligations to society, and lawyers who do so are extolled on the front pages of China's legal press. Legal aid has become a focus of national attention because of what it means for China, not for, or at least not only for, what it means for the rights of individuals who are the recipients of legal aid. It may be precisely because efforts to boost both the legal profession and legal aid are couched in such terms that efforts to expand legal aid have succeeded, that lawyers appear increasingly able to take on cases that were off-limits just a few years ago, and that law is increasingly relevant and useful in the lives of ordinary people. However, reliance on campaigns to implement law reform may not succeed in effecting long-term change in the legal system.

Second, the development of the legal profession is one aspect of a broader recognition of the importance of quasi-external checks on the legal system. In recent years, the press—still government-supervised—has taken on an increasingly active role in exposing legal injustices and in applying pressure on corrupt local officials. Indeed, some Chinese lawyers argue that retaining a lawyer is less useful than cultivating good ties with journalists. As with the legal profession, central government authorities appear increasingly tolerant of this increased press oversight of the legal system—so long as such coverage remains within certain boundaries. Developments in both the press and the legal profession demonstrate the degree to which law has begun to permeate Chinese public discourse, even as most laws continue to go unenforced. Such developments also reflect the degree to which the central government is searching for a means to restrain itself. It remains unclear just how far boundaries around the activities of the press and the legal profession can expand without either inviting government ire or raising more fundamental questions regarding the legitimacy of the legal and political system.

---

61. The majority of state-funded firms are now "self-supporting and self-managed" (BBC 1998a).

V.   Clients

The previous Part suggested caution in reading too much into whether Chinese lawyers are formally classified as state legal workers. This Part urges similar caution in assuming that lawyers' roles will primarily be shaped by their interactions with the state. Very little research in China or abroad has examined how lawyers interact with clients. Such interactions are, however, likely to be of increasing salience for understanding both the roles lawyers are playing and lawyers' relationships to the state. Legal aid programs have developed at least in part because the provision of legal aid is an area in which the interests—in making the legal system more effective and combating local abuses—of the central government and of individuals appear to be largely consistent. The roles lawyers play in the legal aid context may at least partially reveal whether state goals for the legal system are consistent with how individuals use and seek to use the system. Such roles may also indicate whether lawyers' goals are consistent with either those of the central government or of lawyers' clients.

Most people interact with lawyers not in the context of formal representation, but rather through informal consultations; lawyers provide "legal information" far more often than they represent clients in court. Such informal consultations may similarly be undervalued. The provision of legal information in China appears to be occurring in a somewhat different context than elsewhere, as it comes against the backdrop of government campaigns to raise legal consciousness.[62] In providing informal consultations, Chinese legal aid lawyers are assisting clients in protecting their rights, resolving disputes, and navigating the legal/bureaucratic system, and are also assisting the implementation of a government policy of raising legal consciousness. Yet there is little effort to evaluate the importance of such work, or even the types of legal information most in demand. It is similarly unclear just how effective information about law and the legal system will be in a system that remains structurally flawed: increasing knowledge of legally enshrined rights may be meaningless if most disputes are resolved outside the legal system or in a biased system.

The lack of focus on the type or quality of information being provided to clients, or on whether such information will be of use, mirrors a more general characteristic of China's development of both legal aid and the legal profession: a lack of focus on clients. Clients are not wholly absent from Chinese discussions of legal aid.[63] Legal aid regulations suggest the range of people eligible for

---

62. The government's commitment to using law as a tool of sustaining its own legitimacy is further evidenced by the 1999 amendment of China's constitution. At its March 1999 meeting, the National People's Congress amended the constitution to list "governing the country according to law" as a guiding principle (Xinhua News Agency 1999b).

63. This lack of discussion of client interests may, however, simply be one aspect of a general lack of discussion of the actual effects of legal aid. The vast majority of Chinese writings on legal aid have focused on describing what legal aid is and why it is important—with occasional examples of cases in which lawyers have helped particular people in need. The lack of attention to clients may also be one manifestation of the difficulty that officials responsible for legal aid in the Ministry of Justice have observing activities at the local level.

legal aid, and the procedures potential clients must go through in order to receive legal aid. Legal aid centers also often describe clients whose lives have been changed (or saved) by the valiant efforts of lawyers. Additionally, Chinese academic and government writings on legal aid emphasize the importance of improving the circumstances of the least well-off. At least some local governments have recently taken steps designed to protect clients, but such regulations similarly suggest a paternalistic attitude toward clients. Chinese clients are almost always portrayed as passive recipients of lawyer and/or government services.[64] Moreover, authorities responsible for legal aid appear more concerned with the overall number of programs and centers than with the quality of work being performed. Even legal aid centers, while providing anecdotes of individuals who have received help, tend to focus on the total number of people helped, not the substance of the help provided. Client interests appear secondary in a system in which the state is focusing on developing institutions and on raising the number of lawyers, and in which lawyers themselves appear caught up in exploring new opportunities, primarily financial.

Questions regarding the interests and power of lawyers and their clients that have been asked elsewhere (Ellmann 1987, 718; Rhode 1994, 667–86; White 1988, 741–42)[65] are not yet being asked in China. Chinese lawyers litigate on the presumption that their interests and those of their clients are consistent. Yet there is likely as much—or more—disconnect between lawyer and client interests in China as elsewhere, for two reasons. First, successful lawyers in China rely on complicated webs of relationships—legitimate and illegitimate—to pursue their goals. Lawyers in China are as willing as their counterparts elsewhere to sacrifice client interests as they strive to maintain such relationships.[66] Second, many lawyers, in particular full-time legal aid lawyers, are state workers. All lawyers in China have indirect obligations to the state; lawyers working for the state may have stronger obligations. This is best seen in the criminal context,

---

64. China's attempts to limit legal aid to particular classes of deserving clients are not unique. For example, as Michael Grossberg documents, lawyers involved in the early days of legal aid in the United States attempted to limit legal aid to "worthy clients" (1997, 334–35). Similar parallels are also evident between China's treatment of legal aid as charity work and the development of legal aid programs in a number of western countries in the nineteenth century that Cappelletti describes (Cappelletti 1975, 21–23, 29).

65. Legal aid programs elsewhere in the developing world have been criticized for failing to represent the needs of clients adequately: "Where legal services are controlled and allocated by legal professions," lawyers engaged in legal aid work "may tend to monopolize the task of articulating and advocating claims of poor and 'ignorant' clients, or to monopolize the task of identifying the underlying needs of the client and the strategies to address such concerns" (Dias 1988, 63).

66. Although relationships affect the zealousness of advocacy elsewhere (Landon 1985, 105–109; Rhode 1994, 681–82; Schulhofer 1992, 1989–90), such relationships may serve as an even larger constraint in China, where relationships and connections are often more important than the legal issues at stake in a case.

where legal aid lawyers acknowledge that one of their responsibilities is to assist their clients in acknowledging wrongdoing.[67]

Lack of attention to clients may stem in part from the recent growth of the legal profession. Given the recent development of the legal profession, it may be premature to think that Chinese lawyers will soon undertake more client-focused roles. Most lawyers are scrambling for economic opportunities and many legal aid lawyers are focused on expanding their role by increasing the total number of cases handled. Additionally, although some lawyers have represented groups of peasants, such representation has rarely gone beyond arguing cases in court and seeking media coverage of such cases. Lawyers have not attempted to become more involved in representing entire disadvantaged communities as lawyers have done elsewhere in the developing world.[68] Those legal aid providers who have represented the rural poor have largely concentrated their efforts on representing migrant workers who have come to urban areas. Few lawyers in China appear to have made efforts to visit rural communities where legal needs may be particularly acute; those lawyers who have represented the rural poor have generally been sought out by their clients.

The lack of attention to client interests may reflect both a traditional lack of emphasis on individuals in the Chinese legal system, and a government view that legal aid serves the state and that individual and state interests cannot be divorced. Yet the current inattention to clients must also be viewed in the context of a general shift from informal dispute resolution, in particular the use of people's mediation committees, in which lawyers are rarely involved, to more formal resolution of disputes in the courts. The effect of such a shift on client interests in unclear. Mediation in China has often been marked by attempts to impose social norms on participants. To the degree to which a shift toward litigation means that law is beginning to have teeth, it may increase the ability of clients to have their interests protected. Yet dispute resolution in the shadow of an effective court system may in some circumstances result in outcomes that better meet client interests. Moreover, a shift toward a system more hospitable to individual litigants does not necessarily mean that lawyers will do a better job of representing individuals.

Lack of attention to clients may also be the product of a system in which the courts remain deeply flawed. China's embrace both of litigation and legal aid reflects a government desire to steer disputes into the court system at a time when the courts appear not yet capable of resolving many such cases. Even as lawyers are increasingly willing, or forced, to undertake cases on behalf of the disadvantaged, the courts appear unable or unwilling to address difficult cases. The inattention of both government officials and lawyers to the interests of

---

67. For an example of such views, see Li (n.d). See also note 56 above.

68. There appears to be no parallel, for example, to the community representation that Lucie White describes in her discussion of lawyering in South Africa (1988).

clients may be one byproduct of a system in which getting in the courthouse door is a small step toward effective use of the law: lawyers may not pursue client interests if they believe that doing so will be of little use or will jeopardize lawyers' own relationships.

A better understanding of how Chinese lawyers interact with their clients, and how clients perceive the roles lawyers are playing, is essential to further research into the Chinese legal profession. The only conclusion that can be drawn to date regarding client-lawyer interactions is that very little is known. Understanding the relationship of lawyers to the state and society requires understanding not only the levers of control that the government continues to wield over lawyers, and lawyers' willingness to challenge government actors, actions, and interests, but also how lawyers are viewed by the people they are serving. Government press reports have attempted to portray lawyers in heroic terms, working for justice in a corrupt system, but it is too early to determine whether the dramatic rise in the number of lawyers in China will actually translate into increased or more effective access to the legal system for the majority of China's population. Indeed, it is unclear whether potential clients view legal representation by lawyers as important, in particular when viewed in the context of a legal system that is often biased and corrupt. How clients view lawyers will be of increasing importance, however, as the success of government efforts to enhance the role of lawyers and thus law in China is at least partially dependent on increasing popular confidence in the legal system.

Conclusion

This chapter has attempted to question assumptions regarding lawyers in China and to demonstrate that the roles lawyers play are influenced by a range of factors. The role of lawyers cannot be analyzed only in terms of the range of permitted political activity or by distinguishing between the work of lawyers and non-lawyers. Similarly, the increased number of lawyers in China should not be viewed as necessarily resulting in a fairer and more accessible legal system. But the questions discussed above also should not divert attention from the remarkable development of legal aid programs in China. Even if lawyers remain out of reach to most people, the fact that even a relatively small number of centers are providing legal aid is a dramatic, positive step. The development of legal aid demonstrates that government efforts to use lawyers and the legal system to pursue government policies should not necessarily be seen as pernicious.

Very few legal aid lawyers—or lawyers generally—are actually operating at or near the boundaries of what is politically permissible. Nevertheless, it does appear that an increasing number of lawyers, some driven as much by financial incentives as by ethical obligations, are working at the boundaries of what is permissible at the local level—and thus are challenging politically and economically powerful enterprises, departments, and individuals. In so doing, they appear to be working to make the Chinese legal system more effective. At the same time, as this chapter has attempted to suggest, they may also be furthering crucial central government policies designed primarily to sustain the central government's own legitimacy.

The rapid development of legal aid and the legal profession precludes broad conclusions regarding the evolution of the Chinese legal profession. The issues discussed in this chapter do, however, suggest intriguing avenues for further research and a range of observations and questions about the development of the Chinese legal profession and the Chinese legal system.

This chapter has not attempted to provide a richly textured study of the development of legal aid or the legal profession; nor has it attempted to place China's experience in a comparative context. Within China, we still have few answers to a number of fundamental questions. For example, is the Chinese legal profession becoming more or less representative of the population as a whole? We know that there has been a huge increase in the number of lawyers in China; we know very little about the types of people who are actually becoming lawyers. Similarly, it appears that Chinese lawyers are becoming better educated. Yet is this increased emphasis on education resulting in a legal profession that is more heavily representative of China's political and economic elite? We also know very little about the lawyers who are actually carrying out legal aid work and complying with mandatory pro bono obligations: are they, as some lawyers in China claim, lawyers who have been made redundant by the marketization of the legal profession or are they representative of a subset of legal professionals who are dedicated to using their legal skills to address the legal needs of the poor? A better understanding of the people who are becoming lawyers and how lawyers view legal aid and pro bono requirements may be a prerequisite to understanding the effectiveness of such programs.

We also know very little about the influence of lawyers—or law—in the lives of the majority of the Chinese population. The degree to which legal aid becomes more widely available in China may reflect the degree to which the central government's attention to law is actually beginning to have an effect outside of the major cities where the legal profession has developed most rapidly. Indeed, most analyses of lawyers, the courts, and the law more generally in China have focused on urban areas. This is not surprising, for such areas are more accessible to both western and Chinese academics. Likewise, the Ministry of Justice itself appears to find it much easier to obtain information on and evaluate developments in major cities than it does to understand legal development in rural areas. Indeed, as suggested above, difficulties the Ministry of Justice faces in monitoring developments in rural areas may partially explain the lack of attention to basic-level legal workers.

There has also been little attempt as of yet to compare the evolution of the Chinese legal profession to experiences elsewhere. There are numerous avenues for such comparative research. For example, how does China's shift from basic-level legal workers to lawyers compare to developments elsewhere? How do China's efforts to impose mandatory pro bono requirements on lawyers relate to similar efforts in other countries? And how do the agendas and strategies of Chinese legal aid lawyers operating in specific substantive areas—such as women's rights—compare to agendas and strategies that public interest lawyers have pursued elsewhere? Placing the development of public interest law in China in a comparative context may also shed light on the likelihood that China's public interest lawyers will be able to continue to pursue their goals without inevitably treading on more political topics. There is also the need for comparative inquiry into larger themes. For example, do China's efforts to use lawyers as checks on local authorities and the central government's encouragement of lawyers to challenge local authorities parallel experiences elsewhere or is China's use of legal aid and the legal profession as a cornerstone of both China's legal development and of the central government's attempt to maintain control over its regions unique?

A subset of the need to look at developments in China in the comparative context is the need to look at possible international or foreign influences on the evolution of legal aid and the legal profession in China. This chapter has suggested that China has deliberately adopted certain aspects of the U.S. model, in particular a large number of lawyers and wide-ranging economic incentives for lawyers. The Peking University center similarly has embraced a particular model of impact litigation, one that appears similar to that followed elsewhere in the developing world by other Ford Foundation-funded legal aid centers. Understanding how these models evolve in China may shed light on the effectiveness of these models more generally.

The need for further inquiry does not, however, preclude observations and questions about what has been observed thus far. The issues this chapter has examined suggest five concluding observations and questions regarding the evolution of China's legal profession.

First, this chapter, like most writing on Chinese lawyers, has used the term "profession" loosely: China has a significant number of lawyers, hence it has a legal profession. Such usage mirrors Chinese usage. The Ministry of Justice refers to the *lüshi zhiye*, apparently itself a translation from the English "legal profession." Yet does a significant number of lawyers equate to a profession? There is as of yet little evidence that lawyers in China are viewed by consumers of their services as somehow fundamentally different from individuals working in other occupations. Similarly, as discussed above, there is little evidence that lawyers in China are identifying collective interests and no sign of the "professional self-government" that has been a hallmark of the development of legal professions in many liberal states (Halliday and Karpik 1997, 21). It is unclear whether this absence of collective action by lawyers means that the Chinese bar is taking a different historical course than that observed elsewhere,[69] or whether the Chinese legal profession is being hampered by close state oversight. Lawyers'

---

69. For one discussion of the degree to which lawyers have behaved collectively, see Karpik (1997, 122).

associations in China are state-created; many lawyers appear to view such associations with the same skepticism they feel toward other government efforts to regulate their work.

Second, much writing within China on lawyers has portrayed lawyers as aloof from the structural problems that make the courts and legal system ineffective. Yet just as increasing the number of lawyers will not alone result in lawyers being more useful, it is mistaken to assume that the mere presence of lawyers will make the system less biased. Indeed, as Professor Alford points out earlier in this volume, lawyers themselves are active participants in the corruption that undermines the Chinese legal system. The development of legal aid programs demonstrates that lawyers can have positive effects, but the growth of the legal profession does not necessarily lead to such results.

Third, this chapter has discussed lawyers in general terms. As Part II highlighted, however, the term "lawyer" applies to individuals with a wide variety of experiences and training. Lawyers in China have diverse interests. Much scholarship on the Chinese profession has been based almost entirely on research in China's developed cities, in particular in Beijing and Shanghai. There may be significant differences among lawyers within such cities (between western-trained corporate lawyers, for example, and legal aid lawyers or lawyers in government firms), but such differences likely pale in comparison to differences from lawyers in less developed regions.

Although there does not appear to be competition among different segments of the bar akin to that observed elsewhere,[70] it remains to be seen whether divisions develop within the legal profession. This may be particularly relevant in the legal aid context where lines between lawyers in state-run firms and those in legal aid centers may be hazy, in particular in areas of the country where most of the population cannot afford even low officially set legal fees. Such tensions have apparently arisen in the criminal context; some scholars and legal aid workers complain that courts have been slow to reform the system of court-appointed counsel, in part because such reform will shift work away from state-run firms that rely heavily on income from court-appointed cases.[71]

Fourth, the growing importance of the bar exam and recent crackdowns on practice by non-lawyers suggest that the Chinese legal profession may be moving toward assuming a more monopolistic role than that assumed by Chinese lawyers in the past. This shift toward monopoly has primarily resulted from state efforts

---

70. A number of scholars have written about competition among different segments of the bar in western countries. For example, Kenneth Ledford describes the various interest groups in the German bar during the early years of the twentieth century that emerged as a result of the opening of the legal profession to groups that had previously been excluded (1997, 245–46). China may not yet be seeing such competition, but there has been at least some writing in the Chinese legal profession about "unfair competition" within the legal profession, in particular lawyers using illegitimate means to attract clients.

71. To the degree such a trend is occurring, it parallels similar tensions that arose in the early years of the development of legal aid in the United States (Grossberg 1997, 319).

to strengthen the role of lawyers; there is little evidence that lawyers themselves have been advocating tighter controls on who can become a lawyer or on the type of work that non-lawyers can undertake. Such government involvement suggests that the Chinese legal profession's drive toward an economic monopoly may be somewhat different than has been observed by Abel and others in the West (Abel 1989). Government involvement does not mean that lawyers themselves are not interested in monopolizing legal work; government involvement may provide lawyers with a convenient route to expand their influence. But involvement of the Ministry of Justice demonstrates the need to continue to analyze the position of lawyers not only in terms of lawyer autonomy and interests but also in terms of the bureaucratic interests of the Ministry of Justice.

Additionally, non-lawyers continue to engage in an extensive range of work, and thus it is premature to assume that the Chinese legal profession will become monopolistic along the lines of legal professions in western countries. Yet the role of the Ministry of Justice in boosting the role of lawyers highlights both the possibility of such a shift and the degree to which the position of the Chinese bar continues to be defined by complex interactions with the state.

Fifth, lawyers in China today are enjoying increased autonomy. In turn, opportunities for individuals to use lawyers and the legal system to protect their interests are increasing. Such expanded autonomy suggests caution in assuming that government oversight—whether directly via Ministry of Justice regulations or less directly via control of the All-China Lawyers' Association—precludes autonomy. Lawyers' close relationship to the central government—both formally, in the fact that even non-state lawyers continue to be state regulated, and ideologically, as manifest by lawyers pursuing goals consistent with state policy—may actually be facilitating such autonomy. In the legal aid context, for example, lawyers are being encouraged to undertake a range of cases that would not previously have been brought in the formal legal system. The existence and endorsement of such work may also be legitimizing a more general expansion in the range of cases in which lawyers engage.

As law continues to increase in relevance in China, the prominence of individuals providing legal services—be they lawyers or non-lawyers—is likely to increase. Although it is tempting to measure the influence of the Chinese bar in terms of its independence from the Chinese state, this chapter has attempted to highlight the range of questions—from definitions of lawyers and the legal profession to the extent of central and local government control over lawyers to whether lawyers themselves identify common interests with other lawyers— that must be asked first. How these questions are addressed will shape not only the role of lawyers but also the effectiveness of law. Indeed, China provides a remarkable opportunity for observing not only the development of a legal profession but also the evolution of a legal system. The fact that the legal system is undergoing rapid transformation based on a mixture of legal traditions and that the roles of various actors within the legal system are not strictly delineated may itself be the most important factor permitting lawyers to engage in a widening sphere of activity.

Works Cited

Abel, Richard. 1989. *American lawyers.* New York: Oxford University Press.

Association Peru Mujer. 1992. Association Peru Mujer. In *Public interest law around the world,* eds. T. Hutchins and J. Klaaren. New York: Columbia Human Rights Law Review.

BBC Summary of World Broadcasts. 1998k. Article condemns "fascist" practices of "barbaric" cadres. 22 December.

———. 1998a. Legal system booming: State no longer dominant. 4 April.

———. 1998b. Party criticizes "little hot pepper" newspaper for "negative reporting." 22 April.

———. 1998c. Regional paper airs views on freedom to think and speak out. 17 July.

———. 1998d. Regional paper publishes views on awareness of human rights. 17 July.

———. 1998e. Committee established to protect lawyers' rights. 22 July.

———. 1998f. Drunk judges face punishment; jury system to be set up. 19 September.

———. 1998g. Court, procuratorate rectification achieves remarkable results. 22 September.

———. 1998h. Parliament permanent body approves law on village democracy. 4 November.

———. 1998i. Southern newspaper criticizes "farce" of Hainan village poll. 28 November.

———. 1998j. Parliament chairman tells media to increase cover(age) of democratic, legal systems. 16 December.

Beijing Daxue Falü Xi Funü Falü Yanjiu yu Fuwu Zhongxin [The Center for Women's Law Studies and Legal Services of Peking University]. N.d. *Beijing Daxue Falü Xi Funü Falü Yanjiu yu Fuwu Zhongxin.* Beijing: Beijing Daxue Falü Xi Funü Falü Yanjiu yu Fuwu Zhongxin.

Brandt, Hans-Jurgen. 1988. Human rights, legal services and development: Theory and practice. In *Law, human rights and legal services: A neglected field of development cooperation.* Sankt Augustin: COMDOK-Verlagsabt.

Cai Dingjian. 1998. Tigao sifa de wenming shuizhun [Raise justice's standard of civility]. *Nanfang Zhoumo* [Southern weekend]. 24 July.

Cappelletti, Mauro. 1975. The emergence of a modern theme. In *Toward equal justice: A comparative study of legal aid in modern societies,* eds. M. Cappelletti, J. Gordley, and E. Johnson, Jr. Dobbs Ferry, New York: Oceana.

China Business Information Network. 1998a. China: Li Peng on correcting a few judicial workers' law-violating practices. 17 September.

————. 1998b. China approves 15,102 new lawyers. 8 December.

Cohen, Jerome Alan. 1966. Chinese mediation on the eve of modernization. 54 *California Law Review* 1201.

Dias, Clarence. 1988. Human rights and legal resources for development. In *Law, human rights and legal services: A neglected field of development cooperation.* Sankt Augustin: COMDOK-Verlagsabt.

Duan Zhengkun. 1998. Zai shishi yifa zhiguo fanglue zhong jiaqiang lüshi gongzuo [Strengthen lawyers' work in implementing the strategy of ruling the country according to law]. *Zhongguo Lüshi Bao* [China lawyer news]. 16 September.

Eckholm, Erik. 1999. China tightens rein on writers and publishers. *New York Times.* 19 January.

Ellmann, Stephen. 1987. Lawyers and clients. 34 *UCLA Law Review* 717.

————. 1998. Cause lawyering in the third world. In *Cause lawyering: Political commitments and professional responsibilities,* eds. A. Sarat and S. Scheingold. New York: Oxford University Press.

Gao Benhai. 1998. Weihai qingli zhengdun "zhendao shiqiang" [Weihai cleans up and rectifies "with real swords and spears"]. *Zhongguo Lüshi Bao.* 7 October.

Gordley, James. 1975. Variations on a modern theme. In *Toward equal justice: A comparative study of legal aid in modern societies,* eds. M. Cappelletti, J. Gordley, and E. Johnson, Jr. Dobbs Ferry, New York: Oceana.

Grossberg, Michael. 1997. The politics of professionalism: The creation of legal aid and the strains of political liberalism in America, 1900–1930. In *Lawyers and the rise of western political liberalism,* eds. T. C. Halliday and L. Karpik. Oxford: Clarendon Press.

Guo Jianmei. 1997. Yixiang hennan er you yiyi de shiye [Work that is both difficult and meaningful]. In *Beijing Daxue Falü Xi Funü Falü Yanjiu yu Fuwu Zhongxin 1997 niankan* [The Center for Women's Law Studies and Legal Services of Peking University 1997 annual report]. Beijing: Beijing Daxue Falü Xi Funü Falü Yanjiu yu Fuwu Zhongxin.

Halliday, Terence C. and Lucien Karpik. 1997. Politics matter: A comparative theory of lawyers in the making of political liberalism. In *Lawyers and the rise of western political liberalism,* eds. T. C. Halliday and L. Karpik. Oxford: Clarendon Press.

He Weifang. 1998. Fuzhuan junren jin fayuan [Retired soldiers enter the courts]. *Nanfang Zhoumo.* 2 January.

Karpik, Lucien. 1997. Builders of liberal society: French lawyers and politics. In *Lawyers and the rise of western political liberalism,* eds. T. C. Halliday and L. Karpik. Oxford: Clarendon Press.

Landon, Donald D. 1985. Clients, colleagues, and community: The shaping of zealous advocacy in country law practice. *American Bar Foundation Research Journal* 81.

Ledford, Kenneth F. 1997. Lawyers and the limits of liberalism: The German bar in the Weimar Republic. In *Lawyers and the rise of western political liberalism*, eds. T. C. Halliday and L. Karpik. Oxford: Clarendon Press.

Legal Resources Foundation. 1992. Legal Resources Foundation. In *Public interest law around the world*, eds. T. Hutchins and J. Klaaren. New York: Columbia Human Rights Law Review.

Lev, Daniel. 1998. Lawyers' causes in Indonesia and Malaysia. In *Cause lawyering: Political commitment and professional responsibilities*, eds. A. Sarat and S. Scheingold. New York: Oxford University Press.

Li Xiaoling. N.d. *Lüshi zuo hao bianhu gongzuo, cushi beigao renzui fufa* [Lawyers do a good job at defense work, encourage defendants to admit their crimes and follow the law]. Unpublished essay from the Guangzhou Legal Aid Center.

Liebman, Benjamin L. 1999. Legal aid and public interest law in China. 34 *Texas International Law Journal* 211.

———. 1998. Class action litigation in China. 111 *Harvard Law Review* 1523 (Note).

Liu Guangan and Li Cunpeng. 1995. Minjian tiaojie yu quanli baohu [Civil mediation and the protection of rights]. In *Zou xiang quanli de shidai* [Toward a time of rights], ed. Xia Yong. Beijing: Zhongguo Zhengfa Daxue Chubanshe.

Liu Weixing. 1988. Weihu jinrong chengxu, zujin shehui wending [Protect financial procedures, further social stability]. *Zhongguo Lüshi Bao.* 21 October.

Lubman, Stanley B. 1999. Dispute resolution in China after Deng Xiaoping: "Mao and mediation" revisited. 11 *Columbia Journal of Asian Law* 229.

Ma Xueying. 1998. Xinjiang lüshi quanmian kaituo falü fuwu shichang [Xingjiang lawyers fully open up the market for legal services]. *Zhongguo Lüshi Bao.* 30 September.

Meng Baosen. 1997. Falü yuanzhu anjian banan yanjiu baogao [Research report regarding the handling of legal aid cases]. In *Beijing Daxue Falü Xi Funü Falü Yanjiu yu Fuwu Zhongxin 1997 niankan.* Beijing: Beijing Daxue Falü Xi Funü Falü Yanjiu yu Fuwu Zhongxin.

Michalowski, Raymond. 1998. All or nothing: An inquiry into the (im)possibility of cause lawyering under Cuban socialism. In *Cause lawyering: Political commitments and professional responsibilities*, eds. A. Sarat and S. Scheingold. New York: Oxford University Press.

Osiel, Mark J. 1990. Lawyers as monopolists, aristocrats, and entrepreneurs. 103 *Harvard Law Review* 2009.

Pomfret, John. 1999. Chinese officials bare flaws of legal system: Reports to legislature cite growing number of corruption and official abuse cases. *Washington Post.* 24 March.

Qing Feng. 1997. *Zhongguo lüshi zhidu lungang* [A discussion of China's lawyer system]. Beijing: Zhongguo Fazhi Chubanshe.

Rhode, Deborah L. 1994. Institutionalizing ethics. 44 *Case Western Law Review* 665.

———. 1996. Professionalism in perspective: Alternative approaches to non-lawyer practice. *Journal of the Institute for the Study of Legal Ethics* 1:197.

Rojas, Fernando. 1988. A comparison of change-oriented legal services in Latin America with legal services in North America and Europe. *International Journal of the Sociology of Law* 16:203.

Rueschemeyer, Dietrich. 1997. The Prussian bar 1700–1914. In *Lawyers and the rise of western political liberalism*, eds. T. C. Halliday and L. Karpik. Oxford: Clarendon Press.

Sarat, Austin and Stuart Scheingold. 1998. Cause lawyers and the reproduction of professional authority: An introduction. In *Cause lawyering: Political commitment and professional responsibilities*, eds. A. Sarat and S. Scheingold. New York: Oxford University Press.

Schulhofer, Stephen J. 1992. Plea bargaining as disaster. 101 *Yale Law Journal* 1979.

Sifa Bu [Ministry of Justice]. 1991. Xiangzhen falü fuwu yewu gongzuo xize [Provisions on township and village legal services work]. 20 September. Reprinted in *Zhonghua renmin gongheguo falü fagui quanshu* [People's Republic of China compendium of laws and regulations]. 1994. 3:623. Beijing: Zhongguo Minzhu Fazhi Chubanshe.

———. 1997. Guanyu sifa suo he sifa zhuliyuan bixu yange yifa banshi de tongzhi [Notice regarding the need for judicial offices and judicial assistants to carry out work strictly in accordance with law]. September 23. Reprinted in *Zhonghua renmin gongheguo falü quanshu 1997* [People's Republic of China legal compendium 1997]. 1998:959.

Sun Guodong. 1998. Jiceng falü gongzuozhe daili susong yao zhengguihua [Representation in litigation by basic-level legal services workers will be standardized]. *Zhongguo Lüshi Bao.* 22 April.

Wei Xianzhou. 1998. Gongyi chachu feifa sheli de "Wanzhong falü fuwu bu" [Gongyi investigates and discovers the illegally established "Wanzhong Legal Services Department"]. *Zhongguo Lüshi Bao.* 8 July.

White, Lucie E. 1988. To learn and teach: Lessons from Dreifontein on lawyering and power. 1988 *Wisconsin Law Review* 699.

Xinhua English Newswire. 1998. Feature: Public opinions incorporated in law (I). 29 August.

———. 1999. NPC session holds fourth plenary. 10 March.

Xinhua News Agency. 1998a. 142,500 Chinese take exams for lawyer qualification. 10 October.

———. 1998b. Profession of lawyer attracts young, educated people. 12 October.

———. 1998c. Beijing lawyers urged to improve their services. 23 November.

———. 1998d. Township courts should help keep stability in rural China—official. 28 November.

———. 1999a. Supreme People's Court issues new open trial rule. 10 March.

———. 1999b. Chinese legislature adopts constitutional amendment. 15 March.

Yan Lieshan. 1998. Zhuiwen de quanli [The right to question]. *Nanfang Zhoumo*. 21 August.

Zhang Geng, ed. 1998. *Zhongguo falü yuanzhu zhidu yansheng de qianqian houhou* [The ins and outs of the development of China's legal aid system]. Beijing: Zhongguo Fangzheng Chubanshe.

Zhang Xiufu. 1998. Fahui sifa xingzheng jiceng gongzuo zhineng, wei shishi yifa zhiguo jiben fanglue zuo gongxian [Develop the working ability of basic-level justice administration in order to make a contribution to the basic plan of ruling the country in accordance with law]. *Zhongguo Lüshi Bao.* 11 July.

Zhongguo Falü Nianjian Bianji Bu (ZFNBB) [Law yearbook of China editorial department]. 1991. *Zhongguo falü nianjian (1991)* [Law yearbook of China (1991)]. Beijing: Zhongguo Falü Nianjian Chubanshe.

———. 1997. *Zhongguo falü nianjian (1997)*. Beijing: Zhongguo Falü Nianjian Chubanshe.

———. 1999. *Zhongguo falü nianjian (1999)*. Beijing: Zhongguo Falü Nianjian Chubanshe.

Zhonghua Renmin Gongheguo Lüshi Fa [People's Republic of China lawyers law]. 1996. Reprinted in *Zhonghua renmin gongheguo xin fagui huibian* [People's Republic of China collected new laws and regulations]. 1996 (2): 39. Beijing: Xinhua Shudian.

Zhou Shenghuai and Li Fujiang. 1998. Famang dang daili, haisha dangshi ren [Legal illiterate serves as representative, causes harm to litigant]. *Zhongguo Lüshi Bao.* 8 July.

NINE

The Role of Lawyers in Taiwan's Emerging Democracy

JANE KAUFMAN WINN*

Introduction

In recent decades, Taiwan[1] has made considerable strides toward democracy (Tien and Cheng 1997). While its democratic transformation may not yet be complete, it is nevertheless beyond question that political and social institutions in Taiwan are dramatically more open and accountable to the public than they were only ten years ago.[2] At the same time that Taiwan's leaders embarked on a project to open the government to a broader range of political forces than was the case under martial law, the regulation of the economy was substantially liberalized as well.[3] One element of the program of liberalization included increasing

*Professor and Director of the Shidler Center for Law, Commerce and Technology at the University of Washington School of Law.

I wish to thank William Alford, Richard Abel, Jimmy Chi-min Yu and Robert Gordon for their helpful comments on earlier drafts, and the Southern Methodist University Research Council and the John G. Tower Center for the financial support that made the research for this chapter possible. I also wish to thank Jimmy Chi-min Yu for his invaluable research assistance.

1. For purposes of this chapter, "Taiwan" refers to the social institutions and systems associated with the island of Taiwan. This includes, where appropriate, the government of the Republic of China on Taiwan, as well as the social and cultural institutions and practices that can be observed in Taiwan today. The adjective "Taiwanese" refers to things associated with life in Taiwan today, including individuals who arrived or whose families arrived in Taiwan from mainland China in 1949, individuals whose families came to Taiwan from the Fujian province region in the seventeenth or eighteenth century, and individuals who are ethnically distinct from the Han Chinese, such as the Hakka.

2. For example, one criterion for determining that a period of "democratic consolidation" following a period of "democratic transition" has been successfully completed is a peaceful transfer of power that removes the former dominant political group from a position of control over government institutions (Tien and Cheng 1997, 20). This happened in Japan when the Liberal Democratic Party left power following the Socialist Party electoral victory, and in Taiwan in 2000, when the Kuomintang Party was defeated by the Democratic Progressive Party in the ROC presidential election.

3. Taiwan achieved rapid economic growth throughout the 1960s and 1970s through export-oriented economic policies. By the 1980s, Taiwan had achieved such a degree of economic development that it was coming under increasing pressure from trading partners such as the U.S. to open its domestic economy to foreign competition. The liberalization of Taiwan's

the number of attorneys admitted to practice in the Republic of China (ROC). As a result, the number of attorneys in private practice in Taiwan roughly doubled between 1986 and 1996.[4] Such a dramatic increase in the number of lawyers in Taiwan will clearly have some effect on Taiwanese society.

This chapter will suggest what some of those effects might be, especially in light of the experience of some of the other East Asian nations whose legal professions are considered in this volume. This chapter will also discuss some of the new directions Taiwan's legal profession may take in light of the different pressures now being exerted on Taiwanese society, including the consolidation of democratic and liberal reforms in the domestic government and economy, the still unresolved question of Taiwan's sovereignty, and Taiwan's ever greater integration into the Greater China economic region in particular and the global economy in general.

The discussion in this chapter is primarily based on interviews conducted in July 1995 with individuals in, or with some connection to, the legal profession in Taiwan.[5] Those interviews were designed to find out what, if any, connection existed between the major changes the legal profession was undergoing and the progress being made toward liberalization in political and economic spheres at the same time. On earlier trips to Taiwan in 1990 and 1991, I interviewed lawyers in connection with research regarding the operation of Taiwan's informal economy and its relationship to the formal legal system.[6]

In 1994, with Professor Tang-chi Yeh of Chung-Yuan University School of Law, I wrote an article on the legal profession in Taiwan for a symposium on lawyering in repressive states. Professor Yeh and I concluded that the concept of

---

domestic economy that has taken place since the 1980s has opened the local economy to the forces of global competition in a wide range of markets for goods and services.

4. As far as I was able to determine after extensive inquiries in 1995, neither government agencies nor bar associations in Taiwan were maintaining the same kind of extensive statistical data regarding the legal profession that some other East Asian nations discussed in this collection of essays maintain. Individual bar associations maintained membership records, but no one I spoke to could direct me to an organized system for aggregating that information. In 1991, the Ministry of Justice provided me with an estimate of 2,254 for the total number of attorneys in private practice (Winn and Yeh 1995, text at footnote 40). Other observers of the legal system at that time estimated the total number of attorneys in government service as judges or prosecutors to be about the same. Based on the number of attorneys passing the bar, the number of attorneys in private practice would roughly have doubled by 1996, while the number in government service would not have risen so dramatically. During this period, Taiwan had a population of around 20 million.

5. In July 1995, I met with 35 different individuals to discuss their views on the changing role of Taiwan's legal profession under democratization. These individuals included a judge, a prosecutor, 3 legislators, 7 academic social scientists in a range of disciplines, 8 legal academics, and 15 attorneys in private practice. In general, I met these individuals through alumni connections with either Harvard Law School or Southern Methodist University or through the personal contacts of academic colleagues in Taiwan.

6. I published the findings of that earlier research in Winn (1994).

cause lawyering was not well enough developed in Taiwan for the danger of legitimating a regime perceived by the lawyers as illegitimate to have arisen (Winn and Yeh 1995). In this chapter, I use material gathered from interviews in 1995 and on earlier occasions to suggest a range of different possible directions Taiwan's legal profession may take in coming years.

Taiwan's legal profession may continue to expand and may play a more active role in Taiwanese society without necessarily performing the role of the autonomous, disinterested profession mediating conflicts between the state and society that has been described in the sociology of the professions in western societies.[7] While the legal profession in Taiwan has a much greater sense of self-identity and autonomy relative to the state than does the legal profession in the People's Republic of China (PRC),[8] it may not rise to the same sense of self-identity enjoyed by legal professions in many western nations today. The legal system of the ROC never underwent the wholesale devastation inflicted on the PRC legal system during the Cultural Revolution. The greater continuity and integrity of ROC legal institutions, including the private bar, have helped produce a legal profession in Taiwan that is closer to the liberal ideal than the one taking shape in the PRC today.

The sudden increase in the number of lawyers admitted to practice, as well as much of the rapid progress now being made toward the liberalization of political and economic institutions, are very recent changes in Taiwanese society. These changes, in combination with some of the profound social and economic pressures being exerted on Taiwanese society by its growing integration into the Greater China economic region and exposure to the forces of global economic competition generally, may change the character of Taiwan's legal profession. It is possible that these pressures will result in a much stronger embrace by Taiwan's legal profession of the classical liberal ideal of an autonomous professional. I think it is more likely, however, that the legal profession in Taiwan will either move toward an entrepreneurial, commercial notion of law practice or will move toward a hybrid role of mediating between formal and informal coercive orders in order to advance client interests. This is in part because it is difficult to find an actual example of a legal profession today operating according to classical liberal theory even in countries where liberal democratic ideas are part of the indigenous political culture. It is also in part because lawyers in Taiwan might find a strategic advantage in leveraging their legal training and credentials by combining them with more informal methods of representing client interests that resonate with local culture and institutions but that are not reflected in traditional theories of professionalism.

Lawyers in Taiwan today face a range of alternative models for developing their practice or contributing to the further development of Taiwanese society. These alternatives include some models of legal practice that are found in the

---

7. See, e.g., Parsons (1968).

8. For a discussion of the limited sense of self-identity and autonomy of the PRC legal profession, see Professor Alford's chapter and Professor Liebman's chapter, both in this volume.

same western societies that developed the theory of the autonomous professional, where the actual work of lawyers diverges to a significant degree from theoretical models of the legal profession. These alternatives also include combining a license to practice law with other, less formally defined social roles that have been traditionally valued in Taiwanese society. The sociology of the legal profession today does not yet provide robust analytic tools for determining when lawyers as individuals will do a sort of regulatory arbitrage between formal legal representation and mobilizing more informal forms of social capital to represent clients. Should such analytic tools be developed, it might assist in analyzing the roles played by legal professions in developing countries. The ability to predict when a lawyer will select informal processes to advance a client's interest would also be useful in studying the roles played by lawyers in western nations, where such arbitrage is performed as well but where the study of formal institutions and processes may occupy a more central position in the sociology of the legal professional.[9]

As Taiwanese society becomes increasingly open to the social forces exerted by economic activity in global arenas, the legal profession is well placed to play a pivotal role in mediating the interests of local and global actors.[10] Foreign business interests may prefer to work with local lawyers to represent their local interests in Taiwan—lawyers whose style of practice most closely resembles that of attorneys in their home countries. Taiwanese businesses wishing to participate in the Greater China economic region may prefer to work with local lawyers with a knowledge not just of the formal PRC legal system but also an understanding of how to mobilize informal social relations to protect investments in mainland China.[11] Whether in fact Taiwanese lawyers are able to build these kinds of bridges between local Taiwanese interests and interests rooted in the global economy, and if so, what impact that activity would have on processes such as the consolidation of Taiwan's democratic reforms, is not yet clear.

I.   Different Possible Directions for Taiwan's Changing Legal Profession

From the early days of the ROC following the 1911 revolution in China and continuing through its relocation to Taiwan in 1949, a modern legal profession has always been assigned some role in the administration of justice in the

---

9. For example, the emphasis in the "new institutional economics" on identifying criteria for selecting between formal and informal ordering systems and dispute resolution mechanisms could benefit from a study of how attorneys in developed market economies such as the U.S. decide whether to steer clients toward formal or informal systems for protecting their interests.

10. For a discussion of the role the legal profession plays in the process of globalization, see generally Trubek et al. (1994).

11. For an account of the importance of informal networks in business activities carried on in the PRC today, see Wank (1999). See also Yang (1994) and Yan (2000).

ROC.[12] The magnitude of resources allocated to establishing a strong, modern legal profession was limited by the extreme social and political dislocations China suffered in the decades following the founding of the ROC through the triumph of the Chinese Communist Party (CCP) in 1949. The Japanese colonial administration in power in Taiwan from 1895 to 1945 likewise established a modern legal system to aid in its administration of Taiwan (Wang 1992). In a manner similar to that of the governments of Japan (Miyazawa, in this volume), the PRC (Alford, Liebman, both in this volume) and Korea (Kim, in this volume), at various times in recent history, the decision to create a modern legal profession by the ROC government did not necessarily demonstrate a commitment to grant that legal profession any significant powers that could be exercised independently of the political powers of government leaders.[13]

One possible direction that Taiwan's legal profession might take would be to embrace more fully the classical model of the autonomous professional that is associated with a liberal social and political order. Such a professional is uniquely equipped to mediate between the competing interests of the state and civil society, and among the members of a civil society, when its exercise of power is divorced to the greatest extent possible from those exercises of power it is called upon to control. The maintenance of the rule of law requires that those subject to the enforcement of legal obligations believe that enforcement is carried out in a neutral, impartial manner. By shielding the legal profession from both the coercive power of the state and of private institutions such as the market, the interpretation and application of the law may take place dispassionately and fairly.

The role of autonomous professional is one that only in recent years has become theoretically possible for attorneys in Taiwan to adopt. With Taiwan's transition to a multiparty democracy, this role may continue to expand. Taiwan's early success in its transition to democracy was due in considerable part to the efforts of the ruling Nationalist Party (Kuomintang or KMT) that retained power through skillful manipulation of an increasingly open and competitive political process.[14] Although this permitted the KMT to retain power through much of the democratization process, in 2000, Democratic Progressive Party (DPP) presidential candidate Chen Shui-bian achieved a surprise upset victory in a three-way contest against a KMT split into two factions. Competition between the two major parties may well serve to strengthen the autonomy of legal institutions in Taiwan. To some degree, however, the continuous operation of modern legal institutions as part of the ROC government on Taiwan for many decades has laid a foundation for the legal profession to play the role

---

12. This is in marked contrast with the situation that prevailed for centuries prior to the late nineteenth century, in which the representation of others in imperial law courts was generally treated as a crime; see Macauley (1998).

13. The structural limitations on the autonomy of the ROC legal profession are discussed in more detail in the following Part, and also in Winn and Yeh (1995).

14. See Tien and Cheng (1997) for a fuller discussion of this process.

of autonomous professionals. This is in marked contrast with the current situation of the legal profession in the PRC, where modern legal institutions were effectively eviscerated during the Cultural Revolution and only more recently have slowly been rebuilt.

Another possible direction that Taiwan's legal profession might take is that of the entrepreneurial lawyer. An entrepreneurial lawyer is one who self-consciously exploits the license to practice law in a manner calculated to achieve the highest possible economic return for the lawyer. It is beyond the scope of this chapter to consider whether this kind of lawyering is a recent innovation or even an aberration. In any event, commercialization of the legal profession clearly represents a distinct alternative conception to the classical liberal ideal of the legal profession. In the U.S., where this approach to the practice of law is clearly widespread, the discussion of this notion of law practice has questioned whether existing rules governing the legal profession are appropriate or adequate. In addition, the notion of zealous advocacy of the client's interests held by some U.S. lawyers would be seen in some other countries with different standards as a failure to exercise the independent judgment that is supposed to characterize the legal profession.

This model of entrepreneurial lawyering may prove attractive in Taiwan, especially in light of the erosion of the market value of admission to the bar caused by the sudden increase in the number of lawyers in private practice. These economic pressures, combined with an historical lack of autonomy prior to democratization, may mean that the classical liberal idea of the lawyer as exercising judgment independent of both the state and private pressures may never be widely or deeply assimilated by Taiwan's lawyers. Further research would be necessary, however, to determine whether the notion of entrepreneurial lawyering is as popular today in Taiwan as Professor Alford's research in mainland China suggests it is there.

Law can never be the exclusive coercive ordering system in any society, but the boundaries between legal ordering and private ordering are difficult to determine and difficult to analyze. Private ordering systems in a society consist of alternative institutions maintained through the activities of individuals that in turn are in competition to some degree with the legal profession. The sociology of legal professions in countries with strong liberal democratic traditions does not generally focus on the boundaries between informal and formal coercive ordering systems in defining either at a theoretical or normative level the roles played by attorneys.[15] In countries where liberal democratic traditions are not indigenous, as is true for the East Asian societies considered in this volume, defining the relationship between formal and informal ordering systems may be crucial in understanding the roles played by attorneys in those societies.

---

15. Although most research on the sociology of legal institutions may take formal dispute resolution processes and formal legal institutions as its primary focus, there have been also many noteworthy studies that do focus on the boundaries of formal and informal ordering. See, e.g., Wilkins (1990); Merry (1988); Galanter (1981); Moore (1978); Felstiner (1974).

In the English vernacular, the concept of "fixer" is widely recognized, although it has not to date been the subject of any sustained sociological analysis.[16] In this chapter, I use the colloquial term as a general rubric for someone who mediates between competing interests within informal coercive ordering systems. A fixer is offering a service that competes with the kinds of services lawyers offer in administering formalized coercive ordering systems. A lawyer may choose to act as a fixer in achieving his or her client's goals if that lawyer has the ability to invoke the possibility of informal rewards or sanctions to cause another party to meet the client's objectives. The use of personal relationships or other informal forms of social organization may under some circumstances be more effective than addressing the problem in terms of legal rules and institutions. Any sociology of the legal profession in a society in which informal ordering systems create important alternatives to reliance on the legal system should be able to account for decisions by attorneys to take advantage of informal relationships in lieu of legal relationships in pursuing client objectives. As a practical matter, however, analyzing such decisions is problematic because locating and evaluating informal alternatives to law may be more difficult than studying formal legal institutions.

Questions arising out of the interplay between formal and informal coercive systems take on a particular urgency with regard to any country where liberal institutions are not indigenous (Winn 1994). While formal legal institutions operate (or at least appear to operate)[17] with some efficacy in societies where the basic norms of the legal system harmonize with other social norms such as religious values, in societies where legal models have been quite recently imported from foreign legal traditions, formal legal institutions may be less effective. Large-scale reliance on informal ordering is likely to persist in societies with legal systems based on imported models for some time even after liberal institutions have been established. Informal coercive orders may even operate more efficiently in a given society than the ordering created through liberal market institutions, depending on the relationship between imported liberal institutions and competing indigenous social, political, and cultural institutions (Greif 1997).

Researching the proclivity of lawyers to substitute the role of fixer for the role of attorney-at-law first requires identifying when, in fact, informal alternatives compete with liberal institutions in a given society. Ideological filters embedded deep in modern social theory may highlight the functioning of liberal institutions while obscuring the functioning of competing informal social ordering

---

16. See, e.g., the *New York Times* (1998): "In the national G.O.P. [Alfonse D'Amato] was a force too, known as a hard-headed *fixer* and deal-maker and one of the most effective money-raisers in Washington" (emphasis added).

17. The debate over the actual effectiveness of legal institutions as opposed to informal ordering within societies with liberal democratic traditions is beyond the scope of this chapter; see, e.g., Macaulay (1963); *Northwestern University Law Review* (2000).

systems. The presence of such perceptual filters creates a pervasive risk of bias in the collection such facts. Even assuming such biases can be controlled and such information can be collected, it remains unclear whether any appropriate criteria can be found with which to evaluate such informal coercive systems. Conventional liberal notions such as self-determination, transparency, or universality that are used in evaluating the legitimacy of formal legal institutions cannot be applied directly to informal institutions without some difficulty.

While this asymmetry in criteria for evaluating legitimacy makes critical assessment of the interplay between formal and informal coercive ordering systems difficult, such issues should not simply be omitted from the analysis. For example, Yves Dezalay and Bryant Garth try to demonstrate that under certain conditions, elements of traditional East Asian models may be combined with elements of western liberal legality in order to create institutions that repress rather than promote self-determination for the citizens of a country importing the forms of western liberal legality (Dezalay and Garth, in this volume). While Dezalay and Garth's conclusions are very suggestive, they acknowledge that the research they use for support is unclear and amenable to more than one interpretation, and their criteria for recognizing illegitimate exercises of power through informal means are not fully articulated.[18]

The standard problems that arise in any inquiry into the legitimacy of legal institutions, and of competing informal processes, are compounded in a comparative context. It is difficult to identify the objective source of the legitimacy of a legal order within a cultural tradition shared by both the researcher and the research subjects, and it may be difficult to identify objective criteria for evaluating the legitimacy of a legal order operating in a cultural tradition outside the researcher's own indigenous tradition. Given the level of controversy surrounding the appropriate criteria for evaluating the operation of the legal profession within countries such as the U.S. with liberal democratic traditions, it is even more difficult to try to articulate under what circumstances it would

---

18. Because Dezalay and Garth's work is in a neo-Marxian tradition, they tend to presume rather than explain how the social processes they observe produce oppression by some inchoate ruling elite, which in turn may encourage them to gloss over difficult questions about the reliability of certain allegations made by their informants. For example, they conclude that within the legal profession in Korea, admission to Harvard Law School has come to serve as a surrogate for the traditional examination system as a channel for access to participation in government. While graduation from Harvard Law School may be analogized by some members of the Korean legal profession to success in the traditional exam system, such observations may be better understood as metaphors than as a claim that there is a concrete equivalence. The use of such metaphors in speech does not establish that in fact the actual authority conferred on Korean graduates of Harvard Law School is equivalent to the authority of successful candidates of the traditional exam system, or that access to a U.S. legal education at any other leading U.S. law school does not have the same practical effect as a Harvard Law School degree. For a classic study demonstrating how easy it is to jump to fallacious conclusions based on apparent similarities in the deep structure of western and nonwestern societies, see Hamilton (1990).

be appropriate for an attorney in Taiwan to substitute the role of fixer in mediating informal coercive orders for either the role of disinterested autonomous professional or entrepreneurial professional. In his analysis of the contemporary PRC legal profession in this volume, Professor Alford calls for a new sociology of lawyers that can adequately take account of the interplay between lawyers and the state in settings that are more diverse than either a classical western liberal democracy or a modern authoritarian regime. While the relevance of such new directions in the sociology of the profession might be most immediately obvious in the study of legal professions of countries for which liberalism is not an indigenous tradition, they might also provide new insights into the actual operation of legal professions even within countries with liberal democratic traditions.

Within Taiwanese society, it is safe to assume that there will be individuals playing the role of fixer within informal ordering systems for some time, notwithstanding the recent dramatic progress made in democratizing Taiwan's political system and liberalizing its economy. The question with regard to the study of the legal profession is whether those individuals will include a large number of lawyers. Lawyers may find that their membership in the profession can be used as a point of entry into informal ordering systems and that playing the role of fixer is more rewarding, materially or otherwise, than playing one of the roles more commonly assumed by lawyers in western countries. If lawyers migrate in large numbers to a hybrid role of lawyer as fixer, this may have implications for the future character of Taiwan's democracy and the further integration of Taiwan's local economy into global economic arenas.

II. Characteristics of Taiwan's Legal Profession

Specific characteristics of Taiwan's legal profession can only be considered within the larger context of the relationship between Taiwanese society and the ROC legal system. The role of formal legal institutions in Taiwanese society has been affected by a variety of factors, some of which have had the effect of undermining the effectiveness of those institutions. These factors include the unresolved issues surrounding the relationship between Taiwan and mainland China, which place de facto limitations on the sovereignty of the ROC, and the ethnic conflicts among the people of Taiwan, which limits the legitimacy of the KMT regime. In addition, larger social and cultural factors favoring greater reliance on informal ordering systems under certain circumstances have affected the degree to which formal legal institutions are able to achieve their stated objectives.

The ROC constitution dates back to 1947 and purports to apply to all of China, not just the island of Taiwan, but after the 1949 Communist forces victory in the Chinese civil war, it has only been effective in Taiwan.[19] A martial law

---

19. For a discussion of the 1947 constitution and its reforms, see Hwang (1995).

regime was instituted by the KMT regime while it was still in control of mainland China. Justified by reference to the still-unresolved civil war, martial law was retained in Taiwan until 1987. Executive orders suspending the effectiveness of portions of the 1947 constitution were not repealed until 1991. During the period of martial law, political power was concentrated in the executive branch of government, the armed forces, internal security organs, and the KMT party, subverting the division of power set forth in the 1947 constitution. Until 1992, the legitimacy of the national legislature was limited by the suspension of elections to replace representatives elected before the CCP victory from regions in mainland China that came under CCP control in 1949. Many forms of dissent were treated as sedition, and politically sensitive trials were conducted as court-martials.[20] Many attorneys gained admission to the bar following service as a lawyer in the armed forces, which had the effect of minimizing the number of attorneys in private practice who might contest the legitimacy of the KMT regime through the courts.

Relations between the Taiwanese majority and the mainlander minority in Taiwan today remain problematic and may create limits to the further progress of democratization.[21] The majority of the people living in Taiwan today are descendants of Chinese settlers who came to Taiwan before the nineteenth century from Fujian province and who speak a Fujian dialect of Chinese.[22] Although these residents of Taiwan originally welcomed retrocession from Japanese colonial rule in 1945, many swiftly grew disillusioned with the KMT regime. An uprising against the KMT governors in Taiwan in February 1947 was ruthlessly and violently suppressed with thousands of deaths and was followed by decades of exclusion of the Taiwanese from full participation in the government of Taiwan. The refugees who came to Taiwan in 1949 following the defeat of the KMT on mainland China generally speak the standard Mandarin dialect of Chinese, as do their children.

---

20. The most celebrated of these trials is described in Kaplan (1981). In December 1979, a political demonstration organized by the opposition turned violent, with large numbers of police officers suffering injuries. Many leaders of the political opposition were rounded up, court-martialed, convicted on charges of sedition, and given sentences of up to life in prison. See Winn and Yeh (1995) for a fuller discussion of how the Kaohsiung incident and the subsequent trials had the effect of galvanizing Taiwanese opposition to the KMT regime.

21. The relationship between sub-ethnic (see note 22 below) divisions in Taiwan and political transformation is complex, however. While the KMT may resist the transfer of power as a result of sub-ethnic divisions, the divisions may also have motivated the KMT to pursue actively a policy of "Taiwanization" of the KMT in lieu of more formal democratization in an effort to diffuse some of those tensions.

22. Today, there remain on Taiwan few descendants of the original aboriginal inhabitants of Taiwan, although other ethnically distinct groups such as the Hakka people constitute significant minorities. The tension between the Taiwanese and mainlanders in Taiwan is technically sub-ethnic because both groups are members of the same Han Chinese ethnic group who speak different dialects of Chinese, for stylistic reasons. For convenience, the difference between these two groups will be referred to as ethnic in this chapter.

Following its retreat to Taiwan, the KMT regime originally relied heavily on mainlanders, only moving to integrate large numbers of Taiwanese into its ranks in the 1970s. Taiwanese opposition to KMT rule coalesced first into a loose affiliation known as the Tangwai (outside the party) when no opposition parties could be formed, and then into the DPP in the late 1980s, once the formal prohibition on organizing new political parties had been lifted. One of the primary objectives of some members of the DPP has been the declaration of an independent "Republic of Taiwan" and the rejection of the KMT's aspirations to reunite with mainland China at some point in the future. The PRC's opposition to such a move is unequivocal, and it has often reiterated its willingness to use force to prevent Taiwanese secession. With this threat in the background, the degree of public support for the independence of Taiwan is unclear today and is unlikely to be clarified soon. The unresolved tensions between the KMT regime and the CCP regime, and between the two largest ethnic groups inhabiting Taiwan today, put some limits on the full realization of constitutional rule in Taiwan, although the precise dimensions of those limits are impossible to determine.

ROC legal institutions enjoy a distinctive place in Taiwanese society that reflects a particular culturally and historically influenced conception of the appropriate role for legal institutions. Chinese culture and history have been very significant among the many influences on Taiwanese society. The ideological emphasis on the importance of human relationships and ethical behavior in Chinese thought militates against assigning legal institutions the same role they play in legitimating the social order in western societies.[23] Yet no society of the magnitude and complexity of traditional Chinese society could operate without some role for legal institutions.

The Chinese legal historian Ch'u T'ung-tsu (1961) has argued that the resolution of these conflicting impulses in traditional Chinese society was the "Confucianization of law," whereby legal institutions were administered with a view to reinforcing rather than displacing less formal social norms as the basis of the social order. I have argued elsewhere that this same process of preserving a place for legal institutions while subordinating them to the operation of less formal social norms is also operating in contemporary Taiwanese society and can be thought of as the "marginalization of law" (Winn 1994). This process of marginalization can be observed in Taiwanese legal institutions in such processes as the persistent, pervasive use of highly abstract, formalistic language to draft laws that are markedly out of step with local social conditions. Where there is a disconnect between the formal requirements of statutory law and normal social practice, and government officials have inadequate resources to enforce the law, then they may in effect be authorized to use the law selectively to mete out legal sanctions against individuals who have been singled out for enforcement action based on criteria not specified in the law.

---

23. In western societies, the legitimacy of legal institutions is tied up with the evolution of the relationship between church and state from medieval times through the present (see Berman (1983) for an introduction to these issues).

A. Admission to the Bar

Following the reform carried out in the late 1980s, the primary avenue for admission to the ROC bar has been by examination. In the 1990s, of the several thousand candidates who annually sat for the exam, several hundred were admitted to the bar each year. This represents an increase from an average of several dozen each year through 1987. In addition, magistrates or prosecutors who have passed a separate exam still enjoy the right after several years to convert their position as a government legal professional into admission to the private bar. While the large increase in the number of candidates passing the bar exam is having a major impact on the legal profession, these increases nonetheless pale in comparison with the astonishing growth in the legal profession in the PRC. It would be reasonable to expect that in Taiwan, the legal profession may adapt relatively quickly in response to these changes. Changes in Taiwanese society at large occurring as a result of the increased number of attorneys in private practice, however, may be less significant than those occurring in mainland China due to the much larger growth in absolute terms of the legal profession there. Because the magnitude of the change is smaller both in relative and absolute terms, existing ROC institutions may adapt more easily than PRC institutions struggling to accommodate much greater changes.

Before the recent reforms to the bar admission system in Taiwan, there were several avenues to admission to the bar that were at least as important as, if not more important than, the official bar exam. These included service as an attorney for one of the armed forces and passage of a minimal bar exam for those holding positions above a certain rank for a certain period of time within a law faculty in Taiwan. These "backdoors" to admission to the bar were very important when the passage rate for the official bar exam averaged around 1 to 2 percent per year, as it did before 1989. For many years, obtaining a J.D. or other advanced law degree in the U.S. before returning to Taiwan to take up a position teaching part-time in a law faculty was a more certain path to admission to the ROC bar than sitting for the official bar exam, at least for those with the resources to study abroad.

Those who pass the official bar exam are now required to undergo one month of practical training and five months of working under the supervision of an admitted attorney before being permitted to practice independently. In comparison with the quite high incomes newly qualified attorneys could enjoy in the 1980s when only a tiny number of individuals joined the bar each year, pay to new members of the bar during their practical training is now quite modest.[24] In 1995, it was unclear how dramatic the impact of the sudden increase in the number of attorneys admitted to practice ultimately would be on the incomes of attorneys during the early years of their careers. Attorneys

---

24. In 1995, individuals estimated the normal rate of pay during practical training with a law firm to be the equivalent of US$1,000–$1,500 a month. This was less than half of what a newly admitted attorney might have expected to earn ten years earlier.

with large firms reported that newly hired, newly admitted attorneys often had unrealistic expectations regarding the degree of autonomy they should be granted in their work, which might also reflect conflicting ideas regarding an appropriate rate of compensation for newly admitted attorneys working in large firms as well. Many attorneys reported that it was unclear what impact the increasing number of attorneys admitted to local practice would have on the incomes of attorneys generally, because so many newly admitted attorneys had gone to study abroad, had reported for their compulsory military service (in the case of male attorneys), or had moved to the south of Taiwan to establish practices in areas traditionally underserved by the legal profession. Some attorneys speculated that the rising level of demand for legal services caused by the growing sophistication of Taiwan's economy would more than offset the increase in the number of attorneys, so that attorneys capable of delivering the kind of legal services more sophisticated clients were demanding would enjoy rising incomes in any event.

A large amount of legal work is done in Taiwan by legal assistants (*fawu zhuli* or *falü zhuli*), who are individuals who have degrees in law but who have not passed the bar exam. While a bar passage rate of 10 percent is high by historical standards for Taiwan, it is still far below the rate of any state in the U.S., for example. As a result, many individuals wishing to gain admission to the bar must sit for the exam several times before passing, and other individuals fail to pass notwithstanding many attempts to do so. Some of these individuals, and others who are content to work in effect as paralegals rather than aspiring to work as attorneys, do a great deal of legal work in Taiwan either as an employee of a business organization or within a law firm.

A large amount of legal work is also done by individuals admitted to practice law in jurisdictions other than the ROC. Some of these individuals are foreign nationals, and some are Taiwanese who have studied abroad and gained admission to the bar of some other country before returning to Taiwan. Recent reforms in the regulation of foreign-licensed attorneys clarified their right to provide advice to local residents on foreign law (Chiang 1995). These reforms were made in response to pressure from trading partners such as the U.S. for greater openness of the local Taiwanese economy to trade in services, although local attorneys with no connection to foreign law firms or foreign-licensed lawyers had been pressing to restrict their access to the local market. The resistance of local lawyers to any formally recognized role for foreign-licensed lawyers in Taiwan stems in large part from a widespread perception that many of the ROC citizens with law degrees earned in Taiwan who are only admitted to foreign jurisdictions are in fact practicing ROC law in Taiwan. This market for "informal" legal services is possible because clients often do not attach much significance to the fact that an attorney may be advising on local law while he is admitted to practice only in a foreign jurisdiction.

B. Litigation Practice

The ROC legal system was modeled originally on the German and Japanese legal systems, although in recent years legislation from the U.S. and other countries in the common law tradition has been quite influential.[25] One consequence of following the continental European civil law tradition in establishing ROC legal institutions has been a relatively greater emphasis on litigation as the core of private practice rather than the more general business counseling function performed by many U.S. lawyers in private practice.[26] In keeping with the different procedural and evidentiary conventions of the common law and civil law systems, the ROC legal system places less emphasis on oral advocacy, the oral testimony of witnesses, and procedural requirements for introducing evidence in court.

The attorneys interviewed all agreed that most practicing attorneys in Taiwan practice in the Taipei metropolitan region, that most are in solo practice, and that both civil and criminal litigation is a major component of the work of attorneys in solo practice. Attorneys associated with law firms serving major local companies or major foreign investors, including both local law firms and local offices of foreign law firms, reported that local lawyers who had not practiced with the handful of large corporate law offices established in Taipei or received any legal training outside Taiwan had almost exclusively litigation-oriented practices, although this observation was not confirmed by local attorneys. Attorneys in large law firms, whether locally owned or owned by foreign law firms, were also almost uniformly dismissive of the sophistication of locally trained attorneys in solo practice or small firms in dealing with complex business matters.

Attorneys in Taiwan charge clients a lump-sum fee for litigation matters, with representation in each instance subject to a separate lump-sum payment. Local bar associations publish suggested fee rates, but an individual attorney and client are free to negotiate the amount of the fee either up or down using the bar association figures as a starting point. Only attorneys in local branches of U.S. or other foreign law firms, or those in the small number of local law firms that are organized along the lines of U.S. corporate law firms and that service foreign clients, are able to charge hourly fees for their work. Contingent fees are not permitted in Taiwan.

The large number of attorneys in Taiwan whose prior practice experience was in legal work for the military were generally reported to focus on criminal litigation in their private practice, although I was unable to interview any such attorneys to confirm this generalization. I also had no way to evaluate the reliability of reports that attorneys with military backgrounds were more likely

---

25. See generally Abel (1988, 1).

26. For a general discussion of the differences between the legal profession in the U.S. and in continental Europe, including the development of the distinctive U.S. large law firm practice with an emphasis on general business counseling rather than a narrow focus on litigation, see Osiel (1990).

than other attorneys to have clients who expect their attorney to make improper ex parte contacts with magistrates or prosecutors, including offering bribes. In 1994, a survey by the popular newsweekly *T'ien-hsia Tsa-chih* (Commonwealth Magazine) found that the perception that bribery was common and could be effective in influencing the outcome of litigation was widespread in Taiwan, although the perception was more common among people with advanced degrees and less common among those with only primary school education (Shen 1994, 27).

Some individual attorneys in Taiwan take on selected litigation matters on a pro bono basis, although there is no evidence that such efforts are having any noteworthy successes.[27] One attorney with an advanced degree in law from the U.S. working for a large local firm reported to have close ties to the KMT was permitted by his partners to take appellate cases raising important constitutional law issues on a pro bono basis.[28] The attorney was hoping to establish an ROC constitutional law jurisprudence, although by 1995, he had not managed to achieve any precedent-setting cases. The fact that his law firm, which also has very close ties to the foreign investor community, was willing to support his work might be an indication that the classical liberal ideal of autonomous professional is gaining ground in Taiwan.[29]

Another indication that the notion of professional autonomy was gaining some ground came from an attorney who had represented one of the Kaohsiung defendants in 1979[30] and had gone on to represent many more dissidents over the years. This attorney was a recognized expert in maritime insurance law and had enjoyed a successful private practice with a minimum of interference from the government as a result of his work representing political dissidents, even during the period of martial law. He was still active in such organizations as the Human Rights Committee of the Taiwan Bar Association. He also noted, however, that he had not enjoyed any significant successes to date in litigation involving either political dissent under martial law, or more recently, human rights issues following the repeal of martial law. He observed that although the magistrates before whom he has appeared in such cases seem to be taking his clients' claims seriously, the results have always been disappointing. He also observed that while an individual judge might not have any party affiliation or political bias that would affect the outcome of a politically sensitive case, the opinions of individual judges had to be approved by their supervisors

27. In addition, attorneys reported that the Taipei Bar Association has a pro bono program, and some organizations such as the KMT provide financial support to legal aid clinics established to represent the poor. I did not investigate these organizations while I was in Taiwan in 1995.

28. This attorney was also serving as a KMT member of the National Assembly.

29. It might also be evidence of the sophistication of some lawyers at cultivating a liberal public image for the legal profession that distracts from more critical evaluation of the actual social purposes being served by the work of attorneys. See generally Ellmann (1995).

30. See note 20.

(*yuanzhang*) before they could be issued and the risk of political bias among judicial personnel grew at higher levels in the judicial bureaucracy.

C. Legal Counselor

Notwithstanding the insistence of lawyers in Taiwan practicing in large U.S.-style firms that local attorneys in solo practice or small firms handled litigation matters exclusively, there is apparently a long-standing tradition of local attorneys establishing general legal counseling relationships (*falü guwen*) with local businesses and individuals, for which they are paid a sort of retainer fee in monthly installments for this service. One attorney estimated that a well-known attorney with an established practice might receive a fee of NT$100,000 on an annual basis for a *falü guwen* relationship with a business, whereas a young lawyer new to law practice might only be able to ask for NT$10,000 a year to establish a similar sort of relationship with a business.[31] The attorney presents the represented business with a framed plaque announcing the relationship which is hung conspicuously in the client's place of business. In return for the fixed fee, a client might expect to be able to call the attorney without charge and receive answers to simple questions; to receive a discount on the lump-sum fee set in litigation matters, writing opinions, or drafting contracts; to have the attorney write a letter or two on behalf of the client to resolve disputes short of litigating them; or to receive a newsletter discussing recent legal developments.

D. Transactional and Regulatory Practice

Attorneys with a foreign legal education or with practice experience at the large firms in Taipei also generally reported that local attorneys in solo practice could not represent clients in what might be large and complex business transactions. This generalization was not wholly inaccurate, but overlooked the degree to which local attorneys in solo practice or small firms might represent local businesses in business transactions such as real estate developments. Many attorneys reported that with the tremendous growth in Taiwan's economy since the 1950s in general, and the high prices for real estate in recent decades in particular, local businesspeople were recognizing the need for lawyers even in transactions between two local parties. One distinction between the transaction practice of local attorneys in solo practice or small firms and that of attorneys in U.S.-style Taipei firms was the ability to charge clients by the hour for legal work rather than being obliged to negotiate a fixed sum at the time the representation was undertaken. Even transactional work done for fixed amounts was increasing in profitability, however, because clients were generally prepared to base the fee at least in part on the value of the transaction which with rising real estate values, had considerably increased in recent years.

With regard to business transactions involving more complex forms of business regulation, however, there appeared to be a consensus that this work was

---

31. At the time in question, the exchange rate was approximately NT$35:US$1.

done largely by the large, locally owned law firms organized like U.S. corporate law firms or by branches of foreign law firms. This includes work in areas such as securities and bank regulation, foreign investment, intellectual property rights, and international tax. Attorneys working for these firms reported that the increase in the bar passage rate may have been in part a response to the trouble such firms were having hiring local attorneys. In the 1980s, when severe restrictions on the number of attorneys admitted to practice each year were in effect, an attorney who passed the bar exam could immediately set up a solo practice and enjoy a substantial income. Such an attorney joining a U.S.-style firm, whether locally or foreign-owned, would be expected to work as an associate under the supervision of a partner for several years before being allowed to practice independently. The short-term prospect of working under the supervision of partners for a salary, even when the long-term prospect was access to the lucrative market for representing multinational firms in complex corporate and regulatory practice, was simply not appealing enough to attract many licensed attorneys. As a result, U.S.-style firms had an even more hierarchical structure than they have in the U.S., with a tiny number of partners admitted to local practice supervising a very large number of locally educated and foreign-educated legal assistants who were not admitted to practice, and foreign-admitted attorneys who were not admitted locally.

E. Lobbying

Many people recognized the concept of lobbying in general, but very few thought that the western idea of lobbying aimed at producing specific legislative provisions to advance a client's interest had much currency in Taiwan. Most observers felt that individuals in Taiwan were very familiar with the idea of asking an elected representative to intervene in some government process in order to improve the odds of a favorable outcome. Such lobbying was thought to be commonplace and generally not to involve lawyers. The local political culture of Taiwan is very well developed, because for years before the lifting of martial law and recent constitutional reforms went into effect, elections at the county and provincial level were vigorously contested. The political culture of Taiwan has also been influenced by the single nontransferable vote system, which encourages candidates to take whatever actions are necessary to develop a personal following among voters. Allegations of vote-buying and corruption in political processes are widespread in Taiwan, and client-like relationships between individual citizens and their elected representatives are common.[32] The strength of this political culture will mitigate against the development of lobbying as a professional service attorneys could provide to their clients, at least in the short-term.

---

32. For an overview of contemporary Taiwanese political processes and an explanation of how the single nontransferable vote system tends to favor well-known candidates at the expense of internal party discipline, see Tien and Cheng (1997).

The lack of interest among many in Taiwan in the process of lobbying to influence the content of legislation also reflects the relative lack of power of legislative bodies in Taiwan prior to the lifting of martial law and recent constitutional reforms. Until the early 1990s, important political decisions were taken within the KMT and within the executive branch of government, and their formal recognition by the national or provincial legislatures did not involve the exercise of any power independent of KMT controls. With the deepening of democratic reforms in Taiwan, elected representatives have more opportunities to determine the content of legislation within open legislative processes.

A small handful of attorneys with advanced degrees in law from U.S. law schools reported isolated cases of successfully influencing the outcome of legislation through participation in legislative processes. These attorneys reported an uphill battle both in terms of convincing their clients of the value of this form of representation and in terms of gaining effective access to legislators who historically played little or no role in determining the text of legislation. If the success these attorneys enjoyed in persuading lawmakers to reconsider the text of legislation from their clients' perspectives is translated into favorable outcomes for their clients when the legislation is enforced, it stands to reason that this type of lobbying might rapidly gain wider acceptance in Taiwan in the future.

F.   Local Bar Associations

Until the repeal of martial law in the late 1980s and the electoral reforms instituted in the early 1990s, bar associations in Taiwan were little more than agencies of government control over lawyers in private practice. Membership in at least one officially registered bar association was mandatory under the Lawyer Law, although attorneys might join more than one bar association. No bar association as such could be formed without being registered with the government.

An informal independent bar association was formed in the 1970s as the Comparative Law Association. This was a voluntary association of progressive-minded attorneys that included lawyers and law professors, including many individuals that became active in the Tangwai and subsequently, the DPP. More than one attorney recalled that government attorneys who apparently wanted to join were prevented from doing so by pressure from the government. Many members of the association had received some legal education outside Taiwan. One lawyer recalled that the Asia Foundation provided the association with financial support to send a group of lawyers to the U.S. to study legal aid programs there, leading to the establishment of the first legal aid program in Taiwan.

In the late 1980s, after the repeal of martial law, and as the tempo of liberalization accelerated, there was growing pressure within formal bar associations to achieve greater practical autonomy from government or KMT oversight. In 1990, some leading Taiwanese attorneys from major Taipei law firms convinced M. S. Lin, the head of the Taiwan International Law and Patent Office, one of the largest, oldest, locally owned law firms, to lead a successful movement to take control of the board of directors of the Taipei Bar Association away from lawyers with close connections to the government. Following this sudden change in fortunes for the leadership of the Taipei Bar Association, in 1993, progressive lawyers led by M. S. Lin went on to take control of the national federation of bar associations.

While the leaders of this movement clearly felt that they were advancing the cause of an autonomous legal profession, many attorneys with mainlander backgrounds or connections to the KMT noted that M. S. Lin did not seem concerned by the apparent conflict of interest arising from his support of the DPP and the newly autonomous Taipei Bar Association's opposition, under his leadership, to the appointment of General Hau Po-ts'un as prime minister in 1990. Supporters of M. S. Lin's leadership defended the position he took by pointing out that keeping the armed forces and constitutional organs of government separate is an essential element of liberalization and democratization and that the Taipei Bar Association's opposition to Hau's appointment need not be seen as linked to partisan motivations.

III.   Limits to Liberalization Within Taiwanese Society

While considerable progress has been made toward democratizing and liberalizing Taiwanese society, it is also clear that considerable obstacles to further deepening those reforms remain and that those obstacles may prevent the further progress of Taiwan's legal profession toward the classical liberal ideal of an autonomous profession. The most prudent political outcome regarding the unresolved issues surrounding Taiwan's sovereignty and its relationship to the PRC and the unresolved issues surrounding ethnic tensions in Taiwan may be to avoid any resolution of those issues. The leadership of the KMT has already substantially devolved to Taiwanese control under the leadership of Taiwanese politicians such as Lee Teng-hui, a trend that has continued under the DPP presidency of Chen Shui-bian. The threat of the use of military force by the PRC is a powerful countervailing force to any impulse on the part of the Taiwanese majority to declare the formation of the Republic of Taiwan, yet few in Taiwan can see any conditions under which Taiwan would voluntarily reunite with mainland China in the near future. The best prospect for continuing advances in political self-determination and the economic well-being of the people of Taiwan appears to require leaving these major issues unresolved indefinitely.

One force that for decades has pressed for greater autonomy for legal institutions and greater respect for formal law in Taiwan is the foreign investor community in Taiwan, although it is unclear how this pressure correlates with the deepening of democratic reforms. Multinational enterprises that have invested in Taiwan are accustomed to working through law firms in dealing with ROC government agencies and to having their concerns addressed within the framework of current laws and regulations. None of the individuals I spoke with in 1995 made any reference to foreign corporations feeling pressured to resort to bribery or to mobilizing personal relationships in order to accomplish their objectives in Taiwan. Many individuals reported instead that the observance of legal formalities by foreign corporations created an environment within which local businesses might also enjoy the protections of modern laws and regulations. On the other hand, descriptions of bribery, vote-buying or other improper uses of private influence in public processes were common in describing how local people might try to influence the outcomes of legal or political decisions.[33] If these anecdotal descriptions reflect a deeper social reality, it seems likely that legal institutions in Taiwan are stratified to some degree, with some layers embodying the ideals of liberal legality to a much greater degree than others. If such stratification is significant and persistent, it might create an important obstacle to the deepening of liberalizing reforms in Taiwan.

While some participants in Taiwanese society (including more than just foreign investors and political dissidents) may perceive their self-interest to be better-advanced by relying on their formal legal rights than on informal networks of personal relationships, there will inevitably be those in Taiwan who believe their self-interest can be better-advanced by the continued marginalization of legal institutions. Such individuals might include political leaders of whatever party affiliation who believe that the best form of government for Taiwan is one in which the most important powers of government are concentrated in the executive branch with many fewer powers being exercised by the legislative and judicial branches. Such individuals might include those who believe that control of the government by a single party, whether KMT or DPP, is in their best interests as individuals, and who are not particularly concerned about any larger conception of the public interest. A large number of individuals who prefer marginalized legal institutions are likely to be those who feel they can resolve their problems more effectively through informal networks of relationships.

If legal institutions in Taiwan remain marginalized, then some individuals in Taiwanese society will play the role of fixer to mediate between interests defined by the informal coercive systems that perform the functions associated with legal institutions in other societies. These individuals may leverage political, social or economic power in order to perform this function effectively. If attorneys in Taiwan are willing to combine the more traditional role of fixer with the more modern role of attorney, then the legal profession may continue to grow in number and enjoy considerable economic success without promoting the deepening of democratic and liberalizing reforms. For example, hiring a lawyer to bribe a magistrate or prosecutor because the lawyer has personal connections

---

33. None of the individuals I spoke with admitted to any firsthand knowledge of bribery or corruption in the administration of the law in Taiwan, but no one suggested that the widespread reports of such practices were simply false. For example, one lawyer explained that prospective clients knew which lawyers could be expected to help make improper offers to judges and prosecutors and which would not, so an attorney with a reputation for being clean would not receive such offers. The same lawyer noted that judges were referred to as "carnivorous" or "vegetarian" based on their reputation for being amenable to improper influences.

to the magistrate or prosecutor represents hiring the lawyer to act as fixer and tends to subvert the effectiveness of legal processes.

To the extent that Taiwanese society is predominantly composed of individuals with a limited commitment to, or understanding of, classical liberal notions such as individual autonomy, civil society, the public sphere, or the rule of law, it is entirely possible that any attorney who relied too heavily on the classical liberal ideal of disinterested professional might have trouble attracting clients due to a lack of interest among prospective clients in the services such a lawyer would offer. On the other hand, even individuals with a limited appreciation for liberal ideals might appreciate the notion of lawyer as committed, combative advocate or as flamboyant, glamorous agent enough to pay for legal services from such an attorney. Professor Alford has noted the recent rise of this kind of entrepreneurial lawyering in the PRC. As the number of lawyers in private practice continues to grow rapidly in Taiwan, it is possible that this kind of entrepreneurial lawyering will also grow more common there, too, as attorneys seek new ways to enhance the market value of their admission to the bar. If the entrepreneurial model of lawyering gains currency in Taiwan, then the same debate over whether the regulation of the legal profession should be modified to take into account the commercialization of law practice could be expected to spread from western nations to Taiwan.

Many attorneys within Taiwan have shown a commitment to advancing the classical liberal ideal of the rule of law. One attorney was instrumental in establishing the Rule of Law Foundation, which he hoped would become a force for positive change in Taiwanese society. Several attorneys reported having worked in an anti-corruption campaign after martial law was lifted that was aimed at cleaning up the electoral process. One of these attorneys emphasized that in the course of his involvement, he discovered that the stereotype of rural Taiwanese as indifferent to corruption in government was untrue.

Many attorneys, however, still show relatively little interest in or appreciation for the notion of a legal sphere divorced from political pressures. In 1995, the then-current case of Chen Shui-bian was much discussed as an example of the failure of many involved in the administration of law to appreciate this idea. Several years earlier, Chen had torn up some ballots while serving as a DPP legislator in the Legislative Yuan. The Legislative Yuan, apparently acting through the KMT majority, later referred the matter to an investigating magistrate as a possible violation of the criminal law. When the investigating magistrate later subpoenaed Chen, who by then had been elected mayor of Taipei, Chen refused to respond on the grounds that the destruction of the ballots had been a political act and that he should be covered by some sort of theory of legislative immunity. Eventually, the investigating magistrate issued an arrest warrant to try to force Chen to submit to his jurisdiction, but since Chen was the mayor, none of the local law enforcement personnel were willing to execute the warrant. Chen eventually made a voluntary appearance before the magistrate but refused to answer any of the magistrate's questions on the grounds that the matter was political, not legal. The case was extremely controversial at the time and suggests that either the administration of Chen's case was influenced by the party loyalties of at least some of the legal personnel involved or that ROC law on legislative immunity needs to be strengthened to be more consistent with Taiwan's vigorous party politics.

IV. The Effect of Forces for Regional Integration and Globalization on Taiwan's Legal Profession

If Taiwan's lawyers want to play a central role in the next stage of Taiwan's development, that role may differ depending on whether or not the next stage is more dependent on the PRC than on trading partners such as the U.S., the European Union, Australia, and other countries with developed modern legal systems. The historical connection between U.S.-style law firms in Taipei, multinational corporations investing in Taiwan, and the promotion of stable, relatively autonomous legal institutions could play a pivotal role in the future shape of Taiwan's democracy if Taiwan continues to grow closer to countries with western-style legal systems and the foreign interests in Taiwan exercise their influence responsibly. If the interests of foreign corporations in Taiwan are seen as primarily predatory or opportunistic, then their support for more vigorous legal institutions in Taiwan would be limited to protecting their self-interest and not extend to a more general support for liberalization. I raised this possibility with almost everyone I met in 1995 and was unable to find a single individual who would agree that this was a serious concern for the people of Taiwan.

It may have been true at one time that some foreign corporations sought out trade and investment opportunities in Taiwan precisely because of less rigorous law enforcement or dramatically lower legal standards than would apply to their operations elsewhere, but by 1995 such concerns had apparently been allayed. Many individuals argued that far from being a force of oppression, foreign corporations and foreign law firms had been an important force in supporting liberalization. That influence would become less relevant to the political economy of Taiwan if individual Taiwanese perceived their long-term self-interest to be closer relations with mainland China rather than closer relations with North America, Europe, Australia, and New Zealand.

Taiwan's economy is growing ever more intertwined with the economy of the PRC. If Taiwan's investors can protect their interests in the PRC and are allowed to enjoy their profits, they will continue to invest. It is unlikely that in the near future the PRC legal system will attain the same level of integrity and stability as that of the ROC legal system. Therefore, Taiwanese investors must find substitutes for the formal legal protection of their interests, given that the PRC legal system cannot yet provide Taiwanese investors with the same degree of legal recognition they enjoy under the ROC legal system. While the PRC welcomes Taiwanese investors with open arms, individuals with PRC passports do not currently enjoy the same degree of freedom to move to Taiwan and establish operations there. It is therefore unclear what direct impact, if any, the growing involvement of Taiwanese investors in mainland China will have on the integrity and stability of ROC legal institutions so long as there is no formal recognition of PRC sovereignty over Taiwan. The relative underdevelopment of PRC legal institutions may have a considerable indirect impact on the practice of law in Taiwan, however, if Taiwanese lawyers actively seek out opportunities to represent local interests in their activities in mainland China.

Taiwanese investors in mainland China may be relying on networks of personal relationships to protect their investments. If so, Taiwanese investors may be relying on the services of fixers on mainland China for protection rather than depending on PRC or ROC lawyers. ROC lawyers may, nevertheless, be able to play an important role as intermediaries facilitating Taiwanese investment in the PRC where Taiwanese investors are not content to rely on personal connections alone to protect their interests in the PRC. Liberalization in China may be bringing the PRC practice of law roughly into line with the practice of law in Taiwan ten, twenty, or thirty years ago during the heyday of Taiwan's export-led industrialization. Just as many Taiwanese investments in China consist of moving sunset industries from Taiwan to China to take advantage of lower labor costs, ROC lawyers familiar with an earlier generation of more informal business and government practices may find uses in China for skills that may be growing outmoded in Taiwan due to the more rapid pace of its liberalization.

Conclusion

This chapter has identified three possible future directions for Taiwan's legal profession and considered the likely impact each of those three directions would have on the future of Taiwan's current progress toward more liberal economic, political and legal institutions. One future direction would be continued movement toward an independent profession that would enhance the rule of law in Taiwanese society. While Taiwan's legal profession was hindered in the past from playing this role by martial law and one-party rule, the process of democratization and liberalization in Taiwan generally is creating more opportunities for lawyers to move the legal profession further in the direction of autonomy and the ideals of professionalism. However, as long as Taiwan's transition to democracy remains incomplete, whether because of Taiwan's unresolved issues surrounding sovereignty or ethnic relations, or due to the strength of the forces supporting factionalism and corruption in Taiwan's political processes, it seems unlikely that the profession will make dramatic strides in this direction.

Taiwan's legal profession is more likely to embrace the model of the entrepreneurial lawyer. The commercialization of the legal profession may be subversive of many classical liberal political ideals, but it is not inconsistent with further advances in the liberalization of Taiwan's economy and its continued opening to the forces of global competition. Western liberal democracies are struggling with what appears to some to be a rising tide of entrepreneurial thinking within the modern professions, so it seems implausible to think that as Taiwanese society becomes more closely integrated into the global economy, the same forces will not be at work in Taiwan. With less of a history of liberal professionalism to fall back on, the idea of exploiting a professional license as a commercial property may prove very compelling in Taiwan. This is especially true if the number of lawyers continues to increase at a rapid pace, creating a large number of newly licensed attorneys competing in a relatively small market for legal services.

Another possibility is that attorneys will use their license to practice law merely as a point of entry into a relationship with a client and will mobilize a variety of other, more informal forms of coercive social ordering where necessary to achieve a client's objectives effectively. As the sophistication and diversity of Taiwan's connections to the global economy grow, lawyers in Taiwan will have more opportunities to practice law according to modern, western norms. As Taiwan's connections to mainland China grow, however, it is unclear how Taiwanese attorneys will try to define their role in protecting client interests. Taiwanese investors in China will need some form of informal protection of their interests until PRC legal institutions become more sophisticated and more effective. Taiwanese lawyers may be able to parlay their familiarity with both formal legal processes and less formal processes common to both Taiwan and China into a hybrid role as fixer for Taiwanese interests in mainland China.

Works Cited

Abel, Richard L. 1988. Lawyers in the civil law world. In *Lawyers in society: Comparative theories*, eds. R. L. Abel and P. S. C. Lewis. Berkeley: University of California Press.

Berman, Harold. 1983. *Law and revolution: The formation of the western legal tradition.* Cambridge: Harvard University Press.

Chiang, Darryl D. 1995. Foreign lawyer provisions in Hong Kong and the Republic of China on Taiwan. 13 *UCLA Pacific Basin Law Journal* 306.

Ch'u T'ung-tsu. 1961. *Law and society in traditional China.* The Hague: Mouton.

Ellmann, Steven. 1995. Law and legitimacy in Supreme Africa. 20 *Law & Social Inquiry* 407.

Felstiner, William L. F. 1974. Influences of social organization. 9 *Law & Society Review* 1:63–94.

Galanter, Mary. 1981. Justice in many rooms: Courts, private ordering, and indigenous law. 19 *Journal of Legal Pluralism* 1.

Greif, Avner. 1997. Contracting, enforcement and efficiency: Economics beyond the law. *Annual World Bank Conference on Development Economics 1996.* World Bank.

Hamilton, Gary. 1990. Patriarchy patrimonialism and filial piety: A comparison of China and Western Europe. *British Journal of Sociology* 41:77.

Hwang Jau-yuan. 1995. Constitutional change and political transition in Taiwan since 1986: The role of legal institutions. S.J.D. dissertation. On file at Harvard Law School, Cambridge, MA.

Kaplan, John. 1981. *The court-martial of the Kaohsiung defendants.* Berkeley: Institute of East Asian Studies, University of California.

Macaulay, Stewart S. 1963. Non-contractual relations in business: A preliminary study. *American Society Review* 28:55.

Macauley, Melissa Ann. 1998. *Social power and legal culture: Litigation masters in late Imperial China.* Stanford: Stanford University Press.

Merry, Sally Engle. 1988. Legal pluralism. 22 *Law & Society Review* 869.

Moore, Sally Falk. 1978. *Law as process: An anthropological approach.* Oxford: Oxford University Press.

New York Times. 1998. Editorial. Beyond the Schumer victory. 4 November.

Northwestern University Law Review. Spring 2000. Symposium issue on relational contract.

Osiel, Mark. 1990. Lawyers as monopolists, aristocrats and entrepreneurs. 103 *Harvard Law Review* 2009.

Parsons, Talcott. 1968. Professions. In *International encyclopedia of the social sciences,* ed. D. Sills. Vol. XII. New York: MacMillan.

Shen, Hsü-ying. 1994. Hung-bao tan tao, ch'ing-t'ien jang lu? [Will bribery push justice aside?]. *T'ien-hsia Tsa-chih* [Commonwealth magazine]. 1 July.

Tien, Hung-mao and Tun-jen Cheng. 1997. Crafting democratic institutions in Taiwan. *The China Journal* 37:1.

Trubek, David, Yves Dezalay, Ruth Buchanan, and John Davis. 1994. The future of the legal profession: Global restructuring and the law: Studies in the internationalization of legal fields and the creation of transnational arenas. 44 *Case Western Reserve Law Review* 407.

Wang, Tay-sheng. 1992. Legal reform in Taiwan under Japanese colonial rule (1895–1945): The reception of western law. Ph.D. dissertation. University of Washington, Seattle, Washington.

Wank, David L. 1999. *Commodifying communism: Business, trust and politics in a Chinese city.* New York: Cambridge University Press.

Wilkins, David B. 1990. Legal realism for lawyers. 104 *Harvard Law Review* 469.

Winn, Jane Kaufman. 1994. Relational practices and the marginalization of law: Informal financial practices of small businesses in Taiwan. 28 *Law & Society Review* 193.

——— and Tang-chi Yeh. 1995. Advocating democracy: The role of lawyers in Taiwan's political transformation. (Symposium on lawyering against injustice and the danger of legitimation.) 20 *Law & Social Inquiry* 561.

Yan, Yunxiang. 2000. *Liwu de liudang* [Flow of gifts]. Shanghai: Shanghai Renmin Chubanshe.

Yang, Mayfair Mei-hui. 1994. *Gifts, favors and banquets: The art of social relationships in China.* Ithaca: Cornell University Press.

TEN

A Tale of Two Legal Professions: Lawyers and State in Malaysia and Indonesia

Daniel S. Lev*

Introduction

Of the few hundred questions that can be asked about lawyers, the ones posed here concern their relationships with political authority. The conditioning connection between political environment and the practice of law, historically important to both, is often obscured by the mythologies that evolve to legitimate legal and political institutions and rationalize their working orders. Explaining the evolutionary paths of legal institutions anywhere is seldom easy, partly because of the ideological baggage that usually trails the analysis of just about anything we isolate into a compartment labeled "legal."

In this chapter, "legal" is usually intended also to imply "political," "economic," "organizational," and "ideological" in an effort to understand empirically the influences most likely to affect the evolution of private legal professions. By comparing two legal professions, one in Malaysia and the other in Indonesia, I hope to avoid a too simple rendering of either case in an effort to show how and why they differ.

The function of private lawyers most relevant to this analytical perspective is that of intermediary between private economic and social interests, on the one hand, and public institutional authority on the other. With their feet firmly planted in both camps, lawyers have good reason to attend to the disparate claims on their attention. Professional ideology is likely to emphasize lawyers' interests in maintaining an effective legal, especially judicial, process in which the role of lawyers is recognized and respected. But it is also likely to reflect the concerns of the clientele lawyers represent. Given their expertise in relations between state and society, it is not surprising that lawyers often take a special interest in politics, nor that state leaders may find them rather useful or especially irritating. The primary concern of this chapter is with the tensions that

---

*Emeritus Professor of Political Science at the University of Washington.

arise as private lawyers and political leaders circle around one another and with the consequences that mark the evolution of the local legal profession.[1]

The two legal professions dealt with here are as much studies in contrast as the countries in which they work. Malaysia, with a population of about 23 million, is a demographic mix of ethnic Malays, Chinese, and Indians, an amalgam that defines the foundation of the society and its political system. Granted independence peacefully by Great Britain in 1957, it inherited a colonial version of English common law. Indonesia is no less diverse ethnically and religiously but disproportionately and on a much larger scale, with a population of 215 million spread over an immense archipelago. It won its independence from the Netherlands after a revolution (1945–1950) that generated much social and political turmoil thereafter. Its legal heritage from the Netherlands Indies was a continental civil law system replete with constructed fault lines along ethnic and religious divides.

The legal professions of the two countries have followed quite different trajectories of change. Malaysia's is well trained, highly organized, and influential. Nothing could be less true of Indonesian lawyers—mainly advocates, for our purposes, not notaries—who are divided, not always well trained, weakly organized, and professionally only marginally influential. Tracing the postcolonial evolution of the two professions will help to explain the differences.

I. The Malaysian Bar

When Malaya became independent in 1957, one might well have wondered whether the local bar would survive intact.[2] It was quite small, about 300 in a population then of about 7 million—one lawyer per 23,000 people—and badly skewed ethnically. In the colony, where English lawyers dominated, early in the twentieth century Indians first and then Chinese gradually paid their own ways to London and the Inns of Court. The colonial government funded the legal education of a few Malays who, it was assumed, would enter the administrative service, not the private sector. Consequently, by 1957 in a population divided among about 52 percent Malays, 33 percent Chinese, and 10 percent Indians, the bar

---

1. Equally important perhaps is the influence private lawyers have on the evolution of the state. A related matter of secondary interest here, which will not be treated in detail but which deserves more than passing mention, is that the legal profession (like other professions in various proportions) serves through recruitment as a channel that either restricts or promotes social mobility and reflects, in some measure, class interests, ideological directions, and changing social norms. Historically, both the Malaysian and Indonesian professions have tended to notable ethnic and religious diversity in their memberships and have been equally quick to absorb women lawyers over the last several decades.

2. "Malaya" refers to pre-1963 peninsular Malaya. Malaysia, now consisting of peninsular Malaya and the north Bornean provinces of Sarawak and Sabah, came into being in 1963. A solid introduction to law and legal process in Malaysia can be found in Harding (1996).

then consisted of approximately 50 percent Chinese, 40 percent Indians, less than 5 percent Malay, and the rest resident English lawyers.[3]

As ethnicity is basic to Malaysian politics, it is essential to explain how the bar not only survived a precarious ethnic division of labor but in many ways transcended it. An analysis of the conditions that allowed the private legal profession to evolve as a solid institution in Malaysia may throw some light on why it did not in Indonesia.

The Malaysian bar had several advantages from the start. As sovereignty changed hands routinely, there was no sudden political or social upheaval to raise serious questions about existing institutional or political processes. Social stability underlay political stability and continuity. The judiciary left behind by the colonial administration was well organized, and judges were highly educated and accomplished lawyers, many of whom belonged to the national elite; few doubts arose about how the courts exercised their responsibilities. The same was true of the practicing bar. An informed visitor to Malaya before and after independence, even thirty years or so after, would not have noticed many significant differences in the judiciary or, for that matter, the offices of most lawyers. From Daumier prints on the walls to expensive wigs in the courtrooms, not much changed. Until relatively recently, despite pressure to shift to Malay, English was taken for granted in the courts (and still is in higher courts) and is the preferred language among lawyers of every ethnic origin. It is the one language all lawyers comfortably share in common, though pressure is forcing some change in the extent to which Malay is heard in trial.

For the most part, until the 1970s, for reasons both simple and complex, the government left the legal profession to itself. The simpler reason was that key political leaders were themselves trained in the law, knew members of the bar, and regarded most of them, such as judges, as trustworthy familiars. The first three prime ministers were lawyers—one of whom had actually practiced before taking office—which gave lawyers some confidence in the political elite and its respect for the law.

Political leaders took it for granted that the integrity of the legal process had to be maintained, not only because many of them were legally trained, but because it promised the safest means to deal with a perilous ethnic structure in which Malays, Chinese, and Indians doubted one another's intentions in the independent state. The three major parties that emerged during the late 1940s had mobilized along ethnic lines: the United Malay National Organization (UMNO), the Malayan Chinese Association (MCA), and the Malayan Indian Congress (MIC). By 1952, however, leaders of these parties joined forces in the National Alliance (since 1970 it has been called the National Front or *Barisan Nasional*), which reduced the likelihood of violent ethnic conflict. Along with other considerations favoring a strong legal system, it may well have been agreed, at least tacitly, that an effectively neutral legal process offered fuller

---

3. These data are drawn from census reports, the directories of the Bar Society, and gazettes of the period.

assurance of ethnic comity. A parliamentary system, persistently controlled by the Alliance (and within it by UMNO), and a trustworthy legal system promised political stability based on the support of the principal ethnic elites.

The legal profession fit contentedly into this picture. Encased by traditions carried over from the colonial period without contest, the Bar Society and its leadership, the Bar Council, were well organized, respected, autonomous, and untroubled by external interference. New recruits from the Inns of Court and the University of Singapore and then the University of Malaya and the law schools of Australia came in a slow but steady stream; work was adequate for a few long-established and prominent firms and smaller offices, and appointment to the prestigious courts was treasured. Judges, prosecutors, practicing lawyers, and various political prominents in the relatively small country knew one another and mingled comfortably.

Tensions between the bar and political leaders were, then, at first either nonexistent or distinctly subdued. Most private lawyers were in tune ideologically and politically with the parliamentary system, its emphasis on the rule of law, and, significantly, its concern to avoid ethnic conflict. The Bar Council spoke out on issues of principle occasionally, but seldom, if ever, vituperatively. The profession took for granted its responsibility to comment on legal matters, relevant government policies, the courts, and professional questions, and the government usually listened.

During the early years of independence, the Malaysian bar had the substantial advantages of professional autonomy, sound organization, institutional and public respect, and a state commitment to an effective legal process in a workable parliamentary system. By the time political leaders became testy with lawyers during the 1970s, the profession was well enough established and confident to hold its own.

Malaysian lawyers came late to activism in part for the lack of a tradition in it, but also because there seemed little enough about which to be active.[4] Activism, after all, requires a sense that something in the political order or social structure or legal system is fundamentally wrong, professionally disadvantageous, or unjust and in need of righting. Malaysia's share of injustice was greater than the sense of it among lawyers, whose own status and welfare seemed reasonably well assured, but there were few social problems that anyone supposed the government was incompetent to address in good time. The judiciary worked well, with competent, prestigious, and autonomous judges, whose connections in high political and social places disinclined them either to challenge the decisions of political leaders or, on the opposite end, to toe the line too respectfully on institutional issues. With few exceptions, the same was true of private lawyers. In Malaysia, unlike Indonesia, it was the government, not the legal profession, which first took the initiative to establish limited legal aid services.

---

4. Much, but not all, of the remainder of the discussion of the Malaysian bar is imported, with minor revisions, from my chapter "Lawyers' Causes in Indonesia and Malaysia" in Sarat and Scheingold (1998).

The government, moreover, was sensitive to the ethnic structure of Malaysia to which private lawyers also had good reason to be sensitive. In 1970, thirteen years after independence and on the eve of a period of state-driven economic growth that transformed Malaysia (and its professions), the Malaysian bar had more than doubled since 1957 to over 700 members, but still only 38 (5.39 percent) were Malay, 364 (51.70 percent) Chinese, 251 (35.65 percent) Indian, and 52 (7.26 percent) British.[5]

In response to serious ethnic riots in May of 1969, set off by the results of national elections, the government developed a New Economic Policy (NEP) intended to redress economic balances between the ethnic communities, basically by way of direct assistance and encouragement to Malays, on the one hand, and an effort to promote overall economic growth on the other. Although much-criticized and resented, in several respects the NEP had some significant successes on both scores. The legal profession itself offers a prime example.

Public support of legal education for Malays began to change the ethnic structure of the profession, while at the same time the bar grew and flourished with economic growth. From 1970 to 1984, the number of lawyers again more than doubled to 1,658, of whom 48.5 percent were Chinese, 32.25 percent Indian, and 16.25 percent Malay, up from 5 percent.[6] By 1992, the profession more than doubled once more to over 3,800, of whom 1,704 (44.67 percent) were Chinese; Indians and others were about 32 percent; and Malays numbered 865 (22.67 percent).[7] By 2001, the number of lawyers had ballooned to more than 10,500—one per 2,190 citizens—with the change in ethnic distributions probably remaining consistent.[8] By diminishing the ethnic imbalance of the profession, the growing number of ethnic Malay lawyers strengthened the profession politically, or in any case made it less vulnerable to charges of exclusivity. Moreover, without notable difficulty or opposition from all three ethnic groups, the number of women who entered the profession increased markedly, adding a potential dimension of interest and concern that it had previously lacked.[9]

Such rapid change in the size and demography of the profession might have been expected to cause turmoil. Why it did not may help to explain the strength

---

5. From the Bar Council's *Legal Directory* of 1970. The statistical calculations may be slightly off because of the difficulty of distinguishing ethnicity by names alone, particularly between Muslims of Malay and Indian descent.

6. See the Bar Council's *Legal Directory* of August 1984. These figures are by my own count and again may include inaccuracies because of mistaken classification of some names.

7. Calculated from the Bar Council's *Legal Directory* of July 1992.

8. From the Bar Council's *Legal Directory* of 2001. As the copy I examined was on line, which made counting and classifying names tedious and subject to too many errors, I have not done it. So my assumption that the pattern of change in ethnic distribution has been constant may be erroneous, but I doubt it.

9. Unlike ethnic Chinese and Malay women, who have the advantage of potentially substantial ethnic clienteles to make them attractive to law firms, ethnic Indian women are a minority within a minority. Their lack of much more than legal competence to offer renders them exploitable as hired help with fewer chances of partnership.

of the Malaysian bar. For one thing, its organization and competent internal regulation, the expansion of the (executive) Bar Council to reflect change, and its effective socialization of new recruits kept bar affairs and standards steady. As their numbers increased, saturating the capital, Kuala Lumpur, more lawyers opened offices in the provinces, spreading their presence and influence around the country. Ethnic tensions were hardly absent as Malays joined the profession, but neither were they much exacerbated by economic competition, for economic growth proved a huge boon for all private lawyers generally. New construction of large housing estates, for example, provided substantial (and easy) profits from conveyancing work, and there was much other legal work in an active private economy.

The same growth encouraged a measure of ethnic amalgamation in the profession, helped along anomalously by a heritage of colonial ethnic stereotyping. Law offices often brought together ethnic Chinese, Malay, and Indian lawyers, in one combination or another, for the sake of maximizing advantages, such as Chinese commercial abilities, Malay political connections, and Indian litigation skills. The link to reality may be little more than a self-fulfilling prophecy, but the ethnic mixing—again, not entirely without friction—has helped to consolidate corporate and professional relationships and kept the bar whole.[10]

Economic growth from the 1970s onward also generated social and political tensions that ignited some lawyerly fuses and set the stage for serious activism among any so inclined. State-led economic growth naturally strengthened the government, but it also inevitably nurtured those in the middle social strata that fed on it. The result, as in Indonesia too, was more or less predictable: as political leadership and public agencies became more assertive, so did various social groups that grew increasingly conscious of their own private rights and less likely to acquiesce in the face of official initiatives. If most were uninterested in grand state-society issues, enough were—usually professionals and intellectuals of various sorts—to produce a nascent NGO movement.

Not the least sensitive were private lawyers, jealous of their own institutional prerogatives and conscious both of the interests of their clients and of their own ideological commitment to significant legal, constitutional, and political principles. Many lawyers may well have been sympathetic to these principles but no more willing than the middle class generally to engage in open opposition, for to do so was either professionally distracting or politically dangerous. But socially or politically conscious lawyers, who tended also to be active within the profession, often wound up on the Bar Council.

After independence, a few lawyers were occasionally critical of the government on policy matters. One involved the Sedition and Internal Security Acts (ISA), a product of the colonial administration during the 1948–1960 Emergency (as the

---

10. Not entirely, however. During the late 1980s, a small Islamic-oriented law organization was formed around a few Malay lawyers, but it never drew many members or developed much influence.

communist rebellion was called) which proved equally useful later against others whom government leaders found troublesome. During the 1970s, however, the ISA question arose more insistently, as the government resorted to it more often and Bar Council members became more incensed. Other issues accumulated, among them the inclination of the government majority in Parliament to amend the constitution frequently to enhance its own powers or to reduce those of the opposition.

Taking for granted a statutory right to comment and advise Parliament on pending legislation, the Bar Council did so sternly on the constitutional amendments problem. The government lashed back in the Legal Profession Act of 1976, initially intended to rationalize scattered rules. On the assumption that younger lawyers were the problem, provisions of the statute disqualified lawyers from membership on the Bar Council or any bar committee until they had practiced a minimum of seven years.[11] It was not young lawyers particularly, however, but also many of their elders who took a principled view of the constitution and parliamentary institutions. Protests continued, now over the restrictive provision in the Legal Profession Act as well. In an amendment to that act in 1983, the government went further, erasing the Bar Council's right to advise Parliament and extending the attorney general's authority over the profession.[12] Tensions mushroomed.

By the late 1970s and early 1980s, the Bar Council and the government were already frequently at loggerheads when, in 1981, Mahathir Mohamad became prime minister and soon raised the stakes. Mahathir, a medical doctor and Malaysia's first non-lawyer prime minister, had a no-nonsense commitment to efficiency that many lawyers at first found promising (*Insaf* 1981). It was a mistake, for a strong prime minister determined to steer "development" was less likely to brook opposition, dissidence, or even criticism. Tensions rose precipitously as activist lawyers, increasingly politicized, widened their purview.

How far they did so is evident in the Bar Council journal, *Insaf* (Aware), which began in the late 1960s with routine contributions on the profession, legal education, and case commentaries. Not long after, however, the journal began to offer a steady fare of pieces on police behavior, legal aid, the ISA, the responsibilities of lawyers, issues of parliamentary government, and human

---

11. The Legal Profession Act of 1976 (Act 166), Article 46A. Other disqualifications included membership in Parliament or a state legislature, office in a trade union or any political party or "any other organization, body or group of persons whatsoever, whether or not it is established under any law, whether it is in Malaysia or outside Malaysia, which has objectives or carries on activities which can be construed as being political in nature, character or effect, or which is declared by the Attorney General by order published in the Gazette, to be an organization, body or groups of persons which has such objectives or carries on such activities." Moreover, "[a]n order made by the Attorney General under paragraph (c)(iii) of subsection (1) shall not be reviewed or called in question in any Court," which makes quite clear the government's intentions.

12. See the Legal Profession Act of 1983 (Amendment) (Act A567).

rights in and out of Malaysia. The annual conferences sponsored by the Bar Council also broadened both their concerns and their participation beyond formal law and the legal profession. Moreover, the Bar Council itself evolved toward increased appreciation of activism, particularly with the election to chair of Param Cumaraswamy, an articulately engaged Kuala Lumpur lawyer with a major law firm.[13] The profession matched the focus in the journal and the Bar Council on matters of political, social, and legal reform, with a good deal of questioning and rethinking of its role and environment in both state and society.

By the beginning of the 1980s, Malaysian state and society had begun to recognize one another as distinct entities, with state leaders proving rather unhappy about it. Increasingly edgy about the activities of three or four well-known organizations prone to criticize public policy, the government introduced a bill to amend the Societies Act of 1966[14] that required all private organizations to register either as political or nonpolitical, defining "political" as any activity meant to influence the government.[15] The threat, of course, was that the official Registrar of Societies might well refuse or scratch the registration of any organization disapproved of by the government. Unexpectedly, the Societies Bill mobilized for the first time many private organizations against its implications.

The Bar Council, reflecting attitudes shared by many lawyers, took a strong stand against the Societies Act, raising a cry over freedoms of association and speech. It expressed special worries about provisions of the bill that eliminated judicial review of actions by the Registrar of Societies, suggesting a direct threat

---

13. See nearly any issue of *Insaf* through the 1980s. In 1996, Dato' Param Cumaraswamy was appointed United Nations Special Rapporteur on the Independence of Judges and Lawyers and was reappointed twice more for three-year terms. Both as chair of the Bar Council and as a member, Param was extraordinarily active. In late 1996, he was sued by two Malaysian companies on grounds of defamation for his comments suggesting that businessmen were influencing Malaysian courts. In 1999, the International Court of Justice found Dato' Param immune from these actions, and in mid-2001, the Malaysian High Court in Kuala Lumpur dismissed all suits against him. See the "Lawyer to Lawyer Network Action Update," May 1999; press release of the Center for Independence of Judges and Lawyers in Geneva, January 11, 1997; and the letter of UN Secretary-General Kofi Annan to the UN Economic and Social Council of April 26, 2002. In August 2002, Dato' Param set off a few fierce complaints by Indonesian government officials when he made clear, following an investigative trip, his view that judicial and related corruption were extraordinary.

14. See the 1981 amendment (A515) of the Societies Act of 1966 and the discussion of freedom of expression in Harding (1996, 198).

15. One of the best accounts of the events and issues dealt with here and elsewhere in my discussion of Malaysia is in an unpublished paper by Clifford Bob, "State vs. Society in Malaysia and the Judiciary Crisis of 1988" (1993), and a revised version of the same paper, "Courts in Politics/Politics in Courts: The Judiciary and State-Society Conflict in Malaysia, 1987-1999," delivered at the annual meeting of the American Political Science Association in 1999.

to judicial authority and the separation of powers (Bob 1993). So involved in the issues were many lawyers that in April 1981 they did an extraordinary thing for Malaysia then: they mounted a public demonstration at the Parliament building. About two hundred lawyers attended, passing out copies of their objections to the proposed legislation. It was a memorable moment in the history of the profession, about which a few senior members of the bar still enjoy reminiscing. The government compromised slightly on the Societies Bill, but the debate over it helped set a furious stage.

By the mid-1980s, political leaders and the Bar Council were barely on speaking terms, or rather what passed for speech was mainly invective. Ideologically, the two sides had moved miles apart. One sought to make a strong state stronger by extending executive authority and privilege, justified by reference to successful economic development and ethnic justice. The other emphasized the need to protect citizens against executive power by making sure that judicial institutions retained their authority to exercise controls over it. In two tense issues that also arose during the mid-1980s, one over amendments to the Civil Law Act of 1956 and the other over amendments to the Official Secrets Act, the government set out to reduce the authority of the judiciary to interfere with executive discretion, while the Bar Council, supported discreetly by federal judges, stood in outspoken opposition.[16] The principle raised by the Official Secrets Act had to do with freedom of information, but the institutional issue of judicial powers was quite as important, certainly to lawyers, whose own significance and political imagination were inextricably linked to the courts. Inevitably, the judiciary itself became the prime focus of conflict.

Judicial authority had been at issue since at least 1978 when the government began to whittle the Supreme Court's review powers.[17] By the mid-1980s, Prime Minister Mahathir was as determined to subjugate the courts as he was to weaken other institutional, political, or social impediments to his government's freedom of action.[18]

In October 1987, the government stunned the country with a lightning raid, unprecedented since the Emergency, in which more than a hundred assorted figures—NGO activists, a few members of Parliament, journalists, and others—

---

16. See Bob (1993, 25 and following) and just about any issue of *Insaf* through the 1980s.

17. See a long editorial entitled "Further Erosion of Fundamental Rights" and the letter to Prime Minister Mahathir from Ronnie Khoo Teng Swee, then vice president of the Bar Council, in *Insaf*, 1983/84.

18. See Bob (1993, 37 and following) for an illuminating discussion of the rulers' crisis in 1983 as a prelude to the battle over judicial authority. The rulers' issue involved a contest between the government and the sultans who head the nine constituent states of Malaysia over the extent of their authority, which the prime minister was determined to restrict. In this constitutional conflict, many lawyers and liberal reformers supported the sultans, not out of devout loyalty or appreciation by any means, but rather from a wish to prevent the prime minister from accumulating more power. See also Lev (1993, 148 and following).

were detained on the grounds that they had threatened ethnic peace.[19] Most were soon released, but the effect was to cast a pall over Malaysian politics, as many, including some shaken lawyers, retired anxiously from public arenas.

A frontal assault on judicial authority followed not long after, in 1988, as the prime minister sought successfully to remove the lord president of the Federal (Supreme) Court and to replace him with a more compliant judge.[20] A blunt assertion of executive primacy over the judiciary, it was also a slap across the face of the Bar Council and a contemptuous rejection of its view, shared by prominent NGOs and others, of a properly run state. Most Malaysian lawyers were undoubtedly distressed but also cowed by then into quietude. Others were not, and the Bar Council made its outrage elaborately clear. A number of lawyers boycotted sessions of the court chaired by the new lord president. The journal *Insaf* devoted much space to the issue, as well as to human rights and such procedural matters as preventive detention, which lawyers understood to be limited only by autonomous judicial authority.

While the Bar Council sought some political leverage for itself, in part by electing two prominent Malay attorneys in succession as chair, ethnic diplomacy made little difference in the posture of the Bar Council, or activist lawyers generally, on critical issues. That many lawyers decided to withdraw from the struggle, devoting themselves to professional work narrowly defined, is hardly surprising. That others—how many is hard to know—carried on is more interesting and less easy to account for without reference to a combination of professional interest and ideology.

Throughout the 1990s, the Bar Council and individual lawyers persistently questioned the consequences of executive intrusion into the courts, raising the possibility of corruption and collusion among judges now more submissive to political leadership. In September 1998, another serious political crisis arose amid the country's economic problems as Prime Minister Mahathir fired his deputy prime minister, Anwar Ibrahim, and had him arrested on charges of sexual perversion and corruption. Outraged citizens protested on the streets in numbers unheard of since the riots of 1969. Anwar was eventually convicted and imprisoned in a trial that raised many questions still extant. But the sudden

---

19. See Bob (1993, 36) on Operation Lallang, the raid of October 1987. The precipitating issue had to do with the appointment of Chinese school officials who may not have had command of Mandarin Chinese. Given how many of those arrested had nothing to do with ethnic conflict, or had always been critical of it, however, the issue may have been an excuse more than a reason.

20. The judicial crisis generated much commentary and criticism. See especially Abas and Das (1989). Tun Sallah Abas was the lord president (chief justice) forced out by the prime minister. Also see Bob (1993, 47 and following); *Insaf*, all issues following the affair; *Aliran Monthly*, the journal of the reform organization Aliran, whose chair, Chandra Muzaffar, was one of those arrested in 1987; and Lev (1993). What set off the judicial crisis was a string of decisions that went against the government on political issues, culminating in a case that directly involved a split in the dominant Malay party UMNO.

drama of daily protests, police suppression, and political uncertainty had obviously shaken the country badly and raised serious questions about political reform. Indeed, in an odd reversal for Malaysia, whose model has often been cited by Indonesian reformers, Malaysian protesters now picked up the cry of "*reformasi*" from the post-Soeharto reform movement across the straits [in Indonesia—see Part II below]. Among the most prominent critics of Mahathir were lawyers.[21]

The point of this history is not that the Malaysian bar won or lost, but that it acted, often contrary to its own professional interests narrowly understood, in defense of principles—essentially liberal principles—meant to define the institutional responsibilities of the modern state toward its citizens. Not all lawyers agreed, nor did all who agreed make their views known, but the profession as a whole, led effectively by its Bar Council—not all of whose members, perhaps, went along—persistently brought pressure to bear to keep the courts honest and autonomous, opposed the government on issues of constitutional principle, and continues to do so as the government appears to retreat from further interference in the judiciary. Individual lawyers, perhaps with some support within the Bar Council, took the risk of raising the sensitive issue of possible corruption in the courts during the 1990s. One who did so was former Bar Council president Param Cumaraswamy.

At least two conditions made these developments possible. One is that the Malaysian state and its institutions retained a measure of integrity, while political leadership appears to have understood that there are lines too dangerous, or in any case too politically risky, to cross. The other is that the political principles of the Malaysian Bar Society rested on a solid foundation of capable organization, the most impressive lawyers' association anywhere in Southeast Asia. Tightly composed, efficiently run, complete with useful services for its members, along with controls, the Malaysian Bar Society is also a source of information and a forum for interested lawyers. These qualities equip it for political as well as professional action under committed leadership.

II. The Indonesian Advocacy

The Indonesian bar is something else entirely. Comparing the Indonesian with the Malaysian legal profession requires attention to a multitude of variables: Dutch versus English colonial history, civil law versus common law, peaceful transfer of sovereignty versus revolution, a much more versus a much less

---

21. On the Anwar Ibrahim arrest and its aftermath, see *Commentary* (1998). It includes two statements on the political crisis. The first, entitled "Rule of Law Under Threat," was most likely largely the work of lawyers, who were the majority of signatories, including Raja Aziz Addruse and Param Cumaraswamy, both former chairs of the Bar Council, along with the former lord president (chief justice), Tun Mohamed Suffian. See also Bob (1999, 12 and following) and the *Malayan Law Journal*'s issue "The Anwar Ibrahim Judgment" (1999).

authoritarian political system, a population (now) of 215 million versus one of 23 million, and so on. The variables that have counted most, however, are professional organization and state intervention, in which case Malaysian and Indonesian lawyers are at least a light-year apart.

While the Malaysian bar glided smoothly and confidently through much of its history, the Indonesian advocacy has been driving an ancient car without shock absorbers over huge rocks.[22] The first few Indonesian advocates who began to practice in the 1920s, despite the misgivings of colonial authorities, constituted an essentially new group of engaged professionals committed to nationalism and progressive change. Contemptuous of the local customary structures maintained by the colonial administration, they leaned toward an independent state outfitted with the modern legal codes and institutions in which they had successfully made their ways. More than most, they understood the alternative models of state implied by the administrative structure of the Netherlands Indies. In a plural colonial legal system, organized around distinct courts and codes for the different ethnic communities of Europeans, native Indonesians, and "foreign Orientals" (ethnic Chinese, Arabs, and Indians), Indonesian advocates were in a position to explore the whole of its geography.

On the European side of the colonial state, political-legal authority resided in rigorous codes and judicial institutions staffed by highly trained and respected public and private lawyers. Their normative values assumed legal equality, certainty, and predictability. On the Indonesian side, authority was patrimonial more than legal, vested less in courts than in a bureaucracy oriented to social and political hierarchy, not equality, and the privileges of officials, not the rights of citizens. The one side appreciated lawyers; the other did not. In the courts for Europeans, legal counsel was obligatory; in the courts for Indonesians, anyone at all or no one might act as counsel, as is still true (Lev 1976).

Advocates—litigating lawyers on the continental model—decidedly favored the European more than the Indonesian side of colonial administration, which choice implied an interest in refashioning Indonesian social and political organization to suit a state of more or less liberal design. During and after the revolution, politically active private lawyers consistently encouraged institutional reforms toward procedural uniformity and legal equality. In positions of authority, they opposed traditional local privileges, eliminated customary (*adat*) courts, created a nationally unified judiciary, and tried to strengthen courts against executive aggression.

While more influential than their numbers, the size of the profession was limiting. Even among the few legally trained Indonesians, still fewer than

---

22. My discussion of Indonesia draws substantially, often verbatim, from my essays (1998 and 1996).

four hundred when the Japanese army arrived,* advocates were a minority of about 40 percent in 1940.[23] Most indigenous lawyers had joined the colonial government as judges on the superior court for Indonesians, the *Landraad*, or as administrators or scholars whose experience on the Indonesian side of the colonial legal system promoted another perspective.

Tension between the two political-legal orientations broke out openly in July 1945 when the first constitution was drafted, in a debate between Mohammad Yamin and Raden Supomo, the former a West Sumatran who worked briefly as an advocate and the latter a Javanese scholar-official who also taught at the Law Faculty in Batavia (Jakarta). Yamin proposed a constitutional bill of rights, a supreme court with powers of judicial review, and clearly separated legislative, judicial, and executive functions. Rejecting the institutional experience of the colony, his premises—a sharp distinction between state and society, recognition of individual interests and rights, and the need for institutional controls over political authority—challenged head-on the constructs of political authority that underlay the administration of Indonesian society in the Netherlands East Indies (Yamin 1959, 330–37).[24]

Supomo, closely associated with colonial policies intended to preserve local customary law regimes, was the most influential legal technician in the preparatory commissions for independence and largely responsible for drafting the short, executive-heavy constitution of 1945. If some nationalist leaders accepted the institutional heritage of the colony because they were familiar with no other, Supomo consciously preferred it. Against Yamin's radical departure, he insisted that Indonesian jurists had no experience beyond the continental civil law,

---

*Ed. note: The Netherlands East Indies were occupied by Japan from March 1942 until the end of World War II in August 1945. Indonesian nationalist leaders declared independence on August 17 with a new constitution (see note 25 below) and a new president, Soekarno, known to Indonesians as Bung (brother) Karno. After four years of revolution against the Dutch, independence was achieved in late 1949 and a parliamentary government was formed under the provisional (and liberal) constitution of 1950. Unrest in various parts of the archipelago led Soekarno to declare martial law in 1957, which greatly strengthened the political leverage of the army, and in 1959, under army pressure, he re-instituted the 1945 constitution in the regime called Guided Democracy, which lasted until late 1965. Following a complex coup in 1965, power shifted to General Soeharto, who assumed presidential powers in 1966, was named acting president in 1967, and president in 1968. Soeharto's New Order regime lasted until he was forced to resign in May 1998. Succeeding him as president were Bharuddin Jusuf Habibie, 1998–1999; Abdurrahman Wahid, 1999–2001; Megawati Sukarnoputri (Soekarno's daughter), 2001–2004; and Susilo Bambang Yudhoyono, 2004–present.

23. Indonesian advocates, numbering 81 (out of 206 legally trained Indonesians) in 1940, were about evenly divided between ethnic Indonesians and ethnic Chinese, which is relevant here mainly in that ethnic Indonesian lawyers were far more likely to be politically active. Ideologically, however, they were then and remain now much alike. The data is from the 1941 colonial *Regeerings Almanac* 2:56–59. See also Lev (1976).

24. At the time, Yamin's ideas may well have surprised even the advocates in his audience.

which had already been adapted to Indonesian conditions and was known to those who would have to staff the independent state.

Supomo's political agenda was more interesting. Committed to preserving not only the existing legal order but the authority of the aristocracy on which colonial administration had depended, in Java especially, his analysis flowed logically from the ideology of colonial-Javanese patrimonialism (Moertono 1968). Liberal individualism was out of the question, according to Supomo, for the new state was to be conceived as a family, whose interests superseded those of individual members. The constitutional rights against state authority that Yamin wanted were unnecessary, for state and society were indivisible, led by an ascriptive elite responsible for ascertaining and defending the interests of the state-society. The evident superiority of this elite, and the totality of its responsibility, rendered controls superfluous.[25]

The two positions have lasted in a long debate in which Supomo's case has had most of the political advantages, but Yamin's has stayed alive and picked up support in recent decades. Supomo's political ideas lost out for a time during the early parliamentary period of independence, but his legal predilections were consolidated early in the revolution, to the disappointment of many professional advocates. The revolutionary republic sustained the Japanese occupation decision to unify the judiciary around the colonial courts for Indonesians, the *Landraden* (now *Pengadilan Negeri*), rather than the European courts (*Raad van Justitie*), and adopted the procedural code for Indonesians, *Herziene Indoneisisch Reglement* (HIR) (the revised Indonesian regulation of 1926),[26] rather than the European codes of civil and criminal procedure preferred by advocates. Thereafter, the independent state was governed, in effect, by the most repressive side of the colonial procedural regime (Lev 1985).

Even so, if the legal system needed work, the liberal constitution of 1950 and the parliamentary system it supported until 1959 satisfied advocates. The profession was quite thin immediately after independence, perhaps a hundred or so as a guess, in part because many advocates took up positions in the government. Its members were optimistic, however. Constitutionalism and the parliamentary *Rechtsstaat*—a *negara hukum* (law state) in its Indonesian version—seemed promising to the evolution advocates confidently took for granted.

Their confidence was misplaced; what loomed instead was an abyss. Beginning in early 1957, the parliamentary order was swept aside under pressure from the army (particularly) and President Soekarno, who declared martial law as regional dissidence outside of Java, supported for Cold War reasons by the

---

25. Unlike the federal constitution of 1949 and the provisional constitution of 1950, the 1945 constitution provided few institutional controls over executive authority and no stipulated political rights. For Supomo's arguments, see Yamin (1959, 337 and following). An English translation of Supomo's comments on the state can be found in Feith and Castles (1970, 188–92). For the fullest and most sophisticated analysis of Supomo's ideas and influence during the constitutional discussions of mid-1945, see Simandjuntak (1994).

26. See Tresna (1959).

United States, developed toward civil war that broke out openly in February 1958. The successor regime, Guided Democracy, razed all the supports professional advocates thought secure—liberal constitutionalism, an autonomous and effective legal process, and a limited but legitimate private economy. Soekarno dismissed liberal *negara hukum* ideas as an instrument of those who would surrender Indonesian originality to European political fashion, a distraction from his own compelling quest for an independent Indonesia shaped from its own culture and purpose. Jeering at assorted liberals, among them lawyers—with whom (quoting Liebknecht) one could not make a revolution—Soekarno set about erasing the principles of the separation of powers and judicial independence both de facto and de jure.[27]

The Guided Democracy years elated few lawyers of any sort, but advocates suffered the most professionally, politically, and ideologically. Judges and even a few prosecutors regretted their own loss of institutional autonomy and some retired in dismay. Those who stayed retained the rewards of official status, at least, at a time of rising bureaucratic authority. Private lawyers lost clients, professional stature, and more. Their own institutional base and source of professional legitimacy in the judiciary became instead a cause of uncertainty, pain, and indignity. Nakedly unofficial, advocates stood apart from the collegial circle of civil servants in the judicial system. They and their clients paid heavily for it. Professional satisfaction evaporated. Paralyzed and stagnant, the advocacy, then numbering perhaps 250 nationwide, if that, drew scarcely any new recruits. Until 1963, following tradition in the colony, advocates were only organized locally in *balie* (Dutch for "bar")—little more than clubs—here and there in a few major cities. Finally, in March of that year, partly in an effort to save their profession, a dozen or so senior advocates undertook to organize a national association, the Indonesian Advocates Association (*Persatuan Advokat Indonesia* or PERADIN).

When Guided Democracy came to a brutal end following a coup in October 1965, senior advocates were quick to join the forces of reform in and out of the legal system. They helped to frame many of the key issues of New Order politics from 1966 on—restoration of the legal process, institutional reform, constitutionalism, and human rights. Because of the experience of the Soekarno years and because fundamental political features of Guided Democracy also informed the military-dominated New Order, the arguments advocates brought to bear on the state drew support from among a larger and more critically interested audience than ever before. Not formally or exclusively, but unmistakably, reform advocates spoke to and for this audience.

By the time the remaining pockets of the old regime's resistance were mopped up in the late 1960s, a new debate broke out over the shape of the political system and state-society relations, tracing back to the Supomo-Yamin

---

27. See Law 19/1964 on judicial authority and Law 13/1965 on the organization of the civil judiciary.

confrontation of 1945 but enriched by two decades of experience. The protagonists were the army and state bureaucracies, on the one hand, and a small but
expanding universe of self-consciously private groups, on the other. Resting on
military force and jealous of political privilege, the government took for granted
the priority of state interests, which increasingly came to mean the interests of
the New Order elite itself. The other view, emphasizing controls predicated,
inter alia, on autonomous judicial institutions, favored a better balance between
state and private interests. Across the chasm, advocates and their allies insisted
on legal predictability, protection of private interests, and constitutional limits
on state power, while New Order leaders stressed stability for the sake of economic development, fuller control over a diverse society, expansion of state
power, and consolidation of the army's special claim to leadership.[28]

It was hardly a contest. By the time General Soeharto assumed the presidency
in 1967, army leadership had no reason to submit to institutional controls over
political and bureaucratic authority. From the regime's point of view, an
autonomous legal process was not an appropriate means of social and political
management, for it could only diminish the responsibilities (and prerogatives)
of political leadership. Despite occasional public assurances to the contrary, the
legal system was understood to be subordinate to the prior claims of political
authority, as it had been under Guided Democracy.

Legal officials, with a few exceptions, accepted their submerged role. Like the
rest of the civil service, judges needed few explicit reminders that they were subject to the will of the state leaders. Any other view violated the solid political-
bureaucratic ethos of the New Order administration and endangered their
careers. Political authority spoke the language of constitutional guidance but
acted confidently with nearly unrestrained power. At their disposal was a security apparatus staffed by the military, whose extralegal procedures paralleled
and, at will, superseded or subordinated any conventional legal process.[29]

Concessions to demands for administrative and judicial probity were largely
symbolic, unenforceable without useful institutional machinery or political
recourse. The government deflected an effort, led by judges and advocates, to
give the Supreme Court (*Mahkamah Agung*) powers of judicial review over legislative and executive acts (Lev 1978).[30] Complaints against judicial corruption
and prosecutorial or police abuse generated occasional assurances of correction,

---

28. On the politics of the New Order period, see, among other works, Schwarz (1994);
Crouch (1978); and, for comparisons, Alatas (1997).

29. To take the most common example, the Command for the Restoration of Security and
Order (*Komando Operasi Pemulihan Keamanan dan Ketertiban* or KOPKAMTIB) could
arrest and detain people without trial or, alternatively, have the prosecution investigate
accused persons under the Anti-Subversion Act of 1963, which made it easier to convict with
harsher sentences than the HIR procedural code. See, inter alia, Damian (1970) and Kleden
and Walujo (1981). See also Thoolen (1987).

30. Advocates and judges had different purposes. Judges sought improved bureaucratic status,
advocates an autonomous judiciary capable of imposing legal controls over executive authority. The brief alliance did little to moderate the antagonism between judges and advocates.

even a law or two, but went practically unanswered. Government promises to protect citizens from abuse meant little. A new statute on judicial organization (Law 14/1970) was enacted that provided for the legal representation of accused persons from the time of arrest, but the implementing legislation it required was not forthcoming.[31] Every such reform was meant to impose restrictions on bureaucratic privilege, discretion, and prerogative, diminutions of public authority conceded on paper but rejected as long as possible in practice.[32]

Reform interests in the legal process belonged to various segments of a growing professional, commercial, and intellectual middle class, a rigidly controlled working class, and religious and ethnic minorities, among others—whoever lacked useful influence in the regime (Lev 1978). The New Order confirmed the lesson of Guided Democracy that without a share in state power, one needed defenses against it.

No one articulated these views more clearly than the professional advocacy, which itself was transformed by New Order economic growth. Until the late 1960s, the profession consisted of a small group of specialists in litigation in the continental civil law tradition. As foreign and domestic investment grew post-1966, so did the advocacy, as in Malaysia after 1970. But unlike the Malaysian profession, Indonesia's mutated in the process.

Numbering (uncertainly) about 250 in 1965, about the same as (but maybe far fewer than) in the last years of the colony, including both Dutch and Indonesian attorneys, by 1970 the profession had doubled or better. From 1971 through 1984, a total of 1,075 new advocates registered with the Ministry of Justice. Some, but perhaps many more, did not bother to register, which saved them trouble and money but had little other effect for lack of explicit statutory standards and controls.[33] An uncertain estimate of the number of legally

---

31. The same law, like earlier statutes, assumed administrative courts, but these were finally established only twenty years later, in 1991, on the basis of a new law in 1986. The government avoided administrative courts largely because they were intended, after all, to deal with actions against the government itself. Such misgivings proved politically accurate, for in 1995 the State Administrative Court (*Pengadilan Tata Usaha Negara* or PTUN) of Jakarta stunned the country by actually ruling against the minister of information's banning of *Tempo*, an influential weekly, a year earlier in June 1994. The decision, which rested entirely on the black letter of the law, was upheld by the appellate administrative court, at which point Minister of Information Harmoko promptly appealed to the Supreme Court, which obediently overturned the administrative court rulings.

32. A few reform concessions took hold, however. Apart from the administrative courts, a national human rights commission (*Komisi Nasional Hak Azasi Manusia* or KOMNAS HAM) was also created in response to international and domestic pressure, particularly after a massacre of East Timorese by army troops in late 1991. The human rights commission also proved worrisomely unpredictable from the government's point of view, though its authority is only advisory. Legislative reforms, while easily manipulated by the bureaucracy, including courts, nevertheless make promises that activists can put to significant rhetorical use.

33. There is no requirement of professional representation in court. Any litigant can appear with or without counsel, and counsel can be anyone at all, including an utterly untrained friend or "bush lawyer." See note 48 below.

educated private practitioners, both registered and unregistered, might be about 12,000 or so, but perhaps a few thousand or so more; for reasons to be explained shortly, no one knows. Sometime during this period of expansion, the ratio of private lawyers (excluding notaries) to the total population surpassed that of colonial days, about one per 350,000 at best, and now it may be (maybe) in the vicinity of one per 20,000 in contrast to Malaysia's one per approximately 2,200.[34]

At the same time, the average age of advocates declined as seniors died or retired and young law graduates began to find the private sector more attractive than civil service. Once the preserve of fairly high-born sons of Javanese aristocrats or well-established families from Sumatra and Sulawesi, as well as ethnic Chinese, the origins of private lawyers now extended downwards into an also changing middle class and outwards to a more diverse array of ethnic groups from around the archipelago. Women joined the profession in substantial numbers; several are now among the most prominent members of the litigating and commercial bar. For the first time, as a growing economy influenced status values and career choices, the profession attracted lateral recruits from the ranks of retired judges, prosecutors, police officials, other civil servants, and military lawyers.

Moreover, the features of private lawyering were redefined by the emergence of a stratum of non-litigators called "consulting lawyers," who specialized in commercial legal counseling and negotiation. Rather like solicitors or office lawyers who are not notaries but do not fit the traditional mold of advocates, the most successful of them are organized in new multi-member law firms with incomes, often calculated in dollars as well as rupiah, unimaginable only two or three decades ago. Most consulting lawyers, with a few exceptions, did not register as advocates with the Ministry of Justice until compelled to do so during the late 1980s; nor did they join PERADIN, many of whose members refused to recognize them as genuine advocates, which hardly bothered some consulting lawyers.[35] By measures of income and status, consulting lawyers have become the elite of the private legal profession. Such changes affected the social and political outlook of the increasingly diverse profession. Successful consulting lawyers (and a few registered advocates proper who also do commercial advisory work) exist in a lucrative, comfortable commercial stratosphere, well insulated from the

---

34. When comparing Malaysia and Indonesia, however, it should be held in mind that civil law systems tend to generate fewer private lawyers than do common law systems, and divides them up between litigating and notarial specialists, the latter an amalgam of public and private functions.

35. This tension between consulting lawyers and advocates, sometimes quite sharp, sits on top of another between consulting lawyers (especially) and advocates, on the one hand, and notaries, on the other, as the former increasingly wonder whether their own legal skills have not rendered notaries unnecessary. Notaries, understandably, find such views obnoxiously aggressive or worse.

everyday miseries of the courts and of clients who have to deal with them. These lawyers may appreciate reformers, but themselves have long tended to political quiescence, though this posture may be gradually changing since 1998 when Soeharto resigned, inaugurating a period of dramatically uncertain political change. The same has generally been true among advocates who rely on official contacts and do not risk them in critical activism of any sort, whatever their sympathies. In 1978, when the advocates' association, PERADIN, proclaimed itself to be a "struggle organization" dedicated to reform, some members left to found their own organization, the Association of Indonesian Advocates (*Asosiasi Advokat Indonesia* or AAI).[36]

The newfound bulk, prosperity, and public salience of the advocacy, however, also supported the reform efforts of a respectable number of lawyer-activists, both older and younger. Their most influential creation was the Legal Aid Institute (*Lembaga Bantuan Hukum* or LBH) of Jakarta, since 1980 a national foundation with twelve branches around the country. The LBH started a legal aid boom of sorts involving many young lawyers. The brainchild of a former prosecutor, the activist advocate Adnan Buyung Nasution, the LBH was established under PERADIN sponsorship in 1970 and institutionalized the political vision of reform advocates, particularly the most senior among them. More than a provider of legal assistance to the poor, it became for decades Indonesia's most prominent center of social-legal and political-legal criticism and reform activity and remains prominent among the many new legally focused NGOs organized since mid-1998.[37]

Before 1998, private lawyers divided sharply on issues of reform according to professional interests and experience, habits that naturally influenced postures afterwards. Litigating lawyers, who see the shortcomings of any regime in the conditions under which they represent their clients, have always been the most committed reformers. Court work under the New Order was miserable, not only because of the corruption involved, in which many advocates participated—not always with much choice in the matter—more or less equitably: the so-called judicial mafia of collusive prosecutors, judges, and private lawyers. Rather, since the Guided Democracy years, these became just about the only terms on which the role of advocacy in the judicial system was accorded recognition and some respect.

Civil litigation since the 1960s had become invariably difficult. Time-consuming, expensive, often corrupt and professionally depressing, with no assurance that judgments would be executed, advocates avoided it if they could, and some withdrew from it altogether in favor of office practice. But the criminal

---

36. On professional organizations among Indonesian lawyers through the late 1970s, see Abdurrahman (1980). "Legal aid" here refers to both professional counsel and assistance for indigent parties.

37. On the LBH, see Lev (1987) and the sources cited therein.

process incurred the most serious hardships. For advocates, criminal defense became treacherous, filled with abusive police, corrupt and extortionate prosecutors, bureaucratically oriented judges who favored prosecutors as colleagues and regarded defense attorneys as offensive, even illegitimate, interlopers. Unless, of course, a special relationship had been developed. Throughout the New Order period, advocates raised a perpetual din over these problems on behalf of their clients and themselves, leading now and again to open conflict with judges.[38]

Beyond the courts, reform advocates did somewhat better during the New Order years of the Soeharto regime. Paid attention to by the press and by an occasionally sympathetic but powerless parliamentary committee, they had some influence on statutory reforms whose effect, however, was limited.[39] Few legislative improvements were accompanied by the political and institutional changes that might consolidate them.[40] The government did not abide by the spirit or even the letter of a new code of criminal procedure, promulgated in 1980, on any issue of political import. Dissidence remained subject to treatment by the security apparatus, and even common criminality was often dealt with as if the code did not exist.[41]

---

38. Protests had little effect in penetrating the privileged positions of judges, prosecutors, and police, for the government was obliged politically to protect its bureaucratic base. Prosecutors and judges were transferred or even dismissed, occasionally as the result of extraordinary efforts by private lawyers, but their institutions remained essentially unchanged. Reform advocates were frustrated at every turn. See Lubis (1993); Thoolen (1987); Lev (1999).

39. Since 1966, two statutes, pressed for assiduously by reform advocates, have generated especially optimistic though brief public enthusiasm: Law 14/1970 on judicial organization and the new code of criminal procedure of 1981. Advocates were discouraged by the first, because it did not grant review powers to the Supreme Court and because articles favorable to accused persons were not implemented by the supplementary legislation required. The new code of criminal procedure *Kitab Undang-undang Hukum Acara Pidana* (KUHAP) met a few more demands for reform, though again implementation proved to be problematic. That the criminal process was taken so seriously reflects the extent to which political issues, or state-society issues, have dominated public debate about legal change.

40. The new code of criminal procedure punished public prosecutors by turning over responsibility for preliminary investigation to the police, who were made subject to suits for wrongful damages. It also established a new procedure of pre-trial judicial review of arrest and detention and implemented (within limits) the principle of legal representation of accused persons from the time of arrest. Not one of these innovations has worked according to promise, largely because of the resistance of the institutions responsible for them. See Lubis (1993, throughout), and the annual reports on human rights by the Indonesian Legal Aid Institute, *Catatan Keadaan Hak-Hak Asasi Manusia di Indonesia* (Notes on the Human Rights Situation in Indonesia).

41. For one example, in the early 1980s military death squads were detailed to kill petty criminals and the like who were generally regarded as a serious social and political irritation. Soeharto took credit for these *petrus* (mysterious shootings) killings in his memoirs, *Otobiografi* (1988, 364–67).

Even so, the New Order government could not ignore the noise raised by activist lawyers. Particularly outspoken and courageous lawyers—such as senior advocates Yap Thiam Hien and Suardi Tasrif, LBH founder Adnan Buyung Nasution and former LBH directors Mulya Lubis and Abdul Hakim G. Nusantara, and the Surabaya advocate Trimoelya Soerjadi, among many others—captured public attention, as did less well-known younger advocates, for their defense of political detainees and promotion of human rights. Eventually, the government was likely to confront the activist bar not much more subtly than it dealt with the critical press.

New Order leaders domesticated the legal system as they had the rest of the state bureaucracy, in part by imposing military direction, serving the interests both of political security and of patronage for (usually) retired generals. The national police were incorporated into the armed forces in 1967. In 1966, General Sugih-Arto was appointed chief public prosecutor (*jaksa agung*); his successors were also from the military. The Ministry of Justice and Supreme Court were left to civilians for a time, but in the mid-1970s, the ministry went to Lieutenant General Mudjono and then in succession to Generals Ali Said and Ismail Saleh. Finally, the Supreme Court, to which several retired officers were appointed in 1974 and thereafter, was given over to Mudjono in 1981 and, on his death in 1984, to Ali Said.[42] By 1981, retired army officers were in command of the entire core of the official legal system.

Except for Islamic courts, not relevant here, and the politically inert *notariat*, the one significant legal institution not dominated by the military or subdued by political authority was the troublesome, self-governing advocacy. Its only bureaucratic connection was with the Ministry of Justice, which merely registered advocates, from whom a few extralegal fees were extracted in the process; registration had relatively little significance apart from the meager status of *advokat* it bestowed. By the early 1970s, many advocates had come to favor limited government intervention: a law governing practice, for example, to fortify professional legitimacy, define professional rights and responsibilities, and restrict casual competition. Many others were wary of any such public intrusion upon private professional space. PERADIN was interested in a national bar association, however, which would require government support. But hostility to advocates from the courts, prosecution, police, Ministry of Justice, and elsewhere in the administration meant that any official attention might take a bad turn. It did.

It was not legal malpractice, widespread by then, that moved the government to do something about the advocacy. By the early 1980s, New Order leaders were less concerned with protecting public interests than with containing

---

42. The best work on the Supreme Court is Sebastiaan Pompe's extraordinarily detailed and carefully analyzed study in his dissertation "The Indonesian Supreme Court: Fifty Years of Judicial Development" (1996), published in 2005 by Cornell University Southeast Asia Program Publications as *The Indonesian Supreme Court: A Study of Institutional Collapse.*

public criticism and resistance. Beginning in the mid- to late 1970s, a strong NGO movement had taken hold, spawning independent reform organizations with little respect for public policy or officialdom. The original model was PERADIN's legal aid institute, the LBH, which by the early 1980s had grown into a national network with a dozen active branches around the country and which served as an example for others. In the legal system as elsewhere in the public bureaucracy, these challenges reinforced corporatist urges to assert official predominance and eliminate external static.

Antagonism between public and private lawyers added animus. Judges and prosecutors, resenting the independence of professional advocates and plagued by constant charges of corruption, incompetence, and abuse of authority, were eager to silence critics and run a test of prerogatives in which their parent institutions, including the Ministry of Justice and the Supreme Court, had to back them. But there were other political reasons for confining the advocacy. In political trials since 1966, defense attorneys from PERADIN and the LBH had embarrassed the government at home and abroad by challenging the staged affairs, turning them into platforms of political criticism. Private lawyers were prominent among the human rights activists whom state leaders regarded as a threat to the regime, along with hidden communists and assorted other evils.

Consequently, the government initiated a strategy designed to absorb PERADIN and smaller organizations into a single national bar association and to impose disciplinary control over the entire profession. In 1981, at PERADIN's congress in Bandung, Supreme Court Chairman Mudjono, Minister of Justice Ali Said, and Chief Public Prosecutor Ismail Saleh each insisted that the advocacy required a unified organization (*wadah tunggal*). It was left to Ali Said, as minister of justice and later as Supreme Court chairman, to engineer the new Indonesian Advocates Bond (*Ikatan Advokat Indonesia* or IKADIN).

Many advocates were initially receptive, optimistic that an officially sponsored professional association would improve their opportunities and relationships with the bureaucracy. Senior PERADIN leaders, however, were skeptical from the start, assuming that Ali Said was mainly intent upon eliminating PERADIN's influence. At his disposal were numerous retired military law graduates, now practicing, who could be mobilized to take over the new association.

PERADIN delayed but could not avoid IKADIN, which was inaugurated in November 1985, with Harjono Tjitrosubeno of PERADIN as chair.[43] Still, lawyers treated IKADIN cautiously. PERADIN and smaller associations refused to disband, despite official pressure, until IKADIN proved viable and useful. Engaging the government in a tactical struggle for control of the organization, IKADIN leaders fought for organizational autonomy and self-governance, which the Ministry of Justice countered by tightening registration requirements, establishing quotas of advocates (as there were of notaries) in major

---

43. On IKADIN's history, see *Era Hukum* (1987).

cities, and dividing private legal professionals organizationally.[44] Advocates held out; in IKADIN's first elections in 1988, PERADIN's influence remained dominant.

Ismail Saleh and Ali Said meanwhile surrounded the profession with a fence of disciplinary requirements, which advocates contested fiercely. The lawyers argued their case from legal premises, but the norms at work were political, not legal, in which case the advantage lay distinctly with the government. An opportunity to have at the advocacy, and a particularly irritating advocate, arose in 1986 when Adnan Buyung Nasution, founder of the LBH, committed a breach of etiquette in the trial of retired Lieutenant General Dharsono for subversive complicity in riots at the Jakarta port area of Tanjung Priok in September 1984. Minister of Justice Saleh, oblivious to the least subtle legal issues, set about making an example of Nasution. Applying ex post facto a provision from a new law, he accused Nasution of contempt of court, which does not exist in Indonesian (like other civil law) procedure. A first-instance judge, without hearing Nasution, handed down an "administrative decision"—which he later called a "report," though he had granted Nasution the right to appeal from it, but to whom that was never made clear—recommending that the minister of justice revoke the advocate's certification. Ignoring the law, protests from foreign bar associations, and IKADIN's effort itself to deal with the matter, the minister revoked Nasution's registration for a period of one year.[45]

Soon afterwards, in July 1987, the minister of justice and chairman of the Supreme Court promulgated a "joint decision" on procedures for supervising and regulating legal counsel.[46] They construed an article of a new law (Article 54(4) of Law 2/1986, on the lower courts) to grant judges wide authority over private practitioners for the sake of "guiding and developing" the profession.

---

44. Not all advocates joined IKADIN, any more than they had PERADIN or other organizations. By the end of 1986, of 1,125 advocates registered with the Ministry of Justice and practicing, only 645 were enrolled as members of IKADIN (*Era Hukum* 1987, 240). The Ministry of Justice brought pressure to bear by requiring registration of all practicing lawyers and refusing it before registrants joined IKADIN. Although IKADIN was intended at first to incorporate practicing private lawyers of all sorts, except for notaries, tensions among them, as well as the views of the Ministry of Justice, eventually led to separate organizations for registered advocates; unregistered *pengacara praktek* (practical attorneys), including non-degree-holding bush lawyers; and consulting lawyers (see note 48 below). See the July 23, 1988 weekly *Editor* in *Indonesia Reports* (1988).

45. On the Nasution case, see Lev (1986, 4–5). Nasution sued the minister of justice, partly on grounds that Law 2/1986 had been applied ex post facto, but the first-instance court of South Jakarta predictably rejected his claim, ruling, interestingly, that the ex post facto rule did not apply to administrative law, where public interest is the governing consideration (*Kompas* 1988).

46. KMA/005/SKB/VII/1987-M.03-PR.08.05 *tahun* 1987. See also Supreme Court circular no. 8, 1987, dated November 25, 1987, elucidating the joint decision and issuing instructions for its implementation.

The actual purpose of this authority appears in Article 3(c) of the joint decision, which provides that measures may be taken against legal counsel who "act,
behave, bear themselves, speak, or issue statements that indicate lack of respect
for the law, statutes, public authority, the courts, or their officials." Negating the
profession's claim to autonomy, the thrust of the joint decision was to remove
disciplinary powers from the advocates' association to the judiciary and the
Ministry of Justice.

Outraged advocates protested frantically, challenging the joint decision as an
unlawful attempt to destroy their independence and to silence them forever.[47]
Despite criticism from other groups, including legal aid circles and the press,
legal officials stood their ground. Sympathetic members of a parliamentary
commission argued with Ismail Saleh, who conceded little. Promising that the
joint decision would be administered impartially, he also made clear that the
government intended to have its way. Advocates were later denied police permission to hold a retreat to discuss the issue.

One advantage of the advocacy was its own chaotic disunity. In an effort to
consolidate its control over the profession, two years later the Ministry of Justice supported its own candidate for IKADIN chair, setting off a battle in the
organization that led, in early 1991, to an embarrassing brawl between members
of the rival factions within the new organization (*Tempo* 1990). The government's attempt to unify the profession under its own wing failed utterly, as
IKADIN, like PERADIN before it, promptly split in two between the AAI, more
or less amenable to official bidding, and IKADIN proper, largely the old and
still-defiant PERADIN group.

But these organizations represent only advocates registered in the Ministry
of Justice. Two other associations, the Indonesian Legal Defenders Bond (*Ikatan
Pembela Hukum Indonesia* or IPHI) and the Indonesian Legal Practitioners
Association (*Sarekat Pengacara Indonesia* or SPI) encompass some of the huge

---

47. On July 12, IKADIN published a defense of professional independence: "The special character of the advocate and the profession of advocacy, recognized universally in various international conferences and declarations, lies in autonomy . . . in this joint decision no freedom
is left to legal counsel, for every act, attitude, and expression is under the control and authority of the chairmen of the first-instance courts, the chairmen of the appellate courts, the
chairman of the *Mahkamah Agung* [Supreme Court], and the Minister of Justice . . . the wide
authority vested by this joint decision [in the courts and ministry] will cause legal counsel to
lose moral courage to carry out their functions in and out of court in accord with the free
and autonomous character of their profession. In turn legal counsel will always posture and
proceed only according to the taste and whim of the judge, which will greatly damage legal
development in general and particularly those who seek justice." From Central Leadership
Council of IKADIN (*Dewan Pimpinan Pusat, Ikatan Advokat Indonesia*), "Declaration of
IKADIN's view of the joint decision of the Supreme Court chair and Minister of Justice of
the Republic of Indonesia concerning procedures of supervision, measures against, and
defense of legal counsel" (*Pernyataan Pendirian IKADIN atas Keputusan Bersama Ketua
Mahkmah Agung dan Menteri Kehakiman Republik Indonesia tentang Tata Cara Pengawasan,
Penindakan dan Pembelaan Diri Penasihat Hukum*), July 12, 1987.

number of practicing lawyers, generally younger than members of IKADIN and AAI, who have not registered in the Ministry of Justice but are certified to practice by local courts.[48] Still another association is for consulting lawyers, who tend to be too busy to pay it much attention. One or two additional organizations were created after 2001, evidently in order to make it possible for advocates to avoid possible application to them of the ethical rules of the association to which they had belonged earlier.

The condition to which Indonesia's legal profession had been reduced by the 1990s made it much less useful than it might have been to the process of legal reform, such as it was, after Soeharto resigned in May 1998. Indeed, far from being useful, it had been transformed over the previous three decades into a major part of the problem, which is that none of the principal institutions of the state had survived with any measure of integrity in tact. On the official side of the legal system, the courts, prosecution, police, and related bureaucratic institutions were in a shambles beset by deep-set corruption, malfeasance, abuse, and incompetence.[49] A healthier legal profession might have served as a source of pressure for change, of new personnel, of perspectives and ideas essential to fundamental reform. This potential remains in the sense that it may

---

48. The term *pengacara*, literally "procedurer," also means "private lawyer" and is actually interchangeable with *advokat*. But there are important differences that require some explanation. There is a long tradition in Indonesia of untrained "bush lawyers," *pokrol bambu*, who are the bane of professional advocates. Because of the paucity of advocates, the need for legal representation, and the lack of a requirement of professional representation, the government never undertook to abolish them, as many advocates preferred, but in the mid-1960s, did begin to regulate them. They were given the higher status title of *pengacara praktek*, "practical attorneys." Over the last forty years or so, however, many law graduates have refused to register in the Ministry of Justice and simply practiced as *pengacara praktek*. Again, registry confers little advantage other than the title of *advokat* and costs a good deal, often under the table, not only to register but to travel to Jakarta, as one must appear in the ministry. *Pokrol bambu* still exist, but they may well be outnumbered now by formally trained lawyers who do not miss the title *advokat* and even take some pride in lacking it. On *pokrol bambu*, see Lev (1973).

49. Since mid-1998, a great deal of research has been done on legal institutions, particularly the courts and their corruption and related malfunctions. Several reform-oriented NGOs are responsible for making much material available. In English, see the publications of the Partnership for Governance Reform in Indonesia, beginning with *A National Survey of Corruption in Indonesia: Final Report December 2001*. The Indonesian Center for the Study of Law and Policy (*Pusat Studi Hukum dan Kebijakan Indonesia* or PSHK) has established a remarkable online source of legal material, http://www.hukumonline.com, which has become daily fare for lawyers, researchers, and observers. It makes possible, for the first time, public access to draft laws, but also ongoing debates over issues of institutional performance and legal change. The published research of Indonesian Corruption Watch (ICW) is a valuable source of material on institutional corruption. See also Lindsey (1999) for an assortment of perspectives on legal conditions. Hukumonline.com is also an excellent source of daily material on the professional advocacy, while a team of PSHK members conceived, researched, and published by far the best study of the advocacy in Indonesia and one of the most impressive anywhere in the region. See PSHK (2001).

conceivably be easier to remake the private bar than to reform the courts, pros-ecution, and police, but not by much. A brief but explicit comparison with the Malaysian bar makes plain the disabilities of the Indonesian profession.

There is nothing but contrast between the two. On any given day anywhere in Malaysia, one can know, either from the *Legal Directory* or the Bar Council offices, precisely how many lawyers are in practice, who has retired, who has not paid dues, their addresses, telephone numbers, and so on. Two regular publica-tions keep readers up on legal issues at home and abroad, new laws, professional matters, judicial issues, and debates of interest to lawyers. The well-organized central office in downtown Kuala Lumpur is easily accessible on any working day. Annual conferences deal with significant issues and draw crowds. The Malaysian bar is capable of governing itself while undertaking political action for the sake of issues of professional or ideological interest.

In Indonesia, not one of the organizations mentioned above has an up-to-date roster of its members and their estimates of membership vary wildly. Dues are seldom if ever collected, meetings are seldom held, and association chairs or their secretaries administer the offices, which take time to find. From the late 1960s through the early 1980s, PERADIN published a useful and engaging jour-nal, *Hukum dan Keadilan* (Law and Justice); IKADIN published one issue of a journal, but nothing more.

Now the only legal journals are published by various law faculties or related organizations; none directly serve the legal profession. Ethical codes exist in three organizations, and there have been a few—very few—cases of enforce-ment; such efforts may do little more than provoke members to sign up with another organization. Since the fall of Soeharto in May 1998 and the onset of a more open period of debate over reform, two or three of the lawyers' associa-tions have occasionally sponsored seminars or conferences on such problems as an independent judiciary, but have done little to open serious discussions of their own condition.

A few efforts to encourage unification or attention to organizational weak-nesses have achieved thin results. In 2001, two or three of the associations agreed to support a common bar examination of sorts, administered by the Supreme Court. This promising step was weakened, however, by a lack of orga-nizational capacity to impose uniform consequences. The exam was adminis-tered in late 2002, but what effect it had or will have on the younger lawyers who passed it, or did not, is unclear.[50]

Nor, despite the advantages of it, have the several associations undertaken a serious effort to unify the profession—in fact, they have studiously avoided it—let alone provide elementary professional services to their members. A "com-munications forum" meant to maintain contact and supply information has existed for a few years, but appears to attract sparse attention. Organizational

---

50. See reports from 2002 at http://www.hukumonline.com on the Supreme Court's post-ponement of the exam and later reports in the same source on the evident advantage had by young lawyers associated with large firms that provided exam preparation.

rivalries, personal antagonisms, the advantages of professional anarchism to some lawyers, and anxieties among some senior lawyers about the potential of strong professional associations actually to exercise normative controls, all hinder efforts to improve organizational capacities (PSHK 2001, throughout).

This fragmentation and disarray of Indonesia's legal profession is partly the result of direct government intervention and hostile neglect, but it is also due to the profession's rapid expansion and transformation and the inevitable corruption of the advocacy in a corrupt judicial order. For many advocates, as for many—some believe most—judges, prosecutors, and police officials, corruption is so taken for granted that it is understood less as corruption than as custom, simply the way things are done.[51] Somewhere along the way of its history during the New Order years, the profession also lost its ideological identity, defined in distinctly nongovernmental terms by the senior lawyers who established PERADIN in the early 1960s.

By the early 1970s, a few lawyers, troubled by their marginalization and tense relations with judges, supposed that only explicit recognition of the profession by a government statute would repair their sorry condition (Sastrayuddha 1971).[52] Most PERADIN leaders then probably opposed the idea, some out of angry hostility to the New Order government and its legal officials. By the 1990s, however, just about the entire profession supported demands for such a law explicitly recognizing the private legal profession: 99.5 percent according to the only survey done on the matter (PSHK 2001, 93).[53] Some hoped that it would render private lawyers once again a legitimate participant in the legal system, others that such a law would be part of a wider reform of state justice, still others that it would begin to correct the disorder and scars of the profession itself. That the profession is private, a conceptual issue, and that a law would (as in Malaysia) make it vulnerable to further official intervention, a political matter, no longer counted in the imagination of many lawyers.

The Indonesian Ministry of Justice, with a good deal of assistance from advocates, drafted a law that was sent to Parliament in 2001.[54] Long on the narrower

---

51. For many advocates, however, corruption remained corruption pure and simple, but conditions in the courts especially made it depressingly unavoidable if one wanted to remain an active litigator. See Pemberton (1999). Judges and prosecutors are in the habit of blaming advocates for judicial corruption, but few take the ruse seriously. When corruption took serious hold in the judiciary during the late years of Guided Democracy, it began with prosecutors and spread from there to judges. Advocates were the last to join the judicial mafia, but they had no choice. It did not take long for some to become quite comfortable in this procedural route. Others went along but felt demeaned. Still others simply withdrew from litigation altogether and settled into commercial negotiation.

52. Article 38 UU 14/1970, the law on judicial organization, called for a new law on "legal aid" (here meaning primarily professional counsel) but nothing was done about it. See PSHK (2001, 89).

53. The sample consisted of 396 advocates in five major cities of the archipelago.

54. On the history of efforts to achieve a law on the advocacy, see PSHK (2001, 99 and following).

interests of the profession and rather negligent of public interests, ethical controls, and much else, the draft came under hard criticism, particularly in the community of reform NGOs concerned with legal reform. By 2002, the relevant Indonesian parliamentary committee had yet to hold full hearings or bring serious pressure to bear on law association leaders to refine the law or to negotiate prior reforms of the profession.[55] The new law on the professional advocacy was finally promulgated in early 2003, setting off a celebration among many lawyers and a good deal of criticism by others in and out of the profession.

A unified bar in Indonesia of several thousand lawyers might well make a difference in efforts to improve legislation and much else in a legal system desperately in need of both reform and reformulation. A weak legal profession exacerbates conditions, however, by denying useful support to reform efforts and even actively hindering such efforts when "rogue" lawyers join the ranks of resistance to change. The problem is not that lawyers failed to speak out when legal reform became a prime issue after Soeharto's resignation in May 1998. Individual lawyers, as always, have had much to say in public on *negara hukum* issues, the corruption and incompetence of the courts, the abuse of power, human rights, and more. Younger lawyers have been the backbone of law-focused NGOs, including the LBH; the Center for the Study of Law and Policy in Indonesia (*Pusat Studi Hukum dan Kebijakan Indonesia* or PSHK); Indonesian Corruption Watch (ICW) (whose director, however, is not legally trained); ICEL (Indonesian Centre for Environmental Law, which has expanded much beyond its initial concern with mainly environmental issues); Judicial Watch; and others. Prominent commercial and academic lawyers, moreover, staffed the National Law Commission established by President Wahid to initiate the work of legal reform.[56] Absent, however, was (and is) the driving power and political clout of an authoritative association of private lawyers capable of developing the

---

55. The draft law promised little by way of reorganization of the advocacy and provided no convincing sanctions. There was no reason why Parliament should not make passage of a version of the draft law contingent upon the establishment of one or at most two associations, complete with staff, dues collection, a code of ethics, and a professional journal. That it did not do so may have reflected relative disinterest in the problem or, equally serious, the lack of a reform strategy in the parliamentary committee.

56. The National Law Commission (*Komisi Hukum Nasional* or KHN), chaired by the senior lawyer Mardjono Reksodiputro, a former dean of the University of Indonesia law faculty, was composed of several other academic and practicing lawyers. One of its concerns was the legal profession, on which it held one or two days of open meetings in 2000 to call for information, proposals, and so on. Ultimately, however, little came of it, apparently because no strategy was developed either in the government or by the KHN upon which to act once information had been collected. It was never quite clear who was responsible for doing what. The work of the KHN was informed partly by prior research on problems in Indonesia's legal system supported by a World Bank grant, begun in 1996, and carried out by the law firm of Ali Budiardjo, Nugroho, Reksodiputro under the direction of Mardjono Reksodiputro. An English language version of the report is *Law Reform in Indonesia: Diagnostic Assessment of Legal Development in Indonesia* (n.d.). On the legal profession, the report indicated that "Legal

strategies of reform that have been absent from the government, willing to lobby Parliament and the People's Consultative Assembly, and constantly feeding the press significant information. Indonesia has nothing at work equivalent to the Malaysian bar. The movement for legal reform, intimately related, of course, to political reform, has suffered for it.

Conclusion

Several questions arise from this comparison of the legal professions of Malaysia and Indonesia that have not been dealt with here. One, for example, is whether common law and civil law heritages make a substantial difference. It is tempting to answer yes, in part at least because private lawyers are closer to the center in common law than civil law structures and conceptual ideologies. A quick comparison of Malaysian and Indonesian experiences seems to confirm this point, but an equally quick glance at Pakistan, Burma, and Nigeria on the one hand, and Korea on the other, complicates the issues, indicating that legal structures and their assumptions do not explain nearly enough. At most, one can argue a weak *ceteris paribus* case. Or what about local culture as an influence worthy of sustained attention? My answer here is that it is not, partly for the methodological reason that "culture" is too vague a concept to be useful in rigorous analysis, but also because in the Malaysia/Indonesia contrast, an appreciation of Occam's blade renders it only marginally persuasive if at all.

What counts in the analysis developed here is politics on the one hand and organization on the other: the uses of state power and the capability of professional associations. In states of long-standing, where relationships between institutions of governance, society, and economy are so well established as to be taken for granted, it is easy to submerge the battles fought along the way that shape systemic connections, habits, relational patterns, and ideological assumptions. Between legal professions and the modern state, there is an inevitable intimacy filled with comity and conflict, but the dimensions and quality of the relationships vary widely from one state to another and have to be understood by way of local political, economic, and social history. One purpose of this effort to compare two hugely different armies of private lawyers has been to examine critical influences in their early evolution, the issues that will remain important to them, and the experience that will most likely influence their ideological and institutional bearings.

---

services in Indonesia are seen to be inferior in supporting the achievements made in economic development. . . . There is no institution or professional organization which has the power to rectify the misconduct of its members." It proposed creation of a Legal Profession Supervisory Board (*Badan Pengawas Profesi Hukum* or BPPH) as a bridge or "communication forum" between the Supreme Court and lawyers' associations. In the debates over Law 14/1970, PERADIN had proposed a similar board made up of judges and advocates who would help evaluate candidates for the bench and sitting judges. Judges rejected the idea out of hand. Nothing came of the law reform proposal, nor would it have been very useful without prior changes in the Supreme Court and leadership of the lawyers' associations.

Works Cited

Abas, Tun Sallah and K. Das. 1989. *May Day for justice.* Kuala Lumpur: Magnus Books.

Abdurrahman, S. H. 1980. *Aspek-aspek bantuan hukum di Indonesia* [Aspects of legal aid in Indonesia]. Jakarta: Cendana Press.

Alatas, Syed Farid. 1997. *Democracy and authoritarianism in Indonesia and Malaysia.* New York: St. Martin's Press.

Bob, Clifford. 1993. State vs. society in Malaysia and the judiciary crisis of 1988. Unpublished paper, on file with D. Lev.

————. 1999. Courts in politics/politics in courts: The judiciary and state-society conflict in Malaysia, 1987–1999. Paper presented at the annual meeting of the American Political Science Association.

Commentary. 1998. Kuala Lumpur: Just World Trust. October.

Crouch, Harold. 1978. *The army and politics in Indonesia.* Ithaca: Cornell University Press.

Damian, Eddy, ed. 1970. *The rule of law dan praktek penahanan di Indonesia* [The rule of law and detention practices in Indonesia]. Bandung: Alumni.

Era Hukum. 1987. Laporan satu tahun berdirinya IKADIN 10 Nopember 1985–10 Nopember 1986 [First year report on the establishment of IKADIN, 10 November 1985–10 November 1986]. 1 *Era Hukum* 1:1. [This was the first and only issue of the journal of *Ikatan Advokat Indonesia* or IKADIN, the Indonesian Advocates Bond.]

Feith, Herbert and Lance Castles. 1970. *Indonesian political thinking 1945–1965.* Ithaca: Cornell University Press.

Harding, Andrew. 1996. *Law, government and the constitution in Malaysia.* The Hague: Kluwer Law International.

Indonesia Reports. 1988. 36 (November): 27. [This issue cites the *Editor* of 23 July 1988 as well as *Kompas* (see below).]

Insaf [Aware]. 1981. Editorial. The Mahathir administration and the Malaysian bar. December. [*Insaf* is the journal of the Malaysian Bar Council.]

————. 1983/84. Editorial. Further erosion of fundamental rights.

Kleden, Kons and Imam Walujo. 1981. *Percakapan tentang undang-undang subversi dan hak asasi manusia* [A discussion of the subversion law and human rights]. Jakarta: LEPPANAS.

Kompas. 1988. 22 July. Excerpted in the 1998 *Indonesia Reports* 36 (November): 26–27.

Lev, Daniel. 1973. *Bush lawyers in Indonesia: Stratification representation and brokerage.* Berkeley: University of California Law and Society Program.

———. 1976. Origins of the Indonesian advocacy. *Indonesia* 21 (April).

———. 1978. Judicial authority and the struggle for an Indonesian *Rechtsstaat.* 13 *Law & Society Review* 4:37.

———. 1985. Colonial law and the genesis of the Indonesian state. *Indonesia* 40 (October): 57.

———. 1986. Adnan Buyung Nasution. In *Human Rights Internet Reporter* 11 (June): 2. [About Indonesian civil rights lawyer and activist Adnan Buyung Nasution.]

———. 1987. *Legal aid in Indonesia.* Working paper no. 44. Monash University Southeast Asian Studies.

———. 1993. Social movements, constitutionalism, and human rights. In *Constitutionalism and democracy: Transitions in the contemporary world*, eds. D. Greenberg, S. Katz, S. Wheatley, and M. Oliviero. New York: Oxford University Press.

———. 1996. Between state and society: Professional lawyers and reform in Indonesia. In *Making Indonesia*, eds. D. Lev and R. T. McVey. Ithaca: Cornell Southeast Asia Program Publications.

———. 1998. Lawyers' causes in Indonesia and Malaysia. In *Cause lawyering: Political commitments and professional responsibilities*, eds. A. Sarat and S. Scheingold. New York: Oxford University Press.

———. 1999. The criminal regime: Criminal process in Indonesia. In *Figures in criminality in Indonesia, the Philippines, and colonial Vietnam*, ed. V. L. Rafael. Ithaca: Cornell Southeast Asia Program Publications.

Lindsey, Timothy, ed. 1999. *Indonesia: Law and society.* Sydney: Federation Press.

Lubis, Todung Mulya. 1993. *In search of human rights: Legal-political dilemmas of Indonesia's new order, 1966–1990.* Jakarta: Gramedia.

Malayan Law Journal. 1999. The Anwar Ibrahim judgment.

Moertono, Soemarsaid. 1968. *State and statecraft in old Java.* Ithaca: Cornell Modern Indonesia Project.

Pemberton, John. 1999. Open secrets: Excerpts from conversations with a Javanese lawyer, and a comment. In *Figures of criminality in Indonesia, the Philippines, and Colonial Vietnam*, ed. V. L. Rafael. Ithaca: Cornell Southeast Asia Program Publications.

Pompe, Sebastiaan. 1996. The Indonesian Supreme Court: Fifty years of judicial development. Ph.D. dissertation, University of Leiden. Published in 2005 as *The Indonesian Supreme Court: A study of institutional collapse*, Cornell University Southeast Asia Program Publications.

PSHK (Pusat Studi Hukum dan Kebijakan Indonesia) [Center for the Study of Law and Policy in Indonesia]. 2001. *Advokat Indonesia mencari legitimasi: Studi tentang tanggung jawab profesi hukum di Indonesia* [Indonesian advocates in search of legitimacy: A study of legal profession responsibility in Indonesia]. Jakarta: PSHK.

Sarat, Austin and Stuart Scheingold, eds. 1998. *Cause lawyering: Political commitments and professional responsibilities.* New York: Oxford University Press.

Sastrayuddha, S. H. 1971. Hambatan-hambatan bagi advokat dalam melaksanakan tugasnya [Difficulties for advocates in performing their responsibilities]. In *Hukum dan keadilan* [Law and justice] (July/August): 17. [*Hukum dan keadilan* is the journal of PERADIN, *Persatuan Advokat Indonesia*, the Indonesian Advocates Association.]

Schwarz, Adam. 1994. *A nation in waiting: Indonesia in the 1990s.* Boulder: Westview Press.

Simandjuntak, Marsillam. 1994. *Pandangan negara integralistik. Sumber, unsur, dan riwayatnya dalam persiapan UUD 1945* [The integralistic state view: Sources, elements, and their history in the preparation of the 1945 constitution]. Jakarta: Grafiti.

Soeharto. 1988. *Otobiografi* [Autobiography]. [Autobiography as told to G. Dwipayana and K.H. Ramadhan.] Jakarta: Citra Lamtoro Gung Persada. [English edition available as *Soeharto: My thoughts, words, and deeds* (1991).]

Sutherland, Heather. 1979. *The making of a bureaucratic elite.* Singapore: Heinemann.

Tempo. 1990. 4 August.

Thoolen, Hans, ed. 1987. *Indonesia and the rule of law: Twenty years of "new order" government.* London: Frances Pinter for the International Commission of Jurists.

Tresna, R. 1959. *Komentar atas reglemen hukum atjara didalam pemeriksaan dimuka pengadilan negeri atau HIR* [Commentary on the regulation of procedure before the first-instance court or HIR] [(*Herziene Indoneisisch Reglement*), the revised Indonesian regulation, 1926]. Jakarta: Versluys.

Yamin, Muh. 1959. *Naskah-persiapan undang-undang dasar 1945* [Documents from the preparation of the 1945 constitution]. Jakarta: Prepantja.

INDEX